The Fabrication of Labor

Studies on the History of Society and Culture
Victoria E. Bonnell and Lynn Hunt, Editors

The Fabrication of Labor

Germany and Britain, 1640–1914

RICHARD BIERNACKI

University of California Press

BERKELEY   LOS ANGELES   LONDON

University of California Press
Berkeley and Los Angeles, California

University of California Press, Ltd.
London, England

© 1995 by
The Regents of the University of California

First Paperback Printing 1997

Library of Congress Cataloging-in-Publication Data

Biernacki, Richard, 1956–
    The fabrication of labor : Germany and Britain, 1640–1914 / Richard
Biernacki.
        p.   cm.—(Studies on the history of society and culture; 22)
    Includes bibliographical references and index.
    ISBN 0-520-20878-1 (alk. paper)
    1. Working class—Germany—History.   2. Working class—
Great Britain—History.   3. Labor movement—Germany—History.
4. Labor movement—Great Britain—History   I. Title.   II. Series.
HD8448B54   1994
305.5′62′0941—dc20   93-39487
                                                                CIP

Printed in the United States of America
9   8   7   6   5   4   3   2   1

The paper used in this publication meets the minimum requirements of
American National Standard for Information Sciences—Permanence of
Paper for Printed Library Materials, ANSI Z39.48-1984. ∞

To my wife, Robin

Contents

Acknowledgments

The ink now dry on the pages that follow, I can express my gratitude to Victoria Bonnell, who worked long and hard to shepherd the book to completion. Professor Bonnell awakened me to the significance of cultural inquiries in the field of labor studies and offered a reservoir of erudition and counsel as my research unfolded. I can only hope that the results support the ideals of historical investigation that she has endeavored to pass on.

Reginald Zelnik's encouraging spirit and ability to convey his deep appreciation of European labor history were vital for my formulation of the study's direction and its comparative design. Neil Smelser lent his expertise on the British textile industry and challenged me to broaden the scope of my appraisal of social change in Europe. Both of these advisers gave generously of themselves to critique editions early and late of the developing manuscript. Michael Burawoy, Christiane Eisenberg, Jeffrey Haydu, Martha Lampland, William Reddy, Ron Rothbart, Andrew Scull, and Gay Seidman contributed expert criticism of my lettered efforts. The advice offered by Jane-Ellen Long, an erudite text editor for the University of California Press, helped improve the very substance of the book. I hope they will excuse me if in the end I have proven unqualified to incorporate all their wisdom.

In the conduct of research in Europe I burdened many librarians and archivists. In Germany their consideration could not have borne fruit without the instruction in traditional hand scripts I received from Franziska Bunte of Kalkum. She taught me that the droppings of nineteenth-century pens are intelligible signs. The staff of the Stadtbibliothek Mönchengladbach was gracious in organizing the borrowing of materials from so many cities. At the Stadtarchiv Mönchengladbach the librarian Marion Engbarth donated time to my questions philanthropically. I am obliged to Hans

Schmiedhofer for guidance in the lower Rhineland and for preparing delivery of rare books. The historians Karl Ditt, Alan Fowler, Colum Giles, Dermot Healey, Patrick Joyce, Reinhard Schüren, Fritz Soll, Joseph L. White, Jürgen Woelke, and Eduard Westerhoff generously shared their findings from prior historical excavations. For scholarly advice in Saxony and for arranging entrance to archives in the former German Democratic Republic I am indebted to Karin Zachmann, a fellow traveler in the field of textile history. Joanna Bornat, Paul and Thea Thompson, and Elizabeth Roberts kindly granted me access to their painstakingly assembled treasuries of oral history. I also wish to thank two able research assistants, Berit Dencker and Matias Valenzuela, for helping with the analysis of newspapers that appears in Chapter Eight.

I feel exceptionally fortunate to have received, both as student and as professor, the aid necessary for my full plan of research. My first investigations in Yorkshire and western Germany were sustained by the Social Science Research Council International Dissertation Research Program and by the German Academic Exchange Service. The International Research and Exchanges Board sent me to depositories in the former German Democratic Republic. Assistance from the Academic Senate of the University of California at San Diego, the Council for the International Exchange of Scholars Fulbright Fellowship Program, and the National Endowment for the Humanities Fellowship Program for University Teachers permitted journeys to London, Greater Manchester, and Berlin. For indispensable support during a long period of writing I am grateful to the Mabelle McLeod Lewis Memorial Fund and, at the University of California, Berkeley, to the John L. Simpson Research Apprenticeship Program and to the Allan Sharlin Memorial Fund. The Library of the University of California, San Diego, purchased for my work rare journals and factory codes that would otherwise have been unexaminable.

Finally, I am grateful to Robin Fiorelli for her forbearance of my departures and for the encouragement she continued to extend up to the book's last word.

1 Introduction: The Task of Explanation

Do international differences in culture create and sustain decisive, systematic divergences in the formation of manufacturing practices and of industrial relations? In this study I begin with a controlled test to judge with fresh reasoning and evidence whether the answer has been "yes." I endeavor to show that as factory systems took shape in nineteenth-century Europe, contrasting techniques of manufacture emerged in similar economic settings as a result of the cultural premises structuring the producers' conduct. These assumptions concerned an enigmatic transaction whose original strangeness now eludes us: the sale of human labor as a commodity.

In the long and difficult crossing from the feudal and corporate organization of work to a liberal commercial order in Europe, labor became more than an expression of human diligence or a means of generating prosperity. Labor came into public sight as a crude ware. It was objectified as a disposable material with a metric value. To characterize this outcome by means of a generic model of "capitalist development" is to mistake a token for the object. I try to show that during the fateful transition to the new commercial order, a different apparition of labor as a commodity took hold in each of the leading economies of Western Europe. In each country a different solution prevailed for determining just how the precious but subtle thing called *labor* could be calibrated and transferred from hired hands to the employer in the workshop. How could workers sell their ephemeral activity to an employer if the realized output alone bore an exchangeable value? Just how should the "quantity" of labor be measured? At what moment was the labor considered to have been conferred upon the employer? British workers and employers resolved these questions differently than did their German and French counterparts. The diverging specifications of labor as a commodity, inherited from peculiarities in each country's initial transition to a formally free market regime, became entrenched instruments of practice in the succeeding age of the factory. Labor did not serve only as a tool of production; in each economy its symbolic calibration organized in a distinct fashion the experience of industrial work and the use of time and space in the production process.

To isolate the industrial effects of diverging cultural definitions of labor as a commodity, this inquiry starts with a comparison of shop-floor activity in the wool textile mills of Germany and Britain during the nineteenth century. These cases provide an ideal comparison of enterprises that developed under similar circumstances in the early tide of industrial change. German and British wool textile mills developed contemporaneously, installed similar kinds of machines, and competed in the same markets. Such uniformities help to rule out conventional economic explanations for the emergence of divergences in shop-floor procedures. Instead, the fundamental similarity in the immediate economic and technical setting for this branch of textiles allows us to highlight culture as the structuring principle of national differences in factory practice. Differing conceptions of labor as a commodity gave rise to national contrasts in methods of remuneration, calculation of output and costs, disciplinary techniques, rights to employment, and even mill architecture. The dissimilarities pervaded industrial experience, for they were contained within each of the nationally prevailing definitions of the valorization of labor. To speak of "the rise of market culture" or the commodification of "labor" without contextualizing their definitions falsely objectifies our terms of understanding. It might seem that the expressions *labor* and *capital*, as elemental and necessary constituents of commercial bourgeois culture, would naturally take on the same meaning throughout industrializing Europe. But they appeared in varying guises and signified disparate features of human endeavor within the German and the British economies.

Cultural conceptions of labor as a ware do not only illuminate the fixed structures of early factory life. They also aid us in appreciating the strategies and demands of labor movements. Until the classical period of laissez-faire industrialization came to an end in the First World War, German and British workers enacted strikes and protests with different beliefs about what comprised the withholding of the commodity of "labor." They articulated different responses to identical workplace challenges, such as employers' imposition of disciplinary fines. Finally, German and British workers arrived at different explanations for their exploitation based upon their perception of labor as a commodity. In the decades leading up to the First World War, the German labor movement proved more receptive to Marx's analysis of exploitation than did its British counterpart, even among British workers who were convinced of the necessity of dramatic social transformation. I suggest that for each country, the schemas encoded in silent practices within the private factory lent workers the concept of labor they used to voice demands in the public sphere.

If reliance upon a vision of labor as a commodity cast both factory practices and workers' responses in a distinctive image, why did a different apparition of labor prevail in each country? I try to show how conjunctural differences in the timing of the recognition of formally free markets in finished goods, in the abolition of feudal dues in labor, and in the breakdown of guild supervision over urban labor established different motivating conditions for the definition of labor as a commodity. To dissect the combinations of factors that inspired varying cultural outcomes, I investigate the transition to a formally free market in labor not only in Britain and Germany but in France and, more briefly, in northern Italy. The forces at work in these cases show that the understandings of the labor transaction that prevailed in Germany and in Britain, the two chief cases for analysis, resulted from opposite journeys among an array of developmental pathways to wage labor in western Europe.

The discovery that the world of concrete procedures on the shop floor was systematically structured by cultural specifications of labor as a commodity—by practical "theories" about labor, if you will—may open a new avenue of research into correspondences between nineteenth-century practice and the postulates of political economy reigning in that age. I endeavor to show that the contrasts in the apprehension of labor marking the German and British variants of classical political economy matched the differences in the theories about labor operating in German versus British manufacturing. Adam Smith's portrayal of the exchange of labor products recovered the presumptions about the transfer of labor that governed British industrial procedure in his day and long after. Karl Marx's celebrated reflections upon labor power, it turns out, replicated the definition of labor contained in German treatises composed at the beginning of the nineteenth century. Marx's formal economic analysis eerily borrowed from the established cultural schema distinctive to the workers and business people of Germany. Each country's intellectual representatives brought the implicit theory embedded in the quotidian practices of manufacture into the explicit theory of political economy.

In brief, this work examines the national origins of cultural definitions of labor as a commodity, the installation of these specifications into procedures on the shop floor in Germany and Britain, and the ideological consequences for the labor movements of such culturally structured forms of industrial practice. The work's range is broad but its analytic focus precise: it portrays the development of manufacturing to shed light on the explanatory significance of popular understandings of labor as a commodity. My comparative perspective focuses upon the responses of German and British workers that typify the overarching differences in the definition of labor as a ware in each country. Given this cross-national perspective, only occasionally do I dwell upon more specific differences in workers' responses within each country based on occupational, gender, and regional identities. If I manage to encourage further reflection upon the practical effects of labor's reification as a commodity, I will have accomplished my task.

THE INITIAL TEST CASES

Comparative history succeeds when the grounds for juxtaposing cases are specified with precision. My examination of the German and British wool textile industries attempts to single out the effects of culture upon the workplace by providing approximate controls for the confounding effects of differing economic and technical trajectories of development. Britain's reputation for having had a unique experience as the textile pioneer rests on intense, in some respects excessive, attention to the precocious development of cotton factories in Lancashire at the end of the eighteenth century. In Yorkshire, however, the most important center of the country's wool trade, power looms in weaving sheds did not prevail until after the middle of the nineteenth century—by which time the woolen and cotton mills in Germany had also begun to mechanize.[1] Whereas the British enjoyed a head start of half a century in the mechanized treatment of cotton, their lead in the technology for wool was minimal. This consideration simplifies the task of presenting a cultural account of the differences in factory practices that emerged. It helps to exclude explanations of differences that appeal to the timing of development or to the world industrial environment prevailing at the inception of a factory system.[2]

1. Georg Brodnitz, *Vergleichende Studien über Betriebsstatistik und Betriebsformen der englischen Textilindustrie* (Halle: Habilitationsschrift Universität Halle-Wittenberg, 1902), pp. 15–16.
2. John Child and Alfred Kieser conducted an Anglo-German comparison of managers' authority which revealed that, taking into account the size of firms, decision-making was more

Why did the mechanized production of wool cloth appear later than that of cotton in the global textile industry? It was a quirk of nature that placed its mechanization on a deferred time scale. Wool fibers proved more recalcitrant to mechanical handling than cotton. Although some enterprises for the power weaving of cotton succeeded in Britain during the 1790s,[3] experimental power looms for weaving in woolens did not evolve in Britain until the 1830s.[4] By the 1850s these looms could outperform hand looms, and the construction of mechanized weaving mills was begun in earnest.[5] Thereafter change was swift. Employers in the Yorkshire woolen trade had nearly completed the shift to power weaving by the start of the 1870s.[6]

---

centralized in contemporary German than in British companies. Although this finding tallies with stereotypes about German culture, the results could also be explained as adaptations to circumstances under which those firms were founded or to the present conditions of doing business in the branches of manufacture to which these firms devoted themselves. My comparative design takes these alternative economic explanations into account. John Child and Alfred Kieser, "Organizational and Managerial Roles in British and West German Companies: An Examination of the Culture-Free Thesis," in Cornelis Lammers and David Hickson, editors, *Organizations Alike and Unalike: International and Interinstitutional Studies in the Sociology of Organizations* (London: Routledge and Kegan Paul, 1979), pp. 252–271. The most recent influential cross-national study which omitted controls for technology and path of development is that of Gary Hamilton, Nicole Woolsey Biggart, and Marco Orrù, "Organizational Isomorphism in East Asia," in Walter W. Powell and Paul J. DiMaggio, editors, *The New Institutionalism in Organizational Analysis* (Chicago: University of Chicago Press, 1991), p. 366. In an important comparison of workers' attitudes in the French and British oil refining industries, Duncan Gallie set up controls for the contemporary "level of technological development" in these enterprises but not for their developmental trajectory in each country. *Social Inequality and Class Radicalism in France and Britain* (Cambridge: Cambridge University Press, 1983).

3. Neil J. Smelser, *Social Change in the Industrial Revolution* (Chicago: The University of Chicago Press, 1959), p. 147.

4. Frederick James Glover, "The Rise of the Heavy Woollen Trade of the West Riding of Yorkshire in the Nineteenth Century," *Business History* Volume 4, No. 1 (December 1961), p. 9.

5. In 1856 total employment in woolen and worsted textile mills exceeded the number of handweavers in those branches, but statistics for the mills included auxiliary workers. Brodnitz, op. cit., pp. 15–16. In 1860, Samuel Jubb reported that wages for hand weavers in the Batley district had suffered no decline and remained above those for power-loom weavers. *The History of the Shoddy-Trade* (Batley: J. Fearnsides, 1860), pp. 68–70. One-quarter of the looms in Huddersfield in 1868 were still worked by hand. J. H. Clapham, "The Decline of the Handloom in England and Germany," *Journal of the Bradford Textile Society* Volume 11 (1905), p. 45.

6. Handweaving remained an important enterprise at least into the 1880s around Kirkburton, Skelmanthorpe, and Shelley. *Textile Manufacturer,* June 15, 1884, p. 237, and October 15, 1886, p. 447. For an instance of a firm using sixty handlooms in 1891: *Yorkshire Factory Times,* July 10, 1891, Heckmondwike. For other British handweaving towns in the 1890s, see Gerhart von Schulze-Gävernitz, *Der Grossbetrieb: Ein wirtschaftlicher und socialer Fortschritt* (Leipzig: Duncker & Humblot, 1892), p. 272. The Yorkshire worsted textile industry, concentrated in Bradford, used specially combed wool fibers. Worsted weaving was mecha-

In Germany the transition to power looms for woolens occurred more unevenly. A few entrepreneurs experimented with power looms during the 1830s in Berlin and Saxony.[7] By the 1860s, the mechanization of wool weaving was fully underway. In the preeminent textile centers of north-western Germany, such as Elberfeld and Rheydt, the mechanization of weaving with wool materials was nearing completion by 1875—at almost the same time as in Yorkshire.[8] Small wonder Karl Marx commented that "whenever one travels through the Prussian Rhineland and Westfalen, one thinks of Lancashire and Yorkshire."[9] Towns in Saxony, the other leading industrial region in German textiles, lagged about a decade behind.[10]

To be sure, Germany had outlying areas such as upper Lausitz, where isolated hand weavers survived even into the 1890s.[11] Perhaps the decisive condition is that in wool technology, unlike cotton, the German and the

nized about two decades before woolens. Since the cultural principles in the treatment of labor in worsted mills were the same as in woolen mills proper, I include evidence from the worsted branch in my grouping of Yorkshire mills. E. M. Sigsworth, "The Woollen Textile Industry," in Roy Church, editor, *The Dynamics of Victorian Business* (London: George Allen & Unwin, 1980), p. 193.

7. Horst Blumberg, *Die deutsche Textilindustrie in der industriellen Revolution* (Berlin: Akademie-Verlag, 1965), p. 89.

8. Wolfgang Hoth, *Die Industrialisierung einer rheinischen Gewerbestadt, dargestellt am Beispiel Wuppertal* (Köln: Rheinisch-Westfälisches Wirtschaftsarchiv, 1975), p. 200; Alphons Thun, *Die Industrie am Niederrhein und ihre Arbeiter*. Part Two: *Die Industrie des bergischen Landes* (Leipzig: Duncker & Humblot, 1879), p. 197; Horst Matzerath, "Industrialisierung, Mobilität und sozialer Wandel am Beispiel der Städte Rheydt und Rheindahlen," *Probleme der Modernisierung in Deutschland* (Opladen: Westdeutscher Verlag, 1979), p. 23. A useful summary of the mechanization of wool production in northwestern Germany appears in Kathleen Canning, "Class, Gender, and Working-Class Politics: The Case of the German Textile Industry, 1890–1933," Ph.D. diss., Johns Hopkins University, 1988, p. 73.

9. Quoted in Rolf Dlubek and Hannes Skambraks, editors, *"Das Kapital" von Karl Marx in der deutschen Arbeiterbewegung: 1867 bis 1878* (Berlin: Dietz Verlag, 1967), p. 23.

10. By 1880, in such Saxon centers as Glauchau and Gera power looms prevailed even in the fancy goods market. Louis Bein, *Die Industrie des sächsischen Voigtlandes*. Zweiter Theil: *Die Textil-Industrie* (Leipzig: Duncker & Humblot, 1884), pp. 444–445; Enquête-Commission zur Untersuchung der Lage der Glauchau-Meeraner Webwaaren-Industrie, "Bericht der zur Untersuchung der Lage der Glauchau-Meeraner Webwaaren-Industrie berufenen Enquête-Commission," 1881, Stadtarchiv Glauchau, W Abt. 1, Nr. 41; for weaving in Gera, Gera-Greizer Kammgarnspinnerei, *50 Jahre Gera-Greizer Kammgarnspinnerei 1890–1940* (Gera: Karl Basch & Co., 1940), p. 78. In Zittau, the production of half-wool goods was mechanized by 1860. Brigitte Wrobel, *Geschichte der Arbeiterbewegung des Kreises Zittau: Chronik 1830–1945* (Zittau: Kommission zur Erforschung der Geschichte der örtlichen Arbeiterbewegung, 1972), p. 3.

11. See Jean Quataert, "Workers' Reactions to Social Insurance: The Case of Homeweavers in the Saxon Oberlausitz in the Late Nineteenth Century," *Internationale Wissenschaftliche Korrespondenz zur Geschichte der deutschen Arbeiterbewegung* Volume 20, Number 1 (1984). In 1875, only 34 percent of looms in Germany as a whole in the wool branches were mechanized. Horst Blumberg, op. cit., pp. 89 ff.

British engineers were equals from the start.[12] From the first days of mechanization, German wool equipment was usually of domestic design and
manufacture.[13] As early as 1855, at the Paris Exposition, the Germans competed on an equal footing with the British in the design of textile machines
for wool.[14] The German weavers themselves often preferred their own
country's equipment over the British versions.[15] The technical literature
shows that in the decades before the First World War, German and British
looms from the woolen branches typically ran at similar speeds, as measured
by the number of crossings the looms' shuttles could finish each minute.[16]
On the eve of the war, a German business journal even boasted that, ranked
against British factories, "the German woolen industry in its technical and
organizational institutions can be considered in many respects superior."[17]

A focus on wool textiles as a test comparison also simplifies the task of
explanation because it offers basic parallels between the niches in the
world market occupied by the producers. Business journals from the
nineteenth century confirm that German and British fabrics made of
wool and wool mixtures were often of very similar design.[18] The markets
within the British Empire, which were protected for British manufacturers, absorbed primarily cotton, not wool, manufactures.[19] In the wool

12. Herbert Kisch, "The Crafts and Their Role in the Industrial Revolution: The Case of
the German Textile Industry," Ph.D. diss., University of Washington, 1958, p. 35.

13. *Textile Manufacturer*, March 15, 1881, p. 95. Artur Peltzer, "Die Arbeiterbewegung
in der Aachener Textilindustrie von der Mitte des 19. Jahrhunderts bis zum Ausbruch des
Weltkrieges," Ph.D. diss., Universität Marburg, 1924, p. 9. Domestic machinery played a role
in the mechanization of wool weaving in Saxony as early as the 1830s. Horst Blumberg, op.
cit., p. 89; *Gewerbe-Blatt für Sachsen*, June 21, 1838, pp. 197–198.

14. Alfred Schröter and Walter Becker, *Die deutsche Maschinenbauindustrie in der industriellen Revolution* (Berlin: Akademie-Verlag, 1962), p. 186. In worsteds, it seems, German
weavers in the Wuppertal did import looms from Bradford. See *Centralblatt für die Textil-
Industrie* Volume 15 (1884), p. 233. In worsted spinning the Germans disseminated their own
machine designs in the 1860s. F. Orth, *Der Werdegang wichtiger Erfindungen auf dem Gebiete der Spinnerei und Weberei* (Berlin: Verein Deutscher Ingenieure, 1922), p. 81.

15. *Textile Manufacturer*, September 15, 1883, p. 391; *Centralblatt für die Textil-
Industrie* Volume 19 (1888), p. 435.

16. Royal Commission on Labour, PP 1892 XXXV, p. 207. HSTAD Regierung Aachen
1634, report of February 4, 1899.

17. *Seide*, February 1914, pp. 85 ff.; *Die Textil-Zeitung*, Feb. 16, 1897, p. 895.

18. *Das deutsche Wollen-Gewerbe*, August 10, 1884, p. 1285. The product market was
extremely fragmented, however. Sigsworth, op. cit., pp. 185, 190. German wool manufacturers, who began with a reliance on the luxury goods market, pursued a strategy of diversi-
fying their output. They competed in both fancy and plain styles. D. T. Jenkins and J. C. Malin,
"European Competition in Woollen and Cloth, 1870–1914: The Role of Shoddy," *Business
History* Volume 32, Number 4 (October 1990), p. 82.

19. British wool fabric exports were focused on Europe. Gary Firth, "The Bradford Trade
in the Nineteenth Century," in D. G. Wright and J. A. Jowitt, editors, *Victorian Bradford*

trade, however, the British exporters had to compete to a greater degree in noncolonial markets, where entry for British goods was no easier than for German ones.[20] In the wool business, therefore, differences in the market demands satisfied by German and British manufacturers can more easily be discounted as an essential cause for divergences in factory customs.

The German and British wool textile industries resembled each other another way: in both countries, the majority of factories in this branch operated under the principal ownership of family partners.[21] In cotton, by contrast, joint stock undertakings prevailed in some British towns, in particular within Oldham's spinning trade.[22] The sizes of firms in the two countries varied greatly by market specialty, by region, and even by town,[23] but in national comparisons their average sizes were not far apart. In both

---

(Bradford: Bradford Metropolitan Council, 1982), pp. 30–31. Schulze-Gävernitz aptly described the extent to which the British enjoyed a protected market for cotton staples: "It is therefore correctly stated in Lancashire that the demand from India year by year for certain cotton stuffs is as sure as that the English nation requires every year a certain quantity of wheat." *The Cotton Trade in England and on the Continent* (London: Simpkin, Marshall, Hamilton, Kent and Co., 1895), p. 69. At the top end of the scale for fine yarns, British cotton spinners in Lancashire hardly competed with foreign enterprises, for their expertise lent them a virtual world monopoly. John Jewkes and E. M. Gray, *Wages and Labour in the Lancashire Spinning Industry* (Manchester: Manchester University Press, 1935), p. 48.

20. For comments on German competition in the American market for woolens and worsteds, see *Textile Manufacturer*, June 15, 1884, p. 244. On German competition in other markets, see Erich Thal, *Die Entstehung und Entwicklung der Halbwoll- und Wollindustrie im M.-Gladbacher Bezirk bis zum Jahre 1914* (Mönchengladbach: W. Hütter, 1926); and Jenkins and Malin, op. cit., p. 69.

21. *Textile Mercury*, March 28, 1914, p. 253.

22. von Schulze-Gävernitz, *Der Grossbetrieb*, pp. 69, 91; Patrick Joyce, *Work, Society and Politics* (London: Methuen, 1980), p. 340. Karl Emsbach, *Die soziale Betriebsverfassung der rheinischen Baumwollindustrie im 19. Jahrhundert* (Bonn: Röhrscheid, 1982), pp. 407–411. Mike Holbrook-Jones, *Supremacy and the Subordination of Labour* (London: Heinemann Educational Books, 1982), p. 36. Even limited liability firms were sometimes managed by members of a single family. For an example from textiles, see Augustus Muir, *The History of Bowers Mills* (Cambridge: W. Heffer, 1969), p. 35, and, for national overviews, David Landes, "The Structure of Enterprise in the Nineteenth Century: The Cases of Britain and Germany," in Comité International des Sciences Historiques, editor, *Rapports V: Histoire contemporaine* (Uppsala: Almwvist & Wiksell, 1960), pp. 115, 121, and T. R. Gourvish, "British Business and the Transition to a Corporate Economy: Entrepreneurship and Management Structures," in R. P. T. Davenport-Hines and Geoffrey Jones, editors, *Enterprise, Management and Innovation in British Business, 1914–1980* (London: Frank Cass, 1988), p. 26.

23. For example, enterprises in the old textile center of Bocholt were much smaller than elsewhere in the Münsterland. Bernhard Bergmeyer, "Das Baumwollgewerbe im Münsterlande," diss., Bonn, 1921, pp. 87 ff. On the eve of the First World War, the Rhineland had more looms in place than did the Münsterland, but its cotton mills averaged only half as many looms each.

countries, the weaving departments of woolen mills at the close of the century typically employed about sixty looms.[24]

Finally, in wool factories the development of textile workers' unions and collective bargaining show fundamental similarities in the two countries. As is well known, Lancashire's cotton towns sponsored the development of strong and enduring craft unions for spinners and weavers back in the era of artisanal production.[25] This unusual legacy of early organization presents a striking structural difference in an Anglo-German comparison of cotton mills. A comparison of regions with wool mills eliminates this complexity. From an analytic standpoint it is fortunate that unions in Yorkshire for factory weavers and spinners did not become full-fledged standing organizations until after 1881 in the Colne Valley, and not until the 1890s in other localities.[26] The rise of the union movement in Yorkshire therefore coincided with the emergence of formal organization in Germany, where factory textile unions experienced a take-off in membership during the 1890s. In Yorkshire the major union for textile workers embraced both weavers and spinners, establishing another parallel to the German case.[27] The similarities in the timing and structure of collective organization among British and German wool factory workers help us to assess alternative explanations for divergences in shop-floor customs in this branch.

History never duplicates its creations to order. Yet the basic similarities in technology, the timing of mechanization, product lines, proprietorship, and the structure and procession of workers' unionization allow a focus on

24. J. H. Clapham, op. cit., p. 133. *Textile Mercury*, April 8, 1911, p. 271. Germany, *Statistik des Deutschen Reichs*, Volume 214 (Berlin: Kaiserliches Statistisches Amt, 1910), p. 303. Brodnitz found close parallels in the average sizes of the work forces of German and British worsted and woolen weaving mills excluding hand shops. Brodnitz, op. cit., p. 31.

25. Isaac Cohen summarizes the evidence in *American Management and British Labor* (Westport, Connecticut: Greenwood Press, 1990), p. 15.

26. Ben Turner, *Short History of the General Union of Textile Workers* (Heckmondwike: Labour Pioneer, 1920); Ben Turner, *A Short Account of the Rise and Progress of the Heavy Woollen District Branch of the General Union of Textile Workers* (N.p.: Yorkshire Factory Times Press, 1917). Prior associations for weavers in Yorkshire, whose by-laws were printed as early as 1824, were short-lived. *Report from the Select Committee on Combination Laws,* PP 1825 (437) IV, p. 27.

27. *Yorkshire Factory Times*, May 26, 1893, p. 5; Joyce, op. cit, p. 76. The independent local Yeadon textile union, too, emphasized recruitment across professional divides. Archive of General Union of Dyers, Bleachers, and Textile Workers, Bradford, Union minutes, May 13, 1896, and Oct. 28, 1903. For Germany, see Klaus Schönhoven, "Localism—Craft Union— Industrial Union: Organizational Patterns in German Trade Unionism," in Wolfgang J. Mommsen and Hans-Gerhard Husung, editors, *The Development of Trade Unionism in Great Britain and Germany, 1880–1914* (London: George Allen & Unwin, 1985), p. 229; R. M. Dehn, *The German Cotton Industry* (Manchester: Manchester University Press, 1913), pp. 73, 78.

the German and British wool mills to approximate an ideal comparison. This industry also affords a weighty, if relatively neglected, body of evidence. At the turn of this century, the Yorkshire district counted about 180,000 woolen and worsted textile workers.[28] In Germany, there were at this time as many weavers in wool as in cotton.[29] For the German case, much of the primary evidence comes from northwest Germany and Saxony, where mills were renowned for the stiff competition they offered Yorkshire. British technical journals in the nineteenth century selected the German towns of the Wuppertal and of the lower Rhine, such as Düren, as their chief competitors in the woolen market. They also singled out the work forces in these German towns for their ability to rival British textile workers in technical expertise.[30]

Of course, a comparison limited to wool textile factories within narrow geographical regions renders suspect any allegation that findings result from nationally prevailing cultural differences. Where my explanation relies upon the influence of culture, I have an obligation to demonstrate the generality of the outlooks that I hold responsible for divergences in factory customs. In addition to my evidence on the wool mills, which serves as the decisive test example, I therefore include many examples from factories in the major branches of textiles in other regions of each country. At this point I can take advantage of a supplementary kind of comparison. In spite of differences in the timing of mechanization and in the labor and product

28. Data for 1901 from J. H. Clapham, *The Woollen and Worsted Industries* (London: Methuen & Co., 1907), frontispiece. To put Yorkshire employment in perspective, the cotton industry of the time in Lancashire retained about half a million workers. Sydney J. Chapman, *The Lancashire Cotton Industry: A Study in Economic Development* (Manchester: Manchester University Press, 1904), p. 179. The German spinning and weaving mills of the wool branches in 1907 employed over 180,000 workers. Germany, *Statistisches Jahrbuch für das Deutsche Reich* (Berlin: Kaiserliches Statistisches Amt, 1909), p. 80.

29. In 1895, 30 percent of German weavers labored in the wool trade, and 29 percent in cotton; in 1907 the figures were nearly the same. See summary statistics in Karin Zachmann, "Der Mechanisierungsprozess in der deutschen Textilindustrie im Zeitraum von 1870 bis 1914," *Beiträge zur Wirtschaftsgeschichte*, Number One (Dresden: Technische Universität Dresden, 1988), p. 29. In all, the German and British textile workforces were of similar size, each totaling about one million workers. *Textile Mercury*, 1909, p. 330.

30. For the Wupper Valley and Krefeld, see *Textile Manufacturer*, June 15, 1883, p. 217. For Düren, see *Textile Mercury*, August 30, 1890, p. 139. For Mönchengladbach, see *Textile Manufacturer*, February 15, 1906, pp. 37–38, and *Textile Mercury*, December 15, 1883, p. 510. As early as 1828, William Radcliffe focused on Elberfeld as a powerful adversary in the weaving business. *Origin of the New System of Manufacturing Commonly Called "Power-Loom Weaving"* (Stockport: J. Lomax, 1828), p. 92. Although not so famous a pioneer as the Wupper Valley, Düren was distinguished for its centralization of woolen manufacture in large manufactories during the first half of the nineteenth century. Joachim Kermann, *Die Manufakturen im Rheinland 1750–1833* (Bonn: Ludwig Röhrscheid, 1972), p. 155.

markets of the various branches of textile production *within* each country, the practices on the factory shop floor *within* each country tend to display similar traits. This extension increases my confidence that nationally dominant cultural assumptions represent the source of similarity in outcomes within each country.

Even when this study incorporates evidence from cotton, silk, and jute mills to help establish the generality of cultural differences, the comparison of the textile industries as national wholes rests on a prudent criterion. With the maturing of textile machinery in the late nineteenth century, Germany and Britain comprised the premier exporters in the world textile market. As early as the 1880s the professional textile periodicals in Britain focused on Germany, not France, as Britain's most important challenger.[31] By the start of the First World War, British managers complained that the Germans utterly controlled the trade in certain fancy weaves.[32] "We have been lamenting or resenting 'foreign competition,'" the *Textile Mercury* said upon the outbreak of the war, "—meaning by that term almost exclusively German competition in the outside markets of the world."[33] In cotton, to be sure, the British retained a substantial edge in efficiency. They operated their cotton weaving equipment at a speed perhaps 30 percent higher on average than that of German competitors.[34] Yet even in cottons, weaving mills in the two countries were of similar sizes.[35] Outside of wool textiles, the German and British textile producers did not stand at equivalent levels of technical and

31. *Textile Manufacturer*, July 15, 1883, p. 272. For other examples of the British preoccupation with German competition, see *Textile Recorder*, October 15, 1892, worsted branch; *Textile Manufacturer*, September 15, 1889, p. 436; *Yorkshire Factory Times*, February 15, 1912, speech by Swire Smith to the Bradford Textile Society. British textile employers told their workers that German competition in particular prevented them from granting wage increases. *Bradford Labour Echo*, January 28, 1899.

32. *Journal of the British Association of Managers of Textile Works, 1918–1919* (Volume 9), p. 108.

33. *Textile Mercury*, August 22, 1914. The American textile industry hardly competed in the world market. For comparative estimates of national exports of wool manufactures, including those from the United States, see D. T. Jenkins and K. G. Ponting, *The British Wool Textile Industry 1770–1914* (London: Heinemann Educational Books, 1982), p. 294. For a discussion of the lack of American competitiveness in exports of cottons, see Gary Saxonhouse and Gavin Wright, "Stubborn Mules and Vertical Integration: The Disappearing Constraint?" *Economic History Review* 40, n. 1 (February 1987), p. 93.

34. von Schulze-Gävernitz, *The Cotton Trade*, pp. 107–108.

35. Ibid., pp. 67, 79. German cotton spinning mills were typically larger than those of the British, whereas the British cotton weaving factories were larger. See employment figures (excluding self-employed) in Brodnitz, op. cit., pp. 23–24.

professional advance, but at least they occupied closely related stages of development.[36]

At junctures when I consider alternative explanations for factory customs based on market adaptation or "rational choice," I usually must return to the main comparison motivating this study, that of the wool branch, for the most effective controls on sources of variation. Although my comparative framework at these points allows me to consider and reject specific noncultural explanations for differences in factory customs, I never treat culture as a residual category. That is, in no instance do I assume that a practice unexplainable by economic principles is attributable to culture by default. Nor do I suppose that culture clarifies only the variation that remains after applying economic reasoning. The logic of isolating an important cultural cause of differences in outcomes by considering alternative, economic sources of differentiation in no way implies that culture serves only as a supplement for explaining what is left over.

Although the strategy for ruling out alternative explanations for differences in outcomes follows basic comparative logic, the design of my model follows a line of reasoning specific to cultural analysis. Let me preview some findings to illustrate. German owners and workers viewed employment as the timed appropriation of workers' labor power and disposition over workers' labor activity. In contrast, British owners and workers saw employment as the appropriation of workers' materialized labor via its products. These divergent assumptions led to differences in the definition of wages, the calculation of costs, rights of employment, disciplinary fines, and the design of factory buildings. Since the manufacturing practices in each country formed a meaningful constellation, my positive argument is configurational, attached to an overarching pattern of techniques rather than to

---

36. By the late nineteenth century the Germans also became the chief rivals of the British in the export of the textile machinery itself. The *Textile Manufacturer* of Manchester reported that German textile machine makers before 1914 had "built up an export trade of considerable dimensions which meets us in the neutral markets of the world." *Textile Manufacturer*, February 15, 1917, pp. 60 ff. True, in the early decades of mechanization after midcentury, the Germans remained dependent on British machine designs in the cotton branch. Textile machine makers in Germany began modifying British makes by the 1860s. F. Orth, op. cit., p. 81. By the turn of the century the *Textile Manufacturer*, in a report on the looms crafted in Chemnitz by Louis Schönherr, said that "although this country [Britain] still holds the premier position in the building of looms . . . there are many instances where foreign ingenuity has got slightly ahead of us." Foreign loom makers, the journal concluded, "are working abreast of us—not behind us." *Textile Manufacturer*, November 15, 1901, pp. 375–377. The Germans thought even more highly of their equipment. At the turn of the century, the German *Textil-Zeitung* said, "We cannot learn anything from the British, for German loom construction absolutely nothing. We are superior to them." February 16, 1897, p. 126.

a simple outcome. This challenges rival explanations to account for an equally broad range of details in German and British factory customs.

Configurational analyses of factory practices are best executed through comparisons of single industries. By this means the investigator may scan the entire breadth of the practices of production to discern the significance of consistencies which would otherwise go unnoticed. This strategy also permits the researcher to contrast solutions to technical problems that are particular to each branch of capitalist enterprise. As signifying practices, manufacturing techniques create a system of signification from the fixtures specific to each kind of commercial undertaking. It is useless to hold culture constant while varying the economic and technological circumstances—say, by comparing textile and metal factories within the same region—for culture cannot yield uniform effects across industries. For instance, a difference between the fining systems in Germany and Britain was unlikely to appear in industries where a multi-stage production process made the assignment of responsibility for faults impossible or where routine channels for customers to bargain over the price of damaged goods were lacking. In short, the investigator searching for generalities cannot extrapolate from textiles to make inferences about the design of German and British factories across industries as one would extrapolate from a statistical sample. The shop floor furnishes a literal example of a social institution that can be viewed, as Jean Comaroff once expressed it, as a "meeting ground . . . of two distinct orders of determination—one material, the other semantic."[37] In this study I begin generalizing my findings about textiles to characteristic practices in other labor processes, such as coal mining and iron casting. But I do not look for *uniformities* in production methods across businesses in each country. Instead, I search for meaningful *analogies* in practices within each country, considering the technical environment peculiar to each kind of industry. The parallels across economically dissimilar branches of enterprise rebut many economic explanations for nationally prevailing routines.

Comparative analyses of the influence of culture on factory organization have to date chosen contrasting cases with an eye to maximizing the cultural differences in the cases under review. The first landmark study to compare the effect of national traditions on the development of factory systems, Reinhard Bendix's enduring *Work and Authority in Industry*, took Victorian Britain and Tsarist Russia for its primary cases. This gave Bendix a

---

37. Jean Comaroff, *Body of Power, Spirit of Resistance* (Chicago: University of Chicago Press, 1985), p. 4.

pairing of sharply contrasted ideologies used by entrepreneurs to legitimate their authority, and he highlighted this variable to explain differences in the evolution of their systems of industrial relations. Bendix did not assess the independent contribution of cultural or ideological traditions, as opposed to purely economic and technological variables, in the creation of factory institutions.[38]

In recent years the unmatched performance of Japanese firms in the world market has intensified research into the historical origins of their system of industrial relations. The pioneering analyses, such as those by Ronald Dore and Robert Cole, have suffered from the same inability to disentangle cultural and economic influences. They have compared Japan with structurally dissimilar cases such as Britain and the United States.[39] In *Work, Mobility, and Participation,* Cole examines the legitimation of authority with a logic paralleling that of Bendix. In his comparison of Japanese and American employment practices, Cole argues that Japanese employers required a tradition of group loyalty to establish their system of permanent company employment. They used this ideology at the beginning of the century as a means of parrying workers' objections to lifetime dependence on a single employer. In the absence of a comparison with an

38. Bendix conceived his work only with the aim of depicting the interdependencies between the development of legitimating cultures and the play of economic interest. *Work and Authority in Industry* (Berkeley: University of California Press, 1956), pp. 442–443. His selection of cases invites a host of economic explanations for differences between British and Russian factories, based on severe contrasts between their business and technical environments—such as the availability of skilled labor or reliance on a permanent urban work force. Bendix himself lends credence to conventional economic deductions about the pattern of industrial relations when he acknowledges that the Russian company towns, from which he draws much of his evidence, closely resembled communities the British employers established under similar economic circumstances in isolated villages of dependent colonies (p. 183 note).

39. See Ronald Dore, *British Factory, Japanese Factory* (Berkeley: University of California Press, 1973), pp. 401–402. Dore's original study constructed a dual set of arguments to explain the differences between British and Japanese forms of industrial enterprise in the electrical industry. On the one hand, it attributed their differences in work relations and methods of supervision to dissimilarities in the countries' cultural emphases upon individual versus group achievement, to variation in familial values, and to the extent of popular acceptance of the authority exercised by economic elites. On the other hand, Dore connected the differences in work organization to contrasts in the world-economic epochs from which they emerged. By his account, late-industrializing Japan institutionalized its factory practices under economic circumstances that objectively favored the initiation of its lifetime employment systems, for example. After noting some of the congruences between his two lines of causal reasoning, Dore declined to evaluate the relative weight or respective usefulness of the cultural and economic modes of analysis. The same comparative strategy and indecision between these two lines of argument recurs in his more recent book, *Taking Japan Seriously* (London: Athlone Press, 1987), pp. vii, 94–95.

economically similar case, however, even this shrewd view of culture as a legitimizing tool cannot judge whether the institutions would have evolved differently had it not been for the stock of traditions. From Cole's evidence an analyst could conclude just as readily that the needs of capital reinvigorated and sustained an older ideology as that the ideology steered the direction of institutional development.[40]

Since publication of these benchmark comparative studies, advances in comparative description of manufacturing institutions have not taken on the task of delineating with precision culture's separate, systematic effect in the development of workplace organization.[41] The research team of Gary Hamilton, Nicole Woolsey Biggart, and Marco Orrù has forcefully exhibited distinctive national patterns of organizing the financing of manufacture and the exchange of goods among concerns in Japanese, Taiwanese, and South Korean enterprises.[42] But such recent studies have not resolved the

40. Robert Cole, *Work, Mobility, and Participation: A Comparative Study of American and Japanese Industry* (Berkeley: University of California Press, 1979), Chapter One. A more recent study by Shojiro Ujihara likewise outlines the economic preconditions for the vivification of paternalistic tradition. Shojiro Ujihara, "Essai sur la transformation historique des pratiques d'emploi et des relations professionnelles au Japan," *Sociologie du travail* Volume 33, Number 1 (1991), p. 23. Japanese scholars have also stressed the extraordinary economic conditions in Japan as a cause by itself of the development of a distinctive work ethic. Inagami Takeshi, "The Japanese Will to Work," in Daniel Okimoto and Thomas Rohlen, editors, *Inside the Japanese System* (Stanford: Stanford University Press, 1988), p. 33.

41. For a global survey of cultural findings, however, see Raghu Nath, editor, *Comparative Management: A Regional View* (Cambridge, Massachusetts: Ballinger Publishing Co., 1988). Marc Maurice recently outlined an admirably sophisticated strategy of cross-national comparison. Maurice seeks to identify a national influence upon the construction of work practices but defines this effect primarily in terms of the context of societal institutions for certification and training. Marc Maurice, "Méthode comparative et analyse sociétale: Les Implications théoriques des comparisons internationales," in *Sociologie du travail* Volume 31, Number 2 (1989), p. 184. The preliminary results of his research agenda appear in his *The Social Foundations of Industrial Power* (Cambridge: M.I.T. Press, 1986). A more recent examination of the effect of educational systems on workplace organization, following Maurice's lead, appears in François Eyraud and Frédérique Rychener, "A Societal Analysis of New Technologies," in Peter Grootings, editor, *Technology and Work: East-West Comparison* (London: Croom Helm, 1986), pp. 209–230.

Howard Kimeldorf's comparison of the dock workers' union movements on the East versus the West Coast of the United States is founded on similar work institutions but contrasting economic settings, given the differences in the supply of labor. *Reds or Rackets?* (Berkeley: University of California Press, 1988), p. 39.

42. The authors acknowledge that their selection of countries for comparison is not designed to discount or to isolate the effects of contrasting economic trajectories or of differing industrial specialization upon the crystallization of organizational patterns in each society. Hamilton, Biggart, and Orrù, "Organizational Isomorphism in East Asia," op. cit., p. 365. A. Budde and Geert Hofstede have both measured important national differences in the exercise of authority and in the principles of interpersonal conduct in formal organizations. A. Budde, J. Child, A. Francis, and A. Kieser, "Corporate Goals, Managerial Objectives, and

question that Michel Crozier's brilliant study of French organizational culture, *The Bureaucratic Phenomenon*, brought to light three decades ago: how do we show that differences in culture do not merely reflect economic constraints upon the development of institutions but also shape that development? In France, Crozier emphasized, individuals' preference for avoiding face-to-face authority relations and their reticence about creating solidary peer groups correlated with an emphasis in French bureaucracies on the indirect exercise of highly centralized authority through impersonal rules. Whether the organizational structures adapted to the economic context and then created this distinctive culture of interpersonal interaction, or whether they reflected this culture from the start is a question Crozier never tried to resolve.[43]

CULTURE IN LABOR HISTORY

The key issues that must be resolved to specify the effective role of culture have been debated most sensitively in the fast-developing field of labor history. To illuminate the creation of new institutions of work and the development of workers' collective movements, labor historians have devoted increasing attention to the face of culture among both workers and employers. Yet in the main their strategies of research are not designed to respond adequately to the question addressed by this book: whether we can demonstrate and specify culture's *independent effect* upon the construction of factory practices.

The inextinguishable starting point for pondering culture's effect remains E. P. Thompson's *The Making of the English Working Class*. This work, which once served as a charter for cultural inquiries, demonstrated that workers did not acquire a shared class consciousness in early nineteenth-century Britain only in response to the degradation of labor and the rise of factories; workers also depended upon the peculiar legacy of Radical political discourse, carried originally by middle-class shopkeepers and small tradespeople.[44] In *The Making*, the economy moved with a dynamic of its

---

Organizational Structure in British and West German Companies," *Organization Studies*, Volume 3 (Berlin: W. de Gruyter, 1982), pp. 1–32; Geert Hofstede, *Culture's Consequences: International Differences in Work-Related Values* (Beverly Hills: Sage Publications, 1980).

43. Michel Crozier, *The Bureaucratic Phenomenon* (Chicago: University of Chicago Press, 1964), pp. 220–224. Crozier emphasizes at some points that organizational structures adapt to economic circumstances. The pattern of bureaucracy in the United States, he claims, "corresponds to a large extent to the general evolution of industrial society." See pp. 232, 296.

44. E. P. Thompson, *The Making of the English Working Class* (New York: Vintage Books, 1963), pp. 197–198.

own. It established the foundation of change to which workers responded. Culture—in this instance primarily meaning the legacy of political ideas— intervened to mediate workers' reactions to capitalist development. Thompson's argument rested on circumscription: he showed that new economic conditions, typified by the steam engine and textile mill, did not suffice to explain the emergence of class consciousness. Having limited the domain of economic explanation, he celebrated the mysterious indeterminacy of human "agency," for he believed it sufficient for his purpose that culture serve as an indispensable ingredient in workers' responses.

This approach in *The Making*, even if it served at moments only as a device for framing the narrative, has fallen to an objection in principle: it implicitly assumes that workers have an anterior experience of socioeconomic conditions to which popular culture and political discourse respond. The powerful critiques of Gareth Stedman Jones, Patrick Joyce, and Joan Scott have made it commonplace to emphasize instead that culture and language are constitutive of and, in this sense, prior to social and economic experience.[45] From my perspective, Thompson's initial position offers an ineffective defense of the centrality of culture for a very different reason: it does not respond adequately to social investigators who doubt that culture can be called upon to develop rigorous explanatory arguments. In any sequence of change, the number of causes that are necessary for an outcome considered in all its concreteness is unlimited. The issue is not whether cultural components represent necessary ingredients, for almost everything is worthy of that designation; it is, rather, whether cultural elements have an independent and specifiable contribution apart from the influence of other factors. Do they carry a strong, systematic effect which justifies concentrating on them in their own right? Analysts who discount the prominence Thompson lent to culture may justifiably contend that if he probed economic or demographic variables more deeply, the indeterminacy in workers' responses, which he attributed to community culture, would taper off.

Of course, Thompson's own evidence implies that the economy becomes an historical force only as it enters into human experience. He shows that the earnings of the proud artisans, the prices of tools and bread in the countryside, and even wage differentials in the new mechanical

45. Joan Wallach Scott, *Gender and the Politics of History* (New York: Columbia University Press, 1988); Patrick Joyce, *Visions of the People: Industrial England and the Question of Class 1848–1914* (Cambridge: Cambridge University Press, 1991); Gareth Stedman Jones, *Languages of Class* (Cambridge: Cambridge University Press, 1983).

industries conformed to community expectations and notions of social honor.[46] In this sense, the economy itself operated through cultural standards. But in this line of reasoning, too, culture appears as an ingredient whose independent, structuring influence is undemonstrated. The underlying forces of market and technological development might still carry the exclusive principles configuring social change or the form of stability; after all, the "moral economy" of the community eroded as required for the furtherance of capitalist development.[47] As Thompson tells us, lofty artisanal standards suffered earthly degradation: "The form and extent of deterioration relates directly to the material conditions of the industry—the cost of raw materials—tools—the skill involved—conditions favouring or discouraging trade union organisation—the nature of the market."[48] When custom survived, it might do so only as it was selectively appropriated and shaped as a resource by the active, selective logic of market and technological forces.[49]

46. Thompson, op. cit., pp. 235–237.

47. In my view, Thompson's discerning portrayal of the "moral economy" to which crowds appealed at times of food shortage in the eighteenth century illustrates this possibility of the explanatory adequacy of market adaptation alone. The ideal of a "moral economy" was revived periodically so long as it fulfilled a strategic function: in times of crisis it facilitated price bargaining among the common people, the gentry, traders, and local authorities. At the beginning of the nineteenth century, the confluence of interests supporting the fiction of a moral economy disappeared. E. P. Thompson, "The Moral Economy of the English Crowd in the Eighteenth Century," *Past & Present* Number 50 (February 1971), pp. 126, 129. For a discussion of Thompson's more recent work, see p. 36, below. Food rioters requested in advance official permission to fix prices by riot, an occurrence which makes the riot appear as a controlled and institutionalized bargaining strategy. John G. Rule, "Some Social Aspects of the Cornish Industrial Revolution," in Roger Burt, editor, *Industry and Society in the South-West* (Exeter: University of Exeter, 1970), p. 93.

48. Thompson, *Making*, op. cit., p. 258.

49. Patrick Joyce's exemplary study of the paternalist regimes built upon the full-grown textile mills of the late nineteenth century illustrates the same theoretic issue. Joyce shows that workers in the textile communities of the north of England embraced factory life by identifying with their employers. Workers subscribed to folk stories about the family owners, shared membership in religious organizations with employers, and saw the mill and the collective celebrations it sponsored as the epitome of the community. The traditions of deference, religious association, and local attachment called into play for this accommodation in late Victorian Britain were invigorated and manipulated to suit the needs of capital. Despite the richness of his cultural portrait, Joyce's evidence in *Work, Society and Politics* could support the view that community culture had a coherence of its own while it remained subservient in practice to economic requirements. No wonder Michael Burawoy uses Joyce's evidence to emphasize the subjection of culture to the structure of the labor process. *The Politics of Production* (London: Verso, 1985), pp. 97–99. In his more recent examinations of nineteenth-century British workers' representations of the moral community, Joyce shows that popular concepts are not deducible from the logic of capitalism and do not "reflect" an anterior reality (*Visions*, op. cit., pp. 9, 333). Even if these symbols emerge through a distinctive discursive

More recently, William Reddy has transformed the debate on culture's influence by tracing the development of market orientations themselves as cultural forms. In pathbreaking investigations focused upon French textile production, Reddy has demonstrated that dynamic networks of production and distribution in prerevolutionary France promoted the growth of the industry without a model of free market exchange. Only after the Great Revolution did the ideal of pure market transactions, promulgated initially by intellectual elites, gradually became part of economic agents' self-understanding.[50] The new market model was unrealistic. It ignored overwhelming rigidities in the merchandizing of labor power, and it excluded the human interest in honor and autonomy which could not be extinguished in the production process. Yet the model became an effective prescription. It led employers to oversimplify points of contention with workers into plain monetary exchanges and thereby complicated the resolution of labor conflicts.[51] Reddy's *The Rise of Market Culture* is profoundly subversive: rather than treating culture exclusively as a "tradition" separate from and opposed to the market, it turns the market regime itself into a cultural project.

The present study maintains Reddy's emphasis on the cultural construction of economic categories but fully historicizes these forms of practice and experience. In Reddy's narrative, at moments of crisis employers are forced to adopt the postulates of "market culture" to improve production. For example, to cope with mounting commercial challenges in the first half of the nineteenth century, they imagined that they appropriated, not simply a worker's output, but a labor service over which they claimed jurisdiction. When they imposed more exacting rate schedules on mule spinners to gauge labor effort, the design was allegedly determined simply by a need to exploit improved machinery.[52] Reddy inadvertently offers a new cultural teleology: employers acquire market categories through a learning process, but in the end there is only one kind of market culture, and one definition of labor as a commodity, which they are destined to adopt.[53] He collapses

---

lineage and draw upon themes unrelated to the economic categories of capitalism, they may nonetheless be selected, maintained, and indirectly appropriated by the supposedly "instrumental" logic of the marketplace.

50. William Reddy, *The Rise of Market Culture* (Cambridge: Cambridge University Press, 1984), pp. 66–67. Reddy also stresses, however, that commercial change in the eighteenth century stimulated the development of the cultural model of market society (p. 61).

51. Ibid., p. 324.

52. Ibid., pp. 124, 213, 215.

53. Ibid., p. 251; "Here, finally, a step was made toward paying for labor, rather than for its outcome" (p. 124). But, after all, the book does not bear the title "The Rise of *a* Market Culture." Reddy misleadingly portrays Adam Smith as a theorist whose premises about work-

market categories as real forms of experience and as schemata for the use of technology into the generic analytic model of "market society." As an issue of history, this effaces actual cross-national diversity in Europe; as a matter of theory, it reduces the explanatory power of culture. If we rest a cultural argument on the metathesis that the most general building blocks of market-industrial society, such as cost-accounting and the maximization of returns on investment, are cultural creations,[54] this does not enable us to explain variation in realized capitalist practice.

The deciding question is not whether market conduct is culturally acquired and reproduced; the purest economic theorist is justified in ignoring this issue as a philosophical point about the origins of the "capitalist" system or its broadest parameters. The true issue of contention is whether cultural forms of explanation account for variation in historical outcomes on the shop floor better than alternative approaches do. In Reddy's narrative, "market culture" germinates as an intellectual project but disseminates out of practical necessity.[55] From this viewpoint it is all too easy to rest the case for culture's importance upon the comfortable supposition that the most general parameters of conduct are culturally fixed, allowing historical narratives to present as adaptations to economic requirements the specific design of the institutions of work. The comparative strategy of the present study, by contrast, does not merely assert but demonstrates exactly how the cultural construction of economic concepts configured even inconspicuous parts of instrumental practice by symbolic principles that varied in this study's primary cases of Germany and Britain, as well as in Reddy's case, France.[56]

Where, then, may we turn for the theoretical tools to handle such a case demonstration of culture's formative logic upon practice in the factory? In my view, the specification of culture's independent role in the capitalist labor process remains an open problem in contemporary social theory. The most promising theories on the scene that accept the challenge of demonstrating culture's effect, rather than (unconvincingly) taking its influence as an a priori necessity, conceive of culture as a practical schema for organizing

---

ers' conveyance of labor to employers are prototypical and universal to market models (pp. 65, 85).

54. Ibid., p. 70.

55. See above, footnote 53, as well as ibid., p. 99.

56. Rather than contrasting "market culture" with the pursuit of nonmonetary rewards or with less calculative varieties of economic enterprise prior to the rise of market culture, the present study contrasts different incarnations of the fundamental capitalist category of labor as a commodity.

activity.[57] Within this general approach it may be helpful to group into three families the leading attempts to specify the influence of culture upon economic conduct. If we examine each in turn, we may clarify the conditions that must be met to demonstrate satisfactorily the independent, constitutive influence of culture upon the organization of practices at the point of production in capitalist society. Culture's influence is contested in social inquiry in part because the leading cultural theorists have not appreciated the challenge before them.

THE AMBIGUITY OF PRACTICE THEORY

There is, first, the school of analysis that I will call, for lack of a more widely employed term, *cultural practice theory*, in whose development Pierre Bourdieu has played a celebrated role. Although Bourdieu has scarcely applied his approach to the analysis of the capitalist factory, he has established a baseline for discussion of the symbolic and material dimensions of economic conduct. It is therefore incumbent upon me to suggest why his approach does not address the guiding question of this book—and why, perhaps, it should.

Bourdieu's work is intended to overcome the contest between cultural and purely utilitarian accounts of the development of social institutions which divides contemporary theory. The utilitarian approach, consecrated anew in the currently fashionable theories of "rational choice," would explain the visible social order as the outcome of the well-considered activity of individuals pursuing their interests as best they can.[58] Of course, supporters of cultural approaches have long accepted the viewpoint that people conduct themselves as strategizing agents. But adherents of cultural forms of explanation insist that the process by which agents pursue their interests must be situated within a broader perspective upon the operation of human agency and reason. Before people set out in pursuit of their interests, they require an order of cultural symbols that establishes for them a relation to the world. The concepts on which agents rely to accomplish this are an historical product whose constitution and development follow a discipline of their own. Cultural forms of explanation need not exclude the play of

57. Ann Swidler summarizes the reasons for the shift to practice-centered cultural theory in "Culture in Action: Symbols and Strategies," in *American Sociological Review* Volume 51, No. 2 (April 1986), pp. 273–286.

58. By way of illustration, see James S. Coleman, *Foundations of Social Theory* (Cambridge, Massachusetts: Harvard University Press, 1990).

utilitarian calculation, but they are inclined to emphasize that collective concepts give shape to individuals' percepts.

Thus is initiated the cycle of debate between cultural and utilitarian varieties of social explanation. For just as culture can inaugurate the terms for the exercise of instrumental reason, so instrumental reason can establish the conditions for the development of culture. The rational choice theorist may admit that the horizon for agents' conduct is momentarily fixed for them by collective traditions. The question then becomes, what are the forces that lend such a system of shared insights and concepts its distinctive shape? Its formations, too, may follow from simple strategic logic, and its defining features may represent a convenient adaptation to the circumstances of action.[59]

Bourdieu tries to overturn several of the distinctions on which this debate between cultural and purely utilitarian modes of explanation has been founded. Like rational choice theorists, he underscores the agents' unceasing manipulation of their symbolic and material environments. But he contends that agents' strategies are not purely means chosen for the pursuit of interests. The strategies are patterned by implicit principles governing perception and action that are transmitted to the agents by their prior life circumstances in society. The long-term acquisition of these skills enables the agents to compete against others, but in so doing the agents do not rationally follow preestablished interests. They are guided by implicit know-how, and they find themselves dedicated to the very practices through which the competition takes place.[60]

---

59. This is the vision of hard-headed anthropologists such as Marvin Harris, *Cultural Materialism: The Struggle for a Science of Culture* (New York: Vintage Books, 1980), pp. 56–58. The wide variety of ecological explanations are explored in John G. Kennedy and Robert Edgerton, editors, *Culture and Ecology: Eclectic Perspectives* (Washington, D.C.: American Anthropological Association, 1982). Political scientists, ever the philosophers of cynical reason, have also treated culture as a byproduct from the rational pursuit of self-advantage. They have emphasized that political entrepreneurs may manipulate forms of cultural identity in order to create and sustain political alliances between disparate groups. Their stress upon the malleability of culture in the pursuit of self-interest results in a less naturalistic appreciation of culture than that of reductionist anthropologists such as Harris. These political scientists do not treat culture as if it were an adaptation to the physical environment or to the true state of things-as-they-are, but their moral for human society remains the same: culture represents a dependent tool of utilitarian practice. See, illustratively, Abner Cohen, "Symbolic Strategies in Group Organisation," in his *Two-Dimensional Man* (Berkeley: University of California Press, 1974). For a survey of the application of rational choice theory to the formation of political identities, see David D. Laitin, *Hegemony and Culture* (Chicago: University of Chicago Press, 1986), pp. 99–102.

60. Pierre Bourdieu, *The Logic of Practice* (Cambridge: Polity Press, 1990), p. 290.

Bourdieu's insistence that agents organize manufacturing and other kinds of practices in accordance with acquired schemata seems congenial to cultural forms of explanation. But he also suggests that these acquired schemata are "durably inculcated by objective conditions."[61] The agents' accumulated know-how "organizes perception of the world and action in the world in accordance with the objective structures of a given state of the world."[62] What room, then, does Bourdieu leave for the symbolic mediation of social conditions as agents acquire their social skills? Bourdieu adds a proviso that the agents' dispositions do not mechanically mirror social structures. Rather, the agents' prior locations in the social structure decide how they will appropriate and respond to structural conditions of the moment.[63] The historical filtering of "objective" structures does not offer a positive theory for culture's systematic influence. What is more, since Bourdieu views culture as a creation of practice, he insists that it has only partial coherence as a system of meaning. To his mind, cultural principles exist only in the process of getting things done. Their operation appears fuzzy and inarticulable in the light of contemplative reason. Bourdieu's emphasis on culture's inextricability from the ongoing life of practice enjoins us against representing culture as an intellectually coherent structure with a systematic effect of its own.[64]

Yet Bourdieu's refusal to define culture's own structural effects leads him in his histories to embrace economistic explanations that he denies in his theories. In *Distinction*, his wide-ranging investigation of contemporary tastes in France, Bourdieu takes care to show that the dispositions of persons in the working class appear to follow a popular logic of their own but actually reflect the force of economic necessity. He claims, for instance, that "it is possible to deduce popular tastes for the foods that are simultaneously the most 'filling' and most economical from the necessity of reproducing labor power at the lowest cost which is forced on the pro-

61. Pierre Bourdieu, *Outline of a Theory of Practice* (Cambridge: Cambridge University Press, 1977), p. 77.

62. *Logic*, p. 94. Likewise, see Pierre Bourdieu, "Scientific Field and Scientific Thought," in Comparative Study of Social Transformations Working Paper Number 32, University of Michigan, November, 1989, p. 92.

63. Pierre Bourdieu and Loïc Wacquant, *An Invitation to Reflexive Sociology* (Chicago: University of Chicago Press, 1992), pp. 135–136.

64. Bourdieu, *Logic*, pp. 90–91, 261–262. Neil J. Smelser discusses the implications of practice theory for the investigation of cultural systematicity in "Culture: Coherent or Incoherent," in Richard Münch and Neil J. Smelser, editors, *Theory of Culture* (Berkeley: University of California Press, 1992), p. 16.

letariat as its very definition."[65] Such shifts to reductionist forms of explanation are probably unavoidable if Bourdieu wants to account for— rather than merely redescribe—social practices in contemporary societies. In his model, only economic or institutional circumstances (or the agents' transversal of such circumstances over time) offer a specifiable foundation for explanation. Culture is a marker, often misrecognized, of the true arrangement of things. It serves as a model *of* society, not as a model *for* society's creation.[66]

In sum, Bourdieu's work grants culture a prominent but analytically dependent role. To be sure, in *Distinction* Bourdieu makes the survival of the capitalist system dependent upon culture's ability to mystify and legitimate inequality. But if culture serves as a conduit for the expression of economic power, it does not thereby gain independent influence upon the development of institutions or upon historic change.[67] To address the question of whether culture donates a separate constitutive logic to the formation of institutions, we may still preserve one of Bourdieu's insights: namely, culture can be conceived provisionally as the schema that agents employ to orchestrate their instrumental strategies, rather than as a set of revered values.[68] If the principles of a culture are thereby conditioned by the

65. Pierre Bourdieu, *Distinction: A Social Critique of the Judgment of Taste* (Cambridge, Massachusetts: Harvard University Press, 1984), p. 177. Likewise, the culinary styles of other class strata develop from the commercial value of the food preparers' time and from the ethic of deferred or immediate gratification that is instilled by their occupational position.

66. "On Symbolic Power" in his *Language and Symbolic Power*, edited by John Thompson (Cambridge: Polity Press, 1991), p. 169. *Logic*, p. 94; *Outline*, p. 77.

67. In *Distinction*, Bourdieu's exclusive attention to France for illustrations of contemporary capitalist society is integral to his explanatory strategy: it sustains his maneuver of reducing the specificities of French cultural life to a revelation of the generic logic of mature capitalism. He can thus avoid pondering the character of the fit between French culture and the economy, of why certain symbolic goods and practices prevail in France, whereas different ones arise in countries with analytically similar economies. Bourdieu's cross-societal comparisons are limited to gross contrasts between traditional and modern social formations, which protects the implicit reduction of culture to social structure.

68. What other research falls into the subdivision of cultural practice theory? Certainly Ann Swidler's presentation of a new research agenda in her incisive essay "Culture in Action." Swidler grants culture "an independent causal role" because it shapes agents' competencies at assembling enduring strategies of action. Unlike Bourdieu, Swidler does not insist that culture corresponds to the objective institutional environment. But neither does she demonstrate that different cultural complexes can survive in similar structural settings. To the contrary, she emphasizes that institutions distribute resources to decide which cultural ideas will be sustained in the body social. What is more, her definition of culture as a set of skills separates the effectivity of culture from the conventions of an autonomous system of signs. In her view, the capacities that comprise culture are learned rules of purposive action. As for Bourdieu, so for Swidler it is not essential to focus on the mediation of the environment by a set of symbols: the cultural competencies may represent a common-sensical correlate to the surroundings, as

ongoing logic of practice, we can still employ a comparison to search for the means by which culture partially shapes practice into a consistently meaningful structure. If a degree of cultural coherence obtains, it must be identified initially by comparing practices themselves—in our case, everyday solutions to similar manufacturing challenges—rather than by comparing discourse about practice.

TAXONOMIES OF PRODUCTION

A second family of theory that attempts to integrate the meaningful and pragmatic dimensions of economic life while preserving the causal autonomy of culture is that of cultural structuralism. The proponents of this approach share an emphasis on culture as a set of signs whose meanings are fixed only differentially, that is, by their relations to all other signs in a hypothesized system. Starting with the premise that meaning inheres in a coherent, overarching structure of signs, these practitioners tend for the sake of analysis to abstract culture from its contextual uses and to think of it as a formal, systematically interrelated series of terms. Marshall Sahlins is among the distinguished investigators who have applied this specification of culture to the analysis of economic institutions.[69]

In Sahlins's *Culture and Practical Reason*, culture appears to intervene in the same mode in capitalist as in kinship-based social orders: out of an inchoate environment it creates for agents a meaningful order. Only the content of the cultural forms and the site for the invention of the integrative forms of culture—commercial production versus kinship—appear to vary between these social orders.[70] Yet in practice, Sahlins does not faithfully

---

is demonstrated in Swidler's exposition of the culture of poverty. For these reasons, her framework makes it difficult to isolate the independent influence of a symbolic schema upon instrumental conduct (p. 275). Sherry Ortner's initial formulation of practice theory also emphasized this approach's relative disinterest in isolating culture as an analytically separable domain of social life. Sherry B. Ortner, "Theory in Anthropology Since the Sixties," *Comparative Studies in Society and History* Volume 26, Number 1 (January 1984), p. 148. Her recent work, however, returns to the issue of culture's own identifiable influence upon action. See "Patterns of History: Cultural Schemas in the Foundings of Sherpa Religious Institutions," in Emiko Ohnuki-Tierney, editor, *Culture Through Time: Anthropological Approaches* (Stanford: Stanford University Press, 1990).

69. Mary Douglas is also a member of this family of investigators, although her extensive publications reveal important differences from Sahlins. Douglas emphasizes that the classificatory principles that make up a culture reflect social morphology, but she lends culture a measure of autonomy by insisting that diverse symbolic schemata suit the same social structure. *Implicit Meanings* (London: Routledge & Kegan Paul, 1975), p. 314.

70. "The uniqueness of bourgeois society consists not in the fact that the economic system escapes symbolic determination, but that the economic symbolism is structurally determin-

apply his theory to capitalist manufacture. The deviation becomes apparent if we compare his dissection of economies integrated by kinship with those held together by the cash nexus. In traditional Moalan civilization in Fiji, Sahlins shows, the production process itself incarnates an overarching cultural scheme founded on a series of isomorphic, binary distinctions: land/sea, inside/outside, female/male. For instance, men busy themselves in the extremities of the high seas and the distant bush, whereas women work in the interior lagoon and within the village. By the same scheme, villages where the people are designated as belonging to a "land" group do not angle even when they have access to fishing grounds. These binary distinctions governing production are reiterated in the codes of governance, domestic furnishings, and myth.[71]

The logic by which Sahlins demonstrates the economy's dependence upon a symbolic order changes, however, when he turns to "market-industrial society." Here he applies the interrelated distinctions of his formal schemata only to items of consumption such as food and clothing. No application of Saussurean principle emerges for the living execution of production itself. The focus now is on the operation of culture at a remove, as the agents' application of a cultural code identifies for them the kinds of goods worth manufacturing.[72] We observe a cultural structure *for* the production process, not *in* it. In Sahlins's portrayal of the kinship-based society, the divisions of the symbolic order constitute, not just perceptions of production or of goods, nor merely the distribution of particular agents among economic roles, but—the very methods and organization of the production process. What generates this shift in the way Sahlins attempts to demonstrate culture's effect? Is it attributable merely to the misapplication of an adequate theory? Or is capitalist production resistant in principle to this variety of cultural analysis?

ing." Marshall Sahlins, *Culture and Practical Reason* (Chicago: University of Chicago Press, 1976), p. 211.

71. Ibid., pp. 38–41.

72. The conceit that Western society alone is constructed pragmatically arises from ignorance of the symbolic determination of the concrete *ends* of production: "Because it appears to the producer as a quest for pecuniary gain, and to the consumer as the acquisition of 'useful' goods, the basic symbolic character of the process goes on entirely behind the backs of the participants—and usually of economists as well, insofar as the meaningful structure of demand is an exogenous 'given' of their analyses. The differentiation of symbolic value is mystified as the appropriation of exchange-value." At this moment of theoretic synthesis, the symbolic determination of the instrumentalities of production, given a cultural selection of the goods worth producing, recedes from Sahlins's view. Ibid., p. 213.

For one question immediately arises: once capitalist manufacture takes account of the cultural valuation of goods, may it follow an unmediated economic logic in their production? In his more recent studies of Polynesians' contact with Europeans, Sahlins emphasizes that the chiefs' demand for finery by which they could denote their *mana* obviously helped articulate the Polynesian and European economic systems. The demand for particular European goods and therefore their prices were set by native conceptions of *mana*.[73] Yet this acknowledgment of culture's presence does not maintain its explanatory significance. It is theoretically deficient for social investigators who underscore the importance of culture to contend only that culture comprises a necessary ingredient in reconstructing a concrete historical situation.[74] As we know, in the recreation of a sequence of change the number of components whose presence is indispensable for the outcome is inexhaustible if one attempts to appreciate events in all their concreteness. Culture may still operate as a necessary element in a course of change whose fundamental, underlying logic is that of a pristine "capitalist mode of production."

If we oversimplify the task of dissecting the independent contribution of culture to capitalist practice, we subvert the enterprise by making its accomplishment trivial. Even if an investigator must refer to the categorical distinctions of a culture in order to explain agents' conduct, this set of distinctions may change principally in response to the active, directing logic of market and technological pressures. It is not enough to contend that the distinctions themselves can neither register directly nor reflect the bare material logic of economic circumstance. For the forces driving—and necessitating—the redefinition and realignment of cultural categories may still be those of economic imperatives, however much the culture registers the

73. *Islands of History* (Chicago: University of Chicago Press, 1985), pp. 155–156. "To the extent, then, of the Hawaiian market, the European mode of production and trade in the 1820s was organized by the Polynesian conception of *mana*." *Historical Metaphors and Mythical Realities* (Ann Arbor: University of Michigan Press, 1981), p. 31.

Sahlins's shift from culture at the site of production in kin-based societies to culture in the sphere of exchange in capitalist societies is typical of interpretive analysis. In parallel fashion, Mark Gottdiener has asked whether "ideological mechanisms exist at the foundation of capitalist processes or if they are produced only secondarily by the relations of production to promote accumulation." Gottdiener intends to show how ideology constitutes capitalism and does not simply grow out of it. But he focuses only on consumption, the circulation of capital, and the reproduction of labor power outside work—not upon the site of manufacture itself. "Ökonomie, Ideologie und Semiotik," in *Zeitschrift für Semiotik* Volume 10, Numbers 1–2 (1988), pp. 21–23.

74. Sahlins is not the first to locate the effect of culture in the outputs for consumption. See Mary Douglas, *The World of Goods* (New York: Basic Books, 1979).

changes after the fact in modified terms. Few social theorists care to assert that culture has no influence whatsoever upon the concrete events of history. Just as the cultural theorist may accept the actuality (though not the unmediated presence) of material constraint and instrumental adaptation in history, so the rational choice theorist may acknowledge that the cognition of the maximizing agent depends in part upon the orienting assumptions of a culture. Although Sahlins's solution is inadequate for the capitalist production process, he has correctly posed the challenge: the issue is not whether culture represents a social force but whether it bears a constitutive and identifiable logic of its own.[75]

So long as culture is separated from the construction of capitalist manufacture, it surfaces as a decorative frill on the fabric of capitalist development. For if the categorical distinctions of a culture are employed merely to distinguish worthy goods or to *assess* the course of events, culture recedes to the sphere of contemplation. Ought we to suppose that the techniques of machino-facture in the capitalist factory are subordinated to an elegant system of conceptual correspondences such as guides the ritualized procedures of the Moalan economy? The thinking subject under capitalism may impose and reimpose such a comprehensive order upon the free and expressive realm of consumption—and in theory could even draw upon a prior experience of production to do so. But the practitioners of cultural structuralism have not yet shown in a particular setting how the ever-changing, efficiency-driven practices of the capitalist workplace itself correspond to an overarching taxonomy of reiterated classifications. The obstacles to doing so are ones of principle.

In capitalist societies integrated by the mechanisms of commodity exchange, the agents in the labor process have no need to ensure that the categories employed to execute work and to organize social relations at the point of production are aligned with those in other institutional domains. Nor does such a requirement arise at the level of the collectivity. If, as in Moalan society, the institutions of agriculture and manufacture can be contemplated as the fulfillment of a global cultural design, not unlike an intentionally created piece of art, then one can both conceive of culture as a constellation of interrelated categories and see it as constitutive of production. In this setting the process of executing practice also calls that globally integrated culture into everyday experience. But this felicitous application of structuralist theory results from its coincidental

---

75. Culture and Practical Reason, p. 14.

fit with the operation of kinship-based societies. Social reproduction in kinship-based societies depends upon an integrative, overarching cultural schema: or, more exactly, the isomorphism of symbolic relations is a concomitant of the reproduction of institutions that are all centered on kinship relations.[76]

In a society integrated by market relations, by contrast, organizations fulfilling diverse tasks will articulate with one another not by taxonomic design but by commercial function. It causes no surprise, then, that on the single occasion when Sahlins refers to the intervention of culture into the capitalist labor process, he offers only a dissipated form of his characteristic argument: the general economic conditions under which production will proceed always leave meaningful particularities of the manufacturing process unspecified. "An industrial technology in itself," Sahlins contends, "does not dictate whether it will be run by men or women, in the day or at night, by wage laborers or by collective owners, on Tuesday or Sunday, for a profit or for a livelihood."[77] These specificities make of production a realized human endeavor. At this moment, culture illuminates the residual: whatever objective constraints, rational choice, or conventional economic logic leaves undetermined. A system of binary distinctions no longer constitutes the basic form of practice.[78] Advocates of utilitarian explanation could justifiably claim that Sahlins's exposition at this juncture sets up an artificial contrast between the generic and the particular: who would suppose that all the details of production could be explained by introducing only the most basic of economic constraints? By this contrary line of reasoning, the persistence of a residuum is only to be expected, for the conditions for responding to the environment, the appropriation of cultural categories for utilitarian purpose, and the opportunities for profitable adaptation have not been filled in with sufficient detail. Even accepting that inexplicable details are always left

76. Ibid., pp. 39, 41. Similarly, it is no accident that Bourdieu undertakes a study of the schemata used in the production process only for "archaic" societies. For capitalist society, he, like Sahlins, shifts the study of categorical oppositions to the domain of consumption (in *Distinction*) or of personal outlooks upon practice (in Pierre Bourdieu and M. de Saint Martin, "Le Patronat," *Actes de la recherche en sciences sociales* Number 20–21 [March-April 1978]), but abandons analysis of the form of concrete manufacturing procedures themselves. Cf. *Logic*, op. cit., pp. 214–217; "Le Patronat," e.g., p. 56.

77. *Culture and Practical Reason*, p. 208.

78. By Sahlins's own reasoning, the relations between oppositions must be outlined to identify culture in the first place. "It is not that, as some have believed, we have a 'need' to classify. Formal classification is an intrinsic condition of symbolic action." *Islands of History*, op. cit., p. 146.

over, however, small ground remains for attributing to culture the consistent and identifiable effect of a structure or of making it the guiding object of study. For the residuum is precisely that—a haphazard deposit, rather than an ordered constellation.

Cultural structuralism cannot be moved from its original home in kinbased society to the capitalist labor process. If culture is conceived as a global system of categorical distinctions, it cannot order and organize the capitalist labor-process from within. To be sure, interrelated sets of categorical oppositions can be discovered in the agents' outlooks, which in turn influence the way agents *interpret* the operation of the production system. But can we take this as a starting point for the ultimate destination, that is, for elucidating culture's systematic constitution of material practices at the point of production?

The masterful work of Paul Willis inadvertently exposes this path as a blind alley. In his classic study *Learning to Labor*, Willis discovers the classificatory distinctions that organize young working-class men's perception of jobs in Britain. These workers seek their place in the world of labor through a series of parallel cognitive oppositions: manual versus mental exertion; free versus conformist activity; productive versus impotent work; and masculine versus feminine actions.[79] The lads see manual labor as a realm of independence, since it leaves their thoughts unsubordinated, and they esteem it as a demonstration of their manliness. Willis concludes that the culture acquired by the boys in rebellion against the intellectual rigors of school also generates their tragic commitment to a life of toil. If culture thereby serves as a conduit for the reproduction of practices in the capitalist workplace, it does not structure them by its own logic. According to Willis, the commemoration of physical exertion infuses production with an imported meaning that is, in his words, "no part of its intrinsic nature." Willis's emphasis on culture as a superimposition allows him to see it as a distinct component of social reality. It also limits culture's effectivity. The lads' indifference to the particular manual occupation they find and their assumption that work itself is meaningless apart from the detached attitude they adopt in its execution adapt them to any given work environment. Culture is identified merely with the subjective response and adaptation to already given institutions of work.[80]

---

79. Willis calls these parallel oppositions "sets of divisions." *Learning to Labor* (New York: Columbia University Press, 1977), p. 171.

80. Quotation from ibid., p. 150. Willis's positioning of culture resulted from theoretic choice rather than from the thematic commitment of an opus that bridges school and factory.

If the general approach of cultural structuralism fails to demonstrate the cultural constitution of practice at the site of capitalist manufacture, it nonetheless offers important resources for this task. In contrast to the practice theorists, the cultural structuralists do not center their theory upon the confrontation between a singular agent and structural conditions, but upon the invention and use of a cultural schema as an accomplishment of a collectivity. By making the creation of meaning dependent upon the conventionally understood distinctions that stand above the immediate context for action, the cultural structuralists block the reduction of culture to social structure. Yet in their hands this very separation isolates culture and thereby makes it difficult to identify its formative effect. The challenge remains of reattaching culture to the living execution of work while preserving its autonomy. The present study is not engineered to show how diverse concepts articulate and form a kind of architecture in the agents' minds; rather, it is designed to show through comparison that a single concept, that of labor as a commodity, was consistently incarnated in a field of practice.

PRACTICE AND SUBJECTIVE MEANING

In classic sociological theory the paradigmatic demonstration of culture's impact on production is Max Weber's *The Protestant Ethic and the Spirit of Capitalism*. This work founded a third major family of cultural studies of economic practice, one centered upon individuals' understandings of the meaning of their social action. When the cultural structuralists made good on their promise to bridge culture and the shape of institutions in kinship-based societies, they did so by investigating the cultural template embodied

---

This is demonstrated in his essay devoted solely to the site of production, *Human Experience and Material Production: The Culture of the Shop Floor* (Birmingham: Centre for Contemporary Cultural Studies, 1975), pp. 1–3. Here, too, Willis associates culture with the "experiential conditions" of manufacture rather than with the structuring of practice. In the abstract, of course, culture always plays a "role in maintaining the conditions for continued material production in the capitalist mode"—for it sustains the living capacity to work (*Learning to Labor*, p. 171). The parallel distinctions of working-class culture—such as manual/mental, productive/impotent—are not deducible from the logic of capitalism, but they may be used and held in place by that logic all the same. If culture serves as capitalism's transmission belt, even imperfectly, it becomes an ancillary component, not an independent principle in its constitution. Of course one can maintain a hope for radical social transformation by romanticizing the uncertainty of cultural reproduction and by recalling at the last moment its reliance on the human element, as Willis does. But should the capitalist structures fail to reproduce, this may be attributable to their own disarticulation—or even to indeterminacy—rather than to the order of culture by default. Contrast with *Learning to Labor*, pp. 171–172, 176.

in the very form of those institutions. By contrast, Weber sometimes emphasized the disjuncture between culture and organizational forms.

When Weber traced the influence of ascetic Protestantism upon the early development of the Western variety of capitalism, he emphasized that the understanding of the world's significance that Protestant doctrine lent its adherents was subjective, in the sense that agents located in business ventures with the same organizational structure could be motivated by decisively different outlooks about the final import of their actions. This premise guides Weber's comparisons. For example, after Weber examined the enterprises that evolved in Renaissance Italy, he concluded that ascetic Protestantism was not a necessary precondition for the development of "capitalist *forms* of business organization."[81] Prior to the Reformation, entrepreneurs in Italy established the same capitalist business associations and procedures as their dour successors to the north. Therefore the advent of stern Protestantism could not have been necessary for changes in commercial organization. Neither was it sufficient. The rise of this-worldly asceticism may have given its adherents a novel appreciation of the ultimate significance of their actions, but it did not as a matter of course lead them to build new institutional structures. In Weber's depiction, entrepreneurs who ran the putting-out system for the weaving trade and whose conduct was motivated by the Calvinist world view did not have to reshape the organization of their enterprises. They reduced turnover time and introduced a more dynamic pace to the putting-out networks, yet they might well leave the forms of that system intact.[82] Therefore Weber's own evidence identifies a difficulty: an individual's interior assessment of the personally most significant implication of economic practices does not specify with precision how those practices should be outwardly organized. To distinguish the causal influence of culture upon the form of the collective practices of production, it is simpler and more effective to consider the publicly discernible principles immediately organizing their execution.

No wonder theorists who seek to specify and illustrate culture's contribution to social organization have turned away from Weber's concentration on subjective meaning and the agents' evaluation of the ultimate significance of their own existence. As we have seen, theorists have converged

---

81. Max Weber, "Kritische Bemerkungen zu den vorstehenden 'Kritischen Beiträgen,'" in his *Die protestantische Ethik II*, edited by Johannes Winckelmann (Gütersloh: Gerd Mohn, 1982), p. 28.

82. *The Protestant Ethic and the Spirit of Capitalism* (New York: Charles Scribner's Sons, 1958), p. 67.

from different directions onto a conception of culture as the useful set of categories and distinctions on which people rely to organize instrumental practice. Jürgen Habermas has attempted to combine this appreciation of culture with Weber's original concern for analyzing forms of social action and social order in terms of the fundamental types of subjective orientations adopted by the agents. Habermas's imposing philosophy provides a touchstone for metatheoretical reflections upon the relation between culture and capitalist production. Can it provide the tools not just for conceiving but for convincingly isolating culture's historical effects?

In *The Theory of Communicative Action* Habermas uses the term *culture* to indicate "the stock of knowledge from which participants in communication supply themselves with interpretations as they come to an understanding about something in the world."[83] His choice of metaphor—here, culture as a reserve—is precisely motivated. In his view, agents rely upon culture as an inexhaustible and inescapable store of background assumptions that allow them to familiarize themselves with the world. From this starting point, Habermas assigns culture a more powerful inaugurative force than the representatives of practice theory and structuralist theory grant it. He does not think of culture as the set of schemata people employ to order both their conduct and the elements of the world. Rather, culture comprises the surrounding environment of implicit, undissectable assumptions that allow people to employ such schemata.[84]

From Habermas's perspective, instrumental action in the workplace is just as embedded in this indiscernible knowledge as is ritual action at a place of worship.[85] Since he identifies culture with the linguistic resources that erect a stage for action, rather than with the principles that the agents follow in executing their action, Habermas avoids the challenge of specifying the contributions of culture to variation in the relations of production. The influence of culture becomes problematic when he emphasizes that the

---

83. *The Theory of Communicative Action* (Boston: Beacon Press, 1987), Volume Two, p. 138.

84. "Language and culture neither coincide with the formal world concepts by means of which participants in communication together define their situations, nor do they appear as something innerworldly. Language and culture are constitutive for the lifeworld itself." Ibid., pp. 124–125.

85. Culture plays an equally formative role whether the agents are engaging in purposive-rational action—based on the pursuit of specified goals by the most economic and efficient means—or communicative action, which seeks mutual agreement about binding norms. *Theory and Practice* (Boston: Beacon Press, 1974), pp. 158–159. Habermas's most recent formulations respond to the criticism that he separates symbolic communication from work. Cf. John Keane, "Work and Interaction in Habermas," *Arena* Number 38 (1975), p. 65.

mechanisms of the market and of bureaucratic administration have replaced communicative action as the integrative principle of society. The symbols people use in their lifeworlds are subordinated to the functional requisites of the marketplace or to other mechanisms for the impersonal exercise of power. In this instance, cultural resources are constitutive of the lifeworld only in the sense that they represent prerequisites on the level of metatheory for the construction of social institutions; they no longer subject the particular shape assumed by those institutions to a determinant cultural logic.

The disadvantage of Habermas's approach for our purpose is that it defines the role of culture in the organization of production by philosophical decree. It does not contest the predictive power of so-called rational choice theory. It disputes only the conceit that this theory truthfully stipulates the foundations for the agents' execution of their strategies. Surely we must seek a framework that does not simply postulate an overarching cultural dimension for all forms of practice, as Habermas's does, but provides the tools for demonstrating culture's effect. Otherwise we will not be able to battle alternative explanations for institutional practices. Unless allegiance to a theoretical agenda can be debated and disputed in the light of research, the theories with the most commonsense resonance will command the field in much of social research. In this instance, rational choice theory, which suits the ruling power of commerce, will surely become the accepted coin of the realm.[86]

Is it a mistake to let the abstract issues established by theoretical debate shape our own agenda for historical research? E. P. Thompson has suggested that it may be wiser to abandon attempts to make an analytic distinction between practices shaped purely by utilitarian economic strategies and those guided by culture.[87] Thompson's final research into the operation of eighteenth-century law and moral economy in Britain points to the indissoluble concrescence of cultural practices and economic logic.[88] After all, the categories of "the cultural" and "the economic" are imposed by the investigator, not inscribed in the nature of things. Why not acknowledge the palpable merging of their operation and carry on with the investigation of the

86. Habermas does not see his role as that of providing a research agenda that will compete with established programs of theory. Op. cit., p. 375.

87. E. P. Thompson, *The Poverty of Theory and Other Essays* (New York: Monthly Review Press, 1978), pp. 292–295.

88. E. P. Thompson, *Whigs and Hunters: The Origin of the Black Act* (New York: Pantheon Books, 1975), pp. 261 ff.

concrete conditions under which the institutions of manufacture and trade developed?

This solution is deficient because, rather than transforming the field of theoretic debate, it quits the arena altogether. The grand thinkers who champion the self-sufficiency of economic reasoning will always proceed to formulate models founded on the pristine "laws" of necessity within a given mode of production or on individuals' elemental pursuit of self-advantage. These theorists need not assert that culture is absent or irrelevant—only that their hypothetical model captures those fundamental processes about which we can feasibly generalize. Historical investigators who in response draw a series of vignettes showing the intervention of culture cannot dislodge competing heuristic economic models. The historians' scenarios may identify the limitations of a deliberately simplified representation, but they do not displace it. No theory is abandoned in the face of limited discrepancies. No contest can develop as a two-sided struggle between a theory and the facts, only as a many-sided comparison between the evidence and rival *theories*.[89] If the champions of cultural study wish to engage in debate about the causal intervention of culture, they must support culture as a separate analytic category and specify its structure and effects. Otherwise culture becomes a vague residual category—exemplified in Sahlins's localized retreat from a taxonomy for capitalist culture in the labor process—or, alternatively, culture becomes an undissectable background condition whose influence is pervasive in principle but undemonstrable in detail.[90]

The clash between cultural and purely utilitarian forms of social explanation amounts to much more than adjudicating between academic hypotheses. It determines our understanding of how we make ourselves in history. If the cultural order is dismissed as a mere reflection of individuals' utilitarian adaptations to the environment, it is no longer a fateful realm of human contingency—and those who wish to understand and ultimately contribute to the project of our collective self-creation will have to look elsewhere. The comparative logic of this study shows that culture exercised an influence *of its own* but not completely *by itself*. The

89. Of course this is the lesson of Imre Lakatos, "Falsification and the Methodology of Scientific Research Programmes," in Imre Lakatos and Alan Musgrave, editors, *Criticism and the Growth of Knowledge* (Cambridge: Cambridge University Press, 1970), p. 119.

90. The culture/economy divide, haughtily dismissed by some, will have been transcended, if this is possible, only when parsimonious models that go beyond this opposition outdo their rivals in explaining, and not just commenting upon, a range of practical outcomes. All else is merely a play of words.

power of culture arose from its inscription in material practice, a finding which suggests that the influence of discursive struggles upon historical development, often taken for granted in cultural studies, is pivotal but conditional.

A LOOK AHEAD

My approach, which will unfold in the course of this historical study, identifies culture in the order of practice at a single locus, the point of production, not in practices reaching across many institutional domains and not in an overarching world view encompassing social conduct at large. For, in contrast to many other cultural studies, mine does not begin with the philosophical premise that culture enabled people to create a meaningful order. Rather than take such imputed mental processes for granted, I proceed merely from a controlled comparison of outcomes: economic agents in Germany and Britain constructed different techniques for carrying out the same tasks of manufacture under similar business circumstances. These manufacturing procedures tended to be arranged in a consistent constellation around a nationally dominant specification of labor as a commodity. The cultural definition of labor as a commodity was communicated and reproduced, not through ideal symbols as such, but through the hallowed form of unobtrusive practices.

The comparison unfolds in three stages. Part One introduces the differences between the German and the British concepts of labor as a commodity and describes the diverse ways in which the instrumentalities of production communicated these ideas on the shop floor. Part Two considers the historical genesis of the divergences in the cultural specification of labor as a commodity in western Europe. In Part Three the emphasis shifts from settled institutions to movements for change. This last section traces the ways practice on the shop floor provided the templates for workers' understanding of exploitation and choice of tactics for resistance.

The selection of Germany and Britain as the primary countries for comparison grew out of the logic of finding economically parallel cases, but in the end the rewards of study come from the profound differences between the German and the British cultural heritages. This opportunity for comparison was not lost on Thorstein Veblen, who made use of it for his classic Anglo-German study *Imperial Germany and the Industrial Revolution*. The Germans, Veblen observed, lacked "three or four hundred years' experience" of the free play of individuals in commercial intercourse which the

British had gained through their earlier advance to a market economy.[91] Veblen called attention to the Germans' unusual combination of feudal tradition and modern technology:

> The chief distinctive characteristic of the German culture being a re-tarded adherence to certain mediaeval or sub-mediaeval habits of thought . . . this variant of the Western civilization is evidently an exceptionally unstable, transitory, and in a sense unripe phase. Com-prising, rather than combining certain archaic elements—e.g. its traditional penchant for Romantic metaphysics and feudalistic loy-alty—together with some of the latest ramifications of mechanistic science and an untempered application of the machine industry, . . . it makes for versatility and acceleration of change.[92]

Veblen's language is antique, but his choice of cases for comparison remains as compelling as ever—and just as rich for renewed excavation. In the end we will be in a position to appreciate the wisdom behind Veblen's suggestive remarks: in comparison with British development, the merging of feudal and machine-age culture in Germany indeed created a potential for a fateful "acceleration of change."

91. Thorstein Veblen, *Imperial Germany and the Industrial Revolution* (New York: Macmillan & Co., 1915), p. 90.
92. Ibid., pp. 230–231. My excerpt merges two paragraphs from the original.

ENVOI, 1997

As this book passes into its paperback edition, a word of summary may assist new researchers. This study reaches encompassing conclusions about the illusory forms of labor that lay at the center of German and British manufacturing techniques. Its ethnographic evidence reveals why statisticians' superficial indices of commercial method, such as payment of workers by time or by piece, cannot penetrate to the differences in the phantasmic shapes taken by labor as a commodity in each country. The archival record confirms that in Britain, payment by time could rest on the premise that workers conveyed their abstract labor in products; in Germany, payment by product could rest on the premise that workers conveyed the timed disposition of their labor power. To ponder application of this book's conclusions to every terrain of production requires a hum-ble piety for the self-effacing particulars of material practice. *Nosse vol-unt omnes, mercedem solvere nemo.*

Part 1

THE CULTURAL STRUCTURE
OF THE WORKPLACE

2   Concepts and
Practices of Labor

The *senses* have therefore become directly in their practice
theoreticians.

Karl Marx, *Economic and Philosophic
Manuscripts of 1844*

Classical political economy, that garrulous companion to the development
of capitalism in the two centuries that preceded our own, poses a riddle that
anyone would have recognized had they held the means of answering it. On
the eve of the industrial revolution, the British Isles provided a home for the
development of a vigorous economic theory that treated the labor embodied
in products as the determinant of their relative prices. The most notable
contributors to this body of thought in Britain, from Adam Smith to John
Stuart Mill, conceived the purchase of labor from workers as a process
equivalent to the acquisition of labor incorporated in a tangible product.
Adam Smith revealed this assumption in the *Wealth of Nations* when he
theorized the exchange of labor in an "opulent" society, where the division
of labor was far advanced. In this setting, Smith reasoned, "every workman
has a great quantity of his own work to dispose of beyond what he himself
has occasion for; and every other workman being in exactly the same situation, he is enabled to exchange a great quantity of his own goods for a great
quantity, or, what comes to the same thing, for the price of a great quantity
of theirs."[1] Even when Smith, as well as the British economists who followed him, took stock of the sale of labor by subordinate wage-earners
rather than by independent craftspeople, they continued to imagine the
transfer of labor as if it were handed over embodied in a product.

---

1. *An Inquiry into the Nature and Causes of the Wealth of Nations* (Chicago: University
of Chicago Press, 1976), p. 15. Robert Torrens, who was preoccupied with the consequences of
mechanization in the age of the factory, replicated exactly Smith's depiction of the exchange
of materialized labor among autonomous producers. *An Essay on the Production of Wealth*
(London: Longman, Hurst, Rees, Orne, and Brown, 1821), p. 15.

According to influential chroniclers of economic theory, the British economists' understanding of the labor transaction was not definitively exposed and overturned until a foreign initiate, Karl Marx, completed his analysis of the capitalist labor process.[2] Marx himself believed that his greatest contribution to economic analysis lay in his elucidation of the sale of that singular asset he called *Arbeitskraft,* "labor power."[3] The locution indicated that workers transferred not just "labor" to their employer, but the use of their labor capacity. As is well known, Marx claimed that the distinctions attached to his application of the term *labor power* unlocked the secret of the extraction of surplus value under capitalism. By what process of logic and imagination did Marx arrive at his discovery? This is the unsighted riddle. Neither laudators nor detractors have noticed, let alone pursued, the question.[4]

Stranger still, Marx himself never pondered the sources of his revelation. But, in ways never intended, he deposited many clues. To pursue his trail, we must leave the noisy sphere of intellectual exchange and descend into "the hidden abode of production,"[5] where labor is actually set into motion. Marx's expression *Arbeitskraft,* it turns out, was adopted from colloquial German speech, although its equivalent in English, *labor power,* sounds stilted and bookish even to the academician's ear. In Germany the term functioned in the language of the streets as a description of wage labor long before Marx penned it in an economic treatise.[6] In contrast to the British reliance on the indistinct word *labor,* the term *Arbeitskraft* lingers today in German popular usage in descriptions of the employment transaction. Could this timeworn difference in vocabulary mark the appearance of a distinctive concept of labor as a commodity in Germany that remained absent in Britain? More important, is it possible that such differences in

2. Louis Althusser, "Marx et ses découvertes," in Louis Althusser, Etienne Balibar, and Roger Establet, *Lire le capital* (Paris: François Maspero, 1967), Volume Two, p. 19; Ernest Mandel, *The Formation of the Economic Thought of Karl Marx* (New York: Monthly Review Press, 1971), pp. 82–84.

3. Karl Marx and Friedrich Engels, *Marx-Engels Werke* (Berlin: Dietz Verlag, 1974), Volume 32, p. 11. Louis Althusser clarifies Marx's own emphasis upon the intellectual revolution inaugurated by the concept of "labor power" in Althusser, Balibar, and Establet, *Lire le capital,* op. cit., pp. 17–18, 122.

4. Engels said only that Marx's discovery of the mechanism by which employers extracted surplus value from labor power represented "a thunderbolt that struck out of a clear blue sky." Introduction to *Das Kapital* (Berlin: Dietz Verlag, 1980), Volume Two, p. 21.

5. Karl Marx, *Capital* (New York: International Publishers, 1967), Volume One, p. 176.

6. See Chapter Six below, p. 273, and Chapter Nine, p. 412.

concepts of labor accompanied an enduring contrast between the countries in the form of practice down in "the hidden abode of production"?

These high-flying queries can be anchored in the secure ground of material practice by examining procedures on the factory shop floor. A comparison of German and late-developing British textile mills during the nineteenth century shows that the specifications of labor as a commodity did not reflect the labor process, but comprised a constitutive part of its execution. Despite compelling similarities in the settings in which matching German and British textile mills developed, economic agents in the two countries applied different concepts of labor as a commodity to carry out the process of production. German employers and workers indeed acted as if the employment relation comprised the purchase of labor effort and of the disposition over workers' labor activity or, as they termed it, over *Arbeitskraft*. Through quotidian practice British employers and workers defined the factory employment relation as the appropriation of workers' labor concretized in products. By deciphering the hidden language of factory practice we take the first step in a descent to the underground path by which Marx received his remarkable insights into the means by which workers transmitted their labor in the capitalist labor process.

THE LOGIC OF THE WEAVERS' PIECE-RATE SCALES

The occupation of weaving during the second half of the nineteenth century comprised the single largest job category not only in textiles but in the entire manufacturing sector of the British and German economies.[7] The construction of the piece-rate schedules for weavers provides a neglected but

---

7. Germany, *Die deutsche Volkswirtschaft am Schlusse des 19. Jahrhunderts* (Berlin: Puttkammer und Mühlbrecht, 1900), pp. 27–32; United Kingdom, *Census of England and Wales 1891* (London: H.M.S.O., 1893), Volume III, pp. ix, xix, xx. Contemporaries were well aware of the numerical weight of the occupation of weaving. "The weaving sector is far and away the most widespread branch of work," August Bebel said, "and this holds not only for Germany but specifically for England as well." Deutsches Weber-Central-Komitee, *Ausführlicher Bericht über die Verhandlungen des ersten deutschen Webertages abgehalten zu Glauchau in Sachsen vom 28. bis 30. Mai 1871*, transcription in Stadtarchiv Glauchau. In 1895, for instance, the weaving process engaged the majority of German workers in textiles, whereas spinning employed only 18 percent of workers in that business. See summary statistics in Karin Zachmann, "Der Mechanisierungsprozess in der deutschen Textilindustrie im Zeitraum von 1870 bis 1914," *Beiträge zur Wirtschaftsgeschichte*, Number One (Dresden: Technische Universität Dresden, 1988), p. 29.

singularly revealing piece of evidence about the inscription of contrasting suppositions in utilitarian practices. As a tool for extracting labor from weavers, the design of the scales would seem to depend only upon questions of force and pragmatism: How much were employers ready to pay workers for various types of cloth? To what extent could the resistance of weavers lead to modifications in the system's provisions? The physical dimensions of the weaving process and of its products did not provide natural or automatic measures of "how much" a worker produced or of "how much" the employer appropriated. Instead, cultural categories intervened to create contrasting forms of measurement in Germany and Britain. To isolate culture's arbitration, we must first construct a picture of the technical essentials of weaving, for the characteristics of weaving made the design of piece rates in this trade a kind of Rorschach test for industrial culture.

The weaver's job consisted of seeing to it that the weft thread in the loom's shuttle or shuttles moved horizontally back and forth across the vertical threads of the warp.[8] As the shuttles laid their threads, a rotating beam underneath or out to the side of the loom unfolded more of the warp. The speed at which this beam let out the warp largely determined how tightly the weft threads would be woven: the slower the warp moved forward, the denser the weave.

From almost the earliest days of power loom weaving, mill owners in both Germany and Britain preferred to pay weavers by the piece.[9] They maintained that this method of reward gave weavers an incentive to work without close supervision and thereby minimized the costs of superintendence.[10] To be sure, employers in both countries granted time wages for

8. Although there were supplementary tasks, such as refilling the weft supply, weavers themselves quite rightly viewed the insertion of the weft threads as the essence of their occupation, even if the machine itself powered the motion of the shuttles. See Adolf Levenstein, *Die Arbeiterfrage* (München: Ernst Reinhardt, 1912), p. 45; Deutscher Textilarbeiterverband, Hauptvorstand/Arbeiterinnensekretariat, *Mein Arbeitstag—mein Wochenende* (Berlin: Textilpraxis, 1931), p. 24.

9. An employer at a spinning and weaving mill testified, "We always pay by the piece where we can; where it is absolutely impossible to pay by the day." Parliamentary Papers XXXV 1892, Royal Commission on Labour, Nov. 13, 1891, p. 281. The testimony of textile employers in Germany contradicts the assumption of Schmiede and Schudlich that employers preferred payment by time wages until the end of the 1870s. Germany, Enquete-Kommission, *Reichs-Enquete für die Baumwollen- und Leinen-Industrie: Stenographische Protokolle über die mündliche Vernehmung der Sachverständigen* (Berlin: Julius Sittenfeld, 1878), pp. 251, 404–405, 664. Cf. Rudi Schmiede and Edwin Schudlich, *Die Entwicklung der Leistungsentlohnung in Deutschland* (Frankfurt: Aspekte Verlag, 1976), p. 92.

10. For an example of a mill that switched over to piece rates to reduce costs, see *Yorkshire Factory Times*, February 5, 1897. For an example of a manager who converted to piece rates as

weavers if the machinery was untested or if weavers were so unaccustomed to the work that a production norm could not be estimated. But they reverted to remuneration by piece once these conditions passed.[11] "If we did not pay them by piece and by results," a spokesman for Lancashire mill owners claimed in 1891, "the manufacturing concerns would not be able to keep above water twelve months."[12] The economic environment limited the mode of payment, but cultural assumptions precipitated its form.

The mechanics of the weaving activity precluded the application of a unidimensional register of the labor spent on an output. If length of cloth alone were the index of output and criterion of pay, workers on cloth with a dense weave, which required the insertion of many weft threads, would earn no more per yard, and probably less per hour, than workers on looser cloth. Weavers on dense fabric in this hypothetical setting would be *underpaid* and would have an interest in advancing the warp rapidly to produce a looser weave than ordered. But if the number of weft threads inserted by the weaver were measured, weavers on dense fabric would be likely to be *overpaid*. The reason is clear enough: weavers producing loose cloth use up the warp more quickly than weavers on dense cloth. The removal of a finished warp and installation of a new one in the loom creates a major, uncompensated delay.

---

soon as the weavers were competent, consult taped interview with Will Bruce, born 1879, of Bentham Village. (My thanks to E. and J. H. P. Pafford for their willingness to share this recording with me.) See, too, Sydney J. Chapman, *The Lancashire Cotton Industry: A Study in Economic Development* (Manchester: Manchester University Press, 1904), p. 262; *Textile Manufacturer*, October 15, 1910, p. 325. For parallel cases in Germany, see Johannes Victor Bredt, *Die Lohnindustrie dargestellt an der Garn- und Textilindustrie von Barmen* (Berlin: von Bruer & Co., 1905), p. 174; Germany, Enquete-Kommission, *Reichs-Enquete*, op. cit., p. 247; Ludwig Bernhard, *Die Akkordarbeit in Deutschland* (Leipzig: Duncker & Humblot, 1903), p. 125. Benjamin Gott, founder of the first large wool mill in Yorkshire, extended piece payments from overlookers to all operatives and found that "the men consequently feel that they are as much interested as he and cease to look upon him as their master." Cited in Sidney Pollard, "Factory Discipline in the Industrial Revolution," *The Economic History Review* second series, Volume XVI, Number 2 (1963), p. 264.

11. *Textile Recorder*, June 15, 1883, p. 26. *Das deutsche Wollen-Gewerbe*, Volume 18 (1886), p. 32; *Der Christliche Textilarbeiter*, Viersen, October 21, 1899; *Der Christliche Textilarbeiter*, Krefeld, December 9, 1899; Zentrales Staatsarchiv Merseburg, 120 B V 33, Nr. 4, Vol. 1, February 4, 1817, p. 53.

12. William Noble, United Cotton Manufacturers' Association, Royal Commission on Labour, PP 1892 XXXV, June 15, 1891, p. 162. The weavers themselves preferred payment by piece as the only method feasible in their trade for establishing uniform remuneration. Sidney Webb and Beatrice Webb, *Industrial Democracy* (New York: Augustus Kelley, 1965), p. 289.

The predicaments in these two simplified ways of gauging output—length of cloth or number of weft threads inserted—disclose the unique characteristics of the weaving activity and of its product. Production required multi-dimensional gauges. In contrast to other manufacturing processes in which subvarieties of the product differ by gross size or shape, varieties of cloth differ by the mathematical functions that govern their density and pattern. The product is uniform and continuous, and it has a naturally inscribed metric along precisely measurable and equipollent dimensions: length, width, and number of weft threads. The labor activity itself consists of the regulated linkage of actions which have natural metrics as well: the number of times the shuttle crosses the warp, the number of times the beam rotates to let out the warp, the size and number of teeth on the gears that let out the warp, and so forth. Weaving offered the participants multiple and easily coded axes which could be picked out to define units of output and apportion pay, and it required them to combine these dimensions somehow to avoid the problems illustrated with the unidimensional measures. This natural indeterminacy makes weaving an ideal context in which historical analysts can discern the application of the schema by which factory owners and workers decided how they would measure output and outline the otherwise shapeless stuff called labor.

The model of labor in Britain was concretized in the Yorkshire piece-rate system, as illustrated in the schedule introduced in 1883 in Huddersfield and the Colne Valley (Figure 1). As the figure's vertical axis indicates, weavers were remunerated by length of fabric woven, with the standard interval equaling 180 feet of the warp. But the more weft threads woven into each inch of this standard length of warp, the higher the payment. The chart's horizontal axis specifies the requisite weft threads inserted per inch, which in the trade were called the "picks" or, more precisely, the "picks per inch." For basic weaving, with one shuttle and one beam, remuneration for a fixed length of cloth rose linearly as picks per inch rose. For more complicated weaves, with bonuses for extra shuttles, remuneration for a fixed length always rose with increases in density, but not at a constant rate (Figure 2). To calculate weavers' pay, the taker-in of the cloth from the weavers sampled the picks per inch or weighed the total piece to ensure that enough picks had been woven into the warp. (In the discussion which follows, bear in mind that "picks per inch" always refers to cloth density, not to its length. Density, a geometric concept, varies independently of the thickness of the weft yarn.) The Huddersfield

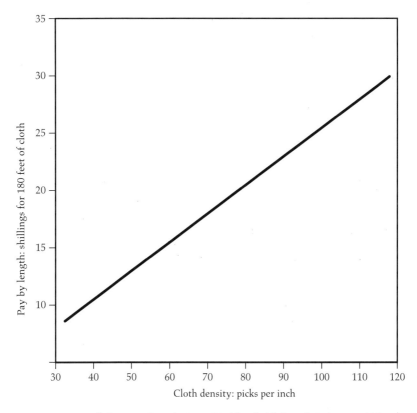

Figure 1.   British Data on British Axes, Huddersfield, Simple Weaves, 1883

scale, the best-known in Yorkshire, served as a benchmark for many others in the woolen trade.[13] Until the First World War, weavers judged the fairness of their pay by this scale's standards.[14]

13. In truth, it represented the maximum renumeration to which owners in the region would consent. Prescriptive its rates were not—only the principles by which it operated. Royal Commission on Labour, PP 1892 XXXV, p. 211.

14. *Yorkshire Factory Times*, September 13, 1889. For examples of strikes to keep the scale's rates in all their particulars, see *Yorkshire Factory Times*, October 25, 1889, and August 21, 1891. For the percentaging of modifications in the Huddersfield scale up to 1892, see Royal Commission on Labour, PP 1892 XXXV, Appendix XII, pp. 501–502. Even in the closing months of the First World War the Huddersfield schedule served as the basis for attempts to negotiate an industrywide price list. Joanna Bornat, "An Examination of the General Union of Textile Workers 1883–1922," Ph.D. diss., University of Essex, 1981, p. 200.

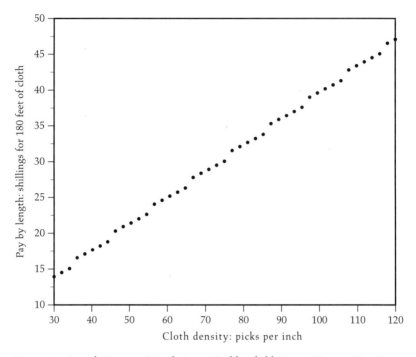

Figure 2.   British Data on British Axes, Huddersfield, Fancy Weaves, Two Beams, Four Shuttles, 1883

To compare basic principles, a German pay table of 1911 from a wool firm in Euskirchen on the lower Rhine is shown in Figure 3.[15] Rather than taking adjacent correlates of the weaver's activity—length and density of cloth—for the criteria of pay, as in Britain, the German system centered its categories directly on the weaver's primary activity of having the shuttle move back and forth. The weavers earned a sum for every thousand times their shuttle shot across the warp—that is, per thousand weft threads woven. The Germans called this system pay by the number of *Schüsse*, literally, pay by the number of "shots" of the shuttle. German managers said they preferred pay by shot over pay by length because it offered a more direct measure of the labor input.[16] As Figure 3 shows, the

15. The scale held only for the regular wool products in which the firm, C. Lückenrath, specialized. Deutscher Textilarbeiterverband, *Jahrbuch des deutschen Textilarbeiterverbandes, 1911* (Berlin: Karl Hübsch, 1912), p. 75. For other comments on pay per shot in this town, see *Die Textilarbeiter-Zeitung*, May 18, 1912.

16. "The calculation of weaving wages by the number of shot threads, for example, ten pfennigs per thousand shots, is the simplest method of labor remuneration," said one German

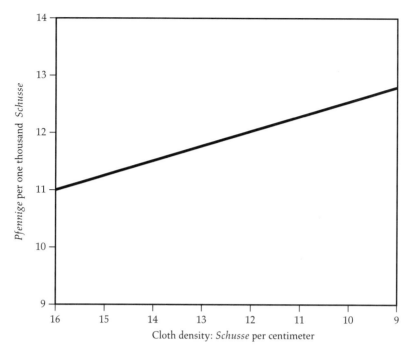

Figure 3. German Data on German Axes, Euskirchen, 1911

remuneration per thousand shots rose linearly with decreases in the shots woven per centimeter. This feature of the scales compensated weavers for more frequent changes of the warp when producing low-density fabrics. On the Huddersfield schedule, one can also identify a linear increase, of course: for basic weaving, remuneration for a fixed length rose linearly as picks per inch rose.

Since the two pay systems manifested their linearity on different axes, they did not "say" the same thing with alternative vocabularies, but concretized fundamentally different statements about the remuneration of labor. On the horizontal axis, Figures 1 and 3 share a common metric, the density of the weave.[17] On the vertical axis, however, the Euskirchen and

director, "since it permits payment of the weaver according to the quantity of executed labor." *Zeitschrift für die gesamte Textil-Industrie,* Volume 14, Number 65 (1910–1911), p. 1126.

17. Notice that on the horizontal axis I have reversed the direction of the metric between the British Figure 1 and the German Figure 3. I did this because the essential point of interest at this stage is the fact that people in both countries used the simplifying assumption that a

Huddersfield scales operated on different dimensions: pay by shot versus pay by length. In both German and English, the referents of ordinary language marked the immediacy of the association between the weft threads and the labor activity, since the words *picks* and *Schüsse* could pertain either to the shuttles' motion or to the product, the woven weft.[18] When practice itself became a concrete form of language in the operation of the piece-rate scales, the choice of referent became unmistakable. Verbal utterances were multivocal, the silent language of production—the piece-rate mechanism—invariable. In comparing types of labor, the German and British systems designated distinct objects. The German piece-rate system centered its comparisons of different ways of weaving on the motion of inserting a pick, without respect to the visible length of the complete product. The British pattern compared the picks in different kinds of finished products rather than in motions.

The dimensions of linearity reveal the core axes of thought inscribed in the techniques of remuneration. It is impossible to translate the data from British weaving price lists onto the German dimensions of thought without altering the intelligibility of the distribution. To demonstrate this, in Figure 4 are shown the values for three types of English cloth on the Huddersfield scale but replotted on the German axes of thought, in pence per one thousand picks or *Schüsse*. Placing the British information on the German dimensions of thought yields two findings. First, the British data lose the shape of a line, in contrast with the German data in Figure 3; instead, as picks per inch decline, the points arrange themselves in a strange curve.[19] The deformation of the line in Figure 1 to the curve in Figure 4 confirms that the British system of measurement embodied a concept of remuneration that began with the length of the materialized

---

linear relation of some kind ought to obtain between pay and changes in cloth density. I did not want to confuse this issue with a contrast in the direction of the lines' slopes. Once I have converted the British data to the German dimensions of thought, I will verify that in both countries, pay per weft thread inserted rises as the density of the cloth declines, although, translated to German axes, the British rise is not linear.

18. In English, the original referent of *pick*, dating back to the time of the handloom, was the throw of the shuttle rather than the inserted weft. F. W. Moody, "Some Textile Terms from Addingham in the West Riding," *Transactions, Yorkshire Dialect Society* Volume 8 (1950), p. 41.

19. The algorithm which explains the new form of the British data is derived as follows: in the British system, pay per length = m (density) + b, or, rephrased in inches, pay per inch = m (picks per inch) + b. To convert to the German system, we need to isolate pay per pick: starting from the initial British equation, pay per pick = $m + b$ (inch per pick), or, rephrased in terms of cloth density, pay per pick = $m + b/$density.

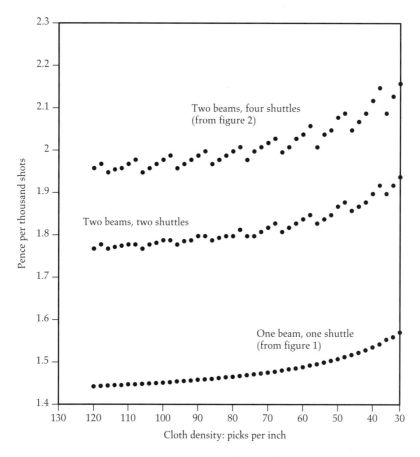

Figure 4.   British Data on German Axes, Huddersfield Scale, Woolens

product as an indicator of labor. The linearity on the native British axes would not have obtained if the producers had reflected upon the exchange of labor for a wage with another combination of axes.

The translation of the British data onto the German dimensions of thought also enables us to understand how the unpretentious language of practice—the concepts incarnated in the weavers' daily labor for a wage— guided the weavers' independent reflections upon the appropriation of labor. When British weavers had more than one shuttle or one warp beam in operation—which was very often the case—their payment per shot did not necessarily increase as the number of shots per inch declined on various weaving jobs. Given a fixed length of cloth, although the net pay rose as the number of shots per inch rose, the pay *per shot* inserted—the measure of pay per effective motion—followed an erratic course. Figure 4 indicates that the more complex the weave, the more irregular and "irrational" the British method appears from a "German" point of view; that is, the more complex the weave, the more the graph deviates from the ideal pattern of higher earnings per shot as the number of shots per inch decreases.[20] For example, on some types of fabric, the British weaver earned less per shot for weaving 56 weft threads per inch than for 62, although 56 weft threads per inch would take longer, *per shot*, to weave (because the warp would have to be changed more often). The difference in the cloth produced was slight; the difference in earnings significant and inequitable.[21] What do these anomalies tell us about the producers' apperceptions?

It would seem that such an "obvious" source of inconsistent earnings in payment per weft thread inserted under the Huddersfield system could not have escaped the notice of the workers themselves. But somehow it did. Weavers in the Colne Valley alleged that the 1883 pay table lowered their wages, especially on the loosely woven cloth. They wrote dozens of letters to newspapers explaining their dissatisfaction with it. These workers astutely analyzed its rates and criticized the *slope* of the straight line on the British axes of thought.[22] They made an effort to analyze the scale mathematically. But since they did not conceive the system in terms of pay per weft thread, they could not identify these inequities or frame them as "irregularities." They looked straight at the problem but did not see it, a remarkable demonstration of how their perception began with the length of the cloth as the basis for pay. Truly, their senses had "become directly in their practice theoreticians."

The weavers were not simpletons who self-effacingly obeyed the dictates of culture:[23] as strategizing actors they knew that their *net* earnings

20. The irregularities are far too large to be explained by the need to calculate total pay in terms of units of pence or halfpence. If this were the origin, furthermore, the more complicated weaves, in which net pay per piece was higher, would show a more regular curve than the simpler weaves, whereas the data reveal exactly the opposite. The scales in effect in the Huddersfield district before 1883 show this tendency to an even greater degree.

21. George S. Wood, "The Theory and Practice of Piecework," *Huddersfield Textile Society Session 1910–1911* (Huddersfield: Huddersfield Textile Society, 1911), p. 11.

22. See, illustratively, *Northern Pioneer*, April 14, 1883; *Huddersfield Daily Examiner*, March 13, March 27, and April 13, 1883.

23. Dennis Wrong, "The Oversocialized Conception of Man in Modern Sociology," *American Sociological Review* Volume 26, Number 2 (April 1961), pp. 183–193.

were higher if they put more picks into cloth of a fixed length (not taking pay *per* weft thread into account!). The workers' recognition of inequity and their resistance to exploitation were not given automatically by their resolve to pursue their interests. Rather, the weavers' very understanding of their interests depended on the cultural suppositions they called upon to interpret their predicament. The assumptions about labor through which they defined their situation derived from the signifying process embedded in the very operation of the piece-rate mechanism. Through the form of their everyday practice, the workers identified their human activity only as it appeared to them in the fantastic shape of the fabric's own properties.[24]

The British weavers could not have perceived the anomalies in their payment per weft thread from the experience of work. The earnings of most British and German weavers fluctuated greatly from week to week. The amount of their weekly pay depended on whether they wove their piece on the warp all the way to the end exactly on pay day or, alternatively, had a small swatch left to do on a large piece which could therefore not be finished and credited until the next pay period.[25] The speed at which a worker finished a piece of cloth depended upon numerous shifting factors which combined in unpredictable ways: the dressing of the warp, the quality of the yarn, how well the warp was wound, the weather, and trouble-shooting by the overlooker. Then, too, weavers turned out a rapidly changing mix of product types.[26] These conditions made it difficult for weavers to move from the phenomenal world of work to expected weekly wages for products of a specific number of picks per inch.

24. Marx, op. cit., Volume One, "The Fetishism of Commodities and the Secret Thereof," p. 86. For an example of the ways in which the types of weaving labor in the putting-out system were distinguished and revalued over the decades by a linear scale corresponding only to the dimensions of the cloth, see testimony of John Kingan, United Kingdom, *Report from Select Committee on Hand-Loom Weavers' Petitions,* 1834, PP 1834 (556) X, p. 16. The proportionate increase in pay as cloth density increased varied to an extraordinary degree, depending upon the absolute pay for cloth of medium density in a given year.

25. According to the Royal Commission on Labour, the weekly wages of an able worsted weaver might fluctuate between two shillings and sixteen shillings. PP 1892 XXXV, p. 222. An experienced woman weaver told the *Yorkshire Factory Times* that her wages lay between five shillings and one pound a week, depending on how many cuts she completed. *Yorkshire Factory Times,* November 14, 1912. Miss W., born 1901, interviewed by Joanna Bornat, said that when she did not finish a whole cut, she took no pay home that week. See also *Yorkshire Factory Times,* March 27, 1891, p. 4.

26. Royal Commission on Labour, PP 1892 XXXV, p. 230; Calderdale Archives, Murgatroyd piece books. A large factory could work on sixty to eighty types of cloth in a day. *Die Textil-Zeitung,* January 19, 1897.

Weavers labored with approximate estimates of what they ought to earn and with only a tacit understanding of how it ought to be reckoned. "Wherever a scale, no matter what its base and no matter how the shuttling was arranged, ran to a good day's wage for a good day's work," said Ben Turner, the union secretary, "the weavers were content with it."[27] Yet when weavers at mills that lacked comprehensive piece-rate charts had an opportunity to devise completely original schedules of their own, their choices revealed their assumptions. They proposed, as a matter of course, that earnings rise linearly for extra picks per inch, and they took pay by length as the unquestioned basis for remuneration. They did so even in regions lacking prior districtwide wage agreements to which they could refer.[28]

The length of cloth operated as the basis for remuneration in nearly all Yorkshire and Lancashire scales, both for the base rates with the simplest weaving and after the addition of more shuttles, beams, and healds to the job.[29] The system of pay by length did not necessarily entail inconsistency in the rates of payment per weft thread inserted; but since British producers did not consciously guard against this defect, their system generated it. On the eve of the First World War, the most capable researcher in Yorkshire, George S. Wood, delivered a lecture to the Huddersfield Textile Society on "The Theory and Practice of Piecework." After finishing an extensive survey of pay systems' consistency, he told the Textile Society that "perhaps the best scale in the woollen trade is the famous Huddersfield Weaving Scale."[30] Wood, in a strange illustration of history's vagaries, worked both as a representative for the employers' association and as an adviser to the textile workers' union. His testimony confirms that the Huddersfield table was no less sound than others in Britain.[31]

27. Ben Turner, *Short History of the General Union of Textile Workers* (Heckmondwike: Labour Pioneer, 1920), p. 46.

28. *Yorkshire Factory Times*, August 16, 1889.

29. For other linear pay scales, see the Standard List issued in the Saddleworth woolen industry in March, 1911, Kirklees Archives; the wage lists preserved for the Bairstow firm, Leeds District Archives; the linear rise in the picks per inch in various Yorkshire towns described in the *Yorkshire Factory Times*, November 22, 1889; the Leeds pay scale reproduced in the *Yorkshire Factory Times*, October 11, 1889. For a truly encyclopaedic collection of piece-rate scales in the Lancashire cotton trade, see British Association for the Advancement of Science, Manchester Meeting of 1887, *On the Regulation of Wages by Means of Lists in the Cotton Industry*, Manchester Meeting of 1887 (Manchester: John Heywood, 1887).

30. Wood, op. cit., p. 11.

31. In addition to the Huddersfield scale, the Yeadon and Guiseley table for woolens, drawn up in 1893, also featured aberrant rates per weft thread woven. Data calculated from scales in the Archive of the General Union of Dyers, Bleachers, and Textile Workers, Bradford. See PP 1909 LXXX, op. cit., p. xl.

The method of comparing types of labor via the linear properties of the product also prevailed in Britain during a formal inquiry by the Bradford Chamber of Commerce into new methods for comparing weaving scales in Yorkshire. The chamber's conclusions reveal that even when British managers, overlookers, and weavers started afresh and reconsidered the principles behind their piece-rate scales, they took pay by length as an unquestioned given. The chamber, with committee representatives from the overlookers' and weavers' unions, considered in 1895 the feasibility of establishing average weaving scales for the various classes of goods in the city.[32] A local journal in Bradford observed that the chamber had set itself a difficult task, because the city's numerous worsted mills produced an "infinite" number of fabric types which could hardly be grouped on a comprehensive schedule.[33] To cope with this challenge, the chamber "set about the classification of the boundless variety of fabrics, from the point of view of the weaving labour involved. . . . It ascertained, availing itself of all obtainable information, the *average price per pick* actually paid for weaving this kind of fabric."[34] The dimensions of the printed scale which the Chamber of Commerce developed as a basis for comparison among firms reveal that it actually took "price per pick" to mean "price per pick per inch" for a fixed length of cloth.[35] When the chamber set out to measure cloth in terms of labor, it ended up measuring labor in terms of cloth (or, more exactly, differences in labor in terms of differences in cloth).[36] The Germans, by contrast, gauged cloth by labor motions. They called a group of one thousand *Schüsse* "the unit of labor," analyzing the product with this unit of activity.[37]

Anomalies in the rates of earnings per weft thread appeared in schedules from Lancashire as well.[38] Shortly after the First World War, a British manufacturers' commission investigated the precision of pay scales in relation to

---

32. Bradford Chamber of Commerce, *Bradford Chamber of Commerce 45th Annual Report* (Bradford, 1895), p. 55.

33. *Bradford*, November 9, 1895.

34. Ibid. Emphasis in original.

35. *Textile Mercury*, November 11, 1896, p. 404; *Bradford Chamber of Commerce 46th Annual Report* (Bradford, 1896), pp. 57–60. Likewise, in Lancashire the piece-rate scales were eventually formulated in terms of the price of one pick, given a standard length of warp. See Uniform List of Prices for Weavers, 1906, LRO, DDHs 83.

36. The attempt to put into effect the general lists of average prices in Bradford failed. See PP 1909 LXXX, Report of an Enquiry by the Board of Trade into the Earnings and Labor of the Workpeople of the United Kingdom in 1906, p. xl.

37. E. Jung, *Die Berechnung des Selbstkostenpreises der Gewebe* (Berlin: Julius Springer, 1917).

38. British Association for the Advancement of Science, *On the Regulation of Wages.*

labor effort. A member of the committee on costs declared that "hardly one single weaving scale in existence is drawn up mathematically correctly in its relation to picks"—that is, in the effective payment per weft thread woven.[39] These discrepancies occurred because the British method of classification captured the labor activity at a remove.[40] Does this mean that the British point of view was backward or primitive? Before we rush to a conclusion, we must consider the disadvantages of pay by shot as the Germans practiced it. Any framework for viewing production also entails its own forms of blindness. The German way of defining the transfer of labor to employers carried distinctive inaccuracies of its own, which, from the British framework, would have seemed intolerable indeed.

Although German weavers received a higher reward per thousand shots if they wove less dense fabrics, their pay scales evaluated the looseness of the fabric only in approximate terms. If an analyst converts the German measure of fabric density—shots per centimeter—to English units, it turns out that the German scales graduated the increase in pay at intervals that were always larger than five picks per inch.[41] Some German scales registered changes in fabric density only at intervals of eight picks to the inch, or by a few bifurcations of yarn types. (This feature represented a specific way of treating labor rather than an incidental feature which resulted from the specifications by which products were sold in the market. The commercial orders German manufacturers filled permitted no leeway in the number of picks per inch.)[42]

---

39. This retrospective comment appears in D. H. Williams, *Costing in the Wool Textile and Other Industries* (Manchester: Emmott & Co., 1946), p. 5.

40. In the days of handweaving, embodied labor was paid according to linear scales that customarily rose by about one penny for each type of cloth. When the base rates for simple cloth rose or declined over the years but the one-penny increments for progressively more complex cloth remained fixed, a curious artifact arose: the payment for one variety of cloth as a portion of another could vary substantially. In 1810 a standard scale for muslin fabric allotted eightpence per standard length of the simplest weave and a supplement of an additional penny per length of the next most simple weave. In 1819 this scale granted threepence for the same, most basic, weave, but the differential for the next grade was still fixed at one penny. Between these dates, then, the original 12.5 percent addition for slightly more complex work increased to 33 percent, whereas no change occurred in the relative labor time embodied in each type of fabric. These unjustified and undiscussed divergences arose from the calculation of labor by the linear comparison of fabrics. See the chart of prices 1805–1834, *Report from Select Committee on Handloom Weavers*, PP 1834 X, testimony of William Buchanan, p. 156.

41. Some scales endorsed by the workers considered only the type of yarn inserted: Stadtarchiv Cottbus, AII 3.3 b 33, pp. 39–42, December 12, 1895.

42. *Centralblatt für die Textil-Industrie*, 1876, Nr. 48, p. 763. See the government specifications for cloth on which it accepted bids, which appeared as a regular feature in textile journals. An example: the cloth needed by a prison that advertised in the *Centralblatt für die Textil-Industrie*, 1876, Nr. 45, p. 808.

In contrast to German methods, British piece-rate scales adjusted the levels of remuneration to the fabric densities by intervals no larger than four picks to the inch, and normally they gauged the rates at intervals of one or two picks to the inch.

Proceedings in the court rolls indicate that English factory inspectors prosecuted mill owners who had their overlookers set the looms to insert two weft threads per inch more than the weavers knew of or were being paid for.[43] A disparity of this magnitude, an issue of legal concern in Britain, made no difference at all in the rate of pay on most German charts. In fact, the odd irregularities in the Huddersfield scale, which turn up after calculating the rates of payment per thousand weft threads woven, fall *in between* the grosser intervals of German pay tables. The British focus on the product allowed them to make fine distinctions in the product to decide upon an appropriate price for it, but did not provide the categories for capturing the labor activity itself. In this affair the Germans were consistent but imprecise, the British the other way around. This contrast originated in the German focus on decomposing the labor activity versus the British focus on decomposing the cloth.

In some instances, the reason that the Germans gave less attention in their pay scales to alterations in picks per inch is that weavers received a small sum for helping to install a new warp. This meant they had less claim on compensation via measurement of looser densities of cloth, because some of the time devoted to more frequent changes of the warp on these orders was taken into account directly.[44] Leaving aside the changing of the warp, there was no readily identifiable difference, on loose versus dense cloth, in the labor exercised to weave a thousand shots, apart from differences in the frequencies of yarn breakages due to the diameters of the yarn used to weave loose versus dense cloth. Thus, from the German view, there was less motivation to register the difference in cloth densities carefully; it was only necessary to capture the time lost in changing the warp and the gross differences in yarn types.[45]

43. Wakefield Library Headquarters, Court Records of July 22, 1891. *Yorkshire Factory Times*, August 3, 1894, p. 8, and April 5, 1901, p. 8.

44. At a firm in Viersen, on the lower Rhine, weavers paid by shot objected in 1908 when a shift to production of cloth of lower densities meant that more frequent changes of the warp were required and thus their pay was reduced. Hauptstaatsarchiv Düsseldorf (henceforth HSTAD), Landratsamt Mönchengladbach 99, pp. 420 ff. Their complaint reveals a drawback of the German system when weavers received no compensation for changing the warps.

45. Of course, under the pure logic of mathematics, payment for installation of the warp would explain only a slower rise in the rates of pay per thousand shot as the density of the pattern declined, not the size of the intervals at which the pay scale recognized changes in the

How are we to account for the emergence of contrasts in the principles used to calculate weavers' earnings in Germany and Britain? The brute, physical fact that workers receive their compensation via piece rates does not reveal what it is about the products that makes them a suitable index for remuneration, or how the products are interpreted to serve as a measure of work. Workers in less commercialized societies, from ancient Greece to prerevolutionary France, received payment by piece rates, but they did not by any means imagine that they sold their labor as a commodity.[46] The mechanism of payment by output does not entail a particular commodity form of labor. To ascertain the definition of labor as a commodity, one must expose the agents' own concepts as embedded in the symbolic form of the piece-rate schedules. A "Statement of Wages" was indeed a statement: the weavers' pay scales in the two countries attempted to combine two elements—the labor activity and the product of labor—in a relation not of mere correlation but of significance. In Germany the relation was conceived metaphorically and the activity of weaving taken as a model or paradigm for identifying and measuring the product. The scale classified the product as a mirror of the activity; cloth comprised the unit of observation, the insertion of the shots the true subject of analysis. As industrial sociologists from Germany have long taken care to emphasize, a piece-rate scale can use the product as a convenient surrogate for measuring the workers' action and need not accept the product as the object of payment itself.[47] Or, as one student of wage forms in the German textile industry expressed it in 1924, the visible output could be

density. But under the practical logic of everyday manufacture, if the slope was lower, payment for changes in picks per inch constituted a smaller proportion of net pay and precision therefore held less significance for the agents.

46. For Greece, see the introduction to Chapter Five below; for France, see Albert Soboul, *Les Sans-culottes parisiens en l'an II* (Paris: Clauvreuil, 1958), pp. 453–454.

47. Herbert Maucher, *Zeitlohn Akkordlohn Prämienlohn* (Darmstadt: Darmstadt Druck- und Verlags-Gesellschaft, 1965), p. 62. Theodor Brauer, *Produktionsfactor Arbeit* (Jena: Gustav Fischer, 1925), pp. 170–179. German sociologists of the time who discussed the piece rate-system still assumed that it was simply an alternate way of valorizing *Arbeitskraft*, not a way of redefining labor as a commodity. "With the modern labor contract the full commitment of the labor power of an individual for a certain time through the employment relation ensues, even if the measurement of compensation proceeds according to labor output." Otto von Zwiedineck-Südenhorst, *Beiträge zur Lehre von den Lohnformen* (Tübingen: H. Laupp, 1904), p. 18. August Löhr, in a study of the metal industry, asked how limits on piece rates were set. The answer, he believed, was "the basic attempt on the part of the factory not to pay the worker substantially more in general for the activation of his labor power than was required at any moment for the relevant category of labor power belonging to the worker." August Löhr, *Beiträge zur Würdigung der Akkordlohnmethode im rheinisch-westfälischen Maschinenbau* (Mönchengladbach: Volksvereins-Verlag, 1912), p. 63.

adopted for the sake of making an "empirical" reading, as distinguished from the actual labor for which the worker was in truth remunerated.[48] If the Germans themselves interpreted the product as a "sign," not as the true object of remuneration, surely we are obligated to take their lead seriously.[49]

In Britain the relation between labor as a concrete activity and its product was conceived metonymically. The British pay scales codified the product as the result of labor but did not identify the value of the product by modeling it on the performance of the weaving. Instead, the product itself became the vessel by which labor was transferred; the materialized labor itself comprised the object of remuneration. The British quantified abstract labor by the substantial dimensions of the complete piece of cloth.[50] As in Germany, workers delivered abstract labor, but in Britain the concrete product functioned as its sign.[51]

48. Alfred Müller, "Die Lohnbemessungsmethoden in der Chemnitzer Textilindustrie," diss., Marburg, 1924, p. 65. If the empirical reading of the product in Germany merely served as an index for the execution of motions, could the reverse situation arise, in which the motions are used to conceive a reading of the product? This was the case with the British spinning scales in Oldham, which were expressed in terms of "draws" of the mule. When this scale was sanctioned in 1876, the "draws" of the machine were a proxy for the length of the product, since the hypothetical length of a draw (63 inches) was chosen to yield easily one hank of yarn. *Textile Mercury*, Nov. 12, 1910, p. 401. Despite the emphasis on the tangible length, the real process of labor consisted in giving the yarn "twists."

49. For references to nineteenth-century German commentators who viewed piece rates as an index of the expenditure of labor power, not as a payment for output, see Schmiede and Schudlich, op. cit., pp. 202–203.

50. Therefore I break with William Reddy's simple opposition between payment for "labor" versus its "outcome." *The Rise of Market Culture* (Cambridge: Cambridge University Press, 1984), p. 124. His distinction is richly suggestive but ultimately insensitive to the new meaning that the conveyance of a product may take on in a capitalist order.

51. Of course, not all British workers were paid by piece rates. But their product could still serve as the sign for abstract labor. In fact, in many trades customary quotas for the amount of work to turn in per day meant that there was no functional difference between piece rates and a timed wage. John Rule, *The Labouring Classes in Early Industrial England, 1750–1850* (London: Longman, 1986), p. 121; James Jaffe, *The Struggle for Market Power: Industrial Relations in the British Coal Industry, 1800–1840* (Cambridge: Cambridge University Press, 1991), p. 2 and sources cited there; David F. Schloss, *Methods of Industrial Remuneration* (London: Williams and Norgate, 1892), pp. 14–16, 20; J. E. Prosser, *Piece-Rate, Premium and Bonus* (London: Williams & Norgate, 1919), p. 1. Overtime, too, could be equated with the delivery of an extra quota of products: *Select Committee on Master and Servant*, PP 1865 (370) VIII, testimony of Alexander Campbell, p. 16. Even the dockworkers could view their employers as purchasers of a kind of tangible "product." When dockworkers began a "go-slow" movement in protest against low wages, they justified their poor work by saying, "If the employers of labor or purchasers of goods refuse to pay for the genuine article, they must be content with shoddy and veneer." *Report of the National Union of Dock Laborers in Great Britain and Ireland*, 1891, cited in Webb and Webb, op. cit., p. 307.

Both ways of conceiving the relation between labor and its product interpret a paradox in the employment relation. The worker's labor may generate the value of the finished product, but this labor, since it consists of an ongoing activity, is not a thing and has itself no exchange value. The weaver's action at the loom, because it does not exist before or after its appearance in the world, cannot as such be either sold or appropriated— although the products of this activity can be. "Labor," Marx wrote, "is the substance and immanent measure of value, but has itself no value."[52] Labor as a visible activity produces but lacks value; labor as a commodity in the moment of exchange has value but does not produce it.[53] To order the disparity between an action without exchange value and its sterling product, the Germans and the British drew upon different fictions. The British, with pay by length, first drew systematic (linear) relations between types of whole cloth and then projected these distinctions onto the weaving activity. The Germans took the *use* of the labor power, or the execution of the activity, as the basis for defining the relative values of fabrics. They did things the other way around from the British: they drew systematic (linear) differences between types of labor and then projected them onto the cloth.

If this interpretation of the contrasting structures of the German and British scales seems incautious, we need only consult the spontaneous evidence offered by the specimens' labels. As early as the 1830s, the tables posted in Germany for remunerating weavers bore the heading "Wage Tariff" or "Wage Table," even when the employees were hand weavers.[54] In 1849, German textile workers called their proposal for a piece-rate system a "Table of Values for Labor Power."[55] The scales for weavers in Britain were entitled "Statement of Prices" or "Weavers' Prices." The phrases hid nothing: the term *price* could just as well have designated the requisition of a product.

To explain the divergence in the structures of the weaving scales, let us start with solutions that treat the methods as naturally prompted adaptations to the immediate circumstances of production. We do not thereby privilege utili-

52. Marx, *Kapital*, op. cit., pp. 65, 559.

53. Karl Marx, *The Poverty of Philosophy* (New York: International Publishers, 1963 [1847]), p. 58. See also Allen Oakley, *Marx's Critique of Political Economy* (London: Routledge & Kegan Paul, 1984), Volume I, p. 118.

54. Stadtarchiv Chemnitz, Protokoll, Verein der arbeitnehmenden Webermeister, August 11, 1848; Eugen Hecking, *100 Jahre J. Hecking* (Neuenkirchen: self-published, 1958); Staatsarchiv Dresden, company records of *Nottroth Textilfabrik*.

55. *Die Verbrüderung*, February 9, 1849, pp. 151–152. The list in question was for the spinning branch.

tarian reasoning and assign the symbolic a residual explanatory burden. Hypotheses that reduce social practice to a "rational" adjustment to the economic environment are neither more fundamental nor more parsimonious than arguments that accept the constitutive role of culture. But their inadequacies throw into relief the advantages of a cultural explanation.

The simplest conjecture, perhaps, is that the differences in the concepts used to construct the scales derived from the implements used to measure cloth. By the turn of the century, it had become a common technique in German firms to install on each loom a so-called *Schussuhr*, or "pick clock," which registered the number of shuttle "shots" as the weavers carried them out.[56] The weavers then received their pay based upon readings of this device rather than upon an examination of their product.[57] Pick clocks were virtually absent in Britain before the First World War.[58] Could the difference between the countries in principles of remuneration have arisen due to the greater readiness or ability of German mill proprietors to install this newfangled gadget? No, because the adoption of pay by shot in the textile factories *preceded* the experimental introduction of the pick clock in the 1880s.[59] Despite general reliance on pay by shot in Aachen, for example, the Free Textile Workers' Union reported in 1902 that only one company there had installed pick clocks.[60] Of the ninety weaving mills which paid by shot that were represented at a national conference of German stuff weavers in 1910, only thirty-five had mounted these gadgets.[61] The German system of pay was not, therefore, originally adopted to take advantage of this mechanical innovation.

Pay by shot did not simplify the determination or recording of wages. Before the introduction of the pick clock, calculating the number of shots in

56. *Der Textil-Arbeiter,* Number 28, 1898, later quoted in the September 1, 1905, edition of this journal.

57. *Centralblatt für die Textil-Industrie,* 1894, Nr. 13, p. 157, and Nr. 43, p. 499; *Die Textil-Zeitung,* September 23, 1907.

58. See below, Chapter Eleven, pp. 492–93.

59. Mill owners concerned about demonstrating to workers that the cloth was measured correctly had their gauges for length certified by authorities for their accuracy, although weavers were paid per thousand shots. See *Das deutsche Wollen-Gewerbe,* June 1, 1877, p. 493; *Das deutsche Wollen-Gewerbe,* Volume 18, 1886, pp. 31–32; Anton Gruner, *Mechanische Webereipraxis sowie Garnnumerierungen und Garnumrechnungen* (Leipzig: A. Hartleben, 1898).

60. *Der Textil-Arbeiter,* June 13, 1902.

61. *Die Textilarbeiter-Zeitung,* August 6, 1910. For the Rhineland, see HSTAD Landratsamt Mönchengladbach 70, p. 204; *Der Textil-Arbeiter,* January 7, 1910, p. 3; my interview with Herr Noisten, Euskirchen, born 1898.

the manufactured cloth was complicated. The German takers-in or production accountants did not measure individually the tens of thousands of shots
woven across the warp. They began with only the length or weight of the
cloth and a sample of the density, in shots per centimeter. Then they reckoned backwards to arrive at the true object of analysis, the number of shots
the weaver had cranked out.[62] Less often, the shots put in were measured by
the weft yarn used up, and weavers' pay tables were based on the length of
this weft yarn consumed.[63] In any case, the German system did not reduce
the requisite calculations.[64] To the contrary, one factory manager who said
that pay by thousand shots was conceptually superior also complained that

62. Landesarchiv Potsdam, Company Records of F. F. Koswig, notebook "Weberei-
Löhne"; *Das deutsche Wollen-Gewerbe*, June 1, 1877, p. 493; *Centralblatt für die Textil-Indu-
strie*, 1878, Nr. 21, p. 241; *Der Christliche Textilarbeiter*, May 11, 1901, Eupen; *Der
Textil-Arbeiter*, January 7, 1910, Aachen, p. 3; Stadtarchiv Chemnitz, Rep. V, Cap. II, Nr. 109,
March 28, 1848; Nicolas Reiser, *Die Betriebs- und Warenkalkulation für Textilstoffe* (Leipzig:
A. Felix, 1903), p. 79. It is critical to remember that this practice of reckoning backwards means
that some piece-rate scales are described in the sources as pay by meter or pay per piece,
whereas the conceptual basis for the allocation of payment was pay per shot. For examples of
this, see Verband Deutscher Textilarbeiter, Gau Brandenburg, *Die Lohn- und Arbeitsbedingungen in der Niederlausitzer Tuchindustrie 1908–1909* (Berlin: Franz Kotzke, 1909), p. 29;
Otto Löbner, *Praktische Erfahrungen aus der Tuch- und Buckskin-Fabrikation* (Grünberg,
Schl.: Das Deutsche Wollen-Gewerbe, 1892), pp. 659–661; *Zeitschrift für die gesamte Textil-
Industrie*, 1910/1911, Nr. 65, p. 1126, and 1912, Nr. 43, p. 955; *Der Textil-Arbeiter*, May 26,
1911, p. 166, Sommerfeld; *Leipziger Monatschrift für Textil-Industrie*, 1910, Nr. 2, "Lohntarife
für die Buntweberei," *Der Textil-Arbeiter*, August 9, 1901, p. 1; *Der Textil-Arbeiter*, December
30, 1904; *Der Textil-Arbeiter*, September 1, 1905. Staatsarchiv Weimar, Landesregierung
Greiz n, Rep. A, Kapitel IXa, Nr. 165, p. 97, 1905: "Die Ausrechnung des eingewebten Schusses
geschieht nach Massgabe der Kettenlänge"; *Der Textil-Arbeiter*, Plauen, June 21, 1901, Firma
Meinhold und Sohn cites pay by meter, then reckons by pay per shot; likewise, *Der Textil-
Arbeiter*, November 15, 1901, Hohenstein-Ernstthal; *Der Textil-Arbeiter*, Elsterberg, April
25, 1902, citing pay per meter, and May 9 issue, showing pay per shot system in effect; *Der
Textil-Arbeiter*, March 14, 1902, pay per shot getting converted to pay per piece; Stadtarchiv
Augsburg, File 1670, firm of Nagler & Sohn. German weavers who were remunerated per
Stück sometimes calculated changes in the work executed by thousand shots inserted in the
piece: *Die Textilarbeiter-Zeitung*, November 19, 1910, Coesfeld.

63. Staatsarchiv Weimar, Landesregierung Greiz n, Rep. A, Kap. IXa, Nr. 165, 1903–1905,
p. 82; Staatsarchiv Weimar, Reuss älterer Linie, Reuss Landratsamt Greiz Nr. 2524, September, 1882. *Der Textil-Arbeiter*, February 22, 1907, Zwickau; *Der Textil-Arbeiter*, November
17, 1905; *Der Textil-Arbeiter*, July 14, 1911, pp. 219–220, Reichenbach.

64. Nor did pay by shot make it easier for the Germans than for the British to calculate
remuneration for short or "odd cuts" of fabric. Although the British scales were formulated
on the basis of a fixed length of cloth, they graduated pay or prorated it for lengths that were
shorter or longer than standard. (See Calderdale Archives, JM646, and pay scales listed above.)
Therefore an analyst could not seek an explanation for the difference in pay systems by
arguing that the German system represented a better method for handling variation in the
lengths of the warps assigned to weavers.

it required more intricate computations.[65] Yet the adoption of the method even among small woolen firms in Aachen and elsewhere which had negligible clerical staffs shows that company investments in accounting do not clarify the reasons for the diffusion of pay by shot in Germany.

Might it have been easier for the weavers to verify the calculation of their receipts under one system or the other? Weavers in both countries complained that they could not easily verify the length of the cloth they wove. The Germans' adoption of pay by shot could not have been intended to alleviate this problem, since they reckoned backwards to the shots after measuring the fabric's length. Often employers and workers even cited wages per meter of cloth turned in, when the evaluation of the value of a meter depended on the analysis of the shots. What is more, many German firms continued to invest in apparatuses which their takers-in used for measuring the length of the cloth, just like the gadgets used in Britain, even after these German companies had converted to pay by shot.[66] The new system of pay did not result from technical convenience or forced adaptation to the physical instruments of calibration.

The divergent principles of the piece-rate systems could not have influenced the weavers' incentive to work. In both countries, once a weaver had a warp in the loom, the ratio of earnings to the cloth turned out remained constant whether the weaver completed the warp quickly or slowly. The marginal returns to effort in a given time period could diverge in the two countries between densities of cloth, not on a given piece of cloth mounted in the loom. Nor did the divergent construction of the German and British schedules lead to differences in the distribution of earnings among weavers in the two countries. True, when one converts the British piece rates to the German dimension of thought, one finds that British weavers earned less on the middle ranges of cloth density in comparison with either endpoint of the British scale than did German weavers on the middle ranges of cloth density in comparison with either endpoint of the German scale. That this formal incongruity created real differences between Germany and Britain in the distribution of earnings among weavers seems unlikely, however, for the range of fabric densities encompassed by the tables varied by company and by town. In other words, German weavers on middle densities of cloth did not always earn more than

65. Löbner, op. cit., pp. 658–662. For Grünberg, Silesia, *Das deutsche Wollen-Gewerbe*, 1892, pp. 659–661.

66. *Der Textil-Arbeiter*, February 3, 1905; September 1, 1905, Euskirchen; November 17, 1905, Sommerfeld.

those on middle densities in Britain, because the range of fabrics covered by each scale, and therefore what counted as the "middle," varied from scale to scale. Within the same town, the endpoint of one piece-rate chart might be the midpoint of the next. In the aggregate, the design of the schedules did not have an appreciable effect upon the distribution of earnings.

In a word, the difference between the principles adopted in Germany and in Britain cannot be explained by the ease or efficiency with which the piece-rate structures served the function of appropriating labor for a wage. The two systems served this purpose equally well; they differed, not in their material function, but in their intelligible form. If there were no concrete obstacles in the immediate environment of the labor process that prevented the British from paying weavers per shot of the shuttle like the Germans, could the difference in pay systems reflect nothing more than the lingering effect of business factors that had operated in the past? The utilitarian arguments considered so far attend only to contemporaneous settings. Suppose institutional inertia had frozen into place pay methods that conformed to the necessities of an earlier period?

Before the rise of the factory system, German weavers who worked at home had their remuneration calculated by a variety of payment systems, including the fabric's weight and, in some instances, its length, just as did their counterparts in Britain.[67] The principle of pay by shot prevailed in Germany contemporaneously with the transition from the putting-out system to factory production.[68] Could this endorsement of pay by shot have reflected the economic conditions under which the German factories initially emerged? By this kind of diachronic reasoning, the British might have transplanted the format of the handweaving scales into the newborn factories, where they took permanent root in collective understandings between employers' and workers' unions; whereas the Germans, who founded their factories later, could have started off with more "modern" thinking, shorn of the legacy of mercantile capitalism. This speculative reasoning merits consideration but collides with the evidentiary record.

---

67. See also Rolf Paas, "Die Beeinflussung der sozialen und wirtschaftlichen Lage der Weber durch die Mechanisierung der deutschen Textilindustrie," diss., Universität Köln, 1961, pp. 56–57; Karl Emsbach, *Die soziale Betriebsverfassung der rheinischen Baumwollindustrie im 19. Jahrhundert* (Bonn: Röhrscheid, 1982), pp. 178–180; Reiser, op. cit., p. 78.

68. For an early example of a factory scale, entitled "Machine Labor," that illustrates the characteristic German logic of linearity per thousand shots and cloth density, see *Chemnitzer Freie Presse*, June 1, 1872. For reference to another pay system established during the 1870s based on the total shots, see *Leipziger Monatschrift für Textil-Industrie*, 1914, Nr. 11, p. 273.

To begin, comparative logic can rule out conjectures based on the timing of development. The Yorkshire woolen trade, unlike the precocious cotton districts of Lancashire, mechanized production no earlier than did many firms in regions of Germany such as the Wuppertal.[69] When the Germans did mechanize, they passed through the same sequence of development as the British, moving from an extensive network of small manufactories and of home weaving under the putting-out system to a full-fledged factory system.[70] The Germans adopted pay by shot whether they set up factories in regions such as Aachen, where small manufactories with handlooms preceded the factory system, or in regions such as urban Mönchengladbach or rural Silesia, where the path of development usually led directly from home weaving to factories.[71] Therefore an analyst cannot explain the national differences in pay systems either by the timing of development or by the forms of the textile labor process that preceded mechanized production. In some areas the shift to pay by shot preceded the development of factories. In the areas around Aachen and in Berlin, for example, it appeared in artisanal workshops for handweavers during the 1860s, *before* these shops gave way to large factories with power looms.[72] The change in methods of pay did not simply mirror changes on the shop floor itself. The close resemblance in the products and markets of firms in Aachen and Huddersfield assures us that no technical factor in Germany, which was absent in Yorkshire, spurred the factories in Aachen to move to pay by shot at an early date.

Nor can one attribute the difference in pay systems to the social origins or acquired business knowledge of the pioneering textile entrepreneurs who founded the earliest factories. As in Britain, so in Germany the largest portion of early mill owners had played a role as middlemen in the putting-

---

69. See Chapter One, at footnote 8, above.

70. Maxine Berg et al., *Manufacture in Town and Country Before the Factory* (Cambridge: Cambridge University Press, 1983); Peter Kriedte, Hans Medick, and Jürgen Schlumbohm, *Industrialisierung vor der Industrialisierung* (Göttingen: Vandenhoeck und Ruprecht, 1977).

71. Herbert Kisch, "The Textile Industries in Silesia and the Rhineland: A Comparative Study in Industrialization," *Journal of Economic History* Volume 19, No. 4 (December 1959), pp. 541–564.

72. Reiser, op. cit., p. 78. In 1857 the weavers in Greiz, although they were not wage workers, calculated the thousands of shots of the loom executed daily in order to justify a certain fee. Staatsarchiv Weimar, Landesregierung Greiz, a Rep. A, Kap. XXI/2c, Nr. 400, Petition of the Guild of Linen and Stuff Weavers of Greiz, May 20, 1857. Workers' remuneration was calculated by thousand shots in the small, cut-rate weaving shops that lived by contracts for quick orders when larger factories were swamped. *Der Christliche Textilarbeiter*, May 26, 1900, Eupen.

out system or had operated workshops for the dyeing, finishing, or fulling of cloth. They had gained an understanding of the organization of trade as mediators between home workers and merchants.[73] The assiduous research of François Crouzet, among others, shows that few of the heads of leading merchant concerns in Britain became factory employers, compared to the preponderance of small workshop owners and of putters-out who had organized the day-to-day operations of domestic production.[74] Such findings make it implausible to surmise that British factory practices based on the appropriation of materialized labor were handed down from the conceptions of employers who had started out as mere traders in finished goods and remained attached to this outlook.[75] The factory pioneers in Britain had the experience of operating small manufactories or of acting as "manufactur-

73. Pat Hudson, *The Genesis of Industrial Capital* (Cambridge: Cambridge University Press, 1986), pp. 75–76; Anthony Howe, *The Cotton Masters, 1830–1860* (Oxford: Clarendon Press, 1984), p. 8; H. Wutzmer, "Die Herkunft der industriellen Bourgeoisie Preussens in den vierziger Jahren des 19. Jahrhunderts," in Hans Mottek et al., editors, *Studien zur Geschichte der industriellen Revolution in Deutschland* (Berlin: Akademie-Verlag, 1960), pp. 146 ff.; Emsbach, op. cit., pp. 343 ff.; Horst Blumberg, *Die deutsche Textilindustrie in der industriellen Revolution* (Berlin: Akademie-Verlag, 1965), pp. 133 ff.; Gerhard Adelmann, "Die wirtschaftlichen Führungsschichten der Rheinisch-Westfälischen Baumwoll- und Leinenindustrie von 1850 bis zum ersten Weltkrieg," in Herbert Helbig, *Führungskräfte der Wirtschaft im 19. Jahrhundert*, Teil II, 1790–1914 (Limburg: C. A. Starke, 1977); Horst Beau, *Das Leistungswissen des frühindustriellen Unternehmertums in Rheinland und Westfalen* (Köln: Rheinisch-Westfälisches Wirtschaftsarchiv, 1959), pp. 61–62; Friedrich Zunkel, *Der Rheinisch-Westfälische Unternehmer 1834–1879* (Köln: Westdeutscher Verlag, 1962), p. 26; Erich Dittrich, "Zur sozialen Herkunft des sächsischen Unternehmertums," in H. Kretzschmar, editor, *Neues Archiv für sächsische Geschichte und Altertumskunde*, Volume 63 (Dresden: Baensch-Druckerei, 1943), pp. 147 ff.; Wolfgang Uhlmann, "Die Konstituierung der Chemnitzer Bourgeoisie während der Zeit der bürgerlichen Umwälzung von 1800 bis 1871," Ph.D. diss., Pädagogische Hochschule Dresden, 1988, pp. 26, 55.

  With the exception of those in upper Silesia, the landowners in Germany who were compensated for the loss of feudal rights invested their receipts in agriculture, not in private factories. Harald Winkel, *Die Ablösungskapitalien aus der Bauernbefreiung in West- und Süddeutschland* (Stuttgart: Gustav Fischer Verlag, 1968), pp. 151–152, 160–161.

74. "I was brought up as a merchant," said Benjamin Gott, the founder of the first large woolen factory in Yorkshire, "and became a manufacturer." Cited in Sidney Pollard, *The Genesis of Modern Management* (London: Edward Arnold, 1965), p. 30. As a man of commerce who had branched out from a very large merchant house, however, Gott was atypical. François Crouzet, *The First Industrialists: The Problem of Origins* (Cambridge: Cambridge University Press, 1985), pp. 106–107, 109–110; Katrina Honeyman, *Origins of Enterprise* (Manchester: Manchester University Press, 1982), p. 81.

75. As mechanized production became widespread, Yorkshire manufacturers rarely occupied themselves with merchanting. Gerald Hurst, *Closed Chapters* (Manchester: Manchester University Press, 1942), p. 3. In Bradford, worsted marketing was dominated by foreign, especially German, agents. Eric M. Sigsworth, *Black Dyke Mills* (Liverpool: Liverpool University Press, 1958), p. 65.

ers," as the directors of the networks of domestic production were called in their day. Conversely, in the German setting both contemporaries and modern historians have emphasized the contributions of small traders and merchants to the founding of textile mills.[76] The industrial commentator Alphons Thun complained in 1879 that German factory managers on the lower Rhine had commercial skills but less knowledge of production technology than their British counterparts.[77] We need not swallow Thun's judgment whole, but the accumulated evidence casts doubt on the hypothesis that the social origins of German businessmen led to a greater focus on production than on relations of exchange.

Still another problem arises with an argument based on the original setting of development. An explanation based on the retention of assumptions about piece-rate schedules from the putting-out system into the late factory age takes it for granted that the principles of the schedules were immutable. What prevented the alteration of the lists? At many Yorkshire mills the weavers were so unorganized that employers could choose their own rules for defining the product and for establishing remuneration.[78] Indeed, some owners chose not to release a pay table at all, but announced the value of a particular piece, as they fancied, *after* the weaver had completed the job.[79] In these cases, obviously, there were no barriers to change in the reckoning of pay. In most regions of Yorkshire, the piece-rate tables

76. For the wool industry of the lower Rhine, see Franz Decker, *Die betriebliche Sozialordnung der Dürener Industrie im 19. Jahrhundert* (Köln: Rheinisch-Westfälisches Wirtschaftsarchiv, 1965), pp. 107, 109–110. Elsewhere: Jürgen Kocka, "Entrepreneurs and Managers in German Industrialization," in *The Cambridge Economic History of Europe,* Volume VII, Part I (Cambridge: Cambridge University Press, 1978), pp. 517–518, 521; Jürgen Kocka, *Die Angestellten in der deutschen Geschichte, 1850–1980* (Göttingen: Vandenhoeck & Ruprecht, 1981), p. 45.

77. Alphons Thun, *Die Industrie am Niederrhein und ihre Arbeiter* (Leipzig: Duncker & Humblot, 1879), Erster Theil, p. 39, and Zweiter Theil, pp. 198, 249–250. For a parallel opinion, Erich Thal, *Die Entstehung und Entwicklung der Halbwoll- und Wollindustrie im M.-Gladbacher Bezirk bis zum Jahre 1914* (Mönchengladbach: W. Hütter, 1926), p. 116.

78. In the Huddersfield woolen district, the weavers' union founded to conduct the 1883 strike could count only 700 members by 1888. James Hinton, *Labour and Socialism* (Amherst: University of Massachusetts Press, 1983), p. 56. By 1891 enrollment had risen to 2,000 members, still less than a quarter of the weavers. PP 1892 XXXV, p. 199. In the Bradford district, only one-sixteenth of the weavers were in the union on the eve of the great Manningham Mills strike. PP 1892 XXXV, pp. 222, 225. On the dismal history of unionization in worsted textiles, see J. Reynolds and K. Laybourn, "The Emergence of the Independent Labour Party in Bradford," *International Review of Social History* Volume 20, Part 3 (1975), p. 316.

79. Royal Commission on Labour, PP 1892 XXXV, p. 230; *Yorkshire Factory Times,* November 1, 1889, Marsh, p. 4; January 10, 1890, Huddersfield; Sept. 18, 1891, Worth Valley, p. 5; May 20, 1892, Mirfield; April 21, 1905, Dudley Hill; and November 22, 1901, p. 4.

were negotiated separately in each factory. In Lancashire, to be sure, the power of a well-organized union movement which regulated the piece rates for weavers made it cumbersome to introduce modifications. But the Lancashire weavers declared their readiness to accept new means of calculating pay, so long as the "aggregate wage fund should not be lowered."[80] The absence of insuperable institutional obstacles to changes in the derivation of rates suggests the operation of another principle: namely, the effect of the lived enactment of the tenet that labor was conveyed as it was embodied in a visible product.

The assumptions about labor that were implicit in the scales were reproduced endogenously by the scales' quotidian use. Not all workers were educated enough to compute exactly the pence or pfennigs owed them for cloth of a given design. No matter: through the scales' material operation they received the ideal definition of the sale of labor. *Facta non verba*: the principles were communicated in action by signifying practice, not by fine phrases. But in ordinary conversation, when British weavers from different factories described their pay scales to one another, they cited the pay for a density at a fixed length, called the "basis," and then stated by how much the pay rose or fell for each increase or decrease in picks per inch.[81] When the British weavers suffered a reduction in rates, they said the factory employer was "pulling pence off" the picks, as if the remuneration inhered in the cloth.[82] Whereas British workers thought in terms of exchanging the length of cloth for payment, the German workers could assert that pay by length was "categorically erroneous."[83] Workers in

80. *Cotton Factory Times*, January 29, 1904, p. 1. See also Chapter Eleven, footnotes 41–43.
81. *Yorkshire Factory Times*, October 11, 1889, and November 22, 1889. In Yeadon the weavers used a "Ready Reckoner" device, 500 copies of which were distributed by the union, to verify their piece rates. Archive of General Union of Dyers, Bleachers, and Textile Workers, Bradford, Minutes, Factory Workers' Union, March 14, 1894. When workers and owners used the phrase, for example, "six pence per pick" to calculate pay, this referred not to each of the picks the weaver wove in but to earnings for so many picks per inch, given a fixed length of cloth. Their language shows that they took the principle of pay by length as a given that regulated their comparisons. See, for example, the wage notes of Bairstow firm, Leeds District Archives, in which listing of picks means picks per inch; *Yorkshire Factory Times*, November 22, 1889; and testimony of Herbert Foster, partner of Fosters of Queensbury, regarding payment "for the picks," Royal Commission on Labour, PP 1892 XXXV, p. 270.
82. *Yorkshire Factory Times*, January 31, 1890, Bingley.
83. *Der Textil-Arbeiter*, July 14, 1911, pp. 219–220. In the Mönchengladbach region weavers asserted that piece rates for the same fabric at various firms could be compared and standardized only on the basis of pay per thousand shots, overlooking the alternative used in British districtwide lists. *Der Christliche Textilarbeiter*, May 16, 1903.

Germany sometimes calculated their output in terms of the number of shuttle motions completed per day, without reference to the length of fabric.[84] They complained about the intensification of work quotas not in terms of cloth delivered, but in terms of the additional shots executed.[85] The secret code embedded in practice became the workers' language of debate and deliberation.

The responses of German weavers to the transition to the principle of earnings per shot in the earliest days of the factory have left no traces. But the discussions of commercial experts, preserved in business newspapers, show that employers preferred this mode of piece rates because it captured the process of carrying out the work. Textile periodicals in the 1870s took pay by shot as a commonplace or described the abandonment of pay by length as a routine occurrence.[86] They spun words around that which practice had already conceived.[87] These journal articles did not mention any instrumental advantage from the shift, but they emphasized that the system seemed logical. Spokespersons for pay by shot considered this method more appropriate once producers had adopted the idea that weavers in the factory sold the disposition over the conversion of labor to labor power. As one proponent summed up his case, only remuneration by shots really paid the weaver "for the quantity of executed labor."[88] When the Chamber of Commerce for the area of Aachen officially rejected pay by length in 1884, it reasoned that pay by shot offered the only "rational" system of measuring labor.[89] Only with this new method, the chairman reported, "is the weaver paid for what he has really carried out."[90] After the turn of the century, a factory owner from Gera, Saxony,

---

84. *Christlicher Arbeiterfreund,* March 17, 1899. See also Deutscher Textilarbeiterverband, Hauptvorstand/Arbeiterinnensekretariat, op. cit., p. 25.

85. Stadtarchiv Cottbus, AII 3.3 b, 34, meeting of February 8, 1903. For instance, weavers in Coesfeld complained that a new pattern required five thousand shots per piece more than the old. *Die Textilarbeiter-Zeitung,* Nov. 19, 1910.

86. *Centralblatt für die Textil-Industrie,* 1876, Nr. 48, p. 863, Nr. 20, p. 226, and 1878, Nr. 21, p. 241. For an example of an owner mentioning his conversion during the 1870s to pay per thousand shots in plain weaving, see *Centralblatt für die Textilindustrie,* 1879, p. 226.

87. In Chemnitz, weavers received payment by the length of weft thread inserted—a measure of the shots—as early as 1848. Stadtarchiv Chemnitz, *Tarif* of June 1, 1848.

88. *Zeitschrift für die gesamte Textil-Industrie* Vol. 14, Nr. 65 (1910/11), p. 1126.

89. Artur Peltzer, "Die Arbeiterbewegung in der Aachener Textilindustrie von der Mitte des 19. Jahrhunderts bis zum Ausbruch des Weltkrieges," Ph.D. diss., Universität Marburg, 1924, p. 10.

90. Reiser, op. cit., pp. 78–79. By 1909, pay by length was derided in Aachen as an "antiquated system." *Die Textilarbeiter-Zeitung,* July 24, 1909. See the factory ordinance of the firm Joseph Kaltenbach, dating from before 1890, HSTAD, Regierung Aachen 1633, and *Der*

reiterated the causes for the triumph of pay by shot. He said in 1905 that among the city's factories, only one continued to pay weavers by cloth length. "The [length of] filled-in warp cannot be taken for the performance of labor by the worker," he explained.[91] In sum, earnings by shot seemed to the employers more coherent, not necessarily more profitable.

By no means did pay by shot become a universal custom in Germany before the First World War. A great many instances can be found of German mills continuing to pay weavers by the piece or by weight. In borderlands such as the Münsterland, where many factory owners before the First World War were of Dutch origin, pay by shot emerged less frequently.[92] Elsewhere, employers whose mills manufactured only coarse, undyed varieties of cloth sometimes did not specify picks per inch to the weaver or measure the total picks, but simply weighed the product and paid the weaver for putting a minimum weight of weft into the warp. Yet to varying degrees, pay by shot encompassed the major types of weaves and materials: wool, linen, cotton, and silk.[93] Even if payment by shot was not universal in

---

Textil-Arbeiter, January 7, 1910, p. 3. For neighboring Eupen, see Zentrales Staatsarchiv Merseburg, Rep. 77, 2525, Nr. 3, Band 1, pp. 6 ff., 1899, and *Die Textilarbeiter-Zeitung*, February 4, 1905. For neighboring Würselen, see *Christliche Arbeiterin*, December 7, 1907.

91. *Der Textil-Arbeiter*, September 1, 1905.

92. Germany, *Jahres-Berichte der königlich preussischen Regierungs- und Gewerberäthe und Bergbehörden, 1905* (Berlin: R. v. Deckers Verlag, 1906), p. 265. For an instance of an important citywide pay scale that paid weavers by length in Meerane as the British did, see Staatsarchiv Dresden, Amthauptmannschaft Glauchau, Nr. 393, 1902, Meerane, pp. 2 ff. (Yet this district converted to pay for the insertion of weft by 1919: Archiv des Volkseigenen Betriebs Palla, Firma Klemm & Co., Nr. 295, "Kalkulationen und Lohntarife.") Pay per shot was also less likely to prevail in German towns that lacked a guild tradition during the eighteenth century, for reasons that in Chapter Six will become obvious. In the silk capital of Krefeld, for instance, where weavers' guilds were not a fixture of the eighteenth century, piece payments based on length per se predominated. Stadtarchiv Krefeld, Bestand 4, Nr. 1117, Königsberger & Co., circa 1906. On the absence of guilds in Krefeld, Franz Wischer, "Die Organisationsbestrebungen der Arbeiter in der Krefelder Seiden- und Samtindustrie," Ph.D. diss., Universität Köln, 1920, p. 13.

93. By way of illustration, cotton: Stadtarchiv Gera, "Mindest-Akkordlohn-Tarif," 1905; Deutscher Textilarbeiter-Verband, Fiale Neumünster, *Jahresbericht für das Geschäftsjahr 1912* (Hamburg: Verlagsgesellschaft deutscher Konsumvereine, 1913), p. 10; Deutscher Textilarbeiterverband; *Jahrbuch des deutschen Textilarbeiterverbandes, 1911* (Berlin: Karl Hübsch, 1912), p. 79; *Der Textil-Arbeiter*, July 14, 1911, Reichenbach and October 27, 1911, Mönchengladbach; *Der Christliche Textilarbeiter*, March 18, 1905, Schneiders & Irmen; *Zeitschrift für die gesamte Textil-Industrie*, 1910/1911, Nr. 65, p. 1126 and Hermann Hölters, "Die Arbeiterverhältnisse in der niederrheinischen Baumwollindustrie mit besonderer Berücksichtigung der männlichen Arbeiter," diss. Heidelberg, 1911, p. 24. Cotton mixtures: HSTAD Regierung Düsseldorf 24706, 1910, pp. 254–255; Deutscher Textilarbeiterverband, *30 Jahre Kampf der Textilarbeiter von Greiz und Umgegend um bessere Arbeits- und Lohnbedingungen* (Greiz: Verlag des Deutschen Textilarbeiterverbandes, n.d.), p. 28; Deutscher Textilar-

Germany, it was predominant there while it was unknown in Britain.[94] In national surveys of German stuff and wool firms in 1910, 75 to 85 percent were found to pay weavers per thousand shots or by a correlate the length of weft used to insert the shots.[95] The prevalence of payment by shot in Germany marked the outstanding difference between the philosophies of

beiterverband, *Jahrbuch des deutschen Textilarbeiterverbandes, 1911* (Berlin: Karl Hübsch, 1912), p. 79; *Die Textilarbeiter-Zeitung*, June 6, 1914. For silk: *Der Textil-Arbeiter* Nov. 15, 1901, Hohenstein-Ernsthal; *Die Textilarbeiter-Zeitung*, August 5, 1911, Süchteln. For pay by shot in linen, see *Der Textil-Arbeiter*, September 6, 1905.

94. For Aachen, Merseburg Rep 120 BB VII Fach 3 Nr. 32, pp. 119–125, 1895; *Die Textil-arbeiter-Zeitung*, September 25, 1909. For Hämmern, *Der Christliche Textilarbeiter*, June 16, 1900. For Aggertal, *Die Textilarbeiter-Zeitung*, April 8, 1911. For northern Germany, *Der Textil-Arbeiter*, Neumünster, June 13, 1902. For firms in Euskirchen, HSTAD Landratsamt Euskirchen 139, 1899, pp. 152 ff; HSTAD Landratsamt Euskirchen 270, July 9, 1906; *Der Textil-Arbeiter*, May 17, 1912; *Textilarbeiter-Zeitung*, May 4, 1912. For firms in Mönchengladbach, see: HSTAD Landratsamt Mönchengladbach 70, p. 204; Landratsamt Mönchengladbach 99, pp. 420 ff.; Stadtarchiv Mönchengladbach, 1c 913, July 2, 1912 report and Bestand 5/660 Schippers & Daniels, October 26, 1910 and Gebrüder Brandts, August 29, 1910; *Der Christliche Textilarbeiter*, March 18, 1905, *Die Textilarbeiter-Zeitung*, May 11, 1907, April 1, 1905, and May 22, 1909; *Der Christliche Textilarbeiter* for Reuter und Paas, May 16, 1903; *Die Textilarbeiter-Zeitung*, January 23, 1909, Busch & Florenz; August 5, 1911, Joest & Pauen; *Der Textil-Arbeiter*, November 25, 1904. For Eupen, *Der Christliche Textilarbeiter*, December 9, 1899; *Die Textilarbeiter-Zeitung*, February 4, 1905; Zentrales Staatsarchiv Merseburg, Rep. 77, 2525, No. 3, Band 1, January, 1899, pp. 6 ff. For eastern Germany, see Stadtarchiv Cottbus, AII 3. 3 b, 33, December 12, 1895; Stadtarchiv Cottbus, AII 3. 3 b, Nr. 34, February 22, 1903, and January 20, 1904; *Die Textilarbeiter-Zeitung*, March 20, 1909, July 10, 1909, and November 20, 1909, Forst (Lausitz); *Der Textil-Arbeiter*, May 16, 1902, and June 13, 1902, Muskau (Oberlausitz); *Der Textil-Arbeiter*, October 20, 1905, Chemnitz; Stadtarchiv Crimmitschau, Rep. III, Kap. IX, Lit. B, Nr. 23, 1901, p. 106; *Der Textil-Arbeiter*, March 7, 1902, and February 10, 1905, Spremberg; *Der Textil-Arbeiter*, April 18, 1902, Görlitz; *Der Textil-Arbeiter*, September 8, 1905, Luckenwalde; *Der Textil-Arbeiter*, January 24, 1902, Nowawes; *Der Textil-Arbeiter*, January 24, 1902, Cottbus; *Der Textil-Arbeiter*, June 21, 1901, Plauen; *Der Textil-Arbeiter*, June 7, 1901, Falkenstein (Voigtland); *Der Textil-Arbeiter*, Grossenhain, May 24, 1901; *Der Textil-Arbeiter*, May 24, 1901, Elsterberg; *Der Textil-Ar-beiter*, March 19, 1909, Sommerfeld; Verband Deutscher Textilarbeiter, *Tariferläuterungen und Statistisches: Bearbeitet nach Aufzeichnungen der Tarifkommission im Sächsisch-Thüringischen Textilbezirk* (Gera: Alban Bretschneider, 1909), p. 15; Staatsarchiv Weimar, Landesregierung Greiz n, Rep. A, Kap. IXa, Nr. 165, 1905, p. 95; Stadtarchiv Crimmitschau, Rep. III, Kap. IX, Lit. B, Nr. 23, Nov. 16, 1901; *Das deutsche Wollen-Gewerbe*, June 1, 1877, p. 122, Forst; Stadtarchiv Werdau, Rep. II, Kap. 4, Nr. 77, Band 2, 1907, p. 13; *Märkische Volksstimme*, Dec. 3, 1905, Neumünster. For southern Germany, see *Der Textil-Arbeiter*, May 16, 1902, Nagold (Württemberg); *Der Textil-Arbeiter*, June 23, 1905, Lambrecht, dating to at least 1900; *Der Textil-Arbeiter*, December 30, 1904, Schiltach (Baden).

95. Of 115 stuff and wool mills polled at a national union conference in 1910, 98 paid by shot. *Die Textilarbeiter-Zeitung*, August 6, 1910. Deutscher Textilarbeiterverband, *Die Tuch-Konferenz in Crimmitschau 26. und 27. Februar 1910: Unterhandlungs-Bericht* (Berlin: Carl Hübsch, 1910), p. 13. A regional survey of 122 weaving mills in the Niederlausitz during 1908 found that 87 percent paid weavers per thousand shots. Verband Deutscher Textilarbeiter, Gau Brandenburg, op. cit., p. 30.

paying weavers presented in the two countries' business press.[96] "Under any circumstances," concluded a German textile journal in 1910, "the wage calculation for fabric by a certain number of weft threads is more proper than by a piece of fabric or by a certain number of pieces."[97]

If the contrasting principles embedded in the operation of German and British piece-rate scales can be explained neither by the mute exigencies of the labor process nor by the legacy of earlier changes at the point of production, where are we to turn for an understanding of their development and significance? To construct weavers' piece-rate scales, managers in both Germany and Britain could not just measure the effort or time taken to weave a single type of cloth. They had to come up with a way of equating the different kinds of labor that went into different kinds of cloth. They could not accomplish this by empirical tests, because weaving was neither a simple process of tending a machine nor a matter of applying one's skill and energy directly as an artisan would, without the interposition of an unmastered technology. Either of these ideal types of production facilitates the empirical measurement of labor in terms of time or, what may amount to the same thing, in terms of the goods it takes a certain amount of time to produce. Weaving, by contrast, consisted of an interaction between the worker, unreliable tools, quirky raw materials, and weather, to turn out a large and changing array of patterns. In a single day a large mill could have over sixty types of cloth in its looms.[98] The enormous variety of patterns and the interaction of such shifting and unmeas-

96. See supporting comments in *Die Textil-Zeitung*, September 23, 1907, and February 27, 1905. For other examples of managers taking pay by shot as the natural method, see *Die Textil-Zeitung*, 1904, Nr. 28, p. 948; *Zeitschrift für die gesamte Textil-Industrie*, 1910/1911, Nr. 65, p. 1126; Max Weber, *Gesammelte Aufsätze zur Soziologie und Sozialpolitik* (Tübingen: J. C. B. Mohr, 1924), p. 185; *Zeitschrift für die gesamte Textil-Industrie*, 1912, Nr. 2, p. 31, and 1912, Nr. 3, p. 52 and 1913, Nr. 13, p. 312; Friedrich Leitner, *Die Selbstkostenberechnung industrieller Betriebe* (3d ed. Frankfurt am Main: J. D. Sauerländer, 1908), p. 179. The *Leipziger Monatschrift für Textil-Industrie* (1914, Nr. 3, p. 82), *Centralblatt für die Textil-Industrie* (1893, Nr. 10, p. 147), and *Christlicher Arbeiterfreund* (March 17, 1899) measured the output of a weaver per day in terms of shots instead of length of product. See also Rolf Paas, op. cit., p. 57.

97. *Zeitschrift für die gesamte Textil-Industrie*, 1910/1911, Nr. 65, p. 1126. The *Leipziger Monatschrift für Textil-Industrie* also recommended pay by shot as "best," without reference to pick clocks: 1910, Nr. 2.

98. Richard Marsden, *Cotton Weaving: Its Development, Principles, and Practice* (London: George Bell & Sons, 1895), p. 471; N. K. Scott, "The Architectural Development of Cotton Mills in Preston and District," Master's thesis, University of Liverpool, 1952, note volume, p. 16. A mill of medium size might turn out three to four hundred types of cloth in the course of a year, Max Weber found. Max Weber, *Gesammelte Aufsätze*, p. 156. Also *Die Textil-Zeitung*, January 19, 1897, "Sprechsaal."

urable factors caused managers in both countries to declare it impossible to gauge from experience or trials the time taken to weave each type of fabric.[99] The weavers themselves scarcely considered such an empirical procedure.[100] British weavers sometimes learned to regret the imprecision: some of them who struck work and succeeded in obtaining a piece-rate schedule of their own design found that the scales they had expected to offer an improvement in rewards led instead to an appreciable decline in compensation.[101] In short, the environment was so chaotic that it could not be mirrored in a coherent scale.

Neither lack of attention to the problem nor a naive wish for simplicity led economic agents to deploy a linear scheme for equating different kinds of weaving whose execution had never been individually timed, but a preference for quantifying labor on a linear scale did. The piece-rate tables incorporated a striking difference between specifications of labor as a commodity: in Germany, workers were remunerated for the conversion of labor power into a product; in Britain, they sold their labor as it was concretized in a product. This explanation not only suits the immediate evidence, but it also explains a whole constellation of differences between the institutions of German and British textile mills. By proceeding to show that other forms of practice, such as fines imposed on workers for defective cloth, the categories for wage records, and the transfer of jobs between workers in a single factory incarnated disparate views of labor as a commodity, we may enhance the plausibility and plenitude of a cultural explanation.

99. *Centralblatt für die Textilindustrie*, 1893, Nr. 12, p. 176. In weaving, managers could not build pay scales by reckoning backwards from the comparative selling prices of the goods in the market, for the patterns of cloth were often produced as unique batch jobs. On the impracticality of pegging piece rates to the market prices of cloth, see J. de L. Mann, "Clothiers and Weavers in Wiltshire During the Eighteenth Century," in L. S. Pressnell, editor, *Studies in the Industrial Revolution* (London: Athlone Press, University of London, 1960), p. 75.

100. The variation in weaving time due to circumstances of the moment was "enormous." Victor Böhmert, "Die Methode der Lohnstatistik," *Der Arbeiterfreund: Zeitschrift des Central-Vereins in Preussen für das Wohl der arbeitenden Klassen* (Berlin: Otto Janke, 1877), pp. 424–46. In 1856 a representative from the board that designed the Macclesfield piece-rate schedules testified that the question of how much time it would take an average weaver to complete a piece of each kind of fabric was never considered. "The question was, what should be paid for a particular article." *Report from the Select Committee on Masters and Operatives*, PP 1856 (343) XIII, p. 167.

101. Andrew Bullen, "Pragmatism Versus Principle: Cotton Employers and the Origins of an Industrial Relations System," in J. A. Jowitt and A. J. McIvor, editors, *Employers and Labour in the English Textile Industries, 1850–1914* (London: Routledge, 1988), p. 32.

DEFINING FINES

Remuneration by piece rates confronted managers with a challenge: how could they ensure that weavers driven to increase the quantity of their output also took care to manufacture cloth of adequate quality? Owners in textiles, as in many nineteenth-century enterprises, found it expedient to impose fines for defective goods—or to hold this sanction in reserve—as a deterrent against workers who might otherwise maximize their earnings by focusing on product quantity alone. But the technology of production made this issue more salient in textiles.[102] The power loom, one of the earliest and inherently clumsiest of mechanical technologies, remained so primitive up to the First World War that under the best conditions it regularly produced defects in the fabric. Managers believed that even well-run machines produced cloth with defects in one out of every ten pieces.[103] Contemporaries therefore agreed that weavers did not have a responsibility to hand in perfect cloth, only to avoid creating severe irregularities or a greater than usual number of errors. Indeed, German and British employers sometimes introduced tolerance limits for the number of flaws that could appear in a run of cloth before fining began.[104]

In both countries, the norms for what factory owners might sell to merchants as premier quality and what they had to sell at a discount as "damaged" fluctuated with the business cycle. Since nearly all cloth was to some extent imperfect, the strength of consumer demand at a given moment influenced the stringency of merchants' standards. A merchant could find after making a purchase from the factory owner that a particular piece was too damaged to satisfy customers and would return the piece to the factory for a refund.[105] Given the indeterminacy of what constituted "bad cloth" in the market, the standard for acceptable quality on the shop floor was estab-

---

102. See the inspectors' results in *Der Textil-Arbeiter,* July 10, 1914, p. 221.

103. *Textile Mercury,* August 8, 1908, p. 106. The proportion of defects varied with the complexity of the pattern, the quality of materials, and the stringency of the firm's standards. At the Epe factory of the firm Gebrüder Laurenz, managers declared fewer than 0.5 percent of pieces defective. Westfälisches Wirtschaftsarchiv Dortmund, F61, Nr. 222.

104. Deutscher Textilarbeiterverband, *Jahrbuch des deutschen Textilarbeiterverbandes, 1913* (Berlin: Karl Hübsch, 1914), p. 113, Aachen; *Der Textil-Arbeiter,* September 1, 1911, Aachen; *Yorkshire Factory Times,* January 17, 1890, Halifax; *Textile Manufacturer,* April 15, 1911, p. 138.

105. *Zeitschrift für die gesamte Textil-Industrie,* Volume 12, Nr. 6, p. 67. In Britain a large number of "job-merchants" specialized in trading slightly defective goods. *Textile Mercury,* 1909, p. 64.

lished through never-ending conflict and negotiation between employers and workers. Fining for bad output ranked as one of the concerns uppermost in textile workers' minds.[106]

The British managers distinguished themselves by sometimes delaying the imposition of a fine for faulty cloth until the effect of the damage had been assessed on the market. They routinely levied a retroactive charge upon the responsible weaver when it finally turned out that a damaged piece fetched a substandard price on the market (in addition to any fines the managers may have levied for faults detected at the moment the weaver handed in the piece). Where the company's cloth examiner was uncertain whether a piece with marginal damage would clear the market, however, he withheld the weaver's wage pending the merchants' inspections. The final deduction might occur many weeks after the weaver had been paid for the piece.[107] A correspondent from Yorkshire, in an exasperated report on the uncertainty weavers experienced over whether they would receive the full price of a piece of fabric, testified, "I have known weavers wait six months for a piece wage."[108] Workers at a firm in Brierfeld reported that their employer followed the market rationale to its conclusion. He notified weavers that they had to cover whatever deductions the merchant buyers in Manchester imposed: "One employer has commenced to give up fining workers for faulty cloth," the *Cotton Factory Times* reported in 1897, "but should anything be deducted from the piece at Manchester, the weaver has to bear the cost."[109]

Did the British system of delayed penalties for defective output arise to provide a special cloak for arbitrary and irregular exactions? This seems unlikely, since it obviously complicated record-keeping and since employers could raise fines even without demonstrating corresponding losses in the

106. See the catalog of major grievances, as reported in textile workers' newspapers, in Table 1, Chapter Four below.
107. *Yorkshire Factory Times,* July 31, 1891; April 8, 1892, Huddersfield; July 7, 1893, Batley. For Lancashire, see LRO, DDX 1274/6/1, Burnley, September 1, 1900, and November 1, 1900; LRO, DDX 1089/8/1, Preston, April 6, 1907, p. 154, and April 22, 1907, p. 158; *Cotton Factory Times,* April 1, 1904, Ramsbottom.
108. *Yorkshire Factory Times,* November 13, 1891. If a piece was to be mended before going to market, the weaver might receive nothing for it until the repairer completed the job and the cost of the remedy was known. *Yorkshire Factory Times,* March 21, 1890, Lindley and Marsh. The wage of the mender often came straight out of that of the weaver.
109. *Cotton Factory Times,* January 29, 1897, Brierfeld. British fining methods did not sit comfortably with all employers. A manager wrote in the businessmen's forum, the *Textile Manufacturer* of Manchester, that "the best of workpeople require a certain amount of restraint, but the fining system is a slovenly and careless method of administering it." September 15, 1905, p. 290.

market. If the system arose because the agents believed that the market functioned as the true arbiter of the value of the weaver's labor product in Britain, might weavers have benefited from the system? Did refunds accrue retroactively to weavers for cloth which, contrary to earlier expectations, managed to clear the market? This would indicate that the system followed an impartial logic that was not uniformly disadvantageous to workers. Refunds of punishments were not unheard of, but they seem to have been rare, as one might imagine. The *Yorkshire Factory Times* reported in 1889 that a weaver in Halifax had received a refund of a cloth fine. The in-house examiner had judged the piece defective, but it later passed muster with the firm's outside distributor.[110]

In contrast to their British counterparts, German owners made their deductions immediately inside the factory, based on their own judgment and, in some cases, on a posted scale of their invention (*Stopf-Tarif*) that codified the withholdings for each variety of damage.[111] Whereas the British employers set fines by the market evaluation of the product, the German employers set fines by in-house assessment of activity at the point of production. Even when German owners complained that customers had sent cloth back as defective, they did not make retroactive deductions.[112] The German fining practices may have been influenced by the concepts of German civil law. The civil law book made a distinction between business contracts for the delivery of a product and employment contracts for the offering of a labor service (*Dienstvertrag*). Jurists in Germany classified textile workers who received piece rates as persons who offered a "service," even if the remuneration system paid workers by the quantity of output.[113] This status as an "employee" established the principles for imposing fines: a textile worker "could not be made responsible for defects in the delivered products, only for such, which he committed by reason of gross negligence or malicious intent."[114] The immediate issue was not

110. *Yorkshire Factory Times*, November 1, 1889, p. 5, Halifax.

111. HSTAD, Regierung Düsseldorf, Regierung Aachen 1634, firm Draemann und Peill, Birkesdorf; *Der Textil-Arbeiter*, September 1, 1911, Aachen, and July 3, 1914, Dresden. The fine was usually levied before the finishing department of the mill received the piece. Stadtarchiv Werdau, Rep. i, Nr. 72, Feb. 21, 1891. German weavers thought the fine should be levied before the piece had even been processed by the mending department, which undertook small corrections on even the best pieces. *Reussische Volkszeitung*, February 18, 1902.

112. *Der Christliche Textilarbeiter*, March 15, 1902; *Der Textil-Arbeiter*, April 23, 1909, p. 131.

113. *Das deutsche Wollen-Gewerbe*, 1911, p. 1457.

114. Ibid.

whether the finished product was less than perfect or had less than the full market value; the issue was whether the work had been executed negligently or recklessly.

British courts never drew a principled distinction in the nineteenth century between the offering of a service by an employee and the delivery of a product by a trader. Accordingly, some employers required weavers to purchase and dispose of damaged cloth themselves.[115] Textile employers in Britain who imposed fines for defects used the same expression as would be applied to contractors who delivered a product and had to make good the errors in workmanship. The employers announced, "All bad work must be paid for."[116]

Yet another aspect of some fining systems in Germany diverged from the principle of the exchange of a labor product in the market. German management journals in textiles declared that the fines levied on workers for flaws could not accurately measure the loss the owner would suffer in the market.[117] The surviving fine books show how this assumption worked itself out in practice. They show that some mills standardized the amount withheld for damaged cloth at fifty pfennigs for every piece, as if the punishment functioned as a signal to workers rather than as a means for assessing the actual value of the damage.[118] Since German owners treated the fines principally as a deterrent to poor-quality production rather than as compensation for a loss suffered in the market, they often chose an alternative method for giving weavers an incentive to maintain high standards of work: they paid a bonus for each unobjectionable piece.[119] In the way they utilized the fines collected, too, German owners showed that they viewed the fine as a disciplinary measure rather than as a means of market compensation. Many German firms voluntarily altered their factory ordinances to give the money collected in dockages for faulty cloth to workers' welfare committees. In the Mönchengladbach factory district, forty-seven companies donated such fines to committees at the

---

115. Royal Commission on Labour, PP 1893–1894 [c.6894-XXIII] XXXVII, Part I, p. 115.

116. *Yorkshire Factory Times*, November 15, 1889, Bingley.

117. *Leipziger Monatschrift für Textil-Industrie*, Nr. 8, 1910, p. 233.

118. Westfälisches Wirtschaftsarchiv Dortmund, F11, Conrad Wilhelm Delius & Co., near Gütersloh; Textilmuseum Apolda, Zimmermann, *Verzeichnis über verhängte Geldstrafen*, 1892 to 1906. For the knitting trade, see Wilfrid Greif, *Studien über die Wirkwarenindustrie in Limbach in Sachsen* (Karlsruhe: G. Braunsche Hofbuchdruckerei, 1907), p. 87.

119. *Zeitschrift für die gesamte Textil-Industrie* Volume 11, Nr. 40 (1907–1908), p. 500; *Der Christliche Textilarbeiter*, August 15, 1898, p. 3; Deutscher Textilarbeiterverband, *Protokoll der 10. Generalversammlung, 1910* (Berlin: Karl Hübsch, n.d.), pp. 300 ff.

turn of the century, although they could perfectly well have pocketed this type of fine.[120]

In sum, the fine for damages in Britain compensated the owner for market losses suffered upon disposing of the workers' labor product. In Germany, the fine disciplined the workers for the careless expenditure of their labor power. In Germany, the practice of assessing fines at the point of production reproduced the belief that workers sold the disposition over "labor power" in the production process; in Britain, the practice of delayed, market-based fining maintained the belief that workers transferred a quantity of labor as it was embodied in finished products. The British method of determining the appropriate fine asked what the product was worth, not how the product came to be.[121]

The implementation of adjustments in some piece-rate lists in Britain tallied with this view that workers were paid for bringing materialized labor to market. At most mills in Lancashire, the prices weavers received for each type of cloth were fixed by districtwide rather than firm-specific schedules. When a new list went into effect, it became valid on fabric delivered to the company warehouse after a specified date. The criterion was not when the labor power was expended, but when the product was brought into the sphere of circulation.[122]

THE CIRCULATION OF LABOR

The divergent German and British specifications of the transfer of labor under the wage contract guided the employers' bookkeeping systems for weavers' earnings. Since British factory proprietors thought of themselves as buying labor as it was embodied in the product, their accounting techniques credited funds only to the loom from which the product was delivered, not to the weaver who executed the labor activity. In both Lancashire and Yorkshire, the employers numbered their looms consecutively by row. Usually the wages books indicated only the number of the loom to which the pay went, not the weaver's name.[123] If a weaver left the mill before

---

120. HSTAD, Regierung Düsseldorf 25017, p. 31, for 1895, and HSTAD, Regierung Düsseldorf 25027, pp. 19 ff., for 1904.

121. Herbert Maucher distinguishes between "causal remuneration," compensation based on the process of creating products, and "final remuneration," based on the products' market value (op. cit., p. 3).

122. LRO, DDX 1123/B/438, Amalgamated Weavers' Association, 1937.

123. For examples, see Robert Clough, Brotherton Collection, University of Leeds; Taylor and Littlewood, Kirklees Archives; West Yorkshire Archive Service, Wakefield, C149/490; W. P. Crankshaw, "The Internal Books of a Weaving Mill," *Journal of the British Association of Managers of Textile Works* Volume 4 (1912–1913), p. 114; Elizabeth Roberts's interviews,

finishing a long piece, the company gave the full amount for the piece to the next weaver who came along and had the loom at the moment of completion.[124] Even if the original weaver and the successor did not know each other, the company left it to the weavers to allocate the pay between themselves.[125] When British employers levied fines for defective fabric, they deducted the penalty from the loom, not necessarily from the weaver who had been in charge of the machine when the work was executed.[126] In the Colne Valley, women on the same looms as men worked at disadvantageous piecerate scales, allegedly because the men could do more tuning of the loom on their own and could carry away the finished pieces.[127] But a man who took the loom of an ill woman as a temporary replacement received only the women's rate, because the loom number remained on the company books as a woman's.[128] Each of these procedures treated the weavers as if they were connected to the mill not by a relation of servitorship but by their occupancy of a machine from which the mill received its deliveries.[129]

Like British employers, the Germans identified each loom by cipher and kept track of each loom's output by code in what they called the "weavers' book." In addition, however, they kept records by which they could ascertain the earnings of each weaver as an employee.[130] In German weaving mills, if

---

Preston, Mrs. B1P, born 1900. When the weavers' union in Preston recorded individual members' requests for intervention in dealing with personal grievances, it took down the weavers' loom numbers. See, illustratively, LRO, DDX 1089/8/1, 1904, p. 2. For the 1840s, see H. S. G., *Autobiography of a Manchester Cotton Manufacturer* (Manchester: John Heywood, 1887), p. 32. British pottery works did not register wages paid to each employee name, either. Royal Commission on Labour, PP 1893–1894 XXXVII, Part I, p. 63.

124. Whether the worker was obligated to finish the piece before leaving or needed only to give notice of his leaving formed a point of legal dispute in Britain. *Yorkshire Factory Times,* May 16, 1890, Marsh and Lindley.

125. *Yorkshire Factory Times,* May 23, 1902, p. 5; LRO, DDX 1274/6/1, Burnley, November 1, 1899, and DDX 1089/8/1, pp. 191–192, Oct. 28, 1907; *Cotton Factory Times,* April 2, 1897, Oldham.

126. *Yorkshire Factory Times,* January 7, 1898, p. 4; LRO, DDC 1274/6/1, Burnley, May 1, 1899. *Yorkshire Factory Times,* September 1, 1893, Batley.

127. Some female weavers working on certain types of looms said that they lacked the strength needed to lift the adjusting weights. Elizabeth Roberts's interviews, Mrs. P1P, born 1898, p. 87. The reduced piece rates for women probably exceeded the actual difference in productivity between men and women.

128. *Yorkshire Factory Times,* July 24, 1891, and September 1, 1893, p. 4. The women's scale had the same structure as the men's scale, but lower rates.

129. For a reference to manufacturers employing "looms" rather than weavers in the putting-out trade, see Minutes of Evidence, John Niblett, Committee on Woollen Bill, PP 1802–1803 (95) VII, p. 38.

130. Barmen, *Beiträge zur Statistik der Stadt Barmen,* Volume 2 (1906), pp. 2–3. *Seide,* July 25, 1900, p. 467. Emil Bittner, *Die Fabriks-Buchführung für Webereien* (Leipzig: Hartle-

one weaver took another's place as a temporary replacement, the firm gave the weavers the choice of allocating the wages themselves or of having the firm do it for them.[131] The German mills directed the compensation to the executor of labor, not merely to the immediate supplier of a good.

The British textile mill owners' bookkeeping faced an unanticipated challenge after Parliament passed the Insurance Act of 1911. Under this law, employers had to transfer weekly deductions from workers' pay to the friendly societies and companies administering the insurance plan. In an address to the Batley Chamber of Commerce in 1912, one manufacturer said that "there was a difficulty arising out of the fact that many manufacturers did not pay the weaver but the loom."[132] How could they know how much to deduct from each weaver's pay when they did not keep track of individual weavers' earnings? To meet the requirements of the act without changing their record system, employers improvised. They subtracted a standard amount regardless of how much the weaver actually earned, "leaving a few odd weavers to claim their penny or two" when the deductions overshot the mark.[133] Despite this unintended intrusion from the state, British employers preserved the integrity of their method of appropriating materialized labor all the way up to the First World War.

The same principles governing the arrangement of numbers on the company ledgers regulated the assignment of workers to machinery. British weavers in charge of a set of looms were responsible for delivering products from the machines, but they did not have to offer their personal labor effort to do so. At many mills weavers escaped punishment for absence from the loom without permission so long as they sent a representative, possibly a family member, to take their place that day.[134] Weaving "sick" became an

---

ben, 1902), p. 27. Since German mill owners in practice were not required to scale their payroll deductions to the weekly earnings of each worker, the difference between German and British accounting methods cannot be attributed to the legal environment. *Die Textilarbeiter-Zeitung,* June 5, 1909, Emsdetten; accounting procedures described in *Der Textil-Arbeiter,* March 3, 1911, Friedland.

131. Stadtarchiv Bielefeld, XII 75, November 13, 1894; Staatsarchiv Weimar, Landesregierung Greiz n, Rep. A, Kap. IX, Nr. 207, 1893, p. 282.

132. *Textile Mercury,* September 7, 1912, p. 182. To fill out the forms for the government's employment censuses, managers sometimes had to ask the individual tuners for information on the current size and composition of the workforce. *Yorkshire Factory Times,* January 18, 1895, and September 12, 1912, p. 6. For Lancashire, see *Yorkshire Factory Times,* April 3, 1908, p. 2, Burnley.

133. Employers could not make insurance deductions from workers who earned under one shilling and sixpence per day.

134. PP 1890–1891 LXXVIII, p. 220. *Yorkshire Factory Times,* November 8, 1889, July 14, 1893, and December 1, 1893. The weavers might also go on vacation if they dispatched substi-

established occupation in Britain; that is, one might not have a permanent loom of one's own, but filled in for friends and neighbors who became ill.[135] In Germany, the firms themselves sometimes kept spare hands around, called "springers"—to "spring in" for ill weavers.[136] It was not unknown in Germany for weavers to dispatch their own substitutes, although the sources mention this much less frequently than in Britain.[137] The meaningful difference, however, is this: the British weavers, unlike their German counterparts, sometimes did not need permission beforehand from the overlooker or manager to send a particular person in their stead.[138] In fact, at mills in the Colne Valley, Yorkshire, the weavers reached arrangements with the factory owners to fetch substitutes of their choosing after the supper break if the machinery had to run overtime.[139]

The British weavers' retention of the disposition over their work capacity, so long as their machines delivered sufficient output, influenced the ordinary assignment of looms to their operators. A single set of looms could regularly be shared among several persons. For example, at a mill in the Buttershaw area of Yorkshire, two women in 1894 who needed only part-time work made a compact to alternate on a single set of looms in the course of the week.[140] They could balance the demands of work with their domestic schedules. In Lancashire, a family as a whole could take on the management of a large group of looms and divide attendance among

---

tutes. *Yorkshire Factory Times,* October 2, 1891, Bradford; December 27, 1889, Kirkstall. For Lancashire: Paul Thompson and Thea Thompson, family and work history interviews, Respondent 336, Keighley, born 1890; LRO, DDX 1274/6/1, December 1, 1900; *Burnley Gazette,* April 14, 1894, p. 8. At some mills, if a weaver became ill the firm gave the loom to someone else unless the weaver sent in a substitute. *Yorkshire Factory Times,* April 7, 1893, Shipley; *Cotton Factory Times,* January 22, 1897, Manchester. For examples of firms waiting only one hour before permanently reassigning an absent worker's loom, see LRO, DDX 1089/8/2, Preston, December 5, 1912, p. 176, and Royal Commission on Labour, Burnley, PP 1892 XXXV, p. 45.

135. Joanna Bornat's interview with Miss V., born 1901; Bradford Heritage Recording Unit, A0087, respondent, born 1903, describes her mother's job of "weaving sick." Also *Yorkshire Factory Times,* December 6, 1889, p. 4; March 4, 1892; March 27, 1903, p. 4.

136. *Die Textil-Zeitung,* March 9, 1897, "Krebsschaden."

137. Factory ordinance of Joseph Kaltenbach, HSTAD, Regierung Aachen, 1633.

138. *Yorkshire Factory Times,* April 25, 1890, Dewsbury and Ravensthorpe. Royal Commission on Labour, PP 1892 XXXV, June 26, 1891, p. 45.

139. *Yorkshire Factory Times,* October 7, 1892, Marsden. Employers denied responsibility for ensuring that the regular weavers paid the substitutes honestly. *Cotton Factory Times,* April 2, 1897, Oldham.

140. *Yorkshire Factory Times,* October 26, 1894. For Lancashire, see Elizabeth Roberts's interview with Ms. L1P, born 1900.

themselves as they wished.[141] At mills where weavers usually operated two looms each, they typically went down to one loom each when business slackened. They believed that under such conditions they had the right to opt instead for a buddy system with a friend. Each weaver doubled up with a partner and worked alternate days for the duration of the depression, each serving two looms during their turn in the mill.[142] These arrangements ensured the provision of finished products to the factory owner without the commitment of the labor capacity lodged in the person of the weaver.[143]

As in weaving, so in spinning. An incident from the spinning department of a mill in Yeadon, Yorkshire, illuminates the British treatment of workers as the deliverers of the output from a machine. When the employer at a Yeadon factory resorted in 1908 to night overtime, he did not require that the daytime mule spinners extend their own hours; instead, he authorized them to "engage the night men" on their own. The daytime spinners received piece rates for the entire output of their machine and themselves decided how to pay the men who tended it during the night shift. When the night-time workers went on strike in 1908, the Conciliation Board defined the day spinners, not the factory owner, as the strikers' "employers."[144] In other situations, when mule spinners hired young assistants known as piecers, the courts recognized the mule spinners, not the mill proprietors, as the piecers' legal employers.[145] The

141. Elizabeth Roberts's interview with Mr. G1P of Preston, born 1903, p. 44. For a similar case in Burnley, see LRO, DDX 1274/6/1, December 1, 1899. For two sisters sharing a set of looms, see Blackburn Library Archives, Minutes, Blackburn Weavers' Association, July 19, 1865. Mrs. E. Brook of Almondbury, Yorkshire, discussed father-daughter sharing in my own interview with her. Weavers on six looms could divide them among assistants as they pleased. See Dermot Healey's interview tape 628, female weaver, Colne, p. 17.

142. *Yorkshire Factory Times*, April 18, 1890, and November 6, 1903, p. 5. In an incident at Great Horton in 1898, the owner said workers could use a buddy system if the manager did not object—but the manager did object. *Yorkshire Factory Times*, February 25, 1898, p. 5.

143. Employers sometimes accepted for a period of months an alternate sent by an ill weaver. See Elizabeth Roberts's interview with Mrs. P1P, born 1898, Preston. For an exception, see Dermot Healey's interview tape 850, male worker from Nelson, born 1907.

144. *Yorkshire Factory Times*, April 3, 1908, p. 1.

145. *Textile Manufacturer*, August 15, 1881, p. 304; *Yorkshire Factory Times*, May 15, 1913, p. 5. When questioned about their attitude toward their "boss," piecers described, not the factory owner, but the spinner. Paul Thompson and Thea Thompson, family and work history interviews, Respondent 122, Bolton, born 1895. Employers thought it was not their business to "interfere" in the supervision of employees' assistants. *Yorkshire Factory Times*, February 28, 1908, p. 6. Mill proprietors had no claim to the piecers' attendance. If piecers rebelliously left the mill "in a body" and shut down production, the owners had no recourse. Report from the Oldham Master Cotton Spinners' Association, Royal Commission on Labour, PP 1892 XXXVI Part IV, p. xxv.

factory spinners became middlemen who contracted to deliver materialized labor to the factory owner. In Germany, by contrast, mule spinners and other workers who directed the use of machinery or even selected their own under-lings were generally viewed as employees who did not have the authority to assume the legal position of an employer.[146] What differed was not the reliance on subcontracting per se but its cultural significance. Workers who selected their assistants in Germany could not assume the status of an employer, because they remained "in a dependent relation to the factory owner."[147]

Is it possible that the contrasts between the countries in the rules for staffing looms can be attributed to differences in the supply of labor? Per-haps British textile firms allowed weavers to send substitutes as a means of attracting workers when labor was scarce. Female workers in particular might have been more willing to undertake mill work if they had some flexibility to attend to family matters on occasion. This explanation does not accord with the economic conditions, however. In Bradford, for instance, companies accepted substitutes of the weavers' choosing even when they enjoyed the benefits of an overwhelming surplus of labor.[148] The availability of labor fluctuated region by region, decade by decade in Britain, whereas the institutions for staffing machinery remained stable. In Germany, com-panies confronted with labor shortages attempted to recruit female workers by another means. They allowed women to leave the mill a half-hour early (and on the eve of some holidays) to manage the household meals.[149] Ger-man employers thereby shortened the expenditure of labor in time but maintained a claim to the labor power lodged in the person of the worker during the worker's hours on duty.

The textile workers' idioms for employment in the two countries be-trayed divergent understandings of the process by which they entered into the wage contract. In the narratives of the textile union newspapers in Germany, weavers who sought employment at a mill asked for "a position." In Britain, however, the weavers asked if the employer "had any looms to let."[150] "Looking for a new pair of looms" stood for going on the job market;

---

146. See Staatsarchiv Dresden, Amthauptmannschaft Flöha, Fabrikordnung Baumwoll-Spinnerei G. Matthes in Leubsdorf.

147. Stadtarchiv Plauen, Rep. I, Kap. VI, Sekt. I, Nr. 90B, March 18, 1873, pp. 123–127. Apart from this difference in their legal positions, subcontractors in Germany had less unquali-fied authority over underlings than did subcontractors in Britain.

148. *Yorkshire Factory Times*, February 26, 1892, and June 4, 1897.

149. Kathleen Canning, "Gender and the Politics of Class Formation," *American Histori-cal Review* Volume 97, Number 3 (June 1992) p. 749; and below, p. 481.

150. *Yorkshire Factory Times*, April 17, 1908, Burnley.

"being given a loom" meant getting hired.[151] British mule spinners who received a job said that they "had taken wheels."[152] To get hired, weavers and spinners in both countries followed the same channels through overlookers and foremen. Yet the expressions of British workers connected them to the company primarily by their use of a machine, as if they were independent operators of equipment for whose output they were paid,[153] whereas the language of the German workers emphasized the occupancy of a social "position" in a relation of servitorship.

The British appreciation of the sale of labor through the delivery of products influenced the language not only of hiring but of joblessness. After British weavers were dismissed from a stint, they said they lacked a loom, not that they were "unemployed." The term *unemployment* acquired wide currency only after the turn of the century, when political analysts launched the expression.[154] To discharge a worker, gestures sometimes proved more powerful in Britain than speech. When a British overlooker or manager fired a weaver, he did not have to utter a word. In a movement which became a standard symbol, understood immediately by the weaver, upon completion of the piece the boss simply yanked the shuttles from the loom.[155] Disabling the *machine* indicated the end of the weaver's tenure at the machine; nothing need be spoken to the *person*.

TRADERS AND CAPITALISTS

Did the differences between the exchange of "labor" in German and British textiles appear in other industries as well? In the mining industry of Britain, which employed more persons than any branch of manufacturing in the country, the understanding of labor delivered as it was materialized in a

---

151. Interview tape with H. Jennings, by Bob Turner, at Centre for English Cultural Tradition and Language, University of Sheffield; *Yorkshire Factory Times*, December 26, 1902; November 1, 1889, pp. 4, 7.

152. Operative Spinners of England, Ireland, and Scotland, *A Report of the Proceedings of a Delegate Meeting of the Operative Spinners of England, Ireland and Scotland, Assembled at Ramsey, Isle of Man* (Manchester: M. Wardle, 1829), p. 44; broadsheet from Henry Wood's Mill, Wigan, Oldham City Archives, TUI 23i.

153. The connection to the firm via title to a machine is illustrated in the reinstatement of workers after strikes. Upon settlement of the extended Huddersfield dispute of 1883, the weavers themselves claimed that if their employers had in the meantime transported some looms out of the shed, those weavers whose machines were missing should seek work elsewhere. *Huddersfield Daily Examiner*, May 8, 1883.

154. Samuel G. Hobson, *Pilgrim to the Left* (London: E. Arnold & Co., 1938), p. 47. For use of the phrase "out-of-work" benefits, see *Yorkshire Factory Times*, January 24, 1908.

155. *Yorkshire Factory Times*, March 4, 1898, and July 4, 1902.

product led to the creation during the nineteenth century of so-called sliding scales. Industrial experts of the time recognized this means of compensating workers as a distinctively British invention.[156] Wage agreements under this system pegged the piece rates that miners received to the price of coal in the raw materials markets. In Cumberland, for example, piece rates in the 1880s rose 1.25 percent for every 1.5 percent rise in the price of coal. In keeping with the logic of transferring materialized labor, the valid selling price was registered at the moment the coal came on board ship or into storage at the colliery, not necessarily when the labor was executed.[157] Calculation of wages as a proportion of the market value of the product had a long tradition in districts where miners and employers could come to agreements.[158] In Germany miners argued that higher coal prices justified an increase in their wage, but no one supposed that a wage should be cast in the form of a standard portion of the selling price realized in the market.[159]

The British iron and steel industry, which employed almost as many persons as the textile trade, used scales that automatically adjusted piece rates to vending prices when circumscribed markets developed for standardized products such as nails and iron bars.[160] Experts have despaired of dating with precision the origin of this institution, but they have concluded that by the 1830s, at the latest, puddlers' remuneration was indexed to the iron's selling price.[161] The endurance of piece-rate scales pegged to the finished article's selling price did not depend on formal collective bargaining or

156. PP 1892 XXXVI, Part 1, February 12, 1892, pp. 259 ff.; C. Colson, *Cours d'économie politique* (Paris: Gauthier-Villars, 1901), Volume 2, p. 68; Bernhard, op. cit., p. 167.

157. J. E. Crawford Munro, *Sliding Scales in the Coal Industry* (London: John Heywood, 1885), p. 6.

158. At the beginning of the nineteenth century, piece rates were determined by the market price of the coal in various cities. Jaffe, op. cit., p. 61. Jaffe shows (pp. 48–49) that employers in the coal industry concerned themselves with the terms of trade in the product markets, not with the conversion of labor power. Cornish miners received a percentage of the value of ore delivered aboveground: see Rule, *Labouring Classes*, pp. 124–125. The challenge of arriving at equitable sliding formulas bedeviled employers and workers. Many scales were canceled and renegotiated. Although coal workers in some regions oscillated on and off the system, they and their employers continued to recommend it as the ideal form of remuneration. Royal Commission on Labour, PP 1892 XXXIV, e.g., pp. 12, 156, 161, 225.

159. *Die Westdeutsche Arbeiter-Zeitung*, January 26, 1901. Prior to the First World War, the factory inspectors could not find instances of the implementation of sliding scales in Germany: see, for example, the report of Bernhard, op. cit., p. 170.

160. J. E. C. Munro, "Sliding Scales in the Iron Industry," Address to the Manchester Statistical Society, December 9, 1885, Manchester Library Archives. PP 1892 XXXVI, Part 1, March 1, 1892, p. 312.

161. Sidney Webb and Beatrice Webb, *The History of Trade Unionism* (London: Longmans, Green and Co., 1894), p. 484.

craft workers' power, since the system remained in place even in periods when the iron workers' unions were nearly extinguished, as in the late 1860s. For members of the steel smelters' union, these sliding scales, based on the selling prices of steel plates, were eventually "extended to practically every class of labour which could directly affect production."[162] Workers supposed that under an adjustable scale they became suppliers of products rather than mere employees. The Association of Iron and Steel Workers, for example, advocated the indexing of piece rates on this ground. The president of this association testified in 1892 that he supported the use of sliding scales for pay because "it has been our custom in the North of England under our board, where it was possible, for every skilled man to be the contractor for his own work."[163] In this respect, the aristocracy of skill did not remain privileged. By the beginning of the twentieth century, less qualified under-hand workers, too, received their compensation as a percentage of the shifting contract rates for iron and steel.[164]

Both workers and employers believed that the indexing of piece rates was founded on the principles by which agents exchanged labor as a commodity. The practice did not represent a form of profit-sharing, for the prosperity of industries did not conform to the selling prices of their products.[165] Workers saw that under the arrangement they sacrificed control over the price at which they disposed of their labor. "In the sliding scale principle," the secretary of the Association of Blast-Furnacemen said in 1891, "when the wages are regulated by the selling price per ton, in a sense a man gives up his right of sale of labor and puts it into his employers' power to sell it at what price he likes."[166] Employers in the iron trade considered the sliding scales a logical means of assessing the value of the labor they purchased.

162. Arthur Pugh, *Men of Steel, by One of Them* (London: Iron and Steel Trades Confederation, 1951), p. 136. German iron workers typically were paid by the amount of raw material they processed as a group. Walter Timmermann, *Entlöhnungsmethoden in der Hannover-schen Eisenindustrie* (Berlin: Leonhard Simion, 1906), p. 25.

163. Royal Commission on Labour, PP 1892 XXXVI, Part 1, March 2, 1892, p. 339. On the use of sliding scales in shipbuilding, see Royal Commission on Labour, PP 1893–1894 [c.6894-VII] XXXII, p. 75.

164. Bernard Elbaum and Frank Wilkinson, "Industrial Relations and Uneven Development: A Comparative Study of the American and British Steel Industries," *Cambridge Journal of Economics* Volume 3, Number 3 (September 1979), p. 292.

165. Robert S. Spicer, *British Engineering Wages* (London: Edward Arnold & Co., 1928), pp. 133–134.

166. Royal Commission on Labour, PP 1892 XXXVI, Part 1, Feb 12, 1892, p. 263. Even when sliding scales lapsed due to disagreement over the rates, they remained the model for selling labor. PP1892 XXXVI, Part I, pp. 259, 309–310.

They claimed that "no better standard existed of the value of labour in the market than the price of the article produced."[167] The system put employers in the role of merchants who resold finished products at a guaranteed margin rather than that of entrepreneurs who sought a profit by combining labor power with other resources.[168] The British system of sliding scales astounded observers in Germany, where workers received wages for the expenditure of their labor power itself. Indeed, to economic agents in Germany, the fluctuating scales in Britain abolished such a thing as a "labor market," given the German understanding of labor as a commodity. "This type of pay agreement," the organ for Christian unions in Germany declared, "is not based on the supply and demand of labor power . . . but on market relations of the product."[169]

Culture does not function as a steel curtain that bends practices into shape. The humble instrumentalities of manufacture result from the intersection of a cultural logic with the tangible materials of production. Accordingly, the assumption in Britain that abstract labor is exchanged as it is objectified in a product appeared under different guises among the country's industries, depending upon the concrete setting of the labor process. Textiles offers a sector of enterprise which, though not representative of industry as a whole, expresses its essential principles. The systems for remunerating workers in mining and iron-making enterprises indicate that the intervention of culture led not to uniformity but to isomorphisms in practice across different sectors of the British economy.

An employer who purchases labor power, rather than materialized labor, will have first claim to the profit that accrues from improvements in the efficient combination and use of the factors of production. But the sliding-scale system in Britain treated labor not as a raw input into a "value-added process" dependent on management and organization but as something purchased as a finished component. Even in British enterprises that did not use sliding scales, the employers could carry this premise into their procedures for keeping the production process in order. Some manuals for cost accounting show that British manufacturers believed their profits came from buying the

---

167. Report of arbitrator for Middlesbrough award of 1882, cited by Munro, "Sliding Scales in the Iron Industry," op. cit.

168. For the application of the sliding-scale tenet in British textiles, see Chapter Nine, below, at footnotes 183 ff. A representative of the jute workers' union endorsed the principle before the Royal Commission on Labour, PP 1892 XXXV, p. 472.

169. *Mitteilungen des Gesamtverbandes der christlichen Gewerkschaften Deutschlands,* November 11, 1901, p. 146.

separate components of a product cheaply and then selling at least one of them dearly. Edward J. C. Swaysland, in an insider's book of advice for commercial success in the boot and shoe trade, claimed in 1905 that manufacturers could turn a profit on an order even if they accidentally purchased labor at a higher price than they could receive by reselling the same labor. Swaysland's guide showed manufacturers how to keep a card for each worker that debited the material and labor costs for each shoe order and credited the worker for the good's selling price: "His credit would be the result of his work, and may be divided into the results from the use of material and the value of his labour. It might happen that a loss on his labour would be more than counterbalanced by the gain on his use of material."[170] Here the labor enters the equation already embodied in the shoe, so that the buying and selling price of that element can immediately be assessed. "The source of profit is too abstruse to be fully considered here," the author explained. "There may be no profit on the estimate of prime cost, but considerable profit on the purchase of material."[171] In this depiction, the manufacturer survives like a mercantile trader who profiteers in the sphere of exchange.

When British textile employers reflected upon the hiring of auxiliary workers with time wages, they conceived this arrangement, too, as the appropriation of the labor materialized in goods, not as the purchase of labor power. From their standpoint, the time wage was only a different measure of the product to be acquired. As the business counsel George Wood put it, "We may define Time-Work as 'A Contract to sell all the produce of labour in a certain time.'"[172] A leading organ for British managers, the *Textile Mercury*, emphasized in 1891 that the employment transaction comprised the renting out of a factory in return for products: "The unexpressed terms of this contract are that the employer shall provide a mill, machinery, motive power, materials to work up into fabrics, and orders for such fabrics; the weaver on his or her side, promising to attend the regulation time for working, and to perform the work given to him or her at the stipulated price."[173]

170. Edward J. C. Swaysland, *Boot and Shoe Design and Manufacture* (Northhampton: Joseph Tebbutt, 1905), pp. 236–237.
171. Ibid., p. 233. "The method of employing labour is also analogous to the purchase of material." Ibid.
172. Wood, op. cit., p. 5. For parallel reasoning in other British industries, see the sources cited above in footnote 51.
173. *Textile Mercury*, September 19, 1891, p. 186. William Marcroft proposed in 1878 that operatives should be able to organize as a group to manage the mill and deliver products to the owner. "If adult operatives by their growing experience show an ability to manage workpeople, and have a desire to contract to do the whole of the practical labour in the mill," he said, "the

The journal's summary cast the employers as investors who get a return by furnishing the means of production, not as innovative organizers and controllers of the use of living labor.

British textile workers acquired a corresponding view of their employers. They expressed this in their response to the problems mill owners encountered at the start of the twentieth century when factories switched production to goods slightly different from those for which the machines had been designed. The owners of these factories in Lancashire requested that weavers accept piece rates lower than the official district wages. Employers in certain neighborhoods said they needed the reduction to cope with their "disadvantages" in the market, since the output on the machines was less than that of competitors. "But why in the world weavers should be expected to pay for local disadvantages is beyond me," a correspondent wrote in 1916 for *The Power Loom*, the journal of the Nelson Lancashire Weavers' Association. "If I own property with certain disadvantages attached to it, I must make allowances for these disadvantages before I can hope to get a tenant."[174] In rejecting the employers' claims, the weavers treated the factory as property that the owner leased to the workers. They could have blamed the owners for poor command of management. Instead they reasoned as if the employers were landlords who rented out a run-down facility, not entrepreneurs who gathered and integrated resources.

The explications of the labor transaction in Britain contrast with the emphasis in the German commercial press upon the employer's purchase of the disposition over the work capacity.[175] The organ of the association of Saxon businessmen, *Sächsische Industrie*, analyzed the transfer of labor in the employment relation in an essay from 1907 entitled, literally, "Labor-'Giver' and Labor-'Taker,'" a play on the German root words for the terms *employer* and *employee* (*Arbeitgeber* and *Arbeitnehmer*). The article took care to define "the modern concept of labor" as "'labor power' or 'labor execution.'" Nowadays, the article explained, "the concept of 'labor' in the modern economy has received another meaning in some contexts than pre-

---

cotton mill operatives, through a committee elected by the adult operatives might undertake to engage those mill operatives whom they thought best calculated to do the work." William Marcroft, *Management of a Company's Cotton Mill* (Oldham: Tetlow, Stubbs & Co., 1878), pp. 7–8.

174. *The Power Loom* (January 1916), p. 4.

175. German employers referred to the workers' labor as a potential that could be valorized. "We do not hold it against any worker if he gives up his service to us," the owners of the Mechanized Weaving Mill of Linden said in 1906, "in order better to valorize his labor power elsewhere." *Volkswille*, Hannover, April 3, 1906.

viously. Labor is the expenditure of power which is supposed to lead to useful results."[176] Given this more exact usage, it said, the German words for employer and employee were not to be taken literally. This journal's sophisticated emphasis on the "modern" definition of labor echoed that of German business economists. Hans Mangoldt, a pioneer in the development of the "theory of the firm," gave a succinct definition of the wage that highlighted the disposition over a potential. "The wage," he explained in his survey of economics, published in 1871, "is the compensation for the use of one's own labor power which has been entrusted to another person."[177] Karl Marx exercised his wit upon the British employers' supposedly crude appreciation of the acquisition of labor. Had Marx turned back to his land of origin and investigated the understanding of labor as a commodity among employers in Germany, he might have experienced the shock of recognition.

THE STRATEGY FOR SPECIFYING CULTURE'S EFFECT

This inquiry did not presuppose that textile factory practices ought to be analyzed as facts of culture. Instead, it used strategic comparisons to rule out alternative explanations that would attribute the shape of factory practices to the survival of customs from earlier stages of development or to forced adaptation to the business environment. The commodity of labor, a fiction of comparatively recent invention, did not assume a natural or generic form in economic exchange with the development of wage labor. It was fabricated out of historically specific concepts that shaped different practices in similar settings. The principle of pay by shot, for example, was rooted in utilitarian practice, but it did not derive from the functional requirements of practice. As a condition for carrying out the "material" exchange of labor for a wage, employers and workers construed the meaning of the transaction with a priori assumptions about what comprised the "labor" transfer.

Social theorists in general and anthropologists in particular have long recognized that agents call upon a symbolic order to organize the material processes of production and exchange. Yet to reaffirm the importance of a

---

176. *Sächsische Industrie*, October 8, 1907, p. 337.

177. Hans Mangoldt, *Grundriss der volkswirtschaftlichen Lehre* (2d ed. Stuttgart: Julius Maier, 1871), p. 149. Carl Friedrich Roesler wrote in 1861, "The wage is the compensation for the use of the productive capacity lodged in the worker, which is directed into the product through the labor process." Carl Friedrich Hermann Roesler, *Zur Kritik der Lehre vom Arbeitslohn: Ein volkswirtschaftlicher Versuch* (Erlangen: Ferdinand Enke, 1861), p. 57.

cultural pattern, some analysts are content to argue that it is a necessary component for the realization of social institutions and for their investigation.[178] The premise that culture provides the indispensable coordinates of conduct, if accepted, by itself reveals nothing about the causal significance of culture. It could well be the case that culture represents a necessary ingredient for the construction of institutions but that it is closely shaped by the demands of economic forces. In this instance, culture need not arise as a "reflection" of economic institutions—for, as a pool of symbolic resources, of ever reconstruable signs, it is not produced by those institutions—yet it is neither directive nor formative in its own right. By comparing factories that developed in similar environments, this study shows not only that culture was *necessary* for building the regimes of the factory but also that it was *independent* of the immediate economic environment and was constitutive of the form of practice. Only a controlled comparison can advance this more decisive point.

Let us be clear about the way in which this study attributes a causal significance to culture. It does not claim that culture set limits to organizational innovation—the business manager's view of culture as an irrational drag upon change.[179] This approach to culture's effect lends it the force of dumb inertia and resistance, not that of a selective social logic. At illuminating junctures, such as the late creation *de novo* of piece-rate scales in Yorkshire or during the breakdown of labor-management institutions in diverse industries, we saw that "institutional inertia" alone cannot be invoked for the reproduction of forms of practice. Nor did this chapter unfold by showing that separate cultural beliefs attached to different domains of conduct fit together to form a consistent world view.[180] This approach, like the structuralist understanding of culture, makes culture in the first instance a way of *interpreting* the capitalist production process rather than a principle *composing* it. Finally, we have not treated culture as a means of legitimating

---

178. Without the concept of culture, Clifford Geertz informs us, we cannot render the agents' conduct intelligible. Clifford Geertz, *The Interpretation of Cultures* (New York: Basic Books, 1973).

179. For an example of the commercial world's understanding of culture as an ingrained "corporate mentality," see Michael Dertouzos, Richard Lester, and Robert Solow, *Made in America: Regaining the Productive Edge* (Cambridge, Massachusetts: The M.I.T. Press, 1989), p. 274.

180. For examples of recent works that critically review the tradition of searching for consistencies across beliefs within a culture, see David Laitin, *Hegemony and Culture* (Chicago: University of Chicago Press, 1986), pp. 17, 19; Robert Wuthnow, *Meaning and Moral Order* (Berkeley: University of California Press, 1987), pp. 45–46.

institutions. Unlike Reinhard Bendix's landmark *Work and Authority in Industry*, this comparative inquiry does not show that ideas justified practices that originated this way or that. It does not show that culture upheld the survival of industrial systems from without; rather, the commodity form of labor constituted from within the form of industrial procedure. In the textile industry the operation of the weavers' piece-rate scales, the assignment of looms, the replacement of absent workers, the recording of earnings—all these instrumentalities assumed their shape and were reproduced by virtue of the definition of labor as a commodity they sustained. In a capitalist order which fragments culture and undermines the coherence of collective belief, we may not be able to show that numerous concepts fit together in the "minds" of the "subjects" to form a consistent world view. But we can examine one concept to see how it composes a consistent province of practice.

The discovery that factory techniques were arranged by cultural definitions of labor as a commodity places several questions on the agenda. How did the specifications of labor influence workers' relations with supervisors in the factory? How did these principles configure the techniques of time discipline and the employers' surveillance of the shop floor? The remainder of Part One resolves these issues. If German producers defined the employment transaction as the sale of the disposition over the expenditure of labor, and British producers defined it as the transfer of materialized labor, what were the historical origins of these opposing assumptions? Part Two, the middle portion of this work, presents the genesis of the cultural differences and advances a model of the creation of labor as a commodity of labor that applies to other European settings as well. Did the contrasting ways of commodifying labor influence the pattern of struggle between textile workers and their employers? Part Three, the study's last segment, shows how the workers' concepts of the sale of labor shaped the formulation of demands, the execution of strikes, and the ideological horizons of the trade unions. We will see that the divergent stipulations of labor organized the most fundamental dimensions of life at the site of production: time and space themselves.

3   The Control
of Time and Space

There is always a mediator between *praxis* and practices,
namely the conceptual scheme by the operation of which
matter and form, neither with any independent existence,
are realized as structures, that is[,] as entities which are both
empirical and intelligible.
                              Claude Lévi-Strauss, *The Savage Mind*

It has become commonplace to assert that the concepts on which we as social
agents rely virtually constitute objects by bringing them into view. The
categories of a culture thereby become instruments of power, for in defining
the setting they demarcate the imaginable courses of action. This view of
culture as a schema for representing the world offers a starting point for
conceiving culture's effectivity. But it is incomplete. If accepted as a terminus, it obstructs our understanding of how culture is situated at the point of
production and of how it is reproduced. By casting culture as a system of
representations, practice appears in the first instance as a referent for signs.

Comparative study of procedures on the factory shop floor reveals that
the micro-practices of production were *constituted* as signs, whether or not
they served as the objects of a system of verbal representations. As the
analysis of the piece-rate scales demonstrated, the bare instrumentalities of
the mill had a representational function incorporated into their material
operation. The commonsensical notion that culture is a schema that agents
own and apply to interpret the environment imitates heroic visions of the
taming of external nature: the environment presents itself as a brute fact
which is mediated and thereby civilized by each individual's use of the
possession of culture. But the factory is culturally constituted through and
through: the producers need only follow its palpable logic. The template of
labor as a commodity came to life not in the subjective outlooks of individuals but in the orchestration of practice to fulfill a signifying function.

Accordingly, the regulation of workers' conduct in time and space at
German and British textile factories did not follow a logic that blindly
multiplied the means of control and surveillance to create a common

"disciplinary regime."[1] Rather, the instrumentalities of the production site were perspicaciously assembled in each country by unique specifications of the valorization of employees' labor time. As with the analysis of the piece-rate scales, so with the measurement of time we need to consider the relevant physical properties of the production process in order to discern the constitutive effect of cultural categories upon industrial institutions. Not only the monetized time of the workers but the very passage of time in the manufacturing process incorporated contrasting guidelines in the two countries.

TIME MEASUREMENTS

The production of the mechanical loom may have been sensible to the naked eye, but it could be intelligibly organized only through its cultural inscriptions. Power looms in England and Germany by the end of the nineteenth century ran at speeds of 70 to over 200 picks per minute.[2] (This means that 70 to over 200 times per minute the looms' shuttles traveled across the warp.) Foremen and overlookers determined the exact rate by adjusting and locking the loom's speed mechanisms.[3] If managers isolated two figures from the flux of production—how long it had taken to weave a length of cloth and the total number of picks that had been woven into it—they could compare the actual total of picks with the hypothetical total the shuttles would have woven if the loom had run perfectly during the time interval,

---

1. In the hands of Michel Foucault, a pioneering investigator of the matter, the division between the content of representations and the techniques of practice became a genuine opposition in the development of contemporary societies in the West. For example, Foucault's well-known *Discipline and Punish* portrays the betrayal of Enlightenment judicial ideals in the eighteenth century by minute disciplinary procedures that were refined and extended without recourse to discursive expressions or representation and without regard for their symbolic form. In his view, the concepts informing social representations may lead to the creation of procedures, to be sure, but these two elements may also remain unconnected. The unobtrusive means of training bodies and shaping their motions in schools, the military, and work proliferated in darkness and silence. Their operations, not their representation, subverted from within the dominant Enlightenment discourse of governance by sanctions that were public and were applied for the edification of autonomous subjects. The absence of a comparative perspective in *Discipline and Punish* is essential. For contrasts in the construction of the micro-apparatuses of discipline based on different systems of representation would undermine the narrative. Or does Foucault mean to say that the micro-apparatuses of discipline have a representational function, but the "topic"—"power"—is universal and the message invariable? Michel Foucault, *Discipline and Punish* (New York: Vintage Books, 1979).

2. *Allgemeine Zeitschrift für Textil-Industrie* (July 1881), p. 2; *Die Textil-Zeitung*, 1912, Nr. 29, p. 678.

3. *Die Textil-Zeitung*, 1911, Nr. 13 p. 313.

without interruption. Comparing the theoretically possible with the actual output revealed the proportion of time that had been "lost" due to stoppages, a ratio of relative "efficiency" (*Nutzeffekt*). In the decades before the First World War, textile journals on both sides of the channel devoted increasing attention to managerial strategies for quickening the tempo of production. Yet only in Germany did the concept of the efficiency ratio gain currency.

The efficiency ratio formed part of both material practice and discourse in Germany. In the "question and answer" columns of the country's textile periodicals, mill directors exchanged their calculations of this percentage for various makes of looms and asked whether customary ratios existed for various classes of goods—even for a product so specialized as "colored, light jute," for instance.[4] The number of published questions points to grass-roots interest in the topic, and the level of responses sent in by mill owners who drew their estimates from practical experience indicates that the efficiency ratio held a place in the conduct of their everyday business. Max Weber, in his neglected study of a Westphalian weaving mill, referred to the efficiency ratio as a statistic in habitual use among textile firms.[5] Samples of German production ledgers contained columns for listing the total number of weft threads actually woven, for recording the maximum that could in theory have been cranked out, and for reckoning the proportion between the two.[6] The underlying content of the question, "How *much* ought particular looms to turn out in practice?" could have been reasoned out and formulated only in terms of the average or expected *length* of cloth, rather than in terms of this percentage. But in Germany the expression of production in terms of

4. E. Pfuhl, *Die Jute und ihre Verarbeitung* (Berlin: J. Springer, 1888–1891), Band II, pp. 253 ff.; *Centralblatt für die Textilindustrie*, 1893, Nr. 10, p. 147, Nr. 12, p. 176, and Nr. 13, p. 191; *Zeitschrift für die gesamte Textil-Industrie*, 1898, Nr. 24, p. 377; *Die Textil-Zeitung*, 1899, Nr. 25, p. 487, and 1900, Nr. 41, p. 802; *Leipziger Monatschrift für die Textil-Industrie*, 1903, p. 163; *Die Textil-Zeitung*, 1903, Nr. 50, p. 1236, Nr. 51, p. 1263, 1904, Nr. 34, p. 849, and 1904, Nr. 38, p. 948; *Zeitschrift für die gesamte Textil-Industrie*, Volume 14, 1910–1911, Nr. 65, p. 1126; *Die Textil-Zeitung*, 1912, Nr. 1, p. 7; *Zeitschrift für die gesamte Textil-Industrie*, September 3, 1913, p. 827. The *Leipziger Monatschrift für die Textil-Industrie*, 1914, Nr. 3, p. 54, set standards for classes of all materials and types of looms.

5. *Gesammelte Aufsätze zur Soziologie und Sozialpolitik* (Tübingen: J. C. B. Mohr, 1924), pp. 131, 187.

6. *Leipziger Monatschrift für Textil-Industrie*, 1902, Nr. 10, p. 683; *Zeitschrift für die gesamte Textil-Industrie*, 1907–1908, Nr. 34, p. 428; Bernhard Bergmeyer, "Das Baumwollgewerbe im Münsterlande," diss., Bonn, 1921. For an example of a firm calculating production equivalent to so many thousands of shots, see Wirtschaftsarchiv Baden-Württemberg, B39-28, Süddeutsche Baumwoll-Industrie A.G., Kuchen, 1882–1929.

length frequently appeared in conjunction with calculations of the efficiency ratio.

In Britain, by contrast, the concept of an efficiency ratio was not endorsed in prewar publications about mill administration.[7] An article about "Weaving-shed Management" in the *Textile Manufacturer* of 1907 furnishes eloquent testimony about its absence. This essay offered technical and managerial advice on productivity and recommended that managers tally the length of cloth woven on each loom, so that variations in work among looms and among weavers could be investigated. Despite its concern with *quantities* of output, with record-keeping, and with precise calculation, the article ventured no definition of *efficiency* and no comparison of the theoretical limit of production with the real level.[8]

Equally instructive is an address which a Lancashire director, H. Dilks, delivered in 1916 to his peers in the British Association of Managers of Textile Works. He asked how the manager could abstract from the details of "daily routine" and represent to himself "the progress of the factory in a broader fashion"—in other words, how he could map factory productivity. Mr. Dilks argued that the graph he labeled Chart 3 (see Figure 5) offers a good way to picture day-to-day changes in efficiency. He explained: "It deals with individual loom stoppages, and indicates the cause of the stoppage and also its duration. It further shows graphically and clearly, by means of one curve, the total amount of loom stoppage in the shed from day to day." This diagram deals only with absolute quantities. It fails to convert these numbers into a ratio or percentage to tell us how much time has been lost, or what portion of possible production time has been lost. The author's description of his Chart 4 has the same feature: "The 'weavers average earnings' form an important measure of the efficiency of the individual loom or weaver, yet it may be high even when a proportion of the looms are stopped. It is therefore desirable to show also the total weavers' earnings for the whole shed—this is a figure that will probably be quite as useful as the other

7. In one instance, a British journal quoted a speech in which a German manufacturer used the efficiency ratio to compare the output of his country's looms with that of Britain. But the journal did not explain the derivation of the term or the exact statistic. *Textile Manufacturer*, September 15, 1881, p. 323.

8. *Textile Manufacturer*, October 15, 1907, pp. 352–353. Other examples of the ratio's absence in appropriate contexts: "Loom Performance and Profits," *Textile Manufacturer*, July 25, 1914, pp. 245 ff., and "The Bonus System in Textile Mills," May 15, 1914, pp. 174–175. Robert Cornthwaite, *Cotton Spinning: Hints to Mill Managers, Overlookers and Technical Students* (Manchester: John Heywood, ca. 1905), Chapter V, "Aids to Efficiency." In the spinning branch, the Gaunt Mill recorded average lost machine time in minutes. General Factory Committee Papers, Leeds District Archives, 1909–1910, Box 12, Twisting Department.

H. Dilks's Chart 3

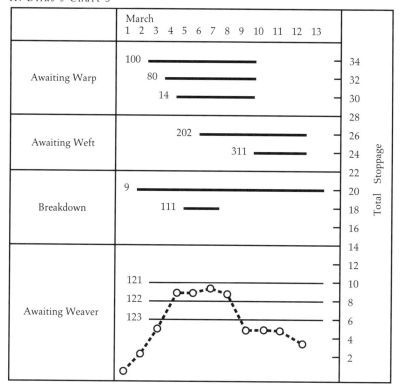

H. Dilks's Chart 4

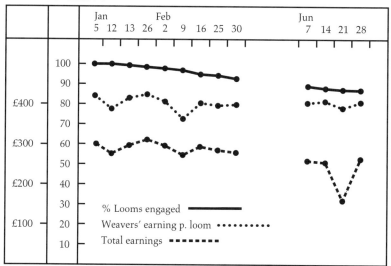

Figure 5.   The Value of Graphical Charts in Weaving Mill Management

in forecasting the colour of the half-yearly balance sheet."[9] Mr. Dilks, in keeping with the treatment of labor as an output rather than a conversion process, saw time not as a continuous function but as a sum of separate days, for he figured how many days each loom runs without breaking, not how much time is lost due to breakdowns. This British manager put into words what the output records of other firms display in their arrangement of numbers.[10] In everyday accounting as well as in prescriptive theory, British managers measured production as a substance, in terms of gross quantities of output.[11]

The negotiations in Lancashire between managers and the powerful textile unions over the establishment of production norms for new varieties of cloth offer another context in which to search for mention of an efficiency quotient. The company managers and leaders of the textile unions met to conduct actual trial runs on the looms. To analyze the results of their tests, however, they measured only the number of threads that broke per hour and the total cloth length.[12] When handbooks for weavers measured productivity, they calculated this in terms of pence per week per loom.[13]

It was impossible for the efficiency ratio used in Germany to remain completely unknown in Britain. The designers and manufacturers of looms,

---

9. "The Value of Graphical Charts in Weaving Mill Management," *Journal of British Association of Managers of Textile Works* Volume VII (1915–1916), pp. 169, 171.

10. For examples of company books measuring productivity by weavers' earnings, see West Yorkshire Archive Service, Wakefield, C149/545, 1888–1891; Burnley Library, Archives, M31, Benjamin Thornber & Sons Ltd, Production and Mill Record Book, February 25, 1909, to July 9, 1938, e.g., week ending February 25, 1909. Likewise, *Yorkshire Factory Times*, March 21, 1890, Dudley Hill. One firm, Christy and Sons of Lancashire, measured output in terms of the weight of the fabric produced by each loom. This seems reasonable enough, but it meant managers could not compare the efficiency of the assorted looms. For at this establishment the width of looms varied, and thus did the weight of the cloth produced at a given efficiency. John Rylands University Library of Manchester Archives, NRA 25970, Box B, production figures 1888–1889. For a spinning mill, see Leeds District Archives, Springfield & Broom Mills, General Factory Committee Papers, 1909–1910, August 12, 1909.

11. The Leicester factory owner John Baines testified that he never measured the number of absent workers or idle looms. "I go by the amount they have earned at the end of the week, and by that I know whether they have worked regularly or not." United Kingdom, *Report on the Select Committee on Stoppage of Wages (Hosiery)*, PP 1854–1855 (421) XIV, May 15, 1855, p. 149.

12. LRO, DDX 1089/14/1, 1917, p. 36; Ashton and District Cotton Employers' Association papers at John Rylands University Library of Manchester Archives, February 3, 1892; D. H. Williams, "Some Suggestions for Factory Organization and Efficiency," *Huddersfield Textile Society Journal* (1918–1919), p. 32.

13. Henry Brougham Heylin, *The Cotton Weaver's Handbook: A Practical Guide to the Construction and Costing of Cotton Fabrics* (London: Charles Griffen & Co., 1908), pp. 204–205. See also the calculation of lost production in terms of yards and pence in ibid.

who sold their machines in the international market, boasted that their inventions could sustain high levels of efficiency under test conditions.[14] But British mill managers rarely adopted such a statistic in their everyday practice or professional conferences. In the exceptional cases where they did, they reformulated it to suit their cultural framework. At the Quarry Bank Mill in Styal, Cheshire, the accountants for the American-designed Northrop looms, installed after 1909, calculated "total efficiency" by comparing the sum of wages the weavers received as a group with their hypothetical earnings at 100 percent efficiency. This weaving department may have been unique in Britain for routine calculation of a version of an efficiency ratio before the First World War. The company records show that managers calculated this figure without considering the number of looms operated, however. Total looms in use at the mill fluctuated, so low earnings by weavers could result either from having fewer machines employed or from low productivity of each loom. The statistic measured success in obtaining a final output, not the *process* of using the equipment.[15]

If German administrators, in the course of computing wages, also had to ascertain every week the number of shots executed on each loom, they had on hand the key figures needed for determining the efficiency ratio. Did the Germans decide to calculate this percentage as an incidental *consequence* of their adoption of the system of pay by shot? After all, their clerks already had a tally of shots carried out that was lacking among the British accountants. Or did use of the ratio carry a meaning of its own, based on the German designation of labor as a commodity? To answer these questions, we need to consider the functions that might have been served by its calculation.

The actual conditions of weaving on the shop floor contradicted the mathematical premises of the ratio in several respects. Given two looms of identical make, supplied with the same yarn and patterns, the loom with a low efficiency ratio could actually produce more than the loom with a high one. This contradiction arose because in the early twentieth century looms remained unreliable contrivances. They presented managers with a trade-

---

14. For American claims, see *Textile Manufacturer*, October 15, 1897, p. 380; W. Bleakly, "Desirable Textile Inventions," *Journal of the British Association of Managers of Textile Works* Volume 4 (1912–1913), p. 94.

15. Manchester Library Archives, C5/1/7/3, "Northrop Loom Account," 1912. What is more, the greatest conceivable and the actual output of the looms were expressed in terms of weavers' wages, not of the actual process of inserting picks. For the background on the introduction of the automatic looms at Quarry Bank, see Mary Rose, *The Greggs of Quarry Bank Mill: The Rise and Decline of a Family Firm, 1750–1914* (Cambridge: Cambridge University Press, 1986), p. 96.

off between speed and stoppages: the higher the picks per minute, the more frequently weft or warp threads broke and became entangled.[16] The efficiency quotient rested on an image of a self-contained machine whose operating speed was regular and given in advance. Looms of the era, in contrast to this ideal, had to be coaxed and felt out.[17] Raising the speed of the shuttles might cause more stoppages and lower the efficiency ratio, yet result in more cloth at the end of the day.[18] Taken too far, however, preoccupation with the shuttles' speed alone might lower output. "I have been in many factories where they pointed to their high speeds," one German manager remarked about his country, "but usually I could reply that I would let the looms run slower and bet that in each loom I would weave more cloth per day."[19]

The efficiency quotient furnished an inaccurate index for a second reason: it supposed that weaving consisted solely of attending to the shuttles. In truth, weaving was not a uniform activity. Up to a quarter of the loom's possible running time could be "lost" while weavers took care of other essential jobs such as twisting in new warps or having the gears that regulated the warp beam changed.[20] The shorter the warp, the greater the proportion of time consumed by these tasks, independent of any efforts of the weaver or the overlooker. The efficiency ratio could not measure different

16. *Die Textil-Zeitung*, 1900, Nr. 40, p. 782. For a detailed examination of the fragilities of the loom, see Richard Biernacki, "The Cultural Construction of Labor: A Comparative Study of Late Nineteenth-Century German and British Textile Mills," Ph.D. diss., University of California, Berkeley, 1988, pp. 223 ff.

17. The skill of the weavers made a contribution of its own to the determination of the optimal number of picks per minute. *Allgemeine Zeitschrift für Textil-Industrie* (July 1881), p. 1, and *Die Textil-Zeitung*, 1912, Nr. 1, p. 7. For the workers' own comments, see *Die Textilarbeiter-Zeitung*, April 9, 1910.

18. Rudolf Weiss, "Entlöhnungsmethoden und ihre Anwendung in der Textilindustrie," Ph.D. diss., München, 1925, p. 94. Conscientious overlookers used trial and error to reestablish the optimal tempo after changes in yarn or pattern. For debates about how to choose the best number of picks per minute, see *Allgemeine Zeitschrift für Textil-Industrie*, 1881, Nr. 1, p. 1; *Zeitschrift für die gesamte Textil-Industrie*, March 24, 1898, pp. 377 ff.; *Die Textil-Zeitung*, 1912, Nr. 1, p. 7, and 1912, Nr. 29, p. 678; *Leipziger Monatschrift für Textil-Industrie*, 1914, Nr. 3, p. 82.

19. *Leipziger Monatschrift für Textil-Industrie*, 1903, Nr. 3, p. 163. For a similar comment from England, see Bradford Technical College, *Report of the Department of Textile Industries, City of Bradford Technical College*, July, 1917, report on meeting held November 13, 1916, Mr. Sowden's remark. At the turn of the century, depending upon patterns and materials, a loom's rate of "efficiency" could lie as high as 85 percent or as low as 45 percent and still turn a profit. *Die Textil-Zeitung*, 1899, Nr. 25, p. 487; Germany, *Jahresberichte der königlich Preussischen Regierungs- und Gewerberäthe und Bergbehörden für 1892* (Berlin: W. T. Bruer, 1893), p. 204.

20. Williams, op. cit., p. 6.

weaving processes with a common yardstick, because the ratios for warps of differing lengths were incommensurable.[21] Even within the same mill, Max Weber concluded, the efficiency ratio was unusable for comparisons of work on different types and lengths of warps.[22]

We cannot leap to the conclusion that British methods remained intellectually backward in contrast with those of the Germans. Since the efficiency ratio mirrored the realities of production so poorly, its use cannot be explained as a rational adaptation to the circumstances of production. When Quarry Bank Mill installed American-designed Northrop looms with pick clocks on the eve of the First World War, and even paid their weavers by the shot, they still did not adopt the German form of the statistic. This indicates that the categories used for measuring production did not derive from convenience of calculation once the mode of payment was in place. Instead, the appreciation of production, too, depended upon the intervention of different concepts of labor as a commodity. But with all the imprecision and misrepresentations it introduced, how could the Germans have maintained an interest in their efficiency quotient at all?

Despite the inaccuracies of the ratio, German accountants used it to distribute production costs. Where the measure of the theoretically possible output embraced net factory time, the ratio served as an approximation in distributing overhead and general expenses to determine the manufacturing costs of various classes of goods. If accountants knew the firm's ratios of efficiency for diverse kinds of cloth, they could estimate how long it would take to weave a particular fabric on a loom and would know what level of general expenses or conversion expenses the cloth should bear. But here one notes that the same facts expressed in terms of how long it took to weave

21. D. H. Williams, *Costing in the Wool Textile and Other Industries* (Manchester: Emmott & Co., 1946), pp. 65 ff.

22. Weber, op. cit., p. 188. For Weber's reasoning, see pp. 186–188. The ratio represented an artificial statistic for yet another reason: there was no well-founded way of determining what time boundaries ought to be taken as the basis for reckoning the maximum or theoretically possible number of shots that could be turned out. A large fraction of time could disappear if weavers had to fetch their own weft, which was the norm, or if they had to wait for new weft bobbins. Some commentators supposed that since this time was extrinsic to weaving itself, it ought to be excluded from the determination of the ratio; others included it, since managers wanted to know the source of all delays. *Leipziger Monatschrift für Textil-Industrie*, 1902, Nr. 8, p. 548. Mill directors sometimes subtracted the time taken to change the shuttles as well, since this did not constitute a stoppage per se but belonged to the regular weaving procedure. Pfuhl, op. cit., "Vorwort." Apparently the German managers were moved by the conviction that they ought to calculate some kind of ratio to express the notion of efficiency in time, even if they were not at all sure what its content ought to be.

cloth of a certain *length* could have served just as well to distribute the costs. As we have seen, the Germans had information about the length of the cloth on hand anyway, since they reckoned the number of shots on this basis. At least in this context, the efficiency ratio was not uniquely suited for the function.[23] Its utility was more apparent than real and rested on the assumption that total output ought to be gauged by the actual versus the maximum possible output in a time period rather than, as the British preferred, by gross quantity of output during that period.

The German agents' use of the efficiency ratio to help construct piece-rate scales furnishes another context in which the ratio's utility was culturally defined. To find a base point for graduating the piece-rate scales for weavers, German business experts believed, the employer ought to proceed by first measuring the normal efficiency ratio of a loom at a certain speed to see on average how many shots weavers performed per day. Then to reach a target wage the managers would choose the pay per thousand shots.[24] An observer outside the system notices, again, that the efficiency ratio remains arithmetically superfluous in this operation: one only needs to compute the average *length* of cloth produced per day to choose the pay per thousand shots. Yet German articles about the construction of weaving scales begin with the need to calculate the efficiency ratio, even those articles written by experienced mill directors who otherwise eschewed elaborate formulas. Here the efficiency ratio does not by itself convey any information or criteria of success that could not have been coded just as accurately in a statement about how much cloth of a certain type could be produced during a certain time interval.[25]

---

23. The periodical literature and accounting handbooks for weaving establishments advised that owners distribute overhead costs, among other ways, as a proportion of the wages paid in producing the cloth or proportionate to all the costs, including weaving. The method recommended depended partly on the extent to which firms specialized in small runs of diverse fabrics. For discussions of overhead relative to selling costs, see *Centralblatt für die Textil-Industrie*, 1887, Nr. 49, p. 1173, Nr. 52, p. 1241, and 1889, p. 30; *Die Textil-Zeitung*, 1904, Nr. 23, pp. 573 ff. For costs relative to wages, see *Leipziger Monatschrift für Textil-Industrie*, 1910, Nr. 9, p. 261; *Die Textil-Zeitung*, 1905, Nr. 38, p. 909, and Nr. 39, p. 933; *Leipziger Monatschrift für Textil-Industrie*, 1914, Nr. 3, p. 65.

24. Examples: *Centralblatt für die Textil-Industrie*, 1893, Nr. 12, p. 176; *Leipziger Monatschrift für Textil-Industrie*, 1902, Nr. 8, p. 548, and 1903, Nr. 3, p. 163; *Zeitschrift für die gesamte Textil-Industrie* Volume 14 (1910/11), Nr. 65, p. 1126; *Leipziger Monatschrift für Textil-Industrie*, 1910, Nr. 2, and 1913, Nr. 5, p. 151.

25. To compare efficiency, an academic observer from outside the industry was content to refer only to absolute levels of production. See Marie Bernays, "Zur Psychophysik der Textilarbeit," *Archiv für Sozialwissenschaft und Sozialpolitik*, Volume 32 (Tübingen: J. C. B. Mohr, 1911), p. 111.

In some instances the Germans employed the efficiency ratio, not to convey information about the known, but as a way of coping with the unknown. When factory owners accepted an order for a pattern of fabric they had not produced before on a large scale, they needed some way of moving from the amount of time taken to weave a similar pattern in the past to estimate how long it would take to weave the novel pattern. They carried out this operation by gathering together their hunches based on prior experience and by estimating then how much down time the new pattern would probably cause in comparison with the similar pattern. Once they had ascertained the picks per minute of the loom, they could calculate how long it would take, in comparison with the similar good, to make the requisite number of shots to fill the order.[26] The fundamental yardstick they used to order their experience about relative weaving difficulty and comparative success was differential down time, not, like the British, simply differential output.[27]

Let us not confound form and content: the Germans' greater concern for a particular concept of efficiency did not denote greater concern for the thing itself. On the eve of the First World War, the "Gospel of Efficiency" had become a standard turn of phrase in Britain.[28] British managers manifested their interest in efficiency in their concern with the small details of production and with the causes of machine stoppages.[29] Germany and Britain competed in the same export markets, especially in those for wool manufactures, where the British more than held their own in the decade before the First World War.[30]

Managers in Britain calibrated output at each loom only between the start of a new piece of cloth and its completion. At some mills, their weavers complained that the warps were not marked with chalk or other signs at

26. *Centralblatt für die Textil-Industrie*, March 21, 1893, p. 176; Otto Both, *Die Bandweberei* (Hannover: Max Jänecke, 1907), p. 227; Pfuhl, op. cit., p. 262; Josef Ittenson, *Das Kalkulations-Buch des Baumwollwebers: Für die Praxis bearbeitet* (Leipzig: Gustav Weigel, 1908), p. 39.

27. John Mackie, *How to Make a Woollen Mill Pay* (London: Scott Greenwood & Co., 1904), "The Importance of Turn-Out," p. 57.

28. *Textile Mercury*, April 11, 1914, p. 294.

29. *Yorkshire Factory Times*, November 22, 1901, Bradford, "Young Men and New Methods." At one British mill, managers kept a log of the causes of loom stoppages. *Cotton Factory Times*, March 11, 1904, Hyde.

30. D. T. Jenkins and J. C. Malin, "European Competition in Woollen and Cloth, 1870–1914: The Role of Shoddy," *Business History* Volume 32, Number 4 (October 1990). D. T. Jenkins and K. G. Ponting, *The British Wool Textile Industry 1770–1914* (London: Heinemann Educational Books, 1982), p. 294.

standard intervals so that the weavers could judge how close they had come to the end of their piece.[31] Managers tied measurement to the discrete events of assigning a fabric order to the loom and receiving delivery. In the German case, by contrast, managers conceived of production as a continuous function. One reason they gave for using the pay-by-shot system was that it permitted them to divide the worker's activity and output into minutely small segments. In later years, the introduction of the *Schussuhr* ("pick clock") permitted the output of the loom to be calculated or read daily.[32] German managers urged workers to work at a regular pace and hoped that workers would even monitor themselves hourly or daily in order to learn how to do so.[33] The workers obliged, but with unforeseen consequences. They became attuned to the manipulation of their labor power and used the efficiency ratio as an index of exploitation. At a meeting to induct weavers into the German Textile Workers' Union in Haan in 1899, a weaver warned that the wages workers received should be compared to the efficiency with which their labor power was used. An increase in take-home pay, he cautioned, might not equal capitalists' added profit "if manufacturers achieve a gain of 12 to 16 percent in efficiency."[34]

It would be simple, but also simplistic, to conclude that the method of pay per shot, the reliance on the efficiency ratio, or, in later years, the use of the pick clock allowed German managers to impose tighter production quotas on workers than could their British counterparts. The timing of the introduction of pay by shot in German factories indicates that the practice did not originate as a strategy to control workers on the shop floor. For the new scales went into effect in Germany well before experts began to advocate "scientific management" or Taylorist methods to monitor the execution of labor. Moreover, the British elaborated their own methods for keeping track of the efficiency of individual workers. Especially in Lancashire, but in Yorkshire as well, British overlookers posted the weekly output of the weavers in their charge.[35] The contrast between the countries arose not from the degree of surveillance but from its form.

---

31. *Yorkshire Factory Times*, October 25, 1889, and November 22, 1889, p. 5.

32. *Centralblatt für die Textil-Industrie*, 1893, Nr. 10, p. 147; *Der Textil-Arbeiter*, January 22, 1904.

33. *Die Textil-Zeitung*, September 23, 1907; *Centralblatt für die Textil-Industrie*, 1876, Nr. 48; *Die Textilarbeiter-Zeitung*, December 10, 1909; Weber, op. cit., pp. 194, 241.

34. Hauptstaatsarchiv Düsseldorf, Regierung Düsseldorf 24691, Haan.

35. *Yorkshire Factory Times*, March 21, 1890. For the northwest, see autobiography of Elizabeth K. Blackburn, born 1902, "In and Out the Windows," Burnley Library, Archives, p. 30; LRO, DDX 1115/1/2, September 17, 1901; *Cotton Factory Times*, December 3, 1886,

For all the inaccuracies the efficiency ratio introduced, the Germans still favored a statistic that they could relate directly to the *execution* of labor during a time period and to the use of a timed potential. When British managers measured output by weavers' wages, they effectively took the *price* of the labor as a marker for the quantity of labor delivered.[36] Had British analysts focused on the process of transforming a labor capacity into an output, however, they might have realized that such an index can be misleading: weavers on fancy patterns can earn high wages with only one loom in operation while they wait for repair of others in their allotment. On these grounds, Max Weber, in his study of a weaving shed, rejected wages as a measure of labor effort.[37] Weber, like German manufacturers, recommended instead computing the total picks inserted. But principles for denoting output through time did not remain sequestered on paper; what bookkeepers wrote in the internal ledgers was externalized on the gates of the factory.

TIME JURISDICTION

British managers marked the beginning and close of the daily cycle of production by subjecting their workers to exceedingly rigid controls on entry into and exit from the factory. The most common, though not universal, practice at mills in Yorkshire and Lancashire was to latch the doors at the start of the workday, compelling latecomers to return home.[38] Only at the

---

Glossop; Paul Thompson and Thea Thompson, family and work history interviews, Respondent 72.

36. The Lancashire director Dilks suggested, "Perhaps the figure which the weaving mill manager is most interested in is that representing the average weekly earnings per loom." Dilks, op. cit., p. 171.

37. Weber, op. cit., pp. 188 ff.

38. Calderdale Oral History Collection, from the heavy woolen district: Maria Shaw, born 1893, mill in Batley; Mrs. Dransfield, born 1896, on Taylor's Cheapside mill; Mr. Robinson, report from year 1916 on a mill in Birkenshaw; Mrs. Hanley, reporting on mother's experience at Mark Oldroyd's mill. Joanna Bornat's interview transcripts from Colne Valley: Mrs. T., born 1896, about first job; Mr. B., born 1901, on John Edward's mill, Marsden; Miss A., born 1897, on "Bruce's mill," Marsden; Mrs. W., born 1900, on Crowther's mill, Marsden; Mrs. B., born 1900, on Robinson's mill, Marsden; Mrs. O., born 1888, on Dewhirst's mill, Elland. My interview with Mrs. E. Brook, weaver at Newsome Mills, Almondbury. My interview with Arthur Murgatroyd, born 1902, halftimer at Crossley's Mill, Halifax. My interview with Mrs. May Broadbent, born 1896, Midgley. Dr. A. H. Clegg, a former half-time worker in Halifax, wrote down his memories of getting locked out: manuscript, Calderdale Archives, MISC 482. For an account by a dialect poet, see James Burnley, *Phases of Bradford Life* (London: Simpkin, Marshall & Co., 1889), p. 45. Newspaper reports include *Yorkshire Factory Times*, December 16, Apperley Bridge; January 28, 1898, Bradford; February 18, 1898, April 25, 1890, Slaith-

breakfast or lunch break several hours after, when the factory as a whole made a ritual of stopping and resuming activity, could latecomers pass through the factory portal and commence work.[39] Interviews with former workers and the complaints published in the union newspapers provide dramatic accounts of workers having the mill door literally shut in their face as they dashed to enter exactly at starting time. Many employers in Britain instructed their porters to secure the gate forcefully even if workers running to it were within sight. "At six o'clock, bang, that's it, shut the gate," remembered a spinner from Halifax. "The man there, his job was to pull it through a yard at once."[40] A female winder in Preston, Lancashire, reported to her union in 1915 that the manager apprehended her entering the mill just as the door began to close. He "mangled and bruised" her arms:

> On Monday morning when I went to work I had just got my foot on the threshold of the door when the door was slammed to and my foot was caught between the door and the door jamb. I pushed the door open with my hand and as I entered the manager was standing there who said to me *"Outside—you are not coming through."*[41]

To be sure, some textile mills, especially in Lancashire, imposed fines for tardiness, generally standard amounts that served as a disciplinary tool

---

waite; July 28, 1893, Batley; January 18, 1901, Greetland; December 13, 1901, Elland; August 28, 1903, Dewsbury; January 13, 1905, Batley; July 21, 1905, Shipley and Saltaire; April 25, 1890, Slaithwaite. The Minutes of the Halifax Overlookers' Society, Calderdale Archives, TU 102/2/1, Mssrs. Martin and Son, February 13, 1897. For the Northwest, *Cotton Factory Times*, February 5, 1897, Darwen; February 12, Stalybridge; March 19, 1897, p. 1. Dermot Healey's interview 628, female weaver, started mill work 1916; Paul Thompson and Thea Thompson, family and work history interviews, Respondent 122, male spinner, born 1895, Bolton, Lancashire; Respondent 140, male worker, Salford, born 1901; *Cotton Factory Times*, February 5, 1897, Darwen; February 12, 1897, Stalybridge; March 19, 1897, p. 1. LRO, DDX 1089, November 4, 1904, p. 194. Sometimes the company books tell the story; Bolton Oral History Collection, Tape 121, mule piecer, born 1899. At Strutt's Belper mill, the grounds for fines logged from 1805 to 1813 do not include tardiness. R. S. Fitton and A. P. Wadsworth, *The Strutts and the Arkwrights 1758–1830* (Manchester: Manchester University Press, 1958), pp. 234–236. For examples of employers bolting latecomers outside hosiery establishments in Nottingham, see Royal Commission on Labour, PP 1893–1894 XXXVII, Part I, pp. 163–170.

39. One female weaver claimed that latecomers were excluded for the entire day. Her report, probably exaggerated in remembrance, indicates all the better her internal experience of the custom. Bornat's interview with Mrs. W., op. cit.

40. My interview with Murgatroyd, op. cit. For an example in which workers were stopped from working for being less than a minute late, see LRO, DDX 1089/8/1, July 1906, p. 106. A female weaver from a village near Halifax recalled as one of the highlights of her working life the day she climbed a wall and clambered through a mill window to get into the mill after starting time. My interview with Mrs. May Broadbent, op. cit.

41. LRO, DDX 1089/8/3, Preston, June 19, 1915.

rather than as a carefully graduated form of recompense for the employer.[42] Yet oral testimony and workers' newspapers show that locking out represented the expected and predominant routine.[43] Mills also combined fines with locking out; workers less than, say, fifteen minutes overdue could pay a penny for admittance, before other latecomers were excluded for good.[44]

42. John Rule, *The Labouring Classes in Early Industrial England, 1750–1850* (London: Longman, 1986), p. 136. For examples of fining in Yorkshire, see Calderdale Archives, Stansfield Mill, "Rules for Piecers and Scavengers," 1833; Leeds District Archives, Springfield & Broom Mills, Factory Committee Minutes, November 11, 1909. For Lancashire, see Manchester Library Archives, F1851/31, Haslingden, 1851. At Marshall's of Leeds, the monetary sanction departed from a time metric because managers retaliated by reducing the overdue workers' official rates of pay for the next weeks. W. G. Rimmer, *Marshalls of Leeds: Flax-Spinners 1788–1889* (Cambridge: Cambridge University Press, 1960), p. 120. Sometimes the latecomers were automatically fined "a quarter"—that is, the fine was not calculated according to minutes lost but was defined as the portion of the daily wage normally earned up to the breakfast break, when the bolted doors opened. *Yorkshire Factory Times*, May 1, 1908, Radcliffe. Analogously, in the carpentry trade workers who arrived five minutes or more overdue lost one hour's pay, as if they had been excluded. Royal Commission on Labour, PP 1892 XXXVI, Part 4, p. viii.

43. In *Kapital*, Marx delights in citing British factory rules setting out excessive fines for late arrival. His selection of anecdotes suited his rhetorical purpose by illustrating the monetarization of human relations. By relying only on the most readily available printed documents, however, he drew a skewed picture of realized practice. *Das Kapital* (Berlin: Dietz Verlag, 1980), Volume 1, pp. 447–448. Few of the mills that administered fines by a time metric kept time-books of hours worked by employees, as one would have expected if they had treated tardiness as a loss from the purchase of time itself. Sidney Pollard, *The Genesis of Modern Management* (London: Edward Arnold, 1965), p. 228. Curiously, the Oldknow papers show that outdoor workers had their labor time recorded to the hour, whereas workers locked inside the mill had their attendance recorded only in approximate quarters of the day—as if their impoundment made superfluous the reckoning of labor time with an accurate metric. Manchester Library Archives, Eng MS 817, 1796–1797.

44. For Yorkshire, *Yorkshire Factory Times*, July 21, 1905, Shipley and Saltaire, and Manningham Mills, July 28, 1905; Royal Commission on Labour, PP 1892 XXXV, p. 309. In the early industrial revolution, too, fining appears to have been combined with locking out: Frederick Engels, *The Condition of the Working-Class in England* (London: George Allen and Unwin, 1892 [1845]), p. 179; United Kingdom, Factories Inquiry Commission, Supp. Rep. Part II, Volume 20 (1834), p. 93; and Jean Lindsay, "An Early Factory Community: The Evans' Cotton Mill at Darley Abbey Derbyshire, 1783–1810," *Business History Review* Volume 34, Number 3 (1960), p. 299. The Royal Commission on Labour's log of fines shows that 10 percent of its sample of Yorkshire mills imposed some kind of fine for lateness, but of these, half appear to have combined fines with locking out. PP 1893–1894 XXXVII, Part I, pp. 103 ff. A union representative testified before the commission that fining for lateness was an exception in Lancashire (PP 1892 XXXV, p. 5). The commission's listing shows that many Lancashire mills claimed the right to fine unpunctual workers, but the maximum equaled only a disciplinary sum for arriving anywhere in the interval from five to fifteen minutes or from fifteen minutes to one-half hour late (PP 1892 XXXV, p. 6). As in Yorkshire (*Yorkshire Factory Times*, Sept. 23, 1892, Apperley Bridge), the penalty could be combined with exclusion after fifteen minutes, a separate matter which the commission did not investigate as a worrisome "fine." For oral testimony to this effect, see Bolton Oral History Collection, interview 121, born 1899; Elizabeth Roberts's interview with Mr. B8P, male spinner from Preston, born 1896, p. 4.

In some instances textile firms carried the practice of locking out to such an extreme that latecomers were prohibited from entering the mill for the day. "This morning I was about five minutes late," a Lancashire weaver complained to the union in 1912. "The watchman would not let me through."[45] Some mills prohibited latecomers from waiting near the mill entrance for access and instead sent them all the way home.[46] In Lancashire the union received several complaints from weavers who were denied entrance to the mill for several days or even a week because of inconsequential tardiness.[47] For example, in Preston a female weaver complained to the union in 1908 that when she arrived late one day the manager spied her as she was "going through the watch-house" and told her to stay home for the week.[48] These severe penalties applied to the Lancashire mule spinners as well, the masculine "barefoot aristocrats" of the mills.[49]

It would be tempting to explain the practice of bolting the gate as an historical residual, a carryover of primitive management technique from the early industrial age. Stories about locked gates abound in the folklore about the days of violent industrial change at the end of the eighteenth century and the beginning of the nineteenth.[50] When a Marsden woolen spinner, born in 1901, complained that the mill gateway resembled "a gaol—with spikes on top," his words echoed the exact comparison that cotton workers in Lancashire had voiced about the gates more than a century earlier.[51] Could the legacy of this earlier transition in England at large have left its traces even in regions such as Yorkshire, which mechanized much later? The historical record does not support such a hypothesis.

So far as the textile unions could tell, during the two decades before the war the practice of locking the gate became more widespread. The *Yorkshire Factory Times* at the beginning of the twentieth century followed the exten-

45. LRO, DDX 1089/9/2, Preston, February 23, 1912, p. 104.

46. LRO, DDX 1089/8/1, Preston, November 4, 1904, p. 194.

47. LRO, DDX 1089/8/1, March 24, 1906, p. 149.

48. LRO, DDX 1089/8/1, June 22, 1908, p. 246. For a similar story in the same source, see Sept. 11, 1905, p. 66.

49. One tardy worker denied entry for a week joined the army out of desperation. Elizabeth Roberts's interview with Mr. B8P. See also Dermot Healey's interview tape 850, born 1907; Calderdale Archives, TU 102/2/1, Mssrs. Martin and Son, February 13, 1897.

50. John Doherty, editor, *The Poor Man's Advocate; Or, a Full and Fearless Exposure of the Horrors and Abominations of the Factory System in England, in the Year 1832* (Manchester: J. Doherty, 1833), p. vii; Pollard, op. cit., p. 183.

51. Joanna Bornat's interview with Mr. B., spinner, born 1901, describing John Edward's mill in Marsden, Colne Valley.

sion of the practice to several mills previously free from its rigidities.[52] One of Yorkshire's most popular dialect poets, James Burnley, in his tour of Bradford textile plants in the late 1880s found one instance in which a firm then shut tardy workers out but in earlier years had fined them.[53] What is more, in these years the new generation of managers who had formal business education sometimes initiated the practice as they took over the reins of directorship.[54] They did so even in neighborhoods where firms suffered from competition for scarce supplies of labor.[55] Locking workers out in Britain thus by no means represented a survival from a previous era.

Could the heads of the British mills have imposed the practice to inculcate time discipline that would pay off in the long run by inducing prompt attendance? In contrast to their predecessors at the dawn of the factory age, mill directors in the late nineteenth century no longer thought it necessary to break an unruly work force to the novel stringency of indoor factory work. The businessmen's forum, the *Textile Mercury*, concluded that over the long term, the "diligence and punctuality of textile workers may be said certainly to have improved, and it is to their credit that their current lapses from perfection still shew favorably against those recorded in some trades."[56] Even so, mill directors might have reasoned that bolting latecomers out would deter workers from arriving even the slightest bit late.[57] It was not unusual for a mill to have a tardy worker every day.[58] Many workers lacked the time-keeping devices necessary for precise adjustment of conduct to the employers' sanctions.

Had mill proprietors in Britain sought only a display of authority or a demonstration of their power to deny wages, they could have used more apt means. They could, for example, have imposed exceptionally severe fines for tardiness, but also have let latecomers onto the premises. This technique

52. *Yorkshire Factory Times*, March 29, 1901, Ravensthorpe; September 28, 1905, p. 5; January 13, 1905, Batley; September 29, 1910, p. 5.
53. Op. cit., p. 45.
54. Oral report from Edward Mercer, weaver, Rawdon. See also the example cited in D. C. Coleman, *Courtaulds: An Economic and Social History* (Oxford: Clarendon Press, 1969), Volume One, p. 251.
55. *Huddersfield Daily Examiner*, September 21, 1910; *Textile Mercury*, March 29, 1913, p. 257, and June 28, 1913, p. 526.
56. *Textile Mercury*, March 21, 1914, p. 230.
57. "The 'pennying process'—that is, the levying of a fine upon all who are five minutes behind time—has been abandoned, punishment now inflicted being to send the delinquents back 'for a quarter,' and thus deprive them of a quarter day's wages, a system which is, I am informed, far more efficient than that formerly in use." Burnley, op. cit., p. 45.
58. For exact records, see, illustratively, Robert Clough company records, Brotherton Collection, University of Leeds.

might have encouraged punctuality without loss of labor power. British mill owners sacrificed some of the labor time available to them, even as they complained of labor shortages.[59] Sometimes the services they cast away remained invisible. If workers were not sure they could get to the mill on time, they might not bother going at all until after the morning break.[60] Shutting workers out also made it more difficult for managers to tell in the morning whether an absent worker had no intention of showing up or had simply met a latched door and might return at lunch time. But the "waste" of labor would have been palpable when, as was sometimes permitted, late-comers waited near the mill for the gates to open rather than make the journey home and back again before breakfast.[61] The excluded labor could reach substantial levels. In Burnley, Lancashire, when the porter at one mill in 1897 allegedly shut the gate two minutes early, sixty-seven weavers who found themselves outside could not work until after the breakfast break.[62] Since employers excluded tardy supervisory workers as well, they denied themselves the vital services of loom tuners who were not instantly replaceable.[63] For example, the minutes of the Halifax Overlookers' Society indicate that in 1897 an overlooker was locked out for arriving a single minute late.[64]

It is conceivable, but undemonstrable, that locking out conferred economic advantages upon British mill employers. If the humiliating experience of total exclusion at the gate stimulated punctuality much better than payment of any fine, locking out may have more than made up for the incidental loss of labor. Whatever the case, the influence of culture cannot be identified automatically in any departure from utilitarian ploys, only in the consistent symbolic forms through which agents strategize.

Could the practice of sending workers home have indicated nothing more than that the British employers did not want the bother of keeping records of fines for lateness or that they did not want to bear the expense of employing a porter to staff the front gate all day long? Oral testimony as well as the tips published in the *Textile Manufacturer* indicate that the porter at-

59. Especially in the last decade before the First World War, employers in Yorkshire and Lancashire complained of a general shortage of labor and did all in their means to attract new recruits. "Work and Wages in the Cotton Trade," *Blackburn Times*, March 2, 1907; *Textile Manufacturer*, May 15, 1906, p. 161; *Yorkshire Factory Times*, November 28, 1912, p. 8; *Textile Mercury*, January 11, 1914, p. 24.

60. LRO, DDX 1274/6/1, Burnley, July 1, 1899.

61. Thompson and Thompson, Respondent 122, op. cit.

62. *Cotton Factory Times*, March 19, 1897, Burnley.

63. *Yorkshire Factory Times*, April 25, 1890, Slaithwaite; August 28, 1903, Dewsbury; July 28, 1893, Batley.

64. Calderdale Archives, TU 102/2/1, Mssrs. Martin and Son, February 13, 1897.

tended the entrance at all hours anyway, to receive salesmen and other visitors. During his free moments he did basic paperwork or small craft jobs such as covering rollers. In sum, a system that monitored workers' exact moment of arrival would have added no significant enforcement costs. Most telling of all, when tramways became a means of commuting to the mill for some workers at the beginning of the twentieth century, factory owners exempted workers from the lock-out rule if they arrived late through no fault of their own but because of transit breakdowns.[65] In view of the administrative complications this exception introduced, it becomes clear that the practice of bolting workers out rested on an ideal standard rather than on a strategy of convenience.

British directors, as well as the workers themselves, viewed the technique of bolting latecomers out as part of the logic of running a factory.[66] One manager from Marsden, who had worked his way up from the position of a simple weaver, formulated an explanation for shutting workers out. "If they're not here on time," he was fond of repeating, "they don't deserve to work."[67] This Marsden manager became known for sending latecomers home even if they were his friends and neighbors. The British technique supposed that the worker had a responsibility to deliver products to the firm in prompt fashion. By locking workers out the British employers did not treat the workers' time itself as a form of property for whose loss they claimed restitution.[68] Shutting workers out did not lay claim to the labor power lodged in the person of the offenders but treated them as though they were contractors who had not taken due care to meet delivery deadlines and therefore deserved suspension of the contract. The struggle was over the acquisition of the product. "Discipline," an early employer declared, "was to produce the goods on time."[69] The ritual of locking workers out diverged

65. Bolton Oral History Collection, Tape 122, female spinner, born 1905; LRO, DDX 1089/8/1, March 24, 1906, p. 149; *Yorkshire Factory Times*, September 29, 1910; Bornat's interview with Mrs. W., op. cit., p. 23.

66. In Rochdale, a union secretary himself intercepted workers arriving more than three minutes overdue and sent them home. Royal Commission on Labour, PP 1893–1894 XXXVII, Part I, p. 115.

67. Interview tape with Joe France, born 1882, courtesy of the France family, Marsden.

68. The Leicester factory owner John Baines testified in 1855, "I have never been able to enforce regular attendance." Rather than impose fines upon workers for their periodic absences, he instituted a mandatory weekly fee for use of the machinery. Thus the workers wasted their machinery "rent" if they did not show up to earn piece rates. United Kingdom, *Report on the Select Committee on Stoppage of Wages (Hosiery)*, op. cit., p. 149.

69. Cited by Sidney Pollard, "Factory Discipline in the Industrial Revolution," *The Economic History Review* second series, Volume XVI, No. 2 (1963), p. 258.

from the artisanal ideal of freedom to choose one's hours of work. Industrial practice did not develop from the habitual carryover of routines from the era of domestic and independent artisanal production but was shaped by the form labor assumed as a commodity in the industrial present.

The British workers themselves may have preferred being locked out to being fined, because the lock-out at least maintained the fiction that workers sold the product of their labor. In the earliest days of the factory system, workers reasoned that since they sold merely their output, the employer had no grounds to impose a penalty for lateness. For example, a writer for *The Poor Man's Advocate* complained in 1832 about the fines for tardiness at a cotton spinning mill: "The machines may not work while the workman is absent; but how can the employer lose, when he only pays for the work that is done?"[70] This reasoning viewed the employment transaction as the delivery of output, not the guarantee of a capacity. At the end of the century, the editorial columns and correspondents' reports of the textile workers' newspaper still maintained that employers had no right to fine workers for lost labor time. The newspapers of the textile unions depicted the hardships imposed by the alternative technique of locking out but did not articulate any objection in principle to the custom. If workers failed to arrive promptly, they lost merely the right to continue the delivery transaction. Fining, by contrast, implied to the workers that the employer controlled the disposition over their labor power and could demand compensation for the loss of the owned time.[71]

On occasion, workers' own actions expressed their acceptance of locking out more clearly than the exclamations of their newspapers did. Workers at a mill in the Colne Valley went on strike in 1910 to demand that latecomers who had been delayed by breakdowns in the public transport system on which they relied be exempted from the shut-out rule. Although the majority of workers there commuted to the mill by foot, they turned out on strike in solidarity with the tram riders until the factory owner granted the riders' demand. The workers never pressed for elimination of lock-outs altogether or for their liberalization by, say, having the employer introduce a grace period for all workers.[72]

70. *The Poor Man's Advocate*, March 3, 1832, p. 51. The reasoning did not depend upon the immaturity of the factory system, for it continued to be voiced through the end of the century. *Yorkshire Factory Times*, July 28, 1893, p. 1, Batley.

71. *Yorkshire Factory Times*, May 8, 1891, Huddersfield; January 13, 1893; July 28, 1893; March 4, 1898. As late as 1901, weavers on piece rates in Saddleworth objected to employers' calculations of their hours of attendance. *Yorkshire Factory Times*, March 1, 1901.

72. *Yorkshire Factory Times*, September 29, 1910.

Whether locking out represented a spontaneous reflex by managers or a calculated policy, its principle did reach formal exposition. A popular Yorkshire handbook of the era, *How to Make a Woollen Mill Pay,* argued that the "enforcement of punctuality at work" represented the first and essential prerequisite for the enactment of a "mill routine."[73] Discipline seemed not to rest on workers' mere presence at work, but on their ceremonial entering and exiting of the premises. In Germany, where the workday was conceived as the elapse of continuous time, not just a temporal succession, time discipline placed more emphasis upon the duration of production than on its beginning and end points.

The German approach could lead to anomalous time accounting. When the introduction of a stricter commercial code in Germany required that manufacturers issue factory rules in 1891 listing exact hours of work, German factory inspectors found that almost all mills already had definite starting and stopping hours. Yet many textile factories did not.[74] They had been content until then with specifying that production would begin "in the morning" or "after sunrise" and last for a certain period. These cases revealed that the organization of a meaningful production process had not required a rigid starting point as an anchor for the passage of time.[75]

German employers treated unpunctual attendance as a denial of labor power whose loss could be calibrated and precisely counterbalanced. Many textile factories applied a sliding scale of fines which either adjusted the penalty to the worker's average earnings or specified percentages of aver-

73. Mackie, op. cit. Mackie's book was reprinted, and it appeared as a serialization in the journal *Textile Manufacturer.*

74. Stadtarchiv Borken, A 539, 1894; Stadtarchiv Mönchengladbach, 25c, Nr. 1754, Greeven & Co. Weberei, 1892. For smaller-scale weaving workshops, see F. Hermann Voigt, *Die Weberei in ihrer sozialen und technischen Entwicklung und Fortbildung* (Weimar: Bernhard Friedrich Voigt, 1882), p. 385. On the maintenance of flexible hours, see Peter Burscheid, *Textilarbeiterschaft in der Industrialisierung: Soziale Lage und Mobilität in Württemberg* (Stuttgart: Klett-Cotta, 1978), pp. 368–369, and Christoph Deutschmann, *Der Weg zum Normalarbeitstag* (Frankfurt: Campus Verlag, 1985), p. 150. In Aachen, workers in needlemaking and spinning could go to the factory when they wished, with no fixed hours: Aachen, Feb. 4, 1817, Zentrales Staatsarchiv Merseburg, 120 B V 33, Nr. 4, Vol. 1, p. 54.

75. Even at the beginning of the twentieth century, after the official posting of factory hours, some German weaving mills in advanced textile towns such as Mönchengladbach did not enforce a particular starting hour. See *Der Textil-Arbeiter,* September 8, 1905, Mönchengladbach, Weberei Pelzer & Droste; November 17, 1905, Eckirch; *Mitteilungen des Arbeitgeberverbandes der Textilindustrie zu Aachen,* April 1903, Stadtarchiv Aachen, 125-45I, p. 6. Some firms offered alternative start times for commuters. Stadtarchiv Krefeld, F1446, C. G. Maurenbrecher, 1909.

age earnings to be levied as fines for various periods of tardiness.[76] This not only graduated the fine to the worker's ability to pay, but it also gauged the value of the lost time.[77] Other mills in Germany applied a standard fine for each fraction of an hour lost.[78] Rather than fixing the penalty at nominal amounts for gross intervals of tardiness—that is, rather than using the fine as a simple tool of discipline—the Germans thereby monetized the lost time itself and froze it with a metric. Due perhaps to their greater interest in minute-by-minute accounting, rather than in marking only gross intervals, textile mills in Germany introduced punch-in clocks on a wide scale at the turn of the century.[79] German managers did not see punctual arrival as an unconditional preliminary for

76. Textilmuseum Apolda, 1857 Factory Rules of Zimmermann firm; Staatsarchiv Detmold, M2 Bielefeld Nr. 760, p. 68, Weberei Elmendorff, 1893; Staatsarchiv Osnabrück, Rep. 610 Lingen, Nr. 124, G. v. Delden & Co., 1901.

77. The model comes from a spinning mill in the Wuppertal in 1838: "Each worker who comes late to work or stays home without permission will receive a fine in the amount of double the value of the time of absence." Reproduced in Karl Emsbach, *Die soziale Betriebsverfassung der rheinischen Baumwollindustrie im 19. Jahrhundert* (Bonn: Röhrscheid, 1982), p. 674. For the lower Rhine woolen industry, see Franz Decker, *Die betriebliche Sozialordnung der Dürener Industrie im 19. Jahrhundert* (Köln: Rheinisch-Westfälisches Wirtschaftsarchiv, 1965), p. 216. Stadtarchiv Bielefeld, Ravensberger Spinnerei 54, Fabrikreglement 1856; Stadtarchiv Bocholt, *Arbeitsordnung* for Franz Beckmann & Co. Spinnerei, 1898; Stadtarchiv Mönchengladbach, *Arbeitsordnung* for Joh. Friedrich Klauser, 1892. Wirtschaftsarchiv Baden-Württemberg, B46–391, Allgemeine Fabrik-Ordnung für die Baumwollspinnerei L. Hartmann Söhne, 1846. The fine at G. Matthes in Leubsdorf was severe: workers paid four times the earnings they would have earned during their minutes of absence. See Staatsarchiv Dresden, Amthauptmannschaft Flöha 2825, Baumwollspinnerei G. Matthes in Leubsdorf, ca. 1846. The ordinance at one firm in Plauen threatened to deduct an hour's pay for each minute of absence. Stadtarchiv Plauen, Rep. I, Kap. VI, Sect. I, Nr. 64, 1863, Weisswaaren-Fabrik.

78. The *Leipziger Monatschrift für Textil-Industrie* considered one pfennig per minute appropriate (1909, Nr. 3, p. 80), although employers charged three pfennigs per minute or more (Stadtarchiv Plauen, Rep. I, Kap. VI, Sect. I, Nr. 64, July 20, 1863, Stickerei, March 17, 1866, Weberei). Textile firms in Greiz applied an invariate fine per quarter-hour: Stadtarchiv Greiz, B 5973, Rep. C, Kap. IV, Nr. 45, companies of Schilbach & Heine, W. Heller, F. Timmel; Stadtarchiv Greiz, B 5975, Kap. IV, Nr. 65, L. Fischer, ca. 1880, and F. Müller, ca. 1867. Likewise, for Aachen, Zentrales Staatsarchiv Merseburg, Rep. 120 BB VII, Fach. 3, Nr. 32, Lequis, Aachen, 1892. Progressively increasing fines per minute were recommended for mills in *Sächsische Industrie-Zeitung*, November 29, 1861. To the workers' chagrin, fining per minute overdue could begin instantly on the hour: HSTAD, Regierung Aachen 1634, February 16, 1899. For women, factories sometimes halved all fines with the exception of those levied for tardiness, suggesting that employers treated fines for lateness as a separate kind of indemnity for stolen time. HSTAD, Landratsamt Grevenbroich 271, 1897 edition of rules for Herrath firm, p. 184.

79. *Die Textilarbeiter-Zeitung*, December 19, 1908, Rheydt; August 26, 1911, Bornefeld & Jansen; November 25, 1911, Mönchengladbach. For the installation of minute-by-minute check-in clocks as early as 1812 in the wool industry of the lower Rhine, see Decker, op. cit., p. 96.

undertaking work in the factory.[80] The time of living labor became a form of property for whose loss employers exacted a refined compensation.

Whereas British textile workers who worked in the textile mills before the First World War drew spontaneously in interviews upon many emotional memories about the lock-outs, former German textile workers described the controls of the threshold in the same period as relatively incidental.[81] One woman's response from the Wuppertal was echoed by others: "Fines? Of course you got fined if you came late. That was not so terrible."[82] Like the first generation of factory workers in Britain, the German home weavers who rebelled against the newly emergent factories labeled the mills "prisons."[83] The derisory term for undertaking factory labor was "going to Spandau." In cultural comparisons, the form in which a grievance is articulated may prove more revealing than the simple occurrence of a complaint. In their indictment of the unprecedented indignities of centralized manufacture, the German workers focused on the state of internment rather than, as the British did, on appurtenances such as the locked doors

80. In the area of the lower Rhine, in the far north, and in Saxony, companies offered small prizes to workers who consistently arrived on time. Contribution by Dr. Moeller, in Otto Dammer, editor, *Handbuch der Arbeiterwohlfahrt*, Volume II (Stuttgart: Enke Verlag, 1903), pp. 351–352; Victor Brants, *Tisserand d'usine de Gladbach*, in Société d'Economique Sociale, ed., *Les Ouvriers de deux mondes*, 3. Série, 6. fascicule (Paris: Au Siège de la Société Internationale, 1902), p. 355; Deutscher Textilarbeiterverband, *Protokoll der Verhandlungen der 6. ordentlichen General-Versammlung des Verbandes aller in der Textilindustrie beschäftigten Arbeiter und Arbeiterinnen Deutschlands* (Chemnitz: Deutscher Textilarbeiterverband, 1902), pp. 41–42; HSTAD, Regierung Düsseldorf 25022, p. 21. For a parallel example from an industry outside textiles, see the article about a metal plant in *Barmer Zeitung*, October 28, 1887.

81. My interviews with Frau Schäfer, weaver, born 1899, Elberfeld; Franz Reidegeld, spinner, born 1900, Rheine; Frau Putz, weaver, born 1900, Elberfeld; Maria Pollman, born 1897, Barmen; Ewald Sirrenberg, born 1897, Barmen; Hans Penz, born 1895, Barmen. Herr Reidegeld reported that the gate was locked beginning a half-hour after starting time but was opened for latecomers, who were fined. This custom also appears in one of the earliest factory codes in Germany, that for the August Jung firm in Hammerstein, 1838, reproduced in Emsbach, op. cit., p. 674.

82. My interview with Maria Pollman, op. cit. Fining may have reduced undelivered labor minutes to a simple exchange of currencies, but in the district of Löbau a strike broke out, not just over wages, but over the size of fines for lateness. Staatsarchiv Dresden, Amthauptmannschaft Löbau, Nr. 3055, p. 9.

83. Willy Brendgens, *Die wirtschaftliche, soziale und communale Entwicklung von Viersen* (Viersen: Gesellschaft für Druck und Verlag, 1929), p. 107. Many of the early manufactories were, of course, actually located in prison houses. Curt Bökelmann, *Das Aufkommen der Grossindustrie im sächsischen Wollgewerbe* (Heidelberg: J. Hörning, 1905), pp. 34, 59; Joachim Kermann, *Die Manufakturen im Rheinland 1750–1833* (Bonn: Ludwig Röhrscheid, 1972), pp. 86–102; Germany, Enquete-Kommission, *Reichs-Enquete für die Baumwollen- und Leinen-Industrie: Stenographische Protokolle über die mündliche Vernehmung der Sachverständigen* (Berlin: Julius Sittenfeld, 1878), p. 663.

and spiked gates encountered in passing across the border.[84] For the German workers, unlike the British, the procedure of entering the mill did not comprise a charged ritual that exemplified the industrial wage-labor transaction.[85]

Can we discern statutory interdictions which prevented German directors from adopting the same practice of locking out as their British counterparts? Employers' work rules offer an answer from the domain of practice. The archives of many German cities safeguard a complete set of the factory rules submitted to the police for obligatory inspection. Of the several hundred work codes available from textile companies before World War One, only a handful exclude latecomers.[86] In one of these rare instances, from a

84. Adolf Levenstein, *Die Arbeiterfrage* (München: Ernst Reinhardt, 1912), pp. 133, 143. Hans Michel, *Die hausindustrielle Weberei* (Jena, 1921), p. 58, and Heinrich Brauns, *Katholische Sozialpolitik im 20. Jahrhundert: Ausgewählte Aufsätze und Reden von Heinrich Brauns*, ed. Hubert Mockenhaupt (Mainz: Matthias-Grünewald-Verlag, 1976), p. 123.

85. It seems doubtful that the contrasting methods of time control can be attributed to national differences in workers' punctuality and self-discipline. German workers were every bit as resistant to the time regime of the factory as were their British counterparts, especially in view of the long survival of "blue Monday" and of unofficial communal festivals in Germany. For the wool industry of the lower Rhine, see Decker. op. cit., pp. 96, 97. Elsewhere, Friedrich Lenger, *Zwischen Kleinbürgertum und Proletariat* (Göttingen: Vandenhoeck & Ruprecht, 1986), p. 174; HSTAD, Düsseldorf, Regierung Düsseldorf 24677, May 1887, pp. 99 ff.; HSTAD, Düsseldorf, Regierung Düsseldorf 25016, 1894, p. 34; HSTAD, Düsseldorf, Regierung Düsseldorf 24684, January 12, 1894; Germany, *Jahres-Berichte der königlich preussischen Regierungs- und Gewerberäthe, 1904* (Berlin: R. v. Decker, 1905), p. 308; Emsbach, op. cit., p. 170. For German textile managers' testimony about workers' early resistance to time discipline, see Germany, Enquete-Kommission, *Reichs-Enquete*, op. cit., p. 67; HSTAD, Regierung Düsseldorf 24677, October 26, 1885, pp. 3–5.

86. Seven exceptional cases among them are: Staatsarchiv Weimar, Reuss älterer Linie, Reuss Landratsamt Greiz, Nr. 4596, mechanische Weberei, Zeulenroda, 1868, shuts latecomers out for a quarter-day; Hauptstaatsarchiv Düsseldorf, Regierung Aachen 13886, N. Scheins & Reiss, May 25, 1892, and Arnold & Schüll, Tuchfabrik, Aachen, 1892, where latecomers had no claims to work for the rest of the day (although in practice they were admitted—Zentrales Staatsarchiv Merseburg, Rep. 120 BB VII 3, Nr. 32, March 18, 1895, p. 8); *Der Christliche Textilarbeiter*, June 23, 1900, Aachen: "Wer ohne Entschuldigung zu spät zur Arbeit kommt, hat erst eine Stunde später Anspruch auf Einlass"; Staatsarchiv Detmold, Regierung Minden I.U., Nr. 425, C. A. Delius & Söhne, 1892, p. 94; Hauptstaatsarchiv Düsseldorf, BR 1015, Nr. 169 II, weaving mill Wilhelm Schroeder & Co, Moers, locks latecomers out until following shift, p. 214. I also found a morning lockout in Augsburg with fines during the first ten minutes, Bernd Flohr, *Arbeiter nach Mass* (Frankfurt am Main: Campus, 1981), p. 106, and in the Aachen area, which the factory inspector viewed as an extraordinary occurrence, HSTAD, Regierung Aachen 1633, 1895 memo, p. 308. Another possible exception comes from Greiz, where the Eduard Brösel factory rules say that latecomers must wait until the doors open again but does not say how frequently the doors are in fact opened. Stadtarchiv Greiz, B 5975, Kap. IV, Nr. 65, Eduard Brösel, November 1, 1882.

For a sample of factory codes that include fines for lateness, see Stadtarchiv Mönchengladbach, 25c, Nr. 1754, which lists fifty-four companies that issued fines for lateness; the collection in HSTAD, Reg. Düsseldorf, BR 1015 169, for examples of factory ordinances issued

silk mill near Bielefeld, the employer revised the ordinance from locking out in 1892 to fining latecomers in 1894.[87] An exception such as this one, studied and approved by inspectors, demonstrates the absence of state constraints upon employers wishing to shut workers out. Legal experts and industrial

---

before they became obligatory and somewhat standardized; HSTAD, Landratsamt Geilenkirchen 88, pp. 1898 ff.; HSTAD, Landratsamt Grevenbroich, Nr. 271, for the following fourteen firms: Emil Quack & Co., 1909; Isaac Falkenstein & Söhne, April, 1909; Adam Breiden, August, 1909; Spinnerei F. Lühl, Wickrath, 1907; Mechanische Weberei Carl Rente, Wickrath, 1892; Peter Sieben, Weberei, 1909; J. A. Lindgens Erben, 1892; Bandfabrik H. G. Schniewind, 1910; Goertz, Kempken & Pongs, 1905; F. W. Barten Weaving, 1892; Weberei Bovenschen, Heerath, 1897; Erckens & Co., 1910; Schwartz & Klein, Jüchen, 1906; Anton Walraf Söhne, 1910; Stadtarchiv Mönchengladbach, *Die Fabrikordnung der Firma F. Brandts zu Mönchengladbach. Ausgabe von 1885* (Mönchengladbach: Stadtarchiv Mönchengladbach, 1974); Klaus Tidow, Hauptstaatsarchiv Düsseldorf, Regierung Aachen 13886, C. Lequis Weberei. Oct., 1892; Staatsarchiv Detmold, M2 Bielefeld, Nr. 760, Bertelsmann & Niemann, 1892, p. 60. The city archives in Forst, Zwickau, and Plauen also have extensive collections of ordinances: Stadtarchiv Forst, Nr. 2382/1 through Nr. 2382/18; Stadtarchiv Zwickau, e.g., Rep. V, Lit. A, Nr. 32; Rep. V, Lit. F, Nr. 22; Rep. V, Lit. G, Nr. 61; EL 4884b 1865; Stadtarchiv Plauen, Rep. I, Kap. VI, Sect. I, Nr. 64, e.g., June 30, 1862, Spinnerei, August 15, 1867, Spindler & Erbert, March, 1867, C. A. Jahn. See also Günter Loose, "Betriebs-Chronik VEB Baumwollspinnerei Zschopautal," in Landesarchiv Potsdam, May, 1956, p. 106 with rules of the cotton spinning mill George Bodemer, 1862; Zentrales Staatsarchiv Merseburg, 120 B V 33, Nr. 4, Volume 2, J. A. Meyer, Brandenburg, 1838; Zentrales Staatsarchiv Merseburg, 120 B II 1 78, Kempten, 1853, Mechanische Baumwoll-Spinn- und Weberei Kempten; Klaus Tidow, *Neumünsters Textil- und Lederindustrie im 19. Jahrhundert* (Neumünster: Karl Wachholtz, 1984), ordinance from 1888, pp. 70–71; Staatsarchiv Weimar, Reuss älterer Linie, Reuss Landratsamt Greiz, Nr. 3861, Mohlsdorf, April 19, 1892; Staatsarchiv Weimar, Reuss älterer Linie, Reuss Landratsamt Greiz, Nr. 4596, mechanische Strumpfwirkerei, Zeulenroda, March 15, 1869; Staatsarchiv Weimar, Reuss älterer Linie, Reuss Landratsamt Greiz, Nr. 4596, mechanische Weberei, Zeulenroda, March 1, 1869, and H. Schopper, May 15, 1869; Zentrales Staatsarchiv Merseburg, Aachen, August 1892, Schwamborn & Classen, 120 BB VII 3 32; Archiv des Volkseigenen Betriebs Palla, 575 Strafbuch, Gebrüder Bachmann, Meerane, fines for lateness, 1901–1918; Wirtschaftsarchiv Baden-Württemberg, B46–391, Allgemeine Fabrik-Ordnung für die Baumwollspinnerei L. Hartmann Söhne, 1846; Wirtschaftsarchiv Baden-Württemberg, B25–316, Arbeitsordnung der Tuchfabrik Lörrach, 1902; Staatsarchiv Dresden, Amthauptmannschaft Flöha, Nr. 2825, Spinnerei G. Matthes in Leubsdorf; Staatsarchiv Dresden, Amthauptmannschaft Flöha, Nr. 2881, Auerswalde Spinnerei, 1882; Staatsarchiv Dresden, Amthauptmannschaft Flöha, Nr. 2925, March 31, 1892, Fuchss Zwirnerei; Staatsarchiv Dresden, Amthauptmannschaft Chemnitz, Nr. 16, "Fabrikordnung," ca. 1858, p. 20; Staatsarchiv Dresden, Kreishauptmannschaft Zwickau, Nr. 1999, Limbach, pp. 156 ff.; Staatsarchiv Dresden, Amthauptmannschaft Löbau, Nr. 3375, C. F. Neumann in Eibau; Staatsarchiv Dresden, Amthauptmannschaft Chemnitz, Nr. 18, K. A. Löhse, 1862; Staatsarchiv Dresden, Amthauptmannschaft Chemnitz, Nr. 10, Thalheim, June, 1889 and August, 1889, p. 20; Stadtarchiv Crimmitschau, Rep. II, Kap. VI, Nr. 61, E. Müller & Renzsch, 1862; *Der Textil-Arbeiter*, May 30, 1902, Kettwig; *Sächsische Industrie-Zeitung*, Sept. 14, 1860, pp. 155–156, Werdau; Seidenzwirnereien der Firma C. U. Springer, 1852, reprinted in Walter Steitz, editor, *Quellen zur deutschen Wirtschafts- und Sozialgeschichte im 19. Jahrhundert bis zur Reichsgründung* (Darmstadt: Wissenschaftliche Buchgesellschaft, 1980), p. 287. See also sources cited in footnote 77, above.

87. Staatsarchiv Detmold, Regierung Minden I.U., Nr. 425, pp. 94 ff.

courts agreed that German employers, so long as they included this provision in their work code, had the right to block entry.[88] In contrast with their British counterparts, however, they generally chose not to do so.[89]

An investigator determined to find a utilitarian explanation for the difference in entrance customs between Germany and Britain might try to explain them by the balance of power between workers and employers. If, say, German textile employers suffered from a relative shortage of labor, this might have discouraged them from locking workers out or from stringently marking the start of the day for fear of provoking workers to transfer to other firms. We can reject this hypothesis by relying on comparisons within Germany itself. A comparison of regions that had surpluses of highly skilled workers, such as Krefeld, with areas such as the Münsterland, where directors complained of shortages, reveals no difference in the entrance customs.[90] Conversely, as was noted above, British mill directors locked workers out even during periods when workers were scarce.

The German directors' rejection of shutting workers out becomes all the more significant when placed in its legal context. After 1891, German law forbade employers from holding in their general till the monies collected through fines. Factory directors in Germany had to put such withholdings into special funds devoted to the welfare of workers, such as factory health insurance funds or welfare committees.[91] The German reliance on fining and the British reliance on locking out are the very reverse of the outcomes that would be expected if the employers had obeyed only the crude monetary incentives of the environment. In truth, the legislation in Germany merely affirmed from above what had already been settled from below: since the era of small shop production under subcontracting systems, German textile employers had deposited workers' fines into insurance and support funds,[92]

88. Philipp Lotmar, *Der Arbeitsvertrag nach dem Privatrecht des Deutschen Reiches*, Volume II (Leipzig: Duncker & Humblot, 1908), pp. 79, 243. Germany, *Die Gewerbe-Ordnung* (Berlin: J. Guttentag, 1878), pp. 108 ff.

89. German textile journals assumed that the only methods possible for influencing punctuality were fining or offering bonuses. *Leipziger Monatschrift für Textil-Industrie*, No. 3, 1909, p. 80.

90. For Krefeld, see Stadtarchiv Krefeld, F1446, C. G. Maurenbrecher, 1909; HSTAD Regierung Düsseldorf, Nr. 24660. Krefelder Seidenfärberei, 1900; *Der Christliche Textilarbeiter*, August 3, 1899, Krefeld. For the Münsterland, see, illustratively, Stadtarchiv Bocholt, *Arbeitsordnung* Franz Beckmann & Co., 1898, and testimony of Herr Reidegeld, cited in footnote 81, above.

91. Carl Koehne, *Arbeitsordnungen im deutschen Gewerberecht* (Berlin: Siemenroth und Troschel, 1901), pp. 219–220.

92. For an example of an agreement from the era of handweaving that allocated fines for bad cloth to a special welfare fund, see Zentrales Staatsarchiv Merseburg, Rep. 120 B I 1 59,

although they knew perfectly well they were not required to do so.[93] German practice ostensibly hearkened back to the guild ideal of depositing fines for infractions of artisanal rules into the association's treasury.[94] British mill owners, under the same circumstances, could pocket disciplinary and restitutive fines as they pleased.[95]

Since employers and workers in Germany conceived of work time as a continuous process of converting labor power into an output, they treated it as something that could be abstracted from its context and transferred. In the earliest days of the factory system, German workers themselves had proposed that tardy arrivals be allowed to make up lost minutes by working late.[96] Many factory directors gave their work force the option of taking off early from work during unofficial religious or communal holidays under the condition that the lost hours be made up by working an hour of over-

---

April 11, 1848, Chemnitz, p. 44. For the wool industry of the lower Rhine, see Artur Peltzer, "Die Arbeiterbewegung in der Aachener Textilindustrie von der Mitte des 19. Jahrhunderts bis zum Ausbruch des Weltkrieges," Ph.D. diss., Universität Marburg, 1924, p. 6; Decker, op. cit., p. 99. Elsewhere, Germany, Enquete-Kommission, *Reichs-Enquete*, op. cit., p. 444; Alphons Thun, *Die Industrie am Niederrhein und ihre Arbeiter* (Leipzig: Duncker und Humblot, 1879), Erster Theil, "Die linksrheinische Textilindustrie," p. 21. For illustrations of early ordinances from textile factories that allocated all fines to a welfare fund, see Zentrales Staatsarchiv Merseburg, 120 B II 1 78, Köcklin & Söhne, Lörrach, 1837, and Mechanische Spinnerei und Weberei Kempten, 1853; Zentrales Staatsarchiv Merseburg, 120 B V 33, Nr. 4, Volume 2, J. A. Meyer, Brandenburg, 1838; "Fabrik-Reglement," 1839, reproduced in Rainer Wirtz, "Die Ordnung der Fabrik ist nicht die Fabrikordnung," in Heiko Haumann, editor, *Arbeiteralltag in Stadt und Land* (Berlin: Argument-Verlag, 1982), p. 63; Stadtarchiv Crimmitschau, Rep. II, Kap. VI, Nr. 61, E. Müller & Renzsch, 1862.

93. Before the revised law was introduced in 1891, business journals informed employers that they were not required to hand over to welfare committees fines for lateness. *Das deutsche Wollen-Gewerbe*, February 22, 1878, p. 171. No wonder Günther Schulz found that in the industry of the Rhineland before the First World War, "the Prussian state was never the motor for the formation of company work relations." Günther Schulz, "Die betriebliche Lage der Arbeiter im Rheinland vom 19. bis zum beginnenden 20. Jahrhundert," *Rheinische Vierteljahrsblätter* Jahrgang 50 (1986), p. 175.

94. *Der Arbeiterfreund*, Sept. 2, 1848; Clemens Wischermann, "An der Schwelle der Industrialisierung 1800–1850," in Wilhelm Kohl, editor, *Westfälische Geschichte*, Volume 3 (Düsseldorf: Schwann, 1984), p. 158. Yet the British employers had institutional precedents similar to those of the Germans for allocating fines to welfare committees. For instance, the Worsted Committee responsible for enforcing cloth specifications at the close of the eighteenth century donated its fines to hospitals and local Sunday schools. Herbert Heaton, *The Yorkshire Woollen and Worsted Industries* (second edition Oxford: Clarendon Press, 1965), p. 434.

95. The practice of depositing the receipts from punishments into welfare committees was not unheard of in Britain but was rare indeed. Large paternalist firms were most likely to adopt the idea. Patrick Joyce, *Work, Society and Politics* (London: Methuen, 1982), p. 138. Whatever they ultimately arranged, the British mill employers had an incentive to impose fines which German employers lacked after 1891.

96. *Zeitung des Arbeiter-Vereins zu Köln*, April 30, 1848.

time during the following days.[97] There was nothing surreptitious about this practice, no attempt by managers in this fashion, at least, to gain hours for the week in excess of those allowed by law. Textile directors had specified in early factory ordinances that they could shift hours among the days of the week, so long as the total remained unchanged.[98] In Britain, production time was anchored in discrete beginning and ending points and remained bound to this concrete setting.[99]

The German managers' floating starting points for the measurement of the workday and their reliance on efficiency ratios both rested on their premise that time was transferable and unfastened. The efficiency ratios attempted an "objective" comparison between the use of time on different days, in different years, or in industrial eras that lay decades apart. Rather than comparing technological progress in terms of the length of the cloth manufactured per loom in the course of a day or of a year, as the English did, the Germans looked at progress in terms of the utilization of time. "If the old weaving mills used to get along with 50 percent efficiency," one journal contributor commented in 1914, "that does not come close to yielding a profit at the end nowadays."[100] A German mill director judged the success of his tenure by looking for improvements in efficiency ratios rather than seeking only an increase in the value of output per loom, as

---

97. HSTAD, Regierung Düsseldorf, 25021, 1899, p. 25; HSTAD, Regierung Düsseldorf, 24677, May 12, 1887, letter from the Handelskammer in Mönchengladbach; HSTAD, Landrats-amt Grevenbroich 271, 1909, J. A. Lindgens Erben; *Der Arbeiterfreund*, Vol. 22 (1884), p. 331; Peltzer, op. cit., p. 29; and the manager's diary from the Schoeller firm in Düren, for example, July 2, 1878. Courtesy Firmenarchiv Schoeller, Düren.

98. Stadtarchiv Mönchengladbach, "Fabrik-Ordnung für die mechanische Weberei, Fär-berei, Schlichterei und Appretur von Böhmer, Ercklentz und Prinzen in Mönchengladbach," November 1, 1862. Not until the 1890s did German factory inspectors, concerned that the shifting of hours between one day and the next made the true total of hours for the week unverifiable by outsiders, consistently intervene to suppress the practice. Germany, *Jahres-Berichte der königlich preussischen Regierungs- und Gewerberäthe, 1897* (Berlin: R. v. Decker, 1898), p. 473; Landesarchiv Potsdam, Rep. 75, Nr. 849, 1893, p. 116. But some years state officials without ado issued permission to extend hours for busy seasons. Landesarchiv Potsdam, company records of Tannenbaum, Pariser & Co., "Zuschriften von Behoerden," 1888–1893, pp. 115–116; HSTAD, Regierung Düsseldorf, 24684, April 15, 1893, Klauser firm; HSTAD, Regierung Düsseldorf, 25015, 1893, p. 18; Germany, *Jahres-Berichte der königlich preussischen Regierungs- und Gewerberäthe und Bergbehörden für 1898* (Berlin: R. v. Decker, 1899), p. 352; *Jahres-Berichte der königlich preussischen Regierungs- und Gewerberäthe und Bergbehörden für 1900* (Berlin: R. v. Decker, 1901), pp. 154, 169, Magdeburg, Merseburg.

99. Hours of labor lost due to stoppages in production were recoverable in Britain under the Factory Acts only in the event of drought, flooding, or other extraordinary disasters at the mill. United Kingdom, *Reports of the Inspectors of Factories*, PP 1836 (78) XLV, half-year ending December 31, 1836, p. 35.

100. *Leipziger Monatschrift für Textil-Industrie*, 1914, Nr. 3, p. 65.

his British counterpart did.[101] In truth, the physical characteristics of the weaving process did not permit any valid comparison of efficiency ratios for looms running at different speeds. The decision to contrast past and present in terms of this ratio therefore derived from an a priori assumption that change ought to be conceived as the differential utilization of abstract time.

The systems for controlling workers' entrances and exits in the textile industry can be generalized to other trades with large work premises. In Germany tardy metal workers and engineers were simply fined,[102] whereas the custom of shutting late workers outside the factory gate emerged in many enterprises in Britain. In the metal-working industry a British manager judged in 1899 that "the usual practice" across the land was to shut latecomers out until breakfast.[103] "The best timekeepers," he added, "are usually retired soldiers, who are accustomed to strict discipline."[104] Likewise, a guide to the "commercial management of engineering works" recommended in 1899 that employers pare their disciplinary rules to keep them simple and memorable. But its author insisted upon the draconian exclusion of latecomers from the premises until the start of the next shift.[105] The adoption of the custom in diverse circumstances—whether the work force consisted predominantly of men or women, whether labor was centralized under one roof early or late in the industrial revolution—implies that the practice embodied a fundamental premise.[106]

101. *Zeitschrift für die gesamte Textil-Industrie,* 1913, Nr. 36, pp. 827–828; *Textile Manufacturer,* October 15, 1908, p. 336.

102. Bernd Flohr, op. cit., pp. 105, 110.

103. Arthur Barker, *The Management of Small Engineering Workshops* (Manchester: John Heywood, 1899), p. 79. Stories about workers shut out in the metal trade can be gleaned from the Dermot Healey interviews of the Regional Studies Department, Oral History Project, Manchester Polytechnic.

104. Barker, op. cit., p. 78.

105. Francis G. Burton, *The Commercial Management of Engineering Works* (Manchester: Scientific Publishing Co., 1899), p. 182. Dyke Wilkinson, a metal worker in Birmingham, reported that when he found he was excluded for arriving one minute late, he took the whole day off. *Rough Roads: Reminiscences of a Wasted Life* (London: Sampson Low, Marston, & Co., 1912), p. 18.

106. In the shoemaking industry, employers locked the doors to deal with workers on piece rates who imagined they could come and go as they pleased. Keith Brooker, "The Northhampton Shoemakers' Reaction to Industrialization: Some Thoughts," *Northhamptonshire Past and Present* Volume VI, No. 3 (1980), p. 154. For locking out unpunctual workers in tailoring and mantle-making, see PP 1893–1894 XXXVII, Part 1, pp. 71, 76; for rope-making, PP 1892 XXXV, p. 331. Tardy workers at slate quarries were regularly excluded from the labor site for one week. PP 1892 XXXIV, p. 369. At a candy factory, an unpunctual female worker was excluded for two weeks. PP 1892 XXXV, p. 344.

FRONTIERS OF DISCIPLINE

The entrance to the textile mill served not just as a regulator of the passage of time but as a marker of territory, the boundary of the employer's domain. In each country the walls of the factory furnished an empty slate on which contrasting messages were inscribed. British mill owners manipulated the doorways of the mill to emphasize their jurisdiction over the borderline of the domain. If workers threatened to strike, the employers impounded them by locking the gate.[107] When an amendment to the Factory Acts in 1902 shortened the legal working hours on Saturdays, an employer in Leeds ordered that the workroom doors, previously locked only from the inside, henceforth be locked from the outside as well.[108] Since only top supervisors had keys to unlock the doors from the inside anyway,[109] his action may have been intended more as a signal than as a real safeguard: if this mill director could not choose the duration of labor as he pleased, he could in this fashion display his claim to prohibit movement across the frontier of the labor space during the workday. Other proprietors responded to the forced reduction in hours with the same tactic of heightened border controls.[110] "Some say it is like being locked in York Castle," the textile union newspaper reported from Ravensthorpe.[111] Command over the entry points represented the critical point of confrontation.

Since the factory proprietors rarely had contact with workers in the course of the daily cycle of production, the entryway itself remained as their primary zone of contact, at once symbolic and material. Both employers and workers viewed the threshold this way.[112] Sir Titus Salt positioned his guests by the mill gate so that they could watch the ceremony

---

107. Dermot Healey's interview tape 628, op. cit., p. 17.

108. *Yorkshire Factory Times*, February 21, 1902.

109. *Yorkshire Factory Times*, November 6, 1903, p. 4.

110. See *Yorkshire Factory Times*, January 17, 1902, for a similar incident in Elland.

111. April 3, 1903, Ravensthorpe. See also April 7, 1893, Shipley, and April 19, 1901, Elland. For Marsden, Bradford, and Eccleshill see the January 10, 1902, issue. Joanna Bornat's interview with Mr. B., op. cit.: "Oh, it were like a gaol." For examples of shutting employees within workrooms in Lancashire, see Mary Brigg, editor, "Journals of a Lancashire Weaver," *The Record Society of Lancashire and Cheshire*, Volume CXXII (1982), p. 3; *The Power Loom* (September 1916), p. 4; LRO, DDX 1628, Nelson and District Power-Loom Weavers' Association, June 10, 1896; Bolton Oral History Collection, Interview 121, mule piecer, born 1899; and Dermot Healey's interview tape 703, male weaver from Burnley, born 1895, line 880.

112. See H. S. G., *Autobiography of a Manchester Cotton Manufacturer* (Manchester: John Heywood, 1887), p. 32; *Yorkshire Factory Times*, February 18, 1898, Dudley Hill, "Scored One"; Dermot Healey's interview tape 664, p. 2.

of the workers leaving.[113] Salt's factory must be counted among the largest in Britain, offering less chance for exchanges between the employer and ordinary workers. For this reason, the ritual of entering Salt's mill took on added importance: if workers arrived late to his mill in the morning, they "knew they dealt not with delegated authority, but with the master himself."[114] Isaac Holden, an owner in Bradford, listed as one of his key management principles for a mill he owned that "the hands going in and coming out must go tranquilly."[115] Among workers at Crossley's Dean Clough Mill in Halifax, the legend persisted that the elderly mother of the owner had had a mirror installed in her room so that she could inspect the crowds of workers daily as they entered and exited the mill. From their countenances, the story maintained, she could deduce their current attitudes.[116] This tale indicates, all the more so if untrue, the way workers at this mill saw entering as a ritual moment of contact with employers and point of exposure to scrutiny.

The everyday experience of the entry controls made the doorway a potent vehicle in popular thought for condensing relations between employers and workers.[117] A tale circulated in the heavy woolen district of Yorkshire illustrates the displacement in folk culture of the mill owner's exercise of authority onto the entranceway:

A Queensbury mill-owner always stood at the mill gate each morning, watch in hand. One morning the carter, who had been at school with the mill-owner forty years before, and had worked at the mill since then, was late. The very next morning the carter was late again, and the mill-owner duly sacked him.

113. Robert Balgarnie, *Sir Titus Salt* (London: Hodder & Stoughton, 1878), p. 251.

114. Op. cit., p. 81. *Capital and Labour*, December 5, 1877, p. 666. "If any of them were late, it was the master's rebuke they feared." Cited by Andrew Yarmie, "Captains of Industry in Mid-Victorian Britain," diss., King's College, 1975, p. 100. Consult also Bolton Oral History Collection, tape 122, female spinner, born 1905, for a description of the inquiries that management made regarding the reasons for lateness.

115. Elizabeth Jennings, "Sir Isaac Holden," diss., University of Bradford, 1982, pp. 53–54. See also *Textile Manufacturer*, March 15, 1883, p. 90. Sometimes overlookers' houses were situated opposite the entrance gate, perhaps to create an effect of unremitting surveillance.

116. *Halifax Antiquary Society* (1950), p. 7.

117. *Yorkshire Factory Times*, February 28, 1908, p. 2. See pp. 338 ff. in D. McKelvie, "Some Aspects of Oral and Material Tradition in an Industrial Urban Area," Ph.D. diss., University of Leeds, 1963. See also the "Socialist Song Sheet," in the Colne Valley Labour Party Archives, Huddersfield Polytechnic, for a comment about entering beneath the eye of the porter: "In his box he sits in state / like a monarch ruling fate."

—"What? Sacking me for being five minutes late—after forty years?"

—"Ah'm not sacking thi for being late, Ah'm sacking thi for defying me!"

—"In that case Ah suppose Ah can go wheer Ah like for a job?"

—"Tha can go just wheer tha likes!"

—"Right," said the Carter, "Ah'm starting here again!"[118]

Former textile workers recalled in their interview that one boss or another always stood at the office window peering out over the mill gate.[119] When workers quit their job in anger or rejected an employer's authority, they cried out, "I'll not be passing through your gateway again!"[120] "The gate" did not just become a familiar turn of phrase but came to signify an opening into the life of the textile worker. A periodical about life in the north of England, which began publication in Manchester in 1905, chose the image of the entryway for its title: *The Millgate.* The editors' column of observations in each issue of this journal bore the heading "From the Mill Window." A magazine edited by a Huddersfield socialist contrasting the factory of the present with the society of the future called itself *The Gateway.*

By comparison with Britain, the form in which labor was commodified in Germany depreciated the importance of the doorway as a zone of contact with employers. At many German mills the managers relinquished central responsibility for recording entry and shifted the onus of keeping track of workers' attendance and punctuality to the individual overlookers.[121] Was

118. Cited in D. McKelvie, op. cit., pp. 338 ff. For another example, see Dermot Healey's interview tape 664, p. 2: "The manager . . . always had his watch in hand standing at the mill door."

119. Joanna Bornat's interview with Mrs. H., born 1895; *Yorkshire Dialect Society, Transactions,* Volume 8 (1950), p. 42; Elizabeth Roberts's interview with Mr. B8P, born 1896, Preston.

120. From my interview with Edward Mercer, weaver, Rawdon. See also Dermot Healey's interview tape 850, male worker from Nelson, born 1907.

121. Wirtschaftsarchiv Baden-Württemberg, B46-391, "Fabrik-Ordnung für L. Hartmann," 1846, and B25-316, 1902; *Der Textil-Arbeiter,* July 19, 1901, Eupen; Stadtarchiv Rheine, 183, "Arbeitsordnung" for Dyckhoff & Stoeveken, 1915; Voigt, op. cit., p. 387; *Arbeiterwohl,* 1881, Nr. 1, p. 48; my interview with Franz Reidegeld, born 1900, Rheine; Stadtarchiv Chemnitz, "Fabrik-Ordnung der Weberei von Ferdinand Waldau," Chemnitz, 1865; Stadtarchiv Chemnitz, Rep. II, Kap. IIIa, Nr. 13 Vol. II, excerpt from *Sächsisches Volksblatt* with dateline March 12, 1910; Textilmuseum Apolda, Fabrikordnung der Firma Zimmermann, 1857; *Der Textil-Arbeiter,* August 27, 1909, Burgstädt; Hauptstaatsarchiv Düsseldorf, Landratsamt Grevenbroich, Nr. 271, Emil Quack & Co., 1909; Tidow, op. cit., p. 70; Alf Lüdtke, "Arbeitsbeginn, Arbeitspausen, Arbeitsende," in Gerhard Huck, editor, *Sozial-*

not the heart of the matter control of the workers' labor power, not of their crossing a line?[122] In some instances the company rules for conduct in Germany defined late arrival as failure to set one's machinery in motion by the specified minute.[123] The overlookers' prospects for keeping their jobs depended on their ability to make sure that the workers in their charge appeared at their machines on time.[124]

The Factory Acts restricting the length of workdays in Britain defined the workers' period of labor by their presence in the factory, defined as including any area within the confines of the mill gates. Space marked the boundaries of employment. In Germany, by contrast, the laws regulating the length of employment in the factory referred to attendance at machines or in manual production. Accordingly, the courts determined that the period of work was determined by use of the employees' labor in the manufacturing process.[125] They reasoned that workers could remain on the premises of the mill for any period if they were not engaged in material production.[126] The courts naturally feared that employers might coerce workers to undertake miscellaneous tasks at all hours, so they were reluctant to exempt all categories of workers from time limits if they were not engaged in manufacture. In contrast to the unambiguous classification in Britain based on the

---

geschichte der Freizeit (Wuppertal: Peter Hammer Verlag, 1980), pp. 100–101. For the wool industry of the lower Rhine, see Decker, op. cit., p. 96; *Sächsisches Volksblatt*, March 12, 1910. For a contrast with Britain, where managers came round to inquire why workers were late, consult Bolton Oral History Collection, tape 122, female spinner, born 1905. The overlookers in Germany were relieved of responsibility for calculating tardiness if punch-in time clocks were installed.

122. *Der Textil-Arbeiter*, February 10, 1911, p. 44, Nordhorn; *Die Textilarbeiter-Zeitung*, November 30, 1901, Hückeswagen; Elisabeth Plössl, *Weibliche Arbeit in Familie und Betrieb: Bayerische Arbeiterfrauen 1870–1914* (München: Schriftenreihe des Stadtarchivs, 1983), p. 243. In the Wupper Valley, for example, a ribbon weaver at a medium-sized firm before the First World War remembered that the lowest overlooker kept track of attendance (my interview with Hans Penz, born 1895; cf. Ewald Sirrenberg, op. cit.). At a large corporation for spinning and weaving in Viersen on the lower Rhine, workers complained in 1905 that whether a worker received a fine for lateness, and the amount of the penalty, varied "according to which overlooker you stood under." *Der Textil-Arbeiter*, March 10, 1905.

123. Staatsarchiv Detmold, Regierung Minden, I.U. Nr. 425, C. A. Delius, Bielefeld, p. 106; Staatsarchiv Dresden, Amthauptmannschaft Flöha 2825, Baumwollspinnerei Matthes in Leubsdorf.

124. HSTAD, Landratsamt Mönchengladbach 710, 1874, pp. 102–103.

125. *Meeraner Tageblatt*, July 21, 1897.

126. *Sächsische Industrie*, October 3, 1905, p. 297. For an example of factory inspectors reporting on the extension of the hours of female workers who were not in buildings with mechanical machinery, see Staatsarchiv Weimar, Landesregierung Greiz, n Rep. A, Kap. IXa, Nr. 303, 1896–1900, p. 16; for a justification of this policy, see Staatsarchiv Weimar, Landesregierung Greiz, n Rep. A, Kap. IXa, Nr. 303, p. 46.

position of the worker in space, however, the German limits on time focused on the use of the labor capacity.

In regulating border crossings, British employers made more of a claim to the workers' presence in the confines of the factory than to their time at the loom. The most popular treatise on "scientific" management published before the war, Edward Elbourne's *Factory Administration and Accounts,* took care to define the worker's arrival as his standing on company property, not as being positioned at the machine.[127] The *Textile Manufacturer* reported in 1901 in a matter-of-fact tone that directors did not force workers to begin work promptly after they were inside the gate. "Most men weavers consider it a disgrace to be in their places waiting for the engines to start," the journal claimed. "They knock the ashes out of their pipes just as the gates are being closed, and then saunter leisurely to their work."[128] In this instance, crossing the border zone between the inside and outside of the mill carried more significance than beginning to produce.

In each country the workers' clothing on factory premises complemented the border controls. In Germany textile workers typically arrived at the mill in their street clothes and changed into work clothes before they reported to their machines.[129] Sometimes the firm designed, procured, and washed the work clothing.[130] The alteration in German workers' exterior signaled

127. *Factory Administration and Accounts* (London: Green & Co., 1914), pp. 31, 92. In emphasizing the importance of the gatekeeper's duties, Elbourne advised that the gatekeeper report directly to the owner, not to any intermediary foreman. Elbourne did not say whether tardy workers should be locked out, however. Using arrival at the perimeter of the factory as the criterion for deciding when an employee was "late," rather than expenditure of labor power, was consistent with the Factory Acts but not determined by them. The acts defined the workers' attendance by presence within the space of the factory, including the grounds if enclosed by a gate. But the Factory Acts allowed several minutes before the start of machinery for workers to arrive at the mill yard and make their way to the work station. Robert Baker, *The Factory Acts Made Easy: Or, How to Work the Law Without the Risk of Penalties* (Leeds: H. W. Walker, 1854), pp. 23, 36.

128. *Textile Manufacturer,* February 15, 1901, p. 38.

129. Minna Wettstein-Adelt, *3½ Monate Fabrik-Arbeiterin* (Berlin: J. Leiser, 1893), p. 16; *Der Christliche Textilarbeiter,* August 15, 1903, Rheydt; Germany, *Jahres-Berichte der königlich preussischen Regierungs- und Gewerberäthe und Bergbehörden für 1900* (Berlin: R. v. Decker, 1901), p. 34, Potsdam. Workers in some departments, such as cloth mending, which was usually conducted in an office apart from the main production process, kept street garments on.

130. For an example from the woolen industry of the lower Rhine, see Decker, op. cit., p. 87. Elsewhere: Hauptstaatsarchiv Düsseldorf, Regierung Düsseldorf, BR1015, Nr. 170, March 10, 1878, M. Lamberts & May, Mönchengladbach; Germany, *Jahres-Berichte der königlich preussischen Regierungs- und Gewerberäthe und Bergbehörden für 1891* (Berlin: W. T. Bruer, 1892), p. 187, Minden. At a firm in Plauen, the time required for changing out of work clothes was considered part of the workday. Stadtarchiv Plauen, Rep. I, Kap. VI, Sect. I, Nr. 64, July 20, 1863, Schnorr & Steinhäuser.

the consignment of their labor power to the factory owner's dominion. British workers, who transferred labor time in products but not the labor power in their person, rarely changed their pants, skirts, or blouses when they entered and exited the mill.[131] Even if work inside the mill coated them with waste, they wore the same clothes home.[132] No wonder the lack of changing rooms was never debated in Britain as it was in Germany, where having to remove clothing in the mill became an important grievance among female workers where facilities for changing in private were lacking.[133] Female textile workers in Britain, like their male co-workers, of course removed their outerwear, such as shawls or vests, but as a rule did not change to a company outfit. In Britain employers emphasized the momentary regulation of workers' bodies as workers stepped over the factory threshold. In Germany the dressing ritual used workers' bodies as a marker of the continuous alienation of the labor power lodged in the person of the worker.

The emphasis on the control of border points that characterized British textile factories prevailed in other trades. The general manager of the Salford Rolling Mills, in an 1896 guide to the administration of iron mills, devoted an

131. *Textile Recorder*, August 15, 1906; E. Blackburn, op. cit., p. 32; Macclesfield Oral History Project, Interview 110a; *Yorkshire Factory Times*, July 26, 1889, p. 4, Elland. Some mule spinners who wanted to put on airs wore bowler hats and top coats on the street, then switched to overalls inside, but this was exceptional. Thompson and Thompson, family and work history interviews, No. 122, Bolton, born 1895; Dermot Healey's interview tape 652, male spinner from Astley Bridge, born 1895, line 400.

132. Dermot Healey's interview tape 702, workers from Oldham, born 1897, p. 12; J. Worthington, "One Day in My Early Working Life," 1918, Bolton Library; *Textile Recorder*, August 15, 1906, reported that the Lancashire operative never has "the chance of cleaning himself before leaving work." For northern Ireland, Betty Messenger, *Picking Up the Linen Threads: A Study in Industrial Folklore* (Austin: University of Texas Press, 1978), p. 62. British managers found the German emphasis on cleaning facilities remarkable: *Textile Manufacturer*, August 15, 1882, p. 280. Ben Turner commented upon the workers' change of clothing in Switzerland, compared with Britain, in *About Myself 1863–1930* (London: Cayme Press, 1930), p. 189. Lancashire weavers might change their clothes when mills artificially raised the humidity of the workrooms by injecting steam into the air. PP 1892 XXXV, p. 76.

133. Like other questions involving the treatment of women, that of dressing rooms depended on more than the intersection of gender and class identities. It took shape through a culturally specific definition of labor as a commodity that is discernible only in a cross-national perspective. German textile-union officials who visited Britain were surprised at the absence of rooms for workers to change clothing. Stadtarchiv Cottbus, A II 4.7i, Nr. 11, July 11, 1906, p. 264. *Der Christliche Textilarbeiter*, February 24, 1900, Dülken; for examples of German workers expecting dressing rooms, see HSTAD, Regierung Düsseldorf, 25022, report for 1900, pp. 13–14; *Der Textil-Arbeiter*, April 25, 1902, Auerbach; *Die Textilarbeiter-Zeitung*, March 13, 1909. On rare occasions male workers, too, presented strike demands for dressing rooms. *Gladbacher Merkur*, May 18, 1899.

entire chapter to the layout and use of "The Entrance Gates." His depiction of the factory perimeter employed the military analogy of a citadel:

> the gates of a factory should be as rigidly watched as those of a fortress, and for this purposes an official, viz. The Gatekeeper, should be appointed. . . . The gates must be absolutely closed at the prescribed time, such, for instance, as when the whistle has ceased blowing. No relaxation whatever must be tolerated.[134]

The ideal of a walled fortress to which this writer referred influenced not only the use of factory buildings but the ponderable design of the structures themselves.

THE PARTITIONING OF SPACE

The differing physical layouts of British and German textile mills in the late nineteenth century furnished contrasting stage settings—true "foundations"—for labor's transmission. Technical manuals of the nineteenth century treated the selection of mill architecture as part of the "science" of manufacturing.[135] Modern British woolen and worsted mills stereotypically were arranged like closed, defensive fortresses: the various rooms for spinning, for assembling the warps, and for weaving formed a ring enclosing a central courtyard or "mill yard." The entrance gate, often set under an archway, offered the only opening from the outside that led into this yard and into the workrooms (see Figure 6). Otherwise, the factory presented a solid barrier to the surrounding world, sometimes with no windows on the ground floor.[136] The layout could also call upon a row of workers' dwellings

134. J. Slater Lewis, *The Commercial Organization of Factories* (London: E. & F. N. Spon, 1896), Chapter XVI, "The Entrance Gates and the Gatekeeper," pp. 141–143.

135. Evan Leigh, *The Science of Modern Cotton Spinning* (London: Simpkin, Marshall and Co., 1873), Vol. II; Elbourne, op. cit., p. 19. For an earlier period, see Andrew Ure, *Philosophy of Manufactures* (London: Charles Knight, 1835), p. 33.

136. See the chapter on "Modern Mill Layout" in D. H. Williams, *Textile Factory Organization and Management* (London: Emmott & Co., 1934). Williams shows that the fortress design could be employed in "rationalized" mills, where each processing room was located around the perimeter for the most efficient throughput and movement of raw materials, as well as in haphazardly organized older mills, where the stages of processing the materials were not necessarily assigned sequentially to adjacent workrooms. Utility for production neither necessitated nor excluded the design. Williams's book deals with smaller mills, but the same design held for such giant enterprises as Titus Salt's Saltaire. For other examples, see Leafield mills, in E. Philip Dobson and John B. Ives, *A Century of Achievement: The History of James Ives & Company Limited* (London: William Sessions, 1948), p. 47; Plan of Bleach Works, Barnsley, 1895, Royal Commission on Historical Monuments, York; Benyon's mill, Holbeck, Leeds, RCHME; Mssrs Blackburn mill, Batley, plan at Kirklees Archives.

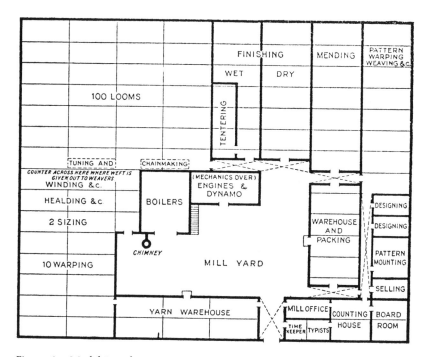

Figure 6.   Model British Weaving Mill
Source: D. R. H. Williams, *Textile Factory Organization and Management* (Manchester: Emmott & Co., 1934)

on one or more sides of its perimeter to form part of the barricaded zone. Naturally, these houses on the boundary had no openings into the mill yard.[137]

The fortress-like enclosure of a mill yard by the workrooms appeared in the design of mills in Lancashire and elsewhere in the northwest, once factory design had come into its own.[138] The arrangement became an emblem not only in the actual conduct of manufacturing but in the fancies of literature. The frontispiece to Andrew Ure's famous tract *The Philosophy of Manufactures*, published in 1835, portrayed a factory whose wings were shaped to enclose a courtyard. The assumptions of this graphic depiction achieved verbal expression. Ure, an advocate of the mill system's satanic regimen during the youthful phases of industrial growth, emphasized the textile workers' encapsulation by referring to the hapless operatives as "factory inmates."[139]

To be sure, the enveloping design occurred more frequently in built-up urban areas, where the need to mark off one's own territory and to guard against intrusions was greater than in the countryside, where isolated mills, which expanded incrementally, sometimes consisted of small, scattered buildings, without a comprehensive model. Therefore the castle design was far from universal and, indeed, was realized in pure form in only a minority of cases.[140] Yet it represented something of an architectural stereotype, a

137. Deepdale mill, Preston, Preston Mill Book, Preston Library Archives.

138. See Manchester Library Archives, William Higgins & Sons, Salford, Manchester, "Plan and Elevation of a Flax Mill," July, 1851. Sylvia Clark, "Chorlton Mills and Their Neighbors," *Industrial Archaeology Review* Volume II, Number 3 (Summer 1978), p. 209; Jennifer Tann, *The Development of the Factory* (London: Cornmarket Press, 1970), pp. 17, 34; Brunswick mill, Manchester, 1838, Houldsworth cotton mill, Stockport, 1867, and Murray's mills, Manchester Archaeology Unit, and annotation to file, p. 21; Brookfield mill, Moor Hall mill, Springfield mill, and Deepdale mill in Preston, Preston Mill Book, Preston Library Archives; for an example of a mill that put warehousing on its ground floor, without windows, see Manchester Archaeology Unit, Brunswick mill.

139. Ure, op. cit., pp. 353, 374, 404. For a similar usage, see Doherty, editor, op. cit., p. vii. The word *inmate* in this era referred to a permanent occupant or indweller of a place. *O.E.D.*, 2d ed., Vol. 5, p. 307. In *The Great Law of Subordination Consider'd*, published in 1724, Daniel Defoe used the workshop portal to classify England's workers into two kinds: "Labourers Without-Doors" and "Labourer Within-Doors." Reprinted in Stephen Copley, editor, *Literature and the Social Order in Eighteenth-Century England* (London: Croom Helm, 1984), p. 144. Among the home weavers, an expression for being in a factory was standing "within the walls." Testimony of Joseph Coope, Committee on Woollen Manufacture, April 23, 1806, PP 1806 III, 1806. The emphasis put on the division between the interior and the exterior of the mill could influence factory bookkeeping. At Strut's mill in Derbyshire, the wages books surviving from the 1870s for those assigned to factory upkeep are divided into two sets, for workers who labored on the exterior of the mill and for those who were inside, although in some instances their tasks were otherwise the same. Manchester Library Archives.

layout which appeared when unprompted by the environment.[141] For instance, Sir Titus Salt in the 1870s built his mill in the middle of an undeveloped parcel of land large enough to accommodate an entire town, yet he, too, adopted the fortress structure.[142] This arrangement struck German observers of British developments as representative of British thinking.[143] Once it was crystallized in factory layouts in the north of England, the British carried it to contexts where land values, the landscape, and the infrastructure were far different. For example, in his treatise on mill construction William Fairbairn presented a blueprint for building a woolen factory in the open countryside of a foreign country, Turkey. He incorporated the classic sealed yard into the design of the U-shaped building itself.[144] The Platt Brothers' plans for integrated cotton mills in Brazil at the beginning of the twentieth century came in various sizes, but they arranged the workrooms in an unbroken circle around a secured yard.[145] The transference of this pattern into such diverse habitats offers a hint that it conformed, not to the physical requirements of the surroundings, but to a cultural model.

Apart from their structural emphasis on control of access points, British mills were distinguished from German ones by the attention they gave to the design of the main portal. The entrance exterior was some-

140. It was not feasible to accentuate control over access points when the building was used for the so-called "room and power system," under which several small businessmen rented out portions of a single mill. See Burnley Library, Archives, Elm Street mill, D74.

141. For examples of enclosed buildings in the shoe trade, see the *Shoe and Leather Record*, January 1, 1892, p. 10, and March 4, 1892, p. 550.

142. See plan of Royal Commission on Historical Monuments, York. On Salt's choice of unoccupied territory, see L. Cooper, *Great Men of Yorkshire West Riding* (London: The Bodley Head, 1955), p. 111. For another example where the design was not intended to conserve land, see LRO, DDX 1129, Kirkham Flax Mill, 1865.

143. Ludwig Utz, *Moderne Fabrikanlagen* (Leipzig: Uhlands Technischer Verlag, 1907), p. 282. Another German manual on industrial architecture, published in 1901, judged that British designers had a distinctive way of breaking up the monotonous lines of factory buildings with adjoining wings: British mills, they concluded, "unite practical considerations with those of taste." Wilhelm Rebber, *Fabrikanlagen: Ein Handbuch für Techniker und Fabrikbesitzer* (2d ed. Leipzig: B. F. Voigt, 1901), p. 94.

144. William Fairbairn, *Treatise on Mills and Millwork* (London: Longmans, Green, 1861). What interests us here is not only the "natural fact" that the castle design occurred with a certain statistical frequency in Britain. We are also interested in the "cultural fact" that the design served as an ideal the builders and owners held before themselves, although they hardly carried out this ideal under all circumstances.

145. Platt Brothers and Company, *Particulars and Calculations Relating to Cotton Ginning, Opening, Carding, Combing, Preparing, Spinning, and Weaving Machinery* (Manchester: Platt Brothers, ca. 1918), pp. 324–325. See also "Plan of Cotton Mill for Abroad," *Textile Manufacturer*, Jan. 15, 1891, pp. 4 ff.

times flanked by imposing towers or crowned by intricate ornamenta-tion.[146] On the inside, the entrance hallway might feature extra doors which managers used as backup devices to seal off access to the main workrooms or, from the other direction, access to the main gate. This design appeared in the very earliest mills. *The Poor Man's Advocate* in-vestigated a spinning mill in 1832 where the gates were "numerous, being placed one within the other, in order, we suppose, that if any of the wretched inmates should escape through the first they may be secured by the next."[147] Similar arrangements appeared in later facilities. At the West Vale textile works near Halifax, constructed during the last quarter of the nineteenth century, owners even installed a special lever for the gate-keeper which ran from his office perch to a second door on the inside of the entry corridor, permitting him to inspect the arrivals a second time in the corridor and decide whether to let them proceed.[148]

What information did the factory's design encode? Let us extract the elementary structure behind the visible architecture by mapping the pas-sages between rooms on the premises. Figure 7 delineates the apertures between the compartments of the illustrative floorplan.[149] The diagrams reveal, first, that the fortress design could turn the mill yard into a nodal point. The yard served not just as an unloading or storage area but as a connector for human traffic. In fact, movement even between work rooms that were contiguous frequently had to flow through the central yard. Each of the major rooms is organized as a self-sufficient space, which opens to the others via an interchange that serves every room in the

146. See sketches and descriptions of entrances to Park mill, Hartford mill, and Alliance mill in the second, documentary volume of N. K. Scott, "The Architectural Development of Cotton Mills in Preston and District," Master's thesis, University of Liverpool, 1952. Charts of Ellar Carr Mills.

147. Doherty, editor, op. cit., p. vii.

148. Royal Commission on Historical Monuments, York, courtesy of Colum Giles. For a description of a similar arrangement in Preston, Lancashire, see Elizabeth Roberts's interview with Mr. G1P, born 1903, p. 96. A machine oil salesman who traveled from mill to mill in the Colne Valley shortly before the First World War described in his memoirs their shuttered atmosphere. On approaching them, he remembered, "You didn't go into an office to be re-ceived decently—you had to rattle a little trap door. A head would come out and say 'What's it about?'" W. Farrar Vickers, *Spin a Good Yarn* (Leeds: MT Co., 1978), p. 19. The style of reception suited a bolted tower more than a modern business concern. Even during this late era, if workers had to stay late on payday to collect their cash, they called this "detention." *Yorkshire Factory Times,* April 25, 1902, p. 4.

149. I owe this technique to Bill Hillier and Julienne Hanson, who present it in *The Social Logic of Space* (Cambridge: Cambridge University Press, 1984), Chapter 4, "Buildings and Their Genotypes."

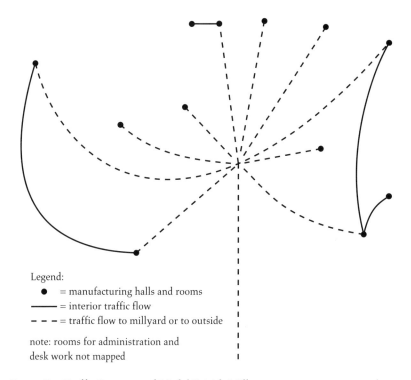

Legend:
● = manufacturing halls and rooms
———— = interior traffic flow
‐ ‐ ‐ = traffic flow to millyard or to outside

note: rooms for administration and
desk work not mapped

Figure 7. Traffic Structure of Model British Mill

complex. In sum, once workers negotiated the entry passage into the facility, the design gave them easy access to every corner of the interior.
This basic principle underlay the design of some mills, such as that of the
Blackburns in Batley, Yorkshire, even when at first glance the mill buildings did not seem to be arranged as a castle, but all of whose rooms nonetheless fed into two courtyard passages.[150] The layout created an
encompassing perimeter while permitting rapid movement in the interior.

Surveillance of the central yard could give a comprehensive view of
important traffic at a glance.[151] To take advantage of this, British textile

150. Plan at Kirklees Archives.
151. William Strutt's Belper Round mill, completed in 1813, divided the circular interior
into eight segments and placed an overseer in the center with a direct view of each part, "like
a spider at the heart of his web." R. S. Fitton and A. P. Wadsworth, *The Strutts and the
Arkwrights 1758–1830* (Manchester: Manchester University Press, 1958), p. 221. But Belper
Round Mill was unique. The British textile mills of classic design differed from Jeremy Bentham's Panopticon because employers sought to control the threshold and observe movement
within the main yard rather than to bind workers to the location of their machines.

directors occasionally incorporated large lookouts or jutting bay windows into their mill offices. These impressive windows did not face away from the factory perimeter for an enjoyable view, but looked instead toward the interior mill yard.[152] At Grecian mills in Bolton, Lancashire, the management offices had such an obtrusive bay window facing the main gate that it may well have shunted entering traffic to the side.[153] At Bean Ing mills in Leeds, Yorkshire, the surveillance windows were placed at the curved tip of a projection that pointed toward the middle of the inner yard.[154] A visitor to a coarse cloth factory at Knightsbridge during the 1840s described a more elaborate contrivance at a rotunda-like factory: "On the summit of the building, at a considerable elevation, is a small square room, provided with windows on all four sides. From this an extensive view may be obtained in every direction."[155] Of course, a simple window peering inward could serve as the observation site almost as well: the strategy was to position the management complex so that it could receive vendors and customers from without but also scan the interned laborers within.[156]

When the Germans constructed their facilities, they consciously imitated other, superficial features of British mill design, such as styles of ornamentation.[157] The Germans also followed the English methods of

---

152. See, for example, Learoyd Brothers, Huddersfield, "A Modern Fancy Worsted Mill," *Textile Manufacturer*, December 15, 1896, p. 457.

153. Bolton Library Archives, ZTA/10, T. Taylor & Son. For another example, see Murray's mills, Manchester Archaeology Unit.

154. Colum Giles, Royal Commission on Historical Monuments, unpublished manuscript, p. 20.

155. George Dodd, *Days at the Factories: Or, the Manufacturing Industry of Great Britain Described* (London: Charles Knight, 1843), p. 285.

156. See E. Blackburn, op. cit., p. 10, and Judy Lown, *Women and Industrialization* (Cambridge: Polity Press, 1990), p. 37. For an example of employers using their office window to observe a confused demonstration in the mill yard, see *Yorkshire Factory Times*, September 25, 1903.

In the north of England the passage to the factory system coincided in some districts with the heyday of violent Chartist conflict, for which there is no close parallel during the industrial transition in Germany. A volatile setting may have increased interest in the control of labor among early British factory employers. But the passing moment of struggle does not clarify the precise modes of spatial control nor the reasons for their reproduction throughout the century; for this, an explanation must call upon the definition of labor as a commodity.

157. Alex Moll, *950 Jahre Oerlinghausen* (Oerlinghausen: Loewe, 1986), p. 50. Gustav Baum, *Entwicklungslinien der Textilindustrie mit besonderer Berücksichtigung der bautechnischen und maschinellen Einrichtungen der Baumwoll-Spinnereien und Webereien* (Berlin: M. Krayn, 1913), p. 83.

transmitting power from the steam engine to the machines.[158] But they incorporated different structural principles into the layouts of the buildings themselves. Their factories did not arrange the workrooms to cordon off the outside world and impound laborers inside. Where German mill owners fenced in their property, as was often the case, this did not form an integral part of the design of the building itself.[159] Rather than arrange workrooms as a fortress to accentuate the frontier between outside and in, the German facilities emphasized the constriction of movement once laborers were engaged in the labor process. Except for the essential transport of materials, the German building layout segregated the principal workrooms from each other and from the ancillary rooms that housed processes such as carding raw cotton or preparing warps for the looms. Moving from one corner of the mill to another required workers to proceed through intermediate chambers of the interior. Figure 8 reproduces the floor plan of a German mill. Figure 9 diagrams its basic structures.[160] In contrast to the British mills, traffic does not converge on a nodal point but flows among links on a chain. There is no "center" from which the privileged observer can inspect traffic on the premises as a whole, yet the lack of central oversight is balanced by greater obstacles to movement between distant points.[161] Counterfeit instances of symmetrical fortress-like structures appear in Germany.[162] With one plan, sketched in 1849 for

158. Wolfgang Müller-Wiener, "Die Entwicklung des Industriebaus im 19. Jahrhundert in Baden," diss., Karlsruhe, 1955, p. 76.

159. The factory rules in German mills frequently specified that workers should enter and leave the factory only through a designated door. The design of the mills, unlike that of those in Britain, did not make the injunction superfluous. Decker, op. cit., p. 213; HSTAD, Landratsamt Mönchengladbach, 703, Kloeters & Lamerz; Germany, *Jahres-Berichte der königlich preussischen Regierungs- und Gewerberäthe und Bergbehörden für 1889* (Berlin: W. T. Bruer, 1890), p. 302.

160. See, too, Stadtarchiv Gera, Schulenburg und Bessler, Zwötzen, 1909; floor plans in Kreisarchiv Karl-Marx Stadt-Land, Stadtrat Limbach III 10d, Nr. 1139.

161. The factory rules issued by textile employers in Germany forbade the hired hands to trespass in rooms outside their own work spot, even when the machinery was turned off and there was no danger of accident. For the lower Rhine wool industry, see Decker, op. cit., p. 214. Elsewhere: Elisabeth Plössl, op. cit., p. 243; Stadtarchiv Greiz, B 5975, Kap.IV, Nr. 65, C. G. Lorenz, ca. 1887; Marie Bernays, "Auslese und Anpassung der Arbeiterschaft der geschlossenen Grossindustrie: Dargestellt an den Verhältnissen der 'Gladbacher Spinnerei und Weberei' A.G. zu Mönchengladbach," *Schriften des Vereins für Sozialpolitik* Volume 133 (Leipzig: Duncker & Humblot, 1910), p. 185; Staatsarchiv Dresden, Amthauptmannschaft Flöha, Nr. 4038, G. F. Heymann Spinnerei, Gückelsberg, 1869.

162. For the absence of the fortress structure, see Utz, op. cit., p. 275, and Ludwig Utz, *Die Praxis der mechanischen Weberei* (Leipzig: Uhlands technischer Verlag, 1907), charts; Stadtarchiv Mönchengladbach, 5/418, floor plan for Buchaly & Herbertz from 1909, and 5/187, floor plan for Bloem & Remy from 1902; *Leipziger Monatschrift für Textil-Industrie*, 1910,

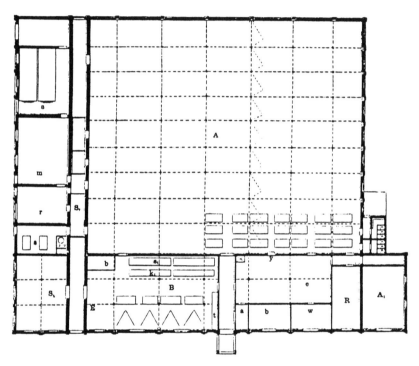

Figure 8.   Model German Weaving Mill
Source: Ludwig Utz, *Moderne Fabrikanlagen* (Leipzig: Uhlands technischer Verlag, 1907)

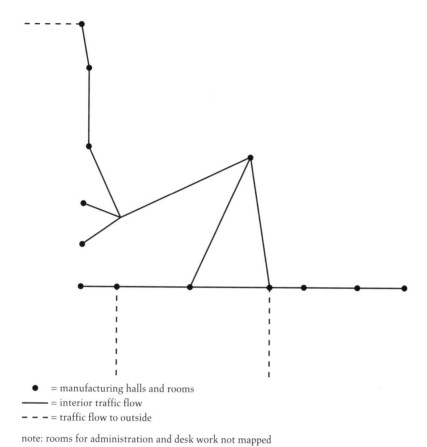

● = manufacturing halls and rooms
——— = interior traffic flow
- - - = traffic flow to outside

note: rooms for administration and desk work not mapped

Figure 9.   Traffic Structure of Model German Mill

Nr. 8, pp. 235 ff.; Edward Beyer, *Die Fabrik-Industrie des Regierungsbezirkes Düsseldorf vom Standpunkt der Gesundheitspflege* (Oberhausen: Spaarmann, 1876), spinning mills in Mönchengladbach; *Allgemeine Deutsche Ausstellung auf dem Gebiete der Hygiene und des Rettungswesens* (Berlin, 1883), M. May & Co. in Mönchengladbach; Hans-Peter Schwanke, "Architektur für Stadt, Gesellschaft und Industrie: Das Werk der Krefelder Architekten Girmes & Oediger 1892–1933," diss., Bonn, 1987, p. 650. For mills in less urbanized areas, see floor plans for L. B. Lühl & Söhne in Gemen, 1913, Heuveldop & Söhne, Emsdetten, at the Westfälisches Textil-Museum. The firm Schulenburg und Bessler in Zwötzen had a factory with multiple entrances (plan from 1909 in Stadtarchiv Gera). The layout of buildings around a central, enclosed yard also typified farm estates in Germany, although these complexes had numerous entrances into the buildings. Schwanke, op. cit., p. 710.

a Saxon village, the castle layout may have fit an aesthetic ideal of a noble court, but it actually contained multiple entrances and was ill adapted for forming an impenetrable perimeter.[163] With another, the Spinning and Weaving Factory Ettlingen in Baden, erected in 1838, the constructor designed the mill according to the same plan he had drawn up earlier for an army barracks.[164] The mill was inserted in a complex that created numerous openings and did not direct traffic through the central court. This was representative: the editor of one set of German mill plans even boasted that an exemplary weaving building was accessible from three separate points after workers had entered the grounds.[165] When large German complexes were erected at once around a central space, such as the Flax Mill of Schoeller, Mevissen, & Bücklers in Düren, they could have emphasized the enclosure of workers and observation of their movement through a central yard. Instead, they opened up onto the adjacent gardens and fields.[166] In Britain, the fortress design could be employed in "rationalized" mills, where each processing room was located around the perimeter for the most efficient movement of raw materials, as well as in haphazardly organized older mills, where the stages of processing the materials were not necessarily assigned sequentially in adjacent work rooms.[167]

German commentators believed that contrasts in building materials and climate could not account for differences in structural design between their country and Britain. Taste, they said, determined the ultimate format.[168] As early as 1844, the engineer Ludwig Kufahl of Berlin observed a crucial difference between British and German plans:

163. Staatsarchiv Dresden, Ministerium des Innern, Nr. 5771. Analogously, see the plan of the Facilides cotton printing and spinning mill with multiple entrances despite the arrangement of rooms around a yard, in Siegfried Kress, "Die Bauten der sächsischen Kattundruck-Manufaktur," diss., Technische Hochschule Dresden, 1958, p. 152.

164. Müller-Wiener, op. cit., p. 21.

165. A. Knäbel, *Die Tuchfabrikation und der Zeugdruck* (Leipzig: Karl Scholtze, 1882), pp. 186–188.

166. The depiction of this factory complex on the company letterhead accentuated its openness and the easy passage from outside. Rheinisch-Westfälisches Wirtschaftsarchiv zu Köln, *Kölner Unternehmer und die Frühindustrialisierung im Rheinland und in Westfalen 1835–1871* (Köln: Rheinisch-Westfälisches Wirtschaftsarchiv, 1984), p. 76. This raises a separate issue for cross-national investigation, to wit, the principles governing not only the construction of the building itself but the perspective by which to represent the completed edifice.

167. See the chapter on "Modern Mill Layout" in Williams, op. cit., p. 3.

168. Der praktische Maschinen-Constructeur, *Bau- und Betriebs-Anlage für Spinnereien und Webereien* (Leipzig: Baumgärten, 1875), p. 1.

I am familiar with the example of an extremely large flax spinning mill in Leeds. . . . With very scrupulous concern this building ensures above all that the workers can be watched over with complete ease. With us this very important point is often neglected. In fact, one could say that our factory buildings often appear to have been deliberately laid out to hinder surveillance of workers. For this one cannot combine every conceivable kind of work process together; but this is by no means necessary, just so the various jobs are grouped in such a way that a suitable control is possible and so that raw materials pass through the hands of the workpeople in the proper order, proceeding in their conversion from a raw condition to a completed manufacture.[169]

Kufahl did not think that work processes should be combined or connected to a single open space simply for the sake of comprehensive oversight of workers from afar. He considered it sufficient to organize traffic to move components through the mill in a logical sequence.[170] The German factory designs were "cellular," with numerous partitions and no centralized pathway for movement between chambers.

The fortress layout in Britain rested upon a combination of technological limits and opportunities. It took the liberty of breaking up the total production space of a factory premises into smaller units to form the fortress wings. Given the engineering techniques of the day, this represented a useful way of partitioning the land parcel. The width of work rooms in multistory spinning mills had in any case been limited by reliance upon iron frameworks to support the weight of the building. Rooms were long and narrow, a shape that was easy to configure around a large court. Beginning in the second half of the nineteenth century, however, an increase in the size of machines and in the scale of production made it preferable to unify floor space.[171] Cotton spinning

---

169. Ludwig Kufahl, "Ueber die Anlage von Fabrikgebäuden," *Zeitschrift für praktische Baukunst*, Volume 4 (Berlin: Allgemeine deutsche Verlags-Anstalt, 1844), p. 30.

170. Of course, as British designers themselves emphasized, the fortress design was also compatible with arrangement of workrooms for efficient throughput. Williams, op. cit., pp. 3 ff. On the relative absence in Britain of textile mills designed from the start for production flow, see Scott, op. cit., p. 104. German technical writers sometimes presented comprehensive plans for large factory estates, in which the production process is fit, not into a single building, but into a number of small structures. German plans for a complete spinning and weaving facility, including dyeing and finishing, laid out the buildings on large grounds with a symmetrical design, but the units were not arranged around a perimeter to enclose the production processes. Knäbel, op. cit., pp. 174, 203.

171. Frank Nasmith, *Recent Cotton Mill Construction and Engineering* (Manchester: John Heywood, 1909), pp. 10–11.

mules, for example, reached a length of 140 feet, so that the width of new buildings had to triple to organize aisle space efficiently.[172] Meeting this requirement became possible only with changes in construction methods. The introduction of steel girders and new techniques for supporting weight in the 1890s permitted the development of huge, squarish rooms that used space efficiently but were no longer arrangeable around a yard.[173]

These innovations in engineering changed the visible edifice of the labor process in newly constructed spinning facilities in Britain. Yet the principles of the underlying structure were preserved and manifested in fresh ways. The cavernous new buildings built in the British towns that were still expanding production were distinguished by an absence of dividing walls between the work processes.[174] Managers in the Bolton cotton trade, for instance, suggested that the preparatory processes be housed on the first floor without boundaries between the drawing, slubbing, and jack frames and the carding engines.[175] At Gil mill, expansion of the mill allowed the preparatory and spinning processes to be installed in the same room as the weaving machines without partitions. By contrast, German mills of equal capacity retained internal walls between departments.[176] This became a characteristic difference between British and German mills that did not escape the notice of contemporaries. A technical writer based in Manchester presented a cotton mill plan in 1897 borrowed from the Continent but made a suggestion on how to adapt the foreign blueprint to British expectations: "The supervision and management of the mill is greatly facilitated," he said, if "the whole of the machinery can readily be

172. Presentation by Harold Hill on "Influences Arising from the Employment of New and Improved Machines," *Official Record of the Annual Conference of the Textile Institute Held at Bolton, June, 1927* (Leeds: Chorley & Pickersgill, 1927), charts following p. 57; Scott, op. cit., p. 72. In spinning departments, a width of forty meters became commonplace: Baum, op. cit., p. 90.

173. Duncan Gurr and Julian Hunt, *The Cotton Mills of Oldham* (Oldham: Oldham Cultural and Information Services, 1989), p. 8. Auxiliary work rooms could also form a perimeter around the main building, as at Hargreaves's Victoria mills, Bolton, plan in Bolton Library Archives.

174. Nasmith, op. cit., pp. 10–11.

175. Presentation by Hill, op. cit., p. 60. Only the scutchers were walled into a separate room, due to the need to isolate the danger of fire. For other examples, see *Textile Recorder*, November 15, 1883, p. 157 for the plan of Stalybridge Mills Co., Oldham.

Of course, not all new mills needed such gigantic rooms or required multistory buildings that used ground space efficiently, so the fortress enclosure could be carried over into some of the latest designs. For examples, see Platt Brothers and Company, op. cit., p. 323; Bolton Library Archives, J. G. & C. Hargreaves, Victoria Mills, p. 11.

176. Baum, op. cit., p. 81; Utz, op. cit., pp. 258, 264.

seen. If desired . . . the internal division walls can be removed and columns substituted."[177] As with the fortress design, the undivided British layout in giant mills depreciated control over the rapid circulation of workers once they were inside the mill, but it lent the observer a sweeping view of their movement.[178] In contrast to the "cellular" design of German factories, the British designs were "circumferential," emphasizing the outer boundary but not partitions within.

The definition of labor as a commodity did not conjure the factory layouts out of thin air, but started from the technical preconditions of building design. Despite changes in these requirements in the late nineteenth century, the tangible materials of production could still be sculpted into shapes that carried the same implications for the treatment of labor as a commodity.[179] Mill architecture and rituals for entering the factory in Germany and in Britain reified contrasting fictions about the employment relation—again, the disposition over labor power versus the appropriation of labor incorporated into products. In Germany, the production process was conceived as the continuous transformation in time of labor power into a product. In this process the worker's labor activity was consumed inside the factory owner's domain, so the divide between inside and out

177. Theodore Sington, "Plan for a Continental Cotton Mill," in his *Cotton Mill Planning and Construction* (Manchester: published by the author, 1897), unpaginated.

178. British managers expounded their jurisdiction over factory workers in expressions involving the "eye." For illustrations, consult "Cotton Mill Organization," *Journal of the British Association of Managers of Textile Works* Volume II (1910–1911), p. 37; autobiographical statement by Joseph Wilson, born 1833, in Joseph Wilson, *Joseph Wilson: Life and Work* (London: Lund Humphries & Co. [1923]), p. 29. Workers referred to the "eagle eye" and "the proverbial 'lynx-eye'" of the employer. *Yorkshire Factory Times*, March 21, 1890, Apperly Bridge and October 12, 1894, p. 5; Dermot Healey's interview tape 655, female weaver from Darwen, born 1890, lines 565 ff. British employers conceived their knowledge and superiority in terms of eyesight: "It should always be remembered that 'the eyes of a master are worth more than the hands of a man.'" Cited in *Textile Manufacturer*, January 15, 1903. See also S. J. Daniels, "Moral Order and the Industrial Environment in the Woolen Textile Districts of West Yorkshire, 1780–1880," Ph.D. diss., University College, London, 1980, p. 249; Burton, op. cit., p. 171. An emphasis on surveillance does not necessarily mark greater management control of the shop floor. British employers sometimes resorted to visual monitoring as an ineffective substitute for direct command over the labor process. See Dyke Wilkinson, *Rough Roads: Reminiscences of a Wasted Life* (London: Sampson Low, Marston, & Co., 1912), p. 19.

179. The taken-for-granted character of the agents' understanding of labor as a commodity froze neither institutional nor architectural forms in place. The same specification of labor could be embodied in a changing technical environment. It did not rule out change, but ordered it. For an analysis of the adaptation of technical requirements to cultural models of space, see Betsy Bahr, "New England Mill Engineering: Rationalization and Reform in Textile Mill Design, 1790–1920," Ph.D. diss., University of Delaware, 1987, p. 19.

did not become marked as the crucial zone of subordination.[180] The layout of the German mills corresponded to an emphasis on the overlooker's responsibility for attaching the worker to the machine and a comparative depreciation of controls at the perimeter of the building. In Britain, by contrast, the workers retained ownership of their labor power but conveyed labor through products that were appropriated; since the workers' labor was not incorporated into the employers' domain through a continuous process in *time*, it was incorporated at a discrete moment through the ritual *event* of entering the factory. Rather than being transformed in the factory, labor was merely circumscribed and observed at a distance, by emphasizing the boundary between the factory and the world outside. Both the centripetal paths for traffic in older British mills and the atrophy of room partitions in the newer cotton spinning mills relaxed controls over rapid movement. Within the German factory, by contrast, the workers were segregated in compartments that curtailed passage between various corners of the mill. Their activity itself was appropriated in space.[181]

Because German and British factory buildings concretized information about the labor transaction, they could take on the task of imparting and reproducing—truly, "holding in place"—definitions of labor among the

180. By the turn of the century, when German rules for discipline in the mills generally followed a standardized format, their titles revealed the center of their interest. Could it have been purely accidental that they were not called "factory ordinances," as in Britain, but "labor ordinances"? Stadtarchiv Rheine, Nr. 183, Gewerbeinspektor Münster.

181. Theft of materials from German textile mills appears to have been a frequent occurrence, partly because home workers in the putting-out system had accustomed themselves to appropriating materials to supplement their official wage. Many late-nineteenth-century German factory ordinances specified that workers suspected of stealing materials or tools were subject to frisking by managers. Despite a similar legacy of domestic production, British codes from the same era seem to have remained silent about such personal examinations. Could the scrutinizing principle incorporated into British mills have obviated body searches? The design of German mills was consistent with an attempt to control the illegal removal of materials from the premises through the ongoing disposition over the body of the worker. The British workers' press considered it rare for workers even to be asked to open their lunch baskets upon exiting. *Yorkshire Factory Times*, October 11, 1889. For references to German workers pilfering materials, see *Gladbacher Zeitung*, May 11, 1871; Ernst Barkhausen, *Die Tuchindustrie in Montjoie, ihr Aufstieg und Niedergang* (Aachen: Aachener Verlags- und Druckerei-Gesellschaft, 1925), p. 102; on the practice of body searches, HSTAD, Geilenkirchen 88, 1899, P. W. Blancke; Emsbach, op. cit., p. 320; Staatsarchiv Dresden, Amthauptmannschaft Chemnitz, Nr. 16, "Fabrikordnung," ca. 1858, p. 230. On the tradition of embezzlement among domestic weavers, see Peter Kriedte, Hans Medick, and Jürgen Schlumbohm, *Industrialization Before Industrialization* (Cambridge: Cambridge University Press, 1981), pp. 53–54; and for both wool and cotton in Britain, see Alfred P. Wadsworth and Julia de Lacy Mann, *The Cotton Trade and Industrial Lancashire 1600–1780* (Manchester: Manchester University Press, 1931), pp. 393, 395, 399.

workers. To receive this knowledge, the participants did not study messages; they enacted and lived them. In the critical mind of the analyst, the tendency for a conformation between architecture and accounting, between spatial and temporal demarcations, makes for a charming coincidence; in the experience of the producers it created an encompassing constellation. For those who lived through the procedures of entry and the partitioning of space under the factory roof, concepts of labor became influential not because they were embodied in literature but because they were literally embodied. The enclosed mill yard and internment of workers in a centripetal space characterized factories in other British trades, including leather-making and sewing.[182] *Vide et crede*: the fictive inventions of labor as a commodity were written in stone.

THEORY IN THE MILL YARD

The present study suggests that powerful impressions of labor as a commodity, which showed prominent variations between countries, were not deliberately generated by formal organizations for the dissemination of ideas. They were not subsidized by the state or by a class but were born in the producers' lived experience at the point of production. Cultural formulations are transmitted through the form of instrumental practice, in addition to conventional verbal communication. For example, the procedures for entering the mill comprised both a humdrum action of individuals' daily routine and a public ritual through which the meaning of labor was communicated and re-endorsed in a shared setting.[183] The ideologies of labor as a commodity were sustained not because they were consistent with or corresponded to everyday procedures but because they were part and parcel of them, brought to life because practice was designed as a mode of communication. Unless analysts reconstruct the signifying function of the forms assumed by the instrumentalities of everyday life, they will pass over the lived context in which verbal discussion assumed its meaning and its power. Furthermore, they will necessarily miss the lucid ideas of a culture that are incarnated in material techniques, transferred from enactment to enactment

182. John Hannavy and Chris Ryan, *Working in Wigan Mills* (Wigan: Smiths Books, 1987), p. 76; W. H. Chalonder and A. E. Musson, *Industry and Technology* (London: Vista Books, 1963), illustration 218; *Shoe and Leather Record*, Jan. 1, 1892, p. 10.

183. On the transmission of discursive ideas in material practice, see Göran Therborn, *The Ideology of Power and the Power of Ideology* (London: New Left Books, 1980), pp. 81–82: "The distinction between a ritual and a material affirmation is an analytical one."

and visibly articulated without passing through a moment of verbal eluci-dation.[184] Individual agents borrowed the specifications of labor but never became their appropriators and owners, for these designs remained lodged in the shared house of public, sensuous practice.

184. Pierre Bourdieu, *Outline of a Theory of Practice* (Cambridge: Cambridge University Press, 1977), p. 87.

4   The Cultural Location
of Overlookers

[Persons] performing the same *motions* side by side, might
be said to be performing different *acts,* in proportion as they
differed in their attitudes toward their work.
                    Kenneth Burke, *A Grammar of Motives*

Investigators who conduct cross-national studies of the labor process take
the "organization" of production as their object of analysis. They assume
that cultural differences are revealed in organizational structures. Marc
Maurice and his colleagues, in their classic studies of contemporary French,
German, and British factories in the 1970s, compared such organizational
features as the chain of command, the proportion of blue collar "works"
employees, and the distribution of workers among maintenance and production departments.[1] The team of Gary Hamilton, Nicole Woolsey Biggart,
and Marco Orrù is bringing this same focus up to date. They have identified
national differences within East Asia in the "organizational characteristics"
of economic undertakings such as the patterns of subcontracting relations
and of social networks for financing.[2] The inquiry at hand diverges from
these prior efforts because it finds national differences not in organizational
structures but in the humble instrumentalities of production, in the micro-
procedures by which workers and employers treated labor as a commodity
that could be registered, manipulated, and accounted for. Consider our initial
exemplar, the construction of the piece-rate scales, which specified the terms
by which weavers' labor was valorized. The piece schedules anchored the
essential terms of the labor transaction. Yet obviously the functioning of the
piece-rate scales—or of the indicators for output, or of accounting for the

1. Marc Maurice, François Sellier, and Jean-Jacques Silvestre, *The Social Foundations of
Industrial Power* (Cambridge, Massachusetts: The M.I.T. Press, 1986), Chapter Two, pp. 59 ff.
Michel Crozier, in *The Bureaucratic Phenomenon,* compared the institutions of collective
bargaining. *The Bureaucratic Phenomenon* (Chicago: University of Chicago Press, 1964), pp.
244–251.
2. "Organizational Isomorphism in East Asia," in Walter W. Powell and Paul J. DiMaggio,
editors, *The New Institutionalism in Organizational Analysis* (Chicago: University of Chicago
Press, 1991), p. 386.

costs of weaving—did not comprise part of the organizational structure of the factory, insofar as they did not by themselves constitute significant differences in job responsibilities or in social interaction among the agents of production in the workplace. They point to a dimension of production separate from face-to-face interaction and distinct from social structure. They mark the formation of inconspicuous but vital micro-procedures for conceiving the valorization of labor.

The constraints of the manufacturing process in nineteenth-century textile mills provide uniquely favorable terrain for illustrating the analytic difference between organizational structure and the instrumentalities of discipline and production on the shop floor. The historian Sidney Pollard, in his distinguished essays on the development of industrial supervision, offered a remarkable comment about the textile business: although this trade included some of the most dynamic enterprises of the first phase of industrialization, it seemed to Pollard that even for the early, "heroic" stage of textile development there was less to be said about administration in this branch of enterprise than in many others. He reasoned that the labor process in the mills was so circumscribed by its essential machinery (in comparison with mining or metal-working) that little scope remained for originality in the layout or design of production.[3] By the latest evidence of the day, some may question Pollard's logic, but we have faint reason to revise his judgment as a statement of historical fact, at least for a comparison of weaving mills.[4] Yet the relative uniformity of industrial organization in this branch of production, far from closing it off to cultural examination, provides a privileged site for highlighting the lodgement of different cultural practices in similar social organizations.

The separability of social organization and micro-procedures becomes evident in the ensemble of practices that defined the activity and the labor contribution of textile factory supervisors. In the weaving branch, overlookers in Germany and Britain had similar training, the same position in the chain of command, and parallel job responsibilities. Yet contrasting procedures were used to conceptualize their wage and to account for its cost to the firm, and the concepts used to compare and distinguish overlookers from workers were different indeed. In other words, although the overlookers had

---

3. Sidney Pollard, *The Genesis of Modern Management* (London: Edward Arnold, 1965), p. 90.

4. For spinning, however, see William Lazonik, "Production Relations, Labor Productivity, and Choice of Technique," *The Journal of Economic History* Volume XLI, Number 3 (September 1981), pp. 491–516.

the same productive functions in each country, these functions received divergent cultural inscriptions.

In the movement of production, weaving supervisors stood in a structurally ambiguous position: they were paid for their labor, in some form, like any other employee; yet in the name of the capitalist they also supervised underlings' performance.[5] Given the overlookers' equivocal status, the definition of the employment transaction in Britain as the delivery of materialized labor could highlight the aspect of the overlookers' activity which corresponded to that of productive agents who incorporated their labor into the product of their subordinates. In Germany, given the same job functions and responsibilities of overlookers, the cultural understanding of employment as the transfer of a service potential framed the overlookers' activity as the execution of the owner's authority over subordinates. The definition of the textile overlookers' role depended upon the template by which labor was commodified, rather than upon differences in the distribution of responsibilities, technology, markets, or societal differences in the style of command in private and public organizations.

IMAGINING THE OVERLOOKERS' CONTRIBUTION

The purchase of labor in the capitalist enterprise confronts social agents with a paradox when they analyze expenses and earnings. The moment workers expend their efforts, their labor no longer belongs to them and cannot be sold. Therefore as a visibly constructive activity, labor lacks an exchange value. It exists as a commodity in the marketplace as a projected activity or as it is materialized in another good—in effect it is brought to market before it is created and remunerated as it disappears into another object.[6]

Yet textile directors had to quantify this apparition. To establish the receipt of labor at a cost, textile employers in Britain and Germany confronted a challenge more difficult than the one they encountered in draw-

---

5. Erik Wright musters an elaborate set of concepts to capture this ambiguity in managers' positions in *Class Structure and Income Determination* (New York: Academic Press, 1979), pp. 39 ff.

6. We prisoners of the twentieth century have lost a sense of the queerness of labor's commodification. But in the nineteenth century, ordinary weavers still pondered at length the baffling process by which labor, which "has not the essentials of any other commodities," was exchanged as a ware. United Kingdom, *Select Committee on Hand-Loom Weavers' Petitions,* PP 1834 (556) X, testimony of William Longson, p. 518.

ing up scales for the weavers. To establish the price of weavers' labor, owners resorted to measuring the product, either as an index of activity or as a vessel for materialized labor, and on either basis compared the value of fabrics that differed only in their formal properties. For the overlookers' pay scales, however, it was not immediately evident to employers and workers whether there was in fact any "product" of the overlookers' activity to take as an emblem for labor. Overlookers assisted in manufacturing but did not accomplish the weaving themselves. Employers relied upon fictive concepts of labor as a commodity to identify the contribution of the overlookers' activity to the company's overall production effort. To isolate the independent effect of these shared concepts on owners' decisions, we must appreciate the overlookers' visible functions in the weaving process.

In contrast with such enterprises as mining or steel, where an owner needed the overlookers to guide and coordinate the labor of work teams, the role of overlookers in weaving rested more exclusively on an immediate technical demand: namely, the need of prewar power looms for frequent repair, for replacement of worn parts, and for adjustment to each change in fabric pattern. Certainly up to the time of the First World War, looms required constant repair. Even for the most experienced weavers, the loom's output in experimental trials varied considerably with the attention given by the overlooker to the instrument's ongoing adjustment.[7] Textile directors in both Germany and Britain assigned each overlooker responsibility for maintaining a number of looms grouped together in a section of the weaving room. Having a team of overlookers take collective responsibility for all the looms in a room proved impossible, for each machine in the mill had its quirks and idiosyncratic history of repairs. Overlookers worked most efficiently on machines they knew individually.[8] At mills that manufactured short runs of different kinds of fabric the overlookers might also take responsibility for assigning warps to particular weavers.[9]

---

7. "A certain mechanical skill is of great advantage to a weaver," the English Board of Trade found, "so that any slight adjustment of the loom can be done immediately, without calling the help of the tuner." United Kingdom, *Textile Trades, Huddersfield* (London: H.M.S.O., 1914). For Germany, see *Der Textil-Arbeiter,* May 14, 1909, p. 155. Weavers, including the women, did their own adjusting of loom chains and tightening of nuts. See Joanna Bornat's interview with Mrs. T., born 1903, pp. 7–8; Hebden Bridge Oral History Project, OH 85/58.

8. *Seide,* January 7, 1914.

9. HSTAD, Regierung Aachen 1634, Birkesdorf, January, 1900.

The weaving overlookers in Germany and Britain also shared the same position in the factory hierarchy. Above them stood the foremen, usually assigned one to a department. Below stood only the weavers themselves. Depending on the difficulty of the pattern and the fragility of the materials, a weaver served from one to four looms: in cotton, four represented the norm; in worsteds, two; and in woolens, one. Any attempt to formulate these averages in a straightforward manner brings out a host of exceptions. Yet in both countries these assignments were the typical ones.

Just as the ratios of looms to weavers corresponded in Germany and Britain, so did the ratios of looms to overlookers. Although employers in both countries saw the overlookers as the key agents responsible for the maintenance of discipline in the mill, the need for adjusting the machinery rather than the need for oversight set the major boundaries for the hiring and allocation of overlookers within the factory. Hardly any manager considered hiring more overlookers than necessary for servicing the looms, although additional superintendents might have offered tighter surveillance over the weavers and greater opportunity to catch faults before weavers ruined a run of cloth. One director of a Yorkshire woolen mill said, "It is far better that the [overlooking] staff should be inadequate rather than too numerous, for men are never so discontented as when they have too little work to do."[10] The precise ratio of overlookers to looms depended primarily on the design of the machine.[11] In both countries, according to oral reports and technical journals, an overlooker for, say, narrow, plain cotton cloth had in his section eighty to one hundred looms and, for checked cotton cloth, fifty to seventy.[12] Due perhaps to relative stagnation in mechanical design in the decades near the turn of the century, these ratios remained stable from at least the 1880s until the

10. John Mackie, *How to Make a Woollen Mill Pay* (London: Scott Greenwood & Co., 1904), p. 43.

11. Wide looms and ones with a complicated mechanism for weaving patterns demanded a great deal more maintenance. *Textile Manufacturer*, January 15, 1913, p. 29. A survey by the Bradford overlookers' union in 1913 found that members on box looms (which changed the color of the weft for pattern effects) served only half as many machines as those on plain looms. Bradford District Archives, 1913 survey.

12. *Der Textil-Arbeiter*, September 6, 1907; *Cotton Factory Times*, February 26, 1897, Norden; Henry Brougham Heylin, *The Cotton Weaver's Handbook: A Practical Guide to the Construction and Costing of Cotton Fabrics* (London: Charles Griffen & Co., 1908), p. 207; LRO, DDX 1115/1/2, February 17, 1897; *Das deutsche Wollen-Gewerbe*, 1912, p. 210, and oral testimony, Herr Schnieders, Rheine. The wage books for the cotton firm Gebrüder Laurenz, in Ochtrup, show that in April of 1912, at nearly full production capacity, when 92 percent of the machines were filled with orders, each overlooker serviced only sixty looms. Their exact model is unascertainable. Westfälisches Wirtschaftsarchiv Dortmund, F61, Nr. 222.

First World War.[13] In silk mills, both German and British businessmen considered fifty looms per overlooker the maximum.[14] In the woolen trade, an overlooker might have charge of fewer than twenty-five looms.[15] The matched numbers of looms per German and English overlooker across the wool, cotton, and silk branches suggests that the actual division of labor in weaving followed down-to-earth technical imperatives in the two countries.

Contemporaries believed that the supply of capable overlookers by far exceeded the demand.[16] Until the First World War, weaving overlookers seldom received specialized technical training, apart from optional attendance at night school.[17] The earliest German investigations into the availability of overlookers, undertaken by the factory inspectorate in 1887, concluded that in Germany as a whole employers very seldom complained of shortages of skilled overlooking applicants.[18] Overlookers' associations in Germany had members on call to fill in or to take up permanent positions.[19]

13. *Textile Manufacturer*, March 15, 1887, and Jubilee Number, December, 1925.

14. *Seide*, January 7, 1914. *Bradford Daily Telegraph*, July 6, 1899.

15. Bradford District Archives, 1913 survey; my interview with Edward Mercer, Rawdon, Yorkshire; Hugo Ephraim, "Organisation und Betrieb einer Tuchfabrik," *Zeitschrift für die gesamte Staatswissenschaft* Volume 61 (1905), p. 607; *Der Textil-Arbeiter*, January 31, 1902, Crimmitschau. *Johann Junkers, 100 Jahre 1852–1952* (Rheydt: n.p., 1952), commemorative book, data for 1895. Usually an overlooker had a variegated mix of loom models in his section, which makes comparisons of assignments between mills, not to mention between nations, merely approximate. In fact, since owners themselves could not compare the burdens of different kinds of looms, they made an effort to give each overlooker in the mill the same mix of loom types.

16. Herbert Kisch, "The Crafts and Their Role in the Industrial Revolution: The Case of the German Textile Industry," Ph.D. diss., University of Washington, 1958, p. 298. For the Wuppertal, see *Der deutsche Meister*, December 21, 1904. For Yorkshire, Minutes of the Overlookers' Union, Calderdale Archives, and Keith Laybourn, "The Attitude of the Yorkshire Trade Unions to the Economic and Social Problems of the Great Depression, 1873–1896," Ph.D. diss., Lancaster University, 1973, p. 314. For information on the employment of Lancashire overlookers, see *Cotton Factory Times*, March 19, 1897, p. 1.

17. Ernst Dietel, *Die Greizer Wollindustrie* (Berlin: Wilhelm Pilz, 1915), p. 89; Franz Decker, *Die betriebliche Sozialordnung der Dürener Industrie im 19. Jahrhundert* (Köln: Rheinisch-Westfälisches Wirtschaftsarchiv, 1963), p. 101. See the enrollment schedules for textile schools in HSTAD, Regierung Düsseldorf 11641, 11652, 21809. In the event of a strike, skilled weavers could immediately fill in for the overlooker. *Textile Mercury*, July 8, 1899, p. 23; United Kingdom, *Textile Trades, Huddersfield*, op. cit., p. 12.

18. Germany, *Jahres-Berichte der mit Beaufsichtigung der Fabriken betrauten Beamten, 1887* (Berlin: Kortkampf, 1888), p. 102. Employers' occasional laments over the lack of qualified supervisors could represent part of a general deficit of labor. Staatsarchiv Detmold, I.U. Nr. 566, Minden, March 26, 1897.

19. For the years 1910–1913, "Stellenvermittlung nach den einzelnen Gewerbegruppen," *Reichs-Arbeitsblatt* Volume 10, 1912, Nr. 4, p. 273; Volume 10, 1912, Nr. 7, p. 516; Volume 10, 1912, Nr. 10, p. 756; Volume 11, 1913, Nr. 1, p. 42; Volume 11, 1913, Nr. 4, p. 280; Volume

In Bradford, Yorkshire, the weaving overlookers' union considered the surplus of overlookers so serious that after the turn of the century it periodically prohibited its members from taking on apprentices, even their own sons.[20] The abundance of qualified overlookers in Yorkshire can also be assessed from the circumstance that some owners there, to take advantage of the competition for overlooking jobs, opened bids from candidates for a position and hired the person making the lowest offer.[21] The overlookers may have dominated their underlings, but above the overlookers there towered a forbidding market.

In view of the parallels in weaving overlookers' technical responsibilities and market predicaments in the two countries, it ought not to occasion surprise that German and British weaving overlookers also shared about the same levels of pay, reckoned as a proportion of that received by an average weaver under them. The Board of Trade in the United Kingdom found in its survey of 1906 that overlookers in the north of England earned 50 to 75 percent more than an average weaver.[22] Local surveys and company wage books in Germany reveal about the same differential.[23]

11, 1913, Nr. 7, p. 518; Volume 11, 1913, Nr. 10, p. 760; Volume 12, 1914, Nr. 1, p. 43; Volume 12, 1914, Nr. 4, p. 302; Volume 12, 1914, Nr. 7, p. 552. A representative to a national convention of foremen in Germany at the turn of the century said younger overlookers joined the union "mainly" because it offered unemployment insurance. Archiv des Deutschen Gewerkschaftsbundes, Deutscher Werkmeister-Verband, "Stenographischer Bericht über die Verhandlungen des Delegiertentages des Deutschen Werkmeister-Verbandes," 1913, p. 201. The German foremen's union reported that in 1908 it paid fifty-five of its members in the textile industry unemployment payments; in 1907, it gave thirty-two members such support. Archiv des Freien Deutschen Gewerkschaftsbundes, Berlin, Deutscher Werkmeister-Verband, "Geschäfts-Berichte des Zentralvorstandes des Deutschen Werkmeister-Verbandes." I cannot say what percentage of the total members in textiles this represented. For Britain, see *Yorkshire Factory Times*, June 12, 1903.

20. Bradford District Archives, Overlookers' Society Minutes 3D86, e.g., February, 1891, June, 1892, July, 1914. On the surplus, see also Kirklees Archives S-PLT, 1912.

21. *Yorkshire Factory Times*, December 12, 1902, Elland. For an example of an unemployed weaving overlooker in Germany being hired at a low salary, see *Zeitschrift für die gesamte Textil-Industrie*, January 8, 1914, p. 2. For an overlooker working as a weaver, see *Der Christliche Textilarbeiter*, June 8, 1901, "Sonderorganisationen."

22. G. H. Wood, "The Statistics of Wages in the Nineteenth Century," *Journal of the Royal Statistical Society* Volume 73 (1910). "Earnings and Hours of Labour of the Workpeople of the United Kingdom," PP 1909 LXXX, p. 83. However, in keeping with the locally segregated labor markets, founded on idiosyncratic types of weaving, the ratios of overlookers' to weavers' pay varied greatly by locality. United Kingdom, *Returns of Wages Published Between 1830 and 1886*, PP 1887 LXXXIX, pp. 91–122; United Kingdom, *Return of Rates of Wages in the Principal Textile Trades of the United Kingdom*, PP 1889 LXX, pp. 69–130.

23. Staatsarchiv Weimar, Landesregierung Greiz, n Rep. A, Kap. IX a, Nr. 326, 1905, p. 330; Barmen, *Beiträge zur Statistik der Stadt Barmen* Volume 2 (1906), p. 7; Klaus Tidow, *Neumünsters Textil- und Lederindustrie im 19. Jahrhundert* (Neumünster: Karl Wachholtz,

If the level of compensation for overlookers was proportionately equal between the two countries, the business procedures for conceiving it followed contrasting principles. In Lancashire, by "universal custom,"[24] an overlooker received the whole of his pay in the form of a commission. It was reckoned as a fraction of all the pay received by the weavers in his section. An overlooker earned a certain amount—from a shilling and twopence up to a shilling and fourpence—on each pound sterling of the weavers' take-home pay. This equaled a commission of 5 to 7 percent.[25] The participants called this the "poundage" system (referring to the unit of currency, of course, not that of weight). Elsewhere in the north of England the methods by which overlookers received their pay varied. In Yorkshire, only 8 percent of overlookers received their wage exclusively in the form of a commission.[26] More often, each received a minimum weekly sum, supplemented by a bonus determined by the earnings of their subordinate weavers.[27]

A variety of payment conventions for textile overlookers also arose in Germany, but remuneration purely by commission was extremely rare.[28] German weaving overlookers, including the lowest loom fixers, generally

---

1984), p. 81; Victor Böhmert, "Weberlöhne einer Fabrik in Meerane," *Zeitschrift des königlich sächsischen statistischen Bureaus* Volume XXIII (1877), p. 64; Marie Bernays, "Auslese und Anpassung der Arbeiterschaft der geschlossenen Grossindustrie: Dargestellt an den Verhältnissen der 'Gladbacher Spinnerei und Weberei' A.G. zu Mönchengladbach," *Schriften des Vereins für Sozialpolitik* Volume 133 (1910), p. 15; *Die Textilarbeiter-Zeitung*, September 25, 1909, Bocholt; *Seide*, February 3, 1904; also Stadtarchiv Mönchengladbach, 1141, Nachweisung.

24.   *Textile Manufacturer*, March 15, 1887.

25.   This rate yielded the overlooker between 45 and 65 percent more pay than that of an average weaver, assuming a complement of twenty-five weavers per overlooker.

26.   "Earnings and Hours of Labour of the Workpeople of the United Kingdom," PP 1909 LXXX, pp. 43 ff. See also *Yorkshire Factory Times*, September 27, 1889, January 23, 1891, Bradford, February 5, 1892, p. 4; July 28, 1893, Batley, p. 1, and June 20, 1912, p. 1. At Dudley Hill in Yorkshire, the firm of J. Cawthra and Co. posted the average earnings of the weavers under each overlooker. *Yorkshire Factory Times*, March 21, 1890.

27.   *Yorkshire Factory Times*, May 9, 1890, p. 1; January 22, 1892, p. 4; April 1, 1898, Oakworth; March 11, 1898, Great Horton; December 6, 1901, p. 5. Calderdale Archives, wage-books of Stott and Ingham, STO 12, 1892–1901, for fluctuations in overlookers' pay. *Bradford Daily Telegraph*, January 1, 1891. Royal Commission on Labour, PP 1892 XXXV, Vol. 1, pp. 223, 303. Respondents to the survey of loom assignments and pay taken by the Bradford tuners' union in 1913 sometimes volunteered information about bonuses. Bradford District Archives, Bradford Overlookers' Society survey of looms, 1913. Mackie, op. cit., p. 45.

28.   For weaving I found several exceptions where German overlookers received a bonus for the output of their underlings. H. Mattutat, "Das Prämiensystem in der Augsburger Textil-Industrie," *Soziale Praxis*, Volume 5 (1895–1896), pp. 210–211. See also Böhmert, op. cit., p. 64. Some firms gave bonuses to overlookers if production exceeded the standard quota. An example: the company records of F. F. Koswig, in Landesarchiv Potsdam, Rep. 75, Nr. 399, Akkordlohnsätze 1907.

worked for a fixed weekly wage.[29] They also received year-end salary bonuses.[30] In contrast to arrangements in Britain, a major portion of the German textile overlookers' compensation seldom fluctuated with the productivity of the immediate underlings they assisted.

How did German and British employers imagine they received the commodity of labor from overlookers? In the case of the overlookers, unlike the weavers, the product could not be decomposed to serve as a model for the activity put into it. For the overlookers we must look beyond the form of remuneration to consider how employers apportioned the cost of overlooking wages in their company books. Since each textile enterprise manufactured a spectrum of products, companies had to estimate the expense of producing each type of fabric. With the maturing of the industry and the consequent crowding of the yarn and cloth markets, cost accounting became increasingly important for the survival of the enterprises in both Germany and Britain. "Many mill men will say with pride that they can tell what it costs to produce a pound of yarn, or a yard of cloth, to a small fraction of a penny," the *Textile Manufacturer* reported in 1907. Although directors and

29. Staatsarchiv Weimar, Landesregierung Greiz, n Rep. A, Kap. VII a, Nr. 90 a, June 26, 1873, pp. 1–2; Stadtarchiv Bocholt, K2/276, September 24, 1896; *Gewerbe- und Kaufmannsgericht,* May 1, 1908, p. 179; *Zeitschrift für die gesamte Textil-Industrie* Volume 13, Nr. 47 (1909–1910), "Wer ist Werkmeister!"; *Bocholter Volksblatt,* January 9, 1901; Decker, op. cit., p. 94. For workers' insights: *Der Textil-Arbeiter,* June 21, 1901, Elsterberg; Jan. 10, 1902, Sonthofen i. Allgäu; *Freie Presse,* July 9, 1873, Lunzenau. Want ads for tuners (*Untermeister* and *Stuhlmeister*) in the professional journals offered both weekly and monthly salaries.

30. The annual supplements usually were not adjusted to the output of individual overlookers. For the woolen industry of the lower Rhine, see Decker, op. cit., p. 88. Elsewhere: Wirtschaftsarchiv Baden-Württemberg, B47-452, Württembergische Leinenindustrie A.G., 1882 ff.; *Der Textil-Arbeiter,* September 1, 1905, Politz, and June 2, 1905, Köpenick; Karl Schmid seems to refer to annual bonuses for overlookers in *Die Entwicklung der Hofer Baumwoll-Industrie 1432–1913* (Leipzig: A. Deichertsche Verlagsbuchhandlung, 1923), p. 76; 2. *Beilage zur Volkswacht,* Bielefeld, Volume 18, Number 255, October 10, 1907. On the prevalence of salary systems for overlookers in other industries, see Jürgen Kocka, *Die Angestellten in der deutschen Geschichte, 1850–1980* (Göttingen: Vandenhoeck & Ruprecht, 1981), p. 37, and Ernst Günther, *Die Entlöhnungsmethoden in der bayrischen Eisen- und Maschinen-Industrie* (Berlin: Leonhard Simion, 1908); Archiv des Deutschen Gewerkschaftsbundes, Deutscher Werkmeister-Verband, "Stenographischer Bericht über die Verhandlungen des Delegiertentages des Deutschen Werkmeister-Verbandes," 1909, p. 225. Yet the methods for paying supervisors varied across German industry. In iron-making and metal-work, for instance, foremen depended more heavily on bonuses for output. See, illustratively, Michael Mende, "Männer des Feuers und der eisernen Kraft," in Wolfgang Ruppert, editor, *Die Arbeiter* (München: C. H. Beck, 1986), p. 232, and Otto Bosselmann, *Die Entlöhnungsmethoden in der südwestdeutsch-luxemburgischen Eisenindustrie* (Berlin: Leonhard Simion, 1906), pp. 44, 51. The method of payment serves as a cultural indicator only in conjunction with the costing system employed for distributing overlooking expenses.

their scriveners tallied labor expenses with great precision, they used contrasting reasoning in Germany and England when they conjectured about
the expense of overlooking for different fabrics.

Managers in Yorkshire who cared to reckon their expenses with precision
used different methods than in Lancashire, yet in both districts they followed a logic that was generically different from that used in Germany. In
Lancashire, the system of pay directly reveals the accounting method in use:
owners automatically lumped the overlooker's wage together with the
weaver's wage in the cost of each piece. If the employer wanted to handle
not only the weaver's labor but also the supervisory and technical contribution of the overlooker as a commodity embodied in the finished product, this
method was the most suitable. It offered a formal advantage in the event of
a downturn: not only did overlookers' wages decline automatically, but they
did so exactly proportionately to weavers' wages, as if to buy exactly so
much "labor" from the overlookers as was necessary for the productive
tasks at hand. In terms of Weber's criterion of formal calculability, this
system of pay ranks as the most rational: it makes supervisory "labor" a
totally flexible production factor.[31] The employer remained free to buy only
so much "labor" as he needed at the moment and could shift all the uncer-
tainties of the demand for labor onto the overlookers themselves.

Although the Lancashire system had a high degree of formal rationality,
its measure of the "labor" purchased had little to do with the substantive
realities of production. Because it piggybacked an overlooker's wages onto
those of the weavers, the Lancashire procedure gave an overlooker a bonus
when the weavers in his section wove cloth with complicated patterns,
which required more skill and thus commanded higher wages. But the overlooker might not be called upon to do proportionately more tuning for the
weavers in this case; he received a bonus for their skill unrelated to his own
input of time or effort.[32] (Furthermore, an overlooker might let the machinery fall into a poor state of repair and then move to another shop, reaping
the pay in the short term for the completed fabric and avoiding the long-
term investment in equipment maintenance.)[33] No matter what the conse-

31. Weber discusses the significance of freely disposable labor for calculability in *Gesammelte Aufsätze zur Sozial- und Wirtschaftsgeschichte* (Tübingen: J. C. B. Mohr, 1924), p. 18,
and in *Economy and Society* (Berkeley: University of California Press, 1968), pp. 162 ff.

32. Since Yorkshire mills had a greater variety of patterns demanding extreme weaving
skill, a pure "poundage" system there would have multiplied the effects of this defect several
times over.

33. For a warning about this possibility, see *Zeitschrift für die gesamte Textil-Industrie*
Number 44 (1913), "Der Webmeister."

quences, the Lancashire system looked at the value of the labor embodied in the product and reckoned backwards to surmise the overlookers' contribution embodied in the product.

The Yorkshire costing method shared the premise of the Lancashire system that the overlookers' wages ought to be figured as if their labor were embodied in the fabric like other workers'. In Yorkshire, the textile book-keepers costed the production expenses of a particular run of cloth by adding the overlooking wages onto the cloth in the same manner as finishing and burling wages: by length of the fabric. The firm took its total cloth production for a year, in yards, and divided this by the overlookers' wage bill for the year. (Less often, the average costs were tallied separately for several major varieties of fabric.)[34] For purposes of costing a particular fabric, Yorkshire mill accountants treated overlookers' salaries as "Productive Wages," together with those of the finishers and burlers and with those of the weavers.[35] Company records show that the overlookers' costs were distributed per piece of fabric, adjusted for length.[36]

In Germany, standard accounting procedures separated the overlookers' wages from those of the subordinate workers. The clerks merged the costs of overlookers' salaries with the costs of machinery, insurance, property taxes, energy, and so forth into a category called *Regiekosten*. A modern accountant might translate this as "administrative overhead," but the term also connotes something like "costs of *directing* production." Having created this general classification, German factory owners relied upon two different methods to distribute the costs of supervision onto a weaving mill's product. With the first method, German accountants calculated how long it took a loom to turn out a particular length of cloth, based on the average efficiency ratio for the firm as a whole or for that particular kind of cloth; then the annual overhead, including the overlookers' salaries, was added to the cloth based on how much of the loom's time, including the changing of the warp, the piece would have been expected to claim.[37] The

---

34. George Pepler Norton, *Textile Manufacturers' Book-keeping* (Bradford: Brear & Co., 1894), p. 254; A. R. Foster, *Weaving Mill Management* (Manchester: John Heywood, ca. 1908), p. 92.

35. Woollen and Worsted Trades' Federation, *Systems of Cost Finding for the Textile Trade* (Bradford, 1921), p. 24. The issue in question is not how the mills tallied net expenses but how they allocated the costs to particular pieces. British and German managers may well have tracked their operating expenses in the same fashion.

36. Calderdale Archives, WAL 3/2–4.

37. *Leipziger Monatschrift für Textil-Industrie*, Nr. 8 (1902), p. 549, "Stimmen der Praxis"; *Die Textilarbeiter-Zeitung*, November 19, 1910. E. Jung testifies about the practice of his company in *Die Berechnung des Selbstkostenpreises der Gewebe* (Berlin: Julius Springer,

German accountants apportioned the wage costs of the ordinary weavers by a different means than they used for the overlookers; they simply read off the amount specified on the piece-rate scales for fabric of a certain grade. But they did not merge overlooking outlays with these expenses, because they did not regard the costs of overlooking as a form of wages (*Arbeitslöhne*).[38]

German accountants also used another system for distributing overlooking costs. This second method distributed weaving overlookers' wages, like other overhead costs, as a percentage of material costs and ordinary workers' wages. The firm recorded its total annual expenditure for ordinary wages and materials and then calculated the ratio of this total expenditure to the yearly overhead expenses, including overlooking. For each piece of cloth, then, the company first considered the cost of the materials that went into it, plus the piece-rate wages for the weaving and warping and the average per meter for burling and finishing. Then the firm assumed that for this particular length and type of cloth, the ratio of these primary costs to overhead costs should be the same as for the mill's output in general, so the firm added on this standard percentage to arrive at the cost of that cloth.[39]

Both German methods merged funds expended on overlooking with general overhead, processing overlooking expenses as part of the underlying cost of maintaining the firm, not, as in England, as an ingredient, like weavers' labor, that was used up and embodied in a length of cloth. Neither German method distributed overlooking outlays as a separate component per length of the cloth, as the Yorkshire and Lancashire systems did. In particular, the first of the German methods considered only the *time* required to turn out a number of shots with a given efficiency ratio rather than the length, that is, rather than the product.[40] This German method

---

1917), p. 131.

38. Germany, Enquete-Kommission, *Reichs-Enquete für die Baumwollen- und Leinen-Industrie: Stenographische Protokolle über die mündliche Vernehmung der Sachverständigen* (Berlin: Julius Sittenfeld, 1878), pp. 403, 453; Landesarchiv Potsdam, uncataloged company records of F. F. Koswig, "Calculation" papers. In comparison with Lancashire, the denominator for calculating overlooking costs was *time* rather than the labor costs of a piece of cloth.

39. *Die Textil-Zeitung*, Nr. 23 (1904), p. 573. *Leipziger Monatschrift für Textil-Industrie*, Nr. 8 (1902), p. 549, and Nr. 9 (1910), p. 261. Nicolas Reiser, *Die Betriebs- und Warenkalkulation für Textilstoffe* (Leipzig: A. Felix, 1903), pp. 133 ff.; *Das deutsche Wollen-Gewerbe*, July 27, 1877, p. 688; Wirtschaftsarchiv Baden-Württemberg, Stuttgart, B25-198, Tuchfabrik Lörrach, 1904.

40. Jung, op. cit., p. 131. Friedrich Leitner, *Die Selbstkostenberechnung industrieller Betriebe* (3d ed. Frankfurt am Main: J. D. Sauerländer, 1908), p. 190.

operated more accurately at a given juncture in the business cycle than the Yorkshire method, in that its focus on the activity also properly measured the time taken up by producing the various densities of cloth, whereas the British either proceeded by length alone or by only a few benchmark densities for which separate yearly tallies could be kept. The Yorkshire method, however, ran with greater accuracy than the German over long time periods, in that overlooking outlays were distributed per length as a separate component rather than as capital investments, which might not behave like overlooking costs through the business cycle.

What, then, were the practical implications of the methods of allocating overlooking expenses? British costing rested on the assumption that overlooking represented a cost that fluctuated with output: under the Lancashire procedure, if a mill turned out more fabric than the previous year and improved its efficiency, overlooking expenses in costing procedures for the following year remained constant per cloth length.[41] This also meant that overlooking costs rose both absolutely and, since capital overhead for machinery would decline per length, as a proportion of total manufacturing costs per length as well. The system treated the overlooker's contribution as an ingredient embedded in the product. Cloth had the same "amount" of this input even if efficiency improved.[42] The Yorkshire costing procedure assumed that overlookers' pay would behave like the pay of other ordinary workers, that is, would remain stable per length of cloth.[43]

41. Or, more exactly, overlooking costs as a ratio of the wages put into the cloth length remained constant.

42. In truth, when the firm was especially busy the weavers themselves had to do more of the loom repairs and adjustments on their own, since the tuner had more warps to install and looms broke more often due to constant operation.

43. Is it possible that the British, in contrast to the Germans, did not add the overlooking costs into their calculations as overhead simply because of the mechanics of the paperwork? It might have been simpler for the British to consider overlooking compensation like other wages since their overlookers received their pay based on those wages. But this hypothesis collides with the evidence, since British accounting manuals and model ledgers also added foremen's salaries onto the cloth with a per-yard average, although foremen received monthly salaries (Woollen and Worsted Trades' Federation, op. cit.). What is more, some of the German overlookers received weekly wages (*Der deutsche Meister*, March 15, 1913), yet this expense counted as overhead, even in the case of overlookers for small departments such as mending. Reiser, op. cit., p. 146. Since in both countries the distribution of costs on particular pieces followed methods based on yearly averages anyway, the form of the overlookers' payment in this respect did not determine cost accounting methods; instead of one element determining the other, both the mode of remuneration and the costing procedure rested on assumptions about the exchange of the overlookers' labor as a commodity.

Under the German accounting system, if the factory improved its efficiency after the course of a year, then for costing purposes in the following year the expenses of overlooking, like other overhead, would decline as a proportion of total manufacturing costs per length. Companies treated overlookers' supervision as a precondition for production, part of the "base" for manufacturing, rather than as a quantity which was incorporated into the product. This procedure incarnated a cultural procedure more than it corresponded to the actual conditions of production; in practice, the Germans dismissed overlookers in the event of a business downturn, so overlookers' pay did not represent a fixed cost like that of a standing loom or like the company's key clerical staff.

Can we derive the difference in these procedures from the demands of the business environment? Is it plausible that the German costing procedures in textiles, which fused overlooking costs with general fixed expenses, resulted from a greater tolerance for high or invariable outlays on supervision? German business manuals argued that if a firm confronted a need to reduce manufacturing costs, it caused less turmoil in the factory to cut the salaries of the overlookers than the piece rates of the workers.[44] German business magazines stressed the need to cap outlays for overlooking.[45] Want ads in German professional journals sometimes specified a preference for unmarried applicants among candidates for overlooking positions, presumably so that the applicant could accept a lower salary or undertake repair work during the evenings as needed.[46] The contrast in accounting logic for overlooking outlays did not mirror thrifty administration in Britain and prodigal management in Germany.

To attribute the difference in modes of payment to Britain's "earlier" industrial development would be fashionable but unduly facile. The British arrangement resembles systems of management which have been called "subcontracting" or "indirect control." In many branches of industry, the pioneering factory owners, unable or unwilling to take direct command of production on the shop floor, started by delegating authority to their foremen, whom they paid by the turn-out of goods (and who in turn hired and

44. *Zeitschrift für die gesamte Textil-Industrie* (1906), p. 11. For the metal industry, see Georg Erlacher, *Briefe eines Betriebsleiters über Organisation technischer Betriebe* (Hannover: Gebrüder Jänecke, 1903), p. 36. German weavers believed that if they organized and succeeded in receiving higher wages, managers would respond by cutting the salaries of loom tuners and overseers. *Die Textilarbeiter-Zeitung*, July 24, 1909, Windelsbleiche.
45. *Die Textil-Zeitung*, January 5, 1897.
46. *Seide*, November 14, 1906.

controlled their own workers). Research in a range of historical settings, from Europe to Japan, has found that in the early industrial era, systems which paid overlookers as subcontractors predominated in many trades.[47] At a time when manufacturing still depended on craft knowledge or on the secret know-how of the overlookers and foremen, graded monetary sanctions gave owners the only feasible check on, and evaluation of, the overlookers' loyalty and efficiency. An explanation of the British method of paying weaving overlookers based on this ground seems especially plausible since Lancashire, the earliest center of the textile industry, also offered the practice's clearest expression.[48]

Yet such an argument based on the timing of development does not apply to the question at hand. The Wuppertal, a forerunner for the rest of Germany, moved only a few decades behind Lancashire in mechanizing its weaving mills; indeed, in wool weaving it kept pace with Yorkshire.[49] But the Wuppertal had a pure salary system for overlookers and allocated overlooking costs as a fixed expense.[50] Even if payment by results first arose in an earlier stage of development, its survival depended on active propagation, not institutional inertia. Management experts contended that the commissions graded by weavers' wages "stimulated" overlookers' interest in efficient production and encouraged them to be punctual.[51] At J. T. and T. Taylor's mill at Batley, Yorkshire, in 1912 managers shifted the overlook-

47. Andrew Gordon, *The Evolution of Labor Relations in Japan* (Cambridge, Massachusetts: Harvard University Press, 1985), p. 40; W. Garside and H. F. Gospel, "Employers and Managers: Their Organizational Structure and Changing Industrial Strategies," in C. Wrigley, editor, *A History of British Industrial Relations* (Brighton: Harvester, 1982), p. 102; for Italy, Carlo Poni, "Mass gegen Mass: Wie der Seidenfaden rund und dünn wurde," in Robert Berdahl et al., editors, *Klassen und Kultur* (Frankfurt am Main: Syndikat, 1982), p. 25; Sanford Jacoby, *Employing Bureaucracy* (New York: Columbia University Press, 1985), p. 15.

48. In Yorkshire, too, the earliest weaving mills relied on subcontracting. Benjamin Gott did not hire the weavers as employees at the mill he built in 1792, but relied upon overlookers to fill the looms. Adrian Randall, *Before the Luddites* (Cambridge: Cambridge University Press, 1991), p. 209.

49. Wolfgang Hoth, *Die Industrialisierung einer rheinischen Gewerbestadt, dargestellt am Beispiel Wuppertal* (Köln: Rheinisch-Westfälisches Wirtschaftsarchiv, 1975), p. 200. By 1861, 30 percent of the looms for lining in Elberfeld were mechanized. Leon Mirus, "Die Futterstoffweberei in Elberfeld und Barmen," diss., Leipzig, 1909, p. 18. See footnote 8, Chapter One, above.

50. My interviews with Ewald Sirrenberg, born 1897, and Hans Penz, born 1895; *Die Textilarbeiter-Zeitung*, May 21, 1910.

51. *Journal of the Department of Textile Industries*, City of Bradford Technical College (September 1918), p. 26; "The Bonus System in Textile Mills," *Textile Manufacturer*, May 15, 1914, pp. 174–175. Edward Elbourne's respected work on "scientific" management, published in 1914, said that "foremen ought to be judged by results only." *Factory Administration and Accounts* (London: Green & Co., 1914), p. 85.

ers to pay based solely on output.[52] The methods British owners used to remunerate overlookers resulted from contemporaneous reasoning rather than unexamined tradition inherited from an earlier phase of development.

A final utilitarian approach to the difference between Germany and England might dissect the consequences of the payment methods for production costs. The textile industry was exposed to price fluctuations on both the input and the output side. On the input side, since the trade's raw materials consisted of vegetable and animal products, their prices varied with the weather and growing conditions. Raw cotton prices could change by as much as 50 percent in a few months, and prices for wool yarn fluctuated even more severely.[53] Merchants and manufacturers alike speculated in the market for these raw commodities.[54] On the output side, the fortunes of many firms and of whole branches depended, season to season, on unforeseeable shifts in clothing fashions.

If a company cut back on production, the Lancashire and Yorkshire systems, by basing the overlookers' wages on those of the weavers, automatically reduced overlooking expenses.[55] At first blush, the German technique would seem to rigidify overlookers' salaries; but in the event of a downturn owners simply laid overlookers off.[56] In 1893 and 1894, members of the German overlookers' and foremen's union (which, to be sure, included nontextile overlookers) reported nearly eight hundred cases of changes of employers; of these, 60 percent were due to the *employer* having given notice.[57]

---

52. *Yorkshire Factory Times,* June 20, 1912, p. 1.

53. HSTAD, Regierung Düsseldorf, 25041, Jahresbericht der Fabrikinspektoren Mönchengladbach, 1911, p. 5; Ernst Meyknecht, "Die Krisen in der deutschen Woll- und Baumwollindustrie," diss., München, 1928. For wool, see R. Isenburg, *Untersuchungen über die Entwicklung der bergischen Wollenindustrie,* Heidelberg, 1906, p. 53; *Die Textilarbeiter-Zeitung,* June 25, 1910, and "Arme Aktionäre," January 12, 1901, as well as J. H. Clapham, *The Woollen and Worsted Industries* (London: Methuen & Co., 1907), p. 182.

54. B. A. Dobson, *Some Difficulties in Cotton Spinning* (Bolton: G. S. Heaton, 1893), p. 62.

55. "Their [the overlookers'] earnings have risen and fallen automatically as a result of the advances or reductions of the weaving rates, or as a consequence of other causes affecting the volume of weavers' earnings." *Textile Mercury,* July 8, 1899, p. 23.

56. Stadtarchiv Gummersbach, Akt 4842, September 14, 1891; *Die Textilarbeiter-Zeitung,* January 29, 1910, Gronau; *Der Textil-Arbeiter,* June 16, 1905, Crimmitschau.

57. This figure unfortunately included overlookers in all industries, but after the metal industry, the largest portion of members came from the textile branch. Archiv des Freien Deutschen Gewerkschaftsbundes, "Geschäfts-Berichte des Zentralvorstandes des Deutschen Werkmeister-Verbandes für 1893 und 1894," p. 12. Textile owners in Krefeld said that laid-off overlookers became weavers for lack of other openings. *Seide,* June 17, 1914, p. 311. See as well the case of a weaving overlooker from Viersen before the Mönchengladbach business court, in *Der deutsche Meister,* January 1, 1911.

Alternatively, mill directors could reduce the days of work and pay of those German overlookers on weekly wages.[58] In short, the German procedure featured a degree of elasticity. The two systems did not diverge greatly in their ability to conform to the business cycle.

Finally, mills in both countries specializing in long runs of fabric for which demand was relatively stable did not deviate from the standards set by firms with fluctuating orders. The same accounting logic prevailed regardless of the market niche in which the firm operated, from simple towel makers to fancy goods manufacturers.[59] It also applied to the spinning branch.[60] This relative invariance *within* each country makes it implausible to contend that the variation in accounting systems evolved to cope with differing business experiences.

The owners' payment of overlookers and their procedures for allocating overlooking expenses fit the commodity forms of labor German and British producers used in carrying out production. As in the construction of weavers' piece-rate scales, so with overlookers the British relied upon the fiction that owners buy the labor embodied in completed products. The employers paid overlookers so much per length of cloth received and calculated the cost as if it represented labor incorporated as a fixed expense in each portion of cloth. As a British textile accountant put it, all machine workers "expend direct labor," because their work is "seen in the finished product."[61] The guidelines for discharging weaving overlookers in Britain also confirmed that overlookers received their payment for materialized labor. In many districts, a weaving overlooker was not to leave his place of employment until the weavers he had supervised had turned in all the cloth he had

---

58. *Bocholter Volksblatt,* January 9, 1901.

59. See the testimony of German weaving manufacturers in a variety of branches, including fancy mixed wool and cotton, Germany, Enquete-Kommission, op. cit., pp. 245, 251, 403, 453.

60. W. M. Christy and Sons, foreman's notebooks, December 30, 1892, John Rylands University Library of Manchester Archives; Reuben Gaunt & Sons, Box 13, Leeds District Archives; J. Brook *A Rational System of Woollen Yarn Costing* (Batley: J. Fearnside & Sons, 1926), p. 57; and, for mule spinning in Yorkshire, *Yorkshire Factory Times,* March 17, 1893.

61. Charles Williams, "Cotton Mill Costings," *Journal of the National Federation of Textile Works Managers Associations* Volume V (1925–1926), p. 87. Likewise, in British shipyard and engineering works, the cost of supervision was charged as a percentage of the labor expended on the material. Dempster Smith and Philip C. N. Pickworth, *Engineers' Costs and Economical Workshop Production* (Manchester: Emmott & Co., 1914), p. 52; "Manager," *Examples of Engineering Estimates, Costs and Accounts, for the Use of Young Engineers* (Huddersfield: C. F. Maurice, n.d.), p. 4.

superintended.[62] Otherwise, the overlooker had not "delivered" his labor and did not receive credit for it.

As in the measurement of weavers' activity, so with the overlookers the German producers relied upon the fiction that employers had the right of disposal over the workers' capacity and effort. The German procedure for adding up production expenses mixed the elements of supervisory labor and capital expenditure in apportioning overhead costs. In an accounting manual written in 1903, a costing expert from Aachen saw no incongruity in combining these elements: he suggested a 50 percent cost addition for a category called "overlookers' salaries, electricity, and steam" and joined together supervisory costs and the depreciation costs of looms.[63] The German accountants handled the overlookers' labor capacity as a kind of "human capital," a *conveyable* resource rather than a substance received in a product.[64]

BELABORED FICTIONS

To trace the construction of a "commodity" out of the ephemeral activity of the overlookers we have so far relied upon the cultural assumptions inscribed in manufacturing practice. In contexts where these suppositions had to be articulated explicitly, they can be found in discursive practice as well. The assumption in Germany that textile supervisors sold the disposition over their work activity, not merely objectified labor, came to light in the judicial interpretation of overlookers' employment contracts. The most arresting legal question for German mill owners in 1911, gauging by the coverage given it by the trade's professional journals, centered on a complaint filed by an overlooker in a town near Düsseldorf. Today the minutiae of this conflict seem, in a word, dull—but not the participants' perception of the facts. The news accounts indicate that the owner of a silk mill hired a certain Herr K. in 1910 to oversee his dyeing department.[65] By the terms of the four-year contract they concluded, the foreman held the title of *Obermeister* (chief foreman) and headed the whole department. He agreed to obey the firm's production directives under all circumstances. Twelve months after the start of the agreement, the owner found it necessary to divide the velvet section from the remainder of the dyeing department, and

62. General Union of Associations of Powerloom Overlookers, *The Almanack and Guide for 1899* (Manchester: Ashton and Redfern, n.d.).

63. Reiser, op. cit., p. 146. Similarly, consult Leitner, op. cit., pp. 93, 179.

64. See HSTAD, Landratsamt Lennep 275, 1865, letter of Bürgermeisterei Radevormwald, for treatment of labor in this fashion.

65. *Seide,* April 10, 1912.

he entrusted supervision of the new section to another person. Herr K. retained his title and salary. Yet he charged the owner with a violation of the employment contract on the grounds that the owner had to let him keep the entire department or dismiss him altogether. Before the provincial court in Düsseldorf, Herr K. demanded payment in full of his remaining (three years') salary, since the contract specified that this was due to him in case of dismissal.

How is it that this course of events, whose unfolding makes today for such pedestrian reading, managed to hold the interest of contemporaries? The manner in which the business community endowed the conflict with significance represents an odd fact; its strangeness offers a riddle about the culture of production.

Although the courts ultimately resolved the suit through an evaluation of the pettiest terms of the employment contract, the business community thought that the case raised a basic question about the nature of the factory staff's employment contract. Owners and staff asked whether Herr K. might not have "the *right* to fully utilize his own capacity for work."[66] One technical journal summed up the issue at stake this way: "A company official, who has bound himself by a contract, naturally has the duty to place his full abilities at the disposal of the enterprise; but it is not so automatic that he also has the right to see that his capacity for work is taken advantage of to the full."[67] Certainly this organ's coverage of the affair threw the foreman's right into question. Yet in its analysis the magazine formulated the possibility of the right as the reverse side of the foreman's contractual obligations. And in so doing the journal, like the foreman's lawyer, revealed something about the business community's understanding of the labor transaction that was set in motion by the employment contract.

In formulating Herr K.'s rights, the press assumed that he offered for remuneration, not the successful turn-out of a quantity of dyed materials, but the disposition of his activity. The business community took the foreman's *Arbeitskraft* as the basis of the exchange, applying the same generic term for the factory official's productive capacities as for those of ordinary workers. This focus on the sale of the capacity for executing work, rather than on its external outcomes, was widespread: in discussions of the legal fine points of hiring factory staff, German business periodicals did not state,

66. *Zeitschrift für die gesamte Textil-Industrie,* January 4, 1912.
67. *Zeitschrift für die gesamte Textil-Industrie,* Nr. 13 (1912), p. 255.

for example, that by accepting a position factory officials obligated themselves to do the best *job* they could for the owner; they said that the staff had to devote all their *abilities and knowledge* to the interests of the owner.[68] Only with the premised sale of "labor power" in view could the foreman's lawyer possibly have articulated his client's complaint in terms of a "right to the full exploitation of his labor power."[69] Since the owner understood that he bought the foreman's full capacity, the argument went, he could not alter that capacity's sphere of operation or application. The contract's provision that the owner still had to pay Herr K.'s full salary even in case of dismissal also follows the supposition that the contract covers the disposition of the activity rather than of the output: Herr K. offered up his full capacities and therefore deserved compensation for having offered them even after he was released from the firm.

In its decision the provincial court of Düsseldorf in 1911 sided with Herr K. The owner appealed the decision on the grounds that it interfered with his prerogative to manage his own business. Finally in 1912 the imperial court at Berlin ruled for the owner; it judged that if the owner had the right to dispense with the foreman's services (at the cost of paying him his full salary), then the owner also had the right to dispense with a part of the foreman's services. In this instance the court ranked the right to full exploitation of one's labor capacity as subordinate to another principle—the owner's management authority. For my cultural analysis the fact of primary significance is simply that the conflict was expressed in terms of the sale of *Arbeitskraft* at all.[70]

My interpretation of the German courts' emphasis on labor power, far from representing a kind of philosophic abstraction, does nothing more than follow the thoughts of the participants themselves. In an age when owners usually regarded the small stratum of professional employees as a species apart from the manual workers under command, the owners nonetheless used the term *labor power* for a factory official's technical services.[71] Only

68. *Zeitschrift für die gesamte Textil-Industrie*, Nr. 17 (1912), p. 346.
69. "Das Recht auf volle Ausnutzung seiner Arbeitskräfte." Ibid.
70. This final decision by the imperial court also seems to contradict the earlier judgments of provincial courts. For example, the Landgericht of Hanau in 1906 ruled that if a foreman were moved to another position, the employer was obligated not just to assure the same level of pay but to provide a setting that suited the foreman's "abilities and skills." *Das Gewerbegericht*, Volume 12, Nr. 9 (June 1, 1907), pp. 199–200, ruling of March 13, 1906.
71. For another instance in which a court—the Prussian Kammergericht—referred to a supervisor's donation as the consumption of *Arbeitskraft*, see *Die Textilarbeiter-Zeitung*, August 7, 1909.

on the basis of logical assumptions about labor activity on behalf of the enterprise in general could they have abstracted this essential similarity between types of action whose overt appearances and prestige seemed otherwise so discrepant.

If the history of Herr K. discloses something about Germans' perception of the labor activity in general, as opposed to something about the status of overlookers, then we ought to be able to find analogous cases for lower grades of workers. This poses a special challenge, since most factory labor codes governing the employment relation specified the owner's right to switch ordinary workers to another machine or task. Yet a German technical journal in 1900 described a dispute involving a lower worker that offers a close parallel to Herr K.'s case.[72]

The facts of the case were these: a regular factory hand in Berlin stayed on the job after a portion of his company's work force began a strike. The management suspected the worker of organizing support for the strikers at the shop. It requested that he cease actual labor but continue to show up briefly at the company's desk twice each day. In this fashion the firm could isolate him from his fellows but avoid freeing him for an entire day to earn money elsewhere. These check-ins were to continue during four weeks, because, according to the factory labor code issued by the owner, both worker and owner had to give four weeks' notice if they wanted to terminate the employment contract. During this period the firm offered to continue paying the worker his full wage. But the worker objected that unless he worked, he was not obligated to check in at the office at all. After the firm fired him, he complained in court that four weeks' pay was due him for his unjustified removal. His employer argued in court that by requesting that the worker check in, he had simply wished to verify the worker's readiness to work (*Arbeitsbereitschaft*). In any event, the employer reasoned, a worker had to report in twice during a regular workday, so the firm was not demanding anything exceptional of him. In the dangerous atmosphere of a strike and at a court which was not known for its support of workers' interests, the judge ruled in favor of the worker. "The plaintiff had a right during the [four-week] interim period not just to payment of his wages," the judge decided, "but to the carrying out of his contractual employment as well."[73]

72. *Seide*, November 14, 1900, p. 728.
73. Ibid.

The Berlin court's decision attached the complex of legal norms to the employee as a bearer of work capacity, not to a person who merely received pay. In a similar case a decade later, the business court of the city of Chemnitz judged that the employment contract required the owner to use the workers' labor capacity and not merely to guarantee compensation.[74] In Britain, by contrast, the laws pertaining to employment were the same as those covering agreements for the delivery of products. Workers could be dismissed without obligation, even if the employment contract required prior notice, so long as they received compensation for the work they could otherwise have completed. The concepts of labor that the manufacturers enacted in practice, the courts sanctified in words.

FORMS OF AUTHORITY

German and British weaving overlookers shared the same dependencies and capabilities with respect to employers above and weavers below. In each country the structure of the production site generated similar conflicts among these parties. Yet due to the understandings of labor as a commodity, the paradigms on which people could draw for interpreting friction varied between Germany and Britain, endowing identical problems with contrasting significance. The British and German definitions of labor as a commodity hold contrasting implications for the owner's authority in the workplace. The German view of employment as the command of "labor power" made the exercise of authority over the execution of work an integral part of the process of earning a profit. The German view unified the relations of appropriation and domination. When capitalists purchased "labor power," their receipt of a profit depended on how successfully they converted that labor capacity into labor itself. Without the immediate domination of the worker, the owner did not appropriate a surplus. Marx believed as a matter of theory, not of rhetoric, that the capitalist organization of work was despotic. Although profit may have been *realized* through exchange on the market, it was generated and appropriated in production.

The purchase of embodied labor in Britain, by contrast, denied any necessary connection between the exercise of authority and the generation of profit. The producers may certainly have believed that the factory proprietor took advantage of his command over capital to pay workers less than he ought. Even so, the owner secured a surplus through an *exchange* relation

---

74. *Das Gewerbegericht,* Volume 15, Nr. 5 (1910), pp. 103–104.

set up by the trade of resources rather than in an immediate relation of domination. The generation and appropriation of surplus were accomplished at a remove, not through the owner's command over the labor potential and person of the worker and not through the owner's authority over social relations in the factory.

Weaving offers an exemplary environment in which to explore the influence of these concepts of labor as a commodity, because the technical characteristics of the labor process made the overlooker's role more ambiguous in this than in many other industries. Weavers worked on their own when all was well with their looms; the overlooker did not coordinate the work of machines or of people, nor was he required to show initiative in leading a team of workers. He did not have to exercise authority as an intrinsic part of his technical function. Furthermore, the overlooker did not contribute to output by *combining* in his department diverse outputs or mechanical procedures; he only aggregated outputs from similar machinery. Production was the sum of the individual loom outputs, a feature which made it easier to think of the overlooker as bestowing his labor upon the lengths of cloth rather than as acting in the capacity of a manager. Textile businessmen in Britain referred to their weaving overlookers as machine "operatives," even when they gave overlookers the right to hire and fire subordinates.[75] Finally, in comparison with a metal-working plant, where each of a company's overlookers might have command over a set of different machine tools and make different kinds of products, a weaving mill had many weaving overlookers, each with a quota of similar kinds of machinery. Because they could compare overlookers who did the identical jobs and they hired many different overlookers for the same job, owners could equate the overlookers' labor and think of it as a homogeneous "input" bestowed upon the fabric.

In this complex situation, how did people on the shop floor define the role of the overlooker? The words used in Britain to designate the overlooker's occupation offer evidence of the participants' emphasis on his role as a technical and productive one. Mill workers in Yorkshire, and on some occasions the owners as well,[76] called their weaving overseers *tuners*, a title which put these employees' technical function before their supervisory one. The word *overlooker* may have appeared in management journals and social

75. *Textile Mercury*, July 8, 1899, p. 24; LRO, Minutes of Blackburn Masters' Association, DDX1115/1/2, February 26, 1900.
76. *Textile Mercury*, July 8, 1899.

scientific descriptions, but not in the ordinary language of the people on the shop floor. Their interviews and their union newspapers' descriptions of mill life used the word *tuner*. In Lancashire the popular term was *tackler*, a metonymic derivative that referred to the overlooker's tools—his tackle— rather than to his authority and place in the chain of command.[77]

The evolution of textile production from home weaving to the central- ized factory allows the analyst to place the dimensions of the overlookers' role—the exercise of a technical skill and the exercise of authority over other people—in a diachronic progression. Loom tuning or tackling had become a recognized occupation in England and on the Continent before the rise of the factory system. By the early nineteenth century handlooms had become complicated enough that special tuners made house calls to fix or adjust them.[78] In this era the fixers were commonly called loomers. (If the fixer specialized in dobby looms, which had parts called witches, the occupa- tion's popular title carried a pun: "witch doctors.")[79] The chore of overseeing workers' conduct was added to the "looming" occupation with the rise of factory production. But when the occupation acquired a new popular name in the transition, the workers did not apply to the overlookers the range of terms, such as *gaffer* or simply *boss*, that they used for persons in higher authority.

In Germany, despite a path of structural evolution similar to Britain's, the overlookers' titles did refer to their supervisory responsibilities rather than to their technical function alone. The lowest-level weaving overlooker, who had responsibility for a certain section of looms, the workers called the *Webmeister* ("weaving master") or *Reviermeister* ("section master"). In contrast to the English weaving overlooker, the German overlooker bore a title that placed him in an integrated system of supervision, part of a hier- archy of officials. The system gave higher-level foremen the title of *Saal- meister* ("room master") or *Werkmeister* ("shop master").

These phrases were not empty punctilios; they betrayed the essence of the overlookers' performance in Germany. German officials articulated

77. *Yorkshire Factory Times*, October 9, 1891. In some cotton districts overlookers were also called loom jobbers. *Cotton Factory Times*, December 3, 1886. When the weavers found that the overlooker bullied them, they called for an investigation. In Blackburn, the town clerk investigated claims that an overlooker should be dismissed for "tyranny," although the weav- ers did not charge the overlooker with brutality. See LRO, DDX1115/1/1, Blackburn, Novem- ber 6, 1895.

78. Healey, op. cit., p. 4.

79. Centre for English Cultural Traditions and Language, University of Sheffield, Bob Turner's interview with respondent A67–72.

the overlookers' role when they were called upon to elucidate a new pension law for "professional technical workers." The law, which took effect in 1913, was based on the longstanding proviso that employers contribute to a comprehensive pension and insurance fund for white-collar workers. It extended this requirement to cover higher-level workers in the workshops as well (*technische Angestellte*). Government administrators had to decide exactly which persons the law admitted to the pension system as professional technical workers. According to the district reports submitted to the German Foremen's Union, the owners of large weaving mills recognized the weaving overlookers (*Webmeister*) as such professionals for insurance purposes without hesitation.[80] But some employers tried to evade requests for insurance coverage by changing the overlookers' occupational titles from *Meister* of various sorts to mere *Vorarbeiter* ("preparatory workers").[81]

To adjudicate the resulting disputes, the imperial insurance bureau in Berlin studied in detail the functions of overlookers in the weaving branch. How could this office decide whom to designate as a professional, not just as a schooled technical expert? In the end officials took the employees' exercise of an oversight function, rather than their level of technical expertise, as the critical requirement for classification as a professional.[82] If weaving overlookers did simple manual work such as installing the warps, they were still higher-level professional workers so long as they also were in charge of watching the weaving process, distributing warps, or enforcing the factory work codes.[83] In another illustration of the importance given to authority, the imperial insurance bureau decided that in departments smaller than the weaving rooms, such as those for carding or dyeing, supervisors had to have at least *two* workers under them to be classified as tech-

80. Archiv des Freien Deutschen Gewerkschaftsbundes, "Geschäfts-Berichte des Zentralvorstandes des Deutschen Werkmeister-Verbandes für 1911 und 1912," p. 17.

81. *Der deutsche Meister,* March 15, 1913; *Geraisches Tageblatt,* October 31, 1912. The courts established, however, that the overlooker's duties, not his title, determined his legal status. *Das deutsche Wollen-Gewerbe,* August 6, 1910, p. 1007. For a discussion by contemporaries of the status implications of the term *Vorarbeiter* versus *Meister,* see *Der Textil-Arbeiter,* August 4, 1905.

82. *Zeitschrift für die gesamte Textil-Industrie,* p. 1163; Stadtarchiv Bocholt, K2/276, case from September 24, 1896.

83. Letter from March 26, 1914, reprinted in *Zeitschrift für die gesamte Textil-Industrie,* 1914, Nr. 14; the periodical *Das Gewerbegericht* cites a decision of the Düsseldorfer *Zivilkammer* of January 2, 1903, in which the court decided that a loom fixer who "merely assists the weavers in installing the warp and who corrects defects is to be regarded as a foreman [technical professional], even when he stands under the supervision of another foreman." See Volume 9, Nr. 7 (1904), p. 198.

nical professionals (*technische Angestellte*).[84] Income levels and the time intervals by which the salary was calculated were judged to be irrelevant.[85] Command over other workers was considered the distinctive part of the overlookers' work role. Even technically trained foremen complained that they were viewed by some employers "only as a driver of the employed workers."[86]

When the German courts were called upon to interpret the overlookers' labor contracts, they too made the exercise of authority delegated by the owner an essential part of the employment relation. By the provisions of the German business law, overlookers, unlike ordinary workers, could be dismissed without the usual notice required by contract if they were proven "disloyal" in their service.[87] What constituted "disloyal" conduct? The construals of the courts discloses the conventional interpretation of the labor transaction. An industry journal, in an article about the legal definition of an overlooker that appeared in 1912, asserted that an overlooker, by the implicit terms of the labor contract, "obligated himself to devote his skills fully and completely to the interests of the employer."[88] In this magazine's view, overlookers became instruments of the owners' will, and to support this claim it cited legal verdicts. The German courts had ruled that overlookers, unlike ordinary workers, could not give notice together at a firm. Giving such notice would amount to an attempt to bargain collectively for better employment conditions and therefore would mean that the overlookers were no longer acting "faithfully" to advance the proprietors' interests.[89]

84. *Zeitschrift für die gesamte Textil-Industrie*, Nr. 48 (1912), p. 1069.

85. *Das Versicherungsgesetz für Angestellte: Vom 20. Dezember 1911.* (Stuttgart: J. Hess, 1912).

86. Archiv des Freien Deutschen Gewerkschaftsbundes, "Geschäfts-Berichte des Zentralvorstandes des Deutschen Werkmeister-Verbandes für 1912–1913," p. 7.

87. Germany, *Gewerbeordnung für das Deutsche Reich* (München: C. H. Beck, 1909), section 133c, point 2.

88. *Zeitschrift für die gesamte Textil-Industrie*, Nr. 17 (1912), p. 346.

89. As an appeals court in Dresden reasoned, "If the professional staff resorts to the threat of collectively giving notice, in order through the planned action to force the employer to be more forthcoming, then the staff has grossly violated the duty inherent in the employment relation to safeguard the interests of the owner and to refrain from anything that could run against those interests, and has thereby proven itself guilty of disloyalty in service." The quotation comes from a case involving white-collar workers but applied to the category of professional technical workers as well. *Zeitschrift für die gesamte Textil-Industrie*, October 1, 1913, p. 264. For an analogous case outside of textiles where an employer could immediately dismiss a technical professional for collaborating with workers, see *Das Gewerbegericht*, September 3, 1903, p. 294, Solingen.

The employment contract was void if the overlookers did not minister to the owners as servants.

This bond of service let the courts designate overlookers as literal agents of the owners. According to German law, if a worker grossly insulted the employer, he or she could be dismissed immediately. The statutes, however, did not specifically address the question of whether overlookers, like owners, enjoyed this privilege. When the courts were called upon for an interpretation, they decided that even the lowest-level overlooker ought to be regarded as an "agent of the employer." On these grounds, disrespect toward an overlooker equaled a direct insult to the owner.[90] The German judicial review for business courts reprinted the rulings of the imperial court in Berlin that emphasized the view that overlookers were agents of the proprietors. The review in 1901 summed up the precedents: "The authority of the employer is transferred to the foreman, for without the accompanying carryover of the 'prestige' of the owner, the transfer of part of the owner's legitimate authority would be unthinkable, otherwise it [the transfer] would directly contradict the interests of the employer, for whose protection the transfer is consummated."[91] The authority of the employer was distilled in the overlooker's everyday activities.

Although the specification of the overlooker's labor as a ware differed between Germany and Britain and the exercise of authority by overlookers carried different implications, the responsibilities of the overlookers in the two countries did not diverge. Even in the most important area in which overlookers exercised authority—in hiring—the German and the British overlookers occupied approximately equivalent positions. To be sure, one finds great variation *within* each country in the weaving overlookers' responsibilities for production. There were two benchmark systems. Under the first, the owners or mill directors took responsibility for recruiting and hiring new workers and assigned them to overlookers as

90. *Seide,* September 16, 1914; *Gewerbe- und Kaufmannsgericht* Volume 19 (1914), pp. 271–272. A weaver unsuccessfully challenged the legality of firing him without notice after he called his tuner a "lazy bum" (*Faulenzer*). *Der deutsche Meister,* May, 1914.

91. *Das Gewerbegericht,* Volume 6, Nr. 9 (1901), p. 183. See also Volume 7, pp. 209–210, for an analogous decision in Mainz. Some of the disciplinary ordinances issued by textile factories treated disrespectful statements to the owners' representatives as direct insults to the owner. See, illustratively, Landesarchiv Potsdam, Rep. 6B, Kreisverwaltung Cottbus, Nr. 1253, regulations issued December 15, 1905, by the Heinrich Linke factory in Guben. The mayor of Fischeln, a town near Krefeld, reported with approval in a letter to provincial authorities in 1891 that overlookers "advocate the views of the employer frequently and with pleasure in personal interaction with their workers." HSTAD, Landratsamt Krefeld 175, p. 35.

they pleased.[92] Under the second system, overlookers or departmental foremen did the hiring entirely on their own.[93] This could lead to extreme decentralization: at a mill near Bradford, a female weaver whom an overlooker fired in 1902 for acting as a ringleader in a "disturbance" immediately found a job under a different overlooker at the same firm.[94] These two pure systems of responsibility for hiring, in which either factory directors or the overlookers themselves took sole responsibility for hiring, formed in both countries the exception rather than the rule. Between the two extremes lay various mixtures of authority between overlookers and higher managers. At many factories, the overlooker did the hiring, but the director exercised veto power or carried out an interview with each worker before the final decision.[95] At others the manager did the hiring but restricted the main field of candidates to people recruited or recommended by the overlooker.

In these mixed systems of hiring the producers never arrived at consistent rules for finding new hires. If a manager happened to see a vacant loom one morning, he might immediately put someone on without asking the overlooker, yet assume that the overlooker as a matter of routine would fill

---

92. Bernays, op. cit., 1910, p. 186. My interview with Arthur Murgatroyd, born 1902, Halifax. Rowland Kennedy, *Westering: An Autobiography by Rowland Kennedy* (London: J. M. Dent and Sons, 1939), p. 95; *Cotton Factory Times*, February 19, 1897, Rochdale.

93. For Lancashire, see *Textile Mercury*, July 8, 1899, p. 23; Bolton Oral History Collection, tape 54, male weaver, born 1898. For Yorkshire, see *Yorkshire Factory Times*, July 26, 1889; July 1, 1892, p. 5; June 21, 1901, Shipley Mary Brown Barrett, "In Her Clogs and Her Shawl: A Working-Class Childhood, 1902–1914," Bradford Library Archives, p. 56. According to a male spinner, born 1896, most overlookers in the Bradford area did their own recruiting, but it was not uncommon for managers to do it. Bradford Heritage Recording Unit, tape A0091. For Germany, see Stadtarchiv Bocholt, K2/276, December 20, 1900, and 6/K1, 1892, Arbeitsordnung Actien-Gesellschaft für Baumwollindustrie, and, for spinning, K2/276, March 6, 1899; Stadtarchiv Rheine, Nr. 183, February 3, 1915, Dyckhoff & Stoeveken; Staatsarchiv Osnabrück, Rep. 610, Lingen, Nr. 125, "Arbeitsordnung Gerrit van Delden," 1901; *Der Textil-Arbeiter*, June 14, 1901, Aachen. In the German case, since the workers had to be entered on the firm's chief roster for the owner to make contributions to the medical and insurance funds (*Krankenkasse*), the overlooker made the offer of employment but could not become an employer of labor on his own right.

94. Not until a higher shop master happened to notice her transfer one day did she finally leave the firm. *Yorkshire Factory Times*, July 4, 1902. The higher supervisor did not himself inform troublesome employees of their dismissal but entrusted delivery of the message to the overlooker. For a parallel example, see *Yorkshire Factory Times*, December 6, 1890.

95. *Yorkshire Factory Times*, October 11, 1889; October 25, 1889; December 13, 1889. For Lancashire, LRO, DDX 1115/1/1, Blackburn and District Managers' Mutual Association, resolution of August 23, 1894. H. Meyer, *Einrichtung und Betrieb einer Seidenstoff-Fabrik* (Zürich: Juchli & Beck, 1908), p. 19. My interviews with Ewald Sirrenberg, born 1897, and with Hans Penz, born 1895 in Barmen.

other empty looms.[96] This vague apportionment of responsibility for hiring at mills in northern England could result in overlookers and managers at a firm promising the same loom to more than one person.[97] Workers in Yorkshire complained that when they wanted to leave the firm they did not know to whom they should give notice.[98] Likewise in Germany the weavers said they were unsure about which of their supervisors was "really the master" and whose permission they needed to take a day off.[99] In Germany, on the one hand the newspapers of the textile workers criticized overlookers for abusing their arbitrary powers of dismissal; on the other, the papers acknowledged that in effect overlookers also needed, but did not always get, upper management's consent to fire a worker.[100] In both countries the compass of the overlooker's jurisdiction was ill-marked and specified more by imputation than by official notice.

If the exact boundaries of the overlooker's responsibility for hiring remained unclear, his influence was nonetheless real. In light of their command over people, how could British producers have crystallized the overlooker's activity as the delivery of materialized labor? Even where British overlookers hired weavers themselves, this could be seen as a technical function, a means of equipping looms with weavers, not weavers with looms. James Burnley, a textile worker and well-known dialect poet, described overlookers' roles in mill life after he revisited a Bradford weaving company: "There are several overlookers in the room, each of whom has the superintendance of a certain number of looms. Their duties are to keep the looms in repair and to supply them with weavers."[101] Burnley, who had a

96. *Yorkshire Factory Times,* May 16, 1890. For cases where the manager overruled the overlooker, see *Yorkshire Factory Times,* August 3, 1894, Horton.

97. *Yorkshire Factory Times,* September 1, 1893, Apperley Bridge.

98. *Yorkshire Factory Times,* August 23, 1901. For other complaints regarding the confusion in responsibility for hiring, see *Yorkshire Factory Times,* October 31, 1890, Bradford and Keighley; March 18, 1892, Ravensthorpe; September 23, 1892, Yeadon; January 2, 1891, Dewsbury; June 19, 1891, Keighley; November 13, 1891, Marsden.

99. *Die Textilarbeiter-Zeitung,* August 13, 1910, and September 14, 1901, Krefeld; *Christlicher Arbeiterfreund,* September 23, 1898, p. 5; *Die Textilarbeiter-Zeitung,* March 15, 1902, Mönchengladbach.

100. *Der Textil-Arbeiter,* October 18, 1901. For Yorkshire, see *Textile Manufacturer* Oct. 15, 1891, p. 456. In part, owners deliberately maintained the ambiguity in responsibility for hiring and firing. They did not always trust their overlookers to hire workers by criteria of efficiency, yet they did not want to diminish overlookers' power to discipline workers. *Centralblatt für die Textil-Industrie,* 1885, p. 791. According to the *Yorkshire Factory Times,* a manager in Batley revoked an overlooker's right to hire due to the favoritism the overlooker showed in hiring. See February 7, 1890.

101. James Burnley, *Phases of Bradford Life* (London: Simpkin, Marshall & Co., 1889), p. 197.

firsthand acquaintance with weaving, expressed himself with precision—
and his choice of words made the looms, rather than the workers, the overlooker's real object of attention.[102] Then, too, the ultimate means by which
overlookers supported or dismissed weavers was not that of official commands but of covert deeds. If a weaver got on the wrong side of the overlooker, he or she might as well leave the firm, even if the overlooker said
nothing. When a piqued overlooker began to withhold prompt technical
assistance, the earnings of the ancillary weaver declined quickly. The
authority of the overlooker could be transmitted through their care of the
machinery as much as through a chain of command.[103]

The specification of the overlooker's transmission of labor did not alter
the overlookers' functions and responsibilities in Germany or Britain, but
it provided the template for workers to formulate their grievances about
superiors. For a ground-level view of workers' complaints, I coded the local
reports that appeared in the newspapers of the textile workers in Britain and
Germany. In Britain, the *Yorkshire Factory Times* focused its coverage on
the everyday concerns of textile workers.[104] This journal, whose premier
edition appeared in 1889, devoted most of its pages to a feature called "Ech-
oes from Mills and Workshops." Each week this revue described incidents
at factories in more than a dozen towns and villages, based on correspondents' reports and on letters and tip-offs sent in by workers. Nowhere else,
the paper boasted, could one find "so true an index of the life of the textile
factory."[105]

In Germany, reports from textile factories reached two newspapers. In
1889 the "free" (or Social Democratic) trade union of the textile workers
began publishing the complaints workers submitted to union officials or
voiced at meetings.[106] The Christian union for German textile workers fol-

102. The overlookers referred to their wages as "monies coming off the looms." LRO, DDX
1151/19/3, July 31, 1908.
103. *Yorkshire Factory Times*, September 19, 1890, p. 4, and March 29, 1901, pp. 4–5.
104. The editor of a sister newspaper, *The Workman's Times*, believed that the *Yorkshire
Factory Times* was "specially dominated" by the textile workers. See his comments, August
29, 1890.
105. *Yorkshire Factory Times*, April 11, 1902. Twenty-five years after the paper's founding, Ben Turner, one of its original staff members, recalled, "It was a real workmen's paper
written by workmen and workwomen for workfolks." Turner described the original network
of contributors in the *Yorkshire Factory Times*, June 25, 1914, p. 4. For an example of an
incomplete report from a correspondent that illustrates the amateur nature of the reporting,
see *Yorkshire Factory Times*, October 23, 1891, Bradford. The paper had the largest circulation
of any weekly journal in the West Riding (June 17, 1892, p. 8, and April 18, 1902, p. 8).
106. See *Der Textil-Arbeiter*, January 17, 1902, Gera, for a reference to the submission
process. The reports were published with major editing. Deutscher Textilarbeiterverband,

lowed suit with a similar publication in 1898.[107] I coded the complaints of workers about practices on the shop floor from the earliest surviving volumes of each of these newspapers. In both countries, these early volumes had the richest and most extensive coverage of problems on the shop floor. The British sample covers the years from 1890 through 1893, the German sample the years from 1899 through 1902. I coded the complaints concretely, with over one hundred separate categories.[108] With such a naive procedure, I could register problems ranging from the cleanliness of the toilets to the timbre of the factory bells used to dismiss the labor force.

The catalog of major complaints listed in Table 1 suggests that in many respects the immediate grounds for conflict were parallel in the two countries. In both, the four most frequent complaints concerned the level of pay, reductions in pay, the fines imposed for allegedly "bad" work, and the disrespectful attitude of supervisors toward their workers. Since the question of interest is how complaints varied within manufacturing processes that were organizationally and technologically alike, I compared the distribution of complaints between countries within the same occupation. The most significant divide is that of the weavers versus those in other textile occupations. In both countries, about two-thirds of the grievances recorded in the newspapers came from the weaving branch (66 percent in Britain, 68 percent

---

Protokoll der vierten ordentlichen General-Versammlung des Verbandes aller in der Textil-Industrie beschäftigten Arbeiter und Arbeiterinnen (Berlin: Deutscher Textilarbeiterverband, 1898), p. 32.

107. For a description of the process by which workers submitted reports to the Christian textile newspaper, see Archiv der Gewerkschaft Textil-Bekleidung, Zentralverband Christlicher Textilarbeiter Deutschlands, "Geschäftsbericht, 1910–1912," p. 120.

108. A word on procedure: since I was interested in using these complaints as a tool to analyze perceptions of relations in the *workplace*, I excluded two kinds of complaints. First, I omitted complaints that referred only to outside agencies such as factory inspectors or the police (these were in any event rare). Second, I eliminated complaints about low wages unless they met one of the following conditions: (a) they attributed the problem to circumstances in the workplace, or (b) they discussed specific rates, modes of payment, or reductions. I excluded general comments about pay that did not meet either of these conditions, on the grounds that they were so vague they could not illuminate workers' perceptions of relations in the workplace. In Britain, where the stories were more numerous, I coded every third issue from these years; in Germany, every issue. If a news story contained multiple grievances, I included each. I am interested in using newspapers for their interpretations of events, not as tools for counting the events themselves. Therefore, where coverage of a strike or protest movement extended across more than a single number of a newspaper, I continued to count each grievance. After all, the same strike could be described in different ways across the weeks. Multiple reports on a single incident were, however, rare. I coded only the weekly local reports, not editorial articles, which were less representative of views on the shop floor. In each country, the sample years included periods of both business recession and prosperity, although I did not find significant differences in the leading complaints generated in good times versus bad.

Table 1. Major Complaints from Textile Workers' Newspapers

Yorkshire Factory Times (n=1385)

	Instances	% of n
Manners and treatment	99	7.1
Pay too low	97	7.0
Fining "bad" work	62	4.5
Pay reductions	59	4.2
Firing for petty cause	53	3.8
False measuring of product	45	3.2
Piece rates not marked[a]	38	2.7
Playing favorites in handing out materials	34	2.5
Blacklisting, firing unionists	30	2.2
Tattling to owner	27	1.9
Job unsafe, unhealthy	27	1.9
Turning engine off late	25	1.8
Dozen top complaints	596	43.0

Combined German samples (n=1238)

	Instances	% of n
Fining "bad" work	91	7.4
Pay reductions	87	7.0
Pay too low	86	6.9
Manners and treatment	76	6.1
Blacklisting, firing unionists	66	5.3
Unpaid auxiliary tasks	41	3.3
Operating more than one loom	39	3.2
Workday too long	30	2.4
Changing work shifts	30	2.4
Bad materials	30	2.4
Waiting for materials	27	2.2
No canteen	24	1.9
Dozen top complaints	627	51.0

Table 1. *(Continued)*

Der Textil-Arbeiter (n =719)

	Instances	% of n
Pay reductions	52	7.2
Manners and treatment	50	7.0
Fining "bad" work	50	7.0
Pay too low	48	6.7
Blacklisting, firing unionists	32	4.5
Waiting for materials	24	3.3
Operating more than one loom	24	3.3
Changing work shifts	23	3.2
No canteen	22	3.1
Unpaid auxiliary tasks	21	2.9
Workday too long	20	2.8
Bad materials	18	2.5
Dozen top complaints	384	53.0

Der Christliche Textilarbeiter (n=519)

	Instances	% of n
Fining "bad" work	41	7.9
Pay too low	38	7.3
Pay reductions	35	6.7
Blacklisting, firing unionists	34	6.6
Manners and treatment	26	5.0
Unpaid auxiliary tasks	20	3.9
Operating more than one loom	15	2.9
Bad materials	12	2.3
False measuring of product	10	1.9
Workday too long	10	1.9
Owner violating work agreement	10	1.9
Short time[b]	9	1.7
Dozen top complaints	260	50.0

Sources: *Yorkshire Factory Times*, 1890–1893; *Der Textil-Arbeiter*, 1901–1902; *Der Christliche Textilarbeiter*, 1899–1901.

[a]Refers to the company's failure to post a standard piece-rate scale.

[b]Refers to reduction in the number of hours worked each week (implying in many cases a reduction in wages).

in Germany). Table 2 compares the twelve complaints that appeared most frequently among weavers alone. The non-weavers were fragmented among so many labor processes that the sample does not allow for such comparisons across other occupations. The figures serve as one piece of evidence among many, not as an arbiter of hypotheses. I cannot derive the meaning of problems as they appeared to the weavers themselves from a set of codings. What appears to have been the "same" complaint for German and British weavers may have come to life in substantially different cultural forms.

To help us begin to appreciate the cross-national differences in the import of complaints, in Table 3 I compare the distribution of persons blamed in the newspapers for workplace problems in all branches of textiles. The Germans assigned blame to the "firm" as a whole for problems nearly twice as often as the British. On the face of it, the meaning of this divergence remains uncertain. It could imply that the German papers considered it less important to censure particular categories of persons, as opposed to the "system," as the cause of problems. Assigning responsibility to the "firm" might also serve as just another way of blaming the firm's owner.[109] If we leave aside complaints about the "firm," the German papers blamed owners and managers in 75 percent of the cases, compared to 54 percent of the cases in the British paper. Rather than looking upward to the top of the company to assign blame, the incidents reported in the British papers stayed closer to the persons with whom workers labored side by side. Among the complaints that blamed particular categories of persons, the British paper blamed the overlookers in 30 percent of the cases, whereas the German paper assigned only fifteen percent of problems to that lower-level party. If we treated complaints about the "firm" as referring to owners and higher managers, the German complaints would appear even more top-heavy. Finally, the same table shows that within the German sample, the Christian and socialist newspapers assigned blame among the factory personnel in almost identical proportions. If these two journals, which originated in markedly contrasting ideological milieus, assign blame to the same categories of persons in the workplace, we have more secure grounds for supposing that the stories to some extent replicated the workers' formulations, not just the agendas of the editors who processed the stories in their offices.

---

109. Blaming problems on the "firm" did not, however, serve as a way of avoiding reprisals for having named particular individuals: other complaints did not always identify even the firm and usually referred only to the position, not the name, of the person blamed.

Table 2. Major Complaints, Weavers Only

Yorkshire Factory Times (n=916)

	Instances	% of n
Manners and treatment	60	6.6
Fining "bad" work	54	5.9
Pay too low	46	5.0
False measuring of product	42	4.6
Pay reductions	39	4.3
Piece rates not marked	36	3.9
Firing for petty cause	31	3.4
Playing favorites in handing out materials	31	3.4
Tattling to owner	23	2.5
Pay not to standard scale	22	2.4
Bad warps	22	2.4
Blacklisting, firing unionists	21	2.3
Dozen top complaints	427	46.6

Combined German samples (n=845)

	Instances	% of n
Fining "bad" work	81	9.6
Pay reductions	63	7.5
Pay too low	52	6.2
Manners and treatment	41	4.9
Blacklisting, firing unionists	37	4.4
Operating more than one loom	37	4.4
Unpaid auxiliary tasks	27	3.2
Bad warps	26	3.1
Waiting for materials	25	3.0
Owner violating work agreement	17	2.0
False measuring of product	16	1.9
Not paid for waiting	14	1.7
Dozen top complaints	436	51.6

Sources: *Yorkshire Factory Times*, 1890–1893; *Der Textil-Arbeiter*, 1901–1902; *Der Christliche Textilarbeiter*, 1899–1901.

Table 3. Persons Blamed in All Complaints*

Yorkshire Factory Times (n=915)

	Instances	% of n
Owner	343	37.5
Manager	153	16.7
Overlooker	280	30.6
Fellow worker	139	15.2
Total	915	

Combined German samples (n=431)

	Instances	% of n
Owner	213	49.4
Manager	111	25.7
Overlooker	67	15.5
Fellow worker	40	9.3
Total	431	

Der Textil-Arbeiter (n=231)

	Instances	% of n
Owner	113	48.9
Manager	59	25.5
Overlooker	37	16.0
Fellow worker	22	9.5
Total	231	

Table 3. *(Continued)*

	Der Christliche Textilarbeiter (n=200)	
	Instances	*% of n*
Owner	100	50.0
Manager	52	26.0
Overlooker	30	15.0
Fellow worker	18	9.0
Total	200	

Sources: *Yorkshire Factory Times*, 1890–1893; *Der Textil-Arbeiter*, 1901–1902; *Der Christliche Textilarbeiter*, 1899–1901. One case from each of the German and British samples remains unlisted here because they assigned no blame.

    *Remainder in each group complained in general terms about the firm.

    Percentages do not equal 100, due to rounding.

The German workers' tendency to focus more often on higher-ups is slightly more pronounced among weavers than among the sample as a whole (Table 4). This only accentuates the question of how factories that appear similar not only from the standpoint of organizational structure and technology but in the sorts of conflicts and disagreements they generate can differ significantly as institutions that "produce" a human experience of the labor activity. We need to rely on contextual evidence to assess the cultural significance of the German assignment of responsibility to overlookers. One of the most frequently voiced complaints, that concerning the supervisors' disrespectful manners, illustrates how British and German workers attached different meanings to complaints that appear categorically similar.

For weavers and for textile workers in general, the British newspaper complained more about the disrespectful treatment workers received from supervisors than about any other difficulty. The late-nineteenth-century factory provided a setting in which overlookers could indulge in severe verbal abuse of their underlings. Employers considered it something of a prerequisite for maintaining discipline that overlookers be able to swear in the local dialect.[110] A reporter from Elland said that some overlookers treated their spot in the mill as a "privileged place." In the overlooker's corner, the reporter said, a female underling might hear "a voice addressing

110. Sidney Webb, *The Works Manager To-Day* (London: Green & Co., 1914), p. 105.

Table 4. Persons Blamed in Complaints from Weavers*

Yorkshire Factory Times

	Instances	% of n
Owner	215	35.8
Manager	93	15.5
Overlooker	194	32.3
Fellow worker	98	16.3
Total	600	

Combined German samples

	Instances	% of n
Owner	147	50.3
Manager	85	29.1
Overlooker	42	14.4
Fellow worker	18	6.2
Total	292	

Sources: *Yorkshire Factory Times*, 1890–1893; *Der Textil-Arbeiter*, 1901–1902; *Der Christliche Textilarbeiter*, 1899–1901. One case from each of the German and British samples remains unlisted here because they assigned no blame.

*Excludes complaints that blame the firm generally.

Percentages do not equal 100, due to rounding.

her in language known as profane, and which, if used on the public streets by a drunken man, would see him taken in hand by the police."[111] The textile workers' unions tried without great success to elicit the cooperation of the overlookers' unions in restraining the corrupt language.[112] They had better

111. *Yorkshire Factory Times*, February 7, 1890, p. 5. A female weaver from the Colne Valley summed up her managers' behavior diplomatically in an interview: "The bosses didn't act like they was educated," she said. "They'd no manners." Joanna Bornat's interview with Mrs. B., born 1887.

112. Bradford District Archives, Minutes of the Overlookers' Society, 3D 86 1/1/11, Spring, 1914; *Textile Mercury*, April 25, 1914, pp. 328–329. The secretary of the Bradford branch of the General Union of Textile Workers said that his association would investigate every case of verbal abuse by overlookers and, if redress were not obtained, would authorize a strike. *Yorkshire Factory Times*, May 7, 1914. For the registration of women's complaints

luck in securing the assistance of the courts. One judge in Dewsbury, Yorkshire, ruled in 1913 that a worker who objected to a supervisor's lewd comments could quit work without waiting to give proper notice.[113]

German workers complained that managers addressed them in military-style, "barracks" language.[114] They claimed that the supervisors' dictionary of abusive terms included "scoundrel" (*Halunke*), "rogue" (*Spitzbube*), and "old ass" (*alter Esel*).[115] At a spinning mill in the Mönchengladbach district, workers testified that a supervisor had "badly cursed even older people." The workers at this mill, trying to discover whether the supervisor could be prosecuted for such conduct, sought the advice of police, who would, they supposed, be knowledgeable about the law.[116]

Not surprisingly, workers picked out their immediate supervisors, with whom they had the most contact, as the most frequent users of humiliating expressions.[117] In both countries, overlookers received a greater share of complaints about rude conduct than about other problems. British workers blamed overlookers for the ill treatment in about two-thirds of the reported incidents in the *Yorkshire Factory Times*. In Germany, overlookers received the blame for harsh manners less frequently, in about 42 percent of such complaints. Yet German overlookers received the blame for poor language more often than did managers or owners (see Table 5).

The raw numbers do not show that British workers reviled their overlookers more than the German their own. Rather, they provide clues whose meaning for the participants can be reconstructed by examining the style of the evidence. The British newspaper framed its comments about the overlookers differently than did the German papers. In Britain, workers criticized the overlookers as individuals; their complaints portrayed the

---

about foul speech, see Archive of General Union of Dyers, Bleachers, and Textile Workers, Yeadon General Union, minutes book April 6, 1911. Female workers were not the only recipients of verbal abuse: in the textile workers' newspapers of both countries that I coded, objections to the insulting speech of supervisors were statistically no more likely to appear in stories featuring women as the complainers than in those featuring men or mixed-gender groups.

113. *Yorkshire Factory Times*, February 13, 1913, Dewsbury Borough Court.

114. Report from the "Sprecher am Niederrhein," reprinted in *Die Textil-Zeitung*, March 20, 1899, p. 226. See also *Der Textil-Arbeiter*, June 11, 1909, Landeshut.

115. *Der Textil-Arbeiter*, April 19, 1901; May 4, 1906, Euskirchen.

116. *Gladbacher Volkszeitung*, July 13, 1899.

117. Even at relatively small firms, workers had little contact with owners. One female weaver in Milnsbridge, born in 1903, said that in twenty-eight years of employment she spoke to the boss, Emmanuel Hoyle, on only two occasions. Joanna Bornat's interview with Mrs. T., born 1896. At Taylor's of Batley, the owner left all the discipline to the foremen: Centre for English Cultural Traditions and Language, University of Sheffield, A73–72, Herbert Chapell, Batley, started work before 1914.

Table 5. Persons Blamed for Harsh Manners*

Yorkshire Factory Times (n=915)

	Harsh manners	% of harsh manners
Owner	13	13.1
Manager	18	18.2
Overlooker	66	66.7
Fellow worker	2	2.0
Total	99	

	Other problems	% of other problems
Owner	331	40.5
Manager	135	16.5
Overlooker	214	26.2
Fellow worker	137	16.8
Total	817	

Combined German samples (n=431)

	Harsh manners	% of harsh manners
Owner	14	20.9
Manager	22	32.8
Overlooker	28	41.8
Fellow worker	3	4.5
Total	67	

Table 5. (*Continued*)

	Other problems	% of other problems
Owner	199	54.7
Manager	89	24.5
Overlooker	39	10.7
Fellow worker	37	10.2
Total	364	

Sources: *Yorkshire Factory Times*, 1890–1893; *Der Textil-Arbeiter*, 1901–1902; *Der Christliche Textilarbeiter*, 1899–1901. One case from each of the German and British samples remains unlisted here because they assigned no blame.

*Excludes complaints that blame the firm generally.

Percentages do not equal 100, due to rounding.

personalities of the overlooker. The epithets applied to the overlookers reproduces this personalistic framework. Many of the insults refer to the physical appearance of the overlooker, such as "Golden Whiskers," "Little Darkey Tuner," or "the fancy-moustache stroker."[118] Others summed up the conduct of the supervisor with nicknames such as "Growler & Howler," "Woman Hater," or "Sleepy."[119] The British workers' conflict with their overlookers rested on a foundation of familiarity. The British complaints also characterized the behavior of the overlookers by comparing them to animals: a "puddledog that can do nothing but bark," a "bull terrier," a "wild bear."[120] These analogies removed the overlookers' conduct from the context of the factory hierarchy. They emphasized the overlookers' personal failings rather than their exercise of the authority that inhered in their office.[121] One story about an unpleasant overlooker (which cited an unfortunate cliché) captured the way workers attributed problems to an unchangeably bad character: "How true it is," the correspondent wrote, "the black man cannot wash his face white, nor a bad-tempered man forget his ways."[122]

118. *Yorkshire Factory Times*, June 13, 1890, p. 4; December 6, 1889, p. 4.

119. *Yorkshire Factory Times*, March 21, 1890; December 6, 1889, p. 4; February 28, 1890, p. 4.

120. *Yorkshire Factory Times*, March 24, 1893, p. 5; April 8, 1892, p. 5.

121. A story from Apperley Bridge said that one must consider the character and intelligence of the overlooker before condemning him. *Yorkshire Factory Times*, May 15, 1891.

122. *Yorkshire Factory Times*, November 17, 1893, p. 4.

German workers also used epithets for their overlookers, but of a less personal sort. They labeled their overlookers with general names in popular circulation, such as "brute" (*Grobian*), "beast" (*Vieh*), and "ape" (*Affe*).[123] These were the impersonal insults that might well be applied to an overbearing stranger. The German newspapers criticized overlookers as the occupiers of an office who insisted on exercising their authority in the name of the owner. Overlookers, they claimed, had nothing better to do than to demonstrate a "service of love" for their employers.[124] "One constantly observes that the overlooker at every moment supports only the interests of his master employer," the *Textil-Arbeiter* reported. "Direct personal contact with the owner," it added, "is suited, like no other practice, to illustrate the superiority of the position of overlooker."[125]

Another major complaint points to different understandings of the exercise of authority in Britain and Germany. As is shown in Table 2, twenty-three complaints about people who squealed to higher-ups in the factory appeared in my British sample for the weaving branch. Sixty percent of these cases identified overlookers as the culprits. A story from a mill in Dewsbury, published in 1893, conveys the spirit of these reports:

> A tuner here is to get married shortly, and the weavers, like good weavers, chaffed him in good fashion. He could not stand it and went and complained in the office. Wasn't it nice to go and complain over a paltry affair like this? I wonder what his affianced will say about it?[126]

The story illustrates the belief that the overlooker's conduct violates the norm against tattling. Its concluding question hints that the overlooker, by snitching on his underlings, will suffer the censure of his friends.[127] The account also suggests that workers and overlookers were co-producers, enough on a level for them to form joking relationships.

---

123. *Der Textil-Arbeiter*, February 13, 1914, p. 55; HSTAD, Regierung Düsseldorf, 24677, p. 153; *Der Textil-Arbeiter*, July 28, 1905, Niederzwönitz. For other generic aspersions, see Stadtarchiv Augsburg, No. 1667, 1903, p. 16.

124. *Der Christliche Textilarbeiter*, May 25, 1901, Mönchengladbach.

125. *Der Textil-Arbeiter*, October 18, 1901. For a complaint about "fawning overlookers" (*liebedienerische Untermeister*) see *Der Textil-Arbeiter*, July 9, 1909.

126. *Yorkshire Factory Times*, August 11, 1893, Dewsbury.

127. This premise appears in other complaints in this category. For example, one story that warned an overlooker about tattling said, "A certain tackler must mend his ways, if he wants people to believe him to be what he represents himself to be." *Yorkshire Factory Times*, March 21, 1890, Skipton.

Most of the tales British overlookers took to superiors concerned the alleged errors weavers made in production or the slow pace of their production. An overlooker who tattled became known as a "greasy" tuner, a "greasehorn."[128] The British complaints regarding tattling about production foul-ups reflect the workers' assumption that the overlooker should not have acted as if he were merely an agent of the owner. The British weavers believed that the lower-level overlookers ought to support their efforts to labor with a degree of autonomy.[129]

In contrast to the frequent complaints about snitching in the British sampling, the German cases revealed only one example. In this exception, from the Bergisches region, the workers had already launched a movement against the authority of the central management. They complained that an overlooker had informed on the weaver who he believed had given a signal to the others to stop work at their looms before the rest period. The account mentioned the overlooker's conduct only as a detail in its narrative of the work stoppage.[130] The significant comparison to draw about tattling is this: in Germany, no grievances appeared regarding overlookers' informing about everyday production errors or about workers' demeanor. Instead, the German workers' comments about the overlookers' "service of love" indicate that workers took it for granted that overlookers would keep the owner informed.

The frequency of complaints about the rude manners of overlookers in Britain suggests that overlookers and workers stood in a closer, more equal relation to each other in Britain than in Germany. British workers, in comparison with their German counterparts, expected overlookers to classify workers as colleagues and were perhaps more sensitized to disrespect. Respondents from Yorkshire said that supervisors and weavers drank at the same pubs.[131] Indeed, the textile workers' newspaper in Yorkshire complained that weavers who shared pub rooms with the overlookers tried to get better warps for themselves or jobs for their relatives by buying drinks for their overlooker.[132] Yorkshire weavers expected their overseers to socialize with them and accused them of "putting on airs" if

128. *Yorkshire Factory Times*, July 1, 1892, Bradford.
129. *Cotton Factory Times*, March 11, 1904, Hyde.
130. The incident occured in Hückeswagen. *Der Christliche Textilarbeiter*, May 25, 1901.
131. My interviews with Mrs. May Broadbent, born 1896, and with Edward Crowthers, both of Midgley. On socializing between overlookers and workers in Lancashire, see Patrick Joyce, *Work, Society and Politics* (London: Methuen, 1982), pp. 101–102.
132. *Yorkshire Factory Times*, September 20, 1889, Slaithwaite; September 27, 1889; October 11, 1889, Bradford; December 4, 1891, p. 5; November 10, 1893, p. 4.

they did not.[133] British weavers were familiar enough with their overlookers to play practical jokes on them without fear of reprisal when the perpetrators revealed themselves.[134] As a weaver correspondent from Bingley expressed it, "Tuners are only workers like ourselves."[135] A spinner from Halifax in an interview put it even more simply: "We was one."[136]

A careful reading of the textile workers' newspapers in Germany provides insight into a different set of relations in Germany. To be sure, the workers there complained that some of their colleagues used all manner of tactics to bribe overlookers for preferential treatment. They alleged, for example, that some workers gave overlookers free pies and turkeys or agreed to buy trinkets from overlookers at inflated prices.[137] In their coverage of these incidents, however, the German newspapers did not mention an equivalent to the British workers' tactic of tipping a drink side by side at the pub, perhaps a relationship more intimate or socially reciprocal than the German overlookers would have tolerated. A respondent from Oerlinghausen in Westfalen, for example, volunteered the insight that the overlookers and weavers in town drank at separate inns and that social mixing would have broken an unspoken law.[138]

The farewell gifts workers gave their overlookers also serve as an index of national differences in relations between these groups. The workers' newspapers in Britain reported that weavers frequently took up collections to provide farewell presents for tuners and managers who were retiring or

133. *Yorkshire Factory Times*, February 22, 1901, and July 8, 1892, p. 5, Oakworth. Russell D. Johnstone, "The Textile Industry in Meltham Fifty Years Ago," Institute of Dialect and Folklife Studies, University of Leeds, p. 13. Workers considered it a universal custom to call overlookers by their first name. See, for example, Joanna Bornat's interview with Mrs. T., p. 17, Miss. B. Nr. 5, born 1887, and Mrs. Q, born 1899; my interview with Arthur Murgatroyd.

134. Elizabeth Roberts's interview with Mr. and Mrs. L1P, born 1894 and 1900; Joanna Bornat's interview with Mrs. H, born 1891, p. 26.

135. *Yorkshire Factory Times*, August 12, 1892.

136. My interview with Arthur Murgatroyd. At the start of the great strike at Manningham mills in 1890, the *Bradford Daily Telegraph* reported, "It is not the wages exactly which has caused the strike, but the sense of inequity. If there is a depression, the wages of all, including foremen and overlookers, should be reduced. Somehow or other there is the feeling among the workpeople that one is as good as another, although there may be a little pomp" (December 22, 1890).

137. Staatsarchiv Münster, Abt. VII, Nr. 52, Bd. 1, March 2, 1910, Gewerbeinspektor Bocholt; Stadtarchiv Gummersbach, Akt 4842, November 26, 1889. *Der Christliche Textilarbeiter*, August 11, 1900, Fischeln; June 16, 1900, Krefeld.

138. My interview with Fritz Soll. Max Weber studied the major mill in this town for his monograph on textile production. See Anthony Oberschall, *Empirical Social Research in Germany, 1848–1914* (New York: Mouton & Co., 1965), p. 115.

transferring between mills.[139] Since the gifts went only to departing supervisors, they could not be reciprocated in favors at work. By all accounts,
British workers offered the gifts spontaneously and apart from those bestowed by management.[140] In Germany, by contrast, stories about unsolic-
ited collective presents from workers to exiting supervisors seem practically
unobtainable.

According to German journals of the textile trade, many German owners
preferred to hire supervisors from distant areas, on the grounds that strang-
ers could better maintain their distance from the lower workers.[141] A respondent from Barmen, who became a loom tuner himself, said weavers
believed that the manager "deliberately" hired outsiders from other towns
as supervisors, with the aim of keeping them separate from the workers.[142]
By comparison with this explicit discussion in Germany, the professional
literature for textiles in Britain remained silent about this tactic. Factory
ordinances issued by German employers warned that each overseer had the
duty "to protect his prestige against the workers."[143] Indeed, the separation

139. *Yorkshire Factory Times*, April 4, 1890, p. 4; October 23, 1891, Ravensthorpe; May
30, 1890, Rastrick; April 25, 1890, Dewsbury; February 5, 1892, p. 4; Sept. 8, 1893,
Thongsbridge; November 17, 1893, Great Horton; *Cotton Factory Times*, Oct. 22, 1886,
Rochdale; January 5, 1912, Stalybridge.

140. *Yorkshire Factory Times*, February 5, 1892, Liversedge.

141. *Centralblatt für die Textil-Industrie*, 1881, pp. 557–558. *Die Textil-Zeitung*, November 21, 1904, Nr. 47, p. 1162. Max Haushofer, *Der Industriebetrieb* (München: E. Koch, 1904),
p. 380. For an example reported in the workers' press, see *Der Christliche Textilarbeiter*, June
11, 1910, Wassenberg. Oral reports from German workers confirm the owners' preoccupation
with dividing the overlookers from the workers. If an employer promoted one of his workers
into the ranks of the supervisors, he took precautions to segregate him from his former peers.
A worker from the Münsterland, for example, reported that after his promotion from mule
spinner to *Meister*, the owner forbade him to let his friends greet him with the familiar form
of address, *du*. My interview with Franz Reidegeld, born 1900, Rheine.

142. My interview with Hans Penz. Weaving overlookers in both countries rose from the
ranks of the weavers. Some overlookers briefly attended textile night schools, but only fore-
men completed a regular course of study. *Yorkshire Factory Times*, February 13, 1891, p. 4;
July 12, 1901, Stainland; April 12, 1901, Bingley; December 18, 1903, Batley. Kirklees Oral
History Project, Miss V., born 1901, p. 23. *Cotton Factory Times*, Sept. 10, 1886, Oldham.
Edward Beyer, *Die Fabrik-Industrie des Regierungbezirkes Düsseldorf vom Standpunkt der
Gesundheitspflege* (Oberhausen: Spaarmann, 1876), p. 135. *Zeitschrift für die gesamte Textil-
Industrie*, Nr. 44 (1912), pp. 966–967. Heinz Potthoff, *Ziele und Erfolge des Werkmeisterstan-
des*, pp. 4–5. *Der Textil-Arbeiter*, June 16, 1905, Beilage, and July 26, 1901, Barmen. Weavers
emphasized that their overseers were not superior in education.

143. Hauptstaatsarchiv Düsseldorf, Regierung Düsseldorf, BR 1015, Nr. 169 I, Gladbacher Spinnerei und Weberei, 1855; Stadtarchiv Rheine, Nr. 183, F. H. Hammersen, 1910;
Stadtarchiv Greven, IV o 30–32, labor ordinance for the Grevener Baumwollspinnerei, issued
1886, reissued for the 1891 Gewerbeordnung; Westfälisches Wirtschaftsarchiv Dortmund, S
8/41 L. & S. Leeser, Dülmen, 1892; Wirtschaftsarchiv Baden-Württemberg, B46–391, 1846,
requires that Meister "ihr Ansehen gegen die untergeordneten Arbeiter zu behaupten wis-

of overlookers from workers in Germany took the most solid form possible: factories' architectural design. A number of mills in Germany provided toilets or eating rooms for supervisors separate from those for workers.[144]

The pattern of fining for indiscipline also betrays the greater emphasis placed on the overlooker's authority in Germany. In both Germany and Britain, workers received petty fines for "misconduct." For example, overlookers and foremen punished workers by withholding earnings for offenses such as looking out the window, talking, or letting bobbing lie on the floor.[145] All of these fines might be explained, perhaps, as measures to ensure high output or to provide greater safety on the shop floor. Beside the fines that bore upon output, however, the German supervisors, unlike their British counterparts, also imposed disciplinary fines for actions they perceived as insults to their authority.[146] At a firm in Mönchengladbach, for example, the foreman fined a weaver who once forgot and twice refused to take off his cap upon greeting the foreman.[147] At a firm in Birgden, near Geilenkirchen, a weaver who expressed irritation at the overlooker for not adjusting the loom received a fine for disrespectful conduct.[148] German managers listed these punishments into "fine books," which include entries for "insolence," "insult," "is always coarse toward me," and "affront."[149]

sen"; Wirtschaftsarchiv Baden-Württemberg, Stuttgart, B46–398 Fabrikordnung, L. Hartmann Söhne, 1846; Stadtarchiv Augustusberg, Clauss firm, ordinance 1910.

144. Ludwig Utz, *Moderne Fabrikanlagen* (Leipzig: Uhlands technischer Verlag, 1907), pp. 133–134; Stadtarchiv Oerlinghausen, Floorplan Carl Weber & Co., Oerlinghausen.

145. *Yorkshire Factory Times*, November 21, 1890, p. 5; June 10, 1892, Leeds; November 4, 1892, Bradford; March 17, 1893, Leeds, p. 5; Kreisarchiv Kempen, Gemeindearchiv Schiefbahn 715, July 30, 1905; my interview with Herr Schnieders of Rheine, who recalled the stories of older weavers; *Der Textil-Arbeiter*, April 25, 1902, Auerbach; March 5, 1909, Rheydt; November 25, 1910, Bautzen, and July 15, 1910, p. 221; HSTAD, Regierung Düsseldorf, 24684, April 27, 1894, report on Klauser firm.

146. On fining for perceived insults, see Wolfgang Ruppert, *Die Fabrik* (München: Verlag C. H. Beck, 1983), p. 211.

147. *Der Textil-Arbeiter*, May 20, 1910. The business court in Mönchengladbach ruled that the employer had been justified in levying the fine, because the worker had disobeyed a supervisor's order. See account in Deutscher Textilarbeiterverband, *Protokoll des 10. Generalversammlung, 1910* (Berlin: Karl Hübsch, n.d.), p. 291.

148. *Der Christliche Textilarbeiter*, January 20, 1900, and *Die Textilarbeiter-Zeitung*, October 15, 1910. In another case, a female worker in Krefeld received a fine for giggling at a manager. *Der Christliche Textilarbeiter*, December 16, 1899. For another fine for disrespectful conduct, see *Der Textil-Arbeiter*, March 21, 1902, Lörrach.

149. Such entries were reproduced in *Der Textil-Arbeiter*, January 20, 1911, for Bamberg. Also see Westfälisches Wirtschaftsarchiv Dortmund, F32, Huesker fine book, 1892–1905; and, at the same archive, F11, Delius fine book, p. 105; Textilmuseum Apolda, Zimmermann firm, "Verzeichnis über verhängte Geldstrafen," 1892 to 1906; Archiv des Volkseigenen Betriebs Palla, Meerane, Gebrüder Bochmann, Nr. 575, Strafbuch, 1905–1906, "Gehorsamsverweigerung." For an example from Göppingen, see Deutscher Textilarbeiterverband, *Protokoll des*

German overlookers also charged their underlings in court with having affronted them. In fact, the records of the local arbiters from textile towns indicate that this was not uncommon. In Odenkirchen, a textile center in the Rhineland, the summary transcripts show that the legal complaints during a twelve-year period at the turn of the century included charges of insult brought against employees by the following supervisors: a spinning overlooker, a weaving overlooker, a carding room supervisor, two foremen, a maintenance overlooker, and a factory director.[150] Where such records also specify the location of the alleged offense, they often refer to the factory itself.[151] The overlookers took seriously the supposition that they shared in the employer's dignity.[152]

The lists of mill complaints in the *Yorkshire Factory Times*, and, less frequently, in the *Cotton Factory Times* might have been expected to mention fining for "affronts" to overlookers' authority. Yet accounts of such incidents are wanting. To the contrary, workers seem to have teased their supervisors to their face. The autobiographies of textile workers describe how workers mocked their overseers. One female weaver from Bradford mentioned her encounter with her overlooker, Harry:

> I have not forgotten how he tried to set Ellen Jaratt's loom right . . . and he had no sooner set it on when the shuttle flew right through the window into the dam, and they never found it yet. I asked him if he had made a goal with that shuttle, and if it counted to his side the other goal, but he pretended not to hear me. . . . I can say a great

---

10. *Generalversammlung,* 1910, p. 289.

150. Stadtarchiv Mönchengladbach, Protokollbücher des Schiedmannes, Odenkirchen, 2769.

151. For example, ibid., p. 93, October 1902; March 2, 1911; March 14, 1912; July 19, 1912. For another town with similar occurrences, see Stadtarchiv Nordhorn, Protokollbuch B42 Schiedsmann zu Bakelde, p. 148.

152. Another complaint from Germany indicates that German workers believed the overlookers identified more with the employer's role as a supervisor of labor than with the worker's role as producer. The overlookers responsible for adjusting and repairing equipment, a German newspaper reported, act "as if they had been appointed to the position of coupon cutters. We are used to seeing them scan their section up and down, with a pencil or cartridge pen behind their ear, in a well-cut blue uniform, ostentatiously carrying their writing book rather than outfitted with a leather bag filled with assorted wrenches and physical instruments." *Der Textil-Arbeiter,* October 11, 1901. The workers' emphasis on the overlooker's task of writing can also be discerned from the surviving fine books. They show that overlookers punished workers who dared glance at their books on the writing pulpits. Stadtarchiv Gummersbach, Nachlass der Gummersbacher Spinnerei Krawinkel & Schnabel, fine for "Gehen auf den Pult"; *Der Textil-Arbeiter,* January 20, 1911, "Eine Strafliste." Protesters in Germany picked out the writing stands (*Pulte*) as targets for vandalism. Werner Rohr, "Die Geschichte der Arbeiterbewegung in Nordhorn," diss., Universität Bremen, 1981, p. 47.

deal more about Harry if he tries to be so witty about me being an old maid again.[153]

Weavers near Baxenden played a game with authoritarian overlookers to shame them. They handed such overlookers the gift of a whip, ridiculing them as slave drivers.[154] Perhaps the most telling demonstration of British workers' assertion of their equality with overlookers came from Great Harwood, Lancashire. The weavers who struck a mill there in 1893 succeeded in having their overlookers sign an apology, which said, "We, the undersigned, do admit that we have been guilty of driving and humbugging the weavers employed under us. . . . We herewith guarantee that in future we will not speak to any weaver when going round with the slate or when fetched to tackle their looms."[155] The autobiographical stories of British workers leave no doubt that they were exposed to tyrannical abuse from some overlookers. At issue is not the degree of cooperation or conflict but the intimate and equalitarian framework British workers used to condemn mishandling.[156]

The factory owner's first motivation for hiring an overlooker, according to the working-class press in Germany, was not to acquire the skills of a technical expert; it was to obtain an agent through which he could exercise his authority

153. *Bradford*, "A Weaver's Notions About Factory Work and Other Work," November 30, 1895. In the original, the last sentence of this quote appeared first. In the representations of complaints in the British textile workers' newspapers I coded, female weavers assigned blame to overlookers more frequently than did male workers, at a statistically significant rate. In Britain, for instance, 40 percent of stories portraying female weavers as the complainers indicted overlookers, versus 29 percent of stories with male or mixed-gender complainers in weaving. In the newspapers' depictions, male or mixed-gender groups of weavers in Britain blamed overlookers twice as frequently as did male or mixed-gender groups in Germany, and female weavers in Britain blamed overlookers two and a half times more frequently than did female weavers in Germany. I plan to publish a separate study contrasting gender distinctions in the two countries. For the present comparison, it is perhaps sufficient to note that the cross-national differences in representations of relations to overlookers traverse the line of gender.

154. *Cotton Factory Times*, September 17, 1889, p. 5.

155. "Strikes and Lockouts in 1893," PP 1894 LXXXI, pp. 625 ff., strike reference number 664, December 14–January 15.

156. Some British supervisors, including female overlookers, left permanent impressions of ill will. Annie Kenney, *Memories of a Militant* (London: Edward Arnold & Co., 1924), p. 16; Hebden Bridge Oral History Project, OH85/59; "Autobiography of Thomas Wood," regarding mill in Bingley, born 1822, *Keighley News*, March 3, 1956 ff.; Sherwin Stephenson, "The Chronicles of a Shop Man," Bradford Library Archives; Jan Lambertz, "Sexual Harassment in the Nineteenth Century English Cotton Industry," *History Workshop* Number 19 (Spring 1985), pp. 29–61. Conversely, many German overlookers had an amiable relation to their underlings within the hierarchical framework. Marie Bernays, "Berufsschicksale moderner Industriearbeiter," *Die Frau* Volume 18, Nr. 3 (December 1910), p. 136.

over the factory.[157] As the *Textil-Arbeiter* said, "The owner of the production shop naturally says to himself that it is in his interest to place the tasks of the workers under control by putting a person there . . . so that a mere glance from this personage will spur workers to the strictest fulfillment of their duties."[158] The German practice of fining workers for mere "affronts" to supervisors reproduced the view that the overlookers' exercise of authority in the name of the owner was essential to the extraction of surplus. In Britain, on the other hand, since the overlookers did not act merely to extend the owners' authority, the extraction of a profit for the owner of the factory was severed from the exercise of authority on the shop floor. The *Northern Pioneer*, a journal for the labor and the "liberal radical" movements in the Colne Valley, expressed the view that the exercise of authority was not an essential aspect of the employment relation and extraction of profit. Textile workers and factory owners, it said in 1883, were merely exchanging their commodities. "Employers should not want to be masters anymore than the men should want to be masters," it concluded.[159] For the British textile workers, as for artisanal workers in an earlier age, the exchange of labor as a commodity could be not only separated from but contrasted with the exercise of authority. "You are no *master* of mine," a rule-maker told his employer in the 1840s, "but only a man who buys my labour for a good deal less than it's worth."[160] The formulation acknowledged a relation that included both formal equality in the marketplace and real exploitation.

It would be simple but superficial to imagine that the differences between practices at the point of production in the two countries resulted from a greater emphasis in general in German society upon authority for building social relations. Such an approach would confuse the ideologies celebrated in the public sphere with actual practice on the shop floor. If the famed tradition of liberalism in British political discourse lent support to notions of individual liberty and autonomy, such ideals did not have any elective

157. *Der Textil-Arbeiter*, February 15, 1907, Augsburg.
158. *Der Textil-Arbeiter*, October 18, 1901. The workers' comments had grounds in reality: some German want ads for overlookers specified that the overlooker, in addition to having technical training, had to know how to control the workers, or, as one ad put it, "possess complete confidence in contacts with workers." *Der deutsche Meister*, January 1, 1913, Betriebsleiter for spinning mill.
159. *Northern Pioneer*, March 3, 1883. The workers' sentiment survives in rarified economic theory even today. For example, the British economic historian John Hicks insists that a hierarchical relation between employer and worker is incongruous with mercantile society. John Hicks, *A Theory of Economic History* (Oxford: Clarendon Press, 1969), p. 122.
160. Dyke Wilkinson, *Rough Roads: Reminiscences of a Wasted Life* (London: Sampson Low, Marston, & Co., 1912), p. 19. Emphasis in original.

affinity with actual use of the British idea of labor as a commodity. After all, the confinement of inmates in fortress-like enclosures scarcely embodied the notion of liberalism. The specification of labor as a commodity in Britain did not inhibit employers from attempting to exercise control episodically in heavy-handed fashion on the shop floor. Although the practice formed no part of the usual organization of production, British employers, if it struck their fancy, fired underlings without warning for looking at them "the wrong way."[161]

The contrasts between factory procedures in the two countries were based not on degrees of authoritarianism but on the modalities by which employers asserted their domination. British employers devoted no less attention to cultivating a paternalist regime in pliant neighborhoods outside the factory as their German counterparts did. Rather than consecrating their mastery of the transformation of labor power into a product at the site of production, British employers displayed their superordinancy in the community, where they could influence workers' mobility and sense of dependency.[162] The Strutt family, acclaimed in the early nineteenth century as factory pioneers, watched over their employees' morality by imposing fines for such mischievous behavior outside the workplace as maltreating a neighbor's dog.[163] In the second half of the nineteenth century, British factory owners did not just support recreational and educational clubs at the mill site. They subsidized workers' clubs, schools, and churches in the community at large.[164] Interviews with former textile workers from Lancashire

---

161. A Huddersfield employer allegedly slapped a female worker in the face. *Yorkshire Factory Times*, April 17, 1908, p. 4. The editor of the *Textile Mercury* trade journal, Richard Marsden, told employers to combat idleness with "instant dismissal." Richard Marsden, *Cotton Weaving: Its Development, Principles, and Practice* (London: George Bell & Sons, 1895), p. 470.

162. David Gadian, "Class Formation and Class Action in North-West Industrial Towns, 1830–1850," in R. J. Morris, editor, *Class, Power and Social Structure in British Nineteenth-Century Towns* (Leicester: Leicester University Press, 1986), p. 50. For the early industrial revolution, see Pollard, op. cit., pp. 201, 205–206; Sidney Pollard, "The Factory Village in the Industrial Revolution," *The English Historical Review* Volume 79, Number 312 (July 1964), p. 527; David Roberts, *Paternalism in Early Victorian England* (New Brunswick, New Jersey: Rutgers University Press, 1979), p. 180.

163. R. S. Fitton and A. P. Wadsworth, *The Strutts and the Arkwrights 1758–1830* (Manchester: Manchester University Press, 1958), p. 236. Similarly, in 1891 a firm in Bradford allegedly fired a "mill girl" for making a face at a fellow worker outside the mill. *Yorkshire Factory Times*, June 19, 1891, p. 4.

164. Anthony Howe, *The Cotton Masters, 1830–1860* (Oxford: Clarendon Press, 1984), p. 285; Joyce, op. cit., pp. 144–145, 168–175; David Russell, "The Pursuit of Leisure," in D. G. Wright and J. A. Jowitt, editors, *Victorian Bradford* (Bradford: Bradford Metropolitan Council, 1982), p. 211; Mike Holbrook-Jones, *Supremacy and the Subordination of Labour* (London:

and Yorkshire towns reveal that into the first decade of the twentieth century many workers still felt compelled to attend the same church or chapel as their employer.[165] Even in large towns with an adequate stock of housing, some British textile employers (like several of their German counterparts) erected company homes and required subordinates to occupy them.[166] British textile workers in employer-provided housing denounced the "tyranny" of their dependency.[167] But the textile industry was in this respect typical of British business.[168]

The prominent commitment of British employers to molding an obedient community outside the point of production attracted the criticism of German employers. As a businessman from the German wool trade judged in 1886, "To encourage the factory director to exercise surveillance over his people even beyond the work hours in order to look after their moral health—this is one English institution that has been taken too far. By this means one develops only empty-headed workers."[169] We should not accede unreservedly to the national contrast this executive wished to draw. But his sentiments undermine the presumption that German employers were automatically more custodial. What differed fundamentally between British and German employers was not the general readiness to supervise or control workers but the catego-

---

Heinemann Educational Books, 1982), p. 93. Sometimes the material basis of employers' hallowed authority was all too flagrant: until at least the end of the nineteenth century, William Hollins Company in Pleasley owned the town church. Stanley Pigott, *Hollins: A Study in Industry* (Nottingham: William Hollins & Co., 1949), p. 91.

165. Paul Thompson and Thea Thompson, family and work history interviews, no. 67, Bolton, born 1901. Joyce, op. cit., pp. 175–176. Joanna Bornat's interview with Mr. L., born 1899, p. 20. Nonconformist employers treated management of workers' personal life as a moral necessity. S. J. Daniels, "Moral Order and the Industrial Environment in the Woolen Textile Districts of West Yorkshire, 1780–1880," Ph.D. diss., University College, London, 1980, pp. 32, 133; Joseph Wilson, "A Private and Confidential Letter from Joseph Wilson to the Workpeople," Bradford Library Archives. *Yorkshire Factory Times*, April 4, 1890.

166. *Cotton Factory Times*, Sept. 10, 1886, Todmorden; J. D. Marshall, "Colonisation as a Factor in the Planting of Towns in North-West England," in H. J. Dyos, editor, *The Study of Urban History* (London: Edward Arnold, 1968), p. 228. Patrick Joyce emphasizes that efforts to build company housing varied: op. cit., pp. 121–123. But the employers themselves confessed that, but for lack of capital, they would have liked to have built more housing, "not for the benefit of the hands exactly, but so that they themselves can be ensured an efficient supply of labour ready at hand as required." *Textile Manufacturer*, June 15, 1901, p. 182.

167. *Blackburn Labour Journal* (February 1898); Royal Commission on Labour, PP 1892 XXXV, p. 223; *Yorkshire Factory Times*, June 21, 1901, p. 5.

168. James Jaffe's *The Struggle for Market Power* shows that in the British coal industry, too, the employers' claims to superordinacy were exerted, not at the point of production, but in the community at large, where employers sought to control housing and commerce. *The Struggle for Market Power: Industrial Relations in the British Coal Industry, 1800–1840* (Cambridge: Cambridge University Press, 1991), pp. 73 ff.

169. *Das deutsche Wollen-Gewerbe*, November 25, 1886, p. 1497.

ries of social consciousness by which they defined the exchange of labor at the point of production. If the emphasis on the disposition over labor power in the German factory had derived from a general cultural emphasis on authority, we would expect the authoritarianism to carry over into all contexts. Instead, in the community, where social relations were mediated by capitalist relations of production but not cast directly in their image, British employers appear no less interested than their German counterparts in controlling subordinates' leisure, religion, and education.[170]

CULTURE'S CONTEMPORANEOUS EFFECT

This chapter has compared structurally equivalent cases to identify the distinct contribution of cultural assumptions to the status of overlookers. In both Germany and Britain, weaving overlookers occupied an ambiguous position between workers and owners. On the one hand, they sold their labor for a wage, like a worker; on the other, they exercised authority over the production process, like an employer. The production process in textile factories was sufficiently standardized by the late nineteenth century that it offers the comparative analyst approximate controls for differences in the social organization of work. Weaving overlookers in Germany and Britain had the same technical roles, similar locations in the factory hierarchy, similar positions in the labor market, matching levels of pay, and the same responsibilities for supervising workers. Given these structural parallels, the divergent cultural definitions of labor as a commodity in Germany and Britain intervened to give overlookers different statuses. In Britain, the view that labor was sold via its products accentuated the aspect of the overlookers' activity that corresponded to that of a productive agent. In Germany, the view that labor was sold as a service placed an emphasis on the overlookers' exercise of authority in the name of the owner rather than on the delivery of a product; in this manner, the German view defined the overlooker's role as essentially unlike that of a worker.[171]

---

170. *Textile Manufacturer*, April 15, 1886, p. 168: "In England, he [the supervisor] is distinctly told by his employer that he must listen, and also that he must keep a look-out upon the conduct of his men after mill hours. . . . I am well informed in a case where a mill manager told his employer that he would not, even at his bidding, have his jurisdiction extended beyond the mill lodge and gates"—accordingly, the manager was fired! In Apperley Bridge, an employer knew his subordinates' habits well enough that when a young male weaver asked for a raise, the employer advised him instead to stop attending the theater. *Yorkshire Factory Times*, Nov. 17, 1893, p. 4; see also April 29, 1892, p. 5.

171. Chapter Ten, below, shows that the cultural classification of the overlooker's role influenced the grounds and goals of workers' collective action.

Historians of late-nineteenth-century factory organization have often emphasized the willingness of British employers to dedicate the real control of production on the shop floor to the workers themselves, particularly to those with craft skills. Compared to capitalists in other countries of the time, economic historians reason, British employers generally enjoyed greater access to pools of highly trained workers who inherited their know-how from the country's generations-long edge in manufacture. Since many British enterprises were founded early in the nineteenth century, when entry costs were lower, British companies in branches of production such as iron and steel production or metal work were smaller and more numerous than counterpart firms in later-developing countries. These circumstances made it more difficult for British firms to muster the great resources needed for investing in new technology and management organization in the course of the century and made it less costly for them to rely instead on the technical and organizational skills of their workers.[172] By this line of reasoning, the British specification of labor as a commodity could well have emerged as a natural reflection of an organizational structure in which employers were compelled to renounce control in reality, not just in ideology, over the conversion of labor power to a product.

A comparative study of the textile industry reveals the limitations of this approach. As we have seen, no prominent organizational differences existed between Germany and Britain in key branches of wool textile production. Yet important cultural differences did arise between them, revealing that the immediate institutional context is not responsible for differences between the materialized specifications of labor as a commodity. At most historical junctures before 1914 in the Yorkshire textile industry, where trade unions were comparatively weak, and at critical moments in the craft trades, such as metal-working after the wholesale defeat of unions in 1898, British employers had *carte blanche* to reorganize practices on the shop floor to match the self-conscious conversion of labor power to a product.[173] They did not try. What is more, analysts' reasoning in terms of adaptation to inherited constraints and opportunities fails to explain the structure of practices in large, recently founded companies in new branches of produc-

172. William Lazonick, *Competitive Advantage on the Shop Floor* (Cambridge, Massachusetts: Harvard University Press, 1990), p. 184; E. J. Hobsbawm, *Industry and Empire: An Economic History of Britain Since 1750* (London: Weidenfeld and Nicolson, 1968), p. 158; Perry Anderson, "The Figures of Descent," *The New Left Review* Number 161 (January–February 1987), p. 72.
173. William Lazonick, *Business Organization and the Myth of a Market Economy* (Cambridge: Cambridge University Press, 1991), p. 143.

tion, such as motor vehicles. The Engineering Employers' Federation successfully combated the establishment of formal collective bargaining in the British auto industry. Despite the freer rein given to employers to reorganize shop-floor practices in this innovative business, especially after 1922, management left control in the hands of craft workers and relied on payment by results to stimulate productivity.[174] Surely the employers' premises about the labor transaction, not just structural constraints, contributed to these outcomes.

In view of the visible decline in competitiveness among most branches of British industry since 1914, it is all too easy to read history backwards, attributing the differences between German and British practice before 1914 to German owners' greater push for efficiency. But certainly up to 1914, German textile mills did not operate more successfully than their British rivals. In the branches of wool textiles in 1907, the length of cloth produced annually from a loom in Germany approximately equaled that produced in Britain.[175] Among the European competitors, Britain's share of world trade in wool fabric rose in the decade before 1914.[176] In the cotton branch, German businessmen who measured output in Britain near the turn of the century had no doubt that British weaving mills produced more cloth

174. Jonathan Zeitlin, "The Emergence of Shop Steward Organization and Job Control in the British Car Industry: A Review Essay," *History Workshop* Number 10 (Autumn 1980), p. 122; Lazonick, *Competitive Advantage*, op. cit., p. 201.

175. Gross national comparisons of wool cloth output are necessarily clouded, since the design of each fabric had a strong bearing on the labor and value added. Nonetheless, annual wool fabric production can be estimated very approximately at 3,850 meters per loom in Britain, slightly less in Germany. For Britain I compared output from 1907 and the loom census from 1904, listed in D. T. Jenkins and K. G. Ponting, *The British Wool Textile Industry 1770–1914* (London: Heinemann Educational Books, 1982), pp. 169, 260. For Germany, see Karl Ballod's calculations in "Die Produktivität der industriellen Arbeit," *Jahrbuch für Gesetzgebung, Verwaltung und Volkswirtschaft im Deutschen Reich*, new series, Volume 34 (1910), p. 732. I also checked this with the loom count from the 1907 census, excluding hand looms. I compared this with the length of fabric the Germans produced, assuming that ratios between the consumption of wool and cloth output remained constant between 1897 and 1907. This procedure may underestimate German efficiency, but the diminution is offset by the fact that the German output included the contribution of hand looms, which survived in fancy weaving. To add to the murkiness, census takers in both countries inconsistently counted looms that wove mixtures of cotton and wool. Germany, *Statistik des Deutschen Reichs*, Volume 214 (Berlin: Kaiserliches Statistisches Amt, 1910), p. 303, and Arthur Spiethoff, *Die wirtschaftlichen Wechsellagen: Aufschwung, Krise, Stockung*, Volume 2 (Tübingen: J. C. B. Mohr, 1955), pp. 4–5 and Table 24. Market share is in the end the only usable indicator of performance.

176. D. T. Jenkins and J. C. Malin, "European Competition in Woollen and Cloth, 1870–1914: The Role of Shoddy," *Business History* Volume 32, Number 4 (October 1990). Jenkins and Ponting, *The British Wool Textile Industry*, op. cit., p. 294.

per loom than German contenders did.[177] The difference in the specification of labor as a commodity did not cause the British to fall behind in production.[178]

In both countries the character of textile technology before 1914 discouraged contemplation of the systematic conversion of "labor power" into a product. The raw materials could not be manipulated by the available technology according to standard rules, only by knack that defied analysis. "The loom of today is practically identical with the loom of fifty years ago," the *Textile Mercury* complained in 1912. "The loom may be ranked today as the crudest piece of widely used mechanism extant."[179] The technician Charles Vikerman remarked in the 1894 edition of his manual on woolen spinning that "no significant technical advance" had occurred in spinning during the preceding fifty years.[180] Technical experts in Germany voiced similar opinions.[181] In the hands of workers with only general experience in a textile branch, the equipment that twisted fiber and finished cloth operated too harshly for satisfactory results. Each town became a specialist in a different range of types of yarn and fabric, due to the mysteriously acquired knack of local labor for pushing obstinate varieties of fibers and yarns through the insensitive machinery. Even in the same neighborhood, however, a manufacturer sometimes failed to turn out a particular weave while the nearest challenger down the street, relying on the same kind of loom and material, succeeded.[182]

The reliance on the workers' knack for product specialties led the participants in the trade to think of fabrics as the result of confecting rather than of manufacturing. Factory managers drew analogies between the spinning

177. Gerhart von Schulze-Gävernitz, *The Cotton Trade in England and on the Continent* (London: Simpkin, Marshall, Hamilton, Kent & Co., 1895), pp. 107–108. On the greater value of British textile production despite the equality in the size of German and British textile workforces, see J. A. Hunter, "The Textile Industries of England and Germany," *Textile Mercury*, January 23, 1915, pp. 68–69.

178. In the 1920s the value of output per worker remained somewhat higher in Britain than in Germany in the textile industry as a whole. The difference was not attributable to price levels alone. Robert Brady, *The Rationalization Movement in German Industry* (New York: Howard Fertig, 1974), p. 268.

179. *Textile Mercury*, December 9, 1912.

180. Charles Vikerman, *Woollen Spinning: A Text-Book for Students in Technical Schools and Colleges and for Skillful Practical Men in Woollen Mills* (London: Macmillan & Co., 1894), p. 223.

181. *Zeitschrift für die gesamte Textil-Industrie*, June 27, 1912; *Zeitschrift für die gesamte Textil-Industrie*, 1910/11, p. 846.

182. Hermann Dornig, *Die Praxis der mechanischen Weberei* (Leipzig: A. Hartleben, 1895), p. 29.

of yarn and the distilling of fine drinks. To produce yarn suited for different kinds of twistings, a director from Bolton explained, "one mill may have five or six different 'mixings,' as they are called, each mixing [of cotton types] more or less skillfully adapted to the requirements of the yarn. This is as important, in its way, as the blending of teas, wines, or spirits."[183] Like the distiller who coped with seasonal variation in the character of the grapes harvested, the spinner dealt with crops of cotton and wool that differed in unpredictable ways, year to year, lot by lot, depending on the season's conditions for growing cotton and raising sheep.[184] Textile production depended on nature in other ways. The direction of the wind affected humidity and temperature and thus yarn breakages, so workers learned to pace their motions in response to the weather. At a mill sheltered behind a hill they learned a different rhythm of work than in a neighboring establishment exposed to the wind.[185]

By reason of this technical foundation, the textile industry developed in both countries into a "folk" trade, dependent on native lore and resistant to systematization.[186] The relatively stagnant design of equipment and the reliance on hit-or-miss tinkering indicates that the specification of labor as a commodity in German textiles did not arise as a consequence of attempts to keep pace with technical change or to rationalize the use of technology.[187] As the introduction of pay by shot first suggested, the German producers imported the definition of labor into the labor process in the early days of the factory system. They maintained their focus on the transfer of labor power to the employer although the surprisingly primitive technology of textile production during the second half of the nineteenth century discouraged employers from methodizing the conversion of labor power into a product. The adoption of a particular concept of labor in Germany did not reflect utilitarian demands but served as a premise for meeting them. The specification of labor was reproduced, not by its conformity with the tech-

183. Dobson, op. cit., p. 27.

184. *Cotton Factory Times*, March 5, 1897, p. 1; *Textile Journal*, 1902, p. 359; Fred Bradbury, *Worsted Preparing and Spinning*, Volume One (Halifax: F. King & Sons, 1910), pp. 19 ff.

185. *Journal of the British Association of Managers of Textile Works* Volume 6 (1914–1915), p. 106. Royal Commission on Labour, PP 1892 XXXV, p. 76.

186. For more particulars, see Richard Biernacki, "The Cultural Construction of Labor: A Comparative Study of Late Nineteenth-Century German and British Textile Mills," Ph.D. diss., University of California, Berkeley, 1988, pp. 223–243.

187. Brady, op. cit., p. 263.

nological environment, but through the symbolic configuration of micro-practices that communicated labor's definition.

In this chapter, as in the two preceding, I have relied on three forms of argument to demonstrate that the cross-national divergences in textile factory institutions had a cultural origin. Most important, I have compared similar business environments in detail to rule out alternative, utilitarian explanations for differences in factory procedures—in this instance, the allocation of overlooking costs—or for differences in the ascription of authority. In particular, my comparisons have excluded explanations based on the timing of the founding of textile mills, on adaptation to the business cycle, or on national variation in the factory directors' commitment to improving efficiency. Second, I have shown that the differing views of labor as a commodity in Britain and in Germany extended into minutiae of factory life where variation did not bear strategic consequences, such as the formal methods for distributing overlooking wages over various types of cloth. The shape of practice in these instances, too, is unamenable to utilitarian explanation. Finally, the contrasting cultural definitions of labor as a commodity in Germany and Britain which found expression in the methods of defining overlookers' remuneration serve as the core principles for interpreting an entire constellation of factory customs. The scope of the instrumentalities elucidated by a cultural principle raises our confidence in the method of analysis and challenges the advocates of purely utilitarian reasoning to account for this range of differences between German and British textile mills. Let them bring their case before the court.

CONCLUDING REFLECTIONS
ON PART ONE

Part One of this study has not attempted to decide which of two forces, culture or material circumstances, was the more powerful. Analysts who conceive of these forces as variables to be laid out side by side might suppose that their effects were conjoined, but their admixture is in fact more fundamental than that. Not only were both prerequisites for the composition of production, but the very operation of each remains inconceivable without the other. Material constraints assume their social effectivity only as they are encoded by culture; culture operates only as it is materialized in the concrete media at hand. The two forces are different moments in the same social process. Nonetheless, we can still isolate the effects of culture if we ask, not which had the most influence, but which comprised a social logic. The brute conditions of praxis in capitalist society, such as the need to compete in a market, did not provide the principles for organizing practices in forms that were stable and reproducible, for by themselves they did not supply a meaningful design for conduct. Rather, practices were given a consistent shape by the particular specifications of labor as a commodity that depended, to be sure, upon the general conditions of praxis for their materials, but granted them social consequences according to an intelligible logic of their own.

The discovery that factory production in Germany and Britain was orchestrated according to its signifying function bears important implications for sociological theories about the distinguishing character of human action in the capitalist order. Many in the tradition of Western Marxism have viewed the increasing salience of exclusively calculative, instrumental conduct as a characteristic developmental tendency of capitalist society.[188] But looking at the sensuous realm of practice on the shop floor from a comparative perspective discloses a more complex process. One can, perhaps, refer to the "rationalization" of the labor process at the very end of the nineteenth century, when formal ideologies of management appeared and the legal system, at least in Germany, elaborated more explicitly the rules governing the transmission of labor in the factory. But the development of capitalism was not marked by the progressive reduction of the activity of labor to the logic of instrumental action alone, without respect for action's communicative function. Instrumental action, rationalized by progressive adjustments

188. See, illustratively, Max Horkheimer, *Eclipse of Reason* (New York: Oxford University Press, 1947), pp. 93, 102.

to end-means logic, was still ordered by its conveyance of meaning and followed the cultural coordinates of a commodity form that varied apart from immediate economic conditions.[189]

If micro-procedures at the site of production were grouped in a meaningful pattern that incarnated different concepts of labor, how did this cultural logic tend to be incorporated consistently into practice? The concept of culture has drawn researchers' attention to the systematicity and global patterning of practices and signs, of strategies and life forms in society. Yet it is too easy to take this patterning as evidence for the influence or presence of something termed *culture* without asking how culture produces this configuration—or this configuration, culture. No social agent craftily designed the constellation of instrumentalities in the factory to embody, across the board, different specifications of labor as a commodity. By what processes did people create and reproduce not just an accidental assemblage of practices and concepts but an undivided cultural *system* based on concepts of labor?

To explain the survival of consistencies in the form of practice we need not invoke the notion of an overarching, harmonized normative order, internalized by the agents, that restrains deviant action. Once practices were installed as a consistent ensemble, their very execution could reproduce the concept of labor they embodied. Adherence to an ideal did not descend downward from contemplative knowledge of the general but percolated upward from practical knowledge of the concrete. It was the encounter with ideas residing in these humble instrumentalities that gave producers a practical knowledge of the ideal form by which labor was transferred as a commodity.[190] The micro-practices contained within themselves the principle that structured the social whole; execution of specific practices could reproduce the structure of the whole from the ground up.

The question that remains unanswered is not how a patterned cultural system was maintained, but, simply, why and how do practices cohere to

189. Habermas makes distinctions among several modes of action, including instrumental action, defined by its focus on the efficacious employment of technical skills to manipulate the environment, and communicative action, which is oriented to reaching reciprocal understanding with other social agents. This philosophical dissection of types of action reflects rather than penetrates the abstractions of capitalist society. For the divides it presents between modes of action, even if intended to be purely analytic, reinforce the separation between technical and communicative functions in the labor process, whereas the use of the impersonal micro-apparatuses of production performed a communicative function.

190. On recent experimental evidence that suggests that abstract concepts can be communicated through forms of practice, see Jean Lave, *Cognition in Practice* (Cambridge: Cambridge University Press, 1988), p. 183.

begin with? The matched comparison of economic environments for British and German factories shows that, in each country, alternative conventions would have met the requirements of the firm in the realm of capitalist competition equally well. If a method for, say, the imposition of fines is installed under one form of labor as a commodity, the choice of form for other techniques is not entailed by practical necessity. What generated the tendency toward consistency of form?

Even if one admits that agents' cultural schemata are arranged into a systematic whole, it by no means follows that the institutions of the factory must themselves incorporate this coherence. Instead, culture could be used by the agents to formulate only a subjective response to practices shaped by external necessities.[191] The built-in requirements of the mind for the production of meaning, which the cultural structuralists present as the ultimate cause of the coherence of culture, may well dictate a kind of formal patterning in language and in conceptual designs.[192] If this holds true for the constitution of language and signification, however, the question—altogether separate—remains of how and why industrial *practice* in the newly emergent capitalist factory methodically embodied such adroit schemata.[193]

Max Weber's sociological perspective offers an advantage in responding to the riddle of systematicity in factory practices because it views cultural patterning as a contingent accomplishment open to historical investigation. As is well known, Weber identifies intellectual specialists as the historical actors who are responsible for the creation of doctrines that make possible the systematic patterning of culture and of conduct.[194] Yet the details of the

---

191. Stephen Gudeman seems to adopt this viewpoint in *Economics as Culture: Models and Metaphors of Livelihood* (London: Routledge & Kegan Paul, 1986). He unearths the underlying structure of peasants' economic concepts in Panama, although their culture serves only as a means for *interpreting* changes in economic practices dictated from without (pp. 23–25).

192. Marshall Sahlins, *Culture and Practical Reason* (Chicago: University of Chicago Press, 1976), p. 55; Marshall Sahlins, *Islands of History* (Chicago: University of Chicago Press, 1985), p. 146.

193. Donald Donham outlines the problems occasioned by the application of models of language to models of practice in *History, Power, Ideology: Central Issues in Marxism and Anthropology* (Cambridge: Cambridge University Press, 1990), p. 211. A valuable analysis of the alleged coherence of culture appears in Neil J. Smelser, "Culture: Coherent or Incoherent," in Richard Münch and Neil J. Smelser, editors, *Theory of Culture* (Berkeley: University of California Press, 1992), pp. 10–13.

194. From Weber's standpoint, the congeries of ideas in a society does not organize social reasoning and conduct by a consistent pattern until an ethical or managerial doctrine has been articulated by experts in symbol-making. Max Weber, *The Sociology of Religion* (Boston: Beacon Press, 1963), pp. 30, 82.

cases at hand disqualify the Weberian approach to the development of a meaningful configuration of micro-practices in the factory. The principle of labor as a commodity did not form part of a formal management doctrine imparted to factory employers. To be sure, general precepts about the mutual responsibilities of the employing and the working classes had wide currency throughout the nineteenth century.[195] But those sanctimonious philosophies about virtuous relations had nothing to say about the organization or execution of manufacturing techniques themselves. "So far as we know," Sidney Pollard concluded for the period of early industrialization in Britain, "the management pioneers were isolated and their ideas without great influence."[196] Since so many factories were family-operated, the technical mysteries of the trade could be passed between generations through firsthand experience in the enterprise. In point of fact, there was as such no formal management doctrine to disseminate during the early development of the factory system. Professional administration of employees did not form an object for sustained reflection and study in either Germany or Britain until approximately the 1880s.[197] Until then the managerial function on the shop floor was not differentiated from that of technical oversight. Accordingly, books on the management of textile mills most often referred to machinery, not people.[198] At least until midcentury, the very term *manager* in Britain lacked a clear referent. The usual title for a supervisor of employees was *clerk*, a locution directed toward the older activity of book-

195. Reinhard Bendix, *Work and Authority in Industry* (Berkeley: University of California Press, 1956), Chapter Two; Judy Lown, *Women and Industrialization* (Cambridge: Polity Press, 1990), p. 96.

196. Pollard, *The Genesis*, op. cit., p. 254. Cf. Peter L. Payne, "Industrial Entrepreneurship and Management in Great Britain," *The Cambridge Economic History of Europe*, Volume VII, Part I (Cambridge: Cambridge University Press, 1978), p. 196.

197. Joseph Litterer, *The Emergence of Systematic Management as Shown by the Literature of Management from 1870–1900* (New York: Garland Publishing, 1986), pp. 65, 68; Introduction by Anthony Tillett to Anthony Tillett et al., editors, *Management Thinkers* (Harmondsworth: Penguin Books, 1970), pp. 48–49. For general reflections on the slow emergence of management as a self-conscious undertaking, see Charles S. Maier, "The Factory as Society: Ideologies of Industrial Management in the Twentieth Century," in R. J. Bullen et al., editors, *Ideas into Politics* (London: Croom Helm, 1984), p. 148, and L. Urwick and E. F. L. Brech, *The Making of Scientific Management* (London: Isaac Pitman & Sons, 1957), Chapter Six. For Germany, see Jürgen Kocka, "Entrepreneurs and Managers in German Industrialization," in *The Cambridge Economic History of Europe*, Volume VII, Part I (Cambridge: Cambridge University Press, 1978), p. 549.

198. When Babbage does refer to workers at the point of production, he limits his observations to the principles of muscular fatigue, as if people *qua* producers entered his discourse as machines. Charles Babbage, *On the Economy of Machinery and Manufactures* (London: Charles Knight, 1835), Chapter Four.

keeping.[199] The crystallization of factory practices based on specifications of labor that varied between Germany and Britain occurred decades before the emergence of management science in either country.

The functioning of the networks of communication in the textile districts also excludes the possibility that similarities in practices across regions arose from the diffusion of formal doctrine about the efficient deployment of labor among machines. Although factory procedures in Yorkshire and Lancashire were based on similar principles, in the formative years of the factory system factory owners in these provinces did not remain in contact with each other to transmit information about those practices.[200] The language of shop-floor life confirms the independence of development. In each of the neighborhoods of Lancashire and Yorkshire counties, managers used distinct vocabularies for parts of the loom and jobs in the mill.[201] Information about technical innovation—a subject of great concern to mill managers—was slow to diffuse. For example, managers in Elland, just outside Bradford, did not acquire for two decades the attachments for automatically changing the weft color on multi-shuttle looms that were standard in the city of Bradford by the 1870s.[202] How much less likely is it, therefore, that communication at length among factory managers about the interior social life of the mill led to the standardization of procedures within each country for managing the purchase of "labor" in the factory. The patterning of conduct according to the specification of labor as a commodity did not reflect a deliberate systematization of administrative rules.

If the patterning did not result from agents orienting themselves to environment with a certain schema and then creating a world in the image of this schema—the solution of idealists—neither was it the trace of the imperatives of the capitalist system imposing their image on people's consciousness. We cannot derive the cultural pattern from the functional requirements of the economy operating behind people's backs, for the

---

199. Pollard, *The Genesis,* op. cit., pp. 59, 104, 125.

200. Payne, op. cit., p. 196. For an illustration of the lack of communication between Lancashire and Yorkshire textile business people at the dawn of the factory era in Lancashire, see the testimony of James Ellis in United Kingdom, *Minutes of the Committee on the Woollen Trade,* PP 1806 (268) III, April 18, 1806, p. 8.

201. Biernacki, op. cit., pp. 244–247.

202. *Yorkshire Factory Times,* November 15, 1889, "Elland"; April 29, 1892, p. 7. The innovation, called a "revolving loom box," was perfected in 1856. Gary Firth, "The Bradford Trade in the Nineteenth Century," in D. G. Wright and J. A. Jowitt, editors, *Victorian Bradford* (Bradford: Bradford Metropolitan Council, 1982), p. 17.

differing specifications of labor were both equally well suited for the reproduction of capitalism. Moreover, they could have been used together indiscriminately in one setting. The conditions of the capitalist system may have sustained a cultural outlook, but they did not by themselves inaugurate it; conversely, a cultural template lodged in concrete practice may have served as a moment in the reproduction of the capitalist system, but it did not create a capitalist economy.

The execution of practice incorporates a cultural schema, as Bourdieu always reminds us.[203] Yet even in his studies of kin-based societies, Bourdieu did not consider seriously the next issue: whence, not just culture, but a cultural *system*?[204] If action requires conception, still there is no requirement emanating from the agents themselves that requires diverse practices to follow a single, generalizable idea. The record of anthropological research shows time and again that agents seem to have an inexhaustible capacity for synthesizing contradictory assumptions into a coherent, though perhaps imperfectly consistent, outlook.[205] The systematicity of practices on the shop floor did not reflect some cognitive necessity lodged in the agents themselves that required them to "think" the structure of society or of the factory with a single principle. Such an explanation would reduce culture to a constraint of the contemplative mind, as if agents engaged in practice so as to gaze upon it from without as upon a work of art—and a simple one at that.

In each country, the operative concept of labor had two guises. Within the rude walls of the factory, the producers transmitted "labor" as an imaginative construct of their lifeworld to their employers through their tangible actions and face-to-face social ties; yet, beyond the realm of lived experience, abstract human labor formed the common denominator by which diverse kinds of products with incomparable use values could be brought into relation with each other and exchanged in the market, awakening to life an impersonal world of commodities in motion. The category

203. *Outline of a Theory of Practice* (Cambridge: Cambridge University Press, 1977), p. 97.

204. To be sure, Bourdieu explains that whatever cultural coherence is observed in the operation of a habitus "has no other basis" than the coherence of the social structure from which the habitus was derived. This of course leads to the Durkheimian circle: the systematicity of culture is a correlate of the systematicity of social structure, which relies upon . . . the operation of culture. Pierre Bourdieu, *The Logic of Practice* (Cambridge: Polity Press, 1990), p. 95.

205. Introduction to *The New Institutionalism*, op. cit., p. 18; Terence Turner, "'We Are Parrots,' 'Twins Are Birds': Play of Tropes as Operational Structure," in James Fernandez, editor, *Beyond Metaphor* (Stanford: Stanford University Press, 1991), p. 156.

of labor did not function as a pivotal concept because it expressed the detached logic of the capitalist system, or, from the other side, because it revealed the supremacy of culture in the producers' negotiation of a meaningful order; instead, it bridged these two realms of a market-integrated social structure and the experienced world. If people monitor and organize their conduct in accordance with the commodity form of labor, they reproduce the networks of exchange and of objectified social relations that constitute capitalist society. Georg Lukács, who insisted on linking the dynamic of the capitalist system to the forms of understanding that people used to constitute their practice and experience, gave this insight a classic formulation long ago. "Objectively, in so far as the commodity form facilitates the equal exchange of qualitatively different objects, it can exist only if that formal equality is in fact recognized—at any rate, in this relation, which indeed confers upon them their commodity character," Lukács wrote. "Subjectively, this formal equality of human labor in the abstract is not only the common factor to which the various commodities are reduced; it also becomes the real principle governing the actual production of commodities."[206]

In capitalist society alone could a concept of labor serve as the organizing principle for a multiplicity of humble practices. Where labor has not been subsumed under the commodity form, it may be recognized as the source of material sustenance but it does not take on the social function of structuring the relation of person to person through the exchange of abstract labor time. Definitions of labor may not surface at all in kin-based or precapitalist societies as a principle for structuring social relations; should they arise, they remain subordinate to other categories coordinating social reproduction.[207] Only in capitalist society is labor both a form of understanding and the integrative principle that regulates social relations in society as a whole; only there does it bridge lived experience and the invisible functioning of a system.

206. *History and Class Consciousness* (Cambridge, Massachusetts: The M.I.T. Press, 1971), p. 87. Jürgen Habermas reformulates this discovery in his reading of Marx, although he frames it in terms of a hypostatized disjuncture between system and lifeworld: "The disposal of labor power by the producers represents a category in which the imperatives of social integration and those of system integration meet: as an action it belongs to the lifeworld of the producers, as accomplished work to the functional nexus of the capitalist enterprise and of the economic system as a whole." Jürgen Habermas, *Theorie des kommunikativen Handelns* (Frankfurt am Main: Suhrkamp, 1981), Volume Two, p. 493.

207. Gudeman, op. cit., pp. 20–21, 24; John L. Comaroff and Jean Comaroff, "The Madman and the Migrant: Work and Labor in the Historical Consciousness of a South African People," *American Ethnologist* Volume 14 (1987), pp. 191–209.

If these considerations render intelligible the patterning of practice by a specification of labor as a commodity, yet they do not explain why the concepts of labor differed between Germany and Britain. To answer this question requires us to uncover the historical genesis of the divergent concepts and the conditions governing their transmission in quotidian practice. That is the task in Part Two of this work.

Part 2

PATHWAYS TO THE
DEFINITION OF LABOR
AS A COMMODITY

5   The Disjoint Recognition
of Markets in Britain

The example of "labor" strikingly shows how even the most
abstract categories . . . are a product of historical conditions and
retain their validity only for and within the framework of these
conditions.
            Karl Marx, *Zur Kritik der Politischen Oekonomie*

What method of inquiry will allow us to account for the historical emergence of contrasting specifications of labor as a commodity in Germany and
in Britain? Pairing German with late-developing British textile mills offered
a synchronic comparison for the sake of highlighting the operation of an
intelligible cultural logic. The riddle of beginnings remains: how did the
contrasting concepts of labor as a ware originate? Formulating a response to
this question requires a shift away from the local industrial setting. Looking
at the whole spectrum of textile factories within each country, we can see
that the distinctive British and German assumptions about labor prevailed
in mills that developed under somewhat different regional circumstances.
For example, in Britain similar definitions of labor organized practices in
early-developing Lancashire and in late-developing Yorkshire. The German
specification of labor appeared both in Silesian towns of the east and in the
Wupper Valley of the west. The broad distribution of similar ideas about the
commodity form of labor in each country suggests that concepts of labor
were decisively influenced by the national historical context, not just by
local conditions of production.

   At the level of the countries as wholes, however, development took such
different paths in Germany and Britain that a comparison of these two cases
alone is ill suited for discovering and singling out the motivating conditions
for divergent impressions of labor. I will proceed by examining these primary cases on their own grounds in order to identify the unique combinations of commercial liberty, feudal authority, and urban corporate
institutions that guided their passage to a formal market in wage labor.
Then, to confirm the consistent influence of these conditions upon the form
of labor as a commodity, I will consider how the same elements interlocked

in France and, in a more summary presentation, northern Italy. These cases illustrate differing timings of similar changes entailed by the European path of capitalist development.

Since the concept of labor as an economic resource appears to have a manifest referent—the performance of work—one might suppose that it arises spontaneously in every society, as a natural reflection of activity in the shop, mine, or farmstead. Yet societies have developed sophisticated networks of trade and techniques for managing the use of labor without generating the idea of labor as a general source of economic value.[1] The ancient Greeks, for example, in their philosophical speculations and political treatises recognized only diverse kinds of concrete work, which they did not compare to uncover labor as a separate, unifying element. Jean-Pierre Vernant demonstrated that the Greeks did not believe the various kinds of artisanal trades shared anything by virtue of carrying out the function of production.[2] Neither Greek nor Latin evolved terms to express "the general notion of 'labor'" for the sake of an economic output.[3] Is this cause for wonder? The ancient world also lacked an extensive, unified market in "formally free" wage labor.[4] Could not the absence of such a market have deprived the ancients of an historical requisite for the concept of labor to emerge as an underlying source of value in popular and scholarly reflections?[5]

1. On the development of methods for the calculated exploitation of slave or serf labor, without the appearance of labor in the guise of a commodity, see Maurice Godelier, *The Mental and the Material: Thought, Economy and Society* (London: Verso, 1986), pp. 197–198.

2. Jean-Pierre Vernant, *Myth and Thought Among the Greeks* (London: Routledge & Kegan Paul, 1983), pp. 258, 262–263. In the *Nicomachean Ethics* Aristotle supposes that the goods artisans produce are comparable, not as the creations of labor, but as products for which there is a demand. See Book V, ch. 5, 1133, lines 15–20, in Aristotle, *Ethica Nicomachea*, trans. W. D. Ross (London: Humphrey Milford, 1925).

3. M. I. Finley, *The Ancient Economy* (Berkeley: University of California Press, 1985), p. 81. On the difficulties Roman jurists had in treating what we call labor, see Finley's notes to p. 66 and also Yvon Garlan, "Le Travail libre en Grèce ancienne," in Peter Garnsey, editor, *Non-Slave Labour in the Greco-Roman World* (Cambridge: Cambridge Philological Society, 1980), pp. 6–22. G. E. M. de Ste. Croix has tried to show that the concept of labor power was alive among the Greeks. The clearest reference to abstract labor de Ste. Croix unearths from ancient sources is a remark from *The Republic*. Plato comments that people not intelligent enough to be accepted as full partners in the Republic must "sell the use of their strength." The phrase does not establish a social equivalence between various kinds of work as productive actions. See de Ste. Croix's *The Class Struggle in the Ancient World* (Ithaca: Cornell University Press, 1981), p. 183.

4. The phrase is Max Weber's, of course. *The Protestant Ethic and the Spirit of Capitalism* (New York: Charles Scribner's Sons, 1958), p. 21.

5. Franz Petry, *Der soziale Gehalt der Marxschen Werttheorie* (Jena: Gustav Fischer, 1916), pp. 24–25.

The experience of Renaissance Italy reveals that the appearance of labor as a separate element of economic discourse coincided with a reliance on free artisanal labor to produce for a dynamic export trade. The Italian peninsula led Europe in dismantling feudal labor dues and in developing an extensive trade in the products of a growing population of urban free persons.[6] As early as the 1470s, Italian administrators who wrote on government policy identified labor as the primary source of a state's wealth.[7] A century later, the noted economist Giovanni Botero reaffirmed the centrality of labor when he said that neither the gold mines of the New World nor the landed estates of the Old produced so much wealth as "the industrie of men and the multitude of Artes."[8] But these early Italian commentators still did not analyze labor as a commodity. They did not theorize its price either as it was transmitted from workers to employers or as it was exchanged among independent traders. This task was first conceived by British thinkers who experienced the consolidation of a liberal commercial order in the seventeenth century. They founded the school of classical political economy that blossomed with Adam Smith. Dare we claim that the formal essays of these economic thinkers, who gave clear expression to new perceptions of commercial development, also depict the process by which the concept of labor as a commodity assumed a central role in organizing manufacturing practice?

Among the enduring analysts of capitalist production, Marx alone considered it essential to uncover the genesis of the concepts he inherited and revised. His *Theories of Surplus Value*, although unpublished in his lifetime, offers a monumental survey of the development of economic theory in Britain, home to perhaps the most influential commercial ideas of his time. Yet in his account economic categories have an equivocal status: sometimes they represent popular forms of social consciousness, sometimes they are analytic devices that capture the true movement of economic forces. By way of illustration, Marx asserts that the notion of labor as a general productive factor emerged when the free circulation of laborers between occupations made the worker's vocation incidental to the universal function of produc-

6. Gino Luzzatto, *An Economic History of Italy from the Fall of the Roman Empire to the Beginning of the Sixteenth Century* (London: Routledge & Kegan Paul, 1961), p. 62.

7. Joseph Schumpeter, *History of Economic Analysis* (New York: Oxford University Press, 1954), p. 163.

8. Botero made this observation in *Della ragion di stato libri dieci,* Venice, 1589. The translation is from *A Treatise Concerning the Causes of the Magnificencie and Greatness of Cities* (London: R. Ockould, H. Tomes, 1606), pp. 48–51.

ing something for exchange.[9] This category of abstract labor represented a form of consciousness bound up with historically specific conditions of social life. Marx believed that he refashioned this popular category to arrive at his own concept of the commodity "labor power," his scientific appreciation of the unique form in which human labor was appropriated in capitalist society. In historicizing economic categories, or at least the ones he revised, Marx set up a realm of mechanical development and one of unprescribed invention: the economic ideas that prevail in everyday life are generated involuntarily by the immediate processes of production and exchange; the elaborations of science, or at least his theory of the valorization of *Arbeitskraft*, may represent original fabrications of the solitary intellect. The underdetermination of his own formal economic innovations and the overdetermination, so to speak, of popular economic notions comprise flip sides of an unresolved problem, that of recovering the historical unity of discursive and manufacturing practice. Part Two of this work shows that by misconceiving this problem in his analyses, Marx cast himself as an actor in a history of ideas that was made behind his back. Not that his ideas were "wrong," as so many have prided themselves in complaining. Rather, Marx's discoveries in the field of economics are pivotal for the understanding of capitalist practices, but for reasons upon which he proved unable to reflect.

THE CODIFICATION OF A MARKET IN PRODUCTS

As in the commercially advanced Italian cities, so in Britain the rise of trade in the products of wage labor coincided with the first reflections on labor as a source of wealth. Clement Armstrong, writing in 1535, concluded in the language of his day that "artificialites"—that is, products manufactured by artisans—provided the mainstay of Britain's foreign-exchange earnings. "Suerly the common weale of England muste rise out of the workes of the common people," he said; " . . . the workes of artificialite encressith plenty of money."[10] Although human industry had emerged as a focus of attention for Armstrong, it did not appear to him as something conveyable as a com-

---

9. Karl Marx, *Grundrisse der Kritik der politischen Ökonomie* (Berlin: Dietz Verlag, 1974), p. 25.

10. R. H. Tawney and Eileen Power, editors, *Tudor Economic Documents* (London: Longmans, Green and Co., 1924), Volume III, p. 127.

modity or as an ingredient that determined the relative prices of goods.[11] When the revolution initiated in 1640 swept away restrictions on internal trade, labor time emerged as a national resource with a metric and as the standard of the value of transmittable goods.[12]

Britain drifted into the waters of a formally free market by default.[13] In the course of the revolution, the executive government lost its arbitrary powers over local authorities.[14] The dismantling of the prerogative courts made economic regulation a matter for Parliament.[15] But Parliament, in contrast to the Privy Council, proved too unwieldy a body to pass significant bills of regulation for the country as a whole.[16] The tortuous history of legislation after the Restoration shows that corporate regulation ended not because of a growing allegiance to laissez-faire but as a result of the deadlock between diverse commercial interests.[17]

Britain's unintended transition to a formally free commercial regime was fundamentally different from the more abrupt entry experienced on the Continent. There the passage to a new order could be debated in some measure and decreed. In France the revolutionary legislation of 1791, which abolished provincial and urban guild restrictions on trade, may not have transformed business mentality overnight; nonetheless, these laws marked

11. Armstrong did not conceive of labor as an item with a cost. The advantage of the growth of trade and industry is that it sets "common people daily to worke in a right ordre of the common weale to kepe theym out of idelnes frome working syne and myschif." Ibid.

12. M. Beer, *Early British Economics* (London: George Allen & Unwin, 1938), pp. 170, 172–174, 215.

13. Harold Laski, *The Rise of Liberalism: The Philosophy of a Business Civilization* (New York: Harper and Brothers, 1936), p. 117. "Private enterprise," Hobsbawm reminds us, "was and is blind." E. J. Hobsbawm, "The Seventeenth Century in the Development of Capitalism," *Science and Society* Volume XXIV, Number 2 (Spring 1960), p. 101. Eric Roll, *A History of Economic Thought* (New York: Prentice-Hall, 1942), pp. 51–52.

14. G. D. Ramsay, "Industrial Laisser-Faire and the Policy of Cromwell," *The Economic History Review* Volume XVI, Number 2 (1946), pp. 108–109.

15. Christopher Hill, "A Bourgeois Revolution?" in J. G. A. Pocock, editor, *Three British Revolutions: 1641, 1688, 1776* (Princeton: Princeton University Press, 1980), pp. 117–118.

16. B. E. Supple, *Commercial Crisis and Change in England 1600–1642* (Cambridge: Cambridge University Press, 1959), p. 231.

17. J. P. Cooper, "Economic Regulation and the Cloth Industry in Seventeenth-Century England," *Transactions of the Royal Historical Society*, Fifth series, Volume 20 (London: Printed for The Society by Butler & Tanner, 1970), pp. 93–99. Lawrence Stone emphasizes the unintended consequences of the revolution in "The Bourgeois Revolution of Seventeenth-Century England Revisited," in Geoff Eley and William Hunt, editors, *Reviving the English Revolution* (London: Verso, 1988), p. 287. Some legislation of local or restricted application continued to stray from the rules of formally free exchange. As late as 1773, Parliament passed an act regulating wages on behalf of the journeymen silk weavers of London and Middlesex. Ephraim Lipson, *The Economic History of England*, Volume III (London: Adam and Charles Black, 1948), p. 270.

a dramatic break in the comprehension of commercial intercourse. In Prussia the bold edicts of 1810 serve as a signpost for the shift to a formal market society. The experience of discontinuity on the Continent versus a prolonged transition in Britain also points to a conjunctural difference in the institutional settings under which tradespeople came to envision the conveyance of labor as a commodity.

THE COMPASS OF THE COMMODITY

The launching of the new market society in England was a work of blindness, an interpretation of the sale of labor that followed one of imagination. William Petty was perhaps the first British economist to combine a focus on labor as a creator of wealth with a systematic account of the determination of a commodity's exchange value.[18] All too often his ideas appear as precursors to more refined theories of labor rather than as signals of abiding features of British commercial thinking. In *A Treatise of Taxes and Contributions*, published in 1662, Petty judged that both land and labor served as "natural denominations" of the value of all goods: "that is, we ought to say, a Ship or garment is worth such a measure of Land, with such another measure of Labour."[19] The dual standards of land and labor remain a part of his thinking even when he focuses upon the more specific question of the principles that determine the relative prices of commodities:

> Suppose a man could with his own hands plant a certain scope of Land with Corn, that is, could Digg, or Plough, Harrow, Weed, Reap, Carry home, Thresh, and Winnow so much as the Husbandry of this Land requires; and had withal Seed wherewith to sowe the same. I say, that when this man hath subducted his seed out of the proceed of his Harvest, and also, what himself hath both eaten and given to others in exchange for Clothes, and other Natural necessaries; that the remainder of Corn is the natural and true Rent of Land for that year. . . . But a further, though collateral question may be, how much English money this Corn or Rent is worth? I answer, so much as the money, which another single man can save, within the same time, over and above his expence, if he imployed himself wholly to produce and make it; *viz.* Let another man go travel into a Countrey where is Silver, there Dig it, Refine it, bring it to the

18. Marx called Petty the founder of political economy. *Theorien über den Mehrwert* (Stuttgart: J. H. W. Dietz, 1919), Volume I, p. 1.

19. Charles Henry Hull, editor, *The Economic Writings of Sir William Petty* (Cambridge: Cambridge University Press, 1899), Volume I, pp. 44, 68.

same place where the other man planted his Corn; Coyne it &c the same person, all the while of his working for Silver, gathering also food for his necessary livelihood, and procuring himself covering, &c. I say, the Silver of the one, must be esteemed of equal value with the Corn of the other.[20]

Commentators unable to divest themselves of prior acquaintance with Marx are wont to assume that Petty anticipates Marx's premise that goods produced with equal amounts of labor have matching values.[21] But Petty asserts only that the value of one commodity, corn, equals the value of another, silver, if the time spent producing them is equal, *after* deducting the expense, in labor and seed, of their production.[22] He adds, "The *neat* proceed of the Silver is the price of the whole *neat* proceed of the Corn."[23] There is no assurance that the prior expenses of the corn farm and the silver business are equal or that the labor expended by the producers for subsistence is on average equal. In fact, Petty's descriptions make this improbable, because the land makes an independent addition to the subsistence of the husbandman. Petty does not offer a theory in which the value of a product can be determined by adding up the costs of its components. He contends that the value of the product is determined by the *surplus* land and labor devoted to its production—a tracer for identifying original features of the British concept of labor as a commodity.[24]

20. *A Treatise of Taxes and Contributions*, in ibid., p. 43.

21. Marx himself misconstrued Petty so. Marx, *Theorien über den Mehrwert*, op. cit., Volume I, p. 1. Shichiro Matsukawa, "An Essay on the Historical Uniqueness of Petty's Labour Theory of Value," *Hitotsubashi Journal of Economics* Volume 5, Number 2 (January 1965), p. 3. Alessandro Roncaglia summarizes Petty's reception by economists familiar with the Marxist tradition in *Petty: The Origins of Political Economy* (Armonk, New York: M. E. Sharpe, 1985), pp. 79, 112. Marx found unresolvable contradictions in Petty's account: on the one hand, Petty seems to imply that the magnitude of a product's value is determined by labor time; on the other, land makes a contribution of its own to exchange value. Marx supposed that this inconsistency appeared because Petty appreciated labor only hazily. In his view, Petty merged two aspects of it which ought to remain separate: "Labour as a source of exchange value," Marx wrote, "is confused with labor as the source of use-value; in this case it presupposes material provided by nature (land)." *Theorien*, op. cit., Volume 1, p. 11.

22. Here I follow the noteworthy lead of David McNally in *Political Economy and the Rise of Capitalism* (Berkeley: University of California Press, 1988), p. 51.

23. Ibid., p. 43. My own emphasis.

24. Petty attempts to equate the value of land and labor in several manuscripts. But in so doing he shifts from looking at labor as the determinant of the relative prices of commodities to looking at labor as the real standard of those prices. See Shichiro Matsukawa, "Sir William Petty: An Unpublished Manuscript," *Hitotsubashi Journal of Economics* Volume 17, Number 2 (February 1977), p. 48.

Most wage earners and petty commodity producers in seventeenth-century Britain derived part of their subsistence from farming their own parcels, as did Petty's father, who combined agriculture with weaving.[25] Analysts of early industrialization and the putting-out system have long observed that laborers in these situations do not receive equal returns on the time they spend on subsistence farming and that spent on manufacture for exchange. Depending on the sufficiency of their holdings, they can earn far more or far less per unit of time devoted to manufacture than to agriculture at home.[26] Adam Smith commented upon one side of the anomaly: where cottagers derived their subsistence from their own agriculture, he said, their manufacture "comes frequently cheaper to market than would otherwise be suitable to its nature."[27] The price of the product need not cover the labor invested in it, because it does not cover the workers' subsistence. Marx, too, observed that production was not governed by the laws of exchange value if independent workers directly produced their own means of subsistence.[28] What seemed an incidental exception in Smith's century and Marx's was still a frequent occurrence in Petty's. Rather than formulate a "law" of value that was anything but, Petty's examples assume that laborers may have an independent means of subsistence outside the market.[29]

25. E. Strauss, *Sir William Petty: Portrait of a Genius* (London: Bodley Head, 1954), p. 20; David Seward, "The Devonshire Cloth Industry in the Early Seventeenth Century," in Roger Burt, editor, *Industry and Society in the South-West* (Essex: University of Essex, 1970), p. 42; John T. Swain, *Industry Before the Industrial Revolution: North-East Lancashire c. 1500–1640* (Manchester: Manchester University Press, 1986), p. 121; Ian Blanchard, "Labour Productivity and Work Psychology in the English Mining Industry," *The Economic History Review* Second series, Volume XXXI, Number 1 (1978), pp. 11, 13.

26. The weavers who set up the first trade union in Lancashire in 1756 complained that the labor of those who relied mostly on inherited farms "can never be reckoned upon an Average with those who have nothing but their Trade to subsist themselves and their family by." Alfred P. Wadsworth and Julia de Lacy Mann, *The Cotton Trade and Industrial Lancashire 1600–1780* (Manchester: Manchester University Press, 1931), p. 317.

27. *An Inquiry into the Nature and Causes of the Wealth of Nations* (Chicago: The University of Chicago Press, 1976 [1776]), pp. 130–131. Smith consigned the division between subsistence farming and manufacture for exchange to "ancient times" and "poor countries."

28. *Das Kapital* (Berlin: Dietz Verlag, 1980), Volume I, p. 184.

29. By far the most thorough and acute analysis of Petty's economic theories appears in Silva Kühnis's *Die wert- und preistheoretischen Ideen William Pettys* (Winterthur: P. G. Keller, 1960). Part of Kühnis's contribution consists in showing that the standard interpretations of Petty start from incorrect premises: Petty, she shows, does not try to establish labor as a measure of relative exchange values, nor does he consider the exchange value of labor equal to the costs of laborers' subsistence, nor does he aim at showing that the value of a product can be deduced by some formula from the cost of the land and labor employed upon it (pp. 161, 190, 81). Instead, in an exhaustive survey of his ideas, she shows that Petty takes on an impossible task, that of arriving at a universal measure of use value based on land, labor, and their products.

The manufacturer of silver in Petty's excerpted paragraph is not a wage earner but an independent producer who covers the expenses of his undertaking.[30] He has the capital on hand for maintaining himself, lays out the capital needed for the production process, and manages the transport of the goods. By comparison, Petty banished the propertyless wage-earner from the liberal commercial order.

> It is observed by Clothiers, and others, who employ great numbers of poor people, that when corn is extremely plentiful, that the Labour of the poor is proportionably dear; And scarce to be had at all (so licentious are they who labour only to eat, or rather to drink). Wherefore when so many Acres sown with Corn, as do usually produce a sufficient store for the Nation, shall produce perhaps double to what is expected or necessary; it seems not unreasonable that this common blessing of God, should be applied to the common good of all people . . . than the same should be abused, by the vile and brutish part of mankind.[31]

Petty dismissed wage labor as something inferior, which ought not be treated as a market commodity at all. He recommended instead that the government fix wage rates by law.[32] "The Law that appoints such Wages," he concluded, "should allow the Labourer but just wherewithall to live."[33] From Petty's standpoint, what an outsider might call labor power has no price set by the market.

In fine, Petty's text marks the emergence of a concept of labor as a commodity restricted to *surplus* labor traded freely in a market, embodied in a product, and vended by independent commodity producers.[34] Petty was not alone among seventeenth-century writers in assuming that labor as a marketable commodity was traded between self-employed workers. Nicholas Barbon, a successful building contractor, is remembered for picturing trade

30. I owe this observation to M. Beer, *Early British Economics* (London: George Allen & Unwin, 1938), p. 168.

31. "Political Arithmetick," originally published 1690, reprinted in Hull, editor, op. cit., Volume 1, pp. 274–275.

32. *A Treatise of Taxes*, op. cit., p. 52.

33. Ibid., p. 87. If the justices allow wages to rise to double the level needed for subsistence, Petty adds, the laborer "works but half so much as he could have done, and otherwise would; which is a loss to the Publick of the fruit of so much labour." Does not Petty exclude the laborer from the "public"?

34. The emphasis upon the free exchange of labor when it is above that required for subsistence appears also in Dudley North's tract of 1690. Beer, *Early British Economics*, op. cit., p. 210.

as "nothing else but an exchange of one mans labour for another."[35] Barbon assumed that this trade took place between independent tradespeople, such as butchers, bakers, and drapers. In the confused succession of oppositional religious and political ideas of the seventeenth century, labor acquired diverse meanings. But the critics of the old order, from worldly critics of idle monks to the Puritan theorists, were united in one supposition: when they contrived explanations for the dignity of labor, they sanctified only the free craftspeople. Their formulations, which amounted to crude versions of a labor theory of value, rested upon the proprietorship of one's person and capacities that the dependent wage laborers, by contrast, had in the popular opinion forfeited once and for all.[36]

These writers may have occupied themselves with general principles, but they did not try to establish a systematic science. Most of the economic thinkers per se were entrepreneurs who wanted to enrich themselves by convincing others of the advantages of adopting certain policies.[37] Petty may have written his most notable work, *A Treatise of Taxes and Contributions*, in the hope of advancing his fortune as surveyor general in Ireland.[38] Petty and the clever marketers of the time drew upon premises that they expected others to understand easily. They did not create, but expressed, the assump-

35. In Nicholas Barbon, *An Apology for the Builder* (London: For Cave Pullen, 1685), p. 67.

36. The preceding comment draws upon Christopher Hill's studies in *Society and Puritanism in Pre-Revolutionary England* (New York: Schocken Books, 1964), pp. 133–134, 143–144, and his comments in "Pottage for Freeborn Englishmen: Attitudes to Wage Labour in the Sixteenth and Seventeenth Centuries," in C. H. Feinstein, editor, *Socialism, Capitalism and Economic Growth: Essays Presented to Maurice Dobb* (Cambridge: Cambridge University Press, 1967), p. 347. See also Beer, *Early British Economics*, op. cit., pp. 174–175. Several interpreters have concluded that John Locke could not admit the contractual sale of labor power, only the sale of the produce or completed service of labor. The servant who sold labor power itself had, like a slave, lost juridical autonomy. Locke also suggested that independent artisans who merchandized their own products were singularly productive for society. *Some Considerations of the Consequences of the Lowering of Interest, and Raising the Value of Money*, 1696, reprinted in Patrick Hyde Kelly, editor, *Locke on Money* (Oxford: Clarendon Press, 1991), Volume One, pp. 241–242; James Tully, *A Discourse on Property: John Locke and his Adversaries* (Cambridge: Cambridge University Press, 1980), pp. 138, 142; Keith Tribe, *Land, Labour and Economic Discourse* (London: Routledge & Kegan Paul, 1978), pp. 48–51.

37. For Josiah Child, Nicholas Barbon, and Dudley North, see William Letwin, *The Origins of Scientific Economics* (London: Methuen and Co., 1963), pp. 37, 54–55, 184–189.

38. Letwin, op. cit., p. 141; Strauss, op. cit., pp. 123, 176. Petty reflected upon a general denominator of values of goods not as a theorist but as an advocate with a practical goal before him. To rebut claims that England's economy was in decline, he sought a measure of value apart from the fluctuating worth of currency.

tions of their age.[39] Their ideas about labor corresponded to those held by many common people, as is confirmed in the popular sentiments that came to the surface following the crisis of 1640.

The Levellers, the most inventive publishers of democratic tracts during the revolutionary period, were united by aspirations for change rather than by a coherent program. Nonetheless, the statements of the Levellers about the franchise reveal that for the common people of Britain, the divide between the sale of wage labor and of products made with labor was fraught with significance. As C. B. Macpherson perceptively observed, the Levellers supposed that the capacity to labor was a form of property "not metaphorically but essentially."[40] People who sold their labor power for a wage lost their birthright and claim to freedom, as if they had permanently alienated a piece of land.[41] They no longer had the right to exclude others from the use and enjoyment of their labor power, and so they had forfeited their property in it altogether. Macpherson adduces evidence that prominent spokespersons for the Levellers used this reasoning to deny the franchise to wage earners.[42] By the same logic, independent artisans, however penurious, sold only the products of their labor and thereby retained a claim to freedom and voice in government.[43]

39. No wonder some of the most notable economic treatises of the seventeenth century have remained anonymous. J. R. McCulloch, editor, *Early English Tracts on Commerce* (Cambridge: Cambridge University Press, 1954 [1856]), p. xiii.

40. C. B. Macpherson, *The Political Theory of Possessive Individualism* (Oxford: Oxford University Press, 1962), p. 153.

41. Christopher Hill, "The Poor and the People," in *The Collected Essays of Christopher Hill* (Amherst: University of Massachusetts Press, 1986), p. 250. Hill, "Pottage for Freeborn Englishmen," op. cit., pp. 342–346. Through the end of the seventeenth century, the term *to employ* applied to the recruitment of an abject servant rather than to the wage-labor relation in general. E. J. Hundert, "Market Society and Meaning in Locke's Political Philosophy," *Journal of the History of Philosophy* Volume XV, Number 1 (January 1977), p. 41.

42. See also Keith Thomas, "The Levellers and the Franchise," in G. E. Aylmer, editor, *The Interregnum: The Quest for Settlement 1646–1660* (London: Macmillan & Co., 1972), p. 68. Christopher Hill has endorsed Macpherson's interpretation, but others contend that the evidence can be read several ways. See the literature cited in ibid., p. 208. Macpherson's interpretation of the franchise proposals supposes that the locution *servants* referred to all wage laborers. He defends his position in "Servants and Labourers in Seventeenth-Century England," in his *Democratic Theory: Essays in Retrieval* (Oxford: Clarendon Press, 1973), pp. 207–223, and in *The Rise and Fall of Economic Justice and Other Papers* (Oxford: Oxford University Press, 1985), p. 153. Christopher Hill unearths evidence in support of Macpherson in "Pottage for Freeborn Englishmen," op. cit., pp. 341–342.

43. The political theorist James Harrington also excluded wage laborers from the franchise on the grounds that they were not "freemen." C. B. Macpherson, "Harrington's 'Opportunity State,'" in Charles Webster, editor, *The Intellectual Revolution of the Seventeenth Century* (London: Routledge & Kegan Paul, 1974), p. 42. J. G. A. Pocock sketches the intellectual setting for reasoning about the franchise in Eugene Kamenka and R. S. Neale, editors, "Early Modern

The outlook of the Levellers, C. B. Macpherson has suggested, reflected their experience of freedom and competition in the market.[44] Among their ranks were many small craftsmen who lacked freehold land or membership in a chartered trading corporation.[45] They learned all too well that workers retained their liberty and self-direction only on condition that they protected their status as independent producers.[46] The semi-servile position of wage earners influenced the vision of the most revolutionary segment of the Levellers' movement. Gerrard Winstanley, a leader of the Diggers, declared it iniquitous for people to work for wages.[47] "We can as well live under a foreign enemy working for day wages," he said, "as under our own brethren." He recommended that the law forbid the institution of wage labor altogether.[48]

When political advisers, merchants, and poor artisans converged upon the view that the only kind of labor sold with a proper commercial value was that of the independent producer, all did so for the same reason: the institutions of work in Britain appeared to reveal labor as a commodity only under this guise. By 1690, according to Gregory King's appraisal, the total of la-

---

Capitalism—The Augustan Perception," in his *Feudalism, Capitalism and Beyond* (Canberra: Australian National University Press, 1975), p. 65.

44. Macpherson, *The Political Theory of Possessive Individualism*, op. cit., pp. 121, 150.

45. Thomas N. Corns, *Uncloistered Virtue: English Political Literature, 1640–1660* (Oxford: Clarendon Press, 1992), pp. 130–131; Christopher Hill, *The World Turned Upside Down* (New York: Viking Press, 1972), pp. 91–94; Fenner Brockway, *Britain's First Socialists: The Levellers, Agitators and Diggers of the English Revolution* (London: Quartet Books, 1980), p. 116; G. E. Aylmer, "Gentlemen Levellers?" *Past & Present* Number 49 (November 1970), pp. 121, 124.

46. George Unwin, *Industrial Organization in the Sixteenth and Seventeenth Centuries* (Oxford: Clarendon Press, 1904), pp. 200–201. Pamphleteers of many sorts commented that people who did not have the working capital needed to maintain their independence could not exchange their labor at its true commercial value. The economist Andrew Yarranton, for example, advanced a plan in 1677 to protect from this abuse laborers who lacked funds. He proposed that a national bank be established from which common people could receive loans. Yarranton told workers that after receipt of some capital, "thy fingers and hands are thy own, and now they are employed for thy benefit and advantage, and not for others." The handicraft makers who lacked sufficient capital could not command the full value of their labor in the market: the "poor Man is forced many times to buy his Materials he makes his Commodity with, with some his own Trade, and is thereby forced to buy dear, and sell cheap. . . . The poor Handicraft Man is forced to let part of that which is gained in the Commodity, go to one of his own Trade." Andrew Yarranton, *England's Improvement by Sea and Land* (London: R. Everingham, 1677), pp. 169, 172. Without sufficient working capital, workers sacrificed the labor they invested in the product.

47. Hill, *World Turned Upside Down*, op. cit., p. 103.

48. Quoted by Christopher Hill in "Discussion," of "Conference Paper" by Keith Thomas, "Work and Leisure in Pre-Industrial Society," *Past & Present* Number 29 (December 1964), p. 63.

boring people and out-servants had reached one-quarter of the population. This group did not on average earn enough, he thought, to cover the price of their subsistence.[49] Latter-day research confirms the dismal view that people who depended only on wages could not maintain themselves. How they survived remains as much a riddle for modern economists as it was for contemporaries.[50] Roger North complained that the clothiers of their day kept dependent laborers "but just alive," so that the desperate employees resorted to theft or escaped starvation only by receiving poor relief.[51] Wage earners were called, not "workers," but "the poor," those in need of benefactory employment or handouts.[52]

The low remuneration for wage earners could not help but shape the development of notions of labor as a commodity. People viewed wage labor not as a means of supporting themselves but as a supplement to a primary source of sustenance such as a smallholding.[53] One retrospective calculation of the incomes of the common people found that a licensed beggar in the seventeenth century could expect higher proceeds than the average wage-

49. See chart in Peter Laslett, *The World We Have Lost* (London: Methuen and Co., 1971), p. 36.

50. Alice Clark, *Working Life of Women in the Seventeenth Century* (New York: Augustus Kelley, 1968 [1919]), pp. 69–90. Historians have corroborated King's estimates of the proportions of the laboring poor among the total population. D. C. Coleman, "Labour in the English Economy of the Seventeenth Century," *The Economic History Review* Second series, Volume VIII, Number 3 (April 1956), p. 283.

51. Cooper, "Economic Regulation," op. cit., p. 94. "Many poor," said Matthew Hale in 1683, "must take such wages as they are not able to live upon." Matthew Hale, *A Discourse Touching Provision for the Poor* (London: H. Hills, 1683), p. 18.

52. David Ogg, *England in the Reigns of James II and William III* (Oxford: Clarendon Press, 1955), p. 34; Gustaf F. Steffen, *Studien zur Geschichte der englischen Lohnarbeiter* (Stuttgart: Hobbing & Büchle, 1901), Volume One, p. 483; J. Haynes, *Great Britain's Glory; Or, an Account of the Great Numbers of Poor Employ'd in the Woollen and Silk Manufactories* (London: J. Marshall, 1715), p. 85. As wage labor and poor relief were fused in public perception, taxpayers feared the introduction of new industries. Roger North, *A Discourse of the Poor Shewing the Pernicious Tendency of the Laws Now in Force* (London: M. Cooper, 1753), p. 62. Christopher Hill, *The Century of Revolution 1603–1714* (Edinburgh: Thomas Nelson and Sons, 1961), pp. 26–27. In Wiltshire, large clothiers had to grant a security deposit for permission to settle employees in a parish. G. D. Ramsay, *The Wiltshire Woollen Industry in the Sixteenth and Seventeenth Centuries* (London: Frank Cass & Co., 1965), p. 129. "Those places, where there are the most Poor," Matthew Hale wrote, "consist for the most part of Trades-men." Op. cit., p. 7. The "Trades-men" themselves were distinguished from their employees by the circumstance that they did not have to depend upon their labor for subsistence.

53. A. L. Beier, *Masterless Men: The Vagrancy Problem in England 1560–1640* (New York: Methuen, 1985), p. 26; Donald Woodward, "Wage Rates and Living Standards in Pre-Industrial England," *Past & Present* Number 91 (May 1981), p. 43; Smith, *Wealth of Nations*, op. cit., p. 130.

earner.[54] Wage laborers as such could not survive as market actors.[55] People in trade and industry who pictured the emerging commercial society saw labor as the wellspring of prosperity,[56] but under these historical circumstances the sale of labor power was ill suited to serve as a model for the exchange of labor as a commodity in general.

The depressed level of wages in England represented a work of political art. The process of enclosing land, which continued through the seventeenth century, deprived people of their livelihood in the countryside faster than new possibilities opened up in urban or rural industry.[57] Where a balance between the labor supply and need for labor did reappear, the employing class used the machinery of local government to restrain any wage increases.[58] The Statute of Apprentices, dating from Elizabeth's reign, gave justices of the peace the responsibility for fixing wage rates for common occupations. These officials were supposed to set minimum levels of remuneration in times of need. In practice, during the seventeenth century they generally confined their efforts to setting maximum rates.[59] Employers who violated the standards by paying a higher wage were subject to fines.[60] The justices set wages at low levels with the expectation that wage earners would find additional support as agricultural tenants or as beneficiaries of poor

54. Beier, op. cit., p. 27.

55. James E. Thorold Rogers, *Six Centuries of Work and Wages: The History of English Labour* (London: George Allen & Unwin, 1884), p. 353. So closely did writers associate poverty with manufacture that they oscillated between asserting that the poor were needed to work up tradespeople's materials and that the materials were important for giving the poor something to do. "Manufacture seems a kind of debt to the laborious part of the people," wrote William Petyt in 1680. William Petyt, *Britannia Languens; Or, A Discourse of Trade* (London: For T. Dring and S. Couch, 1680), pp. 26–27. See also Haynes, op. cit., pp. 83, 85. Robert Reyce said of Suffolk in 1618, "Where the clothiers do dwell or have dwelt, there are found the greatest number of the poor." Quoted by Hill, *The Century of Revolution*, op. cit., p. 25.

56. John Bellers, *Essays About the Poor, Manufactures, Trade, Plantations, and Immorality* (London: T. Sowle, 1699), p. 10; North, op. cit., p. 66.

57. E. C. K. Gonner, "The Progress of Inclosure During the Seventeenth Century," *The English Historical Review* Volume XXIII (July 1908), p. 495.

58. Michael Walzer emphasizes that this legislation was composed in response to the growth of a class of wage laborers who were perceived as "masterless men." *The Revolution of the Saints: A Study in the Origins of Radical Politics* (Cambridge, Massachusetts: Harvard University Press, 1965), p. 200. Dobb shows that diverse legislative measures to lower wages were invoked whenever the supply of labor became inadequate. Maurice Dobb, *Studies in the Development of Capitalism* (London: George Routledge & Sons, 1946), p. 234.

59. Herbert Heaton, *The Yorkshire Woollen and Worsted Industries* (2d ed. Oxford: Clarendon Press, 1965), p. 112.

60. Even during the dislocations of the Interregnum, the machinery of government enforced official maximum wage rates. Margaret James, *Social Problems and Policy During the Puritan Revolution 1640–1660* (London: Routledge & Kegan Paul, 1966), p. 175.

relief.[61] In some instances, local officials did not simply block pay increases; they specified a new standard that fell below the previous average.[62] Alice Clark, after comparing the cost of food with the legislated wages, concluded, "The Justices would like to have exterminated wage earners, who were an undesirable class in the community."[63]

Especially in the fledgling textile industries, employers used the statutory restrictions on wages to impede the development of a market in wage labor. In 1673 the justices of Lancashire supported the employers by republishing maximum legal wage rates in the textile trade "to the end that masters and mistresses of families shall not soe frequently tempte a good servante to leave his service by offering more or greater wages than the law permits."[64] Magistrates responded to employers' reports of workers' dickering over wages by ordering strict enforcement of the maximum rates, which covered men and women regardless of the form of wage.[65] In the textile regions justices issued and revised wage assessments most frequently, and in greatest detail, in areas such as Wiltshire, where the small independent clothier was fast disappearing and the divide between master and journeyman had grown widest.[66] Exactly

61. North, op. cit., p. 43; Rogers, op. cit., p. 422.

62. Unwin, op. cit., pp. 119–120.. W. G. Hoskins, *Industry, Trade and People in Exeter 1688–1800* (Manchester: Manchester University Press, 1968), p. 22.

63. Clark, op. cit., p. 90. See also James E. Thorold Rogers's comparison of living costs with mandated wages in *A History of Agriculture and Prices in England,* Volume V: *1583–1702* (Oxford: Clarendon Press, 1887), pp. 830, 832. Yet some economic theorists cautioned that wage lists should not make laborers destitute. Joyce Oldham Appleby, *Economic Thought and Ideology in Seventeenth-Century England* (Princeton: Princeton University Press, 1978), pp. 147–148.

64. Wadsworth and de Lacy Mann, op. cit., p. 50. The word *industry* remained synonymous with textile manufacture in the seventeenth century. C. H. Wilson, "Trade, Society and the State," in *The Cambridge Economic History of Europe,* Volume IV (Cambridge: Cambridge University Press, 1967), p. 491.

65. The magistrates at the Doncaster sessions received complaints in the 1640s that "servants refuse to worke for reasonable wages, and cannot be hired for competent allowance as formerlye, makeing advantage of the much business of the times." Heaton, op. cit., pp. 111, 114. Herbert Heaton, "The Assessment of Wages in the West Riding of Yorkshire in the Seventeenth and Eighteenth Centuries," *The Economic Journal* Volume XXIV, No. 94 (June 1914), p. 219. In the textile trade, the wages approved by the justices often applied to men and women alike. In agricultural work, women's wages were established below men's. For an example of women spinners appealing for a new official wage, see Buchanan Sharp, *In Contempt of All Authority: Rural Artisans and Riot in the West of England, 1586–1660* (Berkeley: University of California Press, 1980), p. 78. For women's wage assessments in other endeavors, see Clark, op. cit., pp. 66, 72.

66. In Wiltshire wage rates were proclaimed each year and the small, independent textile entrepreneurs comprised a dying class. Ramsay, *The Wiltshire Woollen Industry,* op. cit., pp. 125, 129. On the early demise of the small producer in the West of England, see Wadsworth and de Lacy Mann, op. cit., p. 386.

in the regions where the first groups of people dependent on only their wages emerged, there statutory restrictions ensured that labor power was not treated or conceived of as a market commodity.[67] The mass of rural laborers were "brutally repressed," in Walzer's words, but "they were not integrated into a modern economic system."[68]

The reflections of Rice Vaughan brilliantly illustrate how people of the era segregated labor power from market commodities. In one of the earliest analyses of monetary value, published in 1655, Vaughan sought to measure changes in the worth of money due to changes in its supply over more than a century. The prices of commodities—"Cloth, Linnen, Leather, and the like," he said—varied in response to the oscillations of fashion, the supply of raw materials, and improvements in manufacturing technology. On these grounds, fluctuations in the cost of buying these ordinary goods could not measure changes in the purchasing power of money. Vaughan reckoned that labor was unique because its real price was untouched by supply and demand. The "Wisdom of the Statute" fixed wages at the bare level needed for the necessaries of life. So "there is only one thing, from whence we may certainly track out prices," he concluded, "and that is the price of Labourers and Servants Wages, especially those of the meaner sort."[69] Vaughan reversed the modern technique of consumer price indexing. Instead of recording changes in prices to calculate the real purchasing power of wages, he used adjustments in the money wages of labor over decades to chart the shifting value of money.[70] Labor power served as the only orienting point,

67. Compare C. G. A. Clay, *Economic Expansion and Social Change: England 1500–1700* (Cambridge: Cambridge University Press, 1984), Volume II, pp. 12, 93 with Heaton, *The Yorkshire Woollen and Worsted Industries*, op. cit., p. 114; Rogers, op. cit., p. 428.

68. Walzer's interpretation emphasizes the exclusion of wage laborers from the new regime of disciplined work. Op. cit., p. 230. Macpherson, *The Political Theory of Possessive Individualism*, op. cit., pp. 215–220, presents John Locke as a kind of bourgeois theorist who takes for granted the free marketing of both products and of labor power. E. J. Hundert has convincingly shown that, to the contrary, the concept of a free market in labor power is absent from Locke's writings. Locke assumed that laborers could not conduct themselves as reasonable market actors; coercion and imprisonment were necessary to improve productivity. E. J. Hundert, "The Making of *Homo Faber*: John Locke Between Ideology and History," *Journal of the History of Ideas* Volume XXXIII, Number 1 (January–March 1972), pp. 5, 17; Hundert, "Market Society and Meaning," op. cit., pp. 33–34, 40–44. Perhaps due to the fact of wage regulation, Locke referred to agricultural workers who bargained over the harvest they would accept in lieu of a money wage but not over the money amount of the wage. Locke, op. cit., pp. 237–238.

69. Rice Vaughan, *A Discourse of Coin and Coinage*, 1675, reprinted in J. R. McCulloch, editor, *A Select Collection of Scarce and Valuable Tracts on Money* (London: Political Economy Club, 1856), pp. 58–59.

70. This thought comes from Marian Bowley's article "Some Seventeenth Century Contributions to the Theory of Value," *Economica* Volume XXX, Number 118 (May 1963), p. 137.

because it comprised the only money good excluded from market fluctuations. Until the early eighteenth century, not only people of genius like Vaughan and Petty but almost everyone who speculated about the proper determination of wages endorsed stringent regulation.[71]

By the laws of preindustrial England, persons not lawfully retained, apprenticed, or claiming an agricultural holding were compelled to serve any farmer or tradesman needing labor.[72] Especially if a temporary scarcity of labor arose, the local authorities forced unoccupied men and women into useful occupations.[73] The economic compulsion of a market economy did not suffice for the procurement of labor; extra-economic sanctions made work a legal obligation.[74] Accordingly, Sir William Blackstone, in his famous *Commentaries* on English law, published from 1765 through 1769, treated the relation between the employer and the laborer as one based not on contract but on status. The labor transaction, Blackstone averred, was "founded in convenience, whereby a man is directed to call in the assistance of others, where his own skill and labour will not be sufficient to answer the cares incumbent upon him."[75] Here, as in the remainder of his discussion of the labor transaction, Blackstone fails to specify whether the subordinate satisfying this "call" for aid does so by consent. To the contrary, Blackstone's treatment of the matter, the definitive codification of mid-eighteenth-

71. Edgar S. Furniss, *The Position of the Laborer in a System of Nationalism. A Study in the Labor Theories of the Later English Mercantilists* (Boston: Houghton Mifflin, 1920), pp. 168–169; Roll, op. cit., p. 97; William Sheppard, *Englands Balme* (London: J. Cottrel, 1657), p. 165. Jürgen Kuczynski cites a revealing body of primary sources: *Die Geschichte der Lage der Arbeiter in England von 1640 bis in die Gegenwart* (2d ed. Berlin: Tribüne, 1954), Volume IV, Part One, pp. 226–230.

72. W. S. Holdsworth, *A History of English Law*, Volume IV (Boston: Little, Brown and Company, 1924), pp. 380–381; W. S. Holdsworth, *A History of English Law*, Volume XI (Boston: Little, Brown and Company, 1938), p. 475. The law applied to both men and women. George Howell, *Labour Legislation, Labour Movements, and Labour Leaders* (London: T. Fisher Unwin, 1902), pp. 39 ff.

73. For examples from the second half of the seventeenth century, see Keith Kelsall, *Wage Regulation Under the Statute of Artificers* (London: Methuen & Co., 1938), p. 30. Daniel Defoe thought it advisable that persons be compelled to work in the particular occupations where they were most needed, even if they were not on public relief. See *The Great Law of Subordination Consider'd*, 1724, reprinted in Stephen Copley, editor, *Literature and the Social Order in Eighteenth-Century England* (London: Croom Helm, 1984), p. 147. Dobb supplies examples of coerced labor. Op. cit., pp. 234–235.

74. For evidence of an ordinance in Wiltshire from 1655 requiring young "men and maids" to leave home and "with all convenient speed betake themselves to service for the wages aforesaid, which if they refuse to do the justices shall proceed against them," see James, op. cit., p. 178.

75. Quoted by Otto Kahn-Freund, "Blackstone's Neglected Child: The Contract of Employment," *Law Quarterly Review* Volume 93 (October 1977), p. 511.

century legal thought, created a category of "permanent" servants, a label which referred not to the length of their employment for a particular master but to an inherent condition in their person which compelled them to work for others. According to Blackstone, custom set some standard hours of work, but an employer could require his laborers to do his bidding at any moment, night or day, as if they were serfs with no time unconditionally their own.[76] In practice as in the collective imagination, only independent producers could treat their labor as if it were freely alienable, individual property; otherwise, labor could be commanded.[77]

At least the group of workers coerced by the local justices to work for an employer had one protection denied those who fell into their jobs by other means. If the workers had been drafted into service by statute, local justices who fixed the wage rates had clear authority to issue orders forcing employers to disburse the wages owed to workers.[78] Otherwise, legal remedies were uncertain and numerous masters fell weeks—even months—behind in paying their subordinates.[79] Some masters forced their workpeople to take promissory notes in lieu of wages.[80] Yet there was more to the legal subservience of labor. When an employer accused his workers of having neglected their duty, claiming that they had left their employment or performed unsatisfactorily, the alleged misdeed was classified not as a breach of a civil contract but as criminal misbehavior.[81] If the obligation to serve arose from

76. Kahn-Freund, op. cit., p. 521. See Charles Peard, *The Woollen Labourer's Advocate* (London: Printed by the author and sold by J. Dormer, 1733), p. 4. Naturally contemporaries referred to the sale of "time and labor," but within a relation created by ascribed status. Hundert, "Market Society and Meaning," op. cit., p. 41.

77. The reduction of idle persons to the semi-servile status of a wage earner became not just a legal but a moral injunction. Bishop Berkeley, for example, reasoned in the mid-eighteenth century that public law should sentence lazy persons to a term of "temporary servitude." Quoted by T. W. Hutchison, "Berkeley's *Querist* and Its Place in the Economic Thought of the Eighteenth Century," *British Journal for the Philosophy of Science* Volume IV, Number 13 (May 1953), p. 61. The term did not denote a prison sentence, simply wage labor. Ordinary wage workers in the textile industry who labored on the employer's premises were said to be in "servitude." Anonymous, *The Linnen and Woollen Manufactory Discoursed* (London: G. Huddleston, 1698), p. 11. The term *servitude* was well chosen. Peard complained that some masters in the wool trade compelled dependent employees to "make their Hay, without recompense" Op. cit., p. 4.

78. Holdsworth, op. cit., Volume XI, p. 467.

79. Hill, "Pottage," op. cit., pp. 339–340; Kelsall, op. cit., pp. 47, 52; Julia de Lacy Mann, *The Cloth Industry in the West of England from 1640 to 1880* (Oxford: Clarendon Press, 1971), p. 108; John Rule, *The Labouring Classes in Early Industrial England, 1750–1850* (London: Longman, 1986), p. 117.

80. Lipson, op. cit., p. 278.

81. Daphine Simon, "Master and Servant," in John Saville, editor, *Democracy and the Labour Movement* (London: Lawrence and Wishart, 1954), p. 160.

workers' status rather than by agreement, it was only consistent to enforce the obligation to serve through the mechanism of criminal law. Offenders were incarcerated for weeks or months.[82] The alternative of paying money damages to an employer allegedly injured by a worker's absence, as if the labor power withheld were a commodity like any other, was proscribed.[83] The law denied labor power the status of a simple ware.

Meanwhile the sale of manufactures took place in a comparatively unrestricted market. To be sure, foreign commerce remained the monopoly of government-chartered companies until 1689.[84] But competition in domestic trade, despite the ancient licensing of trading corporations, was opened to almost all challengers during the seventeenth century.[85] During this period, the powerful London merchants succeeded in breaking down provincial barriers against traders from distant cities who wished to contract for work in the countryside.[86] Thus the London merchants expanded to include the whole of the country in their commercial web.[87] This provided the stuff for writers to envision society as a network of market exchanges. "The free circulation of trade among the com.non people," wrote T. Tryon in 1698, "hath made England exceed all here Neighboring Nations in Riches."[88] Catchpenny reasoning was threaded into all layers of the social fabric. "Facts relating to Commerce," opined a commentator in 1680, "branch into almost

82. Kelsall, op. cit., p. 37.

83. Sidney Webb and Beatrice Webb, *The History of Trade Unionism* (London: Longmans, Green & Co., 1894), p. 233.

84. Hill, *The Century of Revolution*, op. cit., p. 213; Dobb, op. cit., p. 176.

85. Unwin says that in London as early as the time of Elizabeth, "As a general rule it was impossible to prevent a citizen who was free of any company from carrying on the trade of any other company, if it seemed in his interest to do so." Op. cit., p. 105. Hill, "A Bourgeois Revolution?" op. cit., p. 118. For the eighteenth century, see Ray Bert Westerfield, *Middlemen in English Business Particularly Between 1660 and 1760* (New Haven: Yale University Press, 1915), p. 347. On the absence of restrictions in Lancashire, see Wadsworth and Mann, op. cit., p. 55. For a contemporary description of free domestic trade, see Joan Thirsk and J. P. Cooper, *Seventeenth-Century Economic Documents* (Oxford: Clarendon Press, 1972), p. 59. The grain trade, on which E. P. Thompson focused his model of the "moral economy," remained a limited exception. Roy Porter, *English Society in the Eighteenth Century* (London: Penguin Books, 1982), p. 207.

86. J. R. Kellett, "The Breakdown of Gild and Corporation Control over the Handicraft and Retail Trade of London," *The Economic History Review* second series, Volume X, Number 3 (April 1958), p. 384.

87. R. H. Tawney, editor, *Studies in Economic History: The Collected Papers of George Unwin* (London: Macmillan and Co., 1927), p. 281. John Lie, "Embedding Polanyi's Market Society," *Sociological Perspectives* Volume 34, Number 2 (Summer 1991), pp. 228–230.

88. T. Tryon, *Some General Considerations Offered, Relating to Our Present Trade. And Intended for Its Help and Improvement* (London: J. Harris, 1698), p. 7.

as many parts as there are humane Actions."[89] The term *market price* no longer referred to the tangible location at which merchandise changed hands, but to the determination of value by abstract forces operating independently of the wills of individuals.[90] In Britain (but not in Germany or France) the development of market thinking followed a separate chronology from the commercialization of labor power.[91]

The views of labor as a commodity invented concurrently with the rise of liberal commercialism in Britain retained their essential form during the eighteenth century. Until the monumental work of Adam Smith appeared, the economist most celebrated by intellectual and financial speculators was Sir James Steuart. Steuart divided the agents of production into two groups: slaves, under either feudal or colonial orders, and workmen. Workmen labored as independent commodity producers. "Those who want to consume," Steuart wrote in his treatise of 1767, "send the merchant, in a manner, to the workman for his labour, and do not go themselves; the workman sells to this interposed person and does not look for a consumer."[92] In Steuart's analysis, the workman covers the entire production expense of the finished ware he sells to the merchant, including tools and materials. This autonomous artisan ordinarily turns a profit for his products above their "prime cost"—that is, beyond the labor and material invested.[93] The laborer who is dependent upon a wage contract is conspicuously absent in this theory. Steuart's division of producers into feudal slaves and masterless workmen illustrates the prevailing assumption that labor entered the market as a free

89. William Petyt, *Britannia Languens*, op. cit., Preface, p. iv. E. P. Thompson presents the claims of the common people in the eighteenth century to a "moral economy" as a paternalist ideal revived principally in times of severe food shortages. E. P. Thompson, "The Moral Economy of the English Crowd in the Eighteenth Century," *Past & Present* Number 50 (February 1971), p. 88.

90. Mann, op. cit., p. 105; Ronald Meek, "Ideas, Events and Environment: The Case of the French Physiocrats," in Robert V. Eagly, editor, *Events, Ideology and Economic Theory* (Detroit: Wayne State University Press, 1968), pp. 48–49.

91. Furniss, in his now classic study of seventeenth-century mercantile writers in England, was forcibly struck by their combination of liberalism in the product market and intrusive legislation in the labor market. Furniss, op. cit., p. 225. G. D. Ramsay remarks upon this combination of product laissez-faire and labor regulation in textiles. Ramsay, *The Wiltshire Woollen Industry*, op. cit., pp. 124–125. Joyce Appleby presents an analysis of the forces that delayed the acceptance of a market in labor power in "Ideology and Theory: The Tension Between Political and Economic Liberalism in Seventeenth-Century England," *The American Historical Review* Volume 81, Number 3 (June 1976), especially pp. 511–515.

92. Sir James Steuart, *An Inquiry into the Principles of Political Oeconomy*, edited by Andrew Skinner (Edinburgh: Oliver & Boyd, 1966), p. 150.

93. Ibid., p. 192.

commodity only when it was incorporated into a finished good and vended by independent manufacturers.

THE INSTITUTIONALIZATION
OF A MARKET IN LABOR

The restrictions on the level of wages which had proven so useful to British employers during the genesis of capitalist relations of production were thrown aside but a few generations later. To be sure, the statutory rates of wages could restrain pay increases. Under altered circumstances, however, they also limited wage reductions. Since the employment relation did not arise through free contract, masters could be required to support dependent laborers both when there was work to be done and when there was not.[94] The employing class that had once welcomed legal intrusions to bind and discipline workers came to find the limitations on their purchase of labor power odious. "The Statutes for regulating wages and the price of labour," wrote Dean Tucker in 1757, "are another absurdity and a very great hurt to trade. Absurd and preposterous it must surely appear for a third person to attempt to fix the price between buyer and seller without their own consents. . . . How can any stated regulations be so contrived as to make due and reasonable allowance for plenty or scarcity of work, cheapness or dearness of provisions, difference of living in town or country?"[95] By the time Tucker and others, including textile entrepreneurs, had formulated their criticisms, however, regulation was becoming superfluous.[96] As the landholdings of wage earners shrank, they became increasingly dependent on wage labor for their subsistence and unable to withhold their labor from the marketplace. To curb wages, manufacturers could rely on the coercive power of the market alone.[97]

94. Kahn-Freund, op. cit., p. 519.
95. Quoted by Laski, op. cit., p. 198. Although Tucker objected to the regulation of wages, he retained the older belief that low wages spurred productivity. George Shelton, *Dean Tucker and Eighteenth-Century Economic and Political Thought* (London: Macmillan, 1981), pp. 55–57.
96. Textile employers in Gloucestershire applied the language of laissez-faire in 1757 to the purchase of labor. In response to a new rating of the weavers' wages, the employers said, "We think it repugnant to the liberties of a free people and the interest of trade that any law should supersede a private contract honourably made between a master and his workman." Quoted by Lipson, op. cit., p. 268.
97. Kelsall, op. cit., p. 100; Joyce Oldham Appleby, *Economic Thought and Ideology in Seventeenth-Century England* (Princeton: Princeton University Press, 1978), p. 274; W. E. Minchinton, "Introduction," in his *Wage Regulation in Pre-Industrial England* (Newton Abbot: David & Charles, 1972), p. 27.

The statutory rating of wages had weakened in some trades when the eighteenth century commenced; by the middle of the century it was moribund in many branches, though not forgotten.[98] The system, Sir John Clapham judged, "died harder than historians used to think—and the memory of it did not die."[99] In the textile trade, as ever the leading department of manufacture, the assessment of wages by the justices became ever more difficult as the varieties of weaving proliferated in response to market enticements.[100] The surviving records do not let investigators date the demise of wage assessments for cloth production with precision.[101] In the West Riding of Yorkshire the steady enforcement of assessments faded after 1732.[102] In Gloucestershire, the clothiers generally ignored the rating of wages issued in 1728.[103] With the slow disappearance of assessments to guarantee minimum earnings, the judicial rationale for compel-

98. North, op. cit., p. 64. In agriculture, to be sure, wage assessments appear to have guided effective wage rates until 1812. "The wages of labour do conform, notwithstanding the continual increase in the price of the necessaries of life, to the assessments of the Quarter Sessions, and the system continued under legal sanction till 1812." Rogers, p. 353. Perkin shows that wage regulation in manufacture was not only unenforced but unthinkable at the end of the eighteenth century, despite the wool workers' brief campaign, initiated in 1802, to revive ancient employment laws. Harold Perkin, *The Origins of Modern English Society 1780–1880* (London: Routledge & Kegan Paul, 1969), pp. 185, 188.

99. J. H. Clapham, *A Concise Economic History of Britain from the Earliest Times to 1750* (Cambridge: Cambridge University Press, 1957), p. 215. For a contemporary reference revealing the survival of wage rating, see P. Colquhoun, *A Treatise on Indigence, Exhibiting a General View of the National Resources for Productive Labour* (London: J. Hatchard, 1806), p. 16. Marx emphasized the extraordinary longevity of wage regulation in Britain. *Kapital*, op. cit., p. 768. For evidence that agricultural workers as late as 1833 believed that Justices of the Peace could fix wage rates, see Howell, op. cit., p. 62.

100. Many statutes were not applied to the new worsted trade, because wage law was considered valid only for occupations existing at the time of its promulgation. Heaton, *The Yorkshire Woollen and Worsted Industries*, op. cit., p. 310. In 1738 Parliament abolished the requirement that narrow cloth manufactured in the West Riding follow standard designs established by statute. Lipson, op. cit., p. 326.

101. Ramsay, *Wiltshire Woolen Industry*, p. 125; for evidence of the survival of fixed customary wages in the textile industry into the mid-eighteenth century, see Robert Malcolmson, *Life and Labour in England 1700–1780* (London: Hutchinson, 1981), pp. 125–126. Local authorities occasionally called regulation back to life when perturbations in the supply of labor threatened to push wages upwards. A. Holderness, *Pre-Industrial England: Economy and Society 1500–1750* (London: J. M. Dent & Sons, 1976), p. 195.

102. Heaton, "The Assessment of Wages," op. cit., p. 232.

103. Lipson, op. cit., p. 266; Mann, op. cit., p. 110. In 1756 Parliament instructed justices in Gloucestershire to rate wages in the textile trade. Mann, op. cit., p. 110. On the Colchester weavers' attempt in the 1740s to preserve locally mandated wages, see A. F. J. Brown, *Essex at Work 1700–1815* (Chelmsford: Tindal Press, 1969), p. 25. In 1757 Parliament repealed the legislation that had enabled justices to govern wool weavers' wages. Lipson, op. cit., pp. 269–271.

ling idle laborers to work for any farmer or tradesperson needing help also faded.[104]

The changes in the institutional framework for determining the price of labor established the background for a momentous change in the appreciation of labor as a marketable ware. During the first century of liberal commercialism in Britain, the belief persisted that workers delivered their labor only under the compulsions of law and hunger.[105] Many enterprises in pottery, mining, and textiles bound their laborers by servile terms of indenture that held them to the same employer for terms of one to twenty years.[106] After the middle of the eighteenth century, employers began to rely upon cash rather than coercive stipulations to secure labor. The opinion slowly and tentatively took hold that workers could be stimulated to work harder by the promise of higher earnings.[107] It required several decades for this viewpoint to become general.[108] By 1776 Adam Smith was able to draw upon it confidently. "Where wages are high," Smith observed, "accordingly, we shall always find the workmen more active, diligent, and expeditious, than where they are low."[109] Indeed, some eighteenth-century employers came to worry that if laborers were remunerated according to the quantity of their output, they would overexert themselves and ruin their constitutions.[110] By the time Smith set down his thoughts, the Statutes of Elizabeth that had mandated terms of apprenticeship as a requisite for legal exercise of ancient craft occupations were dead letters.[111] Labor power was belatedly christened as a commodity.

104. Holdsworth, op. cit., p. 475.

105. N. J. Pauling, "The Employment Problem in Pre-Classical English Economic Thought," *The Economic Record* Volume XXVII, Number 52 (1951), p. 59; Peter Mathias, "Leisure and Wages in Theory and Practice," in his *The Transformation of England* (New York: Columbia University Press, 1979), pp. 150–151; Marx, *Kapital* op. cit., pp. 290–292.

106. Pollard, op. cit., p. 191.

107. A. W. Coats, "Changing Attitudes to Labour in the Mid-Eighteenth Century," *The Economic History Review* second series, Volume XI, Number 1 (August 1958), p. 46. Pollard, op. cit., p. 191.

108. See William Temple, *A Vindication of Commerce and the Arts*, 1758, reprinted in Copley, editor, *Literature and the Social Order in Eighteenth-Century England*, op. cit., p. 154.

109. Smith, *Wealth of Nations*, op. cit., p. 91.

110. *The Monthly Magazine*, "On Taken-Work," by "A Farmer" (May 1799), pp. 273–275; Rule, op. cit., p. 124; L. J. Hume, "Jeremy Bentham on Industrial Management," *Yorkshire Bulletin of Economic and Social Research* Volume 22, Number 1 (May 1970), p. 6.

111. For testimony about long-standing ignorance of the terms of the apprenticeship statutes and about their nonenforcement, see United Kingdom, *Report from the Committee on Woollen Clothiers Petition*, PP 1802–1803 VII, pp. 5–7, March 13, 1803; United Kingdom, *Minutes of Evidence, Committee on Woollen Bill*, PP 1802–1803 (95) VII, pp. 7, 357; United Kingdom, *Minutes of the Committee on the Woollen Trade*, PP 1806 III, pp. 135, 197, 198,

But under what name? The employment of wage labor was assimilated to the prior notion of labor sold as it was embodied in the product of an independent artisan. Strange to say, this continuity is illustrated most vividly in what may otherwise appear to be an historical rupture: the issuance of Smith's *Wealth of Nations*. Smith's formulations about the efficiency of the market may have recast the field of high theory, but his portrayal of labor rested upon the appropriation of simple, long-standing ideas from social practice.

ADAM SMITH'S SUBSTANCE

Smith establishes a foundation for the relative prices of different commodities by extending to the contemporary setting the principles he finds effective in a simplified, archetypal kind of exchange. He seeks the determinants of the values of goods in a situation that "precedes both the appropriation of land and the accumulation of stock."[112] In this original state, where capital investments do not enter into the cost of production, Smith adduces that

> the proportion between the quantities of labor necessary for acquiring different objects seems to be the only circumstance which can afford any rule for exchanging them one for another. If among a nation of hunters, for example, it usually costs twice the labour to kill a beaver which it does to kill a deer, one beaver should naturally exchange for or be worth two deer.[113]

This hypothetical construction lets Smith introduce a set of paired suppositions: the labor the worker applies to the product equals and determines the product's exchange value; and people do not trade their living labor—or, to introduce an anachronism in this context, "labor power"—directly for goods, but instead receive their dues by exchanging the *product* of their labor for other products. Smith also refers at moments to such a society of independent producers as if it were a current reality. In an opulent, well-governed society, he claims, "Every workman has a great quantity of his own work to dispose of beyond what he himself has occasion for; and every other workman being in exactly the same situation, he is enabled to ex-

---

231; Wadsworth and de Lacy Mann, op. cit., pp. 351–352. On the weakening of urban corporations after the revolution and their virtual extinction by the mid-eighteenth century, see ibid., pp. 63–67.

112. *Wealth of Nations*, op. cit., p. 72.

113. Ibid., p. 53.

change a great quantity of his own goods for a great quantity, or, what comes to the same thing, for the price of a great quantity of theirs."[114]

Smith, however, recognized at other moments that not all those who sold their labor in the market did so as independent producers. He commented upon the decay in the statutory restrictions on wages and concluded that people had themselves become wares in the marketplace. "The demand for men, like that for any other commodity," he observed, "necessarily regulates the production of men, quickens it when it goes on too slowly, and stops it when it advances too fast."[115] Whereas Petty and Steuart excluded wage labor from their theory of the market, Smith tries to explain the contribution of labor to the value of goods when the owner of stock invests capital in an enterprise and hires workers for a wage. "In this state of things," Smith reasons, "the whole produce of labor does not always belong to the labourer. He must in most cases share it with the owner of the stock which employs him."[116] When he takes up the question of the source of the capitalist's profit, it seems that Smith alters his initial definition of the determinants of a product's value:

> Neither is the quantity of labour commonly employed in acquiring or producing any commodity, the only circumstance which can regulate the quantity of which it ought commonly to purchase, command, or exchange for. An additional quantity, it is evident, must be due for the profits of the stock which advanced the wages and furnished the materials of that labour.[117]

On the face of it, this passage contradicts Smith's ground premise that labor alone is the source of value. Now the amount of capital applied in the production of the good comprises an independent part of its price. Yet he also contends that the worth of the good can still be translated, by another means, into the universal equivalent, labor, because the finished product has the value of the labor for which it can be *exchanged*. He makes an unacknowledged shift here in the definition of the value of goods between the two cases, from the quantity of labor the goods contain to the quantity of labor that can be gotten in exchange for them.[118]

114. Ibid., p. 15.
115. Ibid., p. 89.
116. Ibid., p. 55.
117. Ibid.
118. David Ricardo was among the first to call attention to this displacement. *On the Principles of Political Economy and Taxation* (3d ed. London: John Murray, 1821), p. 5.

Smith's identification of labor with the delivery of a product permits him to elide this shift in his definition of value while moving from the principles that regulated transactions in the archetypal "nation of hunters" to the conditions when capital has accumulated. In fact, it provides the first occasion for this slippage between the determination of value by the amount of labor a product contains and the determination of value by the amount of labor for which it can be exchanged. A man's fortune is greater or less, Smith says, precisely in proportion to "the quantity either of other men's labour, or, *what is the same thing,* of the produce of other men's labour, which it enables him to purchase."[119] Here Smith equates the employment of wage labor with the purchase of a product, an equation he repeats when he discusses the value of an article produced in capitalist society: "In exchanging the complete manufacture either for money, *for labour, or for other goods,* over and above what may be sufficient to pay the price of the materials, and the wages of the workmen, something must be given for the profits of the undertaker of work, who hazards his stock in this adventure."[120] To lay out the circuit of reasoning here: Smith supposes that if the hiring of a person's labor is the same as buying that person's product, then the owners of goods end up receiving the same amount of labor whether they exchange it for labor in the employment relation or on the market for other products. In the second case, exchanges of merchandise, the value of the owners' goods equals the quantity of materialized labor they contain. In the first case, exchanges in the employment relation, the value of the owners' goods equals the quantity of living labor for which they will exchange. If labor as a commodity is exchanged only via its products, however, these two cases become equivalent.[121]

The import of these equations becomes apparent if we pose the question that Marx did: in capitalist society, do we know whether the quantity of labor in the goods that the worker gets back in the form of wages equals the quantity of labor the worker gives to the employer? To be sure, the restricted

119. *Wealth of Nations,* op. cit., p. 35. Emphasis added. When Smith recognizes a difference between the state of nature and capitalism, he does so not because he recognizes a difference between the sale of living labor and of a labor product. His only problem in making the shift is that he has difficulty in establishing the contributions of labor and of capital to the value of the output in the capitalist order.

120. Smith, *Wealth of Nations,* op. cit., p. 54.

121. In order to make Smith's alternative definitions of value equivalent, Ricardo assumed that Smith believed labor was exchanged in the form of materialized labor. Op. cit., p. 5. Marx, who imagined the sale of labor in the employment relation only in the form of "labor power," could not understand why Ricardo interpreted Smith in this fashion. *Theorien über den Mehrwert,* op. cit., Volume Two, Part One, p. 114.

conditions of the archetypal situation prior to the accumulation of capital permit a comparison between the value of the worker's living labor and the value of the "objectified labor" in the commodities for which it trades. In this restrictive situation, where the worker keeps the whole of his produce, the quantity of labor he invests in the product equals the labor he gets by exchanging it. In the actual situation, however, the wage laborer, as Smith says, cannot keep the whole of the produce. How do we decide what the worker ought to keep? In retrospect it appears that Smith's shift to the determination of value by the amount of labor for which a product will *exchange* makes it impossible to allocate shares to labor and capital based on the value of what they contribute to production. The value of the labor cannot be separated from the capital, because it has a value only when the mixture of the two is conveyed in the market. Smith satisfies himself with the observation that "the real value of all the different components of price . . . is measured by the quantity of labor which they can, each of them, purchase or command."[122] Yet viewing the employment relation as the delivery of labor in the form of a product allows him to assume that it falls under the ethical rules that governed the exchange of products in the archetypal situation. He sees the employer of labor as giving the worker a certain quantity of goods (in the form of wages) in exchange for another quantity of goods (the produce of labor).[123] Even after the accumulation of stock, the product belongs initially only to the laborers who created it, even if they must in the end share portions of it with the owners of capital as a "deduction."[124]

Smith's *Wealth of Nations* reveals the intellectual reproduction of the assumptions about labor as a commodity that originated during the genesis of liberal commercialism in Britain. Abstract human labor was recognized as a transferable ware only as it was incorporated into a product that circulated in the sphere of exchange.[125] This understanding of labor did not sur-

---

122. *Wealth of Nations*, op. cit., p. 56.

123. "The value of any commodity, therefore, to the person who possesses it, and who means not to use or consume it himself, but to exchange it for other commodities, is equal to the quantity of labour which it enables him to purchase or command." *Wealth of Nations*, op. cit., p. 34. Or, again: "The quantity of labor commonly employed in acquiring or producing any commodity is the only circumstance which can regulate the quantity of labor which it ought commonly to purchase, command, or exchange for" (p. 54).

124. On this point see the commentary by E. H. Phelps Brown, "The Labour Market," in Thomas Wilson and Andrew S. Skinner, editors, *The Market and the State: Essays in Honour of Adam Smith* (Oxford: Clarendon Press, 1976), pp. 254–256.

125. Louis Dumont brilliantly captures Smith's inability to think of "value, or surplus value, as already present in the good produced, in anticipation of its future destiny on the

vive in the minds of armchair readers alone. It was sustained in social relations through everyday practice on the shop floor. When journeymen weavers of the eighteenth century worked in the shop of a master rather than on their own account, their payment was often reckoned as "the third part of the cloth"—that is, one-third of the price the material fetched when the master sold it to the merchant clothier.[126] The labor was remunerated by its concretization in cloth brought to market. The concept of labor as a commodity that prevailed in British economic theory did not "reflect" material practices; it was born incarnate in their overall consistencies.

Other circumstances provided suitable material for sustaining the assumption that the commodity of labor resided in a substance. In many trades, artisans' remuneration followed accepted piece scales fixed by custom that reached as far back as workers could recollect. A woolen weaver from the West Country testified in 1802 that the rate for a certain cloth had not changed in his lifetime, "nor yet in my father's memory."[127] When stocking makers struck for higher wages in 1814, they asserted that their rates had changed only twice in two hundred years. The stability in quoted rates veiled the operation of the shifting market, for in times of labor scarcity employers supplemented the rates with perquisites such as a share of the produce or of the work materials. In all events, the compensation did not appear in the form of a simple wage for labor power. Rather, the major, identifiable part of the compensation was fixed in products that had been

---

market." *From Mandeville to Marx* (Chicago: University of Chicago Press, 1977), p. 94. Of course, even Smith remarked that workers who took longer to acquire their skills required higher compensation. *Wealth of Nations*, op. cit., pp. 113 ff. In the nineteenth century, the skilled labor aristocrats among British workers also saw their expertise as a kind of capital. Patrick Joyce, *Visions of the People: Industrial England and the Question of Class 1848–1914* (Cambridge: Cambridge University Press, 1991), pp. 116–117. The issue, however, is not whether economic agents conceive of investment in labor power but how they conceive of and concretely enact the transfer of the commodity of labor to the employer at the point of production.

126. Lipson, op. cit., p. 36. The allocation of shares could vary: United Kingdom, *Report from Select Committee on Handloom Weavers*, PP 1834 (556) X, testimony of Richard Needham, p. 443. Female apprentices were paid by the same method: United Kingdom, *Select Committee of the Petitions of Ribbon Weavers*, PP 1818 (398) IX, testimony of John Carter, p. 5. In Germany, where, however, craft practices were not yet configured by labor's commodity form, payment of artisanal weaving apprentices by giving them a share of the product's selling price was not unheard of, but it was much more common to pay apprentices a time wage. Krefeld comprised an exception. See Peter Kriedte, *Eine Stadt am seidenen Faden* (Göttingen: Vandenhoeck & Ruprecht, 1991), p. 113.

127. Cited by Rule, op. cit., p. 119. Rule provides evidence from other trades as well.

assigned a certain value for decades, as though an established quantity of materialized labor had a self-evident value.[128]

The small instrumentalities of quotidian experience reproduced a specification of labor as a commodity that evolved from the broader context of market development in Britain. The commercialization of artisanal production in Britain since the seventeenth century led to the growth of extensive subcontracting networks and to the separation of master employers, who coordinated the collection of products, from the shops where the manual work was executed.[129] "The employer's role was to initiate the process of production and market the finished goods. What came between," as Clive Behagg recently summed up, "was properly the province of labor."[130] The carpet weavers of Kidderminster expressed this assumption during a long strike in 1828. They collectively sought a new "employer" by advertising in the local press for investors willing to put capital in a weaving undertaking with the strikers as both laborers and, effectively, organizers of the firm.[131] Of course, the decentralized putting-out networks were not sufficient for the *genesis* of the cultural definition of labor as a commodity in Britain. Otherwise, the same understanding would have prevailed everywhere in Europe. The structure of the networks could only reproduce the specification of labor that originated in the broader market context, due to the staggered emergence of formally free markets in products and in labor power itself.

Autobiographies from hand workers of the eighteenth and nineteenth centuries shed additional light on workers' own perception of the wage relationship in these putting-out networks. They emphasize that the employer was rarely to be seen. The typical work group in the eighteenth

128. John Styles, "Embezzlement, Industry and the Law in England, 1500–1800," in Maxine Berg, Pat Hudson, and Michael Sonnenscher, editors, *Manufacture in Town and Country* (Cambridge: Cambridge University Press, 1983), p. 184.

129. Christiane Eisenberg, *Deutsche und englische Gewerkschaften* (Göttingen: Vandenhoeck & Ruprecht, 1986), p. 73.

130. Clive Behagg, "Controlling the Product: Work, Time, and the Early Industrial Workforce in Britain, 1800–1850," in Gary Cross, editor, *Worktime and Industrialization: An International History* (Philadelphia: Temple University Press, 1988), pp. 45–46. See also Clive Behagg, "Secrecy, Ritual and Folk Violence: The Opacity of the Workplace in the First Half of the Nineteenth Century," in Robert D. Storch, editor, *Popular Culture and Custom in Nineteenth-Century England* (London: Croom Helm, 1982).

131. L. Smith, "The Carpet Weavers of Kidderminster 1800–1850," Ph.D. thesis, University of Birmingham, 1982, pp. 224–226. The definition of labor as a commodity did not "reflect" the decentralized organization of craft production, for, after all, such free workers had worked autonomously in mercantile societies of the ancient world. But the subcontracting system provided a site for the incarnation of a specific commodity form of labor in mundane practice.

century consisted of adults of equal rank, with a young helper or two.[132] The organization of production was left to the discretion of workers, who, with the commercialization of the trade, came to see that they were delivering not just tangible products but the commodity of labor materialized in a good. Recent studies of production in early nineteenth-century Britain show that even after industrialization began in earnest and the golden age of Smith's idealized artisans had passed, workers in small shops continued to claim the right to organize the labor process and to control the output until it was delivered to the employer. For example, the workers in a rule shop in Birmingham during the 1840s remained so confident of their control on the shop floor that when their employer tried to spy on them they scared him off by "shying at him rotten potatoes, stale bread, and . . . on occasions, things of a worse description."[133]

Let no one suppose, however, that the permanence of small-scale units of production or the unbroken transmittal of artisanal culture accounts for the formation of the distinct British concept of labor as a commodity.[134] Whereas a superficial continuity appears in the organizational form of production, the cultural code inscribed in work practices changed with the commodification of labor. Even in ancient societies workers sold their products; only in the unique epoch of liberal commercialism could the producers also come to see those products as vessels for the exchange of abstract labor time.[135] Early mercantile businessmen had accepted the delivery of goods from subcontractors at erratic intervals; they had not set down schedules for

132. John Rule, *The Experience of Labour in Eighteenth-Century Industry* (London: Croom Helm, 1981), p. 194; Clive Behagg, "The Democracy of Work, 1820–1850," in John Rule, editor, *British Trade Unionism 1750–1850* (London: Longman, 1988), p. 168.

133. Cited by Clive Behagg, "Secrecy, Ritual and Folk Violence: The Opacity of the Workplace," *op. cit.*, p. 163. G. C. Allen, "Methods of Industrial Organization in the West Midlands," *The Economic Journal* (January 1929), pp. 546, 553.

134. Alas, several analysts have overlooked the profound difference between the simple sale of products as products versus the sale of products as bearers of quantified labor time. These scholars indistinctly contrast the sale of products by independent crafts workers with the sale of labor for a wage by factory workers. Craig Calhoun, *The Question of Class Struggle* (Chicago: University of Chicago Press, 1982), pp. 117–118; William Reddy, *The Rise of Market Culture* (Cambridge: Cambridge University Press, 1984), pp. 124, 251.

135. The employment of small tailors dramatically illustrates the treatment of the product as a container for the transmission of abstract labor time. Tailors in Britain received a piece rate computed by totaling the number of minutes allotted for each stitched component of the complete garment they handed in. The incorporated minutes were remunerated by an hourly standard that varied by city. The Master Tailors' Association attempted to secure a national log book of embodied times that would give "one time for the making of a garment throughout the whole of the kingdom." Royal Commission on Labour, PP 1892 XXXVI, Part II, pp. 115, 117, 160.

delivery that protected their claim to the workers' labor per se.[136] In this blessed era, weavers could work for more than one trader at a time.[137] When traders imposed delivery schedules on workers who depended upon a single contractor for their sustenance, the transaction acquired a new definition: workers delivered, not merely crafts work, but the timed life activity materialized in it, that is, embodied labor.[138] Eighteenth-century legislation compelled male and female domestic workers to meet production deadlines or face prosecution.[139] In parallel fashion, masters at artisanal shops who did not calibrate the hours of attendance still expected each worker to meet delivery quotas.[140] Larger concerns in iron working and in the pottery trades in the eighteenth century also began to insist on the regular delivery of labor products. Long before the installation of powered machinery, they introduced codes that required workers who had once sauntered in and out of workplaces as they pleased to appear instead at fixed intervals on the shop floor.[141]

136. On the merchants' attention to delivery dates, see C. P. Kindleberger, "The Historical Background: Adam Smith and the Industrial Revolution," in Thomas Wilson and Andrew Skinner, editors, *The Market and the State: Essays in Honour of Adam Smith* (Oxford: Clarendon Press, 1976), p. 16.

137. Julia de Lacy Mann, "Clothiers and Weavers in Wiltshire During the Eighteenth Century," in L. S. Pressnell, editor, *Studies in the Industrial Revolution* (London: Athlone Press, 1960), p. 89.

138. Testimony of John Niblett, United Kingdom, *Minutes of Evidence, Committee on Woollen Bill,* op. cit., p. 38. For an example from the eighteenth-century metal file trade, see T. S. Ashton, *An Eighteenth-Century Industrialist* (Manchester: Manchester University Press, 1939), p. 20. For an example from the textile industry of Essex, see D. C. Coleman, *Courtaulds: An Economic and Social History* (Oxford: Clarendon Press, 1969), Volume One, p. 103. When weavers depended on the market for their very subsistence, they contracted debts to putting-out entrepreneurs who then had exclusive claim to the weavers' output. Eric M. Sigsworth, *Black Dyke Mills* (Liverpool: Liverpool University Press, 1958), p. 145. For eighteenth-century cloth traders' calculation of embodied labor times in types of fabric, see Adrian Randall, *Before the Luddites* (Cambridge: Cambridge University Press, 1991), p. 52. In early nineteenth-century Germany, domestic weavers were not only subject to delivery schedules; additionally, some putting-out traders sent agents to the weavers' homes to monitor the execution of the work itself. Kriedte, op. cit., p. 107.

139. *Report from the Select Committee on Master and Servant,* PP 1865 (370) VIII, pp. 3–4. For eighteenth-century reports of male and, especially, female textile domestic workers imprisoned for one month due to failure to complete orders, see Heaton, *The Yorkshire Woollen and Worsted Industries,* op. cit., p. 431. On the evolution of disciplinary codes for home workers, see Wadsworth and Mann, op. cit., p. 397.

140. Rule, op. cit., p. 120. At Crowley's ironworks, one of the largest concerns of the eighteenth century, workers entrusted with orders for a week's worth of labor were paid less than full price for late deliveries. M. W. Flinn, editor, *The Law Book of the Crowley Ironworks* (London: Bernard Quaritch, 1957), p. 138.

141. Llewellynn Jewitt, *The Wedgwoods: Being a Life of Josiah Wedgwood* (London: Virtue Brothers and Co., 1865), pp. 131–132. For supervisors, see Flinn, op. cit., p. 135. E. P.

Labor's progressive envelopment in a commodity form can be traced with flawless clarity in discursive practices as well. Although Petty in the seventeenth century had made labor a standard of value, he had also viewed it as a kind of natural substance, not unlike the raw materials delivered from the land. He observed, for instance, that a calf could increase in value if it grazed unattended. What, he asked, is the general par between the value generated by the land and that created by labor? For him they appeared as equivalent, irreducible sources of wealth.[142] Smith, by contrast, did not suppose that labor created value by making substances equivalent to nature. Human labor represented the sole, independent, and socially generated source of value.[143] Smith made labor constitutive of social relations in high theory at the same time the form of labor as a commodity became a central, organizing principle of micro-practices on the shop floor.[144]

THE TRANSMISSION OF LABOR IN THE AGE OF THE FACTORY

On the clock of the artisanal world, Smith formulated his ideas at the eleventh hour, when the development of a market in labor itself had become inescapably obvious but the commencement of the industrial revolution was as yet perceived only dimly.[145] With the founding of the Ricardian school of economics at the beginning of the nineteenth century, the most widespread form of considered reflection on the economy in Britain moved to an explicitly industrial view of society.[116] Ricardo envisioned a social order with three classes: owners of capital, owners of land, and wage earners in the owners' employ. He saw all workers as dependent laborers, and he

Thompson, "Time, Work-Discipline, and Industrial Capitalism," *Past and Present* Number 38 (December 1967), p. 82.

142. Tribe, op. cit., p. 93.

143. Of course, *The Wealth of Nations* also carried suggestions that labor devoted to cultivation of the land was especially productive. On the reception of this part of Smith, see Tribe, op. cit., pp. 110–112.

144. What is distinctive in capitalist society is not that labor can be bought as a commodity but that labor appears in the first instance as a commodity. Marx, *Kapital*, op. cit., Volume II, p. 114.

145. Hiram Canton, "The Preindustrial Economics of Adam Smith," *The Journal of Economic History* Volume 45 (December 1985), p. 384. On Smith's ignorance of the changes in techniques of production that would later be termed a "revolution," see Kindleberger, op. cit., pp. 6–7.

146. Ricardo influenced trade unionists as well, although his popularity never approached that of Adam Smith. Eugenio F. Biagini, "British Trade Unions and Popular Political Economy, 1860–1880," *The Historical Journal* Volume 30, Number 4 (1987), p. 831 note.

took the mechanization of production for granted.[147] If political economy moved smoothly in the wake of economic change, reflecting and generalizing upon it, would not British thinkers come to discard the notion that wage laborers sold materialized labor? Smith had already found it difficult to reduce the wage contract to the exchange of products. Would not the sale of labor in the form of a product appear increasingly anachronistic in the age of the factory? For social investigators coming after Marx, it may seem more "accurate" to encode labor in the form of "labor power." But this partiality reduces culture to a reflection of social organization. When Ricardo set out to clarify the role of labor in economic life, he did not reject but reinvigorated older suppositions about labor as a commodity.

In his *Principles of Political Economy*, composed more than forty years after Smith's *Wealth of Nations*, Ricardo identified some of the major confusions in his predecessor's work. Ricardo uncovered the surreptitious moves Smith made between two specifications of how labor determines the value of commodities: as Ricardo summarized the difference, sometimes by "the quantity of labour bestowed on the production" of the commodity, sometimes by "the quantity of labour which that commodity would purchase."[148] To set the matter straight, Ricardo declared that only with the first definition could an invariant measure of value be obtained.[149] He reached this conclusion by observing that the value of labor in exchange varied—that is, the quantity of labor in the goods that the worker could buy in return for selling his own labor fluctuated with market conditions.[150] By comparison, Ricardo believed that the quantity of labor the worker bestowed on a product provided a fixed standard for comparing the value of goods in the face of apparent shifts in exchange values. Ricardo reasoned that if a commodity suddenly required a lesser quantity of labor for its production due to technological improvement, that commodity would be exchanged for a lesser quantity of embodied labor.[151]

147. As Marx acutely observed. *Theorien über den Mehrwert*, op. cit., Volume 2, Part Two, p. 346.
148. Op. cit., p. 5.
149. He did not assert that embodied labor provided an absolute measure, only that it allowed for comparisons between commodities. Schumpeter, op. cit., p. 591.
150. Ricardo, op. cit., p. 7.
151. In this example Ricardo apparently believed that the cheapened product would hire or "command" the same amount of living labor. Op. cit., p. 8. In his first chapter, "On Value," Ricardo writes, "If the reward of the labourer were always in proportion to what he produced, the quantity of labour bestowed on a commodity, and the quantity of labour which that commodity would purchase, would be equal, and either might accurately measure the variations of other things: but they are not equal; the first is under many circumstances an

Given the initial trajectory of his thinking, Ricardo might well have arrived at the view that the owner purchased labor as if it were a potential rather than as if it were already materialized in a product. After all, the very first line of his book, by which he definitely announced his entry onto the front stage of the British intellectual drama, sent him on a straightforward path: "The value of a commodity . . . depends on the relative quantity of labour which is necessary for its production, and not on the greater or lesser compensation which is paid for that labor."[152] He could not have chosen a more auspicious starting point for considering discrepancies between labor costs and labor quantities. His emphasis on the *quantity* of labor might have led him to consider how employers derive varying quantities of labor from their workers' potential. Yet he retained the idea that labor was delivered in the form of a product even under penalty of introducing inconsistency into his system.[153]

Whereas Smith resorted to his second definition of value in exchange when he observed that with the advent of reliance upon accumulated stock in production the wage of the worker is no longer equal to the entire value of the products created, Ricardo's approach assumes that the transition to capitalist conditions of production in no way compromises Smith's first definition of value, based on the labor materialized in a product. If the relative prices of commodities are determined by the quantities of labor they contain, this remains true no matter how much of this quantity of labor is reimbursed to the workers as a wage. So Ricardo thinks only Smith's

---

invariable standard, indicating correctly the variations of other things; the latter is subject to as many fluctuations as the commodities compared with it" (p. 5). Notice that Ricardo confuses two issues here: finding an invariant measure of value, and explaining the difference between the quantity of "living labor" a commodity "commands" in the market and the quantity of "embodied labor" it purchases. See Schumpeter, op. cit., p. 591 note. Marx says Ricardo's failure to disentangle these issues shows how insensitive he remained to the difference between living and embodied labor even after he realized that Smith's philosophical equation of the two did not apply to the real world. *Theorien über den Mehrwert*, op. cit., Volume Two, Part One, pp. 113–115.

152. This comprises the introductory heading of Chapter One of his *Principles*. In his notebooks Marx commented that, as far as he could tell, Ricardo asserted here, at the outset of his investigation, that commodities traded not in proportion to the paid labor they contained (the *cost* of the labor) but by the total labor, paid or unpaid. *Theorien über den Mehrwert*, op. cit., Volume Two, Part One, p. 113.

153. Ricardo, unlike Smith, does not consider it his job to explain the origin of profit, only to show that profit's existence does not contradict his initial premises. If finished commodities normally sell in the market for a price higher than the cost of the labor they contain, this remains consistent with his model. Provided that the commodities normally trade in *proportion* to the labor they contain, from his viewpoint nothing more need be said. Keith Tribe comments upon Ricardo's recognition of only embodied labor. Op. cit., pp. 135, 138.

first formulation of value, based on the labor bestowed on a commodity, is accurate: "If the reward of the labourer were always in proportion to what he produced, the quantity of labour bestowed on a commodity, and the quantity of labour which that commodity would purchase, would be equal, and either might accurately measure the variations of other things: but they are not equal." If we impose on this formulation a set of categories alien to Ricardo, we can say that the two quantities represent forms of the same thing, labor, but materialized versus living labor. If the difference between them is only a matter of form, why should they not be equals in exchange? With the help of Marx's tradition, we can pose the question.[154] Ricardo could not. For him they were equal because they were the same. When he observed the inequality he saw, not two different forms of labor, but labor products delivered with the help of capital versus labor traded against labor.

Although Ricardo professes to make a theoretical choice in favor of the *quantity* of labor bestowed on a good as the measure of value, his analysis actually uses the *cost* of labor as that measure. The most obvious evidence for this slippage lies in his arithmetical examples throughout the *Principles*. Ricardo expects the reader to understand that if two owners pay the same amount in wages, they receive the same quantity of labor.[155] If Ricardo identifies the cost of labor with the quantity received, he omits the employer's utilization of the labor as a step that decides how much labor the employer actually receives.[156] Did he ignore this process as a simplifying assumption? Could he not have thought that the variations among employers in the quantity of labor actually extracted from the worker for a certain wage averages out for the economy as a whole? And then, in the aggregate, why could he not equate quantity received with cost? Ricardo's use of the famous "wages fund" theory rules out this interpretation. This doctrine starts from the assumption that capitalists in a society "advance" wages to the workers out of their total

154. Marx himself formulated the question, but he supposed that Ricardo merely failed to inquire into the origins of surplus value. *Theorien über den Mehrwert*, op. cit., Volume 2, Part 2, pp. 116, 126.

155. As he told Malthus, "If my commodity is of equal value with yours, its cost of production must be the same." Cited in Oswald St. Clair, *A Key to Ricardo* (London: Routledge & Kegan Paul, 1957), p. 337. See also Ricardo, op. cit., pp. 46 note, 481. Notice that Ricardo does not say that the cost of production of a single good equals an absolute value. He argues only from comparisons between goods, an important consideration in understanding his treatment of profit.

156. As Marx points out in *Theorien über den Mehrwert*, op. cit., p. 114. For a recent quantitative analysis that includes the process of utilizing labor power, see Samuel Bowles, "The Production Process in a Competitive Economy: Walrasian, Neo-Hobbesian, and Marxian Models," *The American Economic Review* Volume 75, Number 1 (March, 1985).

stock of capital. The capitalists decide in advance what amount of this stock to allocate for the maintenance of productive labor and what part to consume themselves, that is, their budgeting determines the amount of capital "destined" for the payment of wages.[157] Ricardo assumes that if the amount of capital allocated for the payment of wages in a society declines, then, all else being equal, the quantity of labor purchased by employers declines in the same proportion.[158] They cannot use the falling demand for labor to get the real unit cost of labor to decline. (As Marx pointed out, by treating the length of the workday as fixed and irrelevant, Ricardo ignored the process of using labor power itself.)[159] Therefore the reduction of the quantity of labor to its cost does not just represent an averaging out of the use that capitalists can make of labor at the same point in time. It means that even in different circumstances the capitalists cannot make better "use" of or extract more work out of the labor they buy—they purchase it as if it were already embodied.[160]

The second implication of Ricardo's reduction of the quantity of labor to its cost is that it can make his argument appear circular. Samuel Bailey, an early and vociferous critic of Ricardo, called attention to this in 1825:

> Mr. Ricardo, ingeniously enough, avoids a difficulty, which on a first view, threatens to encumber his doctrine, that value depends on the quantity of labour employed in production. If this principle is rigidly adhered to, it follows, that the value of labour depends on the quantity of labour employed in producing it—which is evidently absurd. By a dextrous turn, therefore, Mr. Ricardo makes the value of labour depend on the quantity of labour required to produce wages, or, to give him the benefit of his own language, he maintains, that the value of labour is *to be estimated* by the quantity of labour required to produce wages, by which he means, the quantity of labour required to produce the money or commodities given to the labourer. This is similar to saying, that the value of cloth is to be estimated, not by the quantity of labour bestowed on its production, but by the quantity of labour bestowed on the production of the silver, for which the cloth is exchanged.[161]

---

157. Op. cit., p. 107.

158. At least that is how Ricardo argues in op. cit., Chapter Thirty-One, "On Machinery."

159. *Theorien über den Mehrwert*, op. cit., p. 134.

160. This holds true in Ricardo's famous Chapter Thirty-One, where it is clear that his conclusion does not derive in any way from the notion that real wages, in the long run, tend toward subsistence.

161. *A Critical Dissertation on the Nature, Measures, and Causes of Value; Chiefly in Reference to the Writings of Mr. Ricardo and His Followers* (London: R. Hunter, 1825), pp. 50–51.

Even if Bailey misrepresents Ricardo's argument, he insistently identifies labor with its product at moments when he might well have considered labor power itself as a ware.[162] Read literally, Bailey appears correct in saying that "the value of labour depends on the quantity of labour employed in producing it" is nonsensical. As a declaration in which "labor" actually refers to "labor power," however, the words follow perfect logic and anticipate Marx's conceptual shift. A habitual process of interpretation in Britain reduced "labor" to its exchangeable product and rendered a potentially insightful formulation "evidently absurd."[163]

As is well known, Ricardo's formulation of the labor theory of value became the dominant form of economic reasoning both among specialized theorists and among popularizers of political economy.[164] One of Ricardo's earliest followers, James Mill, imagined the factory worker as the owner of the finished product who negotiated with his employers over how much of his realized output he would yield. Mill classified the wage as a form of payment in advance because the worker received it before the product had actually been disposed of in the market. In *Elements of Political Economy*, Mill wrote that:

> the commodity, when produced, belongs in certain proportions to both [capitalist and laborers]. It may happen, however, that one of these parties has purchased the share of the other, before production

162. For a defense of Ricardo, see Pier Luigi Porta, editor, *David Ricardo: Notes on Malthus's "Measure of Value,"* (Cambridge: Cambridge University Press, 1992), p. xviii, and Mark Blaug, *Ricardian Economics: A Historical Study* (New Haven: Yale University Press, 1958), p. 54 note 56.

163. In the last years of his life Ricardo cogitated furiously on the difficulties that had beset his theory of value. J. H. Hollander, "The Development of Ricardo's Theory of Value," in John Cunningham Wood, editor, *David Ricardo: Critical Assessments* (London: Croom Helm, 1985), Volume II, pp. 33–36. Yet his final writings confirm his earlier definition of labor as a commodity. In an essay on "Absolute Value and Exchangeable Value" he described a worker's wage as a portion of a concrete product in which the worker had materialized his labor. "That part of the value of a commodity which is required to compensate the labourer for the labour he has bestowed upon it is called wages," Ricardo opined; "the remaining part of its value is retained by the master and is called profit." *The Works and Correspondence of David Ricardo*, edited by Piero Sraffa (Cambridge: Cambridge University Press, 1951), Volume IV, pp. 379–380.

164. "Ricardo conquered England as completely as the Holy Inquisition conquered Spain." J. M. Keynes, *The General Theory of Employment Interest and Money* (New York: Harcourt, Brace & World, 1936), p. 32. Donald Winch, "The Emergence of Economics as a Science 1750–1870," in Carlo Cipolla, editor, *The Industrial Revolution 1700–1914: The Fontana Economic History of Europe* (New York: Barnes & Noble, 1976), Volume 3, p. 541; Ronald L. Meek, *Economics and Ideology and Other Essays* (London: Chapman and Hall, 1967), p. 73.

is completed. . . . In point of fact, it does happen, that the capitalist, as often as he employs labourers, by the payment of wages, purchases the share of the labourers. When the labourers receive wages for their labour, without waiting to be paid by a share of the commodity produced, it is evident that they sell their title to that share. The capitalist is then the owner, not of the capital only, but of the labour also.[165]

Here the capitalist cannot even be said to have purchased any labor until he buys a completed product. Mill transformed the transaction between the capitalist and the worker into an ordinary exchange between commodity owners, both of whom trade labor already embodied in products—materialized labor.[166]

The postulate that employers purchased only materialized labor became a standard assumption in British political economy. Peter Gaskell, in his celebrated book on *The Manufacturing Population of England*, suggested that labor had no exchange value until it entered the sphere of circulation as a finished product. "Of itself it [labor] is nothing . . . ," he said, "—it must be stamped or moulded to bring it into a state fit for useful exchange."[167] John Stuart Mill, perhaps the most famous purveyor of the nineteenth century's common sense, supposed that wage laborers received loans from their employers, for they were paid before the finished products which they gave their employer had been disposed of in the market.[168] Were employees

---

165. James Mill, *Elements of Political Economy* (3d ed. London: Henry Bohn, 1844), p. 94; see also pp. 40–41. Mill described this work as a "schoolbook," a codification of accepted principles.

166. Here I call upon Marx's commentary. *Theorien über den Mehrwert*, op. cit., Volume Three, p. 101. Mill's theory follows the logic employed at the dawn of economic speculation about labor: "The Labourer's share of the Cloth is as much in proportion to the whole Cloth as the price of Labour is in proportion to the whole price." Anonymous, *Considerations on the East-India Trade*, 1701, in J. R. McCulloch, editor, *Early English Tracts on Commerce* (Cambridge: Cambridge University Press, 1954 [1856]), p. 588.

167. (London: Baldwin and Cradock, 1833), p. 291. Robert Torrens, who pondered the effect of mechanization on the wages of dependent factory workers, still imagined the transmission of labor as the exchange of output among autonomous producers. "When the divisions of labour, and private property, are established, then each individual lives by giving the surplus produce of his own, for the surplus produce of his neighbour's industry." *An Essay on the Production of Wealth* (London: Longman, Hurst, Rees, Orne, and Brown, 1821), p. 15.

168. John Stuart Mill, *Principles of Political Economy* (London: Longmans, Green & Co., 1920), pp. 417–418. In a footnote Mill argues that the labor invested in helping people acquire work abilities is productive, because these skills represent a kind of durable good. The worker can "transfer" the skills, in the sense that an employer can hire or purchase them. "If the skill itself cannot be parted with to a purchaser, the use of it may." This is the closest Mill comes to seeing labor as a potential the employer uses, but he does not connect this discussion with the

to wait for payment of a wage until their labor products were resold on the market, they would become capitalists like their employers: investment in products for resale, not authority over labor power, defines the capitalist's role in the employment relation.[169]

The conception of the transmission of labor presented in high theory coincided with that presented in the journals of the factory workers' insurgency during the 1830s. When the factory workers' press theorized the employment relation as a kind of economic exchange, it described the purchase of labor as concretized in a ware. For example, *The Poor Man's Advocate* said in 1832 that the mill owner who purchased a "stipulated quantity of labor" from workers was comparable to a customer who bought finished cloth in a store.[170]

The course of development of British political economy poses a genuine riddle when one recalls how the accepted definition of value, the *quantity* of labor embodied, might have caused economists to consider the actual determinants of the quantity of labor delivered. If Adam Smith confused the hiring of labor with the purchase of its product, this might be attributed to the ambiguities that often accompany the founding of a new science.[171] But if Ricardo and his followers, conscious of the need for revision, confused labor with its product, their failure identifies the restricted ways in which the British could imagine abstract labor as an economic factor at all. Of course, British commentators were perfectly capable of describing labor not as a product but as a force. The class of workers supplies "a given quantity of power for the production of commodities," E. S. Cayley wrote in 1830.[172] But remarks such as this define *labor* as a resource at large. They do not retain this formulation when they analyze the mechanisms by which labor is conveyed in a commercial transaction.

---

analysis of profit and exchange in the employment relation (p. 47). Mill also sees that, at the level of the national economy, the ability of labor to produce more than it is paid in a certain time period represents the source of profit, but, again, he does not apply this insight to the capitalist employment relation but says it holds true in societies without the exchange of labor in any form (p. 417).

169. Ibid., p. 417; John Stuart Mill, *Essays on Some Unsettled Questions of Political Economy* (2d ed. London: Longmans, Green, Reader & Dyer, 1874), p. 104.

170. *The Poor Man's Advocate*, January 21, 1832, p. 1. See below, Chapter Nine.

171. Smith sensed his problems. When he sought to explain "wherein consists the real price of all commodities," he apologized that "some obscurity may remain upon a subject in its own nature extremely abstracted." *Wealth of Nations*, op. cit., p. 33.

172. E. S. Cayley, *On Commercial Economy* (London: James Ridgway, 1830), p. 2.

In the analysis of the social mechanisms of capitalism, the signifier *labor* served two functions in classical British political economy. First, it establishes the *medium* for expressing prices, the framework within which prices can mean something. In its second function, *labor* generates the particular messages that the general medium transmits: it specifies the particular values and the movement of values among commodities. In *The Principles* Ricardo moves back and forth without distinction between these two symbolic functions. Thus, when he says that labor "determines" prices, this can mean either that it fixes prices or, at other places, that it lets one ascertain prices. Ricardo conflates these two functions by using the words *regulate* and *measure* interchangeably.[173] In the end, abstract labor came into sight for the British only in the process of exchange. They could not compare labor as a capacity in production or as an activity, only via the finished goods that were traded against each other. The generalizing of labor occurred at the completion of the production process. Nassau Senior, for example, excluded economically productive actions from the category of "labour" unless people performed them for the purpose of exchange.[174]

An emblematic contradiction between form and content runs through the *Wealth of Nations*: the argument makes labor the fount of value, preparatory to sale, whereas the language of analysis treats the labor activity— production—as itself a vending transaction. Smith declares, "Labour was the first price, the original purchase money that was paid for all things. It was not by gold or silver, but by labour, that all the wealth of the world was originally purchased."[175] As the German commentator Theodor Bernhardi remarked in 1847, Smith here equates the original process of production— the creation of a good through the labor activity—with the socially organized way of acquiring goods through monetary exchange.[176] When Smith discusses the determination of the level of wages, he transforms the labor of the isolated worker into a system of trade. "The produce of labour," he

173. This is the insight of Oswald St. Clair, op. cit., pp. 333–335, who diligently traces Ricardo's usages of the terms *regulate* and *measure* in books and correspondence. For an analysis of John Stuart Mill's recognition of this slippage but failure to resolve it, see Blaug, op. cit., pp. 173–174.

174. Nassau William Senior, *An Outline of the Science of Political Economy* (New York: Farrar & Rinehart, 1939 [1836]), p. 57.

175. *Wealth of Nations*, op. cit., p. 35. I am indebted to the astute commentary of Louis Dumont, op. cit., p. 194.

176. Theodor Bernhardi, *Versuch einer Kritik der Gründe, die für grosses und kleines Grundeigentum angeführt werden* (St. Petersburg: Kaiserliche Akademie der Wissenschaften, 1849), p. 101 (written in 1847).

asserts, "constitutes the natural recompence or wages of labour."[177] He frequently uses phrases such as the "labour commonly employed in *acquiring or producing* any commodity," another expression which makes production analogous to acquisition by exchange.[178] Every person who sells his labor, Smith says, "becomes in some measure a merchant," a turn of speech that places the laborer and the tradesman (who merely deals with finished goods) in similar roles.[179]

No wonder Smith's usage makes no distinction between *commerce* and *industry*. He assimilated the process of production to that of exchange. Spokespersons for the common people of Britain in the nineteenth century expressed the same point of view. When they criticized the capitalists' abuse of their power, they defined the capitalists not by their position in production but by their position as manipulative peddlers in the market. The holders of capital, William Heighton explained to trade union members in 1827, "effect exchanges by proxy, without working at all themselves and accumulate the wealth which other people's labour has created through the medium of profit."[180]

The British identification of the commodity of labor in the sphere of circulation left its impression upon the English language. The British, but not the Germans, felt the need to emphasize a single word as the signifier of production undertaken for the sake of exchange. History kindly provided an Anglo-German mediator who noticed this long ago. Friedrich Engels called it to the attention of both German and British readers in translations and annotated editions of *Kapital*. As Engels discovered, the English language in the course of the eighteenth and nineteenth centuries came to rely upon *work* to refer to the qualitative activity of making *use* values; whereas *labor*, the only word that indicated diverse activities as serving a general productive function, became the marker for the activity considered as an abstract creator and quantitative measure of *exchange* value.[181] Certainly

---

177. *Wealth of Nations*, op. cit., p. 72.

178. Ibid., pp. 53–56.

179. Ibid., p. 26. More than a century later, people with factory experience still echoed Smith's words. A spinner, Harold Catling averred, is a "tradesman selling the fruits of his labor." Harold Catling, *The Spinning Mule* (Newton Abbot: David & Charles, 1970), p. 149.

180. William Heighton, *An Address to the Members of Trade Societies and to the Working-Classes Generally* (London: Co-Operative Society, 1827), p. 5, cited in Noel Thompson, *The Market and Its Critics* (London: Routledge, 1988), p. 61. See also footnotes 31 ff. in Chapter Nine, below.

181. See Friedrich Engels's comment in the fourth edition of *Kapital* he edited, cited in *Kapital*, op. cit., pp. 61–62. For references to the same distinction appearing in later writing in English, see Hartmut Graach, "'Labour' und 'Work,'" in Sprachwissenschaftliches Collo-

Smith testified to this usage when he argued that "there may be more *labour* in an hours hard *work* than in two hours easy business."[182]

The difference in meanings between *work* and *labor* in economic discourse did not lie in them as a potential waiting to come to life with the historical development of wage labor; people strove to *create* the distinction in the course of the eighteenth century. Sir James Steuart, for example, had put forward the same conceptual distinction before Smith but had marked it with another arbitrary pairing of terms, that of simple *labor*, production for use, versus *industry*, production for exchange.[183] Steuart's writings show that the need to mark the difference in perspectives on the work activity—the need the terms *work* and *labor* happened later to fulfill—preceded the actual semantic differentiation.[184] Therefore we cannot attribute this differentiation to the stock of words that English, as opposed to German, fortuitously had at its disposal. The Germans had equivalent lexical options available to them.[185] The English term *work* derives from the same source as the German verbs *werken* and *wirken* and, before the rise of liberal commercialism, had a parallel range of meanings.[186] Likewise, the Germans had at their disposal the verb *arbeiten* to correspond to *labor*, inasmuch as the German term, too, was originally associated with the Latin concept of

---

quium Bonn, editor, *Europäische Schlüsselwörter: Wortvergleichende und wortgeschichtliche Studien* (München: Max Hueber Verlag, 1964), pp. 293, 295. Edward Aveling relied on the distinction between labor and work in *The Students' Marx: An Introduction to the Study of Karl Marx' "Capital"* (London: Swan Sonnenschein & Co., 1907), p. 44.

182. *Wealth of Nations*, op. cit., p. 35. My emphasis.

183. "Labour which through its alienation creates a universal equivalent, I call *industry*." Yet Steuart tried to further restrict *industry* to voluntary work in such a way that he overlaid the difference between the work activity as a creator of exchange value and as a creator of use value with other meanings. He left it to Smith to extract the difference in its pure form. Op. cit., Volume I, pp. 146 ff. See Volume II, p. 382, for a definition of *labour*.

184. Authors of the seventeenth century did not treat *work* and *labor* as evident synonyms, but neither did they ascribe indubitable contrasts to them. Petty emphasized that labor was governed by the necessity of maximizing the goods available for exchange. In his table of words he defined *labour* as a person's devotion to the making of commodities "for so many houres as hee is naturally able to endure the same." Sir William Petty, *The Petty Papers*, Volume I (New York: Augustus Kelley, 1967), p. 211. Andrew Yarranton may have supposed that the terms *work* and *labor* had different connotations when he referred to those who "work or labour in Mechanik arts." Op. cit., p. 170.

185. See Hannah Arendt, *The Human Condition* (Chicago: University of Chicago Press, 1958), pp. 79–80.

186. Ortrud Reichel, "Zur Bedeutungswechsel der Worte 'Werk' und 'Wirken' in as, ahd, und mhd Zeit," diss., University of Tübingen, 1952, pp. 92–93; Klaus Grinda, *"Arbeit" und "Mühe": Untersuchungen zur Bedeutungsgeschichte altenglischer Wörter* (München: Wilhelm Fink, 1975), pp. 53 ff.

painful exertion or *molestia*.[187] The Germans did not consecrate the words available to them to differentiate between production for use and production for exchange, although *werken* survived into the first half of the nineteenth century as a verb referring to productive activity.[188] We can conclude that the divergence reflects a difference in the concepts with which people apprehended economic activity, given the original similarity in lexical resources but the final difference between German and British usage. As components of popular languages, these terms and the conceptual operations to which they corresponded were the property in common of economic agents in each country, not the preserve of speculative intellectuals.

THE INSINCERITY OF THE HISTORICAL PROCESS

Social theorists of capitalist development have long characterized Britain as the pioneer society of a liberal market order. In the seventeenth and eighteenth centuries it certainly led Europe in building a nationally penetrating network of trade.[189] In addition, historical analysts of diverse allegiances, from Barrington Moore to Jürgen Kuczynski, have highlighted Britain's early reliance upon market mechanisms rather than upon seigneurial coercion for the extraction of surplus from the agricultural work force.[190] In manufacturing, the separate processes of developing markets in goods and of relaxing administrative controls for the compulsory delivery of labor

187. Günther Drosdowski et al., editors, *Duden Etymologie: Herkunftswörterbuch der deutschen Sprache* (Mannheim: Bibliographisches Institut, 1963), p. 31. Konrad Wiedemann, *Arbeit und Bürgertum: Die Entwicklung des Arbeitsbegriffs in der Literatur Deutschlands an der Wende zur Neuzeit* (Heidelberg: Carl Winter, 1979), p. 255. The word *Arbeit* derives from *arba*, "servant." The verb therefore referred to the activity of a servant. Until the sixteenth century it indicated the activity of feudal workers in agriculture. *Arbeit* in Friedrich Ludwig Karl Weigand, *Deutsches Wörterbuch*, fifth ed., revised by Hermann Hirt et al. (Giessen: A. Topelmann, 1909–1910).

188. The word *werken* still had currency in the countryside at least up to the First World War and had not become archaic even in the cities by 1854, when the Grimms compiled their dictionary. Jacob Grimm and Wilhelm Grimm, *Deutsches Wörterbuch von Jacob Grimm und Wilhelm Grimm* (Leipzig: S. Hirzel, 1854), Volume 14, p. 361.

189. Ellen Meiksins Wood, *The Pristine Culture of Capitalism* (London: Verso, 1991), pp. 95–96. Adrian Randall shows that even the "moral community" of the eighteenth century, which E. P. Thompson so aptly portrayed, was founded upon market relations. Op. cit., pp. 88–89.

190. Kuczynski, op. cit., Volume IV, Part One, p. 225; Barrington Moore, *Social Origins of Dictatorship and Democracy* (Boston: Beacon Press, 1966), pp. 419–420, 424; Robert Brenner, "The Agrarian Roots of European Capitalism," in T. H. Aston and C. H. E. Philpin, editors, *The Brenner Debate: Agrarian Class Structure and Economic Development in Pre-Industrial Europe* (Cambridge: Cambridge University Press, 1985), pp. 297–299.

occurred very early in Britain in world-historical time, but they were staggered far apart in the country's own developmental time. The elimination of guild monopolies on the exchange of wares and of internal barriers to trade, as well as the attachment of the countryside to merchant enterprise in London, were nearing completion by the mid-seventeenth century. The cessation of the requisitioning of labor and of community controls on wages required in some important regions of the country up to a century more.

In terms of its own developmental sequence, then, Britain is distinguished by the relatively late emergence of a formal market in wage labor, given the advanced commercialization of the finished-goods sector.[191] To appreciate this lag one need only compare Sir William Blackstone's definition of the employment relation with that of the Code Napoleon in France. In France the creation of a unified national market in goods occurred later than in Britain, but its definitive recognition coincided with the annihilation of the guilds and, during 1790 and 1791, the formal abolition of corporate controls on the marketing of labor. The Civil Code of Napoleon, promulgated just after the dawning of a liberal market regime in France, recognized "services for rent"—labor power—as a commodity freely exchangeable on the basis of individual contract alone.[192] By contrast, Blackstone, we have seen, treated the engagement of labor power as a transaction founded on the ascribed inferiority of the worker—on status rather than compact. Until 1867, British law treated the worker either as an inferior, subject to imprisonment merely for failure to deliver labor, or as an independent contractor who delivered products.[193] This archaic disjuncture in British law betrayed

191. I do not claim that the actual exchanges in goods or labor in Britain *ever* approached the economists' ideal of a free market. But the institutional structures in place by the mid-eighteenth century recognized labor as a good that in principle was traded according to the unhampered play of the market. Here I adopt the empirical approach to the study of "markets" exemplified in Stuart Plattner's essay "Markets and Marketplaces" in Stuart Plattner, editor, *Economic Anthropology* (Stanford: Stanford University Press, 1989).

192. P. A. Fenet, *Recueil complet des trauvaux préparatoires du Code civil* (Osnabrück: Otto Zeller, 1968 [1827]), Volume 14, p. 339. On the liberality of French labor contracts at the dawn of the new commercial order, see Michael Sonenscher, *Work and Wages: Natural Law, Politics and the Eighteenth-Century French Trades* (Cambridge: Cambridge University Press, 1989), pp. 366–367.

193. The application of the Master and Servant Act, by whose terms failure to work was a criminal offense punishable by imprisonment, did not exclude application of the notion that labor was delivered in a product. The act punished domestic weavers or other home workers who delivered products more than seven days later than scheduled. Testimony of John Strahan, PP 1865 (370) VIII, pp. 3–4. In 1836 the court in Preston ruled that weavers who paid loom rent to a master could not be dismissed from their jobs for coming and going as they pleased, unless they absented themselves more than seven days. In that case, the Master and Servant Act could be invoked. *Preston Pilot*, December 3, 1836. Here, too, the employer was denied a

the legacy of the country's early focus upon the enforced delivery of labor power or the contractual delivery of labor as it was embodied in products.

German commentators found it anomalous that even in the twentieth century the British continued to model the contractual elements of the employment relation upon the delivery of goods. In 1904 Otto von Zwiedineck-Südenhorst compared the German and the British legal classifications:

> With the modern labor contract the full commitment of the labor power of an individual for a certain time through the employment relation ensues, even if the measurement of compensation proceeds according to labor output. The interpretation of this matter seems to differ in England, as emerges from the Labor Department's report on standard piece-rate wages and sliding scales of 1900 (page ten). There the viewpoint is expressed that only the completion of a certain work forms the content of the piece-rate agreement; in other words, that an agreement for a contractor's work, as understood in our civil law, is present.[194]

The British terms for the conveyance of labor might seem less demanding of the worker, but they scarcely derived from the "liberal" British past.

Historical development in Britain cunningly disguised the origins of the commodity form assumed by labor. The concept of labor as a commodity in Britain resembled the exchange of materialized labor between independent petty-commodity producers, or, in more ennobling terms, between freeborn tradespeople. This ideal was sustained in production but did not truthfully reflect its circumstances. Only a fraction of artisans were truly autonomous producers, as Adam Smith himself acknowledged. The toilsome research of modern historians has revealed that even in London, the hub of the artisanal trades, by 1800 only 5 or 6 percent of workers were genuinely self-employed.[195] The understanding of the labor transaction in Britain as the transfer of materialized labor emerged, not from a preponderance of free

---

claim to the workers' labor power, but the act was still enforceable. The act represented a carryover from the enforced sequestering of labor, but after the mid-eighteenth century it was used only to specify the sanctions to be applied if the contractual terms for the transmission of labor were violated. United Kingdom, *Second and Final Report of the Commissioners Appointed to Inquire into the Working of the Master and Servant Act, 1867*, PP 1875 XXX, p. 5.

194. Otto von Zwiedineck-Südenhorst, *Beiträge zur Lehre von den Lohnformen* (Tübingen: H. Laupp, 1904), p. 18.

195. L. D. Schwarz, "Income Distribution and Social Structure in London in the Late Eighteenth Century," *Economic History Review* Volume XXXII, Number 2 (May 1979), pp. 256–257; L. D. Schwarz, *London in the Age of Industrialisation* (Cambridge: Cambridge University Press, 1992), p. 167.

artisans, but from the protracted subjection of labor power itself to social regulation that denied its sellers the contractual and political rights of free, market agents during the economic and cultural formation of a commercial society. Only as it was objectified in products did labor at this critical step of development receive its commodity form. History succeeded in perpetrating a ruse, because coercion itself gave rise to an apparition of freedom: the repressive yoking of wage labor in this era of transition shifted the commercial model to the independent producer as the celebrated, mythologized seller of labor products, the only free vendor of labor in a precociously founded market regime.

6 The Fused and Uneven Recognition of Markets in Germany

> Every serf knows that what he expends in the service of his lord is a definite quantity of his own personal labor power.
>
> Karl Marx, *Das Kapital*

Germany's passage to a capitalist regime differed from Britain's not only in speed and deliberateness but in the conjuncture of institutional changes that helped define the significance of the transition for economic agents. In Britain an extensive free intercourse in manufactured products and a market discourse emerged before "labor power"—if we may use the term here as an analytic category rather than as one recognized by the agents—acquired its specification as a commodity. In Germany, the lifting of statutes that restricted the trade of finished products coincided in many industrial sectors with the shift to the formally free sale of labor power. In contrast to cultural development in Britain, in Germany market discourse included labor power itself from the start. This difference did not suffice to create the definition of labor as a commodity that prevailed in Germany, but it presents the initial fork in the road to be explored. This chapter pursues three dividing points for the German case rather than the single temporal disjuncture which illuminated cultural development in Britain.

Apart from the simultaneous creation of formal markets in merchandise and labor, two additional circumstances fixed the background for German producers to find a cultural destination: the survival of feudal definitions of labor service in the countryside, and the continued corporate organization of artisanal work by the guilds. Marx and Engels contended that these survivals deprived the German economy of a crystalline capitalist form, by comparison with the pure classical model of Britain.[1] It was on Britain, of

---

1. *Das Kapital* (Berlin: Dietz Verlag, 1980), Volume One, pp. 12–15; Friedrich Engels, "Die preussische Militärfrage und die deutsche Arbeiterpartei" (1865), in Karl Marx and Friedrich Engels, *Marx-Engels Werke*, Volume 16 (Berlin: Dietz Verlag, 1973), p. 67.

course, that they fastened their keenest theoretic attention. But if economic change follows a manifest logic, cultural development is the history of the uncanny. The unique articulation of free commercial practices and corporate restraints in the German labor market during the early nineteenth century gave rise to an understanding of the labor transaction which was perhaps more penetrating than that invented by producers in the British setting. At the very least, the German economic agents' appreciation of labor paralleled the key insights Marx developed in his theoretic analysis of the capitalist labor process. The amalgam of formal market intercourse with corporate regulation in Germany did not obscure the essence of the capitalist labor process, but it contributed to a breakthrough in understanding. Marx imagined that capitalist Britain revealed the image of Germany's own future,[2] but who could have dreamed that the less-developed country could show to Britain, the more developed, the image of Britain's true workings?

CORPORATE REGULATION

Was the transition to a liberal commercial order truly less complete in Germany than in Britain, as Marx and Engels claimed? The story of the shift to a juridically free market society in Britain depends upon imperceptible trends; in Germany, where change in the economic constitution was consciously orchestrated from above, it pivots to a greater degree on discrete events. The westernmost regions of Germany entered the era of free commercialism between 1798 and 1810, when the French invaders abolished the guilds and issued the decrees needed to remake economic life in the occupied provinces and towns in their own image of liberty.[3] Official change in the framework of commerce took place very dramatically in Prussia, too, where the government's decrees in 1810 and 1811 attempted to abolish the corporate regulation of trade and occupations almost overnight.[4] Other German states moved more slowly than Prussia. But during the first half of the nineteenth century each of them in a series of grand steps removed legal barriers to trade and to the unhampered exercise of occupations.

2. *Kapital*, op. cit., p. 12.
3. The French abolished guilds in the Rhineland in 1798. T. C. W. Blanning, *The French Revolution in Germany: Occupation and Resistance in the Rhineland 1792–1802* (Oxford: Clarendon Press, 1983), p. 155.
4. Prussia had introduced freedom of trade for cotton and linen production in 1806. Kurt von Rohrscheidt, *Vom Zunftzwange zur Gewerbefreiheit* (Berlin: Carl Heymanns Verlag, 1898), p. 186.

It is easy to exaggerate the suffocation of intercourse prior to these reforms for the sake of creating more vivid contrasts in business life before versus after their promulgation. The most recent historical research has more realistically emphasized the gradual de facto weakening of guild and merchant privileges over many decades. From a cross-national perspective, however, a crucial finding remains: throughout the eighteenth century, enough of the industry and exchange of Germany transpired within corporate institutions to prevent the market from appearing as a force with laws of its own. Although exceptions abounded, guild regulations in the towns assigned specific lines of products to each type of craftsman. Such rules were effective enough that they prevented small masters from switching to new lines of handiwork in response to consumer demands.[5] Of course the statutes controlled not just the manufacture of goods but their conveyance.[6] Before 1787, guild artisans in Prussia were generally prevented from marketing their wares outside their home towns;[7] and even after this date, the protective laws enacted for many localities excluded import of craft goods from neighboring towns and regions.[8] Putting-out merchants in Prussia and Saxony were required to get special approval to sell their goods to the public, rather than to authorized guild merchants who attempted to arrogate the important distribution outlets.[9] A blanket of regulation enveloped the pro-

5. Barbara Vogel, *Allgemeine Gewerbefreiheit: Die Reformpolitik des preussischen Staatskanzlers Hardenberg (1810–1820)* (Göttingen: Vandenhoeck & Ruprecht, 1983), p. 158; Karl Heinrich Kaufhold, *Das Gewerbe in Preussen um 1800* (Göttingen: Otto Schwartz & Co., 1978), p. 426. On the regulation of prices and patterns in textiles in Aachen, see P. Sagnac, *Le Rhin français pendant la révolution et l'empire* (Paris: Félix Alcan, 1917), p. 36.

6. Martin Herbert Pönicke, *Die Geschichte der Tuchmacherei und verwandter Gewerbe in Reichenbach i. V. vom 17. bis Anfang des 19. Jahrhunderts* (Plauen: Franz Neupert, 1929), pp. 32–33, 78; Blanning, op. cit., p. 49.

7. Gustav Schmoller, *Umrisse und Untersuchungen zur Verfassungs-, Verwaltungs- und Wirtschaftsgeschichte* (Leipzig: Duncker & Humblot, 1898), pp. 427–428.

8. Ibid.; Hugo Wendel, *The Evolution of Industrial Freedom in Prussia 1845–1849* (Allentown, Pennsylvania: H. R. Haas, 1918), p. 14; Wolfram Fischer, *Handwerksrecht und Handwerkswirtschaft um 1800* (Berlin: Duncker & Humblot, 1955), p. 37. On the survival of city import taxes, see Rolf Straubel, "Verlage und Manufakturen im Textilgewerbe der preussischen Provinzen Magdeburg und Halberstadt 1763–1800," *Jahrbuch für Geschichte des Feudalismus*, Volume 14 (Berlin: Akademie-Verlag, 1990), p. 212. In Saxony, nonguild producers in the countryside could not sell their wares to the weekly markets in the cities. Paul Horster, *Die Entwicklung der sächsischen Gewerbeverfassung, 1780–1861* (Crefeld: Wilhelm Greven, 1908), p. 27.

9. This barrier to marketing eroded in Prussia during the second half of the eighteenth century but did not disappear until 1794. Hugo Rachel, *Das Berliner Wirtschaftsleben im Zeitalter des Frühkapitalismus* (Berlin: Rembrandt-Verlag, 1931), pp. 166–167; Herbert Kisch, "The Crafts and Their Role in the Industrial Revolution: The Case of the German Textile Industry," Ph.D. diss., University of Washington, 1958, p. 8. In Saxony, which reformed its

curement of raw materials as well. In Prussia, Saxony, and other regions, guild masters had either a monopoly on the purchase of wool or the legal right to purchase it before other traders.[10]

Restrictions on the sale of labor prior to the reforms appeared no less comprehensive. In Prussia, Frederick the Great fixed wages for craft and common labor.[11] In several of the German states, authorities ensured that the use of labor did not fluctuate: they forbade both the sudden firing of home workers and severe cutbacks in piece rates.[12] Home workers could not always vend the products of their industry as they wished, as if they were entrepreneurs. Instead, workers such as spinners, whose product represented an input for weavers, were required to sell their goods to the local weavers' guild.[13] In turn weavers in many regions were required to sell their finished cloth to an authorized entrepreneur or to a local merchant guild, which often had a monopoly on the distribution of the product.[14] In Württemberg the master weavers who had to sell their goods at fixed prices to a

---

business laws more slowly than Prussia did, restrictions on the ability of producers to market their own goods were debated into the 1830s. See *Die Ameise*, January 5, 1838, pp. 11–12.

10. Schmoller, op. cit., p. 425; Günther Kesselbauer, "Einige Probleme des Kampfes der preussischen Bourgeoisie zur Durchsetzung der kapitalischen Produktionsverhältnisse 1789 bis 1806," *Jahrbuch für Wirtschaftsgeschichte* Teil II/III (1964), p. 119; Hans Medick, "Freihandel für die Zunft," in *Mentalitäten und Lebensverhältnisse: Beispiele aus der Sozialgeschichte der Neuzeit*, Festschrift für Rudolf Vierhaus (Göttingen: Vandenhoeck & Ruprecht, 1982), p. 283.

11. Johann Landau, "Die Arbeiterfrage in Deutschland im XVII. und XVIII. Jahrhundert und ihre Behandlung in der deutschen Kameralwissenschaft," diss., Zürich, 1915, p. 129. Marx surveys the history of wage regulation in Silesia in *Das Kapital*, op. cit., Volume One, pp. 767–768. Compared to Britain, however, wage regulation in Germany may not have been so closely tied to a belief in the imposition of poverty to force workers to labor. Cilly Böhle, *Die Idee der Wirtschaftsverfassung im deutschen Merkantilismus* (Jena: Gustav Fischer, 1940), p. 131.

12. Landau, op. cit., p. 223, 237; Schmoller, op. cit., pp. 552, 556. On guild control of wages in Berlin, see Wolfram Fischer, *Handwerksrecht und Handwerkswirtschaft um 1800* (Berlin: Duncker & Humblot, 1955), p. 35.

13. Louis Bein, *Die Industrie des sächsischen Voigtlandes. Zweiter Theil: Die Textil-Industrie* (Leipzig: Duncker & Humblot, 1884), pp. 72–73; Walter Troeltsch, *Die Calwer Zeughandlungskompagnie und ihre Arbeiter* (Jena: Gustav Fischer, 1897), p. 129.

14. Bein, op. cit., p. 232; Medick, op. cit., p. 289–290; Walter Schneider, *Die Apoldaer Wirkwarenindustrie bis zum Jahre 1914* (Jena: Gustav Fischer, 1922), p. 11; Hermann Lehmann, "Die Wollphantasiewaren im nordöstlichen Thüringen," *Schriften des Vereins für Socialpolitik* Volume 40, Part Two (1889), p. 21; Hermann Kellenbenz, "The Organization of Industrial Production," in *The Cambridge Economic History of Europe*, Volume V (Cambridge: Cambridge University Press, 1977), p. 520; Jürgen Schlumbohm, "Seasonal Fluctuations and Social Division of Labour: Rural Linen Production in the Osnabrück and Bielefeld Regions and the Urban Woollen Industry in the Niederlausitz c. 1770–c. 1850," in Maxine Berg et al., editor, *Manufacture in Town and Country Before the Factory* (Cambridge: Cambridge University Press, 1983), p. 94; Landau, op. cit., p. 223.

chartered merchant company protested in 1753 about their dependence. In a petition to the ducal authorities, they complained that officialdom's regulations deprived the small master "of what he could otherwise realize from the ware, so that he stands in severe personal servitude . . . in which he can earn nothing for his own account and for his family."[15] By comparison with Britain, state controls in Germany established an adverse setting during the eighteenth century for idealizing small manufacturers as independent producers whose products were exchanged in accordance with the labor they contained.[16]

The guild and mercantile constraints proved least effective in the countryside, where competition from unauthorized producers, above all in the textile branch, had by the end of the eighteenth century eroded the guild members' monopolies on manufacture in many parts of Germany.[17] Yet

15. Medick, op. cit., p. 291.

16. Of course, petty-commodity producers in eighteenth-century Germany could appreciate mastery over their own labor time without viewing the price of their goods as a measure of their materialized labor. Josef Mooser, "Maschinensturm und Assoziation: Die Spinner und Weber zwischen sittlicher Ökonomie, Konservatismus und Demokratie in der Krise des Leinengewerbes in Ravensberg, 1840–1870," in Karl Ditt and Sidney Pollard, editors, *Von der Heimarbeit in die Fabrik* (Paderborn: Ferdinand Schöningh, 1992), p. 337.

17. Yet the textile trade in the Wupper Valley illustrates the continuing influence of corporate organization even in a region that enjoyed relative commercial freedom. Originally entrepreneurs in this area prospered by avoiding the confines of the guild system in Cologne. The valley was protected under the Duchy of Berg from the impositions of excise officials who patrolled manufactures in Prussia. Despite this comparative liberty, however, manufacturers could still acquire exclusive manufacturing privileges. A cartel of merchants in the towns of Barmen and Elberfeld acquired a legal monopoly on the bleaching of yarn for the region's fabrics. The cartel assigned production quotas for each of its members until 1764. Until its dissolution during the Napoleonic occupation, the organization continued to index wages, supervise the manufacture of cloth, regulate designs, and levy fees for the production and sale of traditional yarns and ribbons. Members of the association were prohibited from bidding for each other's workers and from raising workers' benefits. Herbert Kisch, *From Domestic Manufacture to Industrial Revolution: The Case of the Rhineland Textile Districts* (Oxford: Oxford University Press, 1989), pp. 112, 123, 144; Walter Dietz, *Die Wuppertaler Garnnahrung: Geschichte der Industrie und des Handels von Elberfeld und Barmen 1400 bis 1800* (Neustadt an der Aisch: Ph. C. W. Schmidt, 1957), p. 141. The nearby town of Wermelskirchen, which became dependent upon Wuppertal yarn, also limited textile production by charter. Helmut vom Stein, *Die industrielle Entwicklung der Stadt Wermelskirchen seit Anfang des neunzehnten Jahrhunderts* (Düsseldorf: G. H. Nolte, 1939), p. 2. Krefeld, across the Rhine from the Wupper Valley, offers another example of a town that developed corporate restrictions on manufacture despite the original weakness of the guilds. In this city, which became the center of the Rhineland's silk trade, one merchant family acquired the exclusive privilege to manufacture silk ribbons and handkerchiefs. The family, which employed the largest segment of the region's weavers, also used government sanctions to limit workers' mobility. Kisch, op. cit., p. 182; Peter Kriedte, "Proto-Industrialisierung und grosses Kapital: Das Seidengewerbe in Krefeld und seinem Umland bis zum Ende des Ancien Regime," *Archiv für Sozialgeschichte* Volume 23 (1983), p. 265.

the independent producers in the countryside were not automatically freed of requirements to sell to chartered traders; moreover, in some instances they were officially forbidden to compete with urban producers.[18] In Silesia, new legislation in 1788 required country weavers to bring their products to authorized traders for inspection and pricing.[19] Until the introduction of freedom of trade in the countryside at the close of the eighteenth century, officials in many regions viewed the putting-out system as ancillary to the essential enterprise of agriculture.[20] Entrepreneurs organized their networks according to the privileges granted by mercantilist officials rather than by considerations of transport and resources.[21] Only the Napoleonic invasions and the Prussian response initiated the reforms that cleared away such thickets of official control and gave clear institutional form to the strengthening current of market development in the rural outlands.[22]

The reception of the *Wealth of Nations* in Germany serves as a barometer for the country's economic climate. German was the first foreign language in which Smith's opus was published. The initial volume of its

18. For an example of Saxon prohibitions of rural competition in the textile branch, see Kisch, op. cit., p. 49; for Göttingen, see Walter Höttemann, *Die Göttinger Tuchindustrie der Vergangenheit und Gegenwart* (Göttingen: Göttinger Handelsdruckerei, 1931), p. 56.

19. Hermann Aubin and Wolfgang Zorn, editors, *Handbuch der deutschen Wirtschafts- und Sozialgeschichte*, Volume 1 (Stuttgart: Union Verlag, 1971), p. 537.

20. Uwe Puschner, *Handwerk zwischen Tradition und Wandel* (Göttingen: Otto Schwartz & Co., 1988), p. 179. Johann Heinrich Jung, *Versuch eines Lehrbuchs der Fabrikwissenschaft* (Nürnberg: Grattenauer, 1785), "Vorrede."

21. Jürgen Kocka, "Entrepreneurs and Managers in German Industrialization," in *The Cambridge Economic History of Europe*, Volume VII, Part I (Cambridge: Cambridge University Press, 1978), pp. 504–505. In Göttingen the guild merchants in the late eighteenth century were required to sell a certain amount of cloth fabricated by local chartered manufactories. Klaus Assmann, "Verlag—Manufaktur—Fabrik: Die Entwicklung grossbetrieblicher Unternehmensformen im Göttinger Tuchmachergewerbe," in Wilhelm Abel, editor, *Handwerksgeschichte in neuer Sicht* (Göttingen: Otto Schwartz & Co., 1978), pp. 225, 226. Although manufactories in Prussia were freed of guild regulation upon the use of labor, until the early nineteenth century they relied upon official charters to exclude competition in the marketing of their products. Vogel, op. cit., p. 163. See below, this chapter, p. 291.

22. The putting-out system in Germany dated back to the Middle Ages. Why did this not contribute in Germany to a concept of labor transferred as it is materialized in a ware? The putting-out system in Germany did not create a concept of labor as a commodity similar to the British specification for the simple reason that production for exchange was still segmented and fractured by restrictions and supervision such that a formally recognized market did come into its own. The dominance of trade regulation in the German countryside can be seen in the appeals of rural putting-out entrepreneurs for restrictions on entry into the trade even in the waning days of trade supervision. "Ein Fabrikant," *Praktische Darstellung der Oberlausitzer Leinwand-Fabrikation nebst ihren Mängeln* (Herrnhut: J. D. Schöpfische Buchhandlung, 1837), pp. 49, 66.

translation appeared in Leipzig in 1776, the year of the English publication in London.[23] At this early juncture, however, German critics overlooked its substantive innovations and emphasized instead its incidental similarities to the doctrines of French physiocrats, such as the assumption that agricultural rents rise with prosperity.[24] Smith's ideas were not rejected—they were uncomprehended.[25] For us, the categories Smith used may seem commonsensical and "life-like." But German translators and scholarly reviewers of Smith's work found the main arguments perplexing. "The original is extremely difficult," an early reviewer said, "and the language, by reason of the technical and juridical expressions, difficult and obscure."[26] A translator confessed that he had had to read the book several times over to make sense of it.[27] The German interpreters' attempts to rephrase Smith's expressions illustrates one source of difficulty.[28] The first German translations showed some reluctance to conceive of labor as an abstract category. Where Smith referred to "the demand for labor," his interpreters rendered it as "demand for laboring

---

23. W. Roscher, "Die Ein- und Durchführung des Adam Smith'schen Systems in Deutschland," *Berichte über die Verhandlungen der königlich sächsischen Gesellschaft der Wissenschaften zu Leipzig*, Philologisch-historische Classe Volume 9 (Berlin: Akademie-Verlag, 1867), pp. 4–5. Many German scholars read English, so Tribe surmises that translations were intended for broader professional audiences. Keith Tribe, *Governing Economy: The Reformation of German Economic Discourse 1750–1840* (Cambridge: Cambridge University Press, 1988), p. 134.

24. Roscher, op. cit., pp. 8 ff. Carl W. Hasek, *The Introduction of Adam Smith's Doctrines into Germany* (New York: Columbia University, 1925), pp. 64 ff.; Tribe, op. cit., pp. 145–147.

25. Roscher, op. cit., pp. 17–21; Alfred Nahrgang, "Die Aufnahme der wirtschaftspolitischen Ideen von Adam Smith in Deutschland zu Beginn des XIX. Jahrhunderts, diss., Frankfurt am Main, 1933/34, p. 29; Hugo Graul, *Das Eindringen der Smithschen Nationalökonomie in Deutschland und ihre Weiterbildung bis zu Hermann* (Halle-Saale: Paul Malok, 1928), p. 35. For a partial German rendition of the *Wealth of Nations* in 1779 in which Adam Smith is a person of no consequence for the translator, see Kenneth E. Carpenter, *Dialogue in Political Economy: Translations from and into German in the Eighteenth Century* (Boston: Harvard University Printing Office, 1977), p. 93.

26. Cited in Erik Erämetsä, "Adam Smith als Mittler englisch-deutscher Spracheinflüsse," in Suomalainen Tiedeakatemia, editor, *Toimituksia: Annales*, Series B (Helsinki: Suomalainen Tiedeakatemia, 1961), p. 23.

27. Comments by Christian Garve, in the introduction to Adam Smith, *Untersuchung über die Natur und die Ursachen des Nationalreichtums*, trans. Christian Garve (Breslau: Wilhelm Korn, 1794), pp. iv–v. August Lueder complained that many of the examples Smith introduced to illustrate his argument seemed impenetrable. "Smith becomes unclear out of too great a fear of becoming unclear," Lueder said. *Über Nationalindustrie und Staatswirtschaft*, Part One (Berlin: Heinrich Frölich, 1800), p. xiii.

28. Roscher, op. cit., p. 17: Sartorius said, "Others are preferred, for they can be understood with greater ease." Cited in Hasek, op. cit., p. 67.

hands" or "demand for workers."[29] Smith endowed the category itself with life, whereas German expositors resisted the detachment of the category from concrete persons. These early exegetes, unaccustomed to the reified form of labor as a commodity, thought of labor only as visible work.[30]

The German publishers of the *Wealth of Nations* could not find a significant audience for their intellectual merchandise until the revolutionary market perspective entailed by commercial liberty was introduced.[31] They had not long to wait. The Prussian edict of 1810 made the purchase of a license the only requirement for conducting any form of enterprise anywhere in the state. In 1811 authorities abolished the regulation of wages and lifted requirements that craft entrepreneurs join a guild.[32] These expedients, and the similar ones that followed in the other German states, abruptly revised the conditions for conceiving of transfers of goods and services.[33]

29. This example comes from the neglected dissertation of Gustav Hagan, "Zum sachlichen und sprachlichen Einfluss der englischen politischen Ökonomie auf die deutsche im 18. und 19. Jahrhundert," diss., Humbolt-Universität, Berlin, 1968, pp. 124–125.

30. German and Austrian economic thinkers of the eighteenth century acknowledged that the labor of the population represented a valuable resource. Josef Sonnenfels made the improved use of labor the ultimate goal of economic policy. He sermonized about diverse forms of unfree labor services and work in manufactories, but he did not combine them under the general category of labor. Ernst F. Scheller, *Vorstellung und Begriff der wirtschaftlichen Arbeit* (Erlangen: M. Krahl, 1936), pp. 60–61; Josef von Sonnenfels, *Grundsätze der Staatspolizey, Handlung und Finanzwissenschaft* (2d ed. München: J. B. Strobel, 1801), pp. 259–270. Sonnenfels and other authors discussed means for improving labor's efficiency through machinery, but none conceived of labor as an abstract factor of production voluntarily delivered in a market. Johann Heinrich Gottlob von Justi said that "the blossoming of industry depends in the end on the labor of the lowly rabble." See *Gesammelte politische und Finanzschriften über wichtige Gegenstände der Staatskunst, der Kriegswissenschaften und des Kameral- und Finanzwesens* (Aalen: Scientia Verlag, 1970 [1761]), Volume One, p. 483. See also Hermann Rebel, "Reimagining the *Oikos*: Austrian Cameralism in Its Social Formation," in Jay O'Brien and William Roseberry, editors, *Golden Ages, Dark Ages* (Berkeley: University of California Press, 1991), p. 78.

31. The book reached a significant public audience in Germany only after the opening of debate over land and trade reform in Prussia in 1807. Georg Sartorius declared in 1796, "On this inquiry Smith really has had little or no influence at all among us up to now." *Handbuch der Staatswirthschaft, zum Gebrauche bei akademischen Vorlesungen nach Adam Smiths Grundsätzen ausgearbeitet* (Berlin, 1796), p. ix. On Smith's influence after 1806, see Marie-Elisabeth Vopelius, *Die altliberalen Ökonomen und die Reformzeit* (Stuttgart: Gustav Fischer, 1968).

32. Wendel, op. cit., p. 20; Shulamit Volkov, *The Rise of Popular Antimodernism in Germany* (Princeton: Princeton University Press, 1978), p. 166.

33. German economic thinkers of the eighteenth century wanted to encourage new business initiatives, and they inveighed against the unjust profits that the guilds' abuse of their privileges could create. But they did not appeal to the market as an autonomous force. Unlike their British counterparts, they did not recognize a process so abstract as the formation of natural prices which "the free Market of things will produce." W. Petyt, *Britannia Languens; Or, A Discourse of Trade*, 1680, in J. R. McCulloch, editor, *Early English Tracts on Commerce*

THE RECOGNITION OF LABOR
AS A COMMODITY

In Germany, reflection on market society included from the outset production based on the purchase of labor through the wage contract. It began not just with liberty of trade in manufactures, as in Britain, but with the full regime of capitalism, in keeping with the simultaneous creation of formal markets in wares and in labor power.[34] German economists who interpreted the emergence of industrial liberalism in the first decades of the nineteenth century appropriated many of Smith's insights but resold them by casting the role of labor to conform with the genesis of wage labor in Germany.[35] Long before the extensive development of the factory system in their coun-

---

(Cambridge: Cambridge University Press, 1954 [1856]), p. 512; William Letwin, *The Origins of Scientific Economics* (London: Methuen and Co., 1963), p. 181. Albion Small, *The Cameralists: The Pioneers of German Social Polity* (Chicago: The University of Chicago Press, 1909), pp. 443–447; Kurt von Rohrscheidt, *Vom Zunftzwange zur Gewerbefreiheit* (Berlin: Carl Heymanns Verlag, 1898), p. 186. Justus Christoph Dithmars, in *Einleitung in die Oeconomische Policei- und Cameral-Wissenschaften* (Franckfurth an der Oder: J. J. Friedel, 1745), mentions that "free trade is founded in natural and human law." But he adopts this phrase for foreign commerce to justify the right of states to decide on what terms they will trade with others (p. 118). He makes no reference to a "market."

34. Maurice Dobb, *Studies in the Development of Capitalism* (London: George Routledge & Sons, 1946), pp. 7–9.

35. At first, however, German writers tried to counterfeit his currency. German economists in the opening years of the nineteenth century could acquire a reputation in their country by demonstrating an ability to recapitulate, accurately or not, Smith's expositions. Christian Jacob Kraus, a respected colleague of Immanuel Kant's, was the first of the German professors to give lectures that belong to the modern discipline of economics. Kraus also achieved a measure of prominence for his influence upon the Prussian administrators who eliminated landlords' rights to tithes in labor in 1807. Hasek, op. cit., p. 96. William Reddy emphasizes Kraus's role in *Money and Liberty in Modern Europe* (Cambridge: Cambridge University Press, 1987), p. 82. In *Staatswirtschaft*, his treatise on political economy, Kraus reproduced not only Smith's ideas but his sentences, chapter headings, and anecdotes (including stories which had no particular bearing on Germany). See *Staatswirtschaft*, Volume I, composed before 1807 (Breslau: G. Schletter, 1837): p. xxvi has the same chapter headings; p. 37 revisits the pin factory; p. 22 borrows the same sentences, as well as some vocabulary unusual for German, such as "frivolste Professionen." By our standards he committed plagiarism; for contemporaries who were grappling with this new school of thought, including those who realized Kraus acted only as a transmitter, Kraus seemed brilliant. The two other German economists who published the first treatises on political economy, Georg Sartorius and August Lueder, advertised their debt to Smith by choosing book titles in which they declared that they had "worked out" Smith's ideas. Sartorius, op. cit.; Lueder, op. cit. Johann Heinrich von Thünen described his own excitement on reading Smith for the first time. *Der isolirte [sic] Staat*, Part II (Berlin: Wiegandt, Hempel & Parey, 1875), p. 61. The change in the reception of Smith's ideas indicates the depth of change that economic liberalization since 1776 had effected.

try, German observers of the market were occupied with a distinctive apparition of labor as a commodity which eventually emerged on the factory shop floor itself.

A survey of market theories in Britain can sight the pinnacles of Smith and Ricardo, but the terrain in Germany shows few towering peaks. If German economists of the period did not cast a long shadow, they still serve as indicators of the rise of contrasting economic assumptions. One of the first notable German treatises that presented an alternative to the British appreciation of labor came from the pen of Ludwig Jakob, a professor of philosophy at the University of Halle.[36] In a work published in 1805, Jakob adopted Smith's formulation of the labor theory of value, but already with modification. Smith, he noted perceptively, mistakenly identified the wage for labor with the quantity of labor delivered.[37] "It is not what the worker receives for his labor that forms the measure of exchange value," he wrote in the 1825 edition, "but what it has cost him in the expenditure of power."[38] Jakob was ready to consider the value of a good as determined by the expenditure of labor upon it, apart from the cost of the labor or from its embodiment in the product. In his view, labor did not identify the real values which *inhere* in the goods; it approximated the outcomes of trading between individuals due to individuals' strategizing.[39]

Jakob's work reveals the transcription of British terms for *labor* and *work* into the German field of meanings. When the Germans first transmitted Smith's wondrous ideas into their own language, their translators had had to improvise in two ways: they resorted to the adoption of several words not ordinarily used in German, and they attached more restricted meanings to current words.[40] The word *work*, however, they did not transcribe. It was not that they merged it with their word for *labor* (*Arbeit*) or that they tried out

36. Wilhelm Roscher evaluates Jakob's contribution in *Geschichte der National-Oekonomik in Deutschland* (München: R. Oldenbourg, 1874), pp. 688 ff.

37. Cited in Roscher, op. cit., p. 690. Here Jakob anticipated by fifty years the critique of Smith that Marx offered. See *Grundrisse der Kritik der politischen Ökonomie* (Berlin: Dietz Verlag, 1974), p. 232.

38. Ludwig Jakob, *Grundsätze der National-Ökonomie; oder, Theorie des National-Reichtums* (Halle: Friedrich Ruff, 1825), p. 122. The choice appears in the first edition of 1805: Ludwig Jakob, *Grundsätze der National-Ökonomie oder National-Wirthschaftslehre* (Halle: Ruffscher Verlag, 1805), pp. viii, 68.

39. Jakob reasoned that labor serves as an adequate measure of value because people on average are likely to labor only at occupations through which they can obtain an equivalent amount of labor from others. Op. cit., 1805, pp. 68–72; op. cit., 1825, p. 115. This represented a standard German interpretation of Smith. See Friedrich Hermann, *Staatswirtschaftliche Untersuchungen* (München: Anton Weber, 1832), p. 133.

40. Erämetsä, ibid.

a simple surrogate. They wrote around it. When Smith said, "There may be more labour in an hours hard work than in two hours easy business," the German translator rendered it something like this: "There may be more labor [*Arbeit*] in one hour's difficult manifestation of power [*angestrengten Kraftäusserung einer Stunde*] than in two hours' easy business."[41] Jakob adopted this mode of expression for the work activity as part of his system. In British thinking, work could appear in a system of political economy because it became abstract labor only when examined from the perspective of the later moment of exchange. In Jakob's picture, however, the work activity itself, from the beginning of the process, is seen as abstract labor because it is the expression of a general power. This point of origin, rather than the exchange process, makes heterogeneous kinds of work comparable as abstract labor. Jakob referred to labor as the activation of a latent capacity, defining it as "the activation of human power" and measuring its quantity by "the sacrifice of power."[42]

The difference in Jakob's approach was not only a matter of vocabulary. In his discussion of the employment relation Jakob says that the worker does not merely sell his labor—as Smith, looking at the output, would have expressed it—but "hires out his diligence [*Fleiss*]" to the capitalist or landowner.[43] Jakob's refusal to identify "labor" with a material product showed up as well in the contrast he drew between the functions of factory owners and of landowners. "The whole difference [between them]," he said, "comes down to the simple fact that the landowner is master of external nature, the factory owner master of internal nature."[44] Whereas the landowner made his profit through his control of the goods of the earth, the factory owner made his profit through his control of indispensable human labor. If Jakob had thematized the difference between these economic agents by drawing the conventional distinction between land and capital, as happened in British economics, this would have directed attention to differences in the material resources under their command. He emphasized instead the factory owner's disposal over human powers, which he saw as a "nonmaterial" good of an entirely different dimension.

41. From the translation by Christian Garve, op. cit., p. 53.

42. These phrases occur on op. cit., 1825, pp. 69, 122, 199. "For it [labor] is only an action, not a thing." Op. cit., 1805, p. 30.

43. Op. cit., 1825, p. 140. Jakob also asserted that the worker does not receive a wage from a particular employer merely for his "labor," the actually executed work, but for "the sake of his willingness to labor." Op. cit., 1825, p. 153.

44. Op. cit., 1825, p. 247.

Before long, others used this alternative concept of labor as a commodity to articulate a real theoretic break. Johann Lotz, a contemporary of Jakob's, rejected labor as a measure of the values of goods in the market. In 1811 he emphasized that "the products of labor are always different from the labor itself. . . . Labor," he declared, "is something purely immaterial." The distinction between use value and exchange value, a pairing the British could imagine applying only to finished commodities, he extended to the labor potential hired by the employer. "Viewed as a productive power," Lotz concluded, "it [labor] is always a capacity, a good of high value, but only of use value, not of exchange value."[45] He reasoned that labor could not be used to compare products because the worker's personal expenditure of effort was an immeasurable subjective experience.[46] Lotz's inference, though crudely psychological, betrays the assumption that the value of labor had to be compared at its moment of origin in the production process or not at all. Wilhelm Roscher, in his classic history of German economic theory, completed in 1874, ranked Lotz's rejection of "real" values standing behind prices as an important contribution to the evolution of the country's "national economic grammar."[47] For emphasis on the concrete moment of using labor power led German scholars in the first half of the nineteenth century to abandon Smith's faith that labor establishes a metric for product values.

The insight that labor was conveyed to the employer in the form of a *capacity* became commonplace in the writings of later German economists. Hans Mangoldt, an economist who after midcentury became particularly well known for his analysis of entrepreneurs' organization of the production process, said that "the wage is the compensation for the use of one's personal labor power that has been entrusted to another person."[48] He referred to hiring labor as "acquiring the disposition over another person's labor power," a phrase which, in keeping with Mangoldt's approach, highlighted the entrepreneur's consumption of a potential.[49] Friedrich Hermann,

45. *Revision der Grundbegriffe der Nationalwirtschaftslehre,* Volume One (Leipzig: Sinner, 1811), pp. 101–105; quotation is on pp. 102–103.

46. Op. cit., p. 61.

47. Op. cit., p. 666.

48. *Grundriss der Volkswirtschaftslehre* (Stuttgart: J. Engelhorn, 1863), p. 122. For Mangoldt's subsequently published lectures, see ibid.

49. Op. cit., 1863, p. 122. Sale of "the disposition over [one's] labor power" was a common phrase for employment. Georg Hanssen, "Ueber den Mangel an landwirtschaftlichem Arbeitspersonal," *Archiv der politischen Oekonomie und Polizeiwissenschaft* (Heidelberg: C. F. Winter, 1844), p. 154.

a major expounder of German business economics, distinguished between labor power, the commodity of "the highest-use value," and labor, "the main component of most goods."[50] The Germans' separation of labor from its product was a prerequisite for talking about the "use value" of labor at all. The British could not have theorized about the use value of labor purchased by an employer, because this would have required them to treat the power behind the activity as the actual thing that could be bought and "used" by the employer.

The distinction between labor and labor power which emerged in the Germans' lofty treatises paralleled the development of popular economic thinking in their country. Workers' descriptions of employment highlighted the renting of their labor capacity. For example, *Die Verbrüderung*, the newspaper of the workers' associations during the revolutions of 1848, complained that workers "chained to the power of capital have to hire out their physical or mental powers."[51] In a petition submitted to authorities in 1850, the weavers from a town near Potsdam called employers of wage labor "renters of labor power."[52] The language of formal remonstrance was no different from that of everyday expression, for a textile worker interviewed by the police in 1858 for having left his job described wage labor as "renting yourself out."[53] The assumption that workers put their person in the hands of their employer formed part of the popular understanding of the vending of labor as a commodity.[54]

50. *Staatswirtschaftliche Untersuchungen* (München: Fleischmann, 1870), p. 107 (written in the 1850s but published posthumously). Hermann reserved the term *labor power* (*Arbeitskraft*) for the ability of a worker to produce goods over the duration of his lifetime (p. 13). See also Karl Heinrich Rau, *Grundsätze der Volkswirtschaftslehre* (5th ed. Heidelberg: C. F. Winter, 1847), p. 234. Sartorius had broached the idea of a "use value" of abstract "labor" in Germany as early as 1806. Georg Sartorius, *Elemente des National-Reichtums*, Part One (Göttingen: Johann Röwer, 1806), p. 30. The distinction between labor's value in use and in exchange was to become a stock assumption in Germany even among insipid moneymakers unconcerned with the subtleties of theory. The Chamber of Commerce in the textile town of Greiz proclaimed in 1906 that "although the moral value of labor is the same everywhere, its use value and its exchange value are diverse." *Reussische Volkszeitung*, September 13, 1902.

51. *Die Verbrüderung*, October 3, 1848. Analogously, see *Freiheit, Arbeit*, February 11, 1849, p. 36.

52. See Zentrales Staatsarchiv Merseburg, Rep. 120, D V Fach 1, Nr. 32, Vol. 1, Nr. 605, February 19, 1850. "Bericht der Kommission zur Untersuchung des Nothstandes der Spinner und Weber in Schlesien, auf dem Eichsfelde und in Westfalen" (p. 10 of report).

53. Staatsarchiv Dresden, Amtshauptmannschaft Chemnitz, Nr. 16, p. 92, June 7, 1858. Bebel later made a similar observation: "Insofar as the worker sells his labor power for a certain time period, to a certain extent he includes himself in the sale." August Bebel, *Gewerkschaftsbewegung und politische Parteien* (Stuttgart: J. H. W. Dietz, 1900), p. 14.

54. J. Georg Eccarius, in his discussion of "labor as a commodity," emphasized that the worker "sells his own personal self." *Eines Arbeiters Widerlegung der national-ökonomischen*

The evolution of everyday concepts in economic life can be traced through the introduction of new terms into the German language. The translations of Adam Smith for popular consumption at the beginning of the century lacked the term *Arbeitskraft* ("labor power") to translate the employer's purchase of labor, as well as the plural, *Arbeitskräfte*, to refer to the work force at large.[55] These terms did not appear in dictionaries of the time.[56] Yet by 1854, when the Brothers Grimm released their German dictionary, they included an entry for *Arbeitskraft*. They did not define it, but they illustrated its usage: "One views a person with his labor power as a commodity, whose price rises and falls with the level of supply and demand."[57] The Grimms' example emphasizes that the term is linked to the commodification of labor and did not represent a locution, inherited from the precapitalist era, that highlighted merely a person's natural potential or concrete ability to work.[58] What is more, their explanation specified that the commodity inheres in the person of the seller: the producers themselves, not simply their wares, are inserted into the marketplace. The Grimms' compilation, written to codify the national language, scarcely represents a source that can be faulted for its inclusion of arcane vocabulary. To the contrary, scholars have criticized the work for its admission only of commonplace words.[59]

The public's adoption of the term *labor power* in the first decades of the nineteenth century indicates that the Germans, in contrast to the British, felt a need to mark the workers' contribution in the employment relation by a term more precise than the existing terms for labor available

---

Lehren John Stuart Mills (Berlin: Buchhandlung des 'Vorwärts,' 1888), p. 34. For an early factory ordinance relying on this terminology, see "Dienst-Anstellungs-Vertrag," in *Das Volk: Organ des Central-Komitees für Arbeiter*, July 4, 1848, p. 55.

55. See the Christian Garve edition, op. cit.

56. Johann Adelung, *Grammatisch-Kritisches Wörterbuch der hochdeutschen Mundart* (Leipzig: J. G. I. Breitkopf, 1793), Part One; Theodor Heinsius, *Volksthümliches Wörterbuch der deutschen Sprache* (Hannover: Hahn, 1818); Joachim Heinrich Campe, *Wörterbuch der deutschen Sprache*, Part One (Braunschweig: In der Schulbuchhandlung, 1807); *Encyclopädisches Wörterbuch*, Volume I (Berlin: Zeitz, 1793).

57. Jacob Grimm and Wilhelm Grimm, *Deutsches Wörterbuch von Jacob Grimm und Wilhelm Grimm* (Leipzig: S. Hirzel, 1854), Volume One, p. 545.

58. For another example of passages that use the term *Arbeitskraft* only in the context of business relations, see Versammlung deutscher Gewerbetreibender, *Bericht über die Verhandlungen in der Versammlung deutscher Gewerbetreibender in Leipzig am 7. Oktober 1844* (Leipzig: Friedrich Nies, 1844), p. 13. "The free valorization of free 'Arbeitskraft'" became a philistine cliché. *Allgemeine deutsche Arbeiter-Zeitung*, September 24, 1865, p. 792.

59. Alan Kirkness, *Geschichte des deutschen Wörterbuchs 1838–1863* (Stuttgart: S. Hirzel, 1980), pp. 15–16.

in their language.[60] May we say that thought impressed itself on language, not language on thought? No lexical or semantic obstacles blocked a similar course of development in Britain. Indeed, the British already applied market terms to human qualities by referring to such intangibles as popular "favor" and "opinion" as commodities, since they represented assets that could bring monetary gain.[61] By the nineteenth century the Germans had forgotten lexical resources which they might have employed to designate the contrast between materialized labor and the execution of work. In the period of Middle High German some writers had used the terms *Werk* and *Arbeit* to distinguish between the product of labor and the activity.[62] But in modern German this distinction was no longer sharp enough to enable people to take over the simple word *Arbeit* to signify the disposal of a person's labor power in the market.[63] The economic agents had to start anew.

The German invention of a fresh term rather than rearranging the connotations of an old one was in keeping, perhaps, with the more thoroughgoing break that the simultaneous transition to formal markets in finished articles and in labor power in Germany entailed. Workers themselves used the term *Arbeitskraft* for the commodification of labor. A workers' newspaper published in Chemnitz in the revolutionary days of 1848 said that if property relations were not governed by the market, the workers' "property, labor power" could not be assigned a value.[64] Wurm's German dictionary, published in 1858, emphasized the context of market relations when it asserted that the term *Arbeitskraft* refers "especially to the strength of the commercial worker himself." Wurm also offered a forceful example of usage: "The rich factory masters, who exploit the material labor power of the

---

60. The entry for *Arbeitskraft* in Wilhelm Hoffmann's dictionary emphasizes that it is the "forces or force suitable for carrying out labor." See Wilhelm Hoffmann, *Vollständiges Wörterbuch der deutschen Sprache*, Volume One (Leipzig: A. M. Colditz, 1853), p. 215. For an example of the adoption of the term in popular journals to describe commercial employment, see *Nacht-Eilwagen* Volume XVI, Nr. 28 (July 1845), p. 110. As European scholars were to note, economic agents in Germany also distinguished themselves by using the term *Arbeitslohn* to distinguish the recompense of wage labor from the remuneration received from the sale of labor's products. Riccardo dalla Volta, *Le Forme del Salario* (Firenze: Fratelli Bocca, 1893), p. 62.

61. *Oxford English Dictionary*, Volume III, p. 564.

62. Ortrud Reichel, "Zum Bedeutungswechsel der Worte 'Werk' und 'Wirken' in as, ahd, und mhd Zeit," diss., University of Tübingen, 1952, p. 92.

63. Meta Krupp, "Wortfeld 'Arbeit,'" in Sprachwissenschaftliches Colloquium, editor, *Europäische Schlüsselwörter: Wortvergleichende und wortgeschichtliche Studien* (München: Max Hueber Verlag, 1964), p. 260.

64. *Der Arbeitsfreund*, April 11, 1848, pp. 245–246.

people."[65] German society did not wait for Marx to use *labor power* to describe the extraction of profit; it surfaced in the vernacular beforehand and became commonplace during the revolution of 1848.[66]

The coining of the new term *Arbeitskraft*, its conscious linkage with the new market regime, and the timing of its appearance show that the difference in British and German expressions was not just a matter of linguistic form, of superficial words used to refer to the execution of work in any economic context. It represented a genuine difference in concepts of employment viewed under a capitalist regime. Where labor was not discussed in the context of commercial relations, other terms could be called to service. In Germany, an alternative locution, *Menschenkraft*, referred to the contribution of labor that was not necessarily exchanged as a commodity in the market. For example, a Saxony business journal said that good soil, fine weather, and "human power" (*Menschenkräfte*) went into growing raw materials.[67] The German labor movement during the revolution of 1848 used the general term *labor* to refer to the workers' contribution to society, but the term *Arbeitskraft* to describe the use of labor in production.[68]

65. Christian Friedrich Ludwig Wurm, *Wörterbuch der deutschen Sprache von der Druckerfindung bis zum heutigen Tage*, Volume One (Freiburg in Breisgau: Herder, 1858), p. 509.

66. *Freiheit, Arbeit*, February 22, 1849, p. 48. In 1848 W. Dieterici referred to the "reigning concepts of the threat of capital and its ascendancy over labor power." *Über Preussische Zustände, über Arbeit und Kapital* (Berlin: Ernst Siegfried Mittler, 1848), "Preface." Consider also Deutscher Handwerker- und Gewerbe-Congress, *Entwurf einer allgemeinen Handwerker- und Gewerbe-Ordnung für Deutschland: Berathen und beschlossen von dem Handwerker- und Gewerbe-Congress zu Frankfurt am Main im Juli und August 1848* (Hamburg, 1848), which defines the capitalist as someone who "profiteers from labor power" (p. 5).

67. *Gewerbe-Blatt für Sachsen*, May 16, 1839. See also *Gewerbe-Blatt für Sachsen*, February 9, 1841, p. 61; Zentrales Staatsarchiv Merseburg, Rep. 120, B I 1 60, Volume 7, January, 1849, p. 108; Sächsische Landesbibliothek, Nationalversammlung, Volkswirtschaftlicher Ausschuss über Petitionen von Webern und Spinnern, "Beilage II zum Protokoll der 184. öffentlichen Sitzung vom 12. März 1849." For examples of workers' journals using *Arbeitskraft* only in the context of commercial employment of wage labor, see *Der Arbeitsfreund*, August 19, 1848, title page. Commercial experts who applied the term *Menschenkraft* to labor in general believed workers should learn that the proper designation for labor as a commodity was *Arbeitskraft*. V. Funk, *Arbeiter-Katechismus* (Giessen: Emil Roth, 1881), p. 47. On the other hand, Marx himself used the term *Arbeitskraft* in two senses: to refer not only to the social construct of labor as a commodity but to a person's "natural" ability to work, "an expression of a natural force." "Randglossen zum Programm der deutschen Arbeiterpartei," printed in Karl Marx and Friedrich Engels, *Briefwechsel mit Wilhelm Bracke 1869–1880* (Berlin: Dietz Verlag, 1963), p. 49. In dissecting Marx, however, German exegetes reasserted the distinction between *Naturkraft*, the strength of the human organism, and *Arbeitskraft*, the expenditure of social labor under capitalism. Franz Petry, *Der soziale Gehalt der Marxschen Werttheorie* (Jena: Gustav Fischer, 1916), p. 22.

68. Consider the use of the term *Arbeitskraft* in the *Arbeiter-Blatt* Nr. 3 (October 1848).

The innovative nomenclature for labor as a commodity appeared in the writings of factory directors and other capitalist entrepreneurs concurrently with its appearance in the popular media. On the eve of the revolution of 1848, employers defined the jobless in terms that specified exactly what the subordinates were trying to sell: they were people who "cannot valorize their labor power."[69] Similarly, in 1861 a Saxony newspaper described unemployed wage workers as persons who "let their labor power lie fallow."[70] In the German textile trade the expression *labor power* appeared in the 1860s in the earliest technical guides to the establishment of a mill.[71] Employers and workers moved toward the locution at the same juncture in history, neither ahead of the other.[72] Despite all the differences between them, both groups responded to a shared societal condition, the regulation of social relations through formally free commerce in human work activity.

The basic difference in the way German and British economic agents conceived of the transmission of labor influenced their views of labor's contribution to national wealth and to employers' profits. Adam Smith created a divide between manufacturing labor, which he designated productive because it was fixed in a product, and services, which he called unfruitful because they did not terminate in a durable good.[73] Ricardo excluded serv-

---

69. Gustav Dörstling, *Die Arbeitgeber und die Löhne der Arbeiter* (Chemnitz: J. C. F. Pickenhahn & Sohn, 1847), p. 12.

70. "Seine Arbeitskraft zeitweilig brach gelegt." *Sächsische Industrie-Zeitung*, January 4, 1861, p. 1.

71. J. A. Hülffe, *Die Technik der Baumwollspinnerei* (Stuttgart: J. G. Cotta, 1863), p. 339.

72. German employers could make the same distinction between the value and the price of labor power that workers did. See the discussion of value in *Der Arbeitgeber*, January 6, 1866.

73. Adam Smith, *An Inquiry into the Nature and Causes of the Wealth of Nations* (Chicago: University of Chicago Press, 1976 [1776]), pp. 351–352. For the views of Smith's successors, John Stuart Mill, *Essays on Some Unsettled Questions of Political Economy* (2d ed. London: Longmans, Green, Reader & Dyer, 1874), pp. 84–86. For a history of the distinction, consult Mark Blaug, *Ricardian Economics: A Historical Study* (New Haven: Yale University Press, 1958), pp. 176–177. Mill says that labor devoted to training people is productive even if it does not accumulate in a material product, because the resulting skill has "a certain durability." *Principles of Political Economy* (London: Longmans, Green & Co., 1920), p. 47 note. Senior objects to the division between manufacturing labor and the provision of a service. But his reasoning is significant: he thinks they are ultimately similar because even services create products in some form. *An Outline of the Science of Political Economy* (New York: Farrar & Rinehart, 1939 [1836]), pp. 51–53. John Ramsay McCulloch objected to Smith's claim that only labor deposited in a material ware was productive, but, unlike German theorists, he declined to fuse manufacturing and service employment in a single category as the delivery of a service potential. John Ramsay McCulloch, introduction to Adam Smith, *An Inquiry into the Nature and Causes of the Wealth of Nations* (Edinburgh: Adam Black and William Tait, 1828), Volume One, p. lxxi.

ices from his model altogether. But in the early German reviews of the *Wealth of Nations,* including the very first, in 1777, German commentators took issue with Smith's separation of productive labor from the delivery of a service.[74] Friedrich Hermann, the theorist who built a new renown for German political economy, illustrated in 1832 the German method for equating the two: whether hiring workers or servants, an employer offers money in return for disposition over labor capacity. "The pay of the master [*Brodherr*] goes to the worker, of course; but in return," Hermann reasoned, "the activity [*Tätigkeit*] of the worker comes under the authority [*Gewalt*] of the employer."[75] In the second edition of this book, Hermann said, "We will no longer distinguish rigorously between service and labor."[76] Hermann could carry out this merger of the two categories because he thought that in both instances the worker sold control over the execution of the activity rather than transferring materialized labor.[77]

British economists defined the efficiency of labor in terms of the employer's ability to obtain produce from his workers at a certain price.[78] German economists, by contrast, defined it in terms of the difference between the use value of labor and its exchange value, that is, in terms of the distinct process of converting labor power to an output. The distinction allowed them to see that the production carried out by "labor" could be worth more than the price the employer [*Lohnherr*] had paid for the right to use the "labor." For example, Karl Heinrich Rau, the eminent synthesizer of economic ideas during the 1820s, thought that although labor was not a "material good," it was something from which the employer could acquire unequal amounts of value depending on how he used it.[79] In the case of personal services, Rau said, labor "usually is to be had for a price which stands far under its value."[80] Rau contended here that labor's price in the market could stand below what the employer could get out of the use value of the labor. Such a proposition the British economists could not have entertained, since they did not look at the use made of labor but only at labor's exchange via finished commodities. Rau's own way of interposing a separate

74. Roscher, "Die Ein- und Durchführung," op. cit., p. 7.
75. Op. cit., 1832, p. 33.
76. Op. cit., 1870, p. 167.
77. On the merger of manufacturing labor and services in German economic thought, see Carl Rotteck and Carl Welcker, editors, *Das Staats-Lexikon,* Volume One (Altona: J. F. Hammerich, 1834), pp. 634, 639.
78. *Wealth of Nations,* op. cit., pp. 183–184; Mill, *Principles,* op. cit., p. 419.
79. Rau, op. cit., pp. 234–235.
80. Ibid.

moment for labor's utilization also entailed a theoretical loss, however. In contrast to the British, Rau declined to put forward any important propositions about the relation between wages and the exchange value of the goods produced.[81]

The Germans' conception of the work activity opened up wider possibilities for envisioning the source of the employer's profit. British economists saw labor as a kind of intervening variable that allowed the capitalist to expand his capital. It operated as a requisite that allowed the investment to yield profit, not as an independent source of that profit. The German economists, by contrast, saw the purchase of labor as potentially realizing a profit quite apart from the earnings on the capital invested. Hans Mangoldt, for instance, argued that the employer made a profit not only by putting his capital to work and not only by acquiring part of the worker's produce in return for the use of the capital stock; he also made a profit by renting labor. The employer engages labor, Mangoldt said, only if he "is in a position to turn the hired labor into a value greater than he has to pay for it himself."[82] Roscher believed that workers got less pay for the same output if they sold their labor to an employer rather than directly to consumers in the form of either a product or a service.[83] In the German tradition, the use of labor in the production process, leaving aside the return on capital invested, generated surplus value.

The German economists not only developed their ideas with reference to the British, but they also offered penetrating textual comparisons between the British concept of labor and their own. Theodor Bernhardi, writing in 1847, thought that part of the difference grew out of the infelicities of the English language. The word *production*, he said, had a "double sense" in classical English political economy. It referred to the mathematical function of adding units together to yield a result. This described the process of adding together the market prices of inputs to raise the exchange value of a good. The term could also refer, however, to the physical process of creating a good. By using the word *production* in both these senses, he said, Smith and Ricardo avoided considering labor from the distinct vantage points of commercial exchange value and concrete use

---

81. He said only that the exchange value of those goods had "an influence" on the price of the labor hired to make them, because it set an upper limit against which wages could not rise without bankrupting the employer. Ibid., and Autorenkollektiv, op. cit., pp. 442 ff.

82. *Grundriss*, op. cit., p. 158.

83. Wilhelm Roscher, *Grundlagen der Nationalökonomie* (Stuttgart: J. G. Cotta, 1922), p. 495.

value and overlooked divergences between them.[84] Smith, Bernhardi said, theorized labor only from its appearance in the realm of exchange, so that "labor is immediately conceived as a product."[85] He cited instances from the *Wealth of Nations* where Smith collapsed the process of production into that of exchange by equating the price of labor with the quantity of labor delivered. He objected in particular to Smith's argument that "labour was the first price, the original purchase-money, that was paid for all things."[86] To Bernhardi, this formulation inappropriately turned every producer into a merchant: the employment of natural materials was equated with a commercial exchange. Bernhardi found it incredible that British political economy neither anticipated German innovations nor incorporated them after the fact. "How could reflection on the matter not lead to the distinction between the price of labor and its value?" he concluded. "It seems almost inconceivable that, based on this point, an entire revolution of the whole doctrine did not come about."[87]

Readers in the twentieth century can nod their heads in assent, for they know that Bernhardi foretold the precise route by which classical political economy would finally be subverted. As the inheritors of this historical process, we believe that the perpetrator was another scholar of German origin—Karl Marx. How does the prior evolution of German economic doctrines in the first half of the nineteenth century illuminate the emergence of Marx's seditious theory? Marx did not arrive at his insights purely by applying the force of logic upon British sources. Nor did he knowingly draw upon the traditions of German economic doctrine. History transpires in a more complex and surprising fashion. The answer not only demonstrates how Marx's analysis of labor and profit emerged but helps us recover the historical processes by which the popular concept of labor as a commodity appeared in Germany.

MARX'S REPLICATION OF ECONOMIC THEORY IN GERMANY

In *Kapital* Marx offered an original permutation of economic ideas which had been laid out in advance on both sides of the channel. He combined the

---

84. Theodor Bernhardi, *Versuch einer Kritik der Gründe, die für grosses und kleines Grundeigentum angeführt werden* (St. Petersburg: Kaiserliche Akademie der Wissenschaften, 1849), pp. 87, 91.

85. "Die Arbeit wird hier gleichsam als ein Product gedacht." Ibid., p. 161.

86. Ibid., p. 101.

87. Ibid., pp. 195–196.

British view of circulation with the German view of production. To lay out the terms of the merger, Marx's analysis in *Kapital* of the transactions capitalists made in the sphere of circulation, those by which they purchased inputs (including labor power) and disposed of outputs, proceeded according to the hallowed laws of the exchange of equal values and equal quantities of labor. In his account of the generation of profit Marx reaffirms that on the market "equivalent has been exchanged for equivalent."[88] This is the British view of circulation. Yet Marx argued that, looking at the production process as a concrete activity, the laws that govern the trade of exchange values no longer applied. "The seller of labour power, like the seller of any other commodity," Marx wrote, "indeed realizes its exchange value and parts with its use value. . . . The circumstance that . . . the very same labor power can work during a whole day, that consequently the value which its use during one day creates, is double what he pays for that use—this circumstance is, without doubt, a piece of good luck for the buyer, but by no means an injury to the seller."[89] This insight represents the longstanding German view of the use of labor as a commodity in production. Up to this point Marx followed a trail laid by forgotten predecessors.

Marx completed a narrower innovation. He made a contribution by identifying the double character of labor in its role as a commodity—its determinate exchange value—and in its concrete use as the means for generating a surplus for employers. The purchaser of labor manages to turn a profit only by taking advantage of the use value of the labor in the production process. If the owner at this moment properly uses this labor power, it can yield goods with more exchange value than the exchange value of the labor. (The exchange value of labor power Marx defined as the substantial cost, or amount of labor, needed to maintain the employee's ability to work.) The commodity of labor power is unique because it represents *"a source not only of value but of more value than it has itself.* This is the specific service that the capitalist expects from it."[90] To sum up, the two critical insights which led Marx to this analysis of the source of surplus value in the production process and which appear in earlier German texts were the following: that the owner purchased only

88. *Kapital*, op. cit., p. 209.
89. *Kapital*, op. cit., pp. 208–209. Marx objected to the rhetorical notion that capitalists did not play by the rules of the game or that their profit was a kind of illicit "deduction" from the worker: "The capitalist, having paid the worker the real price of his labor *power,* has the good right—that is, the right in terms of this mode of production—to the surplus value." Karl Marx and Friedrich Engels, *Marx-Engels Werke* (Berlin: Dietz Verlag, 1962), Volume 19, p. 359.
90. *Kapital*, op. cit., p. 208.

"labor power," and that the concepts of "use value" and of "exchange value" can be extended from inert wares to this peculiar human commodity.

Marx's interlacing of German ideas of production with British suppositions of circulation was original but not singular. It represented an intellectual outcome that may have already been in the cards. Karl Roesler published a parallel solution in 1861, six years before the first edition of *Kapital* appeared in the bookstores. He highlighted the dual character of what he termed "labor power" by entitling one chapter of his work "The Use Value of Labor" and the next "The Exchange Value of Labor." He declared that workers' wages depended upon the expense they incurred to develop and reproduce their work capacity:[91]

> One must hold on to the fundamental principle that in the process
> of exchange, including the labor market, values are traded only
> against like values. Without this rule the amount of use value . . .
> would determine the amount of value for the sale of labor power
> and every relation with the general system of other exchanges sun-
> dered. If the free resources in the earth, in the air, or wherever they
> may find themselves cannot be considered in the measurement of
> exchange value, and thus in the price [of a good], so it is not to be
> seen why this is not also or possibly the case with human labor
> power. . . . The use value of labor has no influence on the formation
> of its price.[92]

Roesler retained the classical principle governing equal exchange in the market while acknowledging that the employer could thereby receive a bonus in unpaid use value of the labor power. This acute insight anticipated Marx's analysis of the double character of labor as a commodity in the market and in the production process. Roesler diverged from Marx principally in supposing that capital could make an independent contribution to the exchange value of goods. For this reason, he did not arrive at the conclusion that all profit derived ultimately from the employment of labor. In its explanation of the extraction of surplus value, as in other ways, Marx's contribution remained unique.

Historians of economic theory have often envisioned their task as one of tracing a lineage or sequence of ideas among the known "greats," from

91. *Zur Kritik der Lehre vom Arbeitslohn: Ein volkswirtschaftlicher Versuch* (Erlangen: Ferdinand Enke, 1861), p. 45.

92. Ibid., pp. 47, 54.

Smith to Ricardo to Marx. Within this overall plan of succession, they have, to be sure, identified the discontinuities that Marx introduced into the British line of development. But they have treated this change in the analysis of the valorization of labor as the fortuitous consequence of Marx's genius.[93] To those unfamiliar with German economics Marx's pair of insights into labor might well seem to have come to him in an inspired dream. His voluminous notes and citations reinforce this view, and rightly so. Marx wrote exegetically as a matter of principle. From his perspective, the economic ideas of previous thinkers did not just offer examples of the play of logic, they expressed, sometimes indirectly, the essential social forces and forms of consciousness at work in prior stages of history. By developing his ideas through reflection upon earlier economists, he could join his thought to the central processes of social development.[94] Accordingly, when Marx set out to write *Kapital*—subtitled, of course, a *critique* of reigning views of political economy—he conceived a history of theories of surplus value as an integral part of the project.[95] Most of the theorems he presents in publications or drafts comment upon spirited formulations by other philosophers or pen-pushers. Yet the analysis of the double character of labor power—the undertaking he considered to be his single greatest contribution to the analysis of capitalist production[96]—surfaces in his notebooks and drafts, not to mention in *Kapital* itself, as an invention without precedent, an intellectual creation *de novo*.[97] And so it seemed to him.

Marx, the well-read man of letters, steeped in both the high and vulgar analyses of his day, was in all likelihood unacquainted with formulations of

93. Ernest Mandel, *The Formation of the Economic Thought of Karl Marx* (New York: Monthly Review Press, 1971), p. 83; Claudio Napoleoni, *Smith Ricardo Marx* (Oxford: Basil Blackwell, 1975), p. 99.

94. Allen Oakley, *The Making of Marx's Critical Theory* (London: Routledge & Kegan Paul, 1983), p. 65.

95. Projektgruppe Entwicklung des Marxschen Systems, *Der 4. Band des "Kapital"?* (Berlin: Verlag für das Studium der Arbeiterbewegung, 1975), pp. vi–vii. Even after publication of the first book of *Kapital*, Marx still envisaged a separate volume on the history of theory. Roman Rosdolsky, *Zur Entstehungsgeschichte des Marxschen "Kapital,"* Volume One (Frankfurt: Europäische Verlagsanstalt, 1968), p. 27.

96. Karl Marx and Friedrich Engels, *Marx-Engels Werke,* Volume 32 (Berlin: Dietz Verlag, 1965), p. 11.

97. Engels recounts Marx's discovery of the extraction of surplus value in the Preface to the second volume of *Kapital*. There Engels describes Marx's breakthrough as "a thunderbolt that struck out of a clear blue sky." *Das Kapital,* op. cit., 1989, p. 21. Marx in 1847 cited Proudhon's contention that only labor's potential has value as a commodity, but he dismissed it as unintelligible. Karl Marx, *The Poverty of Philosophy* (New York: International Publishers, 1963 [1847]), p. 58.

labor as a commodity among elite German economists. The value theorems of bourgeois political economy became his central preoccupation only after he fled to Britain. From there he innocently claimed in 1868 that "The economists *without exception* have missed the simple point that, if the commodity is a duality of use-value and exchange value, the labor represented in the commodity must also possess a double-character."[98] In his rough draft, *Grundrisse*, where he presents a full-scale version of the theory of exploitation at the point of production that later surfaced in *Kapital* itself, Marx cites more than one hundred and fifty economic commentators or economic historians. Of these, only fifteen were of German origin, whereas more than ninety came from Britain.[99] Where Marx makes reference to German economic thinkers in this draft and in earlier notebooks, he restricts himself almost entirely to monetary and currency theory or to the surface history of trade and industry.[100]

The neglect was deliberate. In Marx's view, the economically most progressive country could not fail to invent the most advanced economic thought. Conversely, Germany's deficient economic development "ruled out any original contribution to 'bourgeois' political economy." In the Preface to the second German edition of *Kapital*, he said, "Just as in the classical age of bourgeois political economy, so in the age of its decline, the Germans remained mere schoolboys, parroters, and hangers-on—petty retailers for the foreign-owned wholesale business."[101] Marx arrived at this judgment by axiomatic deduction well before he launched his intensive study of economics. As early as 1845—that is, before he had begun his formal-analytic essays on economic theory—he had decided that the late appearance of the German bourgeoisie made it "impossible" for representatives of this class to better

98. Emphasis added. Letter of Marx to Engels, January 8, 1868, in Karl Marx and Friedrich Engels, *Marx-Engels Werke*, Volume 32 (Berlin: Dietz Verlag, 1965), p. 11. "This," Marx added, "is actually the whole secret of the critical view."

99. *Grundrisse*, op. cit. The remainder were French, American, and Italian.

100. Karl Marx, *Exzerpte und Notizen* (Berlin: Dietz Verlag, 1986), pp. 47–55. Johann Heinrich von Thünen, a Prussian author whom Marx indicates he read, approximated Marx's definition of the cost of labor power. Thünen rejected as imprecise the notion that the cost of maintaining the working population determined minimum wage levels. He believed that the cost of reproducing the worker's "capacity to labor" provided a clearer analysis of the determination of various levels of wages. Yet Marx's references to Thünen, as to other German writers, are not intended to clarify the use of labor power in the capitalist labor process. *Das Kapital*, op. cit., 1980, Volume One, p. 649; Thünen, op. cit., p. 82. Marx also cites Roscher and Rau. *Theorien über den Mehrwert* (Stuttgart: J. H. W. Dietz, 1919), Volume Three, pp. 219, 224; *Marx-Engels Werke*, op. cit., Volume 19, p. 367.

101. *Das Kapital*, op. cit., 1980, Volume One, pp. 21, 22.

the political economy expounded in more advanced countries.[102] Marx's subsequent disregard of German sources may seem inexplicable. Only adherence to a powerful theory—in this case, about the social generation of meritable ideas—could have so narrowed his sight.

The retarded evolution of Marx's vocabulary corroborates the supposition that he developed his distinction between labor and labor power independently of the German economists. In the *Grundrisse* Marx makes use of the concept but not the term *labor power*. For example, in some passages he focuses his attention upon the "use value" of what he indifferently terms *labor*. He writes, "The worker exchanges his commodity, labor, the use value, which like all other commodities, also has a price [an exchange value]."[103] In sentences such as this one, for example, Marx could not refer to the use value of labor without implicitly meaning labor power. In a few sections of this draft where the explanation of the generation of surplus value at the point of production is formally identical to that in the renowned final version, *Kapital*, Marx contrives to use instead an unfamiliar scholastic compound, *Arbeitsvermögen* ("labor capacity"), to define labor's commodity form.[104] We have here an extraordinary manifestation of intellectual ignorance: the term *Arbeitskraft* ("labor power"), the indispensable talisman of conventional Marxist economics, is wholly absent from the *Grundrisse* even when Marx makes technical use of the concept,[105] whereas we know that this very locution had already gained currency among German economists as an expression highlighting the difference between the use and exchange values of labor in the capitalist labor process. Engels used *Arbeitskraft* as early as 1843, though without analytic significance or consis-

102. Draft of an article on Friedrich List's book, in *Collected Works* (London: Lawrence and Wishart, 1975–1978), Volume 4, p. 274. In *Kapital* Marx offered a more subtle explanation for German backwardness in matters of economic theory. There he claimed that the prior economic development and maturation of class struggle in Britain provided an example to Germany that deprived the German bourgeoisie of an opportunity to pursue economic theory without vulgar defenses of the capitalist order. *Kapital*, op. cit., 1980, pp. 21–22.

103. Grundrisse, op. cit., p. 185. He repeats the imprecise reference when he says, "Labor, which is sold to capital as a use value, is a good with exchange value for the worker, which he wants to receive" (p. 214; see also pp. 178, 183).

104. See, for instance, ibid., p. 566. "As a use value the labor capacity [*Arbeitsvermögen*] is realized only in the activity of the labor itself, just in the same way as a bottle of wine, which is purchased, is not realized as a use value until the drinking" (p. 946). "The labor capacity [*Arbeitsvermögen*] appears to the free laborer . . . as his property" (pp. 368–369).

105. To be sure, Marx, like German economists of his time, does use the plural term *Arbeitskräfte*, literally, "labor powers," to refer to the supply of workers at large in a society. See, for example, *Grundrisse*, op. cit., p. 408. But neither the singular nor the plural form is used to explicate the purchase and use of labor at the point of production.

tency, in the first essay either he or Marx wrote on economic method.[106] Marx himself later attached great importance to the proper use of terminology about labor to mark what he saw as a momentous revolution, of his making, inaugurated by understanding the purchase and use of *Arbeitskraft*.[107] In hindsight Engels realized that Marx's published analyses of the production process before *Kapital* were absolutely misleading because they used the ambiguous term *labor*.[108] If Marx had borrowed the conceptual distinction between labor and labor power from German economists, he would have used *Arbeitskraft* in the *Grundrisse*.[109]

In the historical unfolding of economic theory, Marx enters the story as a German not because he imparts the legacy of traditional German political economy; rather, his texts reproduce German social experience.[110] How else could he have conceived by separate and independent reflection the same definition of labor as that of the liberal German economists?[111] In his Foreword to the English edition of *Kapital*, Marx introduced himself as a German. "We," the Germans, he told the English readers, "suffer not only from the development of capitalist production but also from the incompleteness of its development. Alongside of modern evils, a whole series of inherited evils oppress us, arising from the passive survival of anachronistic modes of production."[112] Marx's analysis of the commodity of labor came to him as an inspired vision, but the apparition was historically determined: it con-

---

106. "Umrisse zu einer Kritik der Nationaloekonomie," in *Marx/Engels Gesamtausgabe* (Berlin: Marx-Engels Verlag, 1930), Series One, Volume Two, pp. 393, 396, 403.

107. *Das Kapital*, op. cit., pp. 562, 564.

108. "Einleitung zu Karl Marx' 'Lohnarbeit und Kapital' (Ausgabe 1891)," in Karl Marx and Friedrich Engels, *Marx-Engels Werke*, Volume 22 (Berlin: Dietz Verlag, 1963), p. 203; Engels's letter of March 4, 1891 to Adolph Sorge, in Karl Marx and Friedrich Engels, *Marx-Engels Werke*, Volume 38 (Berlin: Dietz Verlag, 1968), p. 45.

109. Ernest Mandel shows that Marx's mature theory of exploitation in the capitalist labor process, known so well from *Kapital*, appears first in the *Grundrisse* even when Marx clumsily uses the indistinct term *labor*. Op. cit., p. 84 note. Roman Rosdolsky's analysis of the intellectual genesis of *Kapital* reaches the same conclusion. Op. cit., p. 230 and Chapter Twelve.

110. In the Preface to *Zur Kritik der politischen Ökonomie*, Marx says that he was motivated to examine the play of material interests in historical development in part due to the polemic he started in the *Rheinische Zeitung* against the condition of the Moselle peasantry. Marx recalled the survival of the use of land in common among peasants near Trier. Cited in Heinz Monz, *Karl Marx: Grundlagen der Entwicklung zu Leben und Werk* (Trier: NCO-Verlag Neu, 1973), p. 370. "Right in my own neighborhood, on the *Hunsrück*, the ancient German system survived until just a few years ago." Letter of March, 1868, in Marx and Engels, *Marx-Engels Werke*, Volume 32 (Berlin: Dietz Verlag, 1974), p. 51.

111. Marx's unpublished "Economic and Philosophic Manuscripts of 1844" said that in the employment relation "the workers are forced to offer their person and their power . . . for a price." *Marx/Engels Gesamtausgabe*, op. cit., Series One, Volume Three, p. 51.

112. *Das Kapital*, op. cit., pp. 12–15.

jured in basic outline the peculiarities of German economic development. We have only to follow its lead.

THE GUILDS' RESIDUAL CONTROL
OVER THE SUPPLY OF LABOR

If the simultaneous emergence of free trade in goods and in labor power in Germany represented a necessary step for the commodification of labor in the cultural form of "labor power," it did not comprise a sufficient condition. After all, judged by this sole criterion, French producers entered the modern world of liberal commercialism by the same door. Yet, as we will see, they reached a different concept of labor as a commodity from that of the Germans. A single contingency is inadequate even for the German case alone. It must be remembered that when freedom of occupation was introduced in Germany, the urban work force consisted primarily of artisanal manufacturers and included many small masters working on their own account. Did they not stand in the same position as the independent tradesmen who typified the sale of materialized labor in Britain? Could they not have evolved the same assumptions about the exchange of labor as a commodity as the British? To stipulate the historical forces that were sufficient to guide the cultural construction of "labor power" in Germany requires a more discriminating analysis of the ensemble of urban and rural institutions of work during the initial decades of liberal commercialism.

Let us turn to the cities. Among thinkers as diverse as Adam Smith and Paul Sweezy, the towns in Europe have been viewed as the nodal points from which capitalist development emanated. In Germany the urban centers with concentrations of artisanal enterprise had once acted as a force for change by sponsoring the growth of mercantile trade. But during the nineteenth century they shrank from the construction of a laissez-faire regime and resigned from a leading role in the development of labor as a commodity.

The introduction of freedom of occupation in Prussia may have destroyed the town guilds' legal monopolies, but it did not obliterate the guilds themselves. They retained many functions in Prussia: they continued to supervise the recruitment and training of apprentices; they retained the right to certify trainees;[113] they still required that masters pass qualifying examinations in

---

113. See the discussion of this issue in the newspaper of Marx's home town: *Trier'sche Zeitung*, February 19, 1845. For Apolda, see Schneider, op. cit., p. 20. For weaving, Zentrales Staatsarchiv Merseburg, 120 B I, 1, Nr. 62 adh. 3, 1860, pp. 3–4.

order to become accepted as full members in the corporation;[114] and they continued to administer workers' insurance funds.[115] Saxony and the southern German states obtained a similar result, for they refused to enforce the guilds' legal monopolies but also declined to abolish the guilds' claims to the allocation of labor.[116] In some German towns craft guilds were to reassert control over workers by controlling their placement in jobs. The guilds issued employment books to workers which documented the holders' training and conduct.[117] Outside Prussia, the guilds generally had more widespread controls: they could regulate access to craft work by imposing residence requirements for licensing and by subjecting new practitioners to severe examination.[118] To be sure, the guilds no longer had clear statutory power to shut down the businesses of interlopers. But, as corporate associations, to the end of the nineteenth century they maintained regulations for the protection and advancement of their trades and for the supervision of labor.[119]

Guild influence was probably weakest in the Rhineland. During the French occupation, the left bank of the Rhine, incorporated into France, had its corporations abolished altogether. After the ejection of the French, however, this zone rejoined the main path of business development as it was being followed in other parts of Germany. In many trades, the artisans in the Rhineland conjured the guild affiliations back from the dead. The Diet of the Rhine province even appealed to the Prussian king in 1826 and 1833 for a partial lifting of freedom of trade and occupation.[120] The craftspeople

114. Jürgen Bergmann, *Das Berliner Handwerk in den Frühphasen der Industrialisierung* (Berlin: Colloquium Verlag, 1973), pp. 51–52.
115. See Manfred Simon, *Handwerk in Krise und Umbruch* (Köln: Böhlau Verlag, 1983), p. 33; Bergmann, op. cit., p. 48.
116. Frank Tipton, *Regional Variations in the Economic Development of Germany During the Nineteenth Century* (Middletown, Connecticut: Wesleyan University Press, 1976), p. 35.
117. Volkov, op. cit., p. 119. Jürgen Kocka emphasizes the guild masters' protracted controls of the craft labor market in his "Craft Traditions and the Labour Movement in Nineteenth-Century Germany," in Pat Thane et al., editors, *The Power of the Past* (Cambridge: Cambridge University Press, 1984), pp. 101, 108.
118. Kocka, op. cit., p. 101.
119. On the guilds' continued influence over technical training into the age of the factory, see Adolf Ipsen, *Neumünster. Ein holsteinischer Fabrikort in seiner Entwicklung während der Jahre 1852–1863* (Kiel: Schröder und Co., 1870), pp. 45, 47; Bergmann, op. cit., p. 82. In 1884 the Reichstag granted guild masters the exclusive right to hire and train apprentices. Kenneth N. Allen, "The Krefeld Silk Weavers in the Nineteenth Century." Ph.D. diss., Stanford University, 1988, p. 130. In 1904 the guilds still counted half a million artisans under their supervision. J. J. Lee, "Labour in German Industrialization," in *The Cambridge Economic History of Europe*, Volume VII, Part I (Cambridge: Cambridge University Press, 1978), p. 456.
120. Theodore S. Hamerow, *Restoration, Revolution, Reaction: Economics and Politics in Germany, 1815–1971* (Princeton: Princeton University Press, 1958), p. 32.

failed in their attempts to restore the old constitution of business with production monopolies, but they succeeded in reinstating the condition that only members of the craft associations could hire apprentices.[121]

Guild membership in Germany remained a sign of social status which complicated the terms by which producers conceived the employment relation for craft production. Christiane Eisenberg's inquiries into the legacy of the guilds in Germany have disclosed that corporate designations of status blunted the adoption of terms descriptive of capitalist relations of production. The locutions *employer* (*Arbeitgeber*, literally, "giver of work") and *employee* (*Arbeitnehmer*) were slow to replace the guild terms *master* (*Meister*) and *journeyman* (*Geselle*). Where the new words appeared to prevail, their usage was sometimes confused with the old: independent producers with guild certification as masters but with no assistants were classified inconsistently as "employers."[122] In contrast to experience in Britain, "no uniform expression developed for the group of independent producers working on their own account."[123] Economic agents in Britain called the producers in this group "free tradesmen" or "undertakers."[124] But in Germany, the public and the craftsmen themselves imposed linguistic distinctions from the guild system upon producers who shared the same market positions. For example, in the mid-nineteenth century they described these independent producers as journeymen working on their own (*selbständige Gesellen*) or as masters working without assistants (*Alleinmeister*).[125] Rather than adopting a terminology based on the exchange of products by independent market actors, as in Britain, the Germans used guild designations that drew upon the prior status distinction between masters and jour-

---

121. *Trier'sche Zeitung*, January 7, February 17, 1845.
122. Ibid.
123. Christiane Eisenberg, *Deutsche und englische Gewerkschaften* (Göttingen: Vandenhoeck & Ruprecht, 1986), p. 49. The formulation of this paragraph relies upon Eisenberg's exemplary comparison.
124. Timothy Shuttle, *The Worsted Small-Ware Weavers' Apology* (Manchester: James Schofield, 1756), p. 14.
125. Ibid. The guild term *master* still marked the status of guild certification even after it came to be applied to people in any position in the production process. For example, during the revolution of 1848–1849, a city association of weavers met in Chemnitz who called themselves "weaving masters in the employ of others" (*arbeitnehmende Webermeister*). Stadtarchiv Chemnitz, IX Za 98a, pp. 94–101. The employment rules issued by factory owners in Werdau during 1860 defined those who would be considered "workers" and then, lest any possibility for confusion remained, said that in factories guild members, too, were "workers." Stadtarchiv Werdau, Rep. I, Cap. 27A, Nr. 26, Vol. III, pp. 59 ff.

neymen.[126] Social forms inherited from the guild system were not modified to conform with the capitalist employment relation, but cross-cut capitalist definitions.[127]

During the revolution of 1848–1849, petitions for the recall of commercial liberty came from small textile masters in all portions of Germany. In Leipzig the craft masters wrote an appeal denouncing free trade as a pernicious "French" principle.[128] "Unrestricted commercial freedom," the artisans of Korschenbroich in the lower Rhineland told the government in 1849, "is the origin of all evil."[129] Every craft worker had a different home remedy for the exotic illness. Some guild petitioners wanted to prohibit merchants from buying goods manufactured by artisanal producers. They would have allowed peddlers to sell machine-made products but not handmade ones—an eloquent indicator of the way craftspeople divided the world of production in two.[130] Craft masters in the textile trade also attempted to prevent the rise of nonguild undertakings by allowing only guild masters to oversee the work of journeymen.[131] Opposition to free trade came not just

126. Artisans employed in a shop said that they "take work with a master" (bei einem Meister Arbeit nehmen). The expression emphasized that employment was defined by relation to a guild superior. See Joachim Heinrich Campe, Wörterbuch der deutschen Sprache, Part One (Braunschweig: In der Schulbuchhandlung, 1807), p. 200; Heinsius, op. cit., Volume One, p. 172.

127. The vocabulary of the bourgeois press during the revolution of 1848 reveals that in craft centers where workers and employers retained membership in corporate groups, terms referring to economic agents' class positions were slower to defuse than in industrial areas such as Elberfeld. Friedrich Lenger, Zwischen Kleinbürgertum und Proletariat (Göttingen: Vandenhoeck & Ruprecht, 1986), p. 168. In Peitz, certified guild "masters" working alone or for others reasoned that they should not enroll in health insurance associations as "workers." Landesarchiv Potsdam, Rep. 6 B, Kreisverwaltung Cottbus Nr. 1256, 1858, pp. 91–98. For many years, the German labor movement refused to classify the guild employers as "capitalists." Kautsky's popularization of Das Kapital, first published in 1887, inserted a section explaining that the "small master" extracted surplus value from subordinate journeymen but nonetheless could not be classified a capitalist. Karl Marx' ökonomische Lehren (Berlin: J. H. W. Dietz, 1980), p. 120.

128. P. H. Noyes, Organization and Revolution: Working-Class Associations in the German Revolutions of 1848–1849 (Princeton: Princeton University Press, 1966), p. 157.

129. Zentrales Staatsarchiv Merseburg, Rep. 120 B I 1, Nr. 62, Band 2, letter in the name of the artisans of Corschenbroich, August 2, 1849; 120 I 1, Nr. 60, Band 2, May 18, 1848, pp. 262 ff. See also Georg Quandt, Die Niederlausitzer Schafwollindustrie in ihrer Entwicklung zum Grossbetrieb und zur modernen Technik (Leipzig: Duncker & Humblot, 1895), p. 31.

130. Zentrales Staatsarchiv Merseburg, 120 B Abt. I, Fach 1, Nr. 60, January 20, 1849, p. 26.

131. Sächsische Landesbibliothek, Nationalversammlung, Volkswirtschaftlicher Ausschuss über Petitionen von Webern und Spinnern, "Beilage II zum Protokoll der 184. öffentlichen Sitzung von 12. März 1849." For attempts by other artisans to limit competition, see Simon, op. cit., pp. 299–303.

from producers in the cities. The operators of rural putting-out systems wanted to restrict entry into the trade as a way of ensuring high-quality workmanship.[132]

The opposition to free trade did not disappear after the revolution was finally suppressed. To the end of their days, members of some of the urban crafts in Germany remained antagonistic to the emergence of liberal commercialism.[133] During the 1850s the weaving guilds continued to send petitions asking the Saxon ministry of the interior to prohibit liberty of trade in their products.[134] For artisans, the development of an unbridled market did not represent a natural progression in contrast to which regulation appeared as an exceptional constraint: as late as 1860, some craft workers saw free business as an artificial invention dreamed up by essayists. "Freedom of trade is a child of the press," the *Magistrat* of Conitz wrote in 1860, "supported by people and judgments that have little insight into the essence of craft work."[135]

In Britain, the cultural commodification of labor took place when artisanal work still enjoyed a vigorous youth. In the eyes of seventeenth-century British observers, small manufacture represented one of the most dynamic sectors of the economy.[136] Given the prolonged suppression of market institutions for wage work in Britain, the exchange of merchandise by independent producers in this branch could provide the context for the commodification of labor as it was objectified in a ware. In Germany, by comparison, the introduction of a formal market in labor power and of

---

132. "Ein Fabrikant," op. cit., pp. 49, 66.

133. The statutes from the founding of the association of silk weavers from Kempen-Schmalbroich in 1881 pledge that the group will "intervene with all legally permitted means for the elimination of freedom of business and the introduction of mandatory corporations." Cited in Allen, op. cit., p. 118. Many urban trades accepted the free-market regime in the 1860s, that is, after the cultural constitution of market-industrial society in Germany. Lenger, op. cit., p. 195.

134. Staatsarchiv Dresden, Ministerium des Innern, Nr. 1385b, 1855. As late as 1850, German weavers in Gera attempted to prevent merchants from placing orders in the guild-free countryside rather than in the city. Staatsarchiv Weimar, Reuss jüngerer Linie a Rep. Gera, Nr. 916, December 17, 1850. The guild masters in Greiz naively said in 1866 that "avarice" was the root of all evil. Their rhetoric still had not accepted the commercial mentality. Staatsarchiv Weimar, Landesregierung Greiz a, Rep. A, Kap. XXI/2c, Nr. 405, Innungsmeister, September, 1866.

135. Zentrales Staatsarchiv Merseburg, Rep. 120 B I 1, Nr. 62, Adh. 3, October 11, 1860.

136. Even Adam Smith believed that independent commodity producers were multiplying. Maxine Berg, "Political Economy and the Principles of Manufacture 1700–1800," in Maxine Berg et al., *Manufacture in Town and Country Before the Factory* (Cambridge: Cambridge University Press, 1983), pp. 47–48.

market discourse coincided with the middle age and deteriorating health of craft enterprise.[137] It accompanied a secular debasement in the conditions of craft labor and a decline in its remuneration. Urban craft work tended to define itself as an opponent of free intercourse in labor rather than, as in Britain, a promoter of its growth within trade-union limits.[138]

The diverging usage of the term *artisan* in German and English illustrates the role of craft work in the cultural commodification of labor in the two countries. In the course of the nineteenth century the German term for artisan, *Handwerker*, came increasingly to refer to self-employed persons outside of large enterprises. It implicitly excluded wage laborers.[139] In Britain, by comparison, the term *artisan* was increasingly used to refer to skilled workers who earned wages in the employ of others. It was applied to the aristocracy of wage laborers, including those in the factory. Unlike the German word, the English term was not shunted to the periphery of capitalist relations of employment but was central to the definition of wage labor. The fates of the terms *worker* and *Werker* also illustrate a divergence in the application of words that derived originally from the world of craft work but were extended to the industrial-capitalist economy. In both languages the term originally applied to those in craft and shop work.[140] In English the term came to refer to the entirety of wage earners, marking the centrality of small manufacture for the definition of commercial labor. In German

137. This is not to say that the eclipse of small units of production was inevitable. Social theorists have of late speculated on the potential viability of small-scale, specialized manufacture in competition with large factory manufacture during the nineteenth century. But to imagine a more vigorous survival of craft production, these theorists change much else in the historical picture. For an example, consider Charles Sabel and Jonathan Zeitlin, "Historical Alternatives to Mass Production: Politics, Markets and Technology in Nineteenth-Century Industrialization," in *Past & Present* Number 108 (August 1985).

138. Toni Offermann offers a nuanced portrait of German artisans' splintered and contradictory attitudes toward the new commercial order. Some partially embraced free enterprise as a means of getting ahead. Yet Offermann also provides many examples from meetings of small masters and craft workers in the 1860s to support the contention that "above all the treatment in political economy of labor as a commodity in a system of supply and demand was opposed." "Mittelständisch-kleingewerbliche Leitbilder in der liberalen Handwerker- und handwerklichen Arbeiterbewegung der 50er und 60er Jahre des 19. Jahrhunderts," in Ulrich Engelhardt, editor, *Handwerker in der Industrialisierung* (Stuttgart: Klett-Cotta, 1984), p. 531. On the precocious dissemination of the market ethos and acceptance of wage labor in British craftwork, see Joyce Oldham Appleby, *Economic Thought and Ideology in Seventeenth-Century England* (Princeton: Princeton University Press, 1978), pp. 145, 151.

139. Jürgen Kocka, "Problems of Working-Class Formation in Germany: The Early Years, 1800–1875," in Ira Katznelson and Aristide Zolberg, editors, *Working-Class Formation: Nineteenth-Century Patterns in Western Europe and the United States* (Princeton: Princeton University Press, 1986), p. 327.

140. Hagan, op. cit., pp. 124–125.

usage, the term *Werker* remained confined to the original context of handicraft production, marking the failure of craft work to provide the template for conceiving of capitalist wage labor. The generic term for worker that prevailed in Germany, *Arbeiter,* came from another domain, that of the serfs on feudal estates.[141]

The urban crafts in Germany did not provide the context for the development of market thinking; instead, the crucible for the cultural specification of labor's commodity form was large enterprise relying upon supervised labor, that is, the manufactory.[142] The employment regulations of Prussia and the other German states had long placed the manufactory and the artisanal workshop in separate worlds. During the eighteenth century, the Prussian state exempted manufactories on a case-by-case basis from the requirement that production of a line of goods rely only upon workers belonging to the guild responsible for that branch of industry. In 1794 Prussia finally arrived at a general rule: manufactories could hire whomever they pleased, including nonguild members and women.[143] In Saxony as well, by the eighteenth century chartered factories were exempt from guild regulations on the use of labor.[144] The German states recognized that the guilds restrained economic development, yet they remained unwilling to abolish them outright, for under the supervision of the masters they provided ready-made organizations for assisting authorities' surveillance and tutelage over workers.[145] Once segmented by state regulation, the two worlds of work, manufactories with unregulated labor and guild craft shops, were never reunited.[146]

141. Hannah Arendt, *The Human Condition* (Chicago: University of Chicago Press, 1958), p. 81.

142. The workers' press associated the appearance of "labor power" as a commodity with the development of the factory system. *Arbeiter-Zeitung,* February 22, 1863, front page.

143. Joachim Kermann, *Die Manufakturen im Rheinland 1750–1833* (Bonn: Ludwig Röhrscheid, 1972), p. 153; Kesselbauer, op. cit., p. 114. In the small states of Thüringen, which contained important textile districts, the authorities segmented factory and craft work by another means. They prohibited factory owners from hiring guild-trained weavers. Staatsarchiv Weimar, Landesregierung Greiz a, Rep. A, Kap. XXI/2c, Nr. 405a, 1866, pp. 12–19. Early use of the term *Fabrik* ("factory") indicated nonguild production, not necessarily production with machinery under a single roof. Vogel, op. cit., p. 162.

144. Horster, op. cit., pp. 20, 34. Wool manufacturers extolled unemployed miners as a source of labor. Curt Bökelmann, *Das Aufkommen der Grossindustrie im sächsischen Wollgewerbe* (Heidelberg: J. Hörning, 1905), p. 49.

145. Kesselbauer, op. cit., p. 116; Puschner, op. cit., pp. 185–188. Small wonder that the state reacted to the revolution of 1848–1849 by attempting to restore those corporative functions of the guilds that would "reestablish the authority of the masters." Bergmann, op. cit., p. 128.

146. As Jürgen Kocka observed, the legacy of separate regulation imparted prominent legal distinctions between craft enterprises and large factories which continue in Germany to the

Prussia and the other German states continued their dual-track policy during the first decades of the nineteenth century. While they allowed guilds to maintain de facto control over labor in traditional workshops, official labor codes all but disappeared from the new and promising sector of large enterprise.[147] Of course, the owners of the prosperous new factories considered their workers to be servants and supposed that the labor laws pertaining to the employment of house servants extended by implication to factory employees. But in Prussia, as elsewhere, these owners found that officials refused to extend the provisions of the laws for servants to factory workers.[148] In the initial decades after the Prussian commercial reforms of 1810–1811, the police also declined to forcibly return workers who had abandoned their employment without notice.[149] To collect compensation from miscreant workers, Prussian factory owners had to take the tedious step of filing claim for damages in court.[150] Prussia, supposedly the land of heavy-handed state supervision, had a consistently laissez-faire policy toward labor contracts during the introduction of liberal commercialism.[151] Enforcing a web of labor regulations in the factories, Prussian officials declared in 1817, "would reduce the natural freedom of people to dispose over their time and talents in the manner that seems most advantageous."[152]

---

present day. Kocka, "Craft Traditions," op. cit., p. 96. Kocka places the nineteenth-century German separation of artisanal work from large-scale manufacture in comparative perspective in "Einführung und Auswertung," in Ulrich Engelhardt, editor, *Handwerker in der Industrialisierung* (Stuttgart: Klett-Cotta, 1984), p. 467.

147. The contrast between guild-controlled craftwork and unshackled factory production was especially sharp in Saxony. Hubert Kiesewetter, *Industrialisierung und Landwirtschaft* (Köln: Böhlau Verlag, 1988), p. 172.

148. Decision of Ministry of the Interior, Zentrales Staatsarchiv Merseburg, 120 B V 33, Nr. 4, Vol. 2, p. 3, January 17, 1839. Journeymen resisted the efforts of the masters to extend guild regulation into the factories during the revolution of 1848. Lee, op. cit., p. 470.

149. Zentrales Staatsarchiv Merseburg, Rep. 120 B V 33, Nr. 4, Vol. 2, 1838, Meyer & Co., Brandenburg, pp. 33–43. Although factory owners in the 1830s called on officials to discipline workers who left without notice, as if it were a matter of public security, the officials refused to intervene until the courts ruled on the employment contracts. Zentrales Staatsarchiv Merseburg, Rep. 120 B, Abt. V, Fach 33, Nr. 4, Volume 1, pp. 240 ff., and Volume 2, p. 11.

150. Zentrales Staatsarchiv Merseburg, Rep. 120 B, Abt. V, Fach 33, Nr. 4, January 17, 1839, p. 3; March 12, 1841, p. 11; August 26, 1843, p. 44.

151. For evidence of the lack of state-sponsored guidelines for factory employment, see Zentrales Staatsarchiv Merseburg, Rep. 120 B V 33, Nr. 4, Vol. 1, March 19, 1816, pp. 43–44.

152. Zentrales Staatsarchiv Merseburg, Rep. 74 K 3 VIII, pp. 50 ff., 1817. Vogel, op. cit., pp. 164, 180. Likewise, even after the riots of 1830, the labor arbitration board run by local business people in Aachen failed to secure authority from Prussian officials to impose jail terms for workers' violations of contracts. Jeffrey M. Diefendorf, *Businessmen and Politics in the Rhineland, 1789–1834* (Princeton: Princeton University Press, 1980), p. 311.

Prussia set a standard for regulation elsewhere. In Saxony, where industrial growth enjoyed an early start, the industrial association reported in 1835 that "a condition of virtual lawlessness" had developed in labor relations.[153] The Saxon state did not issue rules for labor contracts for nonguild factory workers until the 1850s.[154] More remarkable are the steps that authorities there took to prevent town administrators from supplementing those general guidelines with additional disciplinary procedures for workers who left without notice or who damaged machinery. In Saxony provincial officials repeatedly intervened to prevent town administrators from officially sanctioning the employment codes drawn up by factory owners and their Chambers of Commerce.[155] Employers in other regions, too, complained of lack of legal enforcement of employment rules in their mills and shops. "Whereas in other countries the law already regulates labor time, factory ordinances, and rules," the Magdeburg newspaper observed in 1850, "nothing similar occurs with us."[156]

The laissez-faire regime under which factory workers and employers in Germany were left to specify the labor transaction offers a powerful contrast with the fettering of wage labor at the dawn of liberal commercialism in Britain. There, we know, the law in force during the shift to a formal market made labor an exceptional good that employers could requisition by fiat. The law treated the laborer as the holder of an ascribed status rather than as the occupant of a role created through personal contract. In Germany, wage labor outside the guild system was founded on a more thoroughgoing break with the restrictions of the past than was true in Britain.[157]

153. Horster, op. cit., p. 70. In Saxony, as in Prussia, the police were not to intervene to force back to work factory employees who had left without notice.

154. See Staatsarchiv Dresden, Ministerium des Innern, Section XIII, Nr. 140, "Fragepunkte für die Ausschüsse der Gewerbetreibenden und Arbeiter." For a report on Saxony's industrial leadership, see Tipton, op. cit., pp. 30 ff.

155. Stadtarchiv Werdau, Rep. I, Kap. 27A, Nr. 26, Vol. III, April 14, 1860, pp. 40 ff. For other examples where state officials forbade town councils to enforce labor contracts, see Staatsarchiv Dresden, Ministerium des Innern, Nr. 6419, February 1, 1854, pp. 2 ff., and December 22, 1869, pp. 31–32.

156. *Magdeburgische Zeitung*, March 13, 1850. Employers were prevented from claiming in their factory rules that violations carried statutory punishments. Staatsarchiv Dresden, Amthauptmannschaft Flöha, Nr. 2892, draft from year 1862, Gunnersdorf.

157. A spinning-mill director from Viersen complained to a government panel on textiles in 1878 that the laws protecting the freedom of factory workers made it more difficult to control them. The historical novelty of this situation did not escape him. "There is something further to add," he told the board of inquiry, "namely, the effect that our commercial code has on factory workers. The people are free." Germany, Enquete-Kommission, *Reichs-Enquete für die Baumwollen- und Leinen-Industrie: Stenographische Protokolle über die mündliche Vernehmung der Sachverständigen* (Berlin: Julius Sittenfeld, 1878), p. 621.

In this respect the Germans proved themselves more liberal than the British at similar stages in the institutionalization of free exchange and commercialization of social life. Yet the maintenance of corporate organization of work in artisanal undertakings in Germany excluded this sector from a pioneering role in cultural change. The result was a profound division between large, innovative enterprise and small, traditional concerns.[158] As Wolfram Fischer has observed, industrial policy in Germany "discouraged the transformation of the group of conservative artisans into a stratum of modernizing entrepreneurs and helped bifurcate the face of the economy into a static adherence to old forms and a dynamic, unlimited advance."[159]

The historical divide between traditional craft work and the commercialized manufactories in Germany found its theoretical expression in Marx's reflections. Marx excluded urban craft production from his interpretation of the genesis of capitalist relations of production. To be sure, it represented an early island of free labor within feudal society. Despite a propitious start, however, it remained unsuited for the eventual development of capitalist wage labor. "Although urban artisanal production rests essentially upon trade and the creation of exchange values," he acknowledged, "the direct, main purpose of this production is the subsistence of the artisan and of the craft master."[160] Marx assumed that the urban artisans, under the aegis of the guilds, fought successfully against the attempts of merchant capitalists to govern the production process.[161] In *Kapital* he emphasized the limits the guilds placed on the size of work-

---

158. On the regulatory divide between craft and factory production in Göttingen and Westphalia after 1815, see Assmann, op. cit., p. 227. In Saxony "factory" production in the countryside was freed of all corporate approvals in 1840. Bökelmann, op. cit., p. 11.

159. Fischer, op. cit., p. 65. Observers in the early nineteenth century believed that the boundary between guild mastership and factory entrepreneurship was almost impermeable. Vogel, op. cit., p. 160. Johann Raudin, *Praktisches Handbuch der Tuchfabrikation* (Quedlinburg & Leipzig: G. Basse, 1838), p. vi. State requirements in Saxony that guild masters hire only guild workers, whatever the industrial setting, disadvantaged them compared to nonguild entrepreneurs. Stadtarchiv Chemnitz, Kap. V, Sect. II, Nr. 151a, Sept. 18, 1854, letter to Ministry of the Interior.

160. *Grundrisse*, op. cit., p. 411.

161. German artisans, accustomed to controlling the tools of production, were slow to adopt the idea that their labor activity might require capital they did not command. For example, in the 1820s Berlin weavers and other textile workers, so that they might earn their subsistence through labor, considered it reasonable to request looms and carding machines as gifts from the Prussian Ministry of Trade and Industry. See Zentrales Staatsarchiv Merseburg, Rep. 120 D IV, Fach 6, Nr. 13, March 21, 1824, p. 3; February 26, 1827, p. 12; Oct. 17, 1830, p. 25; February 21, 1831, p. 38; August 1, 1832, p. 52.

shops and division of labor in the production process: "The merchant could buy every kind of commodity, with the exception of labor as a commodity. He was tolerated only as a distributor of the artisanal products."[162] The appropriation of materialized labor did not, in Marx's opinion, constitute the purchase of labor as a commodity.[163]

To turn labor into a commodity, from Marx's point of view the capitalist had to take command of the production process in order to control the conditions under which labor power was converted into a product. The creation of a market in manufactures does not suffice to commodify labor; legal restrictions on *both* trade and the use of labor in production had to disappear. This theoretical supposition recapitulated the invention of the market in German history, where the commercialization of exchange in manufactures and the lifting of legal constraints on the use of labor in production were fused. Britain provided the historical laboratory for a model of capitalist development in *Kapital*, but the perspective imposed on Britain came from Germany. By the time internal monopolies on trade in manufactures had decayed in Britain, so had the power of the British guilds.[164] By 1689 only a quarter of the towns in England had guilds with a semblance of organization, let alone ones capable of enforcing business prerogatives.[165] They had lost the ability to impose statutory limits on the size of workshops and the division of labor. Marx's supposition that the urban crafts never allowed labor to crystallize as a commodity badly mis-

162. *Das Kapital,* op. cit., Volume I, p. 380.

163. Ibid., p. 183. A good presentation of the theoretical criteria by which labor can be conceived as a commodity appears in Keith Hart, "On Commoditization," in Esther N. Goody, editor, *From Craft to Industry: The Ethnography of Proto-Industrial Cloth Production* (Cambridge: Cambridge University Press, 1982), pp. 40–41.

164. J. R. Kellett, "The Breakdown of Gild and Corporation Control over the Handicraft and Retail Trade of London," *The Economic History Review* second series, Volume X, Number 3 (April 1958), p. 384; Ray Bert Westerfield, *Middlemen in English Business Particularly Between 1660 and 1760* (New Haven: Yale University Press, 1915), p. 285. For evidence on the nonenforcement of apprenticeship regulations as early as the sixteenth century, see Buchanan Sharp, *In Contempt of All Authority: Rural Artisans and Riot in the West of England, 1586–1660* (Berkeley: University of California Press, 1980), pp. 157–158.

165. Christopher Hill, *The Century of Revolution 1603–1714* (Edinburgh: Thomas Nelson and Sons, 1961), p. 205. By the 1670s, thousands of trespassers had moved without hindrance into occupations formerly reserved for guild members. B. A. Holderness, *Pre-Industrial England: Economy and Society 1500–1750* (London: J. M. Dent & Sons, 1976), p. 106. For London, see L. D. Schwarz, *London in the Age of Industrialisation* (Cambridge: Cambridge University Press, 1992), pp. 216–217. On the expiration of corporations in the woolen trade, see Herbert Heaton, *The Yorkshire Woollen and Worsted Industries* (2d ed. Oxford: Clarendon Press, 1965), pp. 235, 405. Legislation stipulating standards of quality for trade names of woolen cloth remained in effect until the industrial revolution.

judges British experience but fits Germany closely.[166] What appears here in *Kapital* as "theory" represents in fact the displaced historical experience of Germany.

Since Marx excluded urban crafts work from the development of capitalist relations of production, his attention was drawn to centralized manufacture in the countryside: "The original historical form in which capital appeared, first sporadically and locally, next to the old ways of production but gradually undermining them everywhere, was not yet the factory, but Manufacture proper."[167] Historians in our day have emphasized that rural domestic industry based on the putting-out system occupied a larger portion of the work force than did centralized manufacture. David Landes has surmised that Marx's exaggerated estimation of the manufactory's importance stemmed from its role on the Continent as a state-subsidized disseminator of technical knowledge.[168] Marx's accentuation of the manufactory's significance may also have derived from his theorization of social relations at the point of production. Workers in these large undertakings, in contrast to those in the guild-controlled shops, were separated from the tools of manufacture, and the conversion of their labor into a product was subordinated to management decree. To Marx's eye, these workers were the first to sell labor power per se in the emerging capitalist order. The prominence Marx gave to the manufactories was intended to accord, not with their quantitative share of employment, but with their importance as a site of the inception of the social categories of wage labor and capital.

The insight that labor itself became a commodity only when workers were supervised by the owners of large enterprises had become a commonplace observation in bourgeois German economics before it surfaced in *Kapital*. J. C. Glaser, a philistine commentator from Berlin, had adduced such an argument in 1858. He claimed that

> So long as a worker is self-employed and either consumes for his own use the products he created with his labor or exchanges them for others that he can consume, then the wage of labor is the prod-

166. Marx no doubt exaggerated the inability of merchant capital to alter the internal structure of the guilds. Gerald Sider, *Culture and Class in Anthropology and History* (Cambridge: Cambridge University Press, 1986), pp. 189–191. But I am interested only in a negative contention: the guilds failed to sponsor the articulation of labor as a commodity.

167. *Grundrisse*, op. cit., p. 410. There Marx includes rural putting-out industries under manufacture. This disappears in *Das Kapital*. See also Karl Marx and Friedrich Engels, *Marx-Engels Werke*, Volume 3 (Berlin: Dietz Verlag, 1959), p. 55.

168. David Landes, "What Do Bosses Really Do?" *The Journal of Economic History* Volume XLVI, Number 3 (September 1986), p. 601.

uct itself. . . . As soon as the division of labor [in production] is introduced and the individual no longer owns the capital to support his work and therefore no longer works for himself, but for others . . . labor power is rented in return for compensation.[169]

Glaser, in contrast to most economists in Britain, made an explicit contrast in his theory between the selling of mere articles and the offering of labor as a commodity in centralized factories with a division of responsibility. Like Marx, he called labor itself a commodity and applied the term *labor power* only when certain historically specific social relations obtained at the point of production. In addition, however, Glaser took care to say that workers did not sell but merely "rented" their labor power. This marks an understanding of labor power as something lodged in the person of the worker and reveals an understanding of an essential similarity between wage labor and serfdom or slavery. No wonder Glaser chose his words so carefully at this point to demarcate wage labor.[170]

In Britain, economic agents in the nineteenth century supposed that capitalist relations of labor were exemplified in the small craft shop as well as in the factory; in Germany, by contrast, both employers and workers usually focused upon employment in a centralized factory as the exemplary form of wage labor. During the early phases of mechanization in the German textile industry, the very term *Lohnarbeiter*, "wage worker," connoted those who worked in a factory.[171] Remuneration in the factory also acquired a name different from that used in the craft shop. During the 1840s, workers of all sorts in the factories, as opposed to those in outside artisanal shops, were paid what were called "day wages" (*Tagelohn*), as if they were day laborers. This emphasized the diurnal sale of labor power per se, even if the exact amount of the compensation was based on piece rates.[172] In the textile trade, handweavers in trade associations gave their colleagues who entered the factories the contemptuous label of *Tagelöhner*, "day laborer."[173] Employers adopted the same lan-

169. J. C. Glaser, *Die allgemeine Wirtschaftslehre oder Nationalökonomie* (Berlin: E. H. Schroeder, 1858), pp. 182–183.

170. Glaser was not alone. Hermann, too, addressed the issue of whether workers could sell their "labor power," deciding that labor's *permanent* alienation could occur only in slave societies. Hermann, op. cit., 1870, p. 107.

171. Staatsarchiv Dresden, Ministerium des Innern, Nr. 5826, March 24, 1857, pp. 29–32.

172. Zentrales Staatsarchiv Merseburg, Rep. 120 B I 1, Nr. 60, Band 7, January 25, 1849, pp. 1–4. See Chapter Eight below, at footnotes 7–11.

173. Stadtarchiv Chemnitz, IX Za 98a, March 18, 1849, pp. 94–101. Stephan Born's newspaper also used the term *Tagelöhner* for wage-laborers outside small craft enterprise. *Das Volk:*

guage, singling out the factory operative as the true wage laborer. "The so-called day laborers," declared an industry journal in 1861, represented "the worker in the narrowest sense of the term."[174] Conversely, journeymen weavers contended that merely by virtue of the fact that they worked outside the factory system, they were not wage laborers.[175] In Britain, the commodification of labor appeared as a process separate from its impoundment in centralized, mechanized production under the supervision of the owner; in Germany, language testified to the conjunction of the two concepts.

The German view of employment as the purchase of "labor power" made the exercise of authority over the execution of work—that is, the purchase of labor's "use value"—an integral part of the process of securing a surplus from workers. This perspective unified the relations of appropriation and domination. When capitalists purchased "labor power," their receipt of profit depended on how successfully they converted labor capacity into labor. Without control of the production process, the employer did not appropriate a surplus. Profit may have been *realized* through exchange in the market, but it was generated and appropriated in production. There the buyers and sellers of labor as a commodity necessarily entered into relations of domination and subordination. Accordingly, Marx's theory ruled out the possibility of a social formation based on the exchange by independent commodity producers of labor as a commodity.[176]

Organ des Central-Komitees für Arbeiter, July 6, 1848, front page. In industry the paired terms for employer and employee were *Fabrikherr* ("factory master") and *Tagelöhner.* See *Allgemeine deutsche Arbeiter-Zeitung*, September 3, 1865, p. 763.

174. *Sächsische Industrie-Zeitung*, January 4, 1861, p. 1. Gerhard Schildt illustrates the association of the term *wage laborer* with labor outside the urban crafts. *Tagelöhner, Gesellen, Arbeiter* (Stuttgart: Klett-Cotta, 1986), p. 158. For association of *Tagelohn* with remuneration in factories as early as the eighteenth century, see Arno Herzig, "Vom sozialen Protest zur Arbeiterbewegung: Das Beispiel des märkisch-westfälischen Industriegebietes (1780–1865)," in Heinrich Volkmann and Jürgen Bergmann, editors, *Sozialer Protest: Studien zu traditioneller Resistenz und kollektiver Gewalt in Deutschland vom Vormärz bis zur Reichsgründung* (Opladen: Westdeutscher Verlag, 1984), p. 255.

175. Zentrales Staatsarchiv Merseburg, 120 B V 33, Nr. 3, Vol. 6, pp. 128–133.

176. See "Fragment des Urtextes von Zur Kritik der politischen Ökonomie," in his *Grundrisse der Kritik der politischen Ökonomie* (Berlin: Dietz Verlag, 1953), p. 904: "Original production is based on anciently arisen communal entities in which private exchange appears only as a completely superficial and secondary exception. With the historical dissolution of such communal entities, however, relations of domination and subjugation emerge at once. Such relations of violence stand in sharp contrast to mild commodity circulation and its corresponding relations." This was far removed from the British emphasis on the exchange of labor as a product, which confines its gaze to the sphere of circulation, wherein buyer and seller contract as equals. The market in labor, "within whose boundaries the sale and purchase of labor power goes on, was in point of fact," Marx says, "a veritable Eden of innate human rights. Here rule

The unique survival in Germany of corporate labor associations in craft work thus represents the second decisive condition for the development of the German specification of labor as a commodity. The resistance of German guilds to the introduction of liberal commercialism confined them to the margins of cultural development in the commercial economy. Their contribution to the cultural construction of labor was primarily negative. The restriction of the unbridled training and employment of labor to manufacture outside the guild system during the first decades of liberal commercialism in Germany meant that new branches of manufacture and the factory could play a pioneering role in the cultural construction of labor's commodity form. The factory provided a suitable setting for highlighting the supervision of labor and the appropriation of the "use value" of labor in the production process. If the immediate circumstances of production offer material for interpretation, however, they cannot impress themselves automatically upon the social imagination to produce a "corresponding" image of themselves. There is no single concept of labor that conforms most naturally to factory conditions. Instead, German producers drew upon cultural precedents to construct their definition of "labor power."

THE FEUDAL CONTRIBUTION

In Britain feudal tenures had been abolished and agrarian producers separated from the land before the government ceased regulating wages and before labor was formally founded upon contract rather than compulsion. In Germany, by contrast, feudal tenures and compulsory labor dues persisted in the countryside while the state created liberty of occupation and the formally free negotiation of wages for the factories and putting-out shops. This conjunction allowed feudal agricultural labor in Germany to supply a vivid template for the appropriation of labor in the factory during the transition to liberal commercialism.[177] Whereas the contribution of the guilds was negative, that of feudal relations of work in agriculture was positive: they offered a model for the employment of labor on which economic agents could draw to define the labor transaction under the emerging capitalist relations of production.

---

only Freedom, Equality, Property." *Das Kapital*, op. cit., Volume I, p. 189. To the workers' misfortune, production itself took place beyond the gates of Eden.

   177. I use the adjective *feudal* to indicate nothing more than the conveyance of tribute to a superior in the form of days of unpaid labor service.

The original feudalism of the Middle Ages had been founded on the coercive extraction of dues in labor. By the eighteenth century, of course, much of the tribute in labor services in Germany had been commuted to rents in kind or to money rents. This process followed separate tempos in localities from eastern to western Germany. Landowners who had converted most of the obligatory labor services to rents prior to 1810 did not as a rule manage estates of their own where they engaged wage labor.[178] In a word, they did not support the rise of an alternative definition of the labor transaction based on commercial agriculture. Although the offering of labor tribute to seignors had a diminished economic significance in many regions of the country by the early nineteenth century, it remained the principal model for the employment of agricultural labor to accumulate surplus.[179] In comparison to development in Britain, in Germany the introduction of freedom of occupation and of formally unconstrained market determination of wages in shops and factories began before—or in a few areas, barely coincided with—the complete abolition of dues in agricultural labor. We must examine the course of agrarian reform in each of Germany's key regions to show that despite enormous variation within Germany, this represented a general cross-national difference.

For historical analyses of the transformation of feudal relations in Germany, the Prussian heartlands have long served as the locus classicus. Until the reforms of the nineteenth century, most agricultural production here, east of the Elbe, was carried out on large estates with serf labor. Even the minority of peasants who were already legally free were required to give a labor tithe to the lord of their land in return for the use of a holding. Only in 1807, on the very eve of the introduction of freedom of trade, were the serfs themselves freed by law. Even then, many peasants did not satisfy the

---

178. Alexander Conrady, *Die Rheinlande in der Franzosenzeit 1750–1815* (Stuttgart: J. H. W. Dietz, 1922), p. 38; Christof Dipper, *Die Bauernbefreiung in Deutschland 1790–1850* (Stuttgart: W. Kohlhammer, 1980), p. 50. The abolition of labor services on royal estates in Prussia during the 1790s was an exception. But the king had alternative methods for signifying his authority. J. A. Perkins, "Dualism in German Agrarian Historiography," *Comparative Studies in Society and History* Volume 28, Number 2 (April 1986), p. 302.

179. In the first half of the nineteenth century even small farmers who allotted a plot to agricultural laborers (*Heuerlinge*) often did so in return for a certain number of days of labor. The dependent persons, called *Arbeiter* because they stood outside the estates system, were supposed "to stand at disposal for labor at any time" and received no cash wage. Josef Mooser, *Ländliche Klassengesellschaft 1770–1848: Bauern und Unterschichten, Landwirtschaft und Gewerbe im östlichen Westfalen* (Göttingen: Vandenhoeck & Ruprecht, 1984), pp. 248–250; Friedrich Engels, "Zur Geschichte der preussischen Bauern," in *Marx-Engels Werke*, Volume 21 (Berlin: Dietz Verlag, 1962), p. 244.

provisions that in principle would have allowed them to redeem their dues in labor. Indeed, when the German cities experienced the heady days of revolution in 1848, the bulk of the Prussian peasantry still were compelled to deliver a quota of labor tribute.[180] No wonder the entry for *Arbeit* in the German dictionary published in Berlin in 1860 included a feudal illustration of the term's meaning. This compendium, edited by a member of the Society for the Study of Modern Languages in Berlin, listed "going to do compulsory labor at the estate" as an illustration of the word's typical use.[181] At the start of the industrial age, agricultural workers in the east were still bound in feudal relations of work that emphasized the lord's authority over their labor service.[182]

In Saxony, destined to become one of Germany's most heavily industrialized regions, the seignors prior to the era of reform managed only part of their holdings as personal estates.[183] The remaining land had already come into possession of small peasant cultivators who owed the lords money rents as well as labor services. When the value of the money payments depreciated after 1815, however, the lords succeeded in intensifying their subordinates' labor obligations.[184] Not until 1832 did the Saxony government establish a framework for cultivators to release themselves from labor tribute by indemnifying their lords. The peasants who met the eligibility requirements could redeem their obligations by making payments in installments over a span of twenty-five years. When textile mills had become an accepted sight in the Saxony countryside and the mechanized factory an important matter in economic discussions, most of the peasants had not yet paid off their

180. Hanna Schissler, *Preussische Agrargesellschaft im Wandel: Wirtschaftliche, gesellschaftliche und politische Transformationsprozesse von 1763 bis 1847* (Göttingen: Vandenhoeck & Ruprecht, 1978), pp. 92, 107; Reinhart Koselleck, *Preussen zwischen Reform und Revolution* (Stuttgart, Klett, 1975), p. 499. Until 1850, most of Prussia's peasants did not meet the eligibility requirements for redeeming their labor dues. Jerome Blum, *The End of the Old Order in Rural Europe* (Princeton: Princeton University Press, 1978), p. 408.

181. Daniel Sanders, *Wörterbuch der deutschen Sprache*, Volume I (Leipzig: Otto Wigand, 1860), p. 30.

182. Few agricultural workers had become true participants in the money economy by this time. They were lodged in quarters granted to them by the lord and received most of their sustenance through in-kind benefits. Frieda Wunderlich, *Farm Labor in Germany 1810–1945* (Princeton: Princeton University Press, 1961), p. 17.

183. The Oberlausitz comprises an exception to the rest of Saxony. There the lords governed large estates as in East Prussia. Reiner Gross, *Die bürgerliche Agrarreform in Sachsen in den ersten Hälfte des 19. Jahrhunderts: Untersuchung zum Problem des Übergangs vom Feudalismus zum Kapitalismus in der Landwirtschaft* (Weimar: Hermann Böhlaus Nachfolger, 1968), p. 23.

184. Dipper, op. cit., p. 77; Gross, op. cit., pp. 30, 33–34.

feudal obligation to labor.[185] The outposts of factory development were surrounded by a sea of agricultural workers bound by compulsory labor from another era.

As a mechanism for extracting surplus from the agricultural producers, labor dues had less importance in western and southern Germany than in the east. But there were many exceptions to this rule. In some western and central regions, including Paderborn, Hannover, Brunswick, and Magdeburg, feudal rent in the form of labor services absorbed a large portion of the peasantry's workdays.[186] In the districts of Duisburg and Essen, near the centers of industrial expansion, some peasants were still attempting to release themselves from labor dues in the revolution of 1848.[187] In southern Germany the governments of Baden and Württemberg did not earn their liberal reputations for the agricultural reforms they introduced. Only in 1831 did Baden make labor obligations convertible to money payments.[188] In Württemberg small cultivators continued to deliver labor services until the revolution of 1848. The compensation they paid their lords to abolish labor dues was much greater than they paid for release from other fees and rents.[189] Even outside the Prussian heartlands, labor tribute played a role in defining the use of labor in the early nineteenth century.

185. Versammlung deutscher Gewerbetreibender, op. cit., p. 13. For an earlier example of popular economic discussions that placed the development of factories beside the survival of feudal obligations to labor, see *Die Ameise*, April 15, 1836. pp. 182–183.

186. Perkins, op. cit., p. 301. To be sure, cultivators in western Germany had by and large become free in their person and worked without supervision on their allotted parcels. Yet many of these free producers continued to owe at least some services in labor to their lords, who, like their counterparts in the East, also maintained some control of the local administration of justice into the early nineteenth century. In some regions of western Germany, including districts in Brunswick and Bavaria, landholders had aggressively converted labor services into money rents during the eighteenth century. Yet to contemporaries the direction of change was not absolutely clear: the process sometimes reversed itself, as other lords in the same regions happily converted money rents back to days of labor. For a comprehensive survey of labor dues by region, see Friedrich-Wilhelm Henning, *Dienste und Abgaben der Bauern im 18. Jahrhundert* (Stuttgart: Gustav Fischer, 1969), pp. 71, 82, 83, 85–86, 87, 92, 94, 96. The first critique of the system of labor dues did not appear in print until 1752. Blum, op. cit., p. 316.

187. Wilhelm Engels, *Ablösungen und Gemeinheitsteilungen in der Rheinprovinz* (Bonn: Ludwig Röhrscheid, 1957), p. 174. In Westphalia, a center of development in the textile branch, dues in labor were generally substantial until the French invasion. Clemens Wischermann, "An der Schwelle der Industrialisierung (1800–1850)," in Wilhelm Kohl, editor, *Westfälische Geschichte*, Volume 3 (Düsseldorf: Schwann, 1984), p. 62.

188. Dipper, op. cit., p. 84. On earlier reforms that lessened but did not eliminate feudal labor dues, see Sigmund von Frauendorfer, *Ideengeschichte der Agrarwirtschaft und Agrarpolitik im deutschen Sprachgebiet*, Volume I (München: Bayerischer Landwirtschaftsverlag, 1957), pp. 195, 269.

189. Harald Winkel, *Die Ablösungskapitalien aus der Bauernbefreiung in West- und Süddeutschland* (Stuttgart: Gustav Fischer Verlag, 1968), p. 42.

Prior to the French invasion, tithes in labor no doubt had less significance in the Rhineland than in other regions of the country. In this area above all, peasants could not be evicted from their holdings.[190] Most of the services the peasants had once rendered in return for use of the soil had been converted to money rents or to levies on the harvest.[191] The producers came close to enjoying a system of pure land rental.[192]

How, then, could historians conclude that in the Rhineland's system of agriculture prior to the French invasions "medieval survivals certainly still had a wide scope"?[193] One answer is that as a modest supplement to agricultural rents, some days of compulsory labor were still rendered in much of the Rhineland.[194] In rare instances, the obligatory service was rendered in the landowners' small manufactories.[195] Even if the landholders did not rely upon tribute in labor for their economic sustenance, the required services still played an important role in defining farmers' subservience to landowners, as the seignors' reactions to proposed reforms demonstrated. After the French invasion, landholders in western Germany opposed the elimination of labor dues, because they believed they would suffer a "decline of prestige through the future loss of subordinate persons."[196]

190. Engels, op. cit., p. 24. Since the producers remained dependent upon the feudal judicial authority of landowners, they were subject to extra-economic compulsion in the delivery of their rents. For an analysis of the essential similarity between this late system of feudalism and that of classical feudalism based purely on labor dues, see Erik Olin Wright, "What Is Middle About the Middle Classes?" in John Roemer, editor, *Analytical Marxism* (Cambridge: Cambridge University Press, 1986), p. 123.

191. Friedrich-Wilhelm Henning cites an example from Moers on the lower Rhine, where the days of compulsory labor amounted to only eight per year. Op. cit., p. 87.

192. Friedrich Lütge, *Geschichte der deutschen Agrarverfassung vom frühen Mittelalter bis zum 19. Jahrhundert* (2d ed. Stuttgart: Eugen Ulmer, 1967), p. 192. For an analysis of the continuing feudal character of labor under the Grundherrschaft, see Ernst Münch, "Feudalverhältnis—Feudalherrschaft—Feudalstaat," *Jahrbuch für Geschichte des Feudalismus*, Volume 14, op. cit., pp. 123–134.

193. Conrady, op. cit., p. 38. Cf. Blanning, op. cit., p. 137. August Bebel in his autobiography recalled the revolt of small farmers in 1848 against "all kinds of obligations inherited from the feudal period." August Bebel, *Aus meinem Leben*, Part One (Suttgart: J. H. W. Dietz Nachf., 1910), p. 18.

194. Conrady, op. cit., p. 38; Dipper, op. cit., p. 50; Reinhard Feinendegen, *Der niederrheinische Adel der Neuzeit und sein Grundbesitz* (Bonn: Ludwig Röhrscheid, 1961), p. 128. On the survival of labor dues in Mainz until 1792, see Christof Dipper, "Revolution und Reaktion im Jakobinismus," *Quellen und Forschungen aus italienischen Archiven und Bibliotheken* (Tübingen: Max Neimeyer Verlag, 1979), p. 318. On the continuation of some feudal dues in personal services in the Rhineland as a whole until the French invasions, see Joseph Hansen, *Die Rheinprovinz 1815–1915*, Volume I (Bonn: A. Marcus & E. Webers Verlag, 1917), p. 24.

195. Engels, op. cit., p. 82.

196. Von Frauendorfer, op. cit., p. 268. In other regions of Germany as well, landowners opposed the commutation of labor dues even after the economic advantages of wage labor had

Seignors believed that the procurement of labor through dues served as a model of authority relations. Even after some of them began to fathom the inefficiency that accompanied unpaid, coerced labor, they contended that its disciplinary effect was indispensable.[197] Johann Georg Fleischer had put this relation of domination into words in 1775, when he wrote that the dues were "service or labor for the lord" and were "owed as the obligation of a subordinate."[198] For another reason, too, tribute in labor had a significance apart from the bare number of days of work delivered: it could be demanded during the critical harvest period, when the dependent farmer's time was most valuable to himself as well as to the seignor.

The survival of feudal labor services in German agriculture supports the assumption that the labor transaction was based on the offering of a labor potential rather than on the delivery of a product. At the beginning of the nineteenth century, when employers and state administrators first tried to imagine the conversion of dues in labor to a market equivalent, they rejected the view that the dues could be equated with an article of labor. As one adviser, Karl Dietrich Hüllmann, expressed it in 1803, the value of the product delivered could vary, whereas "labor is to be compared only with labor."[199] Hüllmann recommended that landowners replace labor dues with variable money rents indexed by the current price of common day labor. With the funds thereby collected, lords could command the same amount of labor power in the market as they had received by feudal claim. Like others, Hüllmann equated labor dues with the command of living service. Economic theorists put this in a more explicit and commercial form. For example, Fleischer argued in 1775 that the compulsory labor services delivered to the lords represented "active capital,"[200] a living potential that could be used in a way that inert capital could not.

The slow reshaping of the social relations of work in German agriculture in accord with a liberal market regime highlighted the difference between the use value of labor and its price. Commentators observed that the lords extracted far less labor in a day from a vassal than from a free worker.

---

become evident. Blum, op. cit., p. 328.

197. Blum, op. cit., p. 330.

198. Johann Georg Fleischer defined them as "Dienst oder Arbeit . . . aus Unterthanspflicht schuldig" in *Philosophisch-politische Abhandlung von den Naturalfrohndiensten* (Frankfurt am Main: J. G. Fleischer, 1775), p. 37.

199. Karl Dietrich Hüllmann, *Historische und staatswissenschaftliche Untersuchungen über die Natural-Dienste der Gutsunterthanen nach fränkisch-deutscher Verfassung: Und die Verwandlung derselben in Geld-Dienste* (Berlin: Friedrich Nicolai, 1803), p. 171.

200. Fleischer, op. cit., pp. 26, 66.

Fleischer, for example, estimated that the use value of day labor obtained from an unfree subordinate was only half that of a common wage earner; but if both were free laborers in the market, he said, their labor time would have the same exchange value.[201] The conversion of feudal to capitalist institutions of work encouraged German thinkers to determine the distinct moment of converting a labor potential into labor.

Feudal relations of work offered a model for capitalist relations in the eyes of the workers themselves. The recollections of Adam Heuss illustrate their reactions during the critical period of transition. Heuss, born in 1780, worked for a small hand smith in Nürnberg who suffered from a decline in business. He published his observations on this matter in 1845, in a text that was autobiographical in tone and not intentionally political:

> In our age of mighty advance it has perhaps been supposed that it is advantageous to have these tradable wares manufactured in factories with machines. This case probably would follow closely the example of the Mecklenburger estate lords [*Gutsherren*] who released their subject peasants and turned them into day laborers; in this case the necessity of standing up to competition forces the businessman to do this, but truly the people's well-being has gained nothing through this advance.[202]

In Heuss's account, the appearance of wage labor is conjoined with the rise of mechanized factory production, a typical appreciation based on the German path to a market regime.[203] For him, the transition from compulsory labor dues to officially free labor served as a model for the transition from small craft shops to the factory. Heuss's text, focused on private affairs, was not composed for the sake of public dialogue or condemnation. The change from feudalism to capitalism was in his eyes purely formal: it did not alter the substance of employment. He testified to the transfer of feudal models of employment to the factory.

From the early days of factory labor in Germany during the 1830s, popular journals described the unwilling entry of workers into the factory as a

201. Ibid., p. 111.

202. Adam Heuss, *Wanderungen und Lebensansichten* (Jena: Friedrich Frommann, 1845), pp. 173–174.

203. C. Quentin, *Ein Wort zur Zeit der Arbeiter-Koalitionen* (Düsseldorf: J. H. C. Schreiner, 1840), p. 5. German contemporaries viewed the rise of machine production and the official establishment of free markets as separate occurrences whose simultaneous appearance was perhaps distinctive to German history. Ludwig Hoffmann, *Die Maschine ist nothwendig* (Berlin: Naucksche Buchhandlung, 1832), pp. 47–48.

continuation of forced labor under the feudal system.[204] During the revolutions of 1848 and 1849, the workers' newspaper *Die Verbrüderung* restated this judgment. It declared that there was no essential difference between feudal labor dues and "the labor that is demanded from the manual worker today." In both situations, it explained, the worker is compelled to work for his subsistence.[205] Colloquial language also testified to the comparison of industrial and feudal relations of work: during the 1830s, the term *Fröhnerlohn*, the subsistence of the forced laborer, was transferred from agriculture to industry.[206]

The comparison of feudal with capitalist employment relations remained a standard theme into the late nineteenth century. At an assembly of factory laborers and cloth makers in Bautzen in 1873, a speaker for the union movement said that "the serf of the Middle Ages was in a better position than the modern free worker, for the free worker has no means for acquiring the tools for work and thus becomes a vassal of the employer [*Brotherr*]."[207] Joseph Dietzgen, a tanner and early interpreter of Marx's investigation of the capitalist labor process, used the dependent servant's obligation to deliver labor to the lord of the property as a model for the wage laborer's delivery of labor to the capitalist. "Those who are working must do compulsory labor to create a product for the owners," he wrote in 1873, "which in twenty years equals the full value of the invested capital."[208]

204. *Die Ameise*, April 15, 1836, p. 182. In some instances, the introduction of "feudal" relations in the factory was not purely metaphorical. When lords in the eighteenth century built manufactories on their estates, they obtained labor by compelling subordinates to pay their days of tribute in them. Kurt Hinze, *Die Arbeiterfrage zu Beginn des modernen Kapitalismus in Brandenburg-Preussen 1685–1806* (Berlin: de Gruyter & Co., 1963 [1927]), p. 80.

205. *Die Verbrüderung*, Sept. 14, 1849, p. 399. The abolition of compulsory labor and tithes served as a model for the abolition of wage labor. *Die Verbrüderung*, August 10, 1849, p. 361.

206. *Die Ameise*, February 29, 1836, p. 102.

207. Staatsarchiv Dresden, Kreishauptmannschaft Bautzen, Nr. 4333, March 23, 1873, pp. 73 ff. For a similar characterization of the relation, see Ulrich Engelhardt, *"Nur vereinigt sind wir stark": Die Anfänge der deutschen Gewerkschaftsbewegung 1862/63 bis 1869/70*, Volume One (Stuttgart: Ernst Klett, 1977), p. 185. For later examples in the textile industry, see Staatsarchiv Dresden, Polizei-Präsidium Zwickau, Nr. 1404, meeting of German Textile Workers' Union, pp. 47–48, October 21, 1905; *Der Textil-Arbeiter*, March 31, 1911, Langenbielau.

Lassalle drew upon feudal analogies in his critique of capitalism. He said the workers' movement had to fight, not against any bourgeois citizen as a member of an economic class, but against "the citizen insofar as he lays claim to the position of a feudal lord." See Eduard Bernstein, *Ferdinand Lassalle: Eine Würdigung des Lehrers und Kämpfers* (Berlin: P. Cassirer, 1919), pp. 162 ff.

208. Joseph Dietzgen, "Dass der Sozialist kein Monarchist sein kann," in *Der Volksstaat*, August 13 and August 15, 1873, reprinted in full in Cora Stephan, *"Genossen, wir dürfen uns nicht von der Geduld hinreissen lassen"* (Frankfurt am Main: Syndikat, 1977), p. 285.

The long survival of feudal relations of work in Germany influenced the development of an understanding of the capitalist employment relation among elite economists as well. Many German economists saw the offering of feudal labor services as a forerunner to the sale of services by means of the wage contract.[209] Ludwig Jakob was among those who expressed in clear form the carryover of feudal assumptions about labor to the wage contract. In a prize essay on free and servile labor, published in 1814, Jakob said that with wage labor, "the master does not have anything to do with forcing serfs into his service; rather, he selects among persons who seek to rent themselves [*sich vermieten*]."[210] The formulation that free workers compete to "rent themselves" establishes an analogy, suggesting that as serfs confer their person permanently, so wage laborers offer their person to the employer temporarily. Textile workers adopted the same expression. When they looked for work, they said they wanted to "rent themselves."[211]

German economists may have taken liberal commercialism as the foundation for their codifications of economic thought, but they composed their works with many a backward glance at feudal relations of work. Economists such as Jakob, Rau, and Hermann emphasized that labor could be employed most productively if workers received compensation for extra effort and if they remained "free" to bargain for wages that compensated them for their accomplishments.[212] This looks liberal enough, but the writers were not so inured to capitalist relations as to take the officially free labor contract for granted. For the German economists, to say that workers sold their "labor" did not adequately distinguish between feudal and market relations, because

209. Johann Georg Busch, *Abhandlung von dem Geldumlauf in anhaltender Rücksicht auf die Staatswirtschaft und Handlung* (Hamburg: C. E. Bohn, 1780), erstes Buch, erster Abschnitt, pp. 19–41. The very term *relation of dependency (Abhängigkeitsverhältnis)*, used to characterize feudal relations of servitude, was applied by government officials to distinguish the capitalist employment relation from the delivery of goods by petty craftspeople. For an example of its use by officials, see Germany, *Statistik des Deutschen Reiches*, Volume 141 (Berlin: Kaiserliches Statistisches Amt, 1901), p. 5. On its application to feudalism, see, illustratively, Martin Göhring, *Die Feudalität in Frankreich vor und in der grossen Revolution* (Berlin: Emil Ebering, 1934), pp. 9–10.

210. Ludwig Heinrich Jakob, *Ueber die Arbeit Leibeigner und freyer Bauern in Beziehung auf den Nutzen der Landeigenthümer* (St. Petersburg: Akademie der Wissenschaften, 1814), p. 62.

211. Staatsarchiv Dresden, Amtshauptmannschaft Chemnitz, Nr. 16, p. 92, June 7, 1858. Industrial commentators continued to use the curious term *Dienstmiete* ("service rent") for wage labor. Bruno Zeeh, *Die Betriebsverhältnisse in der sächsischen Maschinenstickerei* (Borna-Leipzig: Verlag Noske, 1909), pp. 74–75.

212. Jakob, *Grundsätze*, op. cit., p. 161; Rau, op. cit., p. 138; Hermann, op. cit., 1832, "Ueber die Productivität der Arbeiten," p. 42.

selling one's "labor," in their eyes, could also mean that one bound one's whole person with a feudal obligation to labor.[213] The concept of "labor power," by contrast, identified clearly the commodity the worker sold as something that inhered in the individual but could be separated analytically from the worker's person. At the same time, it maintained the idea that workers sold their labor as if it were a *service* and a resource rather than as if it were materialized in finished articles, as in Britain.[214] The German thinkers did not contrast the person of the worker and the delivered product, as their British counterparts did, to distinguish the commitment of the whole person to labor from the sale of labor as a commodity; rather, the Germans made a distinction between the disposition over the whole person of the worker and the temporary command over the individual's labor capacity.[215] It is telling that even people of business in Germany emphasized that the wage was "the equivalent for *rented* human labor power."[216] Unlike the British, the Germans did not interpose a product between workers and employers but instead established an immediate relation between the two parties by retaining the concept of employment as the offering of a capacity.

Marx called attention in *Kapital* to the continuity between the concepts that ruled the delivery of labor under feudalism and those that operated, in disguised form, in the capitalist factory. In the Middle Ages, Marx claimed, "Every serf knows that what he expends in the service of his master is a definite quantity of his own personal labor power."[217] In the feudal period, "the social relations between individuals in the performance of their labour appear at all events as their own mutual personal relations and are not disguised under the shape of social relations between things, the labor *products*."[218] Under the feudal system, the relations of appropriation and domination were fused in experience. When Marx applied feudal common sense

213. Roscher, *Grundlagen der Nationalökonomie,* op. cit., p. 477.

214. German economic theorists long emphasized the identity of wage labor and unfree labor as subordinate, "dependent" work activity executed under the direction of a superior. Käthe Bauer-Mengelberg, "Zur Theorie der Arbeitsbewertung," *Archiv für Sozialwissenschaft und Sozialpolitik* Volume 55, Number 3 (1926), p. 688.

215. Hermann, op. cit., 1870, p. 168. The notion that workers sold their "labor power" simply to reproduce that power had disturbed German economists long before Marx made it his own. Roscher, for example, found the idea disagreeable because it struck him as the fundamental one governing slave economies. *Grundlagen,* op. cit., p. 477. Hence the need to introduce differences by referring to the "renting" of labor power.

216. Friedrich Leitner, *Die Selbstkostenberechnung industrieller Betriebe* (3d ed. Frankfurt am Main: J. D. Sauerländer, 1908), p. 77. Emphasis added. For parallel expressions among workers, see above, this chapter, footnotes 51 and 52.

217. *Das Kapital,* op. cit., Volume One, p. 91.

218. Ibid., pp. 91–92. The emphasis is my own.

about the delivery of labor to unmask capitalist nonsense, theory recapitu-lated history.[219] For Marx's acquaintance with feudal relations in Germany gave him the historical vantage point needed to use the notion of labor power in a critique of the view of materialized labor that governed British economic thought. Marx, like his contemporaries, emphasized the unusual coincidence in Germany of capitalist relations in the factory with feudal relations in agriculture.[220] The musty German past thereby divulged under-lying truths about the fresh British future.

The distinctive content of the German specification of labor as a com-modity drew in several ways upon the procurement of labor in feudal rela-tions of agriculture. As in the delivery of labor tithes, so in the selling of labor power in a market the German definition of the transaction empha-sized the delivery of labor as a service potential, the employer's authority over the use of the labor, and the challenge of converting the use value of labor into a result. Adelung's dictionary of 1793 highlighted the offering of the worker's own person as a tool to another in its definition of an *Ar-beitsmann* ("workman") as someone who "in everyday life lets himself be used for manual labor."[221] The feudal emphasis on the transfer of labor as a potential at the disposal of a superior was to echo inside the walls of the mechanized factory: at the beginning of the twentieth century, the employ-ment contract was not yet termed a "labor relation" in the German business code but a "service relation."[222]

Even after the ancient system of extracting dues in labor was put to rest, other components of feudalism in agricultural work refused a timely burial. Their spirit animated labor law in the German countryside until the revo-lution of 1918. Up to that year, more than three dozen special ordinances, many dating back to the eighteenth century, condemned the agricultural wage laborer to harsh servitude. For violation of contract, these laborers were still liable to gross physical punishment, imprisonment, and forcible transport by the police.[223] The bondage of agricultural workers to regula-tions outside those of a free mutual contract differs sharply from German

219. Marx also emphasized the historical continuity in laborers' servitude during the transition from feudalism to capitalism. "The transition," he said, "consisted in a change of form of servitude." Ibid., p. 743.

220. Ibid., p. 12.

221. Adelung, op. cit., p. 421.

222. *Sächsische Industrie,* October 10, 1908, pp. 6–7.

223. Wunderlich, op. cit., p. 21. On corporal punishment, see also Robert Wuttke, *Gesin-deordnungen und Gesindezwangsdienst in Sachsen bis zum Jahre 1835* (Leipzig: Duncker & Humblot, 1893), p. 223.

officials' deliberate protection of uncoercive agreements in factories at the dawn of the liberal commercial era. This extreme disjuncture in the pace of liberalization between the factory yard and the landed estate gave German producers an unusual vantage point. They could define the commodity of labor in terms of the underlying similarities between feudal and capitalist work regimes, systems whose principles appeared discordant to countries that had not experienced this coincidence of regimes of labor.

THREE CONDITIONS
FOR THE CULTURAL OUTCOME

This chapter has uncovered three major conditions guiding the construction of labor's commodity form in Germany: the simultaneous creation of juridically free markets in merchandise and wage labor in manufacturing, the prolonged supervision of labor in the urban crafts by guilds, and the compressed transition (amounting in a few regions to a genuine overlap) between the rendering of feudal dues in labor and the offering of labor for a wage in factory manufacture. The presentation has not treated these elements as additive factors; it has assigned them separate locations in an explanatory framework that shows how each established negative limits on the result or positively selected it. The conjoint introduction of formally free trade in manufactures and labor power gave German producers the opportunity of inventing labor's commodity form during the initial period in which market thinking emerged. In Britain the suppression of wage labor during the equivalent phase of the institutionalization of free commercial exchange blocked the discovery of labor as a commodity in the guise of "labor power." The two remaining conditions were still necessary to turn the possible into the actual in Germany. They enabled economic agents to transfer the assumptions surrounding the procurement of labor under feudalism to the labor transaction in the capitalist factory. It is only fitting that the word *Arbeit*, which in capitalist Germany came to designate labor in general, originally referred exclusively to agricultural services rendered by serfs.

To outline the historical origins of the contrasting commodity forms assumed by labor in Germany and Britain, this chapter has unraveled the lost connections between European economic practices lodged in the past and the Marxist analysis of the capitalist labor process debated in the present. We have seen how the categories Marx used to capture the generic logic of capitalist exploitation were unwittingly drawn from the culturally specific concepts used in nineteenth-century German industrial life. The German producers had the pivotal concept of labor power ready to hand. But the parallels are more ample than that. The logical structure of Marx's theory of capitalist production—its exclusion, on analytic grounds, of independent artisanal producers from capitalist relations, its fundamental exemplification of supervised labor in large manufactories—telescopes and freezes the historically unique development of industrial capitalism in Germany.

As is well known, Marx was acutely aware that the concept of labor as a general factor of production arose only with the unhampered circulation of workers among occupations in a capitalist order. He described the historical development of the appreciation of labor as a commodity in his methodological reflections upon his critique of political economy:

> The abstraction of labor in general is not only the intellectual reflection of a concrete totality of kinds of labor. The indifference towards the exact kind of labor corresponds to a form of society in which individuals can transfer with ease from one kind of work to another and the exact type of work is a matter of chance for them, and hence of indifference. Here labor has become a general means for the creation of wealth, not as a category of thought, but in reality. . . . Such a state of affairs is at its most developed in the modern form of existence of bourgeois society—in the United States. Here, then, for the first time, the point of departure of modern economics, namely, the abstraction of the category *labor*, labor as such, labor pure and simple, becomes true in practice.[224]

Marx uses the concept of labor as a commodity not only as an economic but as a social category; it delineates both the systemic laws of capitalism and the culturally specific lifeworld of the producers in bourgeois society. But if Marx brilliantly historicized and humanized a concept that other economists had taken as a gift from on high, at the same time he continued to postulate a single commodity form for labor in all developed capitalist regimes. When he conducted his own interpretive analysis of the causal laws of commodity exchange enunciated by bourgeois economists before him, he still treated capitalism as a general system that stood outside of himself. He failed to reflect upon his own national location within the movement of history and the process by which his experience came to incorporate na-

---

224. *Grundrisse*, op. cit., p. 25.

tional specificities of development. He investigated what was hidden *from* his life experience, not what was hidden *in* it.

The delineation of the three forks in German development led us to the commodification of labor in the form of "labor power," but it left several questions unresolved. What destination does a country reach if it experiences the creation of officially free markets in merchandise and labor simultaneously but lacks the other conditions that prevailed in Germany? Are there other forms in which labor can be molded as a commodity apart from those cast in Germany and Britain? We address these questions in the next chapter.

7 A Conjunctural Model of Labor's Emergence in Words and Institutions

We built an emporium beside a factory of phrases.

Louis Reybaud,
Jérôme Paturot à la recherche d'une position sociale

If labor assumed the commodity form of *Arbeitskraft* in Germany and of materialized labor in Britain, what form did it assume in other countries as they negotiated the transition to a capitalist labor market? This issue does not only arise in the move from a two-case comparison to a theory of broader applicability about the commodification of labor. The question appears on the table the moment the critical variables distinguishing the German and British cases from one another are identified. Since more than one differentiating factor is at work in these two primary examples, we must also view the other conceivable combinations of these variables. Otherwise we can portray but not convincingly demonstrate the influence of the historical conjunctures.

Will every country adopt one or the other of the definitions of labor identified in Britain and in Germany? Now that these concepts of labor as a commodity stand revealed as the lived inventions of the historical actors rather than mere analytic categories imposed from without by investigators, there are no grounds for assuming a priori that in the fabrication of a capitalist regime all countries adopt one or the other definition of labor as a commodity. Within the framework of Marxist discourse the two forms of labor seem analytically exhaustive. That limitation reflects the historical vantage point from which Marx sought to universalize his encounter with the particular. The two economic traditions that in different ways impressed themselves most firmly on him and that he interlaced were none other than those of Germany and Britain. The definitions of labor that developed in these two countries imprinted themselves on succeeding scholars, not as historical exemplifications of social consciousness under capitalism, but as logical essences. The intellectual world, with its habit of sequestered contemplation, reified Marx's portrayal of historical forms of consciousness, restricted them to a deductive economic theory, and thereby deprived them of their capacity to illuminate developmental experience and contingency. The secret power of social theories derives from the inner relation they establish between concepts and historical materials. Now that we have recovered the essential links between Marx's views of labor as a commodity and the progression of economic practice in Germany during his day, not only do we have the foundation to rethink what Marx took for granted—the historical emergence of a cultural specification of labor as a commodity; we can also return his portrayals to the open air of history. They vividly register exactly those circumstances that mark basic divergences in the European routes to the commodification of labor.

In *Kapital* Marx organized his narratives of the historical unfolding of capitalism to highlight as fact, but not as point of theory, the three conditions in Germany and Britain that we found led to different cultural outcomes. First, his tale brilliantly portrays the long statutory regulation of the price of labor power in Britain after the transition to formally free intercourse in articles.[1] By disgraceful legislation, he concluded, "the state employed the police to accelerate the accumulation of capital."[2] Second, Marx dramatized the consolidation of unshackled capitalist relations of labor in large German factories before feudal relations of labor had been dismantled in the rest of that country's economy.[3] Finally, in his eyes, continued guild control of apprenticeship and of the application of labor power ruled out the crystallization of the social categories of wage labor and of capital in the urban crafts. Marx contended in *Kapital* that the survival of the guilds did not just hold in place fragmentary obstructions to the development of the capitalist production process; it actually debarred the operation of the fundamental forms of capitalist activity and consciousness in guild trades.[4] These three parts of his narration of capitalism's emergence in Europe represented for Marx variables that produced only temporary differences among countries; in the end, he believed, these contingencies were outweighed by the fundamental logic of the capitalist system, which produced everywhere the same commercial consciousness. If we set aside Marx's emphasis on a convergent lineage,

1. *Das Kapital* (Berlin: Dietz Verlag, 1980), pp. 767–768.
2. Ibid., p. 770.
3. Ibid., pp. 12, 15.
4. Ibid., pp. 379–380, 533, 743.

however, these variables can be recast into a multilinear model of labor's commodification in Europe.

The investigation of the origins of labor's commodity form in the previous two chapters proceeded by isolating three essential elements at work behind a wealth of empirical material. At this point we can take a more deductive approach and construct a table of permutations using these components. Figure 10 combines the elements into four major types, following the hierarchy of causes operating in Germany as opposed to Britain. The table is admittedly crude, and this chapter correspondingly differs in method from those preceding it. The presentation is exploratory, intended to provide a ladder for more intensive historical examination into branches on the European tree of possibilities. Nonetheless, against the shared background of European feudalism, the basic model captures the essential patterns of cultural development well enough that it enables us to view the concrete historical outcomes as examples of an underlying system of possibilities. Northern Italy and France experienced two so far unillustrated combinations of these variables. By considering development in those two countries in turn we will not only suggest how the explanatory framework for Germany and Britain can be extended to other European nations, but we may also refine our understanding of the contribution each variable made to the cultural construction of labor as a commodity in the two primary cases of Germany and Britain as well.

NORTHERN ITALY: A PREPARATORY APPLICATION OF THE MODEL

The course of development in northern and central Italy, the pioneering regions of the peninsula in the transition to liberal commercialism, shares an essential similarity with development in Britain. Northern Italy, like Britain, began its transition to liberal commercialism cleansed of the legacy of feudal relations in the countryside.[5] As early as the tenth century the

5. Alain Dewerpe, "Politiques, économiques et industrialisation en Italie du Nord pendant la période française," in Gérard Gayot and Jean-Pierre Hirsch, editors, *La Révolution française et le développement du capitalisme* (Lille: Revue du Nord, 1989), p. 163. Northern Italy and Britain share another conjunctural similarity. Both experienced "late" industrialization, by comparison with other institutional changes in their economies. Far more than a century separates the recognition of free intercourse in products in Britain and the launching of the factory system. Likewise, in Italy the factory system did not appear until the end of the nineteenth century, long after the establishment of a liberal market regime. In both instances, then, the networks of putting-out systems of artisanal work provided a suitable terrain for sustaining (though not by themselves creating) the notion that labor was purchased as it was embodied in products.

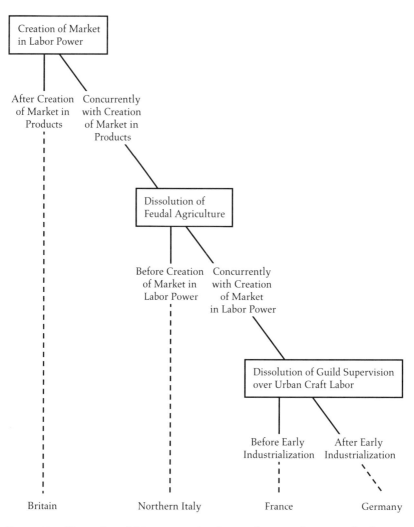

Figure 10. Hierarchy of Motivating Conditions for Specifications of Labor as a Commodity

nobles of northern and central Italy began to abandon manorial agriculture. They converted the obligatory labor services of their subordinates into rents.[6] In the fourteenth century, as the economic influence of the buoyant urban communes encompassed much of the countryside, ownership of the land passed from the ancient nobles to new bourgeois owners.[7] Despite the great variety in the size of holdings in different localities, most agriculture was dominated by small peasant farmers paying rents in money or as a share of the crops.[8] The region was perhaps unique in its prolonged experience with a new rural civilization based on commercial exchange rather than formal legal privilege over persons.[9] Peasants were, to be sure, dependent upon the landowners, but their relation was based originally on contract and did not include a model for the delivery of unpaid labor services.

As the Italian economy in the sixteenth century entered its secular decline, the countryside experienced what some observers have vaguely termed *refeudalization*. The peninsula's many small states, in their quest for revenue, sold rights and functions normally exercised by the central authorities, such as the levying of taxes and administration of justice. The buyers were thereby invested with a "fief." Despite the splintering of authority and the growth of byzantine networks of privilege, this process did not recreate the fusion of property and authority over labor that characterized land ownership in Germany and France. The feudatories received no estate holdings, no right to meddle in the property rights of the people in the fief, and, most important for the development of concepts of labor, no claim to exact dues in work.[10] They acquired the license to levy taxes specified at the time of investiture, to collect fees from public facilities such as grain mills and inns, and to administer justice—although many subjects were exempted from the feudatories' courts or could appeal to central

6. Gino Luzzatto, *An Economic History of Italy from the Fall of the Roman Empire to the Beginning of the Sixteenth Century* (London: Routledge & Kegan Paul, 1961), p. 62.

7. Sigmund von Frauendorfer, *Agrarwirtschaftliche Forschung und Agrarpolitik in Italien* (Berlin: Paul Parey, 1942), p. 22; Guy Fourquin, *Lordship and Feudalism in the Middle Ages* (London: George Allen & Unwin, 1976), p. 225.

8. Von Frauendorfer, op. cit., pp. 13, 16; Marx, op. cit., Volume One, p. 744.

9. Maurice Aymard, "La transizione dal feudalesimo al capitalismo," in Ruggiero Romano and Corrado Vivanti, editors, *Storia d'Italia. Annali I: Dal feudalesimo al capitalismo* (Torino: Giulio Einaudi, 1978), pp. 1169–1170, 1178. But for some public works or in periods of emergency, labor in the service of communal authorities remained obligatory into the sixteenth century. Amintore Fanfari, *Storia del lavoro in Italia dalla fine del secolo XV agli inizi del XVIII* (2d ed. Milano: A. Giuffrè, 1959), pp. 270–273.

10. Here I closely follow Domenico Sella, *Crisis and Continuity: The Economy of Spanish Lombardy in the Seventeenth Century* (Cambridge, Massachusetts: Harvard University Press, 1979), p. 164.

authority.[11] On the whole the peasants remained indifferent to this readjustment of administration, so inconsequential did these changes "on high" seem to them.[12] In the centuries of Italy's economic regression the devolution of responsibility for collecting revenue and for staffing the courts created an interminable maze of privilege but did not alter the reliance in agriculture on contracts for labor rather than on obligatory services.

In the seventeenth century Italy diverged from Britain in its failure to develop a liberal market policy. The weakening of the Italian economy made it increasingly difficult to provision the towns with foodstuffs. Most states controlled prices of grain and imposed tariffs on grain shipments.[13] In textiles, cultivators of raw silk had to dispose of their output to registered merchant guilds.[14] In contrast to Britain's precocious development of an integrated national market, the Italian states regulated trade in such a way as to prevent the formation of interregional markets.[15] The guilds continued to control the training and merchandising of labor power until the mid-eighteenth century.

As in Germany, so in Italy a period of rapid reform orchestrated by the state led to the simultaneous recognition of markets in labor and in other commodities. Venice began the gradual abolition of guild privilege in 1719. In Tuscany the government promulgated freedom of occupation in 1770 and abolished the guilds' exams, courts, and statutes.[16] The administration in Lombardy removed the guilds through a series of bold decrees between 1773 and 1787.[17] This period coincided with the removal of legal restrictions on the free marketing and pricing of goods.

11. Ibid., p. 167.

12. Ibid., pp. 162–163.

13. Price controls on grain survived until the Napoleonic era. Dino Carpanetto and Giuseppe Ricuperati, *Italy in the Age of Reason 1685–1789* (London: Longman, 1987), pp. 24–25. In Lombardy, estate owners and farmers were required to bring an established fraction of their crop for sale in the neighboring city square. Sella, op. cit., p. 33.

14. Sella, op. cit., p. 141; Carlo Poni, "Mass gegen Mass: Wie der Seidenfaden rund und dünn wurde," in Robert Berdahl et al., editors, *Klassen und Kultur* (Frankfurt am Main: Syndikat, 1982), pp. 23, 35.

15. Luigi Dal Pane, *Economia e società a Bologna nell'età del Risorgimento* (Bologna: Zanichelli, 1969), p. 476.

16. Corrado Rainone, *Pensiero e strutture socio-economiche europee e italiane nell'epoca risorgimentale 1748–1861* (Milano: A. Giuffrè, 1975), p. 208. For Bologna, see Dal Pane, op. cit., pp. 271, 331.

17. Commercial law in Lombardy stipulated a laissez-faire regime in labor before the Napoleonic invasions. Anna-Lucia Forti-Messian, "La Législation du travail en Lombardie à l'époque napoléonienne," *Annales historiques de la révolution française* Volume 49 (1977), pp. 637–652.

Northern Italy's conjoint development of formal markets in labor and in finished products and its lack of a feudal legacy therefore combined aspects of the German and the British experiences. The effect upon the construction of labor as a commodity was perhaps foreseeable. First, the absence of a feudal legacy in Italy eliminated the cultural template for imagining that the employer lays claim to a service capacity and has the right of disposal over the person of the subordinate worker. Accordingly, the specification of labor that dominated Italian economic literature during the classical period of political economy bears a generic resemblance to the prevailing concept in Britain: labor was seen as being transferred from worker to employer as it was materialized in a product. Cesare Beccaria's reflections upon the division of labor, perhaps the most celebrated economic discussions from Italy's eighteenth-century bourgeois Enlightenment, are restricted to the example of independent producers exchanging their articles with each other.[18] Yet the conjoint appearance of markets in labor and in finished products created a difference in development between Italy and Britain: when the concept of labor as a commodity appeared in Italy, it was not subsumed under a preexisting concept of material goods exchanged in a market, as happened in Britain. There the antecedent development of formally free intercourse in finished goods that were believed to be exchanged in terms of the value of the materialized labor they contained lent people of commerce the notion that if labor, too, was a commodity it must acquire its calculable value when it entered the market embodied in a ware. In Italy, by comparison, the transfer of labor occurred via the materialized product, but the value of the product was determined by the labor power people were willing to dispense for its acquisition.[19] The simultaneous development of formally free intercourse in both finished products and labor power encouraged economic agents to see the expenditure of labor power and the amount spent on products as determined by the same utilitarian calculus. Since the amount of labor an individual was willing to disburse for a product could differ from the amount of materialized labor received in it, however, labor seemed to be a source of a product's value, but not its determinant.[20] Yet a key similarity

18. Cesare Beccaria, *Elementi di economia pubblica*, in Pietro Custodi, editor, *Scrittori classici italiani di economia politica*, Parte Moderna, Tomo XI (Milano: G. G. Destefanis, 1804).

19. Ibid., p. 54.

20. Graziani, op. cit., p. 121. Francesco Fuoco believed that labor can serve as an index of value because it decides whether something can be easily obtained. "Things that are naturally useful, to put it in rigorous terms, do not have value, because they are not appraised; and they are not appraised because they are lacking one of the principal elements of which an appraisal

between the Italian and British classical economists confirms that the Italians conceived of the conveyance of abstract labor via products: the Italians, like the British, were weak in analyzing the entrepreneurial function. The classical Italian economists, like the British, treated the employer as a capitalist investor rather than as a supervisor of the execution of work.[21]

The development of Italian theories of labor's contribution to the prices of goods may have crested in the work of Francesco Ferrara, who received a chair in political economy at Turin in 1848. Ferrara supposed that labor is transferred between persons in the market via the transfer of articles.[22] He proposed that "labor be considered as a *product* capable of being sold, the price of which is the wage."[23] To be sure, Ferrara acknowledged that the expenditure of labor entered into the calculation of the value of a product, for value is measured by the sacrifice in effort that consumers are willing to make to obtain the product, whether by making it themselves or by working to make an exchange for it.[24] Every person equates the price of something with their "individual appreciation" of the amount of their own "effort" that would be required to obtain that merchandise.[25] Ferrara treated the fact that people hire services as analytically similar to their purchase of a finished ware in an equalitarian exchange:

---

consists. This element is rarity; the things that are hard to obtain call for an extraordinary quantity of labor" ("si ricerca una straordinaria quantità di lavoro"). Fuoco, *Saggi economici*, Prima Serie I (Pisa: Presso Sebastiano Nistri, 1825), p. 176. Fuoco contended that the amount of labor put into a product did not by itself determine the value of the product; yet the amount of labor put into something determines its value because it determines whether it will be rare. Labor serves as an index of value because it expresses the balance of supply and demand for a particular good. But Fuoco does not discuss the transfer of labor except as it is concretized in a product. He has no theory to speak of about labor power's value apart from that of products: "Once the labor becomes a good," he summarizes, "its price will be subject to the laws that regulate the prices of all other goods." Fuoco, *Saggi economici*, Prima Serie II (Pisa: Presso Sebastiano Nistri, 1827), p. 367. Ferdinando Galiani's work expressed a similar view. "Labor," Galiani wrote, "alone gives things value whether they are entirely works of art . . . or such things as minerals, stones, wild fruit trees, and so on." But, in Galiani's view, labor acquires its value by its scarcity according to the balance of supply and demand. *On Money* (Ann Arbor: University Microfilms International, 1977 [1751]), p. 29.

21. Fuoco, op. cit., II, p. 217. Giammaria Ortes could not discover how entrepreneurs who borrowed capital could turn a profit except by stealing from their creditors. See the analysis offered in "Italian School of Economics" in Sir Robert Harry Inglis Palgrave, *Palgrave's Dictionary of Political Economy* (London: Macmillan & Co., 1917), Volume II, note pp. 464–465.

22. G.-H. Bousquet, *Esquisse d'une historie de la science économique en Italie des origines à Francesco Ferrara* (Paris: Marcel Rivière, 1960), p. 83.

23. Francesco Ferrara, *Oeuvres économiques choisis* (Paris: Marcel Rivière, 1938), p. 134.

24. Bousquet, op. cit., p. 80.

25. Graziani, op. cit., p. 167.

> Someone who uses the labor of another will not be disposed to pay
> more for it than he would pay to procure it in another fashion, that
> is to say, to "duplicate" it. . . . The labor that one must pay by
> means of a salary may be "duplicated" personally, just as the pur-
> chaser of a material object may, in certain cases, produce it with his
> own hands rather than purchase it.[26]

As in theories of value, so in theories of practice. Industrial advisers who
discussed the use of piece-rate scales in Italy focused on the employer's
measurement of the materialized labor. In contrast to German commentators upon industrial relations who saw the piece-rate scale as a surrogate
index of the labor activity, the Italian experts saw it as a measure of embodied labor pure and simple.[27] Research in the future must examine the incarnation of labor's commodity form within the instrumentalities of life on the
shop floor in Italy.[28] This preliminary sketch suggests, however, that discourse in Italy about labor was cast in a distinctive mold that followed the
logic of the region's route to liberal commercialism.

FRANCE: A SUGGESTIVE EXTENSION

The French case illustrates the construction of labor as a commodity under
circumstances that display two initial contrasts to those prevailing in Britain. First, the institutional frameworks for the formally free exchange of
manufactures and of labor power were created simultaneously in France
during the Great Revolution, not disjointly as in Britain. Second, France
began the transition to a capitalist labor market with a legacy of feudal
relations of work in agriculture. Both these conditions approximately paralleled the conditions obtaining in Germany during the same process of
transition. But development in France diverged from that in Germany: during the initial transition to a formally free labor market, the guilds in France
were not just stripped of their lawful monopolies over the marketing of

26. "In this case," Ferrara continues, "the calculation of the 'duplication' will take place in
his mind, by comparing that which the laborer demands to the total of sacrifices involved in
personal execution of the work." Op. cit., p. 134. The extraction of a use value through
domination of the worker utterly disappears from this analysis.

27. Riccardo Dalla Volta, *Le forme del salario* (Firenze: Fratelli Bocca, 1893), p. 198.

28. There is evidence that late-nineteenth-century Italian factories bolted latecomers out,
as in Britain, rather than fine them. Luigi Guitto, *La fabbrica totale* (Milano: Feltrinelli
Economica, 1979), pp. 197–198. Factory design in Italy stressed the need for control of border
points as well as total visibility of the production process itself. Carlo Poni, "All'origine del
sistema di fabbrica: Tecnologia e organizzazione produttiva dei mulini da seta nell'italia settentrionale (sec. XVII–XVIII)," *Rivista storica italiana* Volume LXXXVII, fascicolo III (September 1976), p. 489.

goods; they were eliminated altogether. In contrast to development in Germany, urban craftwork in France adapted to commercial liberalism without significant protection and could therefore serve as an institutional locus for the cultural definition of labor as a commodity. The major currents of economic thinking in France in the early nineteenth century gave expression to a distinctive specification of labor as a commodity which was eventually installed on the factory shop floor.

In the decades before the revolution of 1789, the constraints on trade and on the exercise of an occupation eroded in France, but they were not replaced by a formally free market regime in products or labor power. Louis XV's government declared in 1762 that manufacture in the countryside could proceed independently of the guilds, which were centered in the cities.[29] Despite this newly confirmed liberty, exchange in the rural outlands developed under a hodgepodge of shifting local ordinances. At least until 1779, many *intendants* in the provinces enforced requirements that rural textile makers produce only approved varieties of cloth.[30] In the north of France, by order of the *intendant*, inspectors from the textile guilds of Lille tramped through the backwoods districts to seize fabrics that deviated from approved patterns.[31] The surveillance of rural output and the fines levied on aberrant weavers did not halt the rise of outland manufacture, but they helped to attach a portion of that production to the regulated trade of the cities.[32] Urban brokers sometimes retained a statutory monopoly on the marketing of certain lines of fabrics created in nearby villages.[33] In some regions, rural

29. E. Tarlé, *L'Industrie dans les campagnes en France à la fin de l'ancien régime* (Paris: Edouard Cornély, 1910), p. 53.

30. Philippe Guignet, *Mines, manufactures et ouvriers du Valenciennois au XVIIIe siècle* (New York: Arno Press, 1977), pp. 89, 93; for an example of confiscation of cloth in Languedoc in 1773, see J. K. J. Thomson, *Clermont-de-Lodève 1633–1789* (Cambridge: Cambridge University Press, 1982), pp. 422–423; William Reddy, *The Rise of Market Culture* (Cambridge: Cambridge University Press, 1984), p. 36; Harold T. Parker, *The Bureau of Commerce in 1781 and Its Policies with Respect to French Industry* (Durham, North Carolina: Carolina Academic Press, 1979), p. 33. After 1779, textile producers could manufacture cloth by any standard, but unauthorized fabric had to be stamped as such. Parker, op. cit., pp. 36–37, 108.

31. Gail Margaret Bossenga, "Corporate Institutions, Revolution, and the State: Lille from Louis XIV to Napoleon," Ph.D. diss., University of Michigan, 1983, p. 301.

32. Jean-Pierre Hirsch, "Négoce et corporations," in Gérard Gayot and Jean-Pierre Hirsch, editors, *La Révolution française et le développement du capitalisme* (Lille: Revue du Nord, 1989), p. 360. On the attachment of rural production to regulated urban trade, see also Charles Engrand, "Concurrences et complémentarités des villes et des campagnes: Les Manufactures picardes de 1780 à 1815," *Revue du Nord* Volume 61, Number 240 (January–March 1979), pp. 68–69.

33. Bossenga, op. cit., pp. 290, 308, 351. In many branches of manufacture, the state also granted to its favored entrepreneurs exclusive rights within a region to produce a line of textile

spinners and weavers were still required to sell their goods in an approved marketplace, to prevent unlicensed dealers from poaching on the business of the guild brokers.[34] Amid this forest of regulation, the abolition of guild jurisdiction over labor in the countryside represented only a partial clearing.[35]

Within the walls of the municipalities, officials upheld their right to control manufacture. In principle, magistrates in the textile towns remained the "natural judges" of economic activity. They could allocate yarn to various branches of weaving, authorize brokers to serve as intermediaries between producers and merchants, set up appropriate prices to be paid to both male and female workers for products, and decide whether new branches of enterprise should be established.[36] Finally, of course, the urban corporations used their royal charters and judicial rights to buttress their manufacturing privileges and to control the circulation of labor. Guild masters were officially forbidden to compete with colleagues to at-

---

goods. Parker, op. cit., p. 53; Serge Chassagne, "La Diffusion rurale de l'industrie cotonnière en France, 1750–1850," *Revue du Nord* Volume 61, Number 240 January–March 1979, pp. 99–100.

34. Bossenga, op. cit., p. 352; Gay L. Gullickson, *Spinners and Weavers of Auffay* (Cambridge: Cambridge University Press, 1986), p. 64. William Reddy points out that rural outworkers contested these efforts to regulate trade. He describes a riot that occurred in Rouen during 1752 in protest against a royal ordinance restricting trade in yarn to the guild-controlled Cloth Hall. According to Reddy's interpretation of events, the outworkers objected, not to an unwarranted regulation of commerce, but to the expected insufficiency of wages for the procurement of subsistence at a time of high grain prices. See Reddy's brilliant analysis in "The Textile Trade and the Language of the Crowd at Rouen: 1752–1871," *Past & Present* Number 74 (February 1977), pp. 70–74. In their comparison of France and Britain, Wadsworth and de Lacy Mann suggest that the subversion of regulation in Rouen comprised an exception for France. Alfred P. Wadsworth and Julia de Lacy Mann, *The Cotton Trade and Industrial Lancashire 1600–1780* (Manchester: Manchester University Press, 1931), p. 203.

35. Jean-Pierre Hirsch, *Les Deux Rêves du Commerce: Entreprise et institution dans la région lilloise, 1780–1860* (Paris: Ecole des Hautes Etudes en Sciences Sociales, 1991), pp. 159–160. For an account of the climate of uncertainty in the 1780s brought about by policies that combined regulation and market liberty for textile putting-out systems, see Thomson, op. cit., pp. 379, 455.

36. Guignet, op. cit., pp. 43, 78, 80–83, 126–138; Michael Sonenscher, *Work and Wages: Natural Law, Politics and the Eighteenth-Century French Trades* (Cambridge: Cambridge University Press, 1989), p. 67. The judicial authorities of the corporate order may also have discouraged the development of piece-rate lists. Ibid., p. 279. Apart from the prescriptions for textile production, city officials imposed controls on the import of cloth into their domain by checking seals of inspection from brand examiners and certificates proving that the transport duties had been paid on provincial routes. William Reddy, "The Structure of a Cultural Crisis: Thinking About Cloth in France Before and After the Revolution," in Arjun Appadurai, editor, *The Social Life of Things* (Cambridge: Cambridge University Press, 1986), p. 265.

tract journeymen by offering better terms of work.[37] The corporations' fetters on the exercise of an occupation came under increasing criticism from the reform-minded philosophes in the last decades of the old monarchy. Indeed, Turgot suspended the corporations for several months in 1776 after he began his brief tenure as controler-general. But his edict was never enforced.[38] The guilds were swiftly restored and consolidated between 1776 and 1780.[39] As a well-ordered hierarchy of associations subordinate to the monarch, they seemed indispensable to uphold the organization of society.[40] Even when, in the eighteenth century, the de jure monopolies of the guilds became less effective, the model of constitutory corporations remained dominant in popular conceptions of the social order.[41]

The revolution of course swiftly initiated the transition to liberal commercialism. Internal customs and tolls on the transport of goods disappeared in 1790.[42] The Constituent Assembly moved almost immediately to create a formally free market in labor power as well. In the period of the revolution from February to September, 1791, the assembly passed three decrees that demolished the old framework of corporate production. It first eliminated the guild associations of masters and workers. By contrast with the path of reform in Prussia, in France the guilds lost their function as official corporate sponsors of the employment of artisans. They were suppressed as associations for the training of workers, certification of masters, and cultivation of the trade. Then, in June, the Le Chapelier law put an end to all trade associations, including workers' collective organizations. The law provided instead for the establishment of wages by "freely contracted agreements between individual and individual."[43] Finally, in September of that year the

37. Henri Sée, *Economic and Social Conditions in France During the Eighteenth Century* (New York: Cooper Square Publishers, 1968), p. 124.

38. Ibid., p. 135.

39. On the controversial survival of guild regulation for textiles in Lyons, consult L. Trénard, "The Social Crisis in Lyons on the Eve of the French Revolution," in Jeffry Kaplow, editor, *New Perspectives on the French Revolution* (New York: John Wiley & Sons, 1965), pp. 72–77.

40. William H. Sewell, Jr., *Work and Revolution in France* (Cambridge: Cambridge University Press, 1980), pp. 73–74; François Olivier-Martin, *L'Organisation corporative de la France d'ancien régime* (Paris: Librairie du Recueil Sirey, 1938), p. 537; Ellen Meiksins Wood, *The Pristine Culture of Capitalism* (London: Verso, 1991), p. 88.

41. Olivier-Marin, op. cit., p. 537. Even Turgot operated within the assumptions of a corporate order, as Reddy discloses in "The Textile Trade," op. cit., p. 72.

42. Albert Soboul, *The French Revolution, 1787–1799* (New York: Vintage Books, 1975), p. 191.

43. Cited by Sewell, op. cit., p. 89.

assembly set aside the regulations that had prescribed the execution of labor: it dismantled all offices for inspecting the quality and specifications of manufactures.[44] Of course, no perfectly liberated bazaar in articles of commerce or in labor power appeared in France (or elsewhere) that would satisfy the economist's shining ideal of an unbridled play of market forces.[45] But there is a world of difference between community-supported, culturally prominent, foundational restrictions on trade and narrow exemptions from competition or implicit market imperfections such as de facto labor immobility. The revolution brought France across this divide. At one stroke, the outlines of an integrated national market in both products and labor came into view.

The dramatic change in governing economic principle did not allow the concept of labor as a commodity to spring ready-made out of the market stalls and workshops. The current of ideas that surfaced among the *sans-culottes* during the ensuing months of popular organization and insurrection verify that labor's commodity form had not yet taken shape. The *sans-culottes* founded their outlook upon the social contribution of concrete labor itself. As William Sewell's study of the language of labor reminds us, the common people of Paris sanctified those who worked with their hands.[46] In their eyes, manual effort provided the moral foundation of the new French republic. When the radical *sans-culottes* articulated their demands for bread on the morrow or their hopes for greater social equality in times to come, they did not reason from the commercial value of their labor. The dependent artisans and journeymen, Albert Soboul noticed, "did not go so far as to establish a relation between the amount of work and the amount of the wage."[47] They asserted only that their labor made them deserving members of the community and gave them title to a share of its wealth. When they advanced their claims, "wages were not

---

44. Jean-Pierre Hirsch, "Revolutionary France, Cradle of Free Enterprise," *American Historical Review* Volume 94, Number 5 (December 1989), p. 1286.

45. The literature on the efforts of the nineteenth-century French bourgeoisie to fix prices and establish trade cartels is ample. See, illustratively, Bertrand Gille, *Recherches sur la formation de la grande entreprise capitaliste: 1815–1848* (Paris: S.E.V.P.E.N., 1959), pp. 147–162. Jean-Pierre Hirsch has emphasized the conditional and tactical use of a discourse of free enterprise among people of commerce in *Les Deux Rêves*. But he also acknowledges its power to structure practice. "Revolutionary France."

46. Sewell, op. cit., pp. 111–112.

47. Albert Soboul, "Problèmes du travail en l'an II," *Annales historiques de la révolution française* Number 144 (July–September 1956), p. 239.

in the least conceived as representative of labor."[48] Technically labor power might be acquired by contract, but it had not yet been culturally defined as a commodity.[49]

The fashioning of labor's commodity form in France during the first half of the nineteenth century relied upon the understanding of labor services that was inherited from the old regime. Feudal legacies in the countryside and corporate traditions in the towns encouraged French employers and workers to envision the employer's purchase of labor as his requisitioning of the worker's labor activity. The urban corporations of the ancien régime not only ordered French business and industry, but they formed the constituent units of society and were to serve as a model of social relations in France's early commercial society. Their charters and internal organization were similar to those for the universities and learned professions, grouping trade guilds with other associations as upholders of the arts rather than as organizations defined as providers of productive or manual labor per se.[50] "Labor" was recognized as a contributor to social welfare if it was governed by artistic and intellectual discipline.[51] Urban producers supposed that well-ordered activity, not the exchange of materialized labor, bonded society together.

Present-day historians can no longer romanticize the self-consciously corporate organization of the French urban trades by supposing that it ensured stable, communal relations in the workshops. The arduous research of Michael Sonenscher has demonstrated that artisanal manufacture in eighteenth-century France was characterized by rapid turnover in the work force and by reliance on far-flung chains of subcontractors.[52] In these flexible and dynamic networks, however, relations between out-workers and merchants were officially governed by an extensive code that

---

48. Albert Soboul, *Les Sans-culottes parisiens en l'an II* (Paris: Clavreuil, 1958), pp. 453–454. If Sewell judges correctly that the *sans-culottes* had "a clear and consistent conception of labor and its place in society," so does Soboul in saying that they nonetheless lacked a definition of labor as an economic category. Sewell, op. cit., p. 109.

49. What is characteristic about capitalism is not that the commodity labor power can be purchased—which held true even in so-called precapitalist societies such as ancient Greece—but that labor power appears in all events as a commodity. Marx, *Das Kapital*, op. cit., Volume 2, p. 119.

50. Sewell, op. cit., p. 25.

51. Ibid., pp. 22–24.

52. Sonenscher, op. cit. On the omnipresence of subcontracting long before the destruction of the guilds, see Sylvia Thrupp, "The Gilds," in *The Cambridge Economic History of Europe*, Volume III (Cambridge: Cambridge University Press, 1965), p. 280.

prescribed the legitimate exercise of the craft.[53] The British model of independent, self-determining small producers exchanging their wares had little resonance against the background of corporate organization in eighteenth-century France.[54] Instead, the rhetoric of the corporate order portrayed production as the execution of an art which was certified, controlled, and protected by the monarch. Despite their revolutionary sentiments, the *sans-culottes* carried some elements of this outlook forward. They focused on labor executed for the welfare of the community, not on the exchange of contributions produced by autonomous commodity producers. Even as the laws of the corporate order inherited from the ancien régime disappeared, the *sans-culottes* emphasized mutual devotion to the labor activity rather than the exchange among independent manufacturers of products as vessels of materialized labor.

The ancien régime's definition of feudal work relations in the countryside, where by far the greater part of the population toiled, supplemented the emphasis on the delivery of labor services that prevailed in the towns. The feudal legacy in the countryside could play an important role in defining the labor transaction because the urban crafts under the old regime did not define the transfer of labor from dependent worker to employer. In the cities, no term for *employer*, such as *patron*, had yet become current.[55] Most craft masters employed only one or two assistants—or, very often, none.[56] Agriculture offered an important model for large-scale requisitioning of laborers.

Feudal agriculture in eighteenth-century France sustained a view of the transfer of labor as the obligatory delivery of a service. To be sure, the landed elite in France, compared to privileged landowners in German territory east of the Elbe, put scant economic reliance on the receipt of obligatory dues in labor. In the last days of the old regime, dependent peasants by and large tendered no more than twelve days annually of unpaid corvée labor to their landowners.[57] Yet, as in German territory west of the Elbe, these labor serv-

---

53. Reddy, *The Rise of Market Culture*, op. cit., p. 26.

54. Sewell, op. cit., p. 139.

55. Michael Sonenscher, "Le Droit du travail en France et en Angleterre à l'époque de la révolution," in Gérard Gayot and Jean-Pierre Hirsch, editors, *La Révolution française et le développement du capitalisme* (Lille: Revue du Nord, 1989), p. 383.

56. Ibid.; also F. Furet, C. Mazauric, and L. Bergeron, "The Sans-Culottes and the French Revolution," in Jeffry Kaplow, editor, *New Perspectives on the French Revolution* (New York: John Wiley & Sons, 1965), p. 247.

57. Gerd van den Heuvel, *Grundprobleme der französischen Bauernschaft 1730–1794* (München: R. Oldenbourg Verlag, 1982), p. 61.

ices were nonetheless essential in France in defining the relation of the laboring peasantry to persons of rural property. The tribute showed that title to the land conferred a claim not only to rents but to service and to authority over the activity of subordinates.[58] This connotation became explicit in an incident narrated by the abbé Clerget: he claimed that a seigneur at the Parlement of Franche-Comté asserted the right to impose a new corvée on the peasantry in exchange for relinquishing ancient rights over vassals to receive oblations and "lead them in the hunt."[59] Not that the corvée had become purely symbolic: peasants from the village of Haute-Marche in the district of Creuse complained in 1790 that they still sacrificed at least one day weekly to discharge their labor obligations.[60] In the last years of the old regime a few seigneurs tried to reimpose labor tributes that rivaled those of prior centuries.[61] Small wonder that the peasants included the corvées among their humiliating burdens when they compiled lists of grievances on the eve of the revolution.[62]

Memory of the corvées survived well into the nineteenth century. When the reins of power passed again to the Bourbons, the peasants associated the restoration of old political principles with the return of ancient relations in economic life. They feared the resuscitation of the unpaid days of labor.[63] As

---

58. P. de Saint Jacob, *Les Paysans de la Bourgogne du Nord au dernier siècle de l'ancien régime* (Paris: Société "Les Belles Lettres," 1960), p. 115; van den Heuvel, op. cit., p. 64; Ernst Hinrichs, "Feudalität und Ablösung: Bemerkungen zur Vorgeschichte des 4. August 1789," in Eberhard Schmitt, editor, *Die Französische Revolution* (Köln: Kiepenheuer & Witsch, 1976), p. 133. The seigneurs who collected dues in services in the second half of the eighteenth century were reluctant to follow new economic arguments that urged a conversion to money rents. J. Q. C. Mackrell, *The Attack on "Feudalism" in Eighteenth-Century France* (London: Routledge & Kegan Paul, 1973), pp. 14, 146.

59. Mackrell, op. cit., p. 121.

60. Martin Göhring, *Die Feudalität in Frankreich vor und in der grossen Revolution* (Berlin: Emil Ebering, 1934), p. 20.

61. Saint Jacob, op. cit., p. 426.

62. Georges Lefebvre, *Les Paysans du Nord pendant la révolution française* (Bari: Editori Laterza, 1959), p. 137; P.-D. Bernier, *Essai sur le tiers-état rural* (Genève: Slatkine-Megariotis Reprints, 1974 [1892]), p. 137; Mackrell, op. cit., p. 4. The peasantry's resistance to landholders' corvées is described in P. M. Jones, *The Peasantry in the French Revolution* (Cambridge: Cambridge University Press, 1988), p. 52. Peasants complained of being "subject [*sic*] en qualité de prévot à aller où il plaira au dit seigneur, pourvu qu'on puisse retourner en sa maison entre deux soleils." Bernier, op. cit., p. 138. The dues in labor formed part of a larger complex of peasant obligations. A landowner often required peasants to bring their grain to a designated mill, for the use of which they paid a fee. When the peasants delivered rents in kind, such as grain or fowl, they resented not just the amount but the method of the exaction: they had to carry the animals or grain to the lord's estate. This was defined as a kind of service and criticized as an obligation of "servitude." Göhring, op. cit., pp. 112, 226; van den Heuvel, op. cit., p. 64.

63. Mackrell, op. cit., p. 189.

late as 1840 the procurator-general in Bordeaux attributed to the influence of "socialists" the widespread apprehension on the Dordogne about reimposition of the tithes and corvées.[64] The autobiography of the Parisian turner Jacques-Etienne Bédé shows that urban workers, too, used the corvée as a point of comparison. Bédé and his fellow workers on piece rates went on strike in 1819 to protest the unremunerated time they were obliged to spend waiting at the workshop. Their goal, they said, was to abolish "corvées," the supply of unpaid labor.[65]

As employers and workers developed an understanding of the capitalist employment relation in the nineteenth century, they viewed the labor transaction as the offering of a service capacity, paralleling the model of days of service delivered in agriculture. In keeping with the late abolition of feudal relations of work in their respective countries, French workers frequently used *corvée* and German workers applied *Frondienst* to characterize the capitalist employment relation.[66] The English and Italian languages, by comparison, did not retain catchwords referring to the delivery of unpaid dues in labor. Language testified to the fundamental forces at work on the route to the creation of a capitalist labor market.

The vernacular discloses how the specifications of labor as a commodity that prevailed in nineteenth-century France and Germany shared important similarities due to their legacies of feudal relations of work; yet there were also important differences between the countries, which were attributable to the annihilation of the guilds in France. The works of political economists reflect both the parallels and the contrasts in cultural outcomes.[67] Elite economists in France believed that labor was sold as a resource. For example, Jean-Baptiste Say, a former textile manager and one of the earliest economists to draw on French sources to counter some of Adam Smith's proposi-

64. Ibid., p. 190.

65. Cited in Sonenscher, *Work and Wages*, op. cit., p. 31.

66. For France, see Paul Leroy-Beaulieu, *Traité théorique et pratique d'économie politique*, Volume 2 (Paris: Guillaumin, 1900), p. 291; *Le Travailleur*, April 4, 1894, "La Liberté du Travail." For Germany, see the transcript from a textile workers' meeting, Staatsarchiv Weimar, Landratsamt Gera, Nr. 2562, November 27, 1905; Stadtarchiv Cottbus, AII 33b, Nr. 33 Oct. 6, 1896, p. 92, "*Frondienst*"; Staatsarchiv Dresden, Amthauptmannschaft Glauchau Nr. 395, transcript of meeting in Meerane, Nov. 5, 1905, pp. 101–102, regarding "dues in labor services [*Frondienste*] to be carried out for capital." *Der Textil-Arbeiter*, January 20, 1905, Chemnitz; *Beilage zur Volkswacht*, Bielefeld, Nr. 255, Oct. 31, 1907, Spinnerei "Frondienst."

67. The destruction of the ancien régime and the popularization of political economy went hand in hand, as if the science were a natural accompaniment of the new commercial order. Gilbert Faccarello, "L'Evolution de l'économie politique pendant la révolution: Alexandre Vandermonde ou la croisée des chemins," in Maxine Berg, editor, *Französische Revolution und Politische Ökonomie* (Trier: Schriften aus dem Karl-Marx-Haus, 1989), pp. 82–84.

tions, grouped the "industrial services" of workers alongside land and capital in a list of the productive capacities of a nation.[68] He added, "When I hire a laborer by the day, he does not sell me his fund of productive skills; he sells me only the services his capacity can give in the course of a day."[69] Say thereby intended to indicate that renting out any "productive fund," be it capital or labor, equaled the vending of a service.

Say's comment implied that workers were contributing a resource to the production process that had the same status as the contributions of landowners and capitalists. The French concept of labor as a commodity resembled that of the British insofar as both treated the exchange as one that occurred among market equals without necessarily referring to relations of supervision in production itself. But Say's analysis and those of the French economists who followed him differed from those of the British in making a distinction between labor sold as a service and the product of that labor.[70]

The French classical economists highlighted the entrepreneurial function of combining diverse resources to create a product that had a value greater than the sum of its parts. From this perspective, of course, the worker could sell, not a product, but only a resource to be complemented by the employer.[71] To combine the factors of production employers needed only to put tools at the disposal of the workers; they did not require control over the immediate process of production.[72] Pellegrino Rossi, who succeeded Say to the most prestigious chair of economics in France, said that people who put cloth out to tailors to be finished by the tailors' labor bought not a product but a potential. "What do they buy?" he asked in his economics course of 1836–1837. "They buy a force, a means that will produce results whatever

---

68. *Cours complet d'économie politique pratique* (Brussels: Société Belge de Librairie, 1840), p. 55. Say was the first holder of an academic chair for economics in France. Joseph Schumpeter, *History of Economic Analysis* (New York: Oxford University Press, 1954), p. 492.

69. Say, op. cit., p. 55. The workers, he said, "sell their time and their effort, without being interested in the [financial] *result.*" Jean-Baptiste Say, *Catéchisme d'économie politique* (Paris: Guillaumin, 1881), p. 106.

70. In contrast to Ricardo, the French economists who inquired into the origin of profit were able to distinguish between living labor and finished labor. "Il a fallu convenir que toutes les fois qu'il [the worker] échangerait du travail fait contre du travail à faire, le dernier [living labor] aurait une valuer supérieure au premier [materialized labor]." J. C. L. Simonde, *De la Richesse commerciale* (Genève: J. J. Paschoud, 1803), Volume 1, p. 37.

71. Berke Vardar, *Structure fondamentale du vocabulaire social et politique en France, de 1815 à 1830* (Istanbul: Imprimerie de la Faculté des Lettres de l'Université d'Istanbul, 1973), p. 64.

72. *Cours complet*, op. cit., pp. 55–56.

the risks and hazards."[73] Workers sold their potential, but its use was not necessarily under the immediate command of employers and did not form part of the understanding of how the exchange of labor was effected.[74]

Still, the French concept of labor resembled the German concept insofar as it made a contrast between labor and labor power. As in Germany, vocabulary offers a suggestive, if preliminary, indicator of the concepts in operation. In the first half of the nineteenth century, French economists used *labor power (puissance de travail)* as well as *industrial services* to refer to labor as a commodity.[75] Rossi recognized that what the worker sold was the capacity to work, but he felt uneasy about this monetization of the laborers' life process. In his course on political economy, published in 1842, he said, "To conceive of labor power while abstracting it from the means of subsistence of the laborers during the process of production is to conceive of a phantom. Whoever says labor, whoever says labor power, means simultaneously workers and the means of subsistence, the laborer and the salary."[76] In this passage Rossi attempted to shift the emphasis from the sale of living labor to the provision of necessities of life. His discomfort resulted from the perception that workers in a capitalist regime seemed to be selling themselves, an unpleasantry that British economists avoided by focusing on the sale of labor materialized in a product.

If treating the workers themselves as commodities repelled the French economists, why did they not instead take up the British view of labor as a commodity? Where authors can gain a tactical advantage from altering their concept of labor but let the opportunity pass, the constraint laid by

---

73. P. Rossi, *Oeuvres complètes* (5th ed. Paris: Guillaumin, 1884), Volume I, p. 221.

74. This specification of labor's commodity form recurred in later French economics as well. Paul Cauwès, professor of political economy, declared that prices were determined by the need to pay people for their "labor services." He believed the compensation was set neither by the amount of the materialized labor delivered nor by the exchange value of the labor power purchased. Rather, labor services transferred to the employer were rewarded according to how much people were willing to pay for the products delivered—an amount determined only after the product had entered the market. Labor power as such had no determinable value. *Précis du cours d'économie politique* (Paris: L. Larose et Forcel, 1881), Volume One, p. 185. Analogously, see M. Ganilh, *Dictionnaire analytique d'économie politique* (Paris: Imprimerie de Fain, 1826), pp. 432–433, and Théodore Fix, "De la Mesure de la Valeur," *Journal des économistes* Volume 9 (Paris: Guillaumin, 1844), p. 3.

75. Rossi, op. cit., Volume I, p. 237. In the second half of the nineteenth century, the term *force-travail* prevailed. *Le Travailleur,* Lille, February 28, 1894, p. 1.

76. Rossi, op. cit., Volume II, p. 175: "Concevoir la puissance du travail, en faisant abstraction des moyens de subsistence des travailleurs pendant l'oeuvre de la production, c'est concevoir un être de raison. Qui dit travail, qui dit puissance du travail, dit à la fois travailleurs et moyens de subsistence, ouvrier et salaire."

an underlying assumption comes to the surface. A significant example appears in Pierre-Joseph Proudhon's *System of Economic Contradictions*, published in 1846. In the middle of this work's chapter on value, Proudhon wrote as if he were caught between two goals: he wanted to insist, against the prevailing skepticism in France, that embodied labor served as a measure of value; and he wanted to take the moral high ground by refusing to treat the workers themselves as marketable wares. He did not adopt the convenient escape of imagining that the commodity of labor was sold as materialized in a product. Instead, he presented a weak alternative:

> Labor is said to *have value*, not as merchandise itself, but in view of the values supposed to be contained in it potentially. The *value of labor* is a figurative expression, an anticipation of effect from cause. It is a fiction by the same title as the *productivity of capital*. Labor produces, capital has value: and when, by a sort of ellipsis, we say "the value of labor," we make an enjambment which is not at all contrary to the rules of language, but which theorists ought to guard against mistaking for a reality.[77]

With this maneuver Proudhon sacrificed a chance to offer a coherent explanation of how labor determined prices in the contemporary marketplace. He could not compare the value of one person's labor power to another's.[78] Yet he retained the assumption that labor was sold as a potential even as he avoided setting a price tag on the workers themselves.[79]

The French concept of labor as a commodity was embodied not only in words but in legal and economic practice. How to define an employment contract was a difficult question for nineteenth-century French courts. Should home weavers who sold their products to middlemen be considered employees covered by labor law, or were they artisans in charge of an enterprise? Did it make a difference if they supplied their own materials and owned their own tools? The rulings of the French authorities emphasized the character of the market relation rather than the employer's immediate authority over the use of the labor.

77. *Système des contradictions économiques, ou philosophie de la misère* (2d ed. Paris: Garnier Frères, 1850), p. 89. Emphasis in original.

78. When Proudhon is forced to describe how people nonetheless set unequal prices on labor, he says they appraise only the products of this labor, not the labor itself. Op. cit., p. 89.

79. French socialists in the second half of the nineteenth century emphasized that the market could not assign a value to the labor "force" expended by the worker. "Collectivisme et Socialisme," *L'Égalité: Journal républicain socialiste*, July 14, 1878, p. 3.

The employment relation in France received legal clarification when the courts ruled as early as 1836 that wage earners remunerated by piece rates were employees, not entrepreneurial contractors.[80] The courts found that the criterion for identifying an employee was the worker's "state of dependence and subordination," not the mode of payment.[81] Was the laborer who worked at home in such a "state of dependence"? The response that crystallized in France in the nineteenth century was distinctive. French officials defined domestic artisans as employees if they sold their products to one buyer at a time rather than offering them to the general public.[82] Home workers who sold products to a single buyer had the legal status of employees because they entered into an ongoing relation in which they cooperated to deliver labor on a regular basis, rather than formulating a separate contract for each piece of work.[83] When German officials in the nineteenth century were asked to decide the question, they did not see domestic artisans who sold products to a single buyer as dependent employees under the general business code, because they emphasized that these workers labored without supervision, off the premises.[84] True, the Prussian

80. Alexis Martini, *La Notion du contrat de travail* (Paris: Editions des "Juris-Classeurs," 1912), p. 17. Apart from cataloging employment as a freely incurred contract, the Civil Code of 1804 was virtually silent on labor transactions. Jacques Le Goff, *Du Silence à la parole: Droit du travail, société, état 1830–1989* (3d ed. Quimper: Calligrammes, 1989), p. 109.

81. Martini, op. cit., p. 71.

82. Ibid., p. 183. Correlatively, in the revolution of 1848 the bourgeois press defined a *worker* as a person who works "in the account of another." *L'Union sociale*, 1849, p. 94.

83. Charles Goldenberg, *De la Nature juridique des contrats de travail* (Paris: V. Giard & E. Brière, 1908), pp. 39, 53.

84. Philipp Lotmar, *Der Arbeitsvertrag nach dem Privatrecht des Deutschen Reiches* (Leipzig: Duncker & Humblot, 1902, 1908), Volume I, p. 311, and Volume II, p. 476; Otto von Zwiedineck-Südenhorst, *Beiträge zur Lehre von den Lohnformen* (Tübingen: H. Laupp, 1904), pp. 19–20. To be sure, the general German business ordinance offered home workers protection against such abuses as excessive fining. But it excluded them from other safeguards offered to those classified as dependent business employees. The Imperial Statistical Office excluded home workers from some surveys of employees even if they labored for a single contractor. A true "worker," by contrast, was "subject to the control and discipline of the entrepreneur," creating a "personal and economic relation of subordination." Germany, Kaiserliches Statistisches Amt, *Streiks und Aussperrungen im Jahre 1900* (Berlin: Puttkamer & Mülhbrecht, 1901), p. 5*. Lotmar shows that German commentators, in contrast to the French, considered it less relevant whether the home worker had an "ongoing relation" with the employer. Lotmar, op. cit., Volume II, p. 480. The Business Ordinance specified that home workers were "independent trades people," since they maintained their "personal (not economic) independence." Germany, *Die Gewerbe-Ordnung* (Berlin: Carl Heymanns Verlag, 1910), pp. 36–37. For practical rulings, Arbeiter-Sekretriat, Luckenwalde, *2. Geschäftsbericht für die Zeit vom 1. Januar bis zum 31. Dezember 1905* (Luckenwalde: Selbstverlag, 1906), pp. 8–9; *Fach-Zeitung: Organ des Niederrheinischen Weber-Verbandes*, July 16, 1899. In the 1840s, dependent home workers were said to have "no real master" (*keinen eigentlichen Herrn*). Gustav

ministry of trade allowed home textile workers as early as 1856 to enroll as
"factory workers" in the municipal funds for insurance against sickness that
were administered for mill employees. Despite this administrative ruling to
provide social welfare, however, officials noted that home workers, including
those who worked for a single contractor without tools or materials of their
own, did not stand in a "dependent relation of employment" since they
labored "outside the workshop."[85]

In France, by contrast, whether the laborer worked at home rather than
under the employer's eye made no difference "from the moment that a
certain continuity in the relationship between the parties exists."[86] What
defined the exchange of labor in business employment was not the employer's immediate exploitation of the use value of the labor, as in Germany,
but the dedication, via the market, of the worker's labor potential to a single
person. The definition of business employment in France focused on the
offering of a potential but imagined that the employer consumed this potential through market exchanges rather than through immediate relations
of domination, as in Germany.

This difference between the commodity form of labor in France and that
in Germany derived in large measure from the isolation of German artisanal work from the development of commercial liberalism. As we have
seen, even after the revolution of 1848 many German guilds continued their
efforts to reacquire trade monopolies, and they blocked the intrusion of
liberal commercial thought into the urban artisanal economy.[87] By the wiles
of historical process, the very survival of the guilds in Germany placed their

---

Dörstling, *Die Arbeitgeber und die Löhne der Arbeiter* (Chemnitz: J. C. F. Pickenhahn & Sohn,
1847), p. 9.

85. Zentrales Staatsarchiv Merseburg, Rep. 120 BB VII 3 7, May 1, 1856, pp. 25–26. The
Chamber of Commerce in Krefeld reasoned that home workers must be viewed as independent
producers for a second reason: some of them were responsible for apprentices and journeymen
under their supervision. From the chamber's point of view, this position of authority made it
all the more difficult to classify the chief workers as wage laborers. The chamber's rumination
illustrates yet again the emphasis that economic agents in Germany placed on face-to-face
authority relations for the definition of ordinary wage labor. *Jahresbericht der Industrie- und
Handelskammer zu Krefeld*, 1872, p. 27, cited in Kenneth N. Allen, "The Krefeld Silk Weavers
in the Nineteenth Century," Ph.D. diss., Stanford University, 1988, p. 74.

86. Pierre Gerlier, *Des Stipulations usuraires dans le contrat du travail* (Paris: V. Giard
et E. Brière, 1907), p. 24; Le Goff, op. cit., p. 77.

87. Engels captured the fundamental distinctions among the developmental routes trav-
ersed by Germany, Britain, and France (see Figure 10, above). The feudal powers of the landed
elites and of the guild masters, he said, were broken "in England gradually, with one blow in
France, and in Germany it is not yet finished." "Ludwig Feuerbach und der Ausgang der
klassischen deutschen Philosophie" (1888) in Karl Marx and Friedrich Engels, *Marx-Engels
Werke*, Volume 21 (Berlin: Dietz Verlag, 1962), p. 300.

ideas at the periphery of the cultural development of capitalism.[88] In France, by contrast, the annihilation of the guilds meant that some of their collective premises were passed on in new guises, for the urban specialty trades were centrally involved in the development of liberal commercialism and helped shape its course.

Unlike some of their German contemporaries, the small producers in early nineteenth-century France rarely supposed that a refurbished guild system could be reinstated.[89] The corporate idiom inherited from the old regime nonetheless contributed to workers' early visions of an economy founded on association rather than proprietary individualism.[90] As might be expected on the basis of their corporate legacy, French workers in the first half of the nineteenth century sometimes viewed labor as a collective resource rather than as something alienated at a calculable loss or profit to the individual. The journal *La Fraternité* gave expression to this outlook in 1846. "Labor," it philosophized, "is a social act that gives value to the thing processed." This extrapolation from the cooperation of people of diverse talents for the manufacture of a single product bore implications for the claims to compensation that could be pressed by the laborers: "The true claim issuing from labor is the collective force. . . . None of the [individual] men employed on this piece of work can claim proprietorship of this piece, considering that it was made only by uniting his effort with those of others and that it issues only from the union and combination of heads and arms."[91] This emphasis on labor as a collective power could

---

88. "In Germany, one might say, 'archaic' elements of the economy survived longest and strongest in domains that were bypassed by the main process of industrialization." John Breuilly, "Arbeiteraristokratie in Grossbritannien und Deutschland: Ein Vergleich," in Ulrich Engelhardt, editor, *Handwerker in der Industrialisierung* (Stuttgart: Klett-Cotta, 1984), p. 513.

89. German small masters supposed in 1848 that a modified guild system was still viable. Toni Offermann, "Mittelständisch-kleingewerbliche Leitbilder in der liberalen Handwerker- und handwerklichen Arbeiterbewegung der 50er und 60er Jahre des 19. Jahrhunderts," in Ulrich Engelhardt, editor, *Handwerker in der Industrialisierung* (Stuttgart: Klett-Cotta, 1984), p. 529.

90. Sewell, op. cit. The journal *Echo de la fabrique*, edited principally for textile workers in Lyon, counted "love of work, of order" as a requirement for joining a workers' trade association, as did the ancient guilds. November 10, 1833, p. 2.

91. *La Fraternité*, July, 1846, p. 180. See also *Les Droits de l'homme* Number 1 (January 1849), "De l'Association"; *La Fraternité universelle* December 1, 1848, "Organisation du travail." Similarly, *L'Echo de la fabrique* discussed labor as a "social action." March 23, 1834, p. 1. The French emphasis on collaborative social production contrasts with the commercial dream of the early British labor movement, which envisioned "a community of independent small producers exchanging their products without the distortions of masters and middlemen." E. P. Thompson, *The Making of the English Working Class* (New York: Vintage Books, 1963), p. 295.

counter the conclusions offered by those who treated labor as a commodity like any other.[92] Yet the collective assumptions were retained when workers went on to describe, as they had to, the reality of their employment as individuals. They maintained that if the social resource of labor was alienated in practice by the individual, no natural price could be attached to it.[93]

The commodity form of labor in France supported the development of industrial practices that differed from those of both Germany and Britain. To be sure, French textile factory organization in the early nineteenth century superficially resembled that of Britain in several respects. For example, some French employers who made the transition from hand-powered spinning equipment to steam-driven machinery imposed weekly steam fees upon the workers in charge of the new, more productive equipment.[94] The weekly fee held workers responsible for covering the greater capital and operating costs of the powered machines in return for enjoying swifter output and correlatively greater returns from piece rates. This practice lent support to the notion that workers—sometimes called *entrepreneurs d'ouvrage* by the employers—were autonomous renters of the machines, who organized use of the apparatus and delivered finished products to the factory owner.[95] If the French workers were seen as deliverers of products, however, this superficial similarity enables us to ask more precisely what it means to say that labor has taken on a "commodity form."

To place the new form of labor in definitive perspective, let us not forget that even in ancient Mediterranean society, free laborers received payment

92. In France, bourgeois economists emphasized the contribution of "collective labor" to the accumulation of surplus, but they rarely pointed to the empirical fact of cooperation and interdependence in production as grounds for declining to assign values to individual work. See, illustratively, Ganilh, op. cit., p. 410.

93. *La Fraternité*, July, 1846, p. 180.

94. William Reddy, "Modes de paiement et controle du travail dans les filatures de coton en France, 1750–1848," *Revue du Nord* Volume LXIII, Number 248 (January–March 1981), p. 142.

95. Réglement de la filature, Roubaix, Bibliothèque nationale Gr. Fol. Wz 69 (1851). Some French employers gave workers options for how they would divide looms among weavers and assistants, provided, of course, that this did not raise the cost of production. For an example of a firm that constructed various payment plans from which workers could choose, based on how workers decided to divide the looms between weavers and assistants, see Archives départementales du Nord (henceforth cited as ADN) M625/86, February 4, 1908, Estaires. French mill proprietors let responsibility for hiring mule and loom assistants devolve upon each spinner and weaver. For parallel examples from metal-working, see Heinz-Gerhard Haupt, "Frankreich: Langsame Industrialisierung und republikanische Tradition," in Jürgen Kocka, editor, *Europäische Arbeiterbewegungen im 19. Jahrhundert* (Göttingen: Vandenhoeck & Ruprecht, 1983), p. 60.

for their products from regular buyers. But they did not thereby imagine that they were conveying abstract labor time.[96] Likewise, the rich evidence of William Reddy suggests that French textile workers at the start of the nineteenth century believed that they transferred items pure and simple, not that their products were the vessels for abstract labor. (As Reddy hints, the very term *product* may be ill-chosen for this period, since the word designates an article as the "produce" of labor rather than as a mere object suitable for exchange.)[97] This represents a major difference from Britain, where textile workers who saw themselves in part as renters of machinery rather than as employees per se also viewed the products they furnished as signs for abstract labor. French textile workers of the 1830s seem not to have referred to their earnings as wages or to have described themselves as deliverers of "labor." The employers at a spinning mill near Colmar showed that as late as 1842 they could take nothing for granted. They had to remind spinners that workers could not make products of their own choosing in the mill, reiterating in their factory ordinance that the decision as to what type of yarn to spin belonged to the employer.[98] Until labor practices in France embodied labor's commodity form, French factory workers presumed that they should receive the same piece rate for yarn whether it came from an old, short spinning mule or a newer, longer, and more productive one. They overlooked the difference in embodied labor times.[99] After all, from the standpoint of a trader, the goods from the old machine did not differ from the product of the new. The commodity form of labor in France was embodied in factory practice only when workers were conceived of as the sellers of labor services.[100]

With the benefit of a cross-national outlook we can ascertain the unique cultural mode by which labor power was sold in France. As in Britain and Germany, so in France the construction of the piece-rate scales for weavers exemplifies the specification of labor as a commodity. In France, as in Germany and parts of Britain, the mechanization of weaving was undertaken in

96. Arjun Appadurai, "Introduction: Commodities and the Politics of Value," in Arjun Appadurai, *The Social Life of Things: Commodities in Cultural Perspective* (Cambridge: Cambridge University Press, 1986), pp. 8–9.

97. This is the import of Reddy's "The Structure of a Cultural Crisis," op. cit.

98. Règlement de police de la filature de Hausmann, Jordan, Hirn et Cie., August 17, 1842, Bibliothèque nationale, Gr. Fol. Wz 69 (1842).

99. Reddy, *The Rise of Market Culture*, op. cit., p. 211.

100. The textile workers' press referred to the labor transaction as a "contract for the rental of a service." *L'Ouvrier textile*, March 1, 1907, p. 1.

earnest only in the mid-nineteenth century.[101] In the north, which became by far the most important center for mechanized textile production, the weavers in the earliest factories were paid flat day wages.[102] By 1870, however, piece-rate scales applicable to several towns had emerged.[103] Early examples of district piece-rate scales for handweavers set workers' remuneration for a fixed length of cloth. But the schedules, unlike those in Britain during the same period, fail to reveal a linear relation between the increases in the density of the fabric and increases in remuneration.[104]

With the completion of mechanization in weaving during the second half of the nineteenth century, the French made equal use of scales that paid workers per thousand shots inserted in the cloth and of scales that remunerated workers for a fixed length of cloth.[105] But when they used pay per shot, too, they failed to find a linear relation between the density produced and payment for movement of the shuttle, as did German producers.[106] Through the pre–World War One period, the great majority of French lists display irregular rather than linear increases in pay as the density of the fabric increases.[107] Figure 11 plots onto a graph a schedule for merinos from the north of France. The slopes of the French scales, which indicate the rate at which remuneration rises as the density of the cloth increases, change erratically in woolens as in cottons, in moistened linen as in dry.

---

101. Léon de Seilhac, *La Grève du tissage de Lille* (Paris: Arthur Rousseau, 1910), p. 25.

102. Maurice Petitcollot, *Les Syndicats ouvriers de l'industrie textile dans l'arrondissement de Lille* (Lille: Coopérative "La Gutenberg," 1907), p. 299.

103. Petitcollot, op. cit., p. 300.

104. Archives municipales de Roubaix, FII ga(3), 1837; Paul Delsalle, "Tisserands et fabricants devant les Prud'Hommes," diss., University of Lille, 1984, p. 213; ADN M625/55 Seydoux, Sieber & Co., Bousies, 1886; ADN M625/66, Cambrai, 1900; ADN M619/19, Cambrai, 1900; *Le Grand Écho du Nord*, July 10, 1903; *Le Réveil du Nord*, July 11, 1903; ADN M619/32 *Tarif général des façons de la Gorgue-Estaires*, M625/55 pièce 84, 1885–1886. For an exception that displays linear relations on a list covering only three densities, see ADN M625/74, June 6, 1903, Estaires. One segment of the *Tarif général des façons d'Armentières*, for cotton warps, is linear. See ADN M619/32. For an early example of irregular tables from Lyon, see *L'Écho de la fabrique*, July 7, 1833, p. 221.

105. Pay per thousand shots: ADN M625/48 Cambrai, December, 1878; ADN M625/51 St.-Rouplet, July 1, 1882; *Industrie Textile*, September 15, 1903, p. 327, Saint-Quentin; *L'Ouvrier textile*, November 1, 1907, Caudry; ADN M625/66, Bousies.

106. For an early example of nonlinear scales, see *L'Écho de la fabrique*, June 23, 1833, p. 204. For pay per thousand shots, ADN M625/55, pièce 84, 1886; ADN M625/66 Boisies, 1893; ADN M625/56, 1887, Roubaix.

107. The aberrancies appear whether the scales cover a single width or multiple widths of cloth. See ADN M625/55, 1886, Cateau.

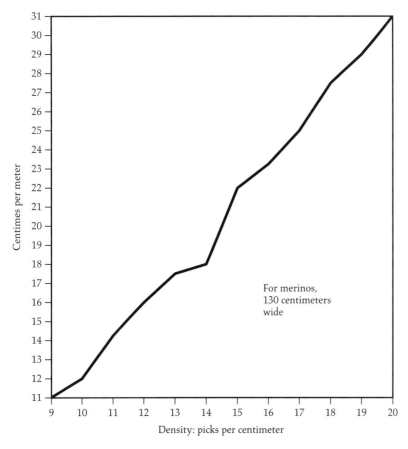

Figure 11.   Tarif of Seydoux, Sieber & Cie., Bousies, 1886
Source: ADN M 625/55

French piece-rate scales based on length of cloth delivered lacked the
linear increases of the British scales because French producers did not view
the product as the vessel of abstract labor incorporated in the material. Of
course, by the second half of the nineteenth century, the fabric delivered
may have represented "labor" effort in the eyes of the French producers. But
that labor was not conceived of as a social substance, materialized in the
product in standard fashion, capable of providing a detectable metric for the
value of the good. Without the notion of an underlying substance corresponding to the physical dimensions of the cloth, the different sectors of the
piece-rate scales were not unified in a linear system. Nor were those French

piece-rate scales that were founded on the unit of one thousand shots unified by linear relations between density and pay, as in Germany.[108] For the
French view of labor as a commodity did not include the employers' appropriation of labor's use value, the supervised use of a concrete activity, which
allows one to valorize each motion delivered to the employer. Instead, piece-
rates for varying densities of cloth in France followed the vagaries of pricing
for each traditional fabric "type" in well-established markets, the nonlinear
tensile strengths of the manipulated yarn, and the readiness of heads of
households to exploit the labor of family members as assistants in producing certain ranges of better-remunerated cloth densities.[109] If the French

108. The Germans thought in terms of linear increases in pay per shot, not just for the
density of the weave but for the breadth of the loom, another dimension French scales did not
incorporate in linear fashion. Staatsarchiv Weimar, Landesregierung Greiz, n Rep. A, Kap. IXa,
Nr. 165, p. 139, "Wechselstuhlarbeit," 1905.

109. William M. Reddy, "Entschlüsseln von Lohnforderungen: Der *Tarif* und der Lebenszyklus in den Leinenfabriken von Armentières, 1889–1904," in Robert Berdahl et al., editors,
Klassen und Kultur (Frankfurt am Main: Syndikat, 1982). Although the customs for entering
French textile factories are not easy to document, evidence suggests that the French often
combined the practices of the Germans and the British. As in Germany, latecomers paid a fine
before they set their labor in motion, in keeping with the principle that the commodity of labor
represented a potential. Georges Duveau, *La Vie ouvrière sous le second empire* (Paris: Librairie Gallimard, 1946), p. 260. As in Britain, the doorway became a symbolic point of contact
between workers and owners and entry into the factory a ritual of submission. French employers used the shutting of the door to mark their authority but opened the door periodically for
latecomers who paid the fine. The French understanding of labor as a commodity, like the
British view, did not highlight the employer's systematic exploitation of the use value of the
labor. Employers accentuated their control at the border zone, the entrance gate. Michelle
Perrot, "The Three Ages of Industrial Discipline in Nineteenth-Century France," in John M.
Merriman, editor, *Consciousness and Class Experience in Nineteenth-Century Europe* (New
York: Holmes & Meier, 1979), p. 157. See Bibliothèque nationale, Gr. Fol. Wz 69, "Règlement
de la fabrique de Blanzat" (Clermont: Typographie Hubler, Bayle et Dubois, ca. 1853); "Règlement de la filature" (Wazemmes: Impr. de Horemans, ca 1854); "Règlement pour la manufacture de Duval, Heurthauz et Cie" (Nantes: Impr. Forest, ca 1857); "Règlement du tissage
mécanique de M. César Piat fils" (Roubaix: Impr. Béghin, 1866); "Règlement du tissage
mécanique S. Willot et Cie" (Roubaix: Impr. Cocheteux, 1880). The concern with control of
the perimeter emerges in another fashion through the printed factory injunctions of French
textile employers: the rules had separate, sometimes extensive sections defining the responsibilities of the gatekeepers. See, illustratively, Bibliothèque nationale, Gr. Fol. Wz 69, Règlement des usines de Auguste Sourd à Tenay (Lyon: Impr. Chanoine, 1851); Règlement pour la
police intérieure des ateliers de filature de M. Ch. Leyberr à Bootz (Laval: Impr. Godbert, 1855);
Tissage mécanique de M. Constant-Delanoë à Barentin (Rouen: Impr. Surville, 1859). In
contrast to Germany, the procedures for entering the factory became a prominent issue for
strikes in France. *Le Grand Écho du Nord,* July 10, 1903. French workers contested the amount
of the fine and the exact time at which the door closed on latecomers. Their strike leaflets
discussed these issues in bold print. ADN M625/64, Armentières, factories of Dulac and Vil-
lard. Whereas in the piece-rate scales the French have neither the British nor the German idea
of linearity, in the control of time and space they combine both techniques of control: employers make the doorway a symbolic divide, and they impose metric fines for loss of time, as if

producers had managed perfectly well without resorting to linear grada-
tions, the design of their scales might seem insignificant, attributable to
simple lack of challenges requiring greater regularity.[110] But in fact linearity
was not invoked as a natural principle even when it could have helped
employers and workers in their efforts to agree upon schedules.[111]

The piece-rate scales held only a nominal status in the eyes of nineteenth-
century French textile employers and their workers. Weavers and spinners
saw them as an initial element in determining their remuneration, not as a
critical measure of labor delivered and an essential yardstick for payment.
Handweavers in the first half of the nineteenth century attempted to rene-
gotiate the piece rate when they turned in the completed fabric, based on
unforeseen difficulties encountered in the weaving process.[112] Even in the
mature factory system it was not unheard-of for weavers to receive a fixed
time wage provided they met a production minimum.[113] In some instances
workers and employers saw the piece-rate scales as temporary conventions,
to be adjusted as necessary to yield a target daily wage.[114] When strikers
demanded higher earnings, on occasion they presented employers with alternatives: either the owners could dispense with fines on damaged fabric,
or they could revise the piece-rate scales upward.[115] This open-ended request
shows that workers looked at the scales as perfunctory contrivances influencing their earnings, not as definitive mechanisms designed to gauge the
appropriation of a real substance, labor.

Workers' appreciation of labor as a commodity in France guided the
formulation of strike demands. In contrast to their counterparts in Germany and Britain, French weavers on strike for higher piece rates focused
their demands on particular densities of cloth, not on the overall construc-

---

they have purchased a labor capacity but do not take for granted their disposition over the labor
activity, as in Germany. When French employers adopted precisely delimited workdays, they
defined the hours of employment by effective work time, as in Germany, rather than by mere
presence within the factory perimeter, as in Britain. Mary Lynn Stewart, *Women, Work, and
the French State* (Kingston: McGill-Queen's University Press, 1989), p. 109.

110. Until about the middle of the nineteenth century, some employers' weaving schedules were imperfectly linear even in Britain. See, illustratively, Kershaw Lees & Co., *Weaving
Prices Paid* (Stockport, 1854).

111. *Le Réveil du Nord*, "Les Grèves de la Gorgue-Estaires," July 11, 1903.

112. Delsalle, op. cit., p. 213.

113. ADN M625/86, February 4, 1908, Estaires.

114. For spinning, see ADN M625/96 May, 1893, Roubaix. For weaving, the employers in
Lille in 1909 declared that "the schedule is nothing, the wage everything." Seilhac, op. cit.,
p. 57. For examples of strikes hinging on whether the scales provide the agreed-upon daily
average, see ADN M625/87, Fiche 1, 1907, Roubaix; ADN M625/86, 1908, Estaires.

115. ADN M625/56, 1887, pièce 27.

tion of the schedules. Even when they lodged complaints about particular densities of many different types of cloth, they concentrated on isolated positions in the overall table.[116] In a strike at Avesnes in 1886, weavers asked for minute adjustments in ten different kinds of cloth rather than calling for an across-the-board revision.[117]

The French specification of labor as a commodity may have influenced not only the conduct of strikes on the ground but the economic theory propounded in the intellectual circles attached to the workers' movement. The chief economists who wrote for the French Workers' Party, a Marxist group supported by Engels, consistently misread Marx's economic theory. For example, Paul Lafargue, the country's most influential expert in Marxist analysis,[118] penned a defense of Marx's theory of surplus value in 1884. Lafargue assumed that production for exchange, including that of domestic workers, gave birth to capital and exploited labor. In his eyes, anyone producing goods for profit in a market (and not only a middleman) became a capitalist. Engels rebuked Lafargue for failing to realize that capitalism was distinguished by the social relations of production, in which ownership of the means of production allowed a proprietor to purchase and supervise another person's labor power. Yet Lafargue's analysis reflected perfectly well the French understanding of labor as a commodity, in which the immediate relations of domination were absent from the concept of purchasing another person's labor activity.[119] Marx's analysis of the extraction of surplus under capitalism resonated with the presumption

116. ADN M625/55, June 17, 1886; ADN M625/66, Bousies; ADN M625/75, June 9, 1903, Tourcoing.

117. ADN M625/55, Avesnes, 17 June 1886. Analogously, see ADN M625/51, March 27, 1882.

118. Claude Willard, *Les Guesdistes* (Paris: Editions Sociales, 1965), p. 146.

119. Friedrich Engels, Paul Lafargue, and Laura Lafargue, *Correspondance* (Paris: Editions sociales, 1956), letter of Friedrich Engels to Paul Lafargue, August 11, 1884, pp. 232–233. For parallel analyses of capitalism, see, illustratively, "Deux Conférences," in *Le Socialiste*, November 10, 1887, p. 2.

Further research is needed to explain why throughout the nineteenth century French workers put so much more emphasis than their counterparts in Britain and Germany on abolishing the subcontracting of labor. In March, 1848, the provisional government abolished "the right of subcontractors to organize labor" as "unjust, vexatious, and contrary to the ideals of fraternity." After the fall of the Second Republic and continuing into the twentieth century, workers demanded that middlemen be prohibited from selling the products of domestic workers to merchants. Perhaps the French drive against *marchandage* grew out of the emphasis on workers being able to conduct themselves as entrepreneurs to get an equitable price for their labor. Bernard Mottez, *Systèmes de salaire et politiques patronales* (Paris: Centre de la Recherche Scientifique, 1966), pp. 21–22, 59–60; P. Hubert-Valleroux, *Le Contrat de travail* (Paris: Rousseau, 1895), p. 62; *Industrie textile*, April 15, 1903, pp. 155–157.

in France that employers purchased a labor activity, but the French assumed that the exploitation of this activity was effected in the market.

THE HIERARCHY
OF MOTIVATING CONDITIONS

This suggestive application of theory to the commercial development of France and, more briefly, to that of northern Italy advances a general model of the development of labor's commodity form while it confirms the individuality of each national case. In France and Italy, as in Germany and Britain, the breakthrough to liberal commercialism was critical for establishing a concept of labor which became an enduring part of national culture. Britain's passage was effected in the second half of the seventeenth century, although its legacy was applied to the free sale of what an outside observer is able to term "labor power" only in the mid-eighteenth century.[120] In France the revolution inaugurated a liberal commercial order that definitively cast labor as a commodity during the bourgeois regime of Louis Philippe.[121] In northern Italy the progression began in the last quarter of the eighteenth century and thereafter followed the rhythm set by France. In Germany the movement extended from approximately 1810 to industrial take-off in the 1850s. During these formative periods, economic agents conceived of and implemented the specifications of the sale of labor that eventually gave shape to the instrumentalities of production in the factory.

These divergent specifications of labor as a commodity developed not from elemental but from conjunctural differences: the four countries in our purview had parallel feudal starting points but contrasting disjunctures and overlaps between major institutional changes in their transition to capitalism. In particular, each country offers its own chronology of change in the demolition of guild constraints on the use of labor, of feudal labor dues, and of local trading privileges in finished articles. The timetable established by the dating of each of these changes in relation to the others in a given country represents the decisive context for the emergence of cultural differences. As delineated in Figure 10, there is a hierarchy in the causal influence of these temporal contrasts. For example, what would have happened in Britain if feudal labor dues had persisted in the countryside after an unfet-

---

120. Here the term *labor power* is obviously a purely analytic concept, not a category of social conciousness.

121. Georges Matoré, *Le Vocabulaire et la société sous Louis-Philippe* (Genève: Slatkine Reprints, 1967), p. 29.

tered national market in finished wares had been introduced? The timing of the dismantling of feudal labor dues in agriculture is irrelevant for the British case. The prior triumph of a commercial discourse centered on products alone ensured that whenever constraints on the unfettered purchase of labor power (which might include feudal dues in labor or guild regulation of laborers) were abolished, the exchange of labor in the resulting market would be assimilated to the established model for the vending of finished articles. The traditional restrictions on the sale of labor power proved irrelevant as a positive model for the shape eventually taken by labor as a commodity in Britain. Their contribution was purely negative, that of allowing a market discourse to identify labor as a substance residing in products. We can infer, therefore, that for Britain the precise form of constraint on the vending of labor power, whether by feudal dues in agriculture, by statutory controls on wages, or by other means, was of no consequence for the final shape of labor as a commodity. When viewed in the European context the disjoint recognition of the free exchange of articles and of labor power is sufficient to explain the British outcome.[122]

A concentration on the development of labor's specification as a commodity in Britain and in Germany offers more than a series of rich historical contrasts. A focus on these primary cases offers a theoretic key, because they represent two extremes among the routes of development: the case with the fewest motivating circumstances versus the case with the most complicated and extreme combination of conditions. Once these cases are laid out, we can see that circumstances in France and northern Italy fill in the alternative permutations between the poles of Britain and Germany. The French-German contrast reveals the difference between conceiving of the labor transaction as the receipt of labor activity through the market and thinking of labor as a service over which the employer exercises immediate command. In France, the annihilation of the guilds meant that the urban trades, with their extensive networks of unsupervised subcontractors and home workers, were included as a setting for economic agents to conceive of the sale of labor to employers. Therefore the emphasis on the employer's direct supervision of the worker, which encouraged a distinction between the use and the exchange

---

122. In the preceding chapter I compared the timing of the dissolution of the guilds with respect to industrialization in Germany and in Britain. The British case illuminated the conservation of precapitalist mentalities in the German guilds. This discussion advanced a theoretic argument about the causes of the specification of labor as a commodity in Germany but used Britain only for empirical material that contrasted with Germany, not to assess the forces leading to the cultural outcome in Britain.

values of labor and on the employer's exploitation of the use value of the labor, was relatively weak. The Italian-British opposition discloses the difference between conceiving of labor as valorized in a product and thinking of labor as a medium for equating the difficulty of procuring products. Yet the outcomes in Italy and Britain share a generic similarity, because feudal dues in agriculture were absent in Italy and irrelevant in Britain.

The investigation of economic thought in Italy suggests that in the European context the disjoint establishment of formally free markets in products and in labor power represents a sufficient but not a necessary cause for the development of the view that labor is acquired only as it is materialized in an article. In Italy the conjoint recognition of markets in products and in labor power meant that the understanding of labor as a commodity was not assimilated to an antecedent market discourse focused upon intercourse in finished articles alone. But the absence of a feudal template for the receipt of labor as a service ensured that the Italians would nonetheless adopt the view that labor is purchased only as it is materialized in a product. Whether the Italians maintained a residual guild system that controlled the labor market for urban craft workers and blocked the operation of capitalist categories was inconsequential for the eventual cultural outcome. Without the feudal constitution of society as the delivery of services, Italians lacked a prerequisite for thinking of the purchase of labor as the appropriation of a labor service. The circulation of products among urban craft specialists located in dense networks of trade does not in itself highlight the appropriation of labor power. The Italian case indicates, however, that the staggered recognition of markets in products versus labor power is necessary for assuming, as the British economic agents did, that labor becomes a calibrated, monetized substance once it is embodied in a ware. For the simultaneous appearance of formally free markets in products and in labor power submits the labor activity and the acquisition of wares to a commercial calculus at the same time, as is illustrated in Italian economic theory. Because the two appear for consideration together, it does not happen, as it does in classical British commercial discourse, that the material articles alone are subjected to such a calculus.

This chapter brings a chain of thought full circle. Part One of the study set out in pursuit of the systematic logic that culture contributed to the organization of capitalist practices in the workplace. Part Two examined the broader commercial framework on which the fabrication of that culture depended. Does this work as a whole thereby follow the bipartite explanatory method that Weber presented in *The Protestant Ethic*, emphasizing culture's causal independence once it was ushered into the world, but its dependence upon the

economy for its birth? Do studies of culture's effect and of its historical genesis represent separate, fragmentable inquiries? The response to this question
closes Part Two.

CONCLUDING REFLECTIONS
ON PART TWO

Of late it has become fashionable among historical investigators to assert
that the social explanation of economic ideologies is inappropriately reductionist because it necessarily treats intellectual ideas as a reflection of underlying social conditions. The new cultural history has emphasized instead
that changes in the social environment make themselves felt—indeed, come
into being—only through the medium of language, which operates with the
power and within the constraints of its own logic and own history.[123] Michael Agnatieff formulated this issue for the history of economics some
time ago by contesting the assumption that agents spontaneously adopt the
language of economics by participating in capitalist development. "Our reflexive, unthinking tendency to assume that the past speaks the same language as our own," he reminded us, "has led us, quite wrongly, to assume
that as 'commercial society' takes shape, in their daily experience and in
their reading, a language of 'markets', 'classes', and 'social relations' is there
at hand to guide them cognitively."[124] Agnatieff and others have suggested
that we examine the development of the categories of capitalist thought as
an autonomous process, guided as much by the discursive resources and
constraints of language as by the imputed economic facts of life. By this line
of reasoning, when the economic surroundings change the process of "generating language adequate to one's conception of social reality" poses a
challenge whose accomplishment is unpredictable.[125]

In raising culture to the status of an independent object of study, however, this variety of cultural history may inadvertently divide language
from the economy. It assumes that the categories of economic analysis belong to the realm of the discursive, outside of which lies "commercial society" proper, whose transactions language tries to grasp. The present study,
by contrast, emphasizes above all that commercial practice was itself struc-

123. For illustrations, consult Joan Wallach Scott, *Gender and the Politics of History* (New
York: Columbia University Press, 1988), pp. 56–57; Keith Tribe, "The 'Histories' of Economic
Discourse," in his *Genealogies of Capitalism* (London: Macmillan & Co., 1981), pp. 124 ff.

124. Michael Agnatieff, "Marxism and Classical Political Economy," in Raphael Samuel,
editor, *People's History and Socialist Theory* (London: Routledge & Kegan Paul, 1981), p. 352.

125. Ibid., p. 351.

tured by categories that communicated the form of the labor transaction. Language did not establish discursive rules for conduct which agents then attempted to follow as a norm: such a viewpoint makes the symbolic order external to practice, insofar as each of the customs of the factory derives its meaning by conforming to "ideal" rules articulated by intellectuals, literate workers, or managers. Instead, practice itself embodied symbolic principles, and the constellation of material instrumentalities on the shop floor served as the elements that conveyed messages independently of verbal analyses. The capitalist economy is a realm of symbolic practice that already contains a language of political economy appropriate for the analysis of social life. The concepts of labor as a commodity did not "reflect" or "express" economic conditions in the two countries—they were part and parcel of those conditions. The political economists' reflections on labor as a commodity, which were debated and discussed outside the shop floor, developed in tandem with the emergence of labor's commodity form as the principle that organized the humblest details of everyday life. In the lived experience of their individual transfers of labor, workers and marketeers sustained the principle of the exchange of abstract labor which, behind their backs, united their society into a functioning whole.

Part 3

THE STRUCTURE OF THE
WORKERS' COUNTERSIGNS

8   The Monetization of Time

Labor is only another name for a human activity which goes
with life itself, which in its turn is not produced for sale. . . .
The commodity description of labor . . . is entirely fictitious.
                    Karl Polanyi, *The Great Transformation*

The rites of practice in which the commodity form was brought to life not
only structured agents' everyday relations to each other, but these conventions also defined the forms of understanding by which people would criticize and attempt to transform their social relations. As for the construction
of practices by which employers and workers effected the transmission of
"labor," so for struggles to modify that transfer the commodity form established the symbolic coordinates of the most fundamental dimensions of
experience at the site of production—those of time and space themselves.
Let us consider in this chapter a single field of effects, those resulting from
the contrasting means of demarcating, exchanging, and consuming time in
Germany and Britain.[1]

Inspired by E. P. Thompson's classic essay on "Time, Work-Discipline,
and Industrial Capitalism," historians have accumulated an imposing body
of evidence about the development of time consciousness in early industrial
societies.[2] Their inquiries have focused on the historical processes by which
individuals came to value the methodical expenditure of time and by which
collective undertakings, including the daily labor activity, came to follow the
rigid and precise cycles of the mechanical clock.[3] For the comparative in-

---

1. In Chapter Ten, the end of Part Three of this work, we will examine the contrasting
uses of space in workers' struggles, based on the disposition of "labor power" in Germany and
of the transmission of "objectified labor" in Britain.

2. E. P. Thompson, "Time, Work-Discipline and Industrial Capitalism," *Past and Present*
Number 38 (December 1967).

3. Thomas Smith, "Peasant Time and Factory Time in Japan," *Past and Present* Number
111 (May 1986); Mark Harrison, "The Ordering of the Urban Environment: Time, Work and
the Occurrence of Crowds, 1790–1835," *Past and Present* Number 110 (February 1986); David
S. Landes, *Revolution in Time: Clocks and the Making of the Modern World* (Cambridge,
Massachusetts: Belknap Press, 1983); Christoph Deutschmann, *Der Weg zum Normalarbeitstag* (Frankfurt: Campus Verlag, 1985). On the development of time discipline in eighteenth-
century agricultural communities, see David Sabean, "Intensivierung der Arbeit und

quiry at hand, we know already that most producers in nineteenth-century Germany and Britain had sensitized themselves to this time economy. The question before us is more precise: how did the cultural definition of labor as a commodity influence workers' perception of the significance of time for remuneration in the labor process? The landmark studies conducted by Thompson and others correlated the differing appreciations of time with the necessities of work. Thompson, for example, associated the imposition of an unremitting time-discipline among the English common people with the transition from independent manufacture at home to supervised, regulated labor at the factory. More recently, in an investigation of the time regime of Tokugawa Japan, Thomas Smith underscored the functional requirements of social relations in agriculture.[4] These studies treat the perception of time as a response to immediate instrumental requirements.

This chapter investigates instead the independent effect of the cultural encoding of practice upon producers' demarcation and manipulation of time. German workers and employers handled labor time itself as a commodity in the employment relation, whereas British workers and employers treated time only as a means for producing commodities. This difference shaped workers' understanding of the source of their income, their rationales for demanding payment from their employers, and, ultimately, the emergence and goals of their strike campaigns.

UNITS OF PAYMENT AND PRODUCTION

A conceptual scheme begins with division and distinction. The segments into which workers partitioned time to gauge their earnings reveals time's meaning for them in the employment relation. Unlike their British counterparts, German weavers calculated their earnings in a temporal framework based on the delivery of abstract work time at the site of production. In both countries, the piece-rate earnings of the weavers fluctuated severely from week to week even when business remained steady. Employers generally paid workers the earnings due at the end of each week, but the workers received credit for work performed only upon completion of an entire piece.

Alltagserfahrung auf dem Lande—ein Beispiel aus Württemberg," *Sozialwissenschaftliche Informationen für Unterricht und Studium* Volume 6, Number 4 (1977), pp. 149 ff.

4. Thompson, "Time, Work-Discipline and Industrial Capitalism," op. cit. In Smith's view, the assumption in Japan that time comprised a collective rather than an individual resource reflected the demands of a farm system that relied upon tight cooperation within the family and community. "Peasant Time and Factory Time in Japan," op. cit.

Table 6. Descriptions of Earnings, British Versus German Weavers

	British weavers		German weavers	
	Instances	*%*	*Instances*	*%*
As rate per piece	47	44.7	45	28.8
As both rate per piece and earnings received over interval of time	9	8.6	24	15.4
As earnings received over interval of time	49	46.7	87	55.8

Sources: *Yorkshire Factory Times*, 1890. *Der Textil-Arbeiter*, 1901–1902 (104 cases), *Der Christliche Textilarbeiter*, 1899–1901 (52 cases): The number of cases from each newspaper corresponds approximately to the proportion of textile workers who belonged to that union. There were no statistically significant differences between the results for the two newspapers.

It required at least several days' effort to come to the end of a piece. If a weaver had not quite finished a piece at the end of a pay period, he or she would take home nothing for it that week. In the following week, however, the weaver might be paid for twice as much work as in the preceding week. The procedure for disbursing wages due was the same in both countries, yet German and British weavers arrived at different interpretations of the relation between remuneration and the passage of time.

Weavers could count their earnings in either of two basic ways: they could quote the wage they received per piece of cloth handed in, or they could convert their pay to a wage received over an interval of time. The reports about wages and working conditions submitted to the textile workers' newspapers in Germany and Britain provide an index of workers' choice of expression. I analyzed weavers' descriptions of their wages from the earliest surviving issues of the textile union newspapers, those from 1890 in Britain and from 1899 to 1902 in Germany. In both countries, the reports, which often quoted verbatim the negotiations over piece rates and the scales for remuneration, often cited wages in terms of earnings per piece without reference to time (see Table 6). This is hardly surprising, since the choice depended on the purpose for which the pay was cited. For example, comparing past and future earnings per piece (without reference to the time required for completion) sufficed to convey the magnitude of a pay hike or decline. The real question of interest, however, is how German and British weavers converted the bare amounts received

Table 7. Time Intervals Cited, British Versus German Weavers

	British weavers		German weavers	
	Instances	%	*Instances*	%
Hour[a]	3	5.2	13	11.7
Day	0	0	29	26.1
Week	54	93.1	55	49.5
Month	1	1.7	0	0
Year	0	0	14	12.6
Total	58		111	

Sources: *Yorkshire Factory Times*, 1890. *Der Textil-Arbeiter*, 1901–1902 (104 cases), *Der Christliche Textilarbeiter*, 1899–1901 (52 cases): The number of cases from each newspaper corresponds approximately to the proportion of textile workers who belonged to that union. There were no statistically significant differences between the results for the two newspapers.

[a]The British weavers who cited hourly rates were "pattern weavers" who were paid for creating fabric samples.

for cloth into a temporal framework to judge their well-being or the returns they received for their effort.

Sharp differences emerge if one considers the specific intervals selected by British and German weavers when they did allude to time. When British weavers put their earnings into a temporal framework, in virtually all cases they chose the week as their unit (see Table 7). They simply followed the cycle of paydays. German weavers were less likely to choose the period of a week, and when they did so they had a specific purpose in mind. They chose the week when they were complaining that the pay was inadequate for the survival of their household, as Table 8 shows. The week was the most meaningful unit for making a comparison between the family's receipts and its expenditures.[5] Workers cited this fraction of time when they wanted to complain that their earnings granted only a beggarly existence or, as they often put it, amounted to "starvation wages."

In contrast to British practice, German weavers who converted their piece-rate earnings to a time equivalent expressed this in the majority of instances in periods other than the week. In more than a quarter of cases, they chose the interval of a day, whereas the British weavers never did so.

5. For examples of German workers paying for their lodging and budgeting other household expenses by the week, see *Der Textil-Arbeiter*, October 1, 1909, "Ein Jammerleben," and *Der Christliche Textilarbeiter*, Düren, January 27, 1900. For British parallels, see Royal Commission on Labour, PP 1892 XXXV, Nov. 11, 1891, hearing, pp. 210, 229, 235.

Table 8. German Weavers' Citations of Time Versus Complaints About
Standard of Living

	No reference to standard of living		Complaint about standard of living	
	Instances	*%*	*Instances*	*%*
Hour	12	14.5	1	3.6
Day	27	32.5	2	7.1
Week	33	39.8	22	78.6
Year	11	13.2	3	10.7
Total	83		28	

Sources: *Der Textil-Arbeiter,* 1901–1902 (104 cases); *Der Christliche Textilarbeiter,* 1899–1901 (52 cases).

When German workers used the unit of a day to express their piece-rate earnings, they were demonstrating their orientation to the daily expenditure of labor power in the production process. If German weavers referred to specific daily earnings, they could relate the pay to the disposition over their activity during this time interval in the production process.[6] For example, in the textile town of Schildesche the weavers who threatened a strike in 1905 informed the owner of their expectation that "a middling worker [should] earn with normal exertion at least two and a half marks a day."[7] In only two out of twenty-six instances in which German weavers converted their piece-rate earnings to a daily average did they also make a reference to the adequacy of this wage for supporting themselves or their families. This indicates that the Germans did not associate the period of a day with the cycle of household expenditure or consumption.

6. *Der Textil-Arbeiter,* Gera, Oct. 4, 1901; Hauptstaatsarchiv Düsseldorf, Regierung Aachen 1634, February, 1900, Düren. See also the discussion of the effort needed to earn an adequate "daily wage" in home weaving, in *Der Rheinische Weber,* September 1, 1899. German weavers who complained about the hard work that defective warps caused them could convert their piece rates to earnings per day. *Der Christliche Textilarbeiter,* Düren, January 27, 1900. Likewise, the German textile unions calculated the exploitation of the worker's expenditure of labor power in terms of the employer's daily profit per worker or per machine. *Der Textil-Arbeiter,* August 8, 1902, Chemnitz.
7. Staatsarchiv Detmold, I.U. 429, March 21, 1905. See also *Die Westdeutsche Arbeiter-Zeitung,* September 17, 1904, Krefeld; *Der Christliche Textilarbeiter,* June 8, 1899, Kempen; Stadtarchiv Velbert VIe 7, Bestand Langenburg, March 25, 1889, strike report.

In adopting diurnal or even hourly intervals to measure their earnings, German weavers applied an abstract time frame to their employment relation, one that was removed both from the tangible cycle of paydays and from the rhythm of finishing a piece of cloth. The vagaries of the weaving process, with unpredictable changes in the speed at which difficult warps could be turned into cloth and fluctuations in earnings over time, did not intrinsically suggest the day or the hour as a convenient measure of earnings, for no piece of fabric could be completed so quickly. German weavers distanced themselves from the delivery of cloth credited per week and from the weekly disbursal of wages, in order to analyze the wage they received as a return for the disposition of hypothetical intervals of time in the production process. For instance, weavers in Gera who required many days to complete a piece of fabric converted the piece-rate earning to a quotidian wage based on what they called the "daily expenditure of time."[8] Even workers who were paid a fixed weekly wage converted their earnings into a remuneration for each day's work.[9] German workers often negotiated with employers for wages measured by a daily calculus, even if the exact amount of remuneration depended on piece rates.[10] German piece-rate workers were so accustomed to looking at the daily cycle of production that they determined average weekly earnings by first considering average daily earnings and then multiplying by the days of the work week. Regardless of the final time frame in which they were interested, they began their reckoning with the unit of a day.[11]

8. *Der Textil-Arbeiter*, March 14, 1902, Gera.

9. *Vorwärts*, May 8, 1908, jute spinning mill.

10. In February, 1900, when weavers in Düren issued an exhortation for strike support, their leaflets averaged out their piece-rate earnings and expressed them as wages per day. HSTAD, Regierung Aachen 1634, Düren. Similarly, the dispute at the town of Emsdetten in 1906 turned on the question of whether weavers' earnings averaged 3.2 marks per day. Stadtarchiv Emsdetten, "Industrialisierung am Beispiel Emsdettens: Ein Rückblick aus dem Jahre 1924." For an example of employers and weavers on piece rates negotiating over wage increases in terms of daily averages, see Deutscher Textilarbeiterverband, *Jahrbuch des deutschen Textilarbeiterverbandes, 1913* (Berlin: Karl Hübsch, 1914), Aachen, p. 113. Even when German piece-rate workers formulated their ideal earnings, without reference to particular employers, they thought in terms of earnings per day. *Der Christliche Textilarbeiter*, July 13, 1901, Krefeld. When the Christian textile union in the area of Krefeld took a survey of members' piece-rate earnings in stuff weaving during 1904, they formulated the results in terms of the average wage per day. *Die Westdeutsche Arbeiter-Zeitung*, September 17, 1904, Krefeld. For a parallel example, see Staatsarchiv Münster, Kreis Steinfurt 1116, December 11, 1910, Neunkirchen.

11. Gauvorstand des Textilarbeiterverbands, *Arbeitszeit und Löhne in der Textilindustrie der Niederlausitz* (Berlin: Franz Kotzke, 1909), pp. 25–27; Deutscher Textilarbeiterverband, *Soziale Gegensätze oder die Lage der Textilarbeiter in Augsburg* (Berlin: Carl Hübsch, 1907), p. 8.

An explanation for the difference in the units of time German and British piece-rate workers used to calculate their earnings is not to be found in the circumstances under which they spent their payments. In both countries, workers on piece-rate systems generally received their wages either weekly or biweekly.[12] German workers did not differ from their British counterparts in the frequency with which they actually paid their rents or in the timeframe, that of the week, that they used for budgeting household expenses.[13] When German workers expressed their earnings per day, therefore, they diverged from a consumption-based framework to orient themselves to the daily cycle of the production process. This assumption shows up in the way German workers expressed their grievances over low rates of pay: when they complained that this remuneration was not commensurate with their skills, experience, or effort, they spoke in terms of daily rates.[14] "As a result of bad warp and

12. In the area of Aachen, to be sure, some weaving mills paid workers immediately upon completion of the warp on which they were working. Artur Peltzer, "Die Arbeiterbewegung in der Aachener Textilindustrie von der Mitte des 19. Jahrhunderts bis zum Ausbruch des Weltkrieges," Ph.D. diss., Universität Marburg, 1924, p. 50. A practice such as this might be expected to have made it more difficult for German workers to adopt the week as their periodic unit for payment of wages. The rich evidence available about payment customs elsewhere, however, indicates that Aachen comprised an exception in this respect. See Germany, Reichskanzler-Amt, *Ergebnisse der über die Verhältnisse der Lehrlinge, Gesellen und Fabrikarbeiter auf Beschluss des Bundesrathes angestellten Erhebungen* (Berlin: Carl Heymann, 1877), p. 235; Karl Emsbach, *Die soziale Betriebsverfassung der rheinischen Baumwollindustrie im 19. Jahrhundert* (Bonn: Röhrscheid, 1982), p. 486 and the sources cited there. And, even in Aachen, some firms paid on a weekly basis: *Jahres-Berichte der Königlich preussischen Regierungs- und Gewerberäthe, 1899* (Berlin: W. T. Bruer, 1900), p. 599.

13. *Der Textil-Arbeiter*, April 8, 1904.

14. For example, the weavers in Greiz in 1857 calculated the number of shots of the loom completed to justify a certain daily wage. Staatsarchiv Weimar, Landesregierung Greiz, a Rep. A, Kap. XXI/2c, Nr. 400, Petition of the Leinen-und Zeugweber-Innung of Greiz, May 20, 1857. For an example of weavers lodging pay demands based upon their calculation of the inserted weft thread per day, see Staatsarchiv Dresden, Amthauptmannschaft Zwickau Nr. 1547, August 18, 1903. The view in Germany that workers alienated their labor through sale of the timed disposition of their activity structured the workers' understanding of employers' attempts to increase work loads. In the three decades before the First World War, German manufacturers in many kinds of wool and silk weaving ordered weavers to tend two looms instead of one. The weavers equated the intensification of effort with an increase in the work time equivalent. Verband Deutscher Textilarbeiter, *Die Tuch-Konferenz in Crimmitschau 26. und 27. Februar 1910: Unterhandlungs-Bericht* (Berlin: Carl Hübsch, 1910), p. 51. German weavers analyzed their cloth as an index of shuttle motions. Then they counted the shuttle motions they could execute each day to estimate daily returns to effort. See, for example, *Der Textil-Arbeiter*, December 10, 1909, p. 397, and July 14, 1911, pp. 219–220. For other references to the expenditure of labor power per day, see *Der Rheinische Weber*, September 1, 1899; HSTAD, Regierung Aachen 1634, February 1900, Düren. For a later example of a worker referring to pay in terms of the daily quota of motions of the loom completed to receive it, see

poor materials," the *Märkische Volksstimme* said in 1906, "a worker can with extremely hard effort earn at the most only 1.5 marks daily."[15]

The preference for the interval of the day as the unit to calculate use of labor power was shared by German employers. When German managers considered the construction of their piece-rate scales, they often began by setting a proposed average daily wage.[16] The in-house memos generated by company clerks on weavers' actual earnings also cited daily averages,[17] and managers founded their calculations of production efficiency upon the unit of a day.[18]

For the British weavers, time was a quantifiable resource but the use of time per se was not what they sold their employer. As would be expected, therefore, when British weavers looked at their earnings over time, they did so only with regard to the cycle of actual paydays. They did not invent an independent framework based on the delivery of abstract labor time; they merely reported what they received in the same units as it came to hand. Does this mean the German weavers (and German employers) were more adept at rational calculation? Did only the German weavers *theorize* receipt of the wage?

The abstractions of a conceptual system can of course take radically different forms. British weavers also calculated their earnings based on abstract theory, but what they considered the object of theory the Germans hardly noted. Rather than figuring the average pay per day, the British weavers calculated the average per loom per week, emphasizing that the total was nothing but the sum of the looms operated. For example, to summarize for its readers the level of earnings for weavers in the town of Hindley in Lancashire, the *Cotton Factory Times* in 1897 said that weavers "are not

Deutscher Textilarbeiterverband, Hauptvorstand/Arbeiterinnensekretariat, *Mein Arbeitstag—mein Wochenende* (Berlin: Textilpraxis, 1931), p. 24.

15. *Märkische Volksstimme*, October 10, 1906.

16. For spinning and twisting, see *Leipziger Monatschrift für Textil-Industrie*, 1913, Nr. 10, p. 286; for mangling, see *Leipziger Monatschrift für Textil-Industrie*, 1911, Nr. 8, "Arbeitslöhne für Mangeln."

17. HSTAD, Regierung Düsseldorf 24692, J. Hellendall memo, October 14, 1899; Wirtschaftsarchiv Baden-Württemberg, Stuttgart, B25-319, 1895–1896.

18. *Leipziger Monatschrift für Textil-Industrie*, 1902, Nr. 9, p. 605; 1902, Nr. 10, p. 683; 1910, Nr. 11, p. 321; *Zeitschrift für die gesamte Textil-Industrie*, 1912, Nr. 37, p. 768; *Centralblatt für die Textil-Industrie*, 1893, Nr. 10, p. 147. German employers who felt compelled to defend the piece-rate scales they had constructed for weavers informed the public about the weavers' earnings in the form of daily averages. See *Viersener Zeitung*, Nr. 102, May 5, 1908; HSTAD, Regierung Düsseldorf 24700, 1904 pamphlet, Deuss & Oetker, p. 288; *Der Christliche Textilarbeiter*, July 18, 1903, front page.

averaging more than three shillings six pence per loom."[19] For weavers assigned several looms at once, as most were, the pay per loom naturally oscillated more than the total take-home pay. Estimating a weekly loom average represented no less a feat of abstraction than the German calculation of daily total averages.[20]

The direction of thought pursued by the British weavers was guided by their understanding of labor's commodity form. The language of the British weavers, as we have seen, revealed the assumption that they took charge of a loom to manage it for a profit, as if they were petty commodity producers. When they sought employment they inquired whether employers "had any looms to let."[21] Once engaged, they were holders of a machine and its output rather than peddlers of labor power.

The British weavers carried into their trade union activities their picture of themselves as entrepreneurs who ought to net so much per loom.[22] Whenever weavers in Yorkshire and Lancashire took up a special collection to provide strike support, to compensate their fellow workers for attending meetings, or to gather the initial funds necessary to support a

19. *Cotton Factory Times*, January 8, 1897. This newspaper also reported that the average in Nelson is "9d per loom" higher than in Burnley: *Cotton Factory Times*, February 19, 1897, p. 6. Unions calculated their members' welfare by earnings per loom: Nelson Weavers' Committee Minutes, LRO, July 2, 1891. For Yorkshire, see *Yorkshire Factory Times*, Feb. 21, 1908, p. 4; February 14, 1890, Bingley.

20. Even when German reports took note of variations in the number of looms per worker, they calculated only the aggregate wage per day given a particular loom assignment, not the pay per loom. Stadtarchiv Mönchengladbach, 5/660, August 29, 1910; Stadtarchiv Mönchengladbach, 1c 913, July 2, 1912.

21. *Yorkshire Factory Times*, November 1, 1889, Leeds, p. 7, December 26, 1902, April 17, 1908, Burnley; interview tape with H. Jennings, by Bob Turner, at Centre for English Cultural Traditions and Language, University of Sheffield. It may be significant that the British textile workers did not use the expressions "piece rates" or "piece-rate system" to describe their wages but used the entrepreneurial phrase that they "kept what they could make." See Joanna Bornat's interview with Miss V., born 1901, p. 21; *Yorkshire Factory Times*, June 12, 1890, p. 4; January 2, 1891.

22. When a report from Rochdale complained about a firm's custom of paying out only full pennies for completed pieces, keeping any halfpennies for itself, the correspondent's way of summarizing the aggregate effect of this measly withholding revealed a significant habit of mind. "This may not look [like] a large matter in itself," the writer reasoned, "but when it comes to be applied to hundreds of looms it multiplies quickly as time goes on." *Cotton Factory Times*, February 26, 1897, Rochdale. Here the correspondent adopted as the basic multiplier not the number of individual employees but the tools they used. Some employers punished weavers for leaving their job without giving notice. Rather than fining each weaver equally for the lost labor power, they levied a fine of sixpence for *each loom* the weaver should have attended. See United Kingdom, PP 1899 XCII, *Strikes and Lock-outs in 1898*, Burnley and Oldham.

union, they imposed a levy on each weaver of so much *per loom*.[23] An analyst might suppose that establishing a contribution on this basis served as a shorthand way of graduating donations to the earnings of weavers. In all likelihood the custom did originate with this purpose. Yet by the late nineteenth century weavers in the West Riding earned less on two looms than on one, because they tended two if they manufactured simpler fabrics.[24] Weavers also charged a levy on each loom when they took up collections in districts or in factories where every weaver served the same quota of looms. In the Huddersfield district, for example, each worker served a single loom.[25] Despite the uniform rate per *person*, weavers there still spoke of levying a fixed sum on each loom.[26] This habit was not confined to fund-raising for the trade unions. Weavers adopted the same unit of calculation when they undertook voluntary subscriptions to charities such as "Indian Famine Relief."[27] In Germany, by contrast, weavers who made special collections simply assessed themselves a certain sum per person.[28]

The British custom of seeking donations *per loom* originated in the era of home manufacture, when weavers operated as independent commodity producers. It began at least as early as the mid-eighteenth century and, despite the changed technical environment, survived into the early twentieth century.[29] In Germany, by contrast, the loom-based view of contributions did not surface in factories which an analyst might suppose would closely parallel the British case. It did not arise in Krefeld or the cities of Thüringen, for example, where handweavers had strong organizational traditions and legacies of collective struggle under the aegis of craft associa-

---

23. Archive of General Union of Dyers, Bleachers, and Textile Workers, Yeadon and Guiseley Factory Workers' Union, Minutes, January 19, 1891, and March 10, 1891, Royal Commission on Labour, PP 1892 XXXV, p. 209; *Yorkshire Factory Times*, February 26, 1892, Yeadon & Guisely; LRO, DDX 1274/1/3, October 14, 1873; LRO, DDX 1274/1/1, March 5, 1872.

24. United Kingdom, *Earnings and Hours of Labour of the Workpeople of the United Kingdom*, PP LXXX, pp. 86 ff.

25. *Textile Mercury*, August 2, 1902, p. 83; United Kingdom, Royal Commission on Labour, PP 1892 XXXV, p. 199; B. Riley, *Handbook, Sixteenth Independent Labour Party Conference* (Huddersfield: Town Hall, 1908), p. 18.

26. *Yorkshire Factory Times*, August 12, 1892, p. 4, Huddersfield.

27. *Cotton Factory Times*, January 29, 1897, Brierfeld, and February 12, 1897, p. 7.

28. *Der Textil-Arbeiter*, March 12, 1909.

29. J. L. Hammond and Barbara Hammond, *The Skilled Labourer* (London: Longman, 1979), p. 169. See, for the mid-nineteenth century, H. Dutton and J. E. King, *"Ten Percent and No Surrender": The Preston Strike, 1853–54* (Cambridge: Cambridge University Press, 1981), p. 34.

tions. The differences in how weavers in the two countries expressed their earnings and dues shows that their understanding of the transfer of "labor" gave weavers different conceptions of the source and denominators of their income over time.

For the purpose of comparing the development of textile labor movements in the two countries, the workers on piece rates represent the key group for investigation. In Germany weavers provided the leadership and the majority of members for the textile unions. The predominance of piece-rate workers in the unions was so great that the Christian newspaper reported in 1908, "For some time now the day-wage workers have planned to found their own organization, because in their opinion the Christian Textile Workers' Union is only for weavers or other piece-rate workers."[30] Where the surveillance records of the police report the job category of a speaker at a textile meeting, it was almost invariably that of weaver.[31]

In Yorkshire, too—that part of Britain which gave birth to the Labor Party and which most resembled Germany in the timing of formal unionization—the textile unions were led by weavers. In Yeadon and Guiseley, for example, the Factory Workers' Union began as the Powerloom Weavers' Association. Not until 1892, when it sought to organize the spinners, did it adopt a more inclusive name.[32] In Lancashire, of course, mule spinners

30. *Die Textilarbeiter-Zeitung,* February 15, 1908, Bocholt. For statistics on the occupations of union members in the Christian textile workers union showing that weavers were a majority of the members, see Archiv der Gewerkschaft Textil-Bekleidung, Zentralverband Christlicher Textilarbeiter Deutschlands, "Geschäftsbericht," 1908–1910, p. 43; 1912–1914, pp. 94–95. For comments from the free textile workers' union about the predominance of weavers and the need to expand the membership beyond this occupational group, see HSTAD, Regierung Düsseldorf, 24691, May 1, 1899, report on meeting in Viersen.

31. To cite a handful of illustrations: HSTAD, Präsidialbüro, 1272, report on meeting of January 8, 1899, p. 42, and January 22, 1899, p. 46; HSTAD, Landratsamt Mönchengladbach, 99, August 25, 1901, p. 180; HSTAD, Regierung Düsseldorf, 24691, March 20, 1899, Neuwerk. Weavers took the leadership posts in the textile unions over other skilled male textile workers. Staatsarchiv Dresden, Amthauptmannschaft Glauchau, Nr. 327, membership list 1891, Hohenstein, pp. 6 ff. Textile employers surveyed by the police reported that the weavers dominated elections to factory committees. Hauptstaatsarchiv Düsseldorf, Regierung Aachen, 13886, October 10, 1895. Dyers in Germany complained that the weavers took the lead over other textile workers. Stadtarchiv Gera, Gemeinde Zwötzen 133, November 19, 1904.

32. Archive of General Union of Dyers, Bleachers, and Textile Workers, Yeadon and Guisely Factory Workers' Union, Minutes Book, March 2, 1892. The evolution of union terminology in the Huddersfield district followed the same path, indicating that the weavers served as the core of the organization there as well. Joanna Bornat, "An Examination of the General Union of Textile Workers 1883–1922," Ph.D. diss., University of Essex, 1981, p. 75. Spinners, the largest occupational group after weavers, accounted for only one-fifth of this

played a key role in the development of unions, but this group, too, was one that depended upon remuneration by piece rates.

While keeping in mind the predominance of piece-rate workers in the union movements, a restriction on the applicability of my comparison to the British and German textile work forces should be noted. For unskilled workers who received a flat day-wage, British employers and workers found it convenient and probably unavoidable to carry over on occasion the same unit, the day, to measure earnings and production.[33] This sometimes happened in ring-frame spinning, for example. In such an environment, however, the calculations of the owners and workers for output and earnings merely copied the temporal unit used for remuneration, a unit owners adopted for an entirely pragmatic reason: by paying a flat wage for each day worked, in place of a flat sum per week, owners could avoid paying workers a full wage during those weeks that included holidays. The position of these day laborers contrasts with that of weavers, who received irregular piece rates and had to rely upon implicit assumptions about the labor activity to *choose* a conventional unit of time over which to average them. However, as we have seen, it was the piece-rate workers who organized and led the labor movements among textile workers. They selected the ideas and planned the programs of the unions. It is they who are of most significance in any comparative analysis of the effect of workplace culture on the development of workers' responses.

THE INFLUENCE OF CONCEPTS OF TIME ON STRIKE DEMANDS

The workers' understandings of the sale of time guided their efforts to protect their interests. Weaving mills in both nations suffered from frequent interruptions in production. Factories usually waited for a merchant house to submit orders for a particular run of fabric before they began its manufacture.[34] If the orders arrived sporadically, weavers found themselves wait-

---

union's members. Compare the figure of five hundred spinners listed by Keith Laybourn, "The Attitude of the Yorkshire Trade Unions to the Economic and Social Problems of the Great Depression, 1873–1896," Ph.D. diss., Lancaster University, 1973, p. 145, with membership figures published in PP 1900 LXXXIII, p. 731.

33. Leslie Marshall, *The Practical Flax Spinner* (London: Emmott & Co., 1885), pp. 198, 234: *Cotton Factory Times*, April 9, 1897, p. 1.

34. Germany, *Jahresberichte der königlich preussischen Regierungs- und Gewerberäthe, 1896* (Berlin: W. T. Bruer, 1897), p. 439; HSTAD, Regierung Düsseldorf, Jahresbericht des Fabrikinspektors, Mönchengladbach, 1902; Hans Botzet, "Die Geschichte der sozialen Verhält-

ing for overlookers to install warps in their looms. Or, if a mill had a full line of orders, it could mishandle the winding of warps and procurement of weft yarn. In this case, too, weavers were left waiting for materials for their work.

The days textile workers lost waiting for materials amounted to a significant portion of work time in both Britain and Germany. In Germany, the union for Christian textile workers kept statistics on the matter, and its reports show that days lost waiting accounted for most of the time that its members spent "unemployed." The union calculated that from 1910 to 1912, for example, 64 percent of the workdays members lost resulted from waiting for materials.[35] In Britain, overlookers' estimates and the report of the secretary of the weavers' union in Yorkshire indicate that Yorkshire weavers normally lost about one-quarter of their work time for lack of warps or weft.[36] Allen Gee, secretary of the union, testified to the Royal Commission on Labour, "A man never expects to be fully employed as a weaver."[37]

British and German weavers developed contrasting responses to this shared predicament. The samples of complaints from the German and British newspapers near the turn of the century (see Tables 1–5, above, Chapter 4) provide one source of evidence of their divergence. In thirty-one cases cited by British weavers from 1890 to 1893, workers complained about higher-ups who distributed work materials unfairly.[38] This grievance thus ranks among the dozen most frequently voiced. In my German sample, by contrast, weavers complained only five times about favoritism in the distribution of materials. This represented about 0.5 percent of the German sample. The relative absence of complaints about favoritism in distributing materials in Germany cannot be dismissed as an artifact of the circumstance that the German weavers minded less about waiting for warp and weft. After all, the list of major complaints shows that they

---

nisse in Krefeld und ihre wirtschaftlichen Zusammenhänge," Ph.D. diss., Köln, 1954, pp. 65 ff. For Britain, see Royal Commission on Labour, PP 1892 XXXV, p. 295.

35. During these years, the union received over nine thousand reports of unemployment due to this cause. The workers who waited for materials lost on average more than ten days of work per year. Archiv der Gewerkschaft Textil-Bekleidung, Zentralverband Christlicher Textilarbeiter Deutschlands, "Geschäftsbericht," op. cit., 1910–1912, p. 112 (b).

36. *Yorkshire Factory Times*, August 5, 1892, p. 8. In its wage census of 1885–1886, the British Board of Trade estimated that "broken time" might reduce the estimated annual earnings of weavers by 13 percent in woolens and by 10 percent in the worsted trade. Laybourn, op. cit., p. 315.

37. Royal Commission on Labour, PP 1892 XXXV, transcript of November 11, 1891, p. 200.

38. In 76 percent of these cases, the British weavers blamed overlookers.

complained about waiting for materials slightly more frequently than did their British counterparts.[39]

Does the lower incidence of complaints about unfair allocation of materials in Germany indicate that German overlookers dispensed the warps and weft more equitably? The possibility cannot be excluded. It seems significant, however, that many of the complaints about waiting for materials that did not blame the overlooker came from districts where mills concentrated on short runs of specialized patterns. Mills in these regions, such as Barmen and Aachen, gave the overlookers responsibility for allocating warps among the weavers so that overlookers could match the skills of individual weavers to specific fabric orders.[40] The lack of blame assigned to the overlooker might indicate that, in reaction to favoritism exercised by overlookers, German weavers who waited for materials simply focused on the more basic issue of losing their time, whereas British weavers particularized the problem and interpreted it as a product of their overlooker's character. What remains certain is the outcome in workers' consciousness: the German workers' relative emphasis on the underlying issue of losing time is in keeping with their view of the employment relation as the sale of the disposition of a labor capacity. The German workers did not attribute lost time to the prejudices of overlookers but addressed it as a basic problem in the employment relation.

Drawing upon their view of employment as the commitment of the use of labor over time, German weavers argued that they had a right to payment for the period they spent waiting without working (*Wartegeld*). "During the period of the labor contract we must place all our labor power [*Arbeitskraft*] at disposal," the workers in Lörrach complained in 1906. "In return the firm is contractually obligated to take care of the prompt delivery of work tools and materials."[41] In Forst, the textile workers issued a statement in 1899 that called the worker's time a kind of capital for which workers had to be paid even while waiting for materials.[42] German workers attached a value to the commitment of time with such precision that when they formulated strike demands for

---

39. German weavers complained about waiting for warp and weft twenty-five times; the British weavers, twenty times. General complaints about waiting for materials comprised 3.0 percent of the German sample and 2.2 percent of the British sample.

40. For similar responsibility for distributing warps in Britain, see *Textile Manufacturer*, October 15, 1907, p. 353.

41. Wirtschaftsarchiv Baden-Württemberg, Stuttgart, B25-319, May 11, 1906. Weavers said that the time lost waiting for materials "curtailed the weaver's natural entitlement to his wage." *Der Christliche Textilarbeiter*, July 7, 1900, Viersen.

42. Stadtarchiv Forst, Kommission der Forster Textilarbeiterschaft, August 8, 1899.

waiting money, they often requested that managers graduate the pay not only for lost days but for fractions of lost hours.[43] From a cross-national perspective, the issue is not simply the lodging of the demand but its design and rationale: the indemnification did not just ensure workers' minimum take-home pay but was finely graduated to lost minutes and was justified as payment for the timed disposal of labor power.[44]

The contestation of uncompensated time was so important to German workers that as individuals they initiated legal complaints against their employers. A weaver from Neugersdorf took the trouble to file a claim in court during 1909 to recover the value of two hours spent waiting. He demanded restitution for the lull caused when a company official had to check the fabric pattern installed on his loom.[45] The difference between the German and the British responses to wasted time cannot be explained by the statutory environment. When textile employers in Germany wanted to be certain that they could escape from threatened litigation over lost time, they merely inserted a disclaimer in their factory rules against providing payment for "canceled time," a tactic which persisted into the 1920s.[46]

43. For examples of strike demands for hourly compensation for waiting, see Stadtarchiv Mönchengladbach, 1c 913, March 26, 1912; Staatsarchiv Detmold, I.U. 429, March 21, 1905, Schildesche; Hauptstaatsarchiv Düsseldorf, Regierung Düsseldorf, 24701, February 23, 1906, p. 223; Hauptstaatsarchiv Düsseldorf, Landratsamt Mönchengladbach, 70, February 22, 1906, p. 103; Hauptstaatsarchiv Düsseldorf, Regierung Düsseldorf, 24699, May 1, 1905, p. 286; Stadtarchiv Wuppertal, Verband von Arbeitgebern im bergischen Industriebezirk, "Bericht des Verbandes von Arbeitgebern im bergischen Industriebezirk,. 01. Januar 1905 bis 31. März 1906," p. 15; Staatsarchiv Münster, Kreis Steinfurt, 1311, July 25, 1906; *Der Textil-Arbeiter*, January 24, 1902, Sonthofen, and February 12, 1909, Mönchengladbach, "Aus der Bewegung in der Textilindustrie"; *Westdeutsche Landeszeitung*, March 7, 1906; *Die Textilarbeiter-Zeitung*, June 27, 1908; for waiting for design cards, *Die Textil-Zeitung*, October 27, 1902, Gera, p. 989; Staatsarchiv Dresden, Amthauptmannschat Chemnitz, Nr. 10, p. 130, Oct. 10, 1889. Another complaint indicates the precision with which German weavers gauged their time: at some mills weavers objected that the waiting time for which they were compensated extended only to the moment when the warp was delivered to the loom, not to the point at which the installers had actually completed putting in the warp. *Der Textil-Arbeiter*, January 4, 1907.

44. In the language of the German workers, the payment for waiting time represented, not an allowance, but an indemnity (*Entschädigung*). *Der Textil-Arbeiter*, February 12, 1904, Elsterberg. It is conceivable that British workers who could not easily demand money for a tangible output (such as railway personnel, perhaps) or those for whom interruptions occurred too irregularly to comprise a normal portion of a product's time of manufacture would resort to demands for waiting time for the sake of minimum take-home pay.

45. *Der Textil-Arbeiter*, February 12, 1909, Neugersdorf. Weavers filed cases to recover small portions of unremunerated time through much of the Wupper Valley as well. HSTAD, Gewerbegericht Elberfeld, 80/47, 1888, case 39; 80/50, 1891, case 225; 80/50, 1891, case 282. *Der Christliche Textilarbeiter*, June 6, 1903, "Wie Fabrikordnungen entstehen."

46. *Der Textil-Arbeiter*, November 26, 1920, p. 201; Landesarchiv Potsdam, Rep. 43, Gewerbeaufsicht Cottbus, Nr. 149, June 18, 1906, p. 8. See also HSTAD, Landratsamt Greven-

Strike demands for reimbursement of waiting time originated in each of Germany's major textile regions, including the Wupper Valley, the lower Rhine, the Münsterland, Saxony, and Silesia.[47] The demands arose both in urban centers and in remote areas where workers supplemented their factory employment with agricultural work.[48] Not only weavers but spinners, beamers, and spoolers demanded "waiting money."[49] The workers enjoyed a measure of success: reports from the textile workers' newspapers and factory rule books show that the custom of paying "waiting

broich, 271, pp. 94 ff., supplement to the "Arbeitsordnung" of J. A. Lindgens Erben, 1909, and p. 192, Erckens & Co; Günter Loose, *Betriebs-Chronik VEB Baumwollspinnerei Zschopautal*, Landesarchiv Potsdam, May, 1956, p. 108; *Kölner Zeitung*, November 18, 1900, Mönchengladbach; *Der Textil-Arbeiter*, Jan. 3, 1902, Saxony. Officials judged that the insertion of the disclaimer into the factory ordinance did not violate labor law. Staatsarchiv Dresden, Amtshauptmannschaft Zwickau, Nr. 2368, pp. 54–55. August 10, 1901. Stadtarchiv Cottbus, A II 4. 7 i, Nr. 11, April 5, 1905. A firm in Bremen that lacked such a disclaimer lost its case. Yet even here the court's reasoning reaffirms the supposition that labor's commodity form structured the debate. The court declared that a worker had a right to materials sufficient for him to "make full use of his labor power." Cited in Deutscher Textilarbeiterverband, *Protokoll des 10. Generalversammlung für das Jahr 1910* (Berlin: Karl Hübsch, n.d.), pp. 286–287. The Berlin industrial court ruled, however, that piece-rate workers who were denied sufficient materials to put their labor power to use had the right to leave their employment but had no claim to restitution. Ludwig Bernhard, *Die Akkordarbeit in Deutschland* (Leipzig: Duncker & Humblot, 1903), p. 224.

47. See the preceding two notes and Hauptstaatsarchiv Düsseldorf, Landratsamt Euskirchen, February 27, 1905, p. 355; Hauptstaatsarchiv Düsseldorf, Regierung Aachen, Birkesdorf, January, 1900; Hauptstaatsarchiv Düsseldorf, Regierung Düsseldorf, 24690, December 3, 1898, p. 148; Hauptstaatsarchiv Düsseldorf, Regierung Düsseldorf, 24692, August 3, 1899; Hauptstaatsarchiv Düsseldorf, Regierung Düsseldorf, 24692, August 16, 1899; Staatsarchiv Detmold, Reg. Minden I.U. Nr. 431, Buntweberei von Knemeyer & Co.; Zentrales Staatsarchiv Merseburg, 77 2524, Nr. 3, Volume 1, p. 13; *Der Christliche Textilarbeiter*, April 6, 1901, Viersen; *Die Textilarbeiter-Zeitung*, March 6, 1909, Münsterthal; March 13, 1909, Mülhausen i. Els.; Stadtarchiv Augsburg, No. 1670, May 16, 1912, p. 11; Staatsarchiv Dresden, Amthauptmannschaft Glauchau, pp. 71–72, July 12, 1910. For other complaints about waiting for warps, see *Der Textil-Arbeiter*, December 28, 1906, Sommerfeld and Mönchengladbach; August 12, 1910.

At the town of Rosenthal in Thüringen, workers went on strike in 1888 after their factory was closed for three days as a result of a breakdown. During the wait for completion of repairs, the factory owner promised one mark daily in restitution. The workers rejected the offer, since it did not equal their usual earnings, and they went on strike. Staatsarchiv Weimar, Reuss älterer Linie, Reuss Landratsamt Greiz, Nr. 2533, Sept. 18, 1888.

48. See the preceding note, as well as Staatsarchiv Münster, Regierung Münster, 718, May 9, 1891, p. 140.

49. *Der Textil-Arbeiter*, March 31, 1905, Mönchengladbach; May 29, 1914, Gronau. For spinners' informal requests for "waiting money," see *Der Textil-Arbeiter*, May 19, 1905, Zwötzen. For examples of spinners who received "waiting money," see *Der Christliche Textilarbeiter*, February 3, 1900, Düren; *Der Textil-Arbeiter*, May 21, 1909, Zwickau; *Die Textilarbeiter-Zeitung*, June 12, 1909. For spoolers and beamers requesting "waiting money," see *Der Textil-Arbeiter*, October 13, 1905.

money" was geographically widespread.[50] In the Wupper Valley, a survey of thirty-nine ribbon-weaving firms near Barmen conducted on the eve of the First World War found that almost half paid weavers for waiting for materials, including sixteen companies that offered restitution calculated to the hour.[51] The payments became a permanent and taken-for-granted procedure.[52] They offered a first step toward demands for payment for vacation time in Germany. The female winders at a firm in Viersen included among their strike demands in 1909 the proposal that they receive their regular pay for labor on days before holidays, when the firm operated only part-time.[53] Workers at a textile mill at Neugersdorf went a step further in 1914 when they asked for compensation for the complete days off for holiday observances.[54]

50. Stadtarchiv Velbert, VI e 7 Bestand Langenburg, December 15, 1893; Hauptstaatsarchiv Düsseldorf, Regierung Düsseldorf, 24692, August 16, 1899; Deutscher Textilarbeiterverband, *Jahrbuch, 1913*, op. cit., p. 134; Archiv der Gewerkschaft Textil-Bekleidung, Zentralverband Christlicher Textilarbeiter Deutschlands, "Geschäftsbericht,' op. cit., 1906–1908, Gronau district, Firma Gaidoel, p. 72; *Bocholter Volksblatt*, October 1, 1901; *Der Textil-Arbeiter*, September 13, 1901, Pennig; May 30, 1902, Kettwig; January 24, 1902, Sonthofen (Allgäu); October 27, 1911, Krefeld; March 2, 1906, Rheydt; May 14, 1909, Neustadt a. d. Orla; August 6, 1909, Viersen; October 29, 1909, Bergisches Land; December 10, 1909, Wuppertal; January 27, 1911, Kunzendorf i. Schl.; May 19, 1911, Hof; August 4, 1911, Unterurbach (Württemberg); *Die Textilarbeiter-Zeitung*, December 9, 1899, Süchteln; February 1, 1902; May 16, 1908, Gronau; July 2, 1910, Grossschönau; September 10, 1910, Bocholt; May 20, 1911, Coesfeld; Hauptstaatsarchiv Düsseldorf, Gewerbegericht Elberfeld, 80/50, 1891, case 225 and cases on p. 2; *Die Textil-Zeitung*, September 11, 1899, p. 734; Stadtarchiv Greiz, B Nr. 5977, Kap. IV, Nr. 97, p. 67, 1909.

51. *Der Textil-Arbeiter*, July 3, 1914, Barmen. An inquiry in Bocholt, taken in 1901 during a severe business downturn in which more than a quarter of the town's looms were taken out of operation, showed that the practice of paying "waiting money" could persist during periods when employers enjoyed an abundance of labor. During this extreme slump in the textile business, nine out of forty-two weaving mills in Bocholt paid workers for lost time. *Der Christliche Textilarbeiter*, August 10, 1901.

52. An article in a German technical magazine took the practice of paying *Wartegeld* as an automatic assumption. In an article published in 1897, for example, a manager said, "It often occurs that looms sit still for two or three days and not only fail to produce anything, but the weavers who are waiting must receive indemnification." *Die Textil-Zeitung*, March 9, 1897, and March 16, 1897, "Krebsschaden." German employers also distinguished themselves from their British counterparts by guaranteeing that workers who were transferred to another job in the same mill would not suffer a reduction in their earnings while they were learning the new job. Having sold the disposition of their labor power, which had a known market value, workers were not to be disadvantaged if the employer put their labor potential into operation in an unanticipated fashion. Stadtarchiv Steinfurt-Borghorst, B379, September 20, 1913 ordinance, A. Wattendorf; HSTAD, Landratsamt Grevenbroich, 271, Anton Walraf Söhne, 1910, p. 243; *Der Textil-Arbeiter*, February 12, 1909, Chemnitz.

53. HSTAD, Landratsamt Mönchengladbach 303, Viersen, 1909, p. 10.

54. *Der Textil-Arbeiter*, April 3, 1914, Neugersdorf. On comparatively early experiments with paid vacation in German textiles, see Jürgen Reulecke, "Die Entstehung des Erholungs-

By contrast with German practice, British textile employers did not offer their piece-rate workers waiting money. Nor did British textile workers ask for it in strike negotiations.[55] In fact, the textile workers' press shows that British workers did not conceive of this as a possible issue of contention. A sampling of the *Yorkshire Factory Times* from 1890 to 1893 uncovered more than twenty complaints from weavers about reductions in earnings due to waiting for materials.[56] Not one mentioned that the employer ought to compensate personnel for unused time. Nor did the complaints up to 1914 voice such a demand. Weavers argued, rather, that prices for fabrics delivered ought to take into consideration time lost waiting.[57] For the intermittent time they spent installing the warp or waiting for a warp, they wished to receive payment via the selling price of the finished good in the market. A beneficent owner in Yorkshire proposed to pay workers for vacation time, but the mouthpiece for the textile union, the *Yorkshire Factory Times*, scorned the notion. For owners to offer money to workers for time not worked would be condescending, the paper claimed. "I should be glad if workers were sufficiently well paid to be independent even of these [payments]," its editorialist wrote on the front page of this journal in 1914.[58] To avoid such "charity" at vacation time, workers had a right to earn enough for the work completed. True, the powerful unions for mule spinners in Lancashire saw to it that owners might pay workers something when the machines were stopped for repairs. But the employers owed such pay only if they needed the spinner's

---

urlaubs für Arbeiter in Deutschland vor dem Ersten Weltkrieg," in Dieter Langewiesche and Klaus Schönhoven, editors, *Arbeiter in Deutschland: Studien zur Lebensweise der Arbeiterschaft im Zeitalter der Industrialisierung* (Paderborn: Schöningh, 1981), p. 261.

55. British miners who complained about idle time (as well as other problems) in the great strike of 1844 requested a minimum of five days' worth of labor out of a work week of six days. These miners were, however, engaged under a yearly "bondage" system that prevented them from switching employers when earnings declined below subsistence. The employers successfully resisted this effort to guarantee a minimum wage, one that would not even have been based upon the full number of workdays miners were expected to show up. Robert Galloway, *Annals of Coal Mining and the Coal Trade*, second series (London: The Colliery Guardian Company, 1904), pp. 167, 176–177.

56. I sampled only every third issue of *The Yorkshire Factory Times* from this era; a full count of the number of complaints appearing about lost time would surely yield a larger number.

57. As an example, see United Kingdom, Royal Commission on Labour, PP 1892 XXXV, pp. 208–210, Nov. 11, 1891. If a spinning mule became unreliable, the spinners negotiated for extra payment for the output. Sidney Webb and Beatrice Webb, *Industrial Democracy* (New York: Augustus Kelley, 1965 [1897]), p. 312. But on lack of compensation for waiting even eight hours in spinning, see *Cotton Factory Times*, Jan. 1, 1897, Stalybridge.

58. *Yorkshire Factory Times*, March 12, 1914.

assistance in carrying out the overhaul.[59] The money served as compensation for extra labor, not, as in Germany, for the commitment of time when weavers were not used for any purpose in the mill.[60]

British textile workers' failure to demand reimbursement for waiting time certainly cannot be attributed to a lack of "time thrift" or to a disregard for time as a resource. Even in Elland, a sleepy village outside Bradford, weavers complained in 1889 that their employer forced them to wait for weft at their shop rather than giving them the chance of "profitably utilising" their time at home.[61] The textile workers' union in Yorkshire reported that some of its members were so concerned about waiting for a warp that they unrealistically expected to qualify for out-of-work benefits from the union.[62] British textile workers sought remedies for the loss of income but did not articulate a demand for compensation from the employer.

Why did the German employers, but not the British, provide "waiting money"? From a comparative perspective, the economic environment does not offer promising ground for generating this variation. A market analyst would be apt to assume that owners paid "waiting money" to discourage the unoccupied workers from seeking employment at another firm. German

59. British Association for the Advancement of Science, *On the Regulation of Wages by Means of Lists in the Cotton Industry*, Manchester Meeting of 1887 (Manchester: John Heywood [1887?]), Spinning, p. 7; Bolton Library Archives, Spinners of Bolton, "Annual Report," 1883, p. 63; Bolton Library Archives, ZGR/7, Taylor & Co. Rules, 1904. The same provision governed the Nottinghamshire lace trade. See W. A. Graham Clark, House of Representatives Committee on Interstate and Foreign Commerce, *Lace Industry in England and France* (Washington, D.C.: Government Printing Office, 1909), p. 27. Analogously, in many British towns the masons and builders who were called to a site outside the locality received compensation for "walking time." The payment covered effort invested, not the commitment of a labor capacity. Webb and Webb, op. cit., p. 313.

60. Wirtschaftsarchiv Baden-Württemberg, B25-319, Tuchfabrik Lörrach, June 18, 1906. Yet British employers shut employees inside at the mill even when, for lack of materials, the employees had no work. For examples of managers restraining workers from leaving even when there was no work to carry out, see Joanna Bornat's interview with Mr. B., born 1901, p. 55; *Yorkshire Factory Times*, January 15, 1892, Golcar. In Wigan, Lancashire, the owners kept the workers' remaining wages if they quit without notice during a period when the mill had no orders to work up and thus no pay for piece-rate workers: *Cotton Factory Times*, May 21, 1897, Wigan.

61. *Yorkshire Factory Times*, November 1, 1889, p. 5.

62. *Yorkshire Factory Times*, January 23, 1891. In Lancashire, too, workers proposed that the unions undertake the task of supporting members who had not been formally laid off but were waiting for materials. In the end the projected expense caused the textile unions to reject such plans. *Cotton Factory Times*, May 28, 1897, Rochdale; Archive of General Union of Dyers, Bleachers, and Textile Workers, Bradford, Yeadon General Union, minutes, Sept. 11, 1908. The unions granted out-of-work pay to weavers who were discriminated against in the distribution of materials. Wakefield Library Headquarters, Local Studies, C 99/585, January 27, 1903.

managers might have had a greater incentive for holding on to their workers under either of two circumstances: if labor resources were scarcer in Germany than in Britain, or if the skills the owners required were so specialized that they could not easily be purchased in the general labor market. The evidence does not support either hypothesis. Factories in Britain that suffered from severe labor shortages paid no waiting money,[63] nor did British companies who relied on unique skills from their workers, such as the isolated silk firms in Bradford and Halifax.[64] In Germany, the incidence of compensation for lost time also contradicts economic logic. The highly paid weaving branch, which offered "waiting money" more often than other textile departments, was the sector least likely to suffer from labor shortages, for spinners, who had lower status and wages, transferred to weaving when they had the opportunity.[65]

The terms under which German firms dispensed waiting money also indicate that the practice was not crafted for the purpose of retaining labor. Companies began crediting the money to workers before the workers had lost enough time to consider changing employers. The payments could begin after as little as two hours of waiting, and almost always began within one workday after the commencement of idleness.[66] If companies wanted to retain labor, moreover, they had other means at their disposal. They could, for example, offer bonuses to workers who stayed in their employ for a long period, a plan implemented by several German textile firms.[67]

---

63. For reports of textile labor shortages in Britain, see *Yorkshire Factory Times,* August 11, 1905, Bradford; *Journal of the British Association of Managers of Textile Works* (1912–1913) p. 93. On May 15, 1906, the *Textile Manufacturer* reported, "More or less through the whole wollen area of Yorkshire the shortage of labour is becoming a serious trouble" (p. 161).

64. Royal Commission on Labour, PP 1892 XXXV, November 11, 1891, hearing, p. 222, and November 13, 1891, p. 282.

65. HSTAD, Düsseldorf, Regierung Düsseldorf, 24652, October 24, 1878, p. 8; Hauptstaatsarchiv Düsseldorf, Grevenbroich, 319, October 28, 1899; Handelskammer Mönchengladbach, *Jahresbericht, 1896* (Mönchengladbach: V. Hütter, n.d.), pp. 5–6; Handelskammer Mönchengladbach, *Jahresbericht, 1897* (Mönchengladbach: V. Hütter, n.d.), p. 5; Hermann Hölters, "Die Arbeiterverhältnisse in der niederrheinischen Baumwollindustrie mit besonderer Berücksichtigung der männlichen Arbeiter," diss. Heidelberg, p. 21.

66. Some managers used tallies of waiting money to monitor lost production time and to check the efficiency of production. The custom provides another indicator of German managers' formal approach to the use of labor time. *Zeitschrift für die gesamte Textil-Industrie* Volume 12, Number 68, p. 68.

67. For the woolen industry of the lower Rhine, see Franz Decker, *Die betriebliche Sozialordnung der Dürener Industrie im 19. Jahrhundert* (Köln: Rheinisch-Westfälisches Wirtschaftsarchiv, 1965), p. 87. Elsewhere: Hauptstaatsarchiv Düsseldorf, Regierung Düsseldorf, 25015, p. 43, for 1893, and Regierung Düsseldorf, 25022, p. 42, for 1900; Hölters, op. cit., p. 23; Staatsarchiv Weimar, Landesregierung Greiz, n Rep. A, Kap. IX a, Nr. 148, reports of factory

If the German employers did not introduce waiting money for their own benefit, then the workers' understanding of labor's commodity form must have comprised the critical force in its introduction. How did the demands for compensation of time originate? Could differences between Germany and Britain in the lodging of time revendications have reflected nothing more than textile union officials' decisions as to which among many grievances to support and articulate? This would be to say that formal organizations for the propagation of ideology intervened to decide whether workers would focus upon and engage the issue. Alternatively, did the claims that attached to time arise as an expression of assumptions about the workday that workers acquired in the labor process? If the specifications of labor as a commodity were imparted to workers by the daily enactment of cultural practices rather than by discursive instruction, then the ideology workers carried into their collective actions could have originated, almost naturally, from the very construction of the labor process. The initiation and distribution of the demands for waiting money allows us to adjudicate between these possibilities.

Weavers in Germany had laid claim to waiting money prior to their incorporation into the factory system. In that era, textile employers had shamelessly enjoyed a gross oversupply of skilled and common labor.[68] They certainly did not institute the payment of waiting money as a response to labor scarcity. In the Wuppertal, for instance, where a surplus of workers in the 1840s led to a disastrous decline in their earnings, handweavers in that decade began to receive money for the time lost between contracts or for the time expended setting up the warps for their next job.[69] Indeed, as early as the 1830s, the entrepreneurs who ran putting-out networks included the weavers' "loss of time" during the changing of the

---

inspectors, 1879–1886, p. 133; *Die Textilarbeiter-Zeitung,* November 26, 1910, Allersdorf; Germany, Enquete-Kommission, *Reichs-Enquete für die Baumwollen- und Leinen-Industrie: Stenographische Protokolle über die mündliche Vernehmung der Sachverständigen* (Berlin: Julius Sittenfeld, 1878), p. 397.

68. Hermann Körner, *Lebenskämpfe in der Alten und Neuen Welt,* Volume I (New York: L. W. Schmidt, 1865), p. 391; Emsbach, op. cit., p. 322; Willi Brendgens, *Die wirtschaftliche, soziale und communale Entwicklung von Viersen* (Viersen: Gesellschaft für Druck und Verlag, 1929), p. 109. In the matter of labor supplies, as in many other respects, the Bielefeld region comprised an exception. Herbert Petzold, "Die Bielefelder Textilindustrie," diss., Rostock, 1926, p. 35.

69. Körner, op. cit., p. 391; Emsbach, op. cit., p. 179. Weavers in France received payment for waiting time as early as the 1830s. *L'Echo de la fabrique,* March 3, 1833, p. 71, and December 29, 1833, p. 6.

loom's fabric patterns as part of the expenses to be covered.[70] In 1848 weavers in the putting-out networks in the Wuppertal, on the left side of the Rhine, in Brandenburg, and in Saxony advanced demands for offi- cially guaranteed compensation for waiting for materials.[71] Cotton print- ers in manufactories also pressed for waiting money during those revolutionary days.[72] But weavers in particular advanced such claims in the first days of the 1848 revolution, before organizations of workers had extended across trade lines and before standing, citywide assemblies of artisans and factory workers had convened.[73] The articulation of claims for waiting time before weavers had come into contact with organizational leaders suggests that the demand emerged as part and parcel of the eve- ryday experience of the employment relation rather than out of a formal discourse imported by intellectual elites.

The demands raised by the British handloom weavers in response to similar predicaments reveal the influence of a different view of the exchange of labor as a commodity. The handloom weavers in Britain proposed all manner of remedies during the early nineteenth century to arrest the de- cline of their earnings, including a legislated minimum wage. Yet they never arrived at the notion that the employer owed them compensation for the simple commitment of time.[74] Their proposals set forth minimum piece

---

70. *Die Ameise*, April 7, 1834, p. 171. For an example of home weavers demanding and, in some instances, receiving compensation for the changing of the warp, see Kenneth N. Allen, "The Krefeld Silk Weavers in the Nineteenth Century," Ph.D. diss., Stanford University, 1988, p. 81.

71. Stadtarchiv Chemnitz, *Tarif* of June 1, 1848; Zentrales Staatsarchiv Merseburg, Rep. 120 I 1, Vol. 2, Nr. 60, March 28, 1848, Berlin, pp. 310–316; Alphons Thun, *Die Industrie am Niederrhein und ihre Arbeiter* (Leipzig: Duncker & Humblot, 1879), Zweiter Theil, p. 195; Peter Kriedte, *Eine Stadt am seidenen Faden* (Göttingen: Vandenhoeck & Ruprecht, 1991), p. 320; Emsbach, op. cit., pp. 648–650.

72. *Die Verbrüderung*, March 16, 1849, pp. 189–190.

73. P. H. Noyes, *Organization and Revolution: Working-Class Associations in the Ger- man Revolutions of 1848–1849* (Princeton: Princeton University Press, 1966), pp. 135–136.

74. Kenneth Carpenter, editor, *The Framework Knitters and Handloom Weavers: Their Attempts to Keep Up Wages* (New York: Arno Press, 1972), pamphlets from 1820 to 1845; Duncan Bythell, *The Handloom Weavers* (Cambridge: Cambridge University Press, 1969), p. 175; United Kingdom, *Report from Select Committee on Hand-Loom Weavers' Petitions*, 1834, PP 1834 X. The *Northern Star* reported in 1841 that two handweavers from Carlisle went to court for compensation "for payment for lost time, on account of their being disappointed of weft." Their complaint rested on the circumstance that the putter-out had them install new warps and then refused to let them take the warps out when the necessary weft did not arrive. The British weavers did not protest about waiting per se, and, unlike German weavers, they did not complain about having to pause between warps. *Northern Star*, September 4, 1841, p. 5.

rates for cloth actually delivered.[75] In keeping with the principle of the exchange of labor via its products, they thought that they ought to earn enough for products delivered during the busy weeks to tide them over slow periods.[76]

We should not suppose that the handweavers in Britain believed they sold their products instead of time; they sold time, but as it was embodied in products. When the putting-out system for home weavers was in its prime, the distributors sometimes assigned a standard piece of fabric a time equivalent, which they used to establish the weaver's payment. If the clothiers in this system altered the remuneration for completion of that cloth, they expressed this as a change in the time investment expected for the work. For example, the clothiers of Wiltshire in 1801 reduced the time allocation for a standard piece of cloth from twenty-three to twenty hours.[77] From the earliest days of radical political economy in Britain, critics of the market system asserted that workers did not get back from their employers all the time they had delivered. In 1805, Charles Hall asserted that the poor enjoyed only "about one-eighth part, or the produce of one-eighth part of their time."[78] But the British workers considered the unfair transfer of time only as it was embodied in products.

75. Frederick James Kaijage, "Labouring Barnsley, 1816–1856: A Social and Economic History." Ph.D. diss., University of Warwick, 1975, pp. 312 ff.

76. Bythell, op. cit., p. 149. In contrast to many of their German counterparts, British handweavers did not seek or receive compensation for the time regularly spent changing the warp. United Kingdom, *Report from Select Committee*, op. cit., testimony of Hugh Mackenzie, p. 60, and of James Orr, p. 95. To the contrary, contractors reduced payments the handweavers received for a variety of cloths after the loom had been adjusted for that fabric pattern. The putters-out knew that the weavers would accept lower rates for additional pieces of cloth of the same type, rather than absorbing the set-up costs to prepare for a different variety. United Kingdom, *Select Committee on Settling Disputes in the Cotton Manufacture*, PP 1802–1803 VIII, testimony of Thomas Thorpe, April 25, 1803, p. 17. In parliamentary hearings British putters-out said they granted weavers an indeterminate bonus under one condition: if a weaver set up a different kind of warp and ended up receiving only one order on that kind of warp. If two or more orders were carried out, the effort invested in the installation was remunerated via the regular piece rate for the cloth. United Kingdom, Committee on Cotton Weavers and Petitions, Minutes of Evidence, *Settling Disputes in the Cotton Manufacture*, PP 1802–1803 VIII, pp. 97–98. Approximately one-eighth of the handloom weavers' time was lost changing from one piece to another. Kaijage, op. cit., p. 144.

77. John Rule, *The Experience of Labour in Eighteenth-Century Industry* (London: Croom Helm, 1981), pp. 137–138.

78. Charles Hall, *The Effects of Civilization on the People in European States* (London: T. Ostell, 1805), p. 118. Perhaps due to their belief that time was transferred as it was incarnated in finished products, English economists such as Hall struck Marx as the originators of a theory of value, but not of a theory of exploitation. Alexandre Chabert, "Aux Sources du socialisme anglais," *Revue d'histoire économique et sociale* No. 4 (1951), p. 382. Bray claimed that "the

Not only the original appearance of claims for waiting money in Germany but its geographical incidence after the establishment of mature factory regimes demonstrates that the demand rested on a popular conviction about the nature of the labor transaction. Weavers demanded restitution for the commitment of time in backwater areas where neither union organizations nor union spokesmen had appeared. A strike in a rural area of the Münsterland offers a telling emblem of German textile workers' belief that they ought to be compensated for the loss of their time. When workers in the village of Neuenkirchen left work to counter a proposed wage reduction in May, 1891, they not only succeeded in maintaining the previous piece rates, but they also drew compensation (*Entschädigung*) from the company for the *time* out of work due to the strike![79] The demand for the reimbursement could hardly have been recommended by union leaders, for organizers did not target this rural area until almost a decade later.[80] German textile workers raised the demand for waiting money in other remote areas where union representatives had not campaigned.[81] Requests for the restitution of time commitments rested on established assumptions that were generated and sustained by the arrangement of workaday practices.[82]

---

workmen have given the capitalist the labour of a whole year, in exchange for the value of only half a year." John Bray, *Labour's Wrongs and Labour's Remedy* (Leeds: David Green, 1839), p. 48. The concept of labor as a commodity in Britain could of course include allocation of compensation for time invested in acquiring skills—cultivating one's "labor power"?—when the products of labor were sold. For an early example based on exchanges among independent commodity producers, see Adam Smith's *Lectures on Justice, Police, Revenue and Arms*, edited by Edwin Cannan (Oxford: Clarendon Press, 1896), p. 174.

79. Staatsarchiv Münster, Kreis Steinfurt, 1311, May 2, 1891, Neuenkirchen, and Regierung Münster, 718, May 14, 1891, p. 146.

80. Karl Hüser, *Mit Gott für unser Recht: Ein Beitrag zur Geschichte der Gewerkschaftsbewegung im Münsterland* (Paderborn: Gewerkschaft Textil-Bekleidung, 1978), pp. 28–29; Heinrich Camps, *Geschichte und Entwicklung des Bezirks Westfalen des Zentralverbandes Christlicher Textilarbeiter Deutschlands* (Münster: Bezirkssekretariat Christlicher Textilarbeiter, 1924), pp. 7–12. Indeed, the initial promoter of textile unions in this region, the Christian textile workers' association, had not yet been established in Germany. Michael Schneider, *Die Christlichen Gewerkschaften 1894–1933* (Bonn: Neue Gesellschaft, 1982), pp. 74 ff.

81. In Eschendorff, a town in the Münsterland, weavers went on strike without notice in 1899 and by all accounts spontaneously demanded an end to waiting without pay for materials or equipment. Staatsarchiv Münster, Kreis Steinfurt 1311, Eschendorff, March 29, 1899; Zentrales Staatsarchiv Merseburg, 77 2524, Nr. 3, Vol. 1, p. 13, April 1, 1899, Amt Rheine.

82. Workers and employers in other branches of enterprise in Germany, including construction and metal work, also battled over compensation for idle time. A contract for Berlin journeymen carpenters and masons in 1870 tried to preclude demands for compensation of unused time. It specified that "the employer is obligated to keep the employee engaged with

The expectation in Germany that employers would provide compensation for the commitment of time also surfaced in the norms for disbursing wages in the event of the temporary closure of a factory. German textile workers successfully demanded that they receive compensation when their mill was shut due to breakdowns or alterations of machinery.[83] British owners failed to offer compensation for disruptions in employment even when they required workers to wait in the vicinity for the mill to reopen.[84] The columns of the textile workers' newspapers in Britain in the decades before the First World War frequently referred to engine breakdowns and stoppages due to the transfer of looms. They never suggested, however, that workers ought to receive compensation from employers during these intervals.

The German workers' readiness to battle for waiting money formed part of a larger struggle over the control and valorization of inappreciable segments of time, a contest in which British workers did not so readily engage. German workers not only complained about the petty ways in which employers controlled their time without compensating them for it, but they went ahead and seized upon that complaint as a cause for launching strikes. Weavers in Mönchengladbach struck with the sole demand of compensation for minutes that some of them lost waiting in line to punch out on the time clock.[85] When the weavers at a mill in the same town went on strike in early 1900, they combined their request for higher wages with a demand related

work; if circumstances force the employer to lay the employee off against the employee's will, the latter cannot request a wage during the time in which he is inactive, but he can in this case request his immediate release." *Der Volksstaat*, February 5, 1870.

83. *Der Textil-Arbeiter*, July 3, 1914, Barmen; *Die Textilarbeiter-Zeitung*, May 8, 1909, Mülhausen i. Els.; *Die Textilarbeiter-Zeitung*, August 20, 1910, Forst, Lausitz; Hölters, op. cit., p. 27; Stadtarchiv Augsburg, No. 1667, p. 1, June 15, 1903; *Die Textilarbeiter-Zeitung*, October 29, 1910, Augsburg. For other complaints about the owner's failure to provide compensation during engine breakdowns, see *Der Textil-Arbeiter*, July 4, 1902, Lörrach; April 23, 1909, Bautzen. The extent to which payment for factory shutdowns became the norm can be judged from the reaction of a mill owner in Mönchengladbach to a momentary break in production. He felt compelled to post an official notice in 1911 *disavowing* compensation to workers for disruptions resulting from the transfer of machinery to a new plant location in town. *Die Textilarbeiter-Zeitung*, March 18, 1911, Peter Brunen. See also HSTAD, Landratsamt Grevenbroich, 271, pp. 94 ff., 1909 factory ordinance.

84. *Cotton Factory Times*, February 19, 1897, Preston; *Yorkshire Factory Times*, October 9, 1903, Dudley Hill. British textile workers who received piece rates as well as those who received time wages, such as dyers and mechanics, were denied compensation by employers for mill closures. *Cotton Factory Times*, February 5, 1897, Mossley.

85. *Die Textilarbeiter-Zeitung*, August 26, 1911, Mönchengladbach. For an example of German weavers complaining about the time lost fetching cops, see *Die Textilarbeiter-Zeitung*, November 27, 1909.

to the expenditure of time. They proposed that the owner cease making the weavers wait to have their spools of yarn weighed (a means of calculating yarn wastage upon completion of a piece),[86] or, alternatively, that the owner "compensate the worker for the resulting time loss."[87] The German workers' enumeration of tasks for which they ought to receive compensation extended to the personal maintenance of their bodies. When the workers at a large silk firm outside of Krefeld in 1905 requested pay for auxiliary chores that consumed their time, they included the task of carrying the coffee water.[88] In Mülhausen, textile workers told their owner in 1909 that for changing their clothing they wanted an extra five minutes' wage credit.[89] If the workers transferred to the employer the labor power lodged in their person, they could expect compensation for sustaining it at the work site.

Even the ritual of handing workers the coins and currency of their pay absorbed time and as such became a contested interval in Germany. As early as 1848, home weavers in Chemnitz asserted that an excessive wait for the processing of their finished warps at the receiving office constituted a violation of the employment contract. When German textile workers negotiated with their employers over wages, they sometimes specified that clerks were to hand the pay out to them during work hours, not during a break or upon the conclusion of the regular workday.[90] In Spremberg, police surveilling workers' meetings at the turn of the century reported that a major complaint of workers concerned the receipt of the pay packet after the close of the workday.[91] In the course of strike negotiations at a mill in Mönchengladbach, the workers requested that their pay be brought to them at their machine.[92] Reports from the *Yorkshire Factory Times* leave no doubt that British workers considered it offensive when employers detained them after normal working hours to dole out pay.[93] Some employers made it a

86. *Seide*, July 25, 1900, p. 466.

87. *Gladbacher Merkur*, January 20, 1900. For another example of the same problem, see HSTAD, Regierung Düsseldorf, 24692, December 27, 1899, p. 160.

88. HSTAD, Regierung Düsseldorf, 24699, May 1, 1905, p. 286.

89. *Die Textilarbeiter-Zeitung*, March 13, 1909.

90. *Der Textil-Arbeiter*, May 21, 1909, Gera. The handweavers in Chemnitz asserted that the time expended waiting at the office of the contractor should be reduced or separately remunerated. Stadtarchiv Chemnitz, *Tarif* of June, 1848.

91. Landesarchiv Potsdam, Rep. 6B, Landratsamt Spremberg, Nr. 490, 1901, p. 34.

92. *Westdeutsche Landeszeitung*, Rheydt, March 7, 1906. German workers also filed court challenges to recover the value of minutes they lost fetching their pay or waiting to exit the factory. *Die Textilarbeiter-Zeitung*, November 25, 1911.

93. *Yorkshire Factory Times*, April 25, 1902, p. 4.

policy to do so.[94] Yet British workers never introduced these lost minutes into strike negotiations; they did not conceive of a small period of waiting as an unauthorized appropriation of their property—their time. British workers were no less vigilant than their German counterparts to protect themselves against the illegal prolongation of work for even a minute or two.[95] In comparative perspective, the issue is not workers' concern about the length of the work shift—or, for employees on time wages, the performance of work without pay. The question is workers' sensitivity to payment for small increments of time in which the labor capacity is unused.

If German workers treated time itself as a kind of currency, so did their employers. They demonstrated this through their handling of the monies withheld from workers for coming to their jobs late. After 1891, German law prohibited factory employers from putting into their general till the funds they collected from disciplinary punishments. They had permission to pocket fines collected from workers for property damage, however. Employers could keep as compensation deductions made for broken windows or for the misuse of equipment, for example. Therefore employers kept two sets of books for the fines they imposed: one for the disciplinary fines, which they transferred to workers' welfare committees, and one for destruction of property. The important point here is that some German owners believed that the fines they levied on workers for tardiness belonged in the category of compensation for property losses.[96]

It would be easy to dismiss the employers' conduct in this instance as underhanded, unprincipled attempts to appropriate funds. But the evidence conflicts with this interpretation for two reasons. The books in which employers recorded their fines, the very records the factory inspectors and the courts used to arraign the avaricious employers, did not group other disciplinary fines, such as those inflicted for socializing away

---

94. LRO, DDX 1274/6/1, July 1, 1900.

95. PP 1892 XXXV, p. 14; *Yorkshire Factory Times*, April 19, 1901, Spen Valley. On convictions for illegal overtime work, see *Yorkshire Factory Times*, April 24, 1908, p. 7. German commentators considered the British to be extremely sensitive to employers' attempts to run the engines a few minutes overtime. *Der Textil-Arbeiter*, March 15, 1907.

96. HSTAD, Regierung Düsseldorf, 24684, May 26, 1894; HSTAD, Regierung Düsseldorf, 25027, printed story on employer from Neersen at Oberlandesgerichts Köln, published December 22, 1904; Germany, *Jahres-Berichte der königlich preussischen Regierungs- und Gewerberäte und Bergbehörden für 1895* (Berlin: W. T. Bruer, 1896), pp. 511–512; Germany, *Jahresberichte . . . 1904* (Berlin: R. v. Deckers Verlag, 1905), p. 433. For brief absences employers also confiscated the deposit workers paid upon beginning employment. *Geraisches Tageblatt*, April 12, 1890.

from one's workstation or for inattentiveness, in the category of damage compensation. In these cases as well, the employers had lost the full use of the labor time they needed for their machinery. But the company books showed that owners did not attempt to profit from these other kinds of disciplinary fines, as they would have been likely to have done if they had merely sought to enrich themselves. Second, the employers whom the factory inspectors accused of misappropriating fines for tardiness presented their reasoning to the courts. Rather than avoid the publicity of a trial—a matter about which employers generally showed acute sensitivity[97]—they supported their practice in public.

In each country, the conflicting expectations of the employers and workers arose from a foundation of cultural agreement, a shared understanding of labor as a commodity. In Germany the transmission of labor via the disposition over workers' time monetized time itself, whereas in Britain the transfer of labor as it was materialized in products meant that time was a resource whose gain or loss was measured in merchandise. In Germany the scales on which employers graduated per minute the amount of the fine they would assess for lateness treated time itself as a form of property—and so workers reciprocated. In Britain employers who locked tardy workers out of the mill enforced their expectation that anyone working for them deliver products at a regular pace, but as a rule employers did not treat the workers' time itself as property for whose loss they claimed a metrically graduated restitution. And, in parallel fashion, neither did British workers. The form of labor as a commodity laid out a distinctive playing field.[98]

---

97. One owner specified in the factory's employment rules that workers had to notify the owner before going public with their complaints in the courts. HSTAD, Landratsamt Grevenbroich, 271, p. 184, circa 1910.

98. The constellation of factory procedures also raises questions about the relation between culture and the actors' pragmatic, manipulative conduct. Did the agents cunningly support certain specifications of labor because they offered advantages lacking in alternative notions? The question has a meaning for social investigators only if they view ideas as an exclusive possession of individuals who appropriate them to act upon the outside world. If, instead, institutions are themselves constituted as symbolic forms, if ideas are materialized in forms of practice, then agents may reproduce these ideas without internalizing or consciously exploiting them. For example, the German weavers who labored under the system of pay per shot and the German employers who calculated weavers' efficiency as a fraction of possible shots executed did not have consciously to endorse and esteem the notion that the commercial transmission of labor depended on the process of converting it from a potential to a product. Their conduct reaffirmed and transmitted the assumption every day. Once the definition of labor was installed, agents employed it to advance their self-interested action, but that definition and the corresponding symbolic form of their action were not created by their private conception of self-interest. Nor did they passively internalize the specification of labor as a

In this culturally mediated struggle, the selection of labor's commodity form never conferred a univocal advantage upon a contestant. For example, the specification of labor in Germany may have enabled employers to justify shifting employees between jobs in the firm, since employers had purchased the disposition over the subordinates' labor power. But for employers it also had an unwanted effect. It immediately led German workers to press far-reaching demands based on the treatment of time as transferable property. Similarly, the specification of labor as a commodity that appeared in Britain may have discouraged textile workers from seeking pay for idle moments; at the same time, however, it encouraged workers to demand the full product of their labor. Even in the first decade of the century, Adam Smith's elaboration of labor's commodity form in *The Wealth of Nations* served as a handbook for working-class radicals who objected to sharing the product of labor with employers. The complex network of response and counterresponse engendered by a particular commodity form shows that the adoption of that form did not offer either side a straightforward instrumental benefit.[99]

The German workers' treatment of time as a form of property guided their articulation of grievances about workloads. In both Germany and Britain, weavers opposed their employers' efforts to have each weaver tend more looms, a contest that reemerged in different periods during the nineteenth century for each kind of fabric manufactured. But in Germany, weavers saw the introduction of more looms per worker not just as an intensification of effort but as a prolongation of work time. For instance, a speaker at the weaving conference in Crimmitschau in 1910 said that if weavers operate an additional loom, it "is indirectly an extension of work time. We must try to combat this with all the strength at our disposal."[100] German weavers converted an issue of concrete effort into a matter of the employer effectively controlling more time.

---

norm; rather, they actively embraced it. The execution of practices in the factory reproduced specifications of labor without agents either cynically choosing which concept of labor to use or helplessly internalizing the concept.

99. The struggles conducted within the regime established by a particular commodity form also show that the shape of labor as a ware provided the signs and cultural definitions out of which those practices were forged through conflict, not a pattern decreed from on high. David M. Schneider, "Notes Toward a Theory of Culture," in Keith H. Basso and Henry A. Selby, editors, *Meaning in Anthropology* (Albuquerque: University of New Mexico Press, 1976), p. 219.

100. Verband Deutscher Textilarbeiter, op. cit., p. 51.

The contest that developed in Germany over the allocation of time did not just concern the total remuneration to which workers could lay claim. It revolved around the point at which the employer converted labor power into a product. Accordingly, strike demands about the use of time followed a different pattern in Germany than in Britain. German workers agitated for adjustments in the partitioning of the workday, not just for changes in its length. A recurring issue for German strikers was how the hours of the day, which as a rule in the late nineteenth century totaled at least ten, would be divided between morning and afternoon. For 1899 through 1906, the years in which official enumerations of the separate demands lodged by German workers in strikes have survived, the textile industry experienced thirty-five outbreaks in which workers lodged requests for changes in the periods for rest pauses, extensions in the lunch break (although this meant workers would labor until later in the evening), or other demands related to the apportionment of the work hours. Workers contested the allotment of time, which sometimes comprised the sole ground for strikes, under many different structures of workdays. Where the lunch pauses lasted an hour, they wanted one and a half; where one and half, they wanted two.[101]

German workers bargained down to the requisitioning of small time fragments. Consider the long strike of weavers in Neumünster in 1888. Over one hundred workers there sustained a labor stoppage for two and a half months because employers refused to extend the lunch hour an extra fifteen minutes.[102] In Luckenwalde the female workers in a weaving room launched a strike in 1904 to gain the right to a ten-minute wash-up break each day.[103] Every fraction of time conceded to workers by, say, extending a

101. HSTAD, Regierung Düsseldorf, 25025, August 8, 1892. Wirtschaftsarchiv Baden-Württemberg, Stuttgart, B25-319, June 15, 1906. When German workers began to voice demands for the ten-hour day, they characteristically attached this to a scheme specifying long breakfast and lunch breaks. For an example from the metal industry in 1872, see Lothar Machtan, "'Es war ein wundervolles Gefühl, dass man nicht allein war': Streik als Hoffnung und Erfahrung," in Wolfgang Ruppert, editor, *Die Arbeiter* (München: C. H. Beck, 1986), p. 264.

102. Klaus Tidow, *Neumünsters Textil- und Lederindustrie im 19. Jahrhundert* (Neumünster: Karl Wachholtz, 1984), p. 32.

103. *Der Textil-Arbeiter*, October 14, 1904, Luckenwalde. Analogously, for negotiations over a five-minute wash break, see Stadtarchiv Crimmitschau, Rep. III, Kap. IX, Lit. B, Nr. 23, Jan. 4, 1904, pp. 298–300. For other accounts of strikes over the timing of brief pauses, Zentrales Staatsarchiv Merseburg, 120 BB VII 1, Nr. 3, Volume 12, 1906, Sommerfeld; *Der Christliche Textilarbeiter*, April 1, 1905, Mönchengladbach. Textile workers in Thalheim struck in 1889 for ten-minute extensions of the lunch and late-afternoon breaks and for receipt of pay earlier on Saturday afternoons. Staatsarchiv Dresden, Amtshauptmannschaft Chemnitz, Nr. 10, June 29, 1889, pp. 4–5.

cleaning break from five to ten minutes comprised in their eyes a significant victory.[104] Not surprisingly, when the textile union in Saxony surveyed the arrangement of workdays in its district, it found some byzantine schedules. The conflict over the apportionment of tiny intervals led to some markedly irregular lunch periods, such as one hour and twenty-five minutes, or to rotating fifteen- and twenty-minute early and afternoon breaks.[105]

Apart from disputing the allocation of work time over the day, textile workers in Germany distinguished themselves by contesting the days of the week when they would deliver their labor power, given a fixed number of hours. For instance, textile workers struck at a mill in Augsburg in 1914 when the employer responded to a downturn by eliminating work on Mondays. The workers demanded that Saturday be free instead. In this instance the struggle was in no way confused with commercial issues of profit and loss, but related solely to authority over time: the employer denied workers their long-held dream of enjoying Saturday off even when the low volume of production could have fulfilled it.[106] When German workers contested the regulation of working hours, they emphasized the delivery of time as an abstract potential that employers consumed. For example, when German workers complained about having to work so many days, they said they "had to put their meager day of rest at the disposal of their employer."[107]

German workers and employers who saw time itself as a kind of property fought at innumerable points, not just over the total amount of time whose ownership would change hands, but when it would do so. In Britain, by contrast, the partitioning of the workday, given a fixed duration, almost never became the touchstone for workers' collective action. The Board of Trade provided a complete enumeration of the strike demands lodged in textiles for the years from 1889 to 1900. In only a single instance did British textile workers request a change in the distribution, given a fixed sum of hours. And even the circumstances surrounding this case seem deviant. It

104. In Werdau, the women workers succeeded in having wash-up time extended from five to ten minutes. Deutscher Textilarbeiterverband, op. cit., p. 41.

105. Verband Deutscher Textilarbeiter, Gau Thüringen, *Tariferläuterungen und Statistisches: Bearbeitet nach Aufzeichnungen der Tarif-Kommission im sächsisch-thüringischen Textilbezirk*, p. 59. It appears that the only British equivalent to this fragmented scheduling was the partial shifts assigned to juveniles in Britain under pressure of the Factory Acts. In this instance, however, employers designed the partitioning of the workday on their own, sometimes with a view to evading the acts. United Kingdom, "Reports of the Inspectors of Factories," PP 1837–1838 XLV, quarter ending June 30, 1838, p. 7.

106. *Der Textil-Arbeiter*, February 27, 1914, p. 66.

107. *Der Textil-Arbeiter*, June 27, 1902, Elberfeld.

occurred at a mill in Dundee whose weavers had been placed on a shortened work week in 1894 due to a business slowdown. They insisted on reducing the number of days they worked each week rather than continuing on brief shifts six days a week.[108] British workers were ready, of course, to protest long workdays. But as a rule, the time sense of British workers paralleled that of the employers: the passage of the workday was not divided into minute increments, with the appropriation of singular moments being contested. Rather, the workday was a block of time during which workers created the products that were to be transferred to employers.

Would it have been more advantageous for British textile workers to have pursued the same demands as did their German counterparts? This question is unanswerable, for the focus among British workers on improving piece rates for cloth delivered may well have given them a higher return for their labor than they would otherwise have enjoyed. Culture guided but in no way blocked workers' struggles for improvements.[109]

REAL ABSTRACTIONS

This chapter calls attention to a new method for attaching workers' articulation of discontent to the structure of the production process and, ultimately, offers a way of linking the domains of social experience and discourse. Cultural historians of labor have recently emphasized that the development of workers' grievances does not parallel the evolution of the conditions of work. These critics have contended that workers' grievances, instead of reflecting the material circumstances or institutional structure of production, depend principally upon discursive resources and the organization of the public sphere in which complaints can be lodged and debated.[110] For instance, in *Work and Wages*, his exemplary study of prerevolutionary artisanal conflicts in France, Michael Sonenscher detaches (changing) discursive practices from the (unvarying) organization of work itself.[111]

108. "Strikes and Lockouts in 1894," PP 1895 XCII, Dundee.

109. For a discussion of the distinction between analyses that treat culture as a set of norms and those, such as that of this study, that view culture as a set of assumptions that facilitate agents' pursuit of interests, see Paul DiMaggio, "Interest and Agency in Institutional Theory," in Lynne Zucker, editor, *Institutional Patterns and Organizations: Culture and Environment* (Cambridge, Massachusetts: Ballinger Publishing Co., 1988), p. 5.

110. Tony Judt, *Marxism and the French Left* (Oxford: Clarendon Press, 1986), pp. 27, 102–103, 112.

111. Sonenscher suggests that artisans' unprecedented complaints about competitive individualism in France during the early nineteenth century represented a new rhetorical strategy

The present chapter shows instead that the signifying processes incorporated into the concrete procedures of work configured the concepts to which workers would have ready access for verbal analyses of the employment relation. Through their experience of the symbolic instrumentalities of production, such as the piece-rate scales, workers acquired their understanding of labor as a commodity and their expectations for its use in the same way that Pascal allegedly would have advised them to acquire religious conviction: "Kneel down, move your lips in prayer, and you will believe."[112] They derived the categories of the discourse of complaint from their lived experience at the point of production, as is confirmed by the very manner in which weavers conceptualized their output. For example, German weavers who worked with piece-rate scales that centered the categories of payment on the execution of the labor activity could judge changes in output by the number of shots inserted in the course of a time interval rather than by the length of cloth delivered. At a meeting of textile workers in Cottbus in 1903, a discussant described in this manner the exploitation of weavers' labor: "Whereas a loom used to give forty-five shots per minute, the new looms have raised this to 105 shots per minute and now three hundred thousand shots are demanded each week from a worker on a new loom."[113] This speaker expressed the additional work extracted in terms of the movements executed in a day—that is, in terms of the metered expenditure of labor power rather than the dimensions of requisitioned fabric.[114] Verbal analysis followed the culturally variable ideas embedded in the execution of work for a wage.

To affirm the symbolic constitution of experience, historians influenced by post-structuralist philosophy, including Joan Scott, have emphasized the

---

to justify allegiance to voluntary business associations. To his mind, the criticism of cut-throat self-aggrandizement after the revolution did not reflect the breakdown of intimate and customary paternal relations in the workshop, for these had corroded under the ancien régime. Michael Sonenscher, *Work and Wages: Natural Law, Politics and the Eighteenth-Century French Trades* (Cambridge: Cambridge University Press, 1989), p. 371.

112. Louis Althusser, *Lenin and Philosophy and Other Essays* (New York: Monthly Review Press, 1971), p. 168.

113. Stadtarchiv Cottbus, A II 33 b, Nr. 34, February 8, 1903. Likewise, the linen weavers of Greiz in 1857 said that they were able to insert nine thousand units of yarn in the course of a year if they had no interruptions, but only eight thousand units if they had responsibility for supervising journeymen. Staatsarchiv Weimar, Landesregierung Greiz, a Rep. A, Kap. XXI/2c, Nr. 400, Petition of May 20, 1857.

114. The conflict of interest between workers and employers was cast in an illusory form, as if the expenditure of labor power could be calibrated as a thing with a value imposed by an objective force. Karl Marx, *Das Kapital* (Berlin: Dietz Verlag, 1980), Volume One, pp. 91–92.

linguistic mediation of social experience. In so doing they have come peril-ously close to severing the nondiscursive from the domain of experience.[115] A focus upon the cultural construction of material practices allows us to reconnect language and social experience without reducing one to the other. Practice is not composed of arbitrary signifiers and does not follow a scripted logic to advance its propositions. This comparative inquiry suggests, how-ever, that as the fixtures of production are employed as signs, they create a shared conceptual experience of the ongoing execution of material practice and thereby supply the constituents—although not the syntax—of formal discourse. Important national differences in workers' experience developed from the immediate execution of practice, apart from the intervention of language—that is, from a symbolically constituted order of reality that is distinct from the mere representation of the world via the divisions of language.

If workers brought into the realm of collective action and trade union struggle that specification of labor as a commodity which is embodied in the material performance of production, this reinforces the importance of the labor process for the formation of workers' discourse about labor, but it does not compel a return to the older view that this discourse reflects the material conditions of production. For if symbolic instrumentalities at the point of production—such as the operation of the piece-rate systems—guided the formation of discourse about exploitation, these instrumentalities are not the outgrowth of adaptation to the actual conditions of the environment. Production is not another order of reality more veracious than discursive practice. If I dare cite the words of Althusser, who has more to contribute to cultural history than most would nowadays admit, what workers' com-plaints express is not "the real conditions which govern the existence of individuals, but the imaginary relation of those individuals to the real rela-tions in which they live."[116]

In both Britain and Germany, the cultural specification of labor's com-modity form rested on preposterous assumptions. British employers and workers supposed that labor could literally be embodied in a product that served as a vessel to transfer it—as if human activity could become a sub-stance. As a matter of principle, the textile workers' labor no more resides

115. Joan Wallach Scott insists that language does not reflect a reality external to it but is "constitutive of that reality." "On Language, Gender, and Working-Class History," in her *Gender and the Politics of History* (New York: Columbia University Press, 1988), p. 57.

116. Althusser, op. cit., p. 165.

in the output than do the other elements that contribute to the creation of the fabric, such as the factory's land.[117] The labor said to be incorporated in the ware reflects a social relation between producers, namely, the relative expenditures of labor time socially necessary for them to create the product—not something materialized in a discrete product. The German specification of labor's commodity form supposed that the employer could purchase time itself and that the expenditure of concrete labor power actually created value. In truth, of course, the use of labor as a factor of production does not create value: the value is conferred by the social relations structuring the activity, not by, say, the observable motions of the shuttle. Likewise, it is absurd to suppose that one can purchase the disposition over workers' time as a thing; time is the medium through which the disposition over human relations is expressed, not an item with a price.[118] Karl Polanyi perspicaciously referred to labor power as an "alleged commodity."[119] But what could only be claimed metaphorically in theory was in the practice of production affirmed as a fact in reality.

117. Marx, op. cit., Volume Three, p. 831.

118. "As far as labor assumes the specifically social character of wage labor, it is not *wertbildend.*" Karl Marx and Friedrich Engels, *Marx-Engels Werke,* Volume 25 (Berlin: Dietz Verlag, 1964), p. 831.

119. Karl Polanyi, *The Great Transformation* (Boston: Beacon Press, 1957), p. 73.

9   Theories of Exploitation in the Workers' Movements

All theory is grey unless it builds upon practical experience.
Fach-Zeitung: Organ des Niederrheinischen
Weber-Verbandes, July 16, 1899

If an analysis of the fabrication of labor as a commodity clarifies the installation of business practices—and thus people's engagement with culture as they come to terms with the commercial universe—it can also elucidate the other side of history: people's engagement with culture as they attempt to transcend that commercial universe. How did the fabrication of labor as a commodity influence workers' understanding of the fundamental sources of economic inequities? Did it guide their reception of formal political ideologies? Did the contrasting notions of labor as a ware that were lived in the humdrum routines of manufacture in Germany and Britain inspire contrasting dreams of the supercession of capitalism?

Historians of nineteenth-century labor and socialist movements have attributed an explanatory significance to culture in two fundamentally different ways. Following the example of E. P. Thompson, many investigators have assigned culture an enabling role as a creator of varying responses among workers. These inquirers associate culture with workers' creative agency. More recently, however, examiners such as Gareth Stedman Jones have assigned culture an explanatory role as a kind of restrictive structure, underscoring its function as an autonomous system of concepts that channel workers' insights and expression.[1] Although both approaches have proven

---

1. *Culture,* the set of collectively shared signs that both structure and create an experience of practice, has become an enigmatic term in social inquiry because it both constricts and broadens human conduct. The mystery stems not from conceptual incoherence but from the multiple effects of signs in social life. This study's examination of manufacturing institutions proceeded by showing that culture limited conduct by selecting the forms that practices on the factory shop floor assumed in economically similar environments. Yet the fictions of labor as a commodity also enlarged the scope of action, for they created multiple and equally viable principles for organizing the labor transaction in nations undergoing a generically similar, epochal process of commercialization. On the one hand, the intervention of culture gave

their fertility, they are both demonstrably inadequate for the task of this chapter, that of explaining why workers in Britain and Germany developed contrasting ideologies of capitalist exploitation. Let us appraise the two prevailing views of culture to see how uncovering the cultural structure of the workplace offers a different means of explaining workers' adoption of specific political ideologies.

THE PLACE OF CULTURE
IN LABOR MOVEMENTS

As a pioneer investigator of workers' embrace of oppositional ideas, E. P. Thompson's writings express in pure form the tensions inherent in cultural analyses of workers' movements that underspecify culture's constitutive role in the labor process itself. In *The Making of the English Working Class*, skilled craftspeople, domestic weavers, field laborers, and the new textile operatives are described as having contrasting social experiences but making common cause by drawing upon the inherited discourses of the "free-born Englishman" and of radical republicanism to interpret their predicaments and to imagine alternatives. Their receptivity to political beliefs comes from their individual experiences of a more ruthless use of labor.[2] But, given this exposure, what match between workers' social being and the political ideologies of the day permitted workers to take up as their own the ideals of cooperative manufacture and political reform that were initially formulated by prosperous artisans and middle-class radicals?

To cast the issue more concretely, does Thompson mean to tell us that given a different political legacy among the middle classes in England, workers in the early nineteenth century would not have acquired a shared class identity? Or, if *some* variety of class consciousness inevitably follows capitalist development (a vexing question for Thompson's argument), how did workers' experience of labor establish the range of ideas they could receive favorably? Thompson, as a man of letters, believed that incertitude suited his humanist goals.[3] The commemoration of indeterminacy fulfills an hon-

---

producers and manufacturers principles for action apart from the exigencies of the immediate economic environment; on the other, it enmeshed these agents in a realm of meaningful practices that constrained their understanding of social relations.

2. *The Making of the English Working Class* (New York: Vintage Books, 1963), p. 258.

3. The extraordinary moral tone of *The Making* resonates with Thompson's analytic insistence that political culture had to transcend workers' social existence; the tenor *is* one of transcendence. The working class fights as a kind of heroic agent that suffers worldly trials, triumphs over ordinary experience, and finally surpasses the world by leaving an imperishable memory of its deeds. *The Making* is emplotted as a "Romance," to borrow the sense for that

orable commitment to human self-making, but it scarcely offers a foundation for a program of research into the forces shaping the adoption of ideologies in workers' collective movements.

Thompson's inexactitude makes a virtue of necessity. It follows unavoidably from his perspective on the labor process. In conceptualizing the generation of work experience, he "humanizes" the point of production in a peculiar fashion. He views the workplace as a site of personal experience, not as a set of practices patterned by culture;[4] he highlights the subjective side of productive relations, not their cultural *structure*.[5] Given this foundation, either the development and endorsement of particular complexes of political ideas appears capricious, an historical miracle in which the common people transcend the limitations of their social existence; or, alternatively, if the historical process is explained by the circumstances of workers' productive life, it is reduced to a mechanical reflection of crude material distress and economic compulsion.

This latter choice, irreconcilable as it seems with the tenor of Thompson's work as a whole, commands the argument of many passages in *The Making*. For example, artisans' sympathetic reception of Paine's *The Rights of Man* fluctuated with their standard of living. "Jacobin ideas driven into weaving villages, the shops of the Nottingham framework-knitters and the Yorkshire croppers, the Lancashire cotton-mills," he says, "were propagated in every phase of rising prices and of hardship."[6] In his account of the Luddite movement's vision of political upheaval and insurrectionary objectives,

---

term that Hayden White chose in *Metahistory* (Baltimore: Johns Hopkins University Press, 1973).

4. See discussion of Thompson above, Chapter One, at footnotes 47–48.

5. Thompson's view of the labor process is aptly described as "experiential" rather than "cultural." The distinction is made by William Sewell, Jr., "How Classes Are Made: Critical Reflections on E. P. Thompson's Theory of Working-Class Formation," in Harvey J. Kaye and Keith McClelland, editors, *E. P. Thompson: Critical Perspectives* (Philadelphia: Temple University Press, 1990), p. 67. Thompson equates culture with "consciousness" in "The Peculiarities of the English," in Ralph Miliband and John Saville, editors, *The Socialist Register* (New York: Monthly Review Press, 1965), p. 351. Although centered more often on the ignominious decline of the labor movement than on its heroic birth, "Alltagsgeschichte" shares this tendency to see culture either as something opposed to structure or as the subjective moment of structure but, in either case, as something that does not comprise a structure in its own right. See, illustratively, Alf Lüdtke, "Rekonstruktion von Alltagswirklichkeit—Entpolitisierung der Sozialgeschichte?" in Robert Berdahl et al., editors, *Klassen und Kultur* (Frankfurt am Main: Syndikat, 1982), pp. 330, 338–339.

6. Op. cit., p. 185. Thompson also cites the Manchester historian Prentice: "'A new instructor was busy amongst the masses—WANT'" (p. 142; cf. p. 184). Or, to cite another instance, the thinking of Thelwall, an interpreter of Jacobinism, appears bound by the artisan's economic interests (p. 160).

Thompson claims, "People were so hungry that they were willing to risk their lives upsetting a barrow of potatoes. In these conditions, it might appear more surprising if men had *not* plotted revolutionary uprisings than if they *had*."[7] Contrary to his own intentions, Thompson resorts to these pictures of mechanical response when he seeks not only to describe but to *explain* workers' reception of new ideas.

In similar fashion, Patrick Joyce adopts reductionist explanations in spite of himself in his sensitive analyses of Victorian factories. He draws correspondences between workers' political visions and the objective features of work. For example, in *Work, Society and Politics* Joyce explains the decline of political radicalism in the textile districts after midcentury as the result of "the power of mechanisation to re-cast the social experience of the worker."[8] The decline of workers' independent political movements, he asserts, mirrored the erosion of their autonomy in the labor process.[9] The supposition that the formulation and acceptance of political ideologies reflects the conditions of production, rejected in his theory, is embraced in his history.[10]

The institutions and manufacturing procedures of the workplace, for Joyce as for Thompson, become technological and economic givens, not because these investigators would assert that work obeys only economic and technical determinations, but insofar as these elements are the only ones they treat as *systemic* forces in the construction of workplace procedures.

---

7. Ibid., p. 592. Consider also Thompson's reference to the pace of capital accumulation and to the stages of technical change in his closing eulogy to a distinguished artisanal culture (pp. 830–831).

8. Patrick Joyce, *Work, Society and Politics* (London: Methuen, 1982), p. 80.

9. Op. cit., ibid., pp. 81–82; Patrick Joyce, *Visions of the People: Industrial England and the Question of Class 1848–1914* (Cambridge: Cambridge University Press, 1991), p. 88. Since the factory workers who occupied the same positions of dependency joined the burgeoning socialist movement in the quarter-century before the First World War, however, this structural explanation for political identities must be incomplete. No wonder another labor historian, Richard Price, adopted the same transition from the "formal" to the "real" subsumption of labor in the workplace to explain precisely the opposite outcome: the *rise* of labor militancy in the late 1880s. "The New Unionism and the Labour Process," in Wolfgang J. Mommsen and Hans-Gerhard Husung, editors, *The Development of Trade Unionism in Great Britain and Germany, 1880–1914* (London: George Allen & Unwin, 1985), pp. 133–149.

10. In *Visions of the People*, Joyce emphasizes in his methodological preface that the ability of language to constitute experience has dissolved "the old assurance of a formative link between social structure and culture." Yet in this recent work, too, the brute fact of mechanization is cited as a cause of workers' new feelings of insecurity and a constriction of their cultural horizons to the established capitalist order. Op. cit., pp. 9, 88. Analogously, see Joyce's inferences from the delegation of authority on the shop floor to populist accommodations to capitalism (p. 119).

Joyce's unwitting reductionism issues from the same source as Thompson's: it results from leaving in place an unreconstructed, implicitly economic view of the development of the factory labor process, which makes possible the explication of determinant connections between the labor process and the acceptance of ideas only by forcing ideas to reflect the economic aspects of work.[11]

Gareth Stedman Jones arrived at an alternative understanding of culture and work by following Thompson's problematic to a different terminus. In the acclaimed essay "Rethinking Chartism," he argued that workers in early industrial Britain discovered their interests through the political language of Chartism, and thus historians ought not to envision social classes with prior economic interests turning to a political medium. Rather, workers' primary experiences in work were constituted from the start by an inherited political language.[12] Yet this linguistic model inhibits explanation of the vitality and acceptance of insurgent ideas. What kept the framework of radical ideas intact in the first half of the nineteenth century despite the proliferation of diverse protest movements and despite great change in the organization of the labor movement? Why did British workers not evolve an alternative discourse of resistance shortly after 1842, if, as Stedman Jones says, the radicals' emphasis on Parliament's responsibility for economic

11. Perhaps I do Thompson and Joyce an injustice here. Thompson in his methodological reflections remains too wary of abstractions to suppose that the "productive process" comprises a merely economic relation. In *The Poverty of Theory*, for example, he insists that economic transactions can also be examined as cultural practices. But few researchers follow their own prescriptions. Even in this methodological essay, Thompson restricts his illustrations of culture in production to ancient customs of exchange in the "moral economy" which industrialization broke apart (op. cit., p. 292) or to the socialization of the actors *outside* of production (p. 294). These very examples rest on implicit contrasts with modern, instrumentally determined practices at the point of production; in *The Making*, those contrasts become explicit. When Thompson contests the formula that steam power plus cotton mills equals a new working class, the variable he wants to include for a more balanced equation, inherited tradition, refers primarily to a culture that is rooted in community relations, relations *outside* of production. The logic of both political resistance movements and Methodism is that they allow people to express, outside of production, that cultural animation which is suppressed, and in Thompson's account, temporarily deactivated, inside the industrial labor process itself. *The Making*, op. cit., p. 446. Likewise, Joyce coins the phrase the "culture of the factory," but this culture is lodged primarily in expressive activities such as social parties and teas or in loyalties that are in some way the offspring of the necessities of work but that do not define the labor process itself. Indeed, culture grows out of the factory when people are not at work, when instead they gossip during breaks or sing "as and when the tasks to hand permitted." *Visions*, op. cit., pp. 131–132.

12. *Languages of Class* (Cambridge: Cambridge University Press, 1983), p. 95. In the introduction to this set of essays, Jones expresses even more forcefully the assumption that identities are shaped in politics rather than through labor: "It is the discursive structure of political language which conceives and defines interest in the first place" (p. 22).

oppression rang increasingly false after that date? Were laborers and their spokespersons incapable of articulating more resonant interpretations of their social predicaments? To address these questions of change and persistence, Stedman Jones would have to consider the connections between political ideas and the workers' lived experience—a divide which brings one back to Thompson's starting point.

By deciphering the signifying processes embedded in the labor process, the present study offers an alternative perspective which bridges workers' experience of production and their reception of public discourse without resorting to economic reductionism. Workers' experience of production did not develop as the subjective side of economic and technological conditions, but emerged through an engagement with the cluster of cultural signs that defined material practices. The definitions of labor that were communicated in the execution of work offered a foundation for the receipt of economic philosophies and radical programs of change.

A PUZZLE IN THE WORKERS' RECEPTION OF IDEAS

During the last decade of the nineteenth century, workers and employers in both Britain and Germany believed they were witnessing a revolution in the labor movement. In Germany this decade was marked by a surge in union membership and by the widespread adoption of a Marxist discourse.[13] In Britain many trade unions during this same period adopted the goal of developing a socialist society. Membership in all trade unions of the United Kingdom rose from 750,000 in 1888 to over two million in 1901. In the country's textile industry, union membership doubled.[14] The endorsement of socialism, though confined to a minority of unions, and rise in membership represented a significant departure from the previous history of British labor.

The textile employers in Britain believed that the new ideology of the unions represented a momentous pullback from their previous support for the settled customs of industrial relations. The businessmen's newspaper

13. Membership in the Social Democratic unions rose from 300,000 in 1890 to 2.5 million in 1913. For an overview, consult Mary Nolan, "Economic Crisis, State Policy, and Working-Class Formation in Germany, 1870–1900," in Ira Katznelson and Aristide R. Zolber, editors, *Working-Class Formation* (Princeton: Princeton University Press, 1986), pp. 378–393.

14. H. A. Clagg, Allan Fox, and A. F. Thompson, *A History of British Trade Unions Since 1889* (Oxford: Clarendon Press, 1964), p. 468.

the *Textile Mercury* took note of the changed atmosphere as early as 1890. This journal said, "The introduction of socialistic principles into English trades-unionism has completely transformed the character of the latter. . . . It is now unrecognizable in its objects, aims, and the means it is using to attain them compared with the trades-unionism of only ten or fifteen years ago."[15] In a column entitled "The Apotheosis of Labour," the journal's editors concluded in the fall of 1890 that "almost everything is being turned topsy-turvy."[16]

During these "topsy-turvy" years of change, continuing up to the First World War, Marxist economic discourse found a ready audience among literate workers in Germany, whereas among workers in Britain it fell on unprepared and partially closed ears. Is it reasonable to conclude that the German workers and their avowed spokespersons, in contrast to their counterparts in Britain, were frustrated by their confrontations with the autocratic German state and found Marxism congenial because they preferred an uncompromising program of change? Professed approval of Marx's analysis of the capitalist production process was neither sufficient nor necessary for support of a strong agenda for social transformation. Although articulate members of the trade unions in Britain proved resistant to Marx's analysis of the extraction of surplus value from labor power, they nonetheless endorsed programs for a dramatic reordering that included the seizure of state power and collectivization of the means of production.[17] Conversely, in Germany some members of workers' organizations who endorsed Marx's economic analyses shrank from attacks upon the state or from calls for the expropriation of capitalist enterprise. The Social Democrat Carl August Schramm offers a well-known example of the divergent political uses to which Marx's economic analysis could be put. Schramm, an early, accomplished initiate into Marx's analysis of the generation of surplus value, combated party members' strengthening endorsement during the 1880s of

---

15. *Textile Mercury*, August 30, 1890, p. 141.

16. *Textile Mercury*, September 27, 1890, p. 210. The members of the Bradford Textile Society also captured the mood of change. In 1895, in an editorial about "Trades Unionism," they remarked, "Everything seems to point out that a great change is about to take place in our commercial and industrial system." *Journal of the Bradford Textile Society* Volume I, Number 5 (February 1895).

17. *Yorkshire Factory Times*, May 13, 1892, Oakworth. The Burnley weavers' union rules in 1892 called for "socialisation of the means of production." Geoffrey Trodd, "Political Change and the Working Class in Blackburn and Burnley 1880–1914," Ph.D. diss., University of Lancaster, 1978, p. 341.

the necessity of political revolution.[18] Likewise, in the 1890s the free trade unions helped disseminate Marx's economic doctrines but at the same time tried to moderate the influence of radicals in the Social Democratic party who were advocating forceful challenges to the political institutions of the old regime.[19] These considerations remind us that Marx's economic analysis could be accepted or repudiated apart from any belief in the need for political revolution.[20] Instead of serving as an index of radicalization, Marx's examination of the capitalist employment relation must be approached for what it is, a system of ideas that can be endorsed or discarded by workers or their avowed spokespersons for its perceived logic and plausibility.

In Marx's analysis of workers' exploitation in the capitalist system of production, as finally presented in *Kapital*, employers adhered to the principles of equitable market transactions. As with the purchase of any commodity, they paid living labor its full exchange value when they appropriated its use value. The degradation of labor did not occur because capitalists added interest and profit to the value of the labor embodied in the finished commodity before they disposed of the commodity in the market, or because capitalists used their power over dependent workers to subvert the operation of a market in labor power. Instead, employers used unpaid labor time at the point of production. If workers did not imagine they sold their labor in the form of "labor power," they could envision that the labor time they put into products for the employer was more than the labor time embodied in the products that they received in return, via their wage. But they could not conceive that employers exploited the difference between the exchange value and use value of labor time at the work site. The cultural constitution of factory practices encouraged members of the labor movement in Britain to focus on the unfair exchange of products in the market, as the histories both of the early socialist movement in Britain and of the reappearance of socialism in the last quarter of the nineteenth century demonstrate. In Germany, by contrast, Marx's dissection of the extraction of surplus at the site of production enjoyed a magnified resonance.

18. Hans-Josef Steinberg, *Sozialismus und deutsche Sozialdemokratie* (Hannover: Verlag für Literatur und Zeitgeschehen, 1967), pp. 17–18. For background on Schramm's continued belief in working toward state aid for producer cooperatives, see Wolf-Ulrich Jorke, "Rezeptions- und Wirkungsgeschichte von Lassalles politischer Theorie in der deutschen Arbeiterbewegung," diss., Bochum, 1973, pp. 17–18.

19. Carl Schorske, *German Social Democracy 1905–1917* (New York: John Wiley and Sons, 1955), pp. 108 ff.

20. Eduard Bernstein, *Von der Sekte zur Partei* (Jena: Eugen Diederichs, 1911), p. 23.

ECONOMIC IDEOLOGIES IN THE WORKERS' MOVEMENTS OF BRITAIN

The recreation of a socialist labor movement in Britain during the last two decades of the nineteenth century invented for a second time the explanation for the exploitation of labor that had developed in the heroic decades of the 1820s and 1830s. In the earlier era, radical political economy supported the rise of a popular conviction that workers could collectively shape their destinies. As a letter writer to the *Co-operative Magazine* in 1826 proclaimed, "Labourers are beginning to think for themselves. And turning their attention to that science, which treats of the production and distribution of wealth."[21] Middle-class educators such as the temperate Francis Place grew alarmed at workers' independent reshaping of this science. Place included Thomas Hodgskin, whose essay *Labour Defended Against the Claims of Capital* grew out of personal experience in the London trades, among those who had caused "incalculable" mischief.[22] During this period political economy became a staple of the labor movement's discourse instead of an esoteric body of theorems.[23]

The view of the labor transaction that prevailed among these early working-class representatives was that of labor being exchanged as it had already taken shape in an object. William Thompson emphasized this mode of conveyance when he wrote in *Labour Rewarded* in 1827, "It is not the differ-

21. *The Co-operative Magazine and Monthly Herald* Volume I, Number 2 (February 1826), p. 64.

22. *The Making,* op. cit., p. 778; quotation on p. 807. Hodgskin edited the *Mechanics' Magazine* before writing *Labour Defended*. Karl-Josef Burkard, *Thomas Hodgskins Kritik der Politischen Ökonomie* (Hannover: SOAK Verlag, 1980), pp. 8, 219. The first clear point of contact between the working-class movement and the labor economists is publication of a review of Hodgskin's *Labour Defended* in *Trades Newspaper* in 1825. See the copious documentation of the popular appreciation of Hodgskin in Noel Thompson, *The People's Science: The Popular Political Economy of Exploitation and Crisis 1816–1834* (Cambridge: Cambridge University Press, 1984), pp. 12–13. This exemplary study of the British economists' focus on the mechanisms of exchange provides the foundation for the following section.

23. Jones, op. cit., pp. 114–115, 133–134 note. For other references to the importance of political economy for workers' formulations, see H. Dutton and J. E. King, *"Ten Percent and No Surrender": The Preston Strike, 1853–54* (Cambridge: Cambridge University Press, 1981), pp. 55–56; T. W. Hutchison, *On Revolutions and Progress in Economic Knowledge* (Cambridge: Cambridge University Press, 1978), p. 59; Simon Dentith, "Political Economy, Fiction and the Language of Practical Ideology in Nineteenth-Century England," *Social History* Volume 8, Number 2 (May 1983), pp. 183–199; Max Goldstrom, "Popular Political Economy for the British Working Class Reader in the Nineteenth Century," in Terry Shinn and Richard Whitley, editors, *Expository Science: Forms and Functions of Popularisation* (Dordrecht: D. Reidel, 1985), p. 270.

ences of production in different laborers, but the complicated system of exchanges of those productions *when made*, that gives rise to . . . frightful inequality of wealth."[24] The "higgling of the market," not the subordination of labor in production, denied workers the full produce of their labor.[25]

This view of the exchange of materialized labor did not arise from observers whose horizons were limited by the world of small craftshops. The press of the common people, which regularly surveyed and elaborated upon the ideas of Thompson, Hodgskin, and other economists, was perfectly cognizant of the new regimens and tactics of control deployed in the large textile mills. Popular writers in the industrial North formulated economic principles based on the conveyance of materialized labor as they studied the centralization of production under the eye of the mill owner. *The Poor Man's Advocate*, which covered problems in textile mills, drew an analogy between the consumer who bought finished cloth in a store and the mill owner who bought a quantity of labor from his workers.[26]

The popular economists were capable of describing a difference between labor and its product when they discussed the manufacture of goods, but they did not theorize about the meaning of this difference for the wage contract. William Thompson, in *An Inquiry into the Principles of the Distribution of Wealth*, drew a pregnant distinction between the products of labor and labor itself, defined as "that productive energy which called wealth into being."[27] Seldom did British authors distinguish so carefully between the two as Thompson did.[28] But in this work, printed in 1824, Thompson's very identification of the difference showed that in the end he did not imagine that under the regime of commercial liberalism surplus was appro-

---

24. William Thompson, *Labour Rewarded* (London: Hunt & Clarke, 1827), p. 12. Emphasis added. Thomas Hodgskin described the capitalist as someone who has "power over the produce of labor." Thomas Hodgskin, *Popular Political Economy* (New York: Augustus Kelley, 1966 [1827]), p. 245.

25. W. Thompson, op. cit., pp. 12, 36.

26. *The Poor Man's Advocate*, January 21, 1832, p. 1. *The Operative*, which catered to the interests of factory workers, also emphasized the market as the site of exploitation. See discussion of economics on February 3, 1839. We cannot deduce workers' understanding of the exchange of labor for a wage from the brute fact that they are inserted into large-scale industry, as one analyst has unfortunately assumed. Craig Calhoun, *The Question of Class Struggle* (Chicago: University of Chicago Press, 1982), p. 117.

27. *An Inquiry into the Principles of the Distribution of Wealth* (New York: Burt Franklin, 1968 [1824]), p. 88.

28. John Bray briefly refers to the sale of labor and products of labor but says both amount to the sale of "labour for labour." Then the example immediately following illustrates only the exchange of finished products. *Labour's Wrongs and Labour's Remedy* (Leeds: David Green, 1839), p. 48.

priated from the labor activity itself, only from labor's products. For example, in his chapter entitled "Labour Must Receive Its Full Equivalent," Thompson pondered the seizure of "labor itself":

> Take away what labour *has* produced, or anticipate and seize on, as it were beforehand, what labor is *about* to produce: where is the difference in the operation? Where the difference in pernicious effects? If any, the difference would be in favor of seizing the products after production rather than anticipating them, because the relaxation of the producing industry is avoided where the products already exist, and the effect of discouragement would be only against *future* productions. But where the labour is compelled, the product itself to be seized upon is raised and completed with diminished energy.[29]

Thompson equated the appropriation of the workers' labor capacity with reliance upon "compelled," slave labor, not the incentives of marketed wage labor.[30] From his standpoint, employers under the new regime of capitalism sequestered, not labor itself, but its products.

With this appreciation of labor as a commodity in mind, the early British socialists formulated a coherent set of propositions that placed the capitalist in the role of a middleman. "Betwixt him who produces food and him who produces clothing, betwixt him who makes instruments and him who uses them," wrote Thomas Hodgskin, "in steps the capitalist, who neither makes nor uses them, and appropriates to himself the produce of both."[31] William Heighton defined the holders of capital in 1827 as those who "effect exchanges by proxy."[32] The nomenclature *middleman* that denoted the capitalist also embraced such disparate groupings as small retailers, peddlers,

---

29. Emphasis in original. *An Inquiry*, op. cit., p. 89.

30. On William Thompson's periodization of history by the transition from compelled labor to labor organized by individual competition, see J. E. King, "Utopian or Scientific? A Reconsideration of the Ricardian Socialists," *History of Political Economy* Volume 15, Number 3 (1983), p. 358.

31. Thomas Hodgskin, *Labour Defended Against the Claims of Capital* (London: Labour Publishing Company, 1922 [1825]), p. 71. Likewise, the broadside "A Riddle" calls a capitalist a "rogue [who] steps in between to make the exchange" (Manchester Library Archives). The British workers moved beyond the ancient view that profit is simply the difference between purchase and sale prices, for in the liberal-capitalist order products appeared as the incarnation of quantified labor. Profit now emerged from labor appropriated from the worker. For a sophisticated commentary, see Burkard, op. cit., p. 58.

32. William Heighton, *An Address to the Members of Trade Societies and to the Working-Classes Generally* (London: Co-Operative Society, 1827), p. 5, cited in N. Thompson, op. cit., p. 61. Italics in original.

merchants, and master manufacturers. The odious term drew boundaries between laborers and their exploiters based not on the ownership of capital per se but on a market position as an intermediary.[33] "[Middlemen] get their living by buying your labour at *one* price and selling it at *another*," the *Poor Man's Guardian* warned its readers. "This trade of *'buying cheap and selling dear,'* is of all human pursuits the most anti-social."[34] Producers equated the capitalist with the trader and imagined his metier not as the control of production but as the manipulation of exchange.[35]

In the periodicals aimed at the new factory operatives, the workers' exploiters were reduced to the "landowner and money-monger," a pairing that ignored the use of capital at the point of production.[36] *The Operative* said in 1839 that "all the tyranny and misery in this world are the work of landlords and profit-mongers . . . that is to say, the man who lives by lending the use of land, which ought never to be individual property, and the man who

---

33. N. Thompson, op. cit., p. 61. The *Poor Man's Guardian* referred in 1833 to the middle-class supporters of the Reform Bill as "middlemen." See Jones, op. cit., p. 105.

34. *Poor Man's Guardian*, No. 80, December 15, 1832, p. 641. Emphasis in original. On the influence of this newspaper among workers, see Frederick James Kaijage, "Labouring Barnsley, 1816–1856: A Social and Economic History." Ph.D. diss., University of Warwick, 1975, p. 470, and Patricia Hollis, *The Pauper Press* (London: Oxford University Press, 1970), p. 293.

35. The stress on the "defalcations of exchange" in the workers' press was overwhelming. As a writer for the *Poor Man's Advocate* expressed it, "The value of all commodities is the amount of human labour it has taken to procure them . . . but the merchant or agent between buyer and seller, being able to conceal the real state of the transaction, contrives with scarcely any labour to charge . . . one quarter above the value which he calls profit." January 21, 1832, p. 8. "Remember friends and brethren, that you and you alone produce *all* the real wealth of the country . . . middlemen . . . trick you out of the greater part of the wealth which you create." *Poor Man's Guardian*, No. 4 (1831), p. 25. Or, as John Bray said, it was "an inevitable condition of inequality of exchanges—of buying at one price and selling at another—that capitalists shall continue to be capitalists and working men be working men." Op. cit., pp. 48–49. The economy contained an *"error,"* John Gray claimed, a "defective system of exchange." John Gray, *The Social System* (London: Longman, Rees, Orme, Brown & Green, 1831), p. 23. Emphasis in original. See also Stedman Jones, op. cit., p. 119.
Employers reciprocated the workers' emphasis on the sphere of circulation. The textile manufacturers were slow to theorize the difference between profitable exchange as a merchant and the generation of returns through investment in plant and equipment. Sidney Pollard shows that during the formation of factory practice in Britain, textile managers rarely distinguished between capital and revenue or between fixed and circulating capital. Their accounting followed the logic of commercial rather than of industrial capitalism. "The rise of modern cost accounting," Pollard concluded, "dates from the 1880's only." "Capital Accounting in the Industrial Revolution," *Yorkshire Bulletin of Economic and Social Research* Volume 15, Number 2 (November 1963), p. 79.

36. *The Operative*, Nov. 4, 1838. "Aggregation of property into large masses" means "unjust preference given to the land-owner and money-monger that are the heaviest curses of the English Operative."

lives by the use of money, which ought never to be any thing more than a mere symbol of value."[37] The journal's correspondent viewed money as a fraudulent token, for instead of allowing goods to exchange at their value in labor, it itself becomes the measure of value. The control of money leads to exploitation not because the owners invest in and control the production process but because it facilitates deceitful exchange.

Given this diagnosis, the corrective, too, lay in the marketplace. In *Labour's Wrongs and Labour's Remedy*, published in 1839, Bray located the problem and its solution. "Inequality of exchanges, as being the cause of inequality of possessions, is the secret enemy that devours us," he wrote.[38] The introduction of trading cooperatives would short-circuit the market, allowing goods to be exchanged according to the value of labor they contained. "The general equality of condition which would be induced by equal exchanges," Bray said, "is, to the capitalist and economist, the last and most dreaded of all remedies."[39] Bray, like other authors, acknowledged that the ultimate goal was to secure workers' ownership of the means of production. "To free Labour from the dominion of Capital," he said, "it is necessary that the land and reproducible wealth of the country should be in possession of the working class."[40] The establishment of equal exchanges represented a sufficient means for this end.[41] Fair exchange would lead to an adequate reform of production, not the reform of production to the establishment of fair exchange.[42]

The focus of the socialist economists on the distribution of wealth insofar as this impinged upon equitable market exchange made it all too easy for the purification of exchange to become not only the means but the goal of reform. John Gray, for example, said that once the system of commerce was purified of distortion and the labor embodied in goods determined prices, it

37. *The Operative*, February 7, 1839.

38. Bray, op. cit., p. 52. Bray also says that the infraction of the law of equal exchanges oppresses the working man more than accumulation of capital (p. 48).

39. Ibid., p. 199. See his comments on p. 110 as well. Although Robert Owen lacked an economic theory to explain the exploitation of labor, he said that articles in his reformed communities would exchange "with reference to the amount of labour in each." *Report to the County of Lanark of a Plan for Relieving Public Distress* (Glasgow: Wardlaw & Cunninghame, 1821), p. 21.

40. Op. cit., p. 127.

41. Association for the Dissemination of the Knowledge of the Principles of an Equitable Labour Exchange, *Production the Cause of Demand* (Birmingham: Radcliffe & Co., 1832), p. 5.

42. Employers without large quantities of capital were seen as victims of market exchange just as much as wage laborers were. Submission in market exchange, not the position of authority conferred by the employment of labor power, marked class boundaries. Jones, op. cit., pp. 131–132.

was proper to sanction any inequalities of wealth that resulted.[43] He endorsed "unrestricted competition between man and man," once prices had been cleansed of distortions.[44] Likewise, William Thompson said that wherever the principle of "free interchange" of equivalents was respected, there property had been distributed in the most useful fashion.[45] The socialist economists imagined that the concentration of the means of production in the hands of a few may have resulted from, but did not necessarily cause, inequitable exchange.[46]

The work of Thompson, Gray, and Hodgskin received considerable popular attention and endorsement as the labor movement matured in the 1830s. "When Marx was still in his teens," E. P. Thompson wrote in *The Making*, "the battle for the minds of English trade unionists, between a capitalist and a socialist political economy, had been (at least temporarily) won."[47] With the decline of agitation after 1848, popular political economy lost its bite and its critical legacy was forgotten. The theories' internal logic may have accelerated and completed their eclipse. As Noel W. Thompson has remarked, a preoccupation with the mechanism of exchange, rather than with the power of capital to shape workers' productive lives, could easily give way to a limited, conservative focus on the proceeds of wage agreements negotiated in the labor market.[48]

43. John Gray, *Lectures on the Nature and Use of Money* (London: Longman, Brown, Green, and Longmans, 1848), p. 97.

44. Ibid., p. 159. For Hodgskin's praise of a cleansed market, see N. Thompson, *The Market and Its Critics*, op. cit., pp. 71–73.

45. *An Inquiry*, op. cit., p. 103. By "free" interchange Thompson did not necessarily mean market exchange.

Owen's doctrines are not analyzed in this chapter because they do not offer an economic theory of labor exploitation. Yet Owenite thinking, too, rested on the assumption that the inauguration of fair exchange and the subsequent prosperity of cooperative societies would be sufficient to eliminate disparities of wealth. See *The Making*, op. cit., p. 805, and N. Thompson, *The People's Science*, op. cit., p. 81.

46. Bray, op. cit., p. 110.

47. *The Making*, op. cit., p. 829. On the early influence of formal theories of labor's value in Bradford, see Jonathan Smith, "The Strike of 1825," in D. G. Wright and J. A. Jowitt, editors, *Victorian Bradford* (Bradford: Bradford Metropolitan Council, 1982), p. 75.

48. N. Thompson, *The People's Science*, op. cit., p. 224. Sidney Pollard suggests that the theories of the early socialists were forgotten so completely because the process of industrialization made it increasingly unrealistic to imagine that workers could accumulate enough capital to replace the capitalists. But if this is granted, the question arises of why the socialists did not recast their economic solutions; once again, the answer may be found in their preoccupation with the market exchange of products. Sidney Pollard, "England: Der unrevolutionäre Pionier," in Jürgen Kocka, editor, *Europäische Arbeiterbewegungen im 19. Jahrhundert* (Göttingen: Vandenhoeck & Ruprecht, 1983), p. 26.

The heritage of this critical political economy was never reappropriated by the labor movement as a native intellectual growth. The advocates for the socialist revival of the 1880s, including Beatrice Potter Webb, attempted to place the new movement in context by tracing the succession of prior socialist movements in the land. On the whole their surveys overlooked the early popular economists entirely; some, like H. M. Hyndman's *The Historical Basis of Socialism in England*, made passing reference to them in notes.[49] Until nearly the end of the century, the labor organizers remained out of touch with early socialist economic theory from their own soil, regarding socialist economic conjectures as an alien import. Not until the issuance in 1899 of an English translation of Anton Menger's original German volume, *The Right to the Whole Produce of Labour*, with H. S. Foxwell's extended preface about British socialist works, were the popular British economists recognized again in their country of origin.[50]

The rescue occurred due to the combined and uneven development of theory across the European landscape. Among the leading economic theorists of the second half of the nineteenth century, Marx was almost alone in taking notice of the contributions of the early British economists. The prestige of Marx's ideas in Germany led economists there to reexamine the British philosophers of labor who had long been forgotten by the British themselves. When the Austrian scholar Anton Menger wrote his history of *The Right to the Whole Produce of Labour*, he set out to discredit Continental Marxists by showing that Marx had disguised the true magnitude of his debt to these early British predecessors.[51] Menger asserted that many of Marx's consequential assertions, including those concerning the mechanisms by which surplus value was generated and appropriated, had been anticipated, sometimes in embryonic form, by earlier French and British socialists, and in particular by William Thompson.[52]

---

49. H. M. Hyndman, *The Historical Basis of Socialism in England* (London: Garland Publishing, 1984 [1883]), p. 120. But the perception of a new start for socialism can be seen in Hyndman's claim that his book *England for All* "was the first Socialist work that appeared up to 1881 in English." Henry Mayers Hyndman, *The Record of an Adventurous Life* (London: Macmillan & Co., 1911), p. 248. Sidney Webb, *Socialism in Great Britain* (London: Swan Sonnenschein & Co., 1890), refers to Marx and Engels but not to the early British socialists (pp. 19, 85).

50. See H. S. Foxwell's introduction to Anton Menger's *The Right to the Whole Produce of Labour* (New York: Augustus Kelley, 1962 [1899]), p. cii; Dona Torr, *Tom Mann and His Times*, Volume One (London: Lawrence & Wishart, 1956), p. 183. The idea for this paragraph heavily relies upon the research of Noel Thompson in *The People's Science*, op. cit., p. 83.

51. Menger, op. cit., p. cxv.

52. Ibid., pp. 101–102.

The English translation of Menger's work about Marx earned broad attention. In this circuitous manner the British became aware of their own early socialists. These pioneering socialists were brought back from the dead by the writings of the dead, through Menger's excavations of the deceased Marx.[53] The roundabout rediscovery left its trace in language. When Foxwell highlighted the similarities between Ricardo's theory and those of the early British socialist economists,[54] he helped establish the appellation "Ricardian socialists" for the popular British economists, following Marx's categorization of economic history.[55] As everyone knows, Marx's commentary and elaborations on Ricardo lauded him as the most important advocate of the labor theory of value on which the early British socialists seemed to build. The label "Ricardian socialists" became a permanent, though deceptive, term of reference.[56] It was misleading insofar as the British socialist economists rarely alluded to Ricardo, but made frequent reference to Adam Smith.[57] Their preoccupation with the process of exchange resonated more strongly with Smith's rich descriptions of commercial transactions than with Ricardo's abstract models of the costs of production.[58] By looking at their early writers as "Ricardian socialists," the British rediscoverers viewed their heritage from the standpoint of Marx, who, more than the early Brit-

53. See the earliest known reference to "Ricardian socialists" in N. Thompson, *The People's Science*, op. cit., p. 84 note 5. See also Beatrice Webb, *The Co-operative Movement in Great Britain* (London: S. Sonnenschein, 1891), p. 47; Foxwell in Menger, op. cit., pp. iii–iv. Engels placed even the Owenite movement among the Ricardian school. Karl Marx, *Das Kapital* (Berlin: Dietz Verlag, 1980), p. 20.

54. Foxwell in Menger, op. cit., pp. xl–xlii.

55. N. Thompson, *The People's Science*, op. cit., p. 84.

56. Joseph Schumpeter, *History of Economic Analysis* (New York: Oxford University Press, 1954), p. 583.

57. I am indebted to Noel Thompson for this observation. See "Ricardian Socialists/Smithian Socialists: What's in a Name," in his *The People's Science*, op. cit., Chapter Four. Esther Lowenthal was among the first to remark upon the discrepancy between appellation and content in *The Ricardian Socialists* (Clifton, New Jersey: Augustus M. Kelley, 1972 [1911]), p. 103.

58. King, op. cit., p. 346. Yet the British socialists could perhaps have found just as much support in Ricardo as in Smith for their view that exploitation occurred in the market. The notion that exploitation took place when exchanges did not properly balance the quantities of labor being traded rested on a comparison of the quantities of labor expended on the product—an analysis thoroughly consistent with Ricardo. Ricardo's theory also set up the exchange of equals for equals as a standard. That the early British socialists developed Smith's ideas more than Ricardo's has perhaps more to do with the possibilities of development opened up by these two founders' presentation than with their respective definitions of how labor determined values. Cf. Gregory Claeys, *Machinery, Money and the Millennium: From Moral Economy to Socialism, 1815–60* (Cambridge: Polity Press, 1987), p. xxv.

ish socialists themselves had done, proceeded by developing the problematic suggested by Ricardo's theory.[59]

Whereas Marx overlooked what was distinctively German about his thinking by deriving his conclusions from English economic history, the later British socialists overlooked what was distinctively British about the thinking of the early socialists in their own land by looking at them through the legacy of Marx. In a sense, Marx was a more faithful successor to Ricardo than the early British socialists were, since only he rigorously pursued Ricardo's emphasis on the labor invested at the point of production as the ultimate determinant of value. It was by a process of cross-cultural development, in which thinkers in each country expressed their own life experience in how they appropriated concepts from another land, that the later British socialists came into contact with their native predecessors.

More specifically, by accepting Marx's view of himself as a successor to the heritage of British political economy, the British socialists at the end of the nineteenth century failed to appreciate how Marx's account of the extraction of surplus from labor power at the point of production diverged from the early British socialists' preoccupation with exchange in the marketplace. They therefore acted as though they were condemned to rebuild an edifice that had been erected by their forebears. They supposed that Marx, like themselves, believed that the market comprised the site of exploitation and that labor was transferred as if it were concretized in a ware.[60] Foxwell said that after a half-century of neglect, the ideas of the original socialists survived because they "remained germinating in the minds of Marx and Engels."[61]

If the popular political economy of the newly emergent socialism in Britain at the end of the century and that created near its beginning contained parallel concepts of labor, how are we to explain this family resemblance? The similarity cannot be explained by a continuity of intellectual tradition or by the inertia of ideas among a literate elite. Instead, it points to similarities in the social environments. In particular, the specification of labor as a commodity, reproduced in everyday practice on the shop floor, came to the fore in both British movements' understanding of capitalist

59. Ernest Mandel, *The Formation of the Economic Thought of Karl Marx* (New York: Monthly Review Press, 1971), p. 45.

60. Stuart Macintyre, *A Proletarian Science* (Cambridge: Cambridge University Press, 1980), p. 161.

61. Cited in Richard Pankhurst, *William Thompson* (London: Watts & Co., 1954), p. 217.

exploitation. What the British labor movement had forgotten about its past it was bound to repeat.[62]

The rebirth of socialist movements in the textile towns of Yorkshire and Lancashire illustrates the popular footing of the movements and the distinguishing features of their understanding of wage labor. Yorkshire served as the home base of the Independent Labour Party, perhaps the most influential propagator of a renewed socialism. The organization was tied to the textile mills from the start, for the first group of workers in Yorkshire to propose the establishment of a union in order to run independent labor candidates in local and parliamentary elections was assembled during 1891 in the weaving town of Slaithwaite. The earliest meetings of this group, the predecessor of the Independent Labour Party, were attended largely by weavers.[63] As its name suggested, the association began with the simple objective of breaking with the Liberal Party to secure autonomous representation for workers. Many of its elected committee members, however, were already convinced socialists, as were the speakers at the local labor clubs sponsored by the new organization.[64] When the delegates from like-minded committees in other provinces assembled in Bradford in 1893 to found the Independent Labour Party as a national organization, they counted "socialism" and the communal ownership of production among their goals.[65]

The ideals of this labor party emerged through grass-roots debate, not through the speculations of a few intellectuals. The independent labor movement in Yorkshire inspired the growth of an extensive network of

62. The immobility of theory in Britain rests upon the continuity, not of ideas, but of practices. Ideology has no history in its own right.

63. Archive of the Huddersfield Polytechnic Labour Collection, "Jubilee Souvenir: History of the Colne Valley Labour Party," p. 5. Textile workers also dominated the executive committee elected at the meeting. David Clark, *Colne Valley: Radicalism to Socialism* (London: Longman, 1981), p. 19.

64. Clark, op. cit., p. 33.

65. See the transcript of the debate at the founding meeting of the Independent Labour Party reprinted in Henry Pelling, editor, *The Challenge of Socialism* (London: Adam & Charles Black, 1968), pp. 187–189; James Hinton, *Labour and Socialism* (Amherst: University of Massachusetts Press, 1983), pp. 58, 75; Stanley Pierson, *British Socialists: The Journey from Fantasy to Politics* (Cambridge, Massachusetts: Harvard University Press, 1979), p. 37. Bradford's significance in the rise of this party can be gauged from its share of national membership dues. In 1895 Bradford provided one-sixth of the party's affiliation fees. J. Reynolds and K. Laybourn, "The Emergence of the Independent Labour Party in Bradford," *International Review of Social History* Volume 20, Part 3 (1975), p. 315. E. P. Thompson makes a strong case for the dynamic of local factors and for the contribution of Yorkshire to the development of the Independent Labour Party in "Homage to Tom Maguire," in Asa Briggs and John Saville, editors, *Essays in Labour History* (London: Macmillan & Co., 1960), p. 277.

neighborhood labor clubs, especially in textile towns.[66] The clubs competed with taverns as places where workers could meet to talk after work. In them, workers were able to discuss socialist ideas. In 1892, twenty-three labor clubs, with about three thousand members, operated in Bradford alone. By 1895, the Independent Labour Party claimed thirty-five thousand members.[67] Before the First World War, the Yorkshire textile districts provided the setting for some of the party's most significant electoral successes.[68] By 1907 the party had managed to elect Labour M.P.'s from Bradford, Leeds, Halifax, and the Colne Valley, as well as representatives to municipal and county government in the region.[69]

The textile unions were linked to the socialist campaigns not by geographic coincidence but by personnel. The leaders of the principal textile union in Yorkshire, the West Riding Power Loom Weavers' Association, also worked for the new labor party. Ben Turner, Allen Gee, and J. W. Downing, for example, worked for the committee for labor representation in Slaithwaite as early as 1891.[70] The textile workers in Yorkshire adopted socialist ideas as their own during the 1890s.[71] In Yeadon, the Factory Workers' Union, a purely local association whose membership consisted of weavers, dyers, and spinners, adopted the songbooks and message of the independent labor movement. The union's goal, the secretary said, was to help workers find their "social salvation."[72] A correspondent to the *Yorkshire Factory Times* in 1914 assumed that the textile unions were vehicles for social trans-

---

66. Ben Turner, *About Myself 1863–1930* (London: Cayme Press, 1930), p. 80.

67. Hinton, op. cit., pp. 58, 60.

68. Keith Laybourn, "The Attitude of the Yorkshire Trade Unions to the Economic and Social Problems of the Great Depression, 1873–1896," Ph.D. diss., Lancaster University, 1973, p. 451.

69. Frank Bealey and Henry Pelling, *Labour and Politics 1900–1906* (London: MacMillan & Co., 1958), p. 292; T. L. Jarman, *Socialism in Britain: From the Industrial Revolution to the Present Day* (London: Victor Gollancz, 1972), p. 89. On local representatives, see Turner, op. cit., p. 176, and Keith Laybourn, "'The Defence of the Bottom Dog': The Independent Labour Party in Local Politics," in Wright and Jowitt, editors, *Victorian Bradford*, op. cit., p. 224. For George Garside's early election to the County Council in Slaithwaite in 1892, see *Yorkshire Factory Times*, February 26, 1904.

70. Clark, op. cit., p. 23. Ben Turner also lists members of the early Socialist Club in Leeds who later became trade union leaders. Op. cit., p. 79. See also Robert Brian Perks, "The New Liberalism and the Challenge of Labour in the West Riding of Yorkshire 1885–1914," Ph.D. diss., Huddersfield Polytechnic, 1985, p. 53.

71. *Yorkshire Factory Times*, May 13, 1892, Oakworth speech, p. 7; speech at Batley by Ben Turner, *Yorkshire Factory Times*, December 21, 1894, p. 8. In some towns of Lancashire, too, the organizers of the Independent Labour Party also worked for the local textile union. Elizabeth Roberts's interview with Mr. C1P, born 1894, Preston, p. 20.

72. Archive of General Union of Dyers, Bleachers, and Textile Workers, Headquarters, Yeadon and Guiseley Factory Workers' Union, Minutes, January 25, 1899.

formation, not just effective negotiation. "Organized working men," he said, "wish to use Trade Unionism as a means for ending the present conditions of society."[73]

In Lancashire the admission of socialist ideas was more localized. They were perhaps received most enthusiastically in the Clitheroe district, which originally represented an outpost of liberalism in a large region captive to the Tory party. The district included the textile centers of Nelson, Burnley, and Colne. The quarterly report of the Nelson weavers for 1902 expressed the break that textile workers in this region had made with the bread-and-butter politics of conservative unions in other Lancashire districts. "Therefore, let us workers sink our little differences and go hand in hand and return representatives to Parliament and on all public bodies from our class," the Nelson union stated in the conclusion of its report, "and show the capitalist class that we are determined not to have them as our representatives any longer."[74] To be sure, the textile workers in the unions of the Clitheroe district belonged to the United Textile Factory Workers' Association, one of Lancashire's ossified, conservative unions. At the same time, however, the local textile unions could affiliate themselves with a political party without receiving approval from the central office.[75] The Nelson weavers attended the founding conference of the Labour Party in 1900. In 1902 the parliamentary constituency of Clitheroe elected the vice-president of the Weavers' Amalgamation as the first Labour M.P. in the north of England.[76]

Blackburn represented another outpost of the socialist movement in Lancashire. Many weavers there were tied to the Social Democratic Federation, an avowedly Marxist league founded in 1881.[77] If the best indicator of a movement's influence is the number of attempts to organize an

---

73. *Yorkshire Factory Times,* January 1, 1914, p. 4. Similarly, see *Yorkshire Factory Times,* May 13, 1892, Oakworth.

74. Bealey and Pelling, op. cit., p. 105.

75. Town branches also elected socialist spokespersons: a member of the Social Democratic Federation served as vice-president of the Burnley Weavers' Association in 1895. Chushichi Tsuzuki, *H. M. Hyndman and British Socialism* (Oxford: Oxford University Press, 1961), p. 99.

76. Alan Fowler and Lesley Fowler, *The History of the Nelson Weavers Association* (Nelson: Burnley, Nelson, Rossendale & District Textile Workers Union, 1989), p. 16. For the weavers' support of an independent labor party in the conservative Preston district, see Michael Savage, *The Dynamics of Working-Class Politics* (Cambridge: Cambridge University Press, 1987), p. 154.

77. In 1895 the Social Democratic Federation claimed 10,500 members in the United Kingdom. Hinton, op. cit., pp. 41, 60.

opposition, then the socialists in the textile unions were becoming a power with which to reckon. Textile workers in Blackburn who wanted to distinguish themselves from the socialists, who allegedly controlled the main textile union in town, founded a separate city union in 1912.[78] Before the First World War, the Lancashire and Yorkshire textile regions provided the major base of support—the votes, the financing, and the ideas—for the emerging socialist groups.[79]

The recreated socialist movement in Britain propagated what its members considered a novel, reinvigorated political economy. The socialist journals of the textile communities published regular columns, sometimes composed in simple language, that analyzed the origin of profit. The *Bradford Socialist Vanguard* even adopted the graces of dialect: in 1908 it told its readers, "Capital is nobbut stored up labour."[80] In the wool districts even the staple *Yorkshire Factory Times* recounted the lectures and debates over labor theories of value that were sponsored by the workers' clubs.[81] The autobiographies of former textile workers describe workers' eager consumption of economic theory.[82]

In the populist newspapers' rejuvenated discussions of the exploitation of labor, the portrayal of the capitalist evolved but did not depart from the essential form it had assumed in early British socialism. The capitalist became a financier who received a profit by charging interest on industrial investment or by coercing the worker to pay a rent for the use of the tools of production. The cause of the exploitation, the *Blackburn Labour Journal* said in 1900, is that "the capitalists permit you to use the means of production on certain terms."[83] The workers paid a surcharge to *use* the means of production, but in this theory the capitalist did not occupy a special role as

---

78. *Blackburn Times,* June 15, 1912.

79. Deian Hopkin, "The Membership of the Independent Labour Party, 1904–1910," *International Review of Social History* Volume 20, Part Two (1975), p. 182; Bealey and Pelling, op. cit.; Pierson, op. cit., p. 46. For statistics on the geographic concentration of Labour's vote in municipal elections, see M. G. Sheppard and John L. Halstead, "Labour's Municipal Election Performance in Provincial England and Wales 1901–13," *Society for the Study of Labour History* Bulletin Number 39 (Autumn 1979), p. 56. It may also be true, however, that among the textile labor force only a minority of workers supported socialist causes.

80. *Bradford Socialist Vanguard* (December 1908).

81. *Yorkshire Factory Times,* October 10, 1912; February 1, 1895, Bradford.

82. Isaac Binns, *From Village to Town* (Batley: E. H. Purchas, n.d. [ca. 1882]). Sherwin Stephenson, "The Chronicles of a Shop Man," Bradford Library Archives, pp. 94, 197. For other references to popular beliefs about political economy, see R. V. Clements, "British Trade Unions and Popular Political Economy 1850–1875," *Economic History Review* Volume XIV, Number 1 (August 1961), p. 102.

83. *Blackburn Labour Journal* (June 1900).

the director of production.[84] Although workers in their concrete complaints criticized their subordination to the mill owners, in their discourse of economic reform the capitalist's organization of work and his exercise of authority at the point of production did not appear as essential conditions for the extraction of profit.[85] Instead, the surplus extracted by the capitalist was secured like a kind of rent: the capitalist, like the landowner, secured profit at a remove as a deduction from the product of the worker.[86] The "explanation" for exploitation, the *Blackburn Labour Journal* said, is simple: "We allow a certain class to own all the land in the country. These landowners do not allow the land to be used unless a large share of what is produced is given up to them in the form of rent. The same remark applies to machinery. Unless a big profit can be made for the capitalists who own the machinery, they refuse to allow it to be used."[87] By this reasoning, laborers who had no need of tools owned by another person were fortunate indeed, for even if these laborers were subordinated to an employer they could escape exploitation.[88]

In the resuscitated socialist movement the capitalists were portrayed as usurious lenders, empowered by the unequal division of wealth to manipulate exchange relations in the market.[89] In this respect, just as in the economic theories of early British socialism, so in those of the century's end the

84. See, for example, the discussion at a meeting of workers in 1894, where the capitalist was portrayed as a usurious lender who bargains thus: "I will allow you to use these tools on condition that you keep me without working." *Keighley ILP Journal*, February 4, 1894. The formulation is not essentially changed from that presented by Adam Smith, who thought that the workers "stand in need" of the capitalist to "advance them the materials of their work, and their wages and maintenance till it be compleated." *An Inquiry into the Nature and Causes of the Wealth of Nations* (Chicago: University of Chicago Press, 1976 [1776]), pp. 73–74.

85. These British formulations contrast with those of the German literature, such as Kautsky's widely read popularization of Marx, which emphasized that "the means of production serve above all the goal of absorbing into themselves the labor power of the worker." *Karl Marx' ökonomische Lehren* (Berlin: J. H. W. Dietz, 1980), p. 121.

86. The rich were those "who monopolise the land and capital, who thereby control labour and compel it to surrender to them its products, saving a bare pittance." *The Labour Journal,* October 14, 1892. Sometimes the analogy between the rent of the landowner and the interest paid to the capitalist allowed workers to conceive of the control of land as the original source of profit. The program of the Independent Labour Party in 1895 called for nationalization of land, not of industry.

87. *Blackburn Labour Journal* (September 1898). Even the British Socialist Party judged that "agriculture is most important and most valuable of all industries." *The Pioneer* (February 1914), "Socialist Land Policy."

88. *Bradford Labour Echo*, November 19, 1898.

89. Philip Snowden, *Socialism and Syndicalism* (Baltimore: Warwick & York), p. 167.

capitalist could be likened to a middleman.[90] The capitalist controlled the marketing of products by forcing laborers to use the means of production that he owned. The *Burnley Gazette*, in a column intended to explain why the attainment of higher wages represented an inadequate solution to workers' poverty, also exposed its understanding of exploitation. Socialism offers the only solution, it said, because a rise in wages does not "catch the profit-monger in the labour market."[91] The *Bradford Labour Echo*, organ of the Bradford Independent Labour Party, told workers in 1898 that they were exploited because "all sorts of middle-men" cut workers out of the full value of the product.[92] Robert Blatchford's *Merrie England*, published in 1894, one of the most widely distributed books that sought to revive the theoretic analysis of the exploitation of labor, succinctly identified the extraction of profit: "As a rule, profit is not made by the producer of an article, but by some other person commonly called 'the middleman' because he goes between the producer and the consumer; that is to say, he, the middleman, buys the article from the maker, and sells it to the user, at a profit." Blatchford went on to define all middlemen as capitalists.[93]

Even the Social Democratic Federation, an organization which saw itself as the most loyal disseminator of Marxist ideas, supposed that the market was the site of exploitation. James L. Joynes, who translated into English Marx's *Lohnarbeit und Kapital* ("*Wage Labour and Capital*"), also wrote "The Socialist Catechism," a sixteen-page pamphlet that served as perhaps the most influential introduction to socialist economic theory in Britain during the 1880s. In it Joynes argued that capitalism was distinctive because

90. Allen Clarke's description of the operatives of Bolton in 1899 treated the source of profit as in "trade" rather than "manufacture." The workers, Clarke said, "think that the masters build factories and workshops not to make a living for themselves by *trading* but in order to find the people employment." Quoted in Joyce, *Work, Society and Politics*, op. cit., p. 90, emphasis added. Ben Turner said he did not condemn employers, only "the system under which employers in the district *traded*." *Yorkshire Factory Times*, December 11, 1903, p. 6. Emphasis added.

91. *Burnley Gazette*, August 5, 1893.

92. *Bradford Labour Echo*, April 9, 1898. Sometimes the revived socialist movement supposed that the stabilization of wages at subsistence level represented, not the sale of labor (power) at the cost of its reproduction, but the remainder left to workers after miscellaneous middlemen completed their thievery. "Before getting his poor wages home, however, he [the worker] is systematically waylaid by robbers, each one taking various amounts till the last one, the leader, takes all he has left except just sufficient to keep him and his family at work." *Bradford Labour Echo*, May 9, 1896.

93. Robert Blatchford, *Merrie England: A Series of Letters to John Smith of Oldham—a Practical Working Man* (New York: Monthly Review Press, 1966 [1894]), pp. 82–83, 84.

exploitation arose from market forces rather than custom.[94] Even the leader of the Social Democratic Federation, Hyndman, who was attempting to follow Marx's account of the generation of surplus value, tellingly misrepresented it in *The Historical Basis of Socialism in England*, published in 1883. To clarify the word *Arbeitskraft*, Hyndman introduced the clumsy translation "force of labour," which of course never acquired currency.[95] Hyndman did not present the difference between the use value and the exchange value of labor power or the fact that the capitalist paid the worker the full exchange value of his ware. Stripped of these ideas, the elaborate phrase "force of labour" served no function in his presentation. Instead, he emphasized that the capitalist was able to buy labor power, in contrast to machinery and raw materials, "on the cheap," due to the competition among workers for subsistence. As a result, the fact that the capitalist can earn a surplus from this "human merchandise" appears to result from overcompetition among workers, which prevents labor from fetching its fair "market price."[96] Thus the leading British proponent of Marxist economics transformed the theory of exploitation into market cheating.[97]

94. Henry Collins, "The Marxism of the Social Democratic Federation," in Asa Briggs and John Saville, editors, *Essays in Labour History 1886–1923* (Hamden, Conn.: Archon Books, 1971), p. 52.

95. Hyndman, *The Historical Basis of Socialism*, op. cit., pp. 113, 114, 116.

96. Ibid., pp. 119–122. "Everything else which is needed for the purposes of production—raw material, machinery, &c.—have been bought by the capitalist at their actual market value and paid for at their actual market price. It is from labour only, the labour-force of human beings compelled to compete against one another for a bare subsistence wage, that the actual employer derives his surplus value, and the merchant, &c., his profit" (pp. 119–120). The British Marxists, including Hyndman, retained a belief in the iron law of wages even when the writings by Marx available to them repudiated it. This follows from their interpretation of Marx as a theorist of market exploitation. In their understanding, the capitalist realizes a profit only if the competition among workers forces the price of labor down to subsistence, thus to below its real value. Their adherence to the iron law of wages results not from ignorance of Marx but from the internal logic of the market-based understanding of exploitation which they derived from Marx. For explicit reference to the "iron law of wages" and the logic behind its retention, see ibid., pp. 118–119. For evidence that the British Marxists retained a belief in this iron law after they most certainly must have known that Marx rejected it, see Collins, op. cit., pp. 52–53.

97. In *The Economics of Socialism*, written a decade later, Hyndman renders Marx's theory more cogently. He emphasizes that the employer purchases labor power at its full exchange value. But again he fails to make a distinction between labor's value in use and in exchange. Instead, he reasons that unlimited competition among workers forces wages down to subsistence level, whereas workers produce more than they need for the reproduction of their labor power. Since the moment of the employer's exercise of authority to exploit the use value of labor at the point of production disappears from Hyndman's analysis, in his view the extraction of surplus depends upon the power of market forces to depress wages. *The Economics of Socialism* (London: The Twentieth Century Press, 1909), pp. 83, 97. In his memoirs

The socialist press emphasized that the capitalist's purchase of labor was in essence like that of the home consumer's purchase of finished products. The only difference was that the capitalist used his ownership of the implements of production and his position in the market to devise an unfair exchange. "Every child who buys a pennyworth of nuts or toffee in a tuckshop is, in one and a true sense, an employer of labour," the *Bradford Labour Echo* claimed in 1898. "But, though every buyer, as such is, like this child, an employer of labor, he is not an interceptor of part of his employees' earnings, nor therefore an earner of 'employers'' profits."[98] The products the capitalists purchased at an unfairly depressed price they resold at an inflated one. The emphasis on the "seizure" of profits by controlling the price at which finished goods were sold in the market tallied with the view prevailing among British socialists that labor was transferred to the capitalist as it was concretized in a ware.[99]

As in the original socialist movement, so in the second a significant body of workers looked upon the assurance of fair exchanges not as the result of socialism but as socialism's very goal. *The Labour Journal* of Bradford imagined that variations in individuals' work effort would lead to variations in their income under socialism. But unequal income would no longer result from unequal exchange. "The sum of socialism," it claimed in 1892, "is equal economic opportunities for all, and then the reward proportioned to the use individually made of such equal opportunities."[100] Many socialists' vision of the future rested on the presumption that both the injuries of capitalism and the justice of the coming order rested on equitable transfers in the sphere of exchange.[101]

Hyndman again focuses on the market as the locus of exploitation: British workers would continue to live in poverty, he said, "as long as competition for mere subsistence ruled in the labour market. . . . The dominant classes are no fools. They know perfectly well that if sweating were abolished and unemployment ceased to be, the whole capitalist system would be doomed." Henry Hyndman, *Further Reminiscences* (London: Macmillan & Co., 1912), p. 18.

98. *Bradford Labour Echo*, November 26, 1898.

99. The *Bradford Labour Echo* said that capitalists confiscate "the annual produce of the workers." *Bradford Labour Echo*, April 13, 1895. Correlatively, Ben Turner, an early convert to socialism and a leader of the Yorkshire textile unions, said that the profit was made on cloth, not labor. Turner, op. cit., p. 105.

100. *The Labour Journal*, December 2, 1892, Bradford.

101. The understanding of the labor transaction as the sale and resale of materialized labor, born in the British experience of commercialization, also informed the later elaborations of British academics. Richard H. Tawney exemplified it in his misinterpretation of Marx, imposing on him the British understanding of the exploitation of labor. Marx, he said, did not castigate the honest merchant. According to Tawney, Marx believed that "the unpardonable sin is that of the speculator or the middleman, who snatches private gain by the exploitation

ECONOMIC IDEOLOGIES IN THE
WORKERS' MOVEMENTS OF GERMANY

Workers' debates about political economy in Germany during the revolution of 1848–1849 did not inspire the formation of a group of thinkers so renowned as the so-called Ricardian socialists in Britain. Due perhaps to the legacy of corporate regulation in the urban crafts trades in Germany, the artisans who spearheaded the workers' movement there never expressed the degree of interest in formal theories of capitalist exploitation that their counterparts in the early British socialist movement did.[102] When the labor periodicals which blossomed in the revolution analyzed the sources of workers' impoverishment, however, their portrayal of the labor transaction varied from the start from that of the British. The revolutionary press in Germany generally viewed the concentration of capital not as the *result* of ruinous exchange in the market but as its *cause*.[103] It acknowledged that market forces reshaped the landscape, but market transactions themselves did not appear to it to comprise the site of exploitation.[104] For example, the Cologne newspaper *Freiheit, Arbeit* declared in 1849 that the wealthy profited not just through trade but by "the administration of work" and by "guiding the manufacture" of products.[105] It portrayed the subordination of labor in the workshop as a mechanism in its own right for extracting profit. In *Die Verbrüderung* the correspondent Oskar Stobek declared in 1850 that workers engaged in the workshops of superiors were exploited because they

---

of public necessities." *Religion and the Rise of Capitalism* (New York: New American Library, 1954 [1926]), p. 38.

102. Only upon the reestablishment of political movements in the 1860s did urban artisans begin to adopt the discourse of liberal political economy. Friedrich Lenger, *Zwischen Kleinbürgertum und Proletariat* (Göttingen: Vandenhoeck & Ruprecht, 1986), p. 195.

103. P. H. Noyes, *Organization and Revolution: Working-Class Associations in the German Revolutions of 1848–1849* (Princeton: Princeton University Press, 1966), pp. 240–241.

104. *Arbeiter-Blatt*, from the textile district of Lennep, edited by members of the local workers' association, portrayed the market as a medium that reflected circumstances disadvantageous to workers, not as the cause of unequal exchange. The newspaper cited wage-depressing factors in Germany, including the abundance of landless, dependent laborers and the stiffening competition that hand workers faced from domestic and foreign machine production. December 3, 1848. In these dire circumstances, the newspaper believed, society needed to protect workers' only property, their labor, from exploitation in the workplace. It did not focus on the moment of exchange itself. *Das Arbeiter-Blatt*, October 29, 1848.

105. The wealthy controlled the "valorization" of "talent and labor power." "Materielle Noth," in *Freiheit, Arbeit*, February 11, 1849, pp. 36–37. For a discussion of workers' contributions to the content of this journal, see Michael Vester et al., editors, *Gibt es einen "Wissenschaftlichen Sozialismus"?* (Hannover: SOAK Verlag, 1979), p. 64.

were paid only for elapsed time on the premises, not for the value of the output.[106]

When the German workers' press referred to commercial investment, it revealed some fundamental differences from the British. German writers offered a prescient distinction between money and capital. In 1850 the national organ of the German workers' associations asked, "By what do the people live, who claim that they pay taxes for support of workers? Simply by the circumstance that they use the labor power [*Arbeitskraft*] of the worker to get the greatest possible use from their money and to elevate the money to the status of capital."[107] In a word, money became capital when it employed labor in the production process.[108] In Britain, by contrast, some writers in the same era made no distinction between money and capital,[109] whereas others supposed that capital referred to any material holding, such as a house, without necessarily entailing an intervention in production.[110] The definition of capital that prevailed in the German workers' press during the revolution emphasized its engagement with labor at the point of production, a necessary step for conceiving of the appropriation of surplus at this site. The convention of masters and business persons that met in Frankfurt during July and August, 1848, defined a capitalist not as a shady dealer in the realm of exchange but as a "producer who profiteers with labor power."[111]

In Britain the emphasis on the realm of exchange as the locus of exploitation led spokespersons for workers to devote great attention to the use of money as a form of trickery. Reliance on the artificial symbols of pounds and pence, John Bray averred in *Labour's Wrongs and Labour's Remedy*, allowed people to avoid exchanging equal quantities of labor for labor.[112]

---

106. *Die Verbrüderung*, December 5, 1850, p. 74.

107. *Die Verbrüderung*, April 13, 1850, p. 114.

108. "Grundzüge eines Systems, um Kapital zu sammeln," *Arbeiter-Zeitung*, February 22, 1863.

109. *The Operative*, February 3, 1839.

110. Bray, op. cit., pp. 140–141. John Gray said that the difference between money and capital is between the currency and physical items, including consumer goods. Gray, *Lectures*, op. cit., pp. 196–197.

111. Deutscher Handwerker- und Gewerbe-Congress, *Entwurf einer allgemeinen Handwerker- und Gewerbe-Ordnung für Deutschland: Berathen und beschlossen von dem Handwerker- und Gewerbe-Congress zu Frankfurt am Main im Juli und August 1848* (Hamburg, 1848), p. 5.

112. Bray, op. cit., p. 153. In the 1830s leaflet "The Workings of Money Capital," an anonymous author explains that capital yields a profit because it "buys goods dishonestly obtained." Manchester Library Archives.

Workers believed they could eliminate exploitation by effecting their transactions in labor notes denoting time rather than resorting to currency, as their support for the ill-fated labor-exchange movement illustrated.[113] German workers, by comparison, did not focus on the use of money per se as a contributor to exploitation, since they did not see the mechanism of exchange as the crucial arbiter of their fate.

The chronology of the development of socialist ideas in Germany nonetheless displays a basic parallelism with that of Britain: in both countries, an early socialist movement was extinguished in the first half of the nineteenth century and a new one born in the second half. During the repression of the 1850s the German states succeeded in dismantling most of the labor organizations, such as Stephan Born's German workers' association, which had introduced workers to socialist ideas during the revolutionary years of 1848–1849. When the German labor movement reemerged in the 1860s, the leaflets about the exploitation of labor with which workers were most likely to come into contact were those of Ferdinand Lassalle.[114] In his autobiography August Bebel testified that, "Like almost all others who were socialists back then, I came to Marx by way of Lassalle. Lassalle's writings were in our hands long before we knew one writing of Marx and Engels."[115]

Lassalle emphasized that the use value of a good regulated its distribution in precommercial society, whereas its exchange value regulated its distribution in capitalist society.[116] Consequently, he could not seize upon the *difference* between the use value and the exchange value of labor in the capitalist epoch to specify the extraction of surplus at the point of production, as Marx did. Unlike the early British socialists, Lassalle did not envision that the exploitation of labor occurred in the marketplace. He supposed

113. The outlook of the labor exchange movement can be gleaned from the very title of William King's pamphlet: *The Circulating Medium and the Present Mode of Exchange the Cause of Increasing Distress Amongst the Productive Classes: and an Effective Measure for Their Immediate and Permanent Relief Pointed Out in the Universal Establishment of Labour Banks, in Which All the Business of Life May Be Transacted Without Money* (London: William Dent, 1832). For the statutes governing the exchange of labor time certificates at such an organization, see Equitable Labour Exchange, *Rules and Regulations of the Equitable Labour Exchange, Gray's Inn Road, London: for the Purpose of Relieving the Productive Classes from Poverty, by Their Own Industry and for the Mutual Exchange of Labour for Equal Value of Labour* (London: Equitable Labour Exchange, 1832).

114. Jorke, op. cit., p. 10, 18; Roger Morgan, *The German Social Democrats and the First International 1864–1872* (Cambridge: Cambridge University Press, 1965), p. 124.

115. August Bebel, *Aus meinem Leben*, Part One (Stuttgart: J. H. W. Dietz Nachf., 1910), p. 131.

116. Tatiana Grigorovici, *Die Wertlehre bei Marx und Lassalle* (Wien: Ignaz Brand & Co., 1910), pp. 63–64.

that the capitalist made a profit by controlling, like a feudal lord, "the will and acts" of workers under his authority.[117] Lassalle and his followers, like British socialists, believed the capitalist employer made a profit by buying cheap and selling dear, but in addition they supposed that the employer's ability to do this depended upon his authority at the point of production.

In keeping with this outlook, Lassalle supposed that profit represented merely a deduction from the labor output. The Lassallians demanded that workers receive the full "return" of their labor, but they used the ambiguous term *Ertrag*, which did not refer clearly to either the product or the value of the work.[118] In contrast to the early socialist movement in Britain, which had supposed that the workers' retention of the value of their labor through equal exchange would lead to the workers' acquisition of capital, the Lassallian movement made the acquisition of capital by the workers' cooperatives the necessary starting point for workers to receive the value of their labor.[119] Lassalle's theory shows that even when the German labor movement lacked Marx's striking elucidation of the appropriation of surplus value in production, it did not focus upon unequal exchange in the product market as the locus of exploitation.

After the publication of *Kapital,* Lassalle's followers quickly adopted Marx's analysis of the capitalist employment relation, even though Marx had modified Lassalle's earlier presentation.[120] The *Social-Demokrat,* organ of the Lassallians, succinctly identified Marx's innovation: the worker, this journal explained, "instead of being able to incarnate his labor into a ware,

117. *Lassalles Reden und Schriften,* ed. Eduard Bernstein (Berlin: Verlag des 'Vorwärts,' 1893), Volume 3, p. 180 and, correlatively, p. 798.

118. On the imprecision of the term *Ertrag,* see Karl Marx, *Kritik des Gothaer Programms* (Moskau: Verlag für fremdsprachige Literatur, 1941), p. 20.

119. Lassalle assumed that the production cooperatives he advocated would develop with the support of a socialist state, not simply through workers' frugality and the retention of labor's produce. Ulrich Engelhardt, *"Nur vereinigt sind wir stark": Die Anfänge der deutschen Gewerkschaftsbewegung 1862/63 bis 1869/70,* Volume One (Stuttgart: Ernst Klett, 1977), p. 329.

120. Hannes Skambraks, *"Das Kapital" von Marx—Waffe im Klassenkampf* (Berlin: Dietz Verlag, 1977), p. 104; *Social-Demokrat,* February 23, 1868, reprinted in Rolf Dlubek and Hannes Skambraks, editors, *"Das Kapital" von Karl Marx in der deutschen Arbeiterbewegung: 1867 bis 1878* (Berlin: Dietz Verlag, 1967), p. 180. Von Schweitzer deduced from Marx's analysis that even a "just" employer, who paid labor power its full value in the market, nonetheless appropriated surplus value from the worker. Therefore demands for market "justice" would not protect workers. Cora Stephan, *"Genossen, wir dürfen uns nicht von der Geduld hinreissen lassen!"* (Frankfurt am Main: Syndikat, 1977), p. 212. German analysts adopted Marx's appreciation of the sale of labor power even when they did not accept other portions of Marx's political agenda and diagnosis. Skambraks, op. cit., pp. 104, 106, 126–127, 142–143.

must consequently sell his *labor power* itself. The value of this labor power itself is determined not by the value that it *creates* and *can create*, but by the value required to *produce and maintain it*."[121] The columns of the *Social-Demokrat* emphasized that the site of production, not the market, represented the locus of exploitation. In 1870 the journal said that "the exchange of commodities in proportion to the labor they contain does not at all rule out the exploitation of labor power by capital; rather, it provides the basis on which it [exploitation] can develop."[122] After the appearance of *Kapital*, the Lassallian journal also highlighted the significance that could be attached to the locution *Arbeitskraft* even when the subject matter was not economic theory. For example, an article on commercial development said that labor had become a commodity, but then added a clarification: "To put it more exactly, *labor power* is a commodity."[123] By comparison with British misperceptions of Marx, the ready absorption of Marx's analyses and swift revision of Lassalle's economic tenets in Germany suggests that Marx's theory resonated with German experience.[124]

Of course, only a small minority of the members of the free unions and of the Social Democratic party in Germany concerned themselves with matters of economic theory. Even some of the organizations' top officials, whose time was taken up by party business, paid no attention to Marx's analysis.[125] In the first decade after the publication of *Kapital*, party members treated as savants those able to expound the theory at length.[126] But the creed did not remain occult. In subsequent decades workers interested in Marx's examinations could find abbreviated summaries of his analysis of the production process in popular tracts published by Johann Most, Carl August Schramm, and, after 1887, Karl

121. *Social-Demokrat*, February 23, 1868, in Dlubek and Skambraks, editors, op. cit., p. 180. Emphasis in original. Schweitzer's long reviews of *Kapital* in the *Social-Demokrat* pivoted on the difference between the exchange value and the use value of labor power. Johann Baptist von Schweitzer, "Das Werk von Karl Marx," *Social-Demokrat*, no. 25, February 26, 1868, reprinted in Dlubek and Skambraks, editors, op. cit., p. 181.

122. *Social-Demokrat*, May 25, 1871, cited in Dlubek and Skambraks, editors, op. cit., p. 80.

123. *Neuer Social-Demokrat* (Berlin), July 10, 1874. Dlubek and Skambraks, editors, op. cit., p. 80.

124. Wilhelm Bracke, once a follower of Lassalle, keenly propagated Marx's concept of the sale and use of labor power. See *Der Lassallesche Vorschlag*, 1873, reprinted in Dlubek and Skambraks, editors, op. cit., p. 241.

125. Morgan, op. cit., pp. 132–133; Stephan, op. cit., p. 202. But Stephan catalogues a lengthy roster of Social Democrats who did read *Kapital* soon after its appearance.

126. Steinberg, op. cit., p. 17.

Kautsky.[127] Unlike the popularizations of Marx published in Britain, those in Germany remained true to his distinctive conception of labor as a commodity and to his theorization of exploitation at the site of production.[128] The records of the libraries of workers' associations and of party libraries around the turn of the century show that Kautsky's popularization of the new theory of exploitation, *Karl Marx' ökonomische Lehren* ("Karl Marx's Economic Theories"), was frequently borrowed.[129] Over 40 percent of the textile and metal workers who responded to the survey of workers' attitudes initiated by Adolf Levenstein in 1907 reported that they read socialist and trade union literature, including several who said they had read *Das Kapital* or other economic writings by Marx in the original edition.[130]

How well could workers comprehend Marx's prose? The libraries of the workers' associations and of the Social Democratic party lent many copies of Marx's *Kapital*, but clerks at the lending institutions claimed few readers succeeded in digesting the material.[131] Not all workers were mystified by the thinker in the original, however. In her luminous autobiography, Ottilie Baader reports that Marx's *Kapital* was the first socialist book with which she came into contact as a sewing machine worker during the period of the anti-socialist laws. Baader said she studied it to great profit, first with family

127. Ibid., pp. 17, 130. For a discussion of other influential popularizations of *Kapital*, see Rolf Dlubek, "Die Rolle des 'Kapitals' bei der Durchsetzung des Marxismus in der deutschen Arbeiterbewegung," in *Beiträge zur Marx-Engels Forschung*, Institut für Marxismus-Leninismus (Berlin: Dietz Verlag, 1968), p. 47. Members of the Allgemeiner Deutscher Arbeiter-Verein, Lassalle's organization, wrote extensive reviews of *Das Kapital* for popular newspapers. Heinrich Leonard, *Wilhelm Bracke: Leben und Wirken* (Braunschweig: H. Rieke & Co., 1930), p. 16. The secondhand discussions of *Kapital* saved the book from the oblivion into which the low sales of the original would have cast it. On the original's marketing, see Steinberg, op. cit., p. 21 note.

128. August Geib's pamphlet on the *Normalarbeitstag* also uses the term *Arbeitskraft* to distinguish between the use value and the exchange value of the workers' only commodity. Dlubek and Skambraks, editors, op. cit., p. 211. See also the 1873 edition of Johann Most's *Kapital und Arbeit: "Das Kapital" in einer handlichen Zusammenfassung* (Frankfurt am Main: Suhrkamp Verlag, 1972), p. 27, reprinted in Dlubek and Skambraks, editors, op. cit., pp. 276–279. Although the 1873 edition captured the distinction between use and exchange values of labor, it contained other misrepresentations, which Marx corrected in the edition of 1876. Dlubek, op. cit., p. 27.

129. Steinberg, op. cit., pp. 130–139. On the influence of Kautsky's popularization of the first volume of *Kapital*, see Erich Matthias, "Kautsky und der Kautskyanismus," *Marxismus-Studien*, second series (Berlin: Institut für Marxismus-Leninismus, 1957), p. 156, and Hans-Josef Steinberg's introduction to Karl Kautsky, *Karl Marx' ökonomische Lehren* (Berlin: J. H. W. Dietz, 1980), p. xiv.

130. Adolf Levenstein, *Die Arbeiterfrage* (München: Ernst Reinhardt, 1912), pp. 393–403.
131. Steinberg, op. cit., pp. 130–137.

members and later in reading groups of socialist women.[132] Testimony such as hers, in conjunction with the pattern of library lendings, suggests that a significant minority of educated workers had a serious encounter with Marx's theory of exploitation in the capitalist labor process.[133]

Workers did not absorb Marx's ideas only in solitude, through texts. Members of workers' associations discussed *Kapital* soon after its publication. In Magdeburg, the cooper Julis Bremer announced a lecture to the workers' education club in Magdeburg on Marx's *Kapital* just five months after the book's appearance. In the next three years, programs of the Social Democratic workers' association there included the work frequently enough that the local liberal newspaper, the *Magdeburgische Zeitung*, took fright at the "propositions" of Karl Marx that "were interpreted and demonstrated."[134]

During the period of union expansion in the two decades before the First World War, the newspapers and conferences of the Social Democratic (or "free") textile unions faithfully adopted the Marxist theory of the extraction of surplus. Local branches held meetings for workers on such topics as "The Value of Labor Power."[135] The journal of the German textile union, *Der Textil-Arbeiter*, used the general term *labor* to describe the factors necessary for production but referred to *labor power* in the context of the employment relation.[136] *Der Textil-Arbeiter* also emphasized that workers were exploited separately as "producers" at work and as "consumers" in the

132. Ottilie Baader, *Ein steiniger Weg: Lebenserinnerungen einer Sozialistin* (Berlin: J. H. W. Dietz, 1979 [1921]), pp. 23, 25, 36.

133. Workers' letters to Marx upon reading *Kapital* are listed in Eike Kopf, "Die Ideen des 'Kapitals' von Karl Marx werden zur materiellen Gewalt: Zur Wirkungsgeschichte des 'Kapitals' in Deutschland bis 1872," *Wissenschaftliche Zeitschrift der Friedrich-Schiller-Universität Jena*, Gesellschafts- und Sprachwissenschaftliche Reihe, Volume 17, Number 2 (1968), p. 150.

134. Hans Bursian, "Über den Einfluss des 'Kapitals' von Karl Marx auf die Magdeburger Arbeiterbewegung, 1869–1871—Forschungsprobleme und Ergebnisse," *Beiträge zur Geschichte der deutschen Arbeiterbewegung*, Volume 10 (Berlin: Institut für Marxismus-Leninismus, 1968), pp. 115, 117–118. In 1868 at the general conference of the ADAV the representatives heard a presentation of Marx's theory of surplus value and passed a resolution praising Marx's analysis of "the capitalist production process." Jutta Seidel, *Wilhelm Bracke: Vom Lassalleaner zum Marxisten* (Berlin: Dietz Verlag, 1966), pp. 40–42.

135. *Der Textil-Arbeiter*, August 1, 1902, Adorf. For references to other unions' discussion of terms such as "the commodity of labor power," see Dlubek, op. cit., p. 41.

136. *Der Textil-Arbeiter*, November 4, 1904, "Produktion." The "free" unions' newspapers referred to the extraction of unpaid labor time and described the profits of companies as "surplus value." *Fach-Zeitung*, July 16, 1899, Krefeld; *Der Textil-Arbeiter*, October 8, 1909, Bautzen.

market who paid taxes and higher prices due to tariffs.[137] By comparison, the press of the British labor movement did not distinguish so carefully between these two modes of exploitation, but, rather, combined them under the general rubric of unfair exchange in the market.

The assumption that the worker transferred labor to the employer in the form of labor power shaped literate workers' descriptions of their productive activity. *Der Textil-Arbeiter* treated "labor power" as a detached *thing* which the capitalist tried to seize. For example, the newspaper enjoined its readers in 1901, "Above all, [your] labor power and [your] very selves must be protected from exploitation."[138] The phrasing treated labor power as an entity apart from the concrete person and identified its use as the cause of exploitation. At a conference of workers from the jute textile industry in 1906, a representative complained that "the piece rates are arranged so that to achieve the pay of 1.6 marks, the labor power is fully absorbed [by the capitalist]."[139] Labor power was seen as comprising a real substance which the employer "consumed." The choice of expression shows that even when textile workers did not engage in abstract discussions of political economy, they assumed that their struggles pivoted around the calibrated use of "labor power" in the production process.[140]

THE PRACTICAL FOUNDATIONS FOR THE RECEPTION OF IDEOLOGY

Where are we to turn for an explanation of the success of the dissemination and development of Marx's theory of exploitation in Germany, but its weakness in Britain? Could the difference in outcomes have resulted merely from

137. *Der Textil-Arbeiter*, April 26, 1901, p. 1.

138. *Der Textil-Arbeiter*, April 5, 1901. A representative to the textile workers' national conference in 1891 reported that some workers were shying away from the textile labor market but conveyed this by saying that workers were "witholding their commodity of labor power from the market." Deutscher Textilarbeiterverband, *Protokoll des ersten deutschen Textilarbeiter-Kongresses* (Berlin: Deutscher Textilarbeiterverband, n.d.), p. 46. For parallel expressions, see *Der Textil-Arbeiter*, April 23, 1909, Aachen. In their discussion of women's labor, the papers likewise objectified the "labor power" as a thing apart from its owner. The organ of the union of German workers' associations reduced female workers to "bearers of purchased labor power." *Demokratisches Wochenblatt*, January 2, 1869, p. 6. "Capital," said the *Textil-Arbeiter*, "has in the labor power of the woman found a choice object of exploitation [*Ausbeutungsobjekt*]." Sept. 6, 1901.

139. Verband Deutscher Textilarbeiter, "Die Sklaven des Jute-Kapitals, Protokoll," Jutearbeiter-Konferenz Braunschweig, Oct. 7, 1906, pp. 8–9, Archiv des Freien Deutschen Gewerkschaftsbundes, Berlin.

140. For an example of a metal worker referring specifically to the appropriation of "labor power," see Levenstein, op. cit., p. 108.

a difference in the supply and dissemination of ideas? Marx's initial volume of *Kapital* appeared in Germany in 1867, but did not appear in English until the journal *To-day*, under Hyndman's editorship, began to serialize it in 1885. *Kapital* lacked an English translation in one volume until the publication of Engels's edition in 1887.[141] As is well known, Marx remained in contact with key intellectuals of the German labor movement during his long exile in Britain.[142] Perhaps his ideas triumphed in Germany due to their more vigorous propagation by this intellectual elite, which was in place before the trade union movement took off in Germany. Is it possible that the difference in outcomes had little to do with the cultural horizon of the workers but resulted from differences in the trade union elites and publishing organizations responsible for diffusing ideas?

This line of reasoning does not match the circumstances of ideological development in either Britain or Germany. In Britain the failure of Marxist economic theory resulted, not from ignorance or rejection of Marx, but from misinterpretation. Marx was the single most important writer on economic theory for the revived socialist movement in Britain at the end of the nineteenth century, so much so that opponents of the labor movement in Britain criticized its members for inviting "German" theory into the land.[143] At his

141. Tsuzuki, op. cit., p. 60. Apart from stray copies of pamphlets issued by the First International, none of Marx's works were available in English in full until James L. Joynes's edition of *Wage-Labour and Capital* (London: The Modern Press, 1886) appeared. On the introduction of translations of Marx's works, see also Torr, op. cit., p. 326; Collins, op. cit., p. 59.

142. Georg Adler, *Die Geschichte der ersten sozialpolitischen Arbeiterbewegung in Deutschland* (Frankfurt am Main: Sauer & Auvermann, 1966 [1885]), pp. 299–300. Yet Marx also had an extensive network of contacts with British trade unionists. See Henry Collins and Chimen Abramsky, *Karl Marx and the British Labour Movement* (London: Macmillan & Co., 1965), especially pp. 93 ff.

143. As Eric Hobsbawm has put it, "Marxism—or at all events some sort of simplified version of marxism—was the first kind of socialism to reach Britain during the revival of the 1880s, the one most persistently propagated by devoted pioneers at a thousand street corners, and the one most persistently and ubiquitously taught at a thousand classes run by socialist organizations, labour colleges or freelance lectures." E. J. Hobsbawm, "Karl Marx and the British Labour Movement," in his *Revolutionaries: Contemporary Essays* (London: Weidenfeld and Nicolson, 1973), p. 105. For an extensive list of sources of testimony by British socialists about their engagement with Marxian economic literature, consult Duncan Tanner, "Ideological Debate in Edwardian Labour Politics: Radicalism, Revisionism and Socialism," in Eugenio F. Biagini and Alastair J. Reid, editors, *Currents of Radicalism: Popular Radicalism, Organised Labour and Party Politics in Britain, 1850–1914* (Cambridge: Cambridge University Press, 1991), p. 280. On the influence of professed Marxists in Yorkshire, see Tom Mann, *Tom Mann's Memoirs* (London: Labour Publishing Company, 1923), pp. 39 ff., 129; for the role of other Marxists in Yorkshire see Bernard Barker, "Anatomy of Reformism: The Social and Political Ideas of the Labour Leadership in Yorkshire," *International Review of Social History* Volume 18, Part 1 (1973), p. 8, and Laybourn, op. cit., p. 234. For the availability of

speech in Burnley in 1893, William Morris rebutted this attack upon the introduction of ideas from abroad, asserting, "It was said that Socialism was a German import. It was nothing the worse for that. And Socialism is English now."[144] If, as Morris insisted, British workers gave socialist theory a native hue, much of the materials they used came from Germany. Some members of the Social Democratic Federation and founders of the Labour Party, such as the trade unionist Jem Macdonald, said they received the ideas of *Kapital* from European acquaintances, including German artisans. "When *Das Kapital* appeared in English," Macdonald later wrote, "it was to me as a book that I had read over and over again."[145] Tom Maguire, who said he had studied Marx intensively, organized for the Socialist League in Leeds after 1884. Many of the leaders of the Independent Labour Party in the textile districts of the north, including Margaret McMillan, an elected member of the Bradford school board, boasted that they had studied *Kapital*.[146] Tom Mann used *Wage Labour and Capital* as his basic text for the socialist economics course he gave in Bolton in 1888.[147] In Burnley, Lancashire, which had a long tradition of open-minded debate in workers' clubs, skeptical liberals pressed the socialists to demonstrate the feasibility of their blueprints for the future. The local socialists responded in 1894 that they believed, not in the discredited Owen, but in Marx.[148] The letters from many Burnley workers published in the *Burnley Gazette* during the 1890s cite the descriptive portions of Marx's *Kapital*, though not segments defining the transmission of labor in the form of a commodity.[149] In sum, Marxist economic analysis was both well-represented in Britain and, in predictable ways, misunderstood.[150]

Marxist economic theory in Britain generally, see Pierson, op. cit., pp. 28, 255; Eric Hobsbawm, editor, *Labour's Turning Point 1880–1900* (London: Lawrence & Wishart, 1948), pp. 23, 41; Hinton, op. cit., p. 94; E. P. Thompson, *William Morris: Romantic to Revolutionary* (New York: Pantheon Books, 1976), pp. 332–333.

144. *Socialist and N.E. Lancashire Labour News*, December 15, 1893, p. 5. For a similar comment from Tom Mann, see Trodd, op. cit., pp. 328–329.

145. Torr, op. cit., p. 183. See also Collins and Abramsky, op. cit., p. 303; Hinton, op. cit., p. 53.

146. *Keighley ILP Journal*, December 30, 1894. On McMillan's election and tenure, see Laybourn, op. cit., p. 226.

147. Torr, op. cit., p. 253. But compare his understanding of workers' retention of "the full fruits of their labor" in Chushichi Tsuzuki, *Tom Mann, 1856–1941* (Oxford: Clarendon Press, 1991), p. 146. Eleanor Marx also spoke at socialist meetings in Bolton. Neil Duffield, "Bolton Socialist Club," *Bolton People's History* Volume 1 (March 1984), p. 3.

148. *Burnley Express and Advertiser*, January 24, 1894.

149. *Burnley Gazette*, e.g., August 5, 1893, and April 11, 1894.

150. The work that faithfully presented Marx's theory of exploitation in Britain was written by Edward Aveling, translator of *Kapital*. See Edward Aveling, *The Students' Marx: An Introduction to the Study of Karl Marx' "Capital"* (London: Swan Sonnenschein & Co., 1907), p. 46.

Whereas the reborn English movement misinterpreted its chosen step-father, the German labor movement grew up in its early years an orphan. There is no evidence of a network of communication between Marx and the largest workers' movement of the revolution born in 1848, the Arbeiterverbrüderung ("Workers' Brotherhood").[151] The members of workers' clubs in the 1860s had little acquaintance with Marx's early writings. In his autobiography, Bebel stressed the disconnection during this period between Marxist ideas and the workers' associations, for which Leipzig served as a traditional center:[152] "That there were workers who were familiar with the *Communist Manifesto,* for instance, or who knew something about Marx's and Engels's activity during the revolutionary years in the Rhineland, of this I saw absolutely no indication at this time in Leipzig." In sum, the German labor movement after the repression of the 1850s did not begin with an established Marxist heritage.[153] Marx had been sorely disappointed by the lack of response to his early *Critique of Political Economy.*[154] His ideas did not gain an audience in the workers' movement until the publication of *Kapital.*[155] Although the British workers' movements were exposed to Marxist ideas more than a decade later than their German counterparts were, the involvement, once it began, was intense. How, then, are we to explain the long-lasting divergences in Britain and in Germany in the interpretation of Marx's theory of exploitation?

If Marx's analysis of the exploitation of labor was widely distributed in Britain but systematically misrepresented, and if this analysis was transmitted more successfully to the German labor movement despite the absence of a standing Marxist tradition leading back to 1848, then the supply of ideas among intellectuals does not represent the critical variable for differentiating between the German and British outcomes. The differentiating circumstance is not the depth of engagement with Marx but the variations in

151. Frolinde Balser, *Sozial-Demokratie 1848/49–1863,* Volume One (Stuttgart: Ernst Klett Verlag, 1962), pp. 211, 233.

152. Adler, op. cit., p. 299. The founding congress of the General German Workers' Association took place in 1863 in Leipzig.

153. Bebel, op. cit., pp. 49–50. For Bebel's assessment of the lack of continuity in socialist ideas between the 1848 revolution and the 1860s in the German labor movement at large, see August Bebel, *Gewerkschafts-Bewegung und politische Parteien* (Stuttgart: J. H. W. Dietz, 1900), p. 8.

154. Stephan, op. cit., p. 199; Dlubek and Skambraks, op. cit., p. 34.

155. The works of Marx, according to Bebel, were not known in the Social Democratic Party until the end of the 1860s. August Bebel, *Aus meinem Leben,* op. cit., pp. 131 ff.

response among those who came into contact with Marx's propositions. Intellectual elites may serve as the tentative formulators of an explicit system of ideology, but that ideology will be received sympathetically by workers and sustained from below only if it resonates with portions of the conduct of everyday practice. Lloyd Jones, a prominent member of the co-op movement, noted the limits on workers' readiness to take up economic theories. "The working man accepts such of these views as his experience in the world and workshops justify to him," Jones wrote in 1877. "Where his experience does not do so, he rejects them."[156]

A comparison of the textile industries of Yorkshire with those of early industrializing regions of Germany is well suited for comparing the reception of ideologies, because it proceeds from structural parallels in the environment in which the textile unions acquired their economic philosophies before the First World War. The characteristics sometimes used to label the British labor movement—early craft unionization based on occupational exclusivity, and delayed affiliation with a political party—do not fit Yorkshire textiles. In Yorkshire the first unions for factory weavers and spinners did not emerge until 1881 in Huddersfield and until the 1890s in other districts.[157] The emergence of unions in Yorkshire well after the completion of mechanization matched experience in Germany, where textile union membership expanded rapidly after 1890. As in Germany, trade unions in Yorkshire developed in tandem with an independent workers' party with which union organizers were affiliated.[158] Still another feature of the textile associations in Yorkshire makes it parallel to the German case. The major union for textile workers in Yorkshire admitted all workers in the trade, not just those in select occupations.[159] This practice resembled the industrywide

156. Quoted in Clements, op. cit., pp. 93–104.

157. H. A. Turner, *Trade Union Growth Structure and Policy* (Toronto: University of Toronto Press, 1962), pp. 175–178. Local textile unions for factory workers founded earlier in the century disbanded shortly after the conclusion of the strike movements to which they owed their birth. E. E. Dodd, *Bingley: A Yorkshire Town Through Nine Centuries* (Bingley: T. Harrison & Sons, 1958), p. 164; Sheila Lewenhak, *Women and Trade Unions* (London: Ernest Benn, 1977), pp. 86, 92. See also Chapter One, footnote 26.

158. Even contemporaries noticed the parallels in the timing and political sponsorship of unionization between Yorkshire and Germany. Joyce, *Work, Society and Politics*, op. cit., pp. 76, 226.

159. The Weavers' and Textile Workers' Association sponsored meetings for willeyers, fettlers, rag grinders, and packers. *Yorkshire Factory Times*, March 17, 1993, p. 5. In some towns, workers in dyeing, combing, and finishing shops maintained their own craft unions, however. Joanna Bornat, "An Examination of the General Union of Textile Workers 1883–1922," Ph.D. diss., University of Essex, 1981, p. 8. These small societies did not form regional craft associations, but survived as local clubs. Laybourn, "The Attitude," op. cit., p. 140.

recruitment practiced by German unions.[160] The example of Yorkshire shows that the boundaries of unionization and the legacy of past organizational development do not account for the differential reception of analyses of the exploitation of labor.

The reception of ideas depended upon something more profound than the environment for union growth. Upon the publication of *Kapital*, attention in Germany focused on Marx's analysis of labor as a commodity, and the ready absorption of a Marxist vocabulary into the expression of ordinary problems shows that Marxism resonated with German producers' everyday experience of micro-practices on the shop floor. For the workers, cultural practice led theory: they lived out the Marxist specification of labor on the shop floor before intellectuals presented those categories to them as a formal body of propositions. Workers without advanced education could grasp the importance of the distinction between labor and labor power, Marx claimed, and could thereby prove themselves sharper economists than vulgar analysts were.[161] But in Britain, despite the contacts between British trade unionists and their German counterparts,[162] and despite the availability of Marxist-inspired discourse from British intellectuals, the trade unions resanctified a theory of exploitation based on the transfer of materialized labor.

The lived experience of the transfer of "labor power" represented a necessary but not a sufficient condition for the adoption of the belief that the owner's extraction of unpaid labor time was intrinsic to the employment relation. On the eve of the First World War, about one-quarter of the textile workers in Germany who joined unions chose the Christian textile workers' union.[163] The Christian (predominantly Catholic) associations did not seek

160. In Germany only a few local societies, such as the relatively short-lived Weavers' Association of the Lower Rhine, centered in Krefeld, limited membership by textile occupation. On the exclusion of auxiliary cloth workers from that union, see Kreisarchiv Kempen, Stadt Lobberich, 1444, August 22, 1899. See also Chapter One, note 27.

161. Karl Marx and Friedrich Engels, *Marx-Engels Werke*, Volume 6 (Berlin: Dietz Verlag, 1961), p. 594. The article by Engels is entitled "Einleitung zu Karl Marx *Lohnarbeit und Kapital*, Ausgabe 1891."

162. *Yorkshire Factory Times*, January 3, 1908; Yorkshire Textile Workers' Deputation, *Official Report of the Yorkshire Textile Workers' Deputation: An Enquiry into the Conditions of the German Woollen Cloth Operatives* (Batley: News Office, 1908).

163. In 1910, the Christian textile workers' union counted more than 32,000 members and the "free" German textile workers' union more than 113,000 members. Deutscher Textilarbeiterverband, *Jahrbuch des deutschen Textilarbeiterverbandes, 1910* (Berlin: Karl Hübsch, 1911), and Zentralverband Christlicher Textilarbeiter Deutschlands, "Geschäftsbericht," 1908–1910, Archiv der Gewerkschaft Textil-Bekleidung, Düsseldorf.

to overthrow the capitalist system; they simply sought better treatment and higher earnings for workers.[164]

Despite the self-proclaimed limits of the Christian movement, however, their deliberations about economic affairs revealed the distinctive influence of German experience of labor as a commodity. The Christian unions did not simply vindicate the noble character of work or its social value. They advanced a crude labor theory of value and reasoned in terms of abstract labor time. "Money is the representation of human labor," the Christian textile newspaper concluded in an editorial on economic principles, "minted, tangible, metallicized human power."[165] The Christian unions adopted the German notion of the sale of labor power to portray the workers' insertion into the capitalist economy.[166] In an article entitled "Is Labor a Commodity?" their *Textilarbeiter-Zeitung* made explicit in 1900 the telling and characteristic German distinction: employers, it explained, "regard labor *or, rather, labor power* as a commodity."[167] This journal also identified labor power as an entity "alienated" by the worker: "Conceiving of labor as merely a commodity, which the owner of the *labor power* sells," it explained, "makes the worker dependent on the purchase offer that the employer makes to him."[168] Christians also referred to the owner's exploitation "of the [labor] power of the worker"—though not, of course, with Marx's conclusion that the exploitation of labor represented the ultimate source of profit.[169]

164. The flavor of the Christian movement can be appreciated from a speech a secretary, Johann Giesberts, gave before a meeting of nine hundred textile workers in Mönchengladbach in 1898. "The Christian workers demand only an adequate existence, and if one grants them this, then their will to labor and conscientiousness, of which the employer will have the use, will grow." HSTAD, Präsidialbüro 1272, p. 40.

165. *Der Christliche Textilarbeiter*, February 24, 1900.

166. Workers, *Der Christliche Textilarbeiter* stated, "own just a single commodity, namely their labor power." December 16, 1899, Mörs. Of course, some Christian commentators insisted that labor could never truly become a commodity, but when they discussed its treatment as such, they defined it as the sale of labor power. See the discussion of this doctrine in *Die Textilarbeiter-Zeitung*, January 11, 1908. Even if Christian organizers accepted the labor contract as a worthy mechanism for regulating social relations, they threw a worried glance back at the feudal commitment of the whole individual, just as German economists had. For example, in its delineation of the sale of labor, the *Christlicher Arbeiterfreund* showed that it could take nothing for granted: "The personage [of the worker] with all its intellectual and physical capabilities," it concluded, "is the inviolable property of the worker." *Christlicher Arbeiterfreund*, May 27, 1898.

167. *Der Christliche Textilarbeiter*, June 30, 1900, emphasis added.

168. Ibid. Emphasis added.

169. *Die Textilarbeiter-Zeitung*, July 28, 1900, Borken. The Christians' emphasis on the creative power of human labor nonetheless led them to radical critiques of the profit accruing to owners of capital. "The Christian unions are an enemy of the false economy based on

Similar worker demands emerged on the left bank of the Rhine, where Christian unions dominated most of the Catholic cities, as appeared in districts where Protestants and the socialist-affiliated "free" unions were ascendant: the same rationale for the payment of waiting time, the same contestation of the distribution of hours over the workday. In view of the pervasive differences between the experiences of Catholic and Protestant workers *outside* the workplace in the period before the First World War and between the intellectual roots of their leaders,[170] the convergence in the underlying view of labor in the Christian and Social Democratic labor movements suggests the influence of something else their members shared in common: namely, the workers' everyday experience of the conveyance of "labor power" at the point of production.

In part, of course, the Catholic movement consciously distanced itself from the prevailing discourse of political economy in Germany, for both the established bourgeois economists and those of the Social Democratic movement accepted the commodification of everyday life and of labor as accomplished facts. Catholic intellectuals, by contrast, remained uncomfortable with these premises and developed an alternative discursive tradition based on the contributions to the social whole of organically related "estates." Yet when elite speakers for the Catholic labor unions reflected upon the essentials of the capitalist labor transaction, they, too, adopted the view that labor was sold in the form of labor power.[171] Even when they rejected the world view of socialist and bourgeois economics, their social experience lent them much the same specification of labor as a commodity as circulated among their ideological opponents.

PRACTICAL ANALYSES OF EXPLOITATION

The contrasting forms of signifying practice in the workplace did not only support contrasts in the formal ideologies of exploitation; they correlated as

capital," said one leader at a textile union meeting in Rheine in 1904. Speech by Herr Pesch of Krefeld, cited in Staatsarchiv Münster, Kreis Steinfurt, 1116, February 1, 1904.

170. Eric Dorn Brose, *Christian Labor and the Politics of Frustration in Imperial Germany* (Washington, D.C.: The Catholic University of America Press, 1985), Chapter One and pp. 146, 148; Jonathan Sperber, *Popular Catholicism in Nineteenth-Century Germany* (Princeton: Princeton University Press, 1984), pp. 296–297.

171. "Through the labor contract the entrepreneur receives likewise a certain sway over the person of the worker . . . over the expenditure of his physical and intellectual powers." Heinrich Brauns, "Die Notwendigkeit der Gewerkschaften," in his *Katholische Sozialpolitik im 20. Jahrhundert: Ausgewählte Aufsätze und Reden von Heinrich Brauns,* edited by Hubert Mockenhaupt (Mainz: Matthias-Grünewald-Verlag, 1976), p. 12.

well with differences in workers' impromptu articulation of complaints about exploitation on the shop floor. Contrasts in the workers' immediate apperception of exploitation appeared in weavers' responses to fines imposed for fabric that the employers alleged to be defective, one of the problems about which workers complained most frequently. The British workers analyzed the amounts of the fines assessed in terms of the market cost of repairing the defect in the finished product. "3d per yard is deducted for ends down," the *Yorkshire Factory Times* reported of one mill. By the newspaper's reckoning, this totaled "three times more than it costs to sew them in."[172] In its account of a fine imposed on a woman weaver from Batley, the newspaper claimed that the cloth checker "had fined her 4s 6d for a damage that could be mended in three hours, and that would not cause the piece to be sold for any less in the market."[173]

The British weavers viewed fining as a violation of the rules of fair exchange of finished products in the market. "I think it is a burning shame," wrote a correspondent for the *Yorkshire Factory Times*, "that employers cannot be satisfied with the profit they make at market out of the goods they manufacture without taking a portion of an employee's hard-earned money from him to further swell their coffers."[174] Comments such as this rested on the idea that exchanges in the market, not labor alone, generated ordinary profits. The fine constituted a separate, unusual means of making a profit from labor. The *Yorkshire Factory Times* expressed a female weaver's view that fining comprised a kind of additional profit for the employer this way: "The masters smoke a tremendous lot of four-penny cigars, and the two piece wages [fines] last week were for cigars."[175]

Given the British weavers' treatment of fining as a deviation from the rules of fair market exchange, the solutions they proposed ought not to occasion surprise. First, they insisted that textile workers on piece rates be treated as contractors who delivered a product. "They are piece workers," the *Yorkshire Factory Times* claimed, and therefore "by law" could not be

---

172. *Yorkshire Factory Times,* October 31, 1890, Shipley.

173. *Yorkshire Factory Times,* January 2, 1891, Batley. For other examples of such comparisons, see January 17, 1890, Halifax, and July 10, 1891.

174. This writer contended that fining was "nothing better than second-hand pocket picking." *Yorkshire Factory Times,* April 29, 1892, Bingley. This reliance on reasoning about the sale of finished products in the market became evident in other contexts as well. British workers articulated the right of women workers to equal pay with men on the ground that the finished products were indistinguishable: "When a manufacturer sells a piece he does not tell the merchant that it has been woven by a woman." *Yorkshire Factory Times,* September 25, 1891, p. 4.

175. *Yorkshire Factory Times,* April 4, 1890, Bingley.

fined simply for violating the mill's standards for cloth.[176] By the workers' reasoning, if the employer wanted to fine them for bad cloth he had to prosecute them as he would a contractor who delivered a defective product. The British weavers' opposition to any form of fining for spoiled work led them to resist institutions that would regulate the fining system. For example, Parliament in 1896 passed a factory act that required employers to post a notice about all forms of fines to which employees at the site were subject. This legislation would have protected weavers by requiring employers to standardize the penalties imposed for each kind of defect. Yet the weavers' unions lobbied to have Parliament exempt textiles from the act's provisions—they preferred to suffer fining without safeguards than to recognize the legitimacy of the practice.[177]

In contrast to the British weavers, who held up an ideal of the exchange of products in the market as a way of assessing the injustice of fines, German weavers included fines for purportedly flawed cloth in a list of more general abuses. They saw the imposition of fines as another expression of the owners' disposition over their labor. "Fines are always the order of the day," declared a union speaker at a shop meeting in Württemberg. "The workers at this firm are fined twice, for actually it is already a punishment if someone has to work at a plant with this kind of poor ventilation."[178] This complainant drew a parallel between two grievances: just as submission to unhealthy air represented a kind of exploitation that resulted from the employers' domination of the production process, so did the payment of a fine. That is, German workers treated fines as just another strategy by which the owner could use his authority over the workplace to extract unpaid labor. They called the fines "pay deductions" (*Lohnabzüge*), the phrase that referred to any lowering in the pay scale or in the amount workers actually earned.[179]

176. *Yorkshire Factory Times*, January 13, 1893.
177. *Cotton Factory Times*, April 8, 1904, "'Reasonable' Fines." The M.P. from Darwen, speaking in 1896 for the textile workers, said, "The operatives wished to do away with fines altogether; and they objected to this Bill which recognises and regulated fines." See speech by John Rutherford in United Kingdom, *Parliamentary Debates*, Series Four, Volume 43, 1896, July 17—August 6, pp. 767–770.
178. This is the union's report of the address. *Der Textil-Arbeiter*, August 4, 1911.
179. See almost any issue of *Der Textil-Arbeiter*—for example, May 2, 1902, Ostritz; May 9, 1902, Rendsburg; May 16, 1902, Elsterberg. The widespread practice of offering workers a bonus for cloth of perfect quality, which could be withheld in its entirety for any faults, also discouraged German workers from adopting market-based criticisms like those of their British counterparts. Under the German bonus system, whether the piece had one fault or many, the worker suffered the same loss. The withholding of the gratuity, which represented a substan-

In contrast to the British workers' refusal to bargain over fines for allegedly spoiled work, German workers at some mills formed committees to
negotiate with the owners on this issue.[180] They also composed lists specifying how much weavers ought to be fined for each defect and included such
charts among their strike demands. This difference between German and
British reactions to fining cannot be dismissed by assuming that German
textile workers were invariably more cooperative than their British counterparts. As we have seen, the German workers pressed ambitious demands
concerning many facets of mill life.[181] The example of fining shows that the
contrasting "theories" of the labor transaction hidden in the disciplinary
regime of German and British factories generated their counterpoints in

---

tial loss, departed from the idea that the cloth had a determinant "market value" from which
the fine constituted a deduction. *Der Textil-Arbeiter,* April 30, 1909, Bocholt; July 6, 1909,
Oelsnitz; March 6, 1914, p. 79.

180. *Der Textil-Arbeiter,* March 31, 1911, Peilau-Eulengebirges; February 27, 1914,
Langenbielau.

181. British workers' attention to the sale of their labor as product in a market exchange
showed up in another complaint as well. Table 2, above, Chapter 4, which compares the
distribution of complaints from weavers, shows that British weavers distinguished themselves
from their German counterparts by focusing on mispayments for delivered pieces. Nearly
5 percent of complaints (42) from the British sample for weavers concerned the deceptive
measuring of fabric, making it the fourth most frequent complaint. This grievance arose under
two conditions: when company clerks paid the weaver for a shorter length of cloth than the
weaver actually manufactured, and when the weaver received credit for fewer picks per inch
than he or she had executed. Under 2 percent of complaints (16) from the German sample
concerned the mismeasurement of pieces, making it only the eleventh most frequent complaint. Yet the deception in those cases that came to light in Germany was egregious (Staatsarchiv Münster, Kreis Steinfurt, 1116, January 19, 1904, Rheine; HSTAD, Regierung
Düsseldorf, 25029, p. 2, for 1906; *Der Textil-Arbeiter,* May 30, 1902, Elsterberg). Academic
writers described the mismeasurement of cloth as a fact of life in Germany; they arrived at
averages for the rate at which owners shortchanged weavers in whole districts. Karl Schmid,
Die Entwicklung der Hofer Baumwoll-Industrie 1432–1913 (Leipzig: A. Deichertsche Verlagsbuchhandlung, 1923), p. 76.

Whether this difference in the salience of mismeasuring resulted purely from workers'
interpretations of similar settings or whether it was determined partly by the honesty of
German employers, I am unable to say. The outcome, however, was consistent with the
difference in the ways workers defined the commodity of labor in the two countries. Complaints about the false measurement of pieces originated in the era when handloom weavers
sold their goods to putters-out. This grievance centered on whether the employer, as a kind of
merchant, was obeying the rules of fair market exchange for finished goods. The *Yorkshire
Factory Times,* in its appeals for workers to change factory conditions, placed a fair market at
the center of its vision. It declared in 1891, "The textile industry in Yorkshire can be raised
from commercial depravity, as at present, to commercial honesty." *Yorkshire Factory Times,*
March 27, 1891, Pudsey. As with the theme of fining, so with measuring: the British textile
workers formulated their responses by focusing on deviations from the ideal of equitable trades
of products in the market.

workers' formulation of grievances: in each country, workers relied upon a corresponding theory of exploitation to criticize capitalist practice. When the concrete procedures of everyday manufacture "directly possess the naked and abstract form of the commodity," then workers are in immediate possession of economic theory.[182]

The pervasive effect of the contrasting theories of the hiring of labor also emerged when German and British textile workers attempted to reach industrial bargains with their employers. In Lancashire representatives of the spinners' unions proposed that workers be paid according to piece-rate scales that would fluctuate to allow employers a stipulated percentage of return on their invested capital. For example, at a meeting in 1900 with the Federation of Master Cotton Spinners' Associations, the operatives said they preferred that "wages be adjusted on a net margin allowing for the fluctuations in the prices of cotton, coal, etc."[183] The workers suggested that negotiators agree on the average capital invested in a spinning factory per spindle, figure the cost of depreciation, grant the owners a shifting allowance for working capital, and then assign a rate of return. The "net margin" between all these sums and the proceeds from disposing of the finished product in the market would provide workers with their wages fund. The representatives of the employers acceded to the workers' idea, provided that owners receive at least a 5 percent rate of return. According to the workers' research, for yarn of standard fineness mill owners needed a profit on average of one farthing per pound of cotton spun in order to realize an annual return of over 5 percent on investment.[184]

More important than the figures, perhaps, are the principles they illustrate. The conduct of the negotiations shows that both the workers and the employers conceived of the factory proprietor as an investor in the marketplace rather than as a manager of labor power.[185] For if the selling prices of the finished product were far above the cost of production, the owners were not entitled to reap the benefit of efficiently converting the raw materials

---

182. Georg Lukács, "Reification and the Consciousness of the Proletariat," in his *History and Class Consciousness* (Cambridge, Massachusetts: The M.I.T. Press, 1971), p. 172.

183. Goldsmiths' Library, University of London, Federation of Master Cotton Spinners' Associations, *Report of Negotiations 1899–1900*, p. 16.

184. *The Leader*, March 22, 1901, "Textile Tattle."

185. Language itself could betray the understanding of profit as the reward of trade: "The manufacturer feels that if he lays out capital on improved machinery, or supplies extra good material, and thus enables his workpeople to produce more in a given time, he ought to get a trading profit." John Watts, "Essay on Strikes," *British Association for the Advancement of Science: The Workman's Bane and Antidote* (Manchester: A. Ireland, 1861), p. 7.

and labor power into a completed ware. Like bankers, they received only interest on investment. The workers, conversely, were not selling a resource, labor power, which had a fixed market value prior to being converted to a product. Rather, the operatives handed their labor over as if they were traders in products, who paid a rent on the mill, purchased supplies, and then delivered yarn at its current market appraisal. In the event, workers and employers could not reach agreement on the average capital invested per spindle and on the grade of yarn to take as a standard, but they did not fail for lack of effort. The spinning employers and their operatives sought for more than a dozen years to reach an accord on the "net margin" principle.[186] To certify actual expenditures, mill owners offered to open their accounting books to the workers' inspection.[187] Weavers, too, negotiated for piece rates by "net margin."[188] The complications of putting the workers' "net margin" proposal into effect were so daunting that only well-established assumptions about the nature of the labor transaction could have kept employers and spinning operatives engaged with the idea for so long.

Although the "net margin" proposal legitimated the mill owners' rates of return, British workers in many industries were ready to let their wages fluctuate according to the selling price of their product because this index seemed to eliminate the most odious form of profit-taking, that appropriated by the "middleman" in the market for finished wares.[189] In the coal trade, the miners at Newcastle declared as early as 1831 that they wanted to peg their earnings to product markets. "The Men and Boys are willing to abide the Risk of Fluctuations of the Coal Trade," their handbill declared.[190] The miners' response showed, of course, that they saw their labor as a commodity and imagined the organization of work as a market relation. But their reaction did not entirely accept the commercial system, for it resisted

186. *Textile Mercury*, January 15, 1910, p. 43. Card room workers were included in the plans. *Burnley Gazette*, Nov. 14, 1908, p. 3.

187. Federation of Master Cotton Spinners' Associations, op. cit., p. 18. The negotiations failed in part because the employers themselves still lacked an adequate method for determining the cost of depreciation. M. W. Kirby, "The Lancashire Cotton Industry in the Inter-War Years," *Business History* (July 1974), p. 153.

188. *Nelson Chronicle*, March 29, 1901, p. 4; *Burnley Gazette*, Nov. 14, 1908, p. 3.

189. Sometimes the operative spinners seemed to view speculators in the product markets, not the employers, as the real exploiters. Mawdsley, the Lancashire spinners' leader, attacked the "middlemen bloodsuckers" who took the profit out of the cotton industry. Joyce, *Visions of the People*, op. cit., p. 120. Likewise, weavers sometimes blamed merchants, not employers, for low wages. *Bradford Observer*, January 25, 1894, Shipley.

190. James Jaffe, *The Struggle for Market Power: Industrial Relations in the British Coal Industry, 1800–1840* (Cambridge: Cambridge University Press, 1991), p. 115. The miners believed that unmanipulated trade in products would break the power of their employers.

the middleman predator. Near the turn of the century, the president of the miners' federation in Leicester endorsed sliding scales with a similar line of reasoning: "The giving away of value to middlemen," he said, "should not determine the rate of wages."[191] In Germany the initiative for pegging wages to the selling prices of products came only after the First World War, and then not from workers but from employers, who adopted it to cope with the country's runaway inflation.[192]

THE LABOR PROCESS
AS AN ANCHOR FOR CULTURE

The flow of ideas between German and British analysts of the exploitation of labor confirms the persistence of fundamental differences in the nationally prevalent concepts of labor. Cross-cultural exchange did not soften the contrasts in definitions of labor as a commodity, but, rather, demonstrated their rigidity. If a correspondence emerged in each country between the labor movement's concept of labor as a commodity and the definition of labor incorporated into manufacturing procedures, how can we ascertain that the production process served as the original source of these concepts? Is it not possible that the political and union movements acted as a precursory cradle of ideas that in turn shaped the institutionalization of factory practices?

In the case of Germany we can confirm that the conceptions of labor were lodged in the production process before they circulated in a trade union movement or in workers' political parties. The inscription of concepts of labor on the piece-rate scales, on the rules of employment, and on the measurement of time for factories was in place by the 1860s, before substantial numbers of workers had enrolled in the labor or political movements and, more particularly, before the dissemination of Marxist economic theory. The movements of artisanal workers that flowered during the revolution of 1848–1849 in Germany were suppressed and disabled in the 1850s.[193] When the labor movement began to take shape again in the 1860s, it engaged a tiny segment of workers incapable of changing the face of mechanization. The process of industrialization, considered in terms of quantity of output, was at this time far from complete. In qualitative terms, however, the transformation was well under way, for the installation in the factory of the cultural

191. *Bradford Labour Echo*, Jan. 9, 1897.
192. *Der Textil-Arbeiter*, April 23, 1920; March 10, 1922, p. 37.
193. Adler, op. cit., pp. 297–298.

concept of labor that would govern production was in large measure accomplished.[194]

In Britain the distinctive procedures by which textile factory employers received materialized labor—the accounting methods, techniques of remuneration, and factory layouts—coincided with the development of early socialism and the labor organizing of the 1820s and 1830s. In this instance we cannot exclude the possibility that the philosophies of commerce in the insurgent workers' movements contributed to consistencies in the shape of factory practice. But we have also seen that the stereotypical understanding of labor as a ware in Britain had been articulated by elite economists in the second half of the eighteenth century and had already been experienced in the practices of the handweavers.[195] Theories of value and exchange in the original socialist movement of the first half of the nineteenth century replicated and sometimes actively drew upon this antecedent intellectual and industrial heritage. In the British case, then, the early labor movement may have served as a momentary transmitter of ideas put into practice on the factory shop floor, but not as their originator.

Even if the cultural formation of manufacture was established before the labor movements developed their own economic outlooks, another question remains. Once manufacturing procedures are in place, if workers inventively call upon the resources of their culture as a whole to construct their experience of production, there is no original source or ultimate center to that experience. By this reasoning, the discursive resources deployed in civic politics, religion, family networks, or other contexts may also intervene firsthand in workers' (and employers') understanding of life at the point of production. On these grounds, cultural analysts of labor who emphasize the role of discourse in constituting workers' experience of production have

194. Similarly, the timing of the emergence of the German specification of labor as a commodity makes it implausible to view the state as its critical shaper. Even in Germany, where government supervision of the workplace became strongest, the state did not assume an active role in overseeing industrial relations for adult workers until after the crystallization of the distinctive German forms of work practice and of the correlative understanding of labor as a commodity in the German labor movement. For example, Prussia did not mandate inspections of factory sites until 1878. Günther Schulz effectively discloses the state's nonintervention on the shop floor in "Die betriebliche Lage der Arbeiter im Rheinland vom 19. bis zum beginnenden 20. Jahrhundert," *Rheinische Vierteljahrsblätter* Jahrgang 50 (1986), p. 175.

195. To the extent that the workers' movements of the 1820s drew upon a preceding ideology of British protest movements, it was that of a political radicalism which had much to say about the construction of political relations among citizens but very little to say about the construction of production relations between workers and employers. The practices of the factory system were structured by concepts of production more precise than those to be found in the political discourse of the eighteenth-century British radicals and republicans.

effected a decisive shift in the agenda that guides research in social history. Not only have they removed the institutions of the workplace from their pride of place as the original generator of workers' experience; they have discounted as tunnel vision the attempt to trace determinate connections between the structure of work and the development of workers' economic or political outlook.[196] In so doing, they take two steps backward. By treating the dissection of the structure of political ideas as a self-sufficient enterprise, they return to old-fashioned intellectual history. But if we drop the supposition that the economic base dictates an ideological superstructure—resorting for the sake of exposition to this anachronistic vocabulary—the workplace can still play a central role in the generation of experience and in the reception of ideologies.[197] We may grant to the signifying practices of the labor process (rather than to the economic and technological conditions of production) an unwavering influence upon the development of collective movements and political organizations.[198]

Further, the uncanny stability in the understanding of the transmission of labor despite profound shifts in other aspects of public discourse indicates that this understanding was rooted in an immediate and unchanging experience, that is, in the exposure to labor's conveyance at the work site. The course of development in nineteenth-century German and British industry suggests that ideas which are incorporated into and reproduced through forms of manufacturing practice have greater permanence than those that float in the realm of civic politics. In Britain in particular the idioms of politics, religion, education, and domestic culture underwent significant change between the start of industrialization and 1914.[199] Yet in cross-

196. Tony Judt, *Marxism and the French Left* (Oxford: Clarendon Press, 1986), p. 27 note. "Marxists and anti-marxists alike are going to have to abandon their anachronistic obsession with the workplace and the shop-floor," Tony Judt has written, "with everything described in terms of its effect upon or as the result of work relations or work-related attitudes" (p. 114). Ernesto Laclau and Chantal Mouffe, who emphasize the constitutive power of discourse, have put the conclusion in simple form: "There is no logical connection whatsoever between positions in the relations of production and the mentality of the producers." *Hegemony and Socialist Strategy* (London: Verso, 1985), pp. 84–85.

197. My approach differs from that of labor historians of Britain who emphasize that radical political economy "revealed the fractured reality of social relations in production." The cultural shape of practice, not the structural features of the social organization of production, provided the template for workers' formulations of exploitation by "middlemen." Richard Price, "Structures of Subordination in Nineteenth-Century British Industry," in Pat Thane et al., editors, *The Power of the Past* (Cambridge: Cambridge University Press, 1984), p. 123.

198. Laclau and Mouffe, op. cit., p. 77.

199. For a sketch of religious fluidity, see Hugh McLeod, *Class and Religion in the Late Victorian City* (London: Croom Helm, 1974), p. 283. Gareth Stedman Jones discusses changes

national perspective the definition of labor as a commodity remained relatively fixed. It provided a stable point of reference that informed the diagnoses and prescriptions of the labor movement from the commencement of the nineteenth century and at its end. Upon the break-up of the early workers' movements in each country the distinctive appreciation of labor faded from the public sphere, only to resurface there, unchanged, because it had been preserved in the practices of production.

Ideas incarnated in a constellation of manufacturing techniques can be reproduced with less variance than ideas whose transmission depends principally upon discursive formulations. The definition of labor as a commodity was recreated day in, day out by a cluster of micro-procedures that did not require the producers to lend their attention to the meaning of labor in order to preserve its shape. The concept was received through experience rather than instruction; it was lived before it was turned to account. The specification of labor escaped those vagaries of constant reinterpretation and reappropriation to which verbal formulations are subject. Verbal formulations draw upon language's modulation of register, its interminable ability to inflect and ironize statements. These communicative resources discourage the stable transmission of concepts.[200] Although the concepts of labor could be put into words for political and theoretic excursus, there was no need of words for their social reproduction. They survived through the arrangement of industrial practices and through the relative univocality of their material operation.[201] Unlike the leading myths and narratives deployed in the realms of civic politics and religion, the manufacturing practices did not derive their power from their ability to act as a reservoir of multiple and potentially inconsistent meanings.

This chapter has not sought to explain workers' choices of conservative versus socialist parties. It does not account for marginal variation in rates of participation in the socialist movement by occupation or geographic region. Rather, with a cross-national perspective, it shows why ideologies of exploi-

---

in domestic and neighborhood culture, op. cit., pp. 217–218. The immobility of labor's specification as a commodity poses a challenge to alternative explanations of its foundation that would appeal to household or community structures subject to dramatic change.

200. This comment draws upon Paul Connerton, *How Societies Remember* (Cambridge: Cambridge University Press, 1989), p. 59.

201. A new generation of cognitive scientists have begun to show that concepts are reproduced through their employment in limited and concrete settings. The experimental evidence disqualifies the alternative view that culture is transmitted through the agents' deliberate, formal acquisition of a set of general principles that can be applied across contexts. Jean Lave, *Cognition in Practice* (Cambridge: Cambridge University Press, 1988), p. 43.

tation were apt to take a certain shape among those workers who affiliated themselves with a socialist movement. In none of the domains outside work could practice have so vividly incarnated differing forms of labor as a commodity. As a cultural apparatus the workplace seemed to uphold, without perturbation, a specification of labor as a commodity despite tremendous change in workers' educational, religious, and electoral experiences.

10   The Guiding Forms
of Collective Action

> Meaning is not decreed: if it is not everywhere, it is nowhere.
> Claude Lévi-Strauss, *Totemism*

Strikes have entered sociologists' imagination as if they were events prefabricated for numerical analysis. They seem to present themselves with ready-made dimensions such as number of participants, duration, and frequency. Yet before strikes can be enumerated, they must be identified, and doing so requires that one define the cessation of the transfer of labor. In every society labor and its exchange are conceived before they are perceived. Accordingly, the occurrence of a labor stoppage, like the transmission of the social force called *labor*, takes place in the imagination of the agents themselves.

In *The Rise of Market Culture*, William Reddy compellingly demonstrated the symbolic constitution of strikes in early nineteenth-century France. The operative principles of culture become visible only by descending to the particulars of practice. Consider one of Reddy's examples. In 1839 the employer at a spinning mill near Rouen asked his workers to pay for illuminating oil so he could extend the hours of manufacture into the evening. The operatives consigned themselves to the prolongation of work but rejected the surcharge for lighting. They made no concerted effort to abstain from labor, but at starting time each morning they mounted a demonstration against the new exaction for oil, causing the insulted owner to shut them out day by day afresh. "They were ready to work, they wanted to work; 28 centimes per kilogram of yarn was acceptable to them," Reddy concludes. "This was not a strike, so much as a state of refusal to pay for oil that resulted each morning in a new closing of the mill."[1] Attaching the term *strike* to the event may suit a blind statistical vision of such events, since the *result*, to be sure, was a labor stoppage of quantifiable dimensions. But the workers did not intend to withhold their

---

1. William Reddy, *The Rise of Market Culture* (Cambridge: Cambridge University Press, 1984), p. 190.

labor in order to bring the employer to terms. French industrial workers of this era had not yet adopted the concept of the strike or coined a locution for it.[2] For the investigator to label it as such results in an anachronistic generalization; it effaces the character of the event and falsely abstracts the human agency that created it.

The agents' cultural schema determines not only whether a strike is a conceivable course of action but the forms the strike could imaginably take. The meaning and constitution of strikes assumed their contrasting forms in late-nineteenth-century Germany and Britain in accordance with those of the commodity of labor. What were hallmarks of a strike in one country were extraneous in the next. The workers' understanding of the labor transaction shaped the goals of strikes, the means by which strikes were executed, and, indeed, whether workers' collective action could be classified as a strike at all.

SCRIPTS ON STAGE AND ON PAPER

The workers used their definition of labor as a commodity to orchestrate the unfolding of a work stoppage in space. When British workers had a grievance they wanted corrected, they typically filed out of their workrooms into the central mill yard, which served as a theater for their demonstration. The tactic was habitual, as the documentary sources as well as oral history collections in Britain show. Textile workers from both Yorkshire and Lancashire, asked in interviews what they did to correct a workplace problem, responded, "We went out to the mill yard."[3] The workers in some instances transformed this action into a raucous assembly, singing and shouting slogans in the yard.[4] For example, at Glossop, just southeast of Lancashire, the

2. Ibid., p. 129. French urban journeymen of the time attached multiple meanings to the term *faire grève*, which eventually came to signal "strike" but as yet could include looking for new employment in general, apart from a campaign against a master employer. William Reddy, "Skeins, Scales, Discounts, Steam, and Other Objects of Crowd Justice in Early French Textile Mills," *Comparative Studies in Society and History* Volume 21, Number 1 (January 1979), pp. 205–206.

3. Bradford Heritage Recording Unit; Dermot Healey's interview tape 667, pp. 11–12, Lancashire. *Yorkshire Factory Times*, November 22, 1889, Birstall; May 2, 1902, Dewsbury, p. 5; June 27, 1902, Broadfield mill; Sept. 25, 1903, Birstall, p. 5; February 8, 1912, M. Oldroyd & Sons; February 8, 1912, Dewsbury district, p. 4. Even youngsters knew the tactic: *Yorkshire Factory Times*, April 29, 1898, Dudley Hill. Blackburn Library Archives, M31, Nr. 5403, Blackburn Weavers' Minutes, August 16, 1865. An employer narrating the course of a strike told the Royal Commission on Labour that he had received no prior notice: "The first I was aware of was seeing all the workpeople out in the yard." PP 1892 XXXV, p. 93.

4. *Yorkshire Factory Times*, January 10, 1902, Marsden.

weavers at one mill who filed into their yard delivered a message that merged rebellion and patriotic conformity when they commenced singing "Rule Britannia" as loudly as possible.[5]

The British textile workers also imported community traditions of demonstration into the factory. At the end of the nineteenth century, textile workers in urban areas, especially women, still subjected miscreant supervisors to the proverbial ceremony of "rough music." At a mill in Bradford, for example, the female workers in 1893 condemned the advances of their overlooker by preparing an effigy of him. They banged on cans and shouted.[6] In 1891 at Great Horton, near Bradford, weavers who were "members of the weaker sex" jeered and hissed on the shop floor at a team of new overlookers with whom they were supposed to work. When the overlookers informed the employer of the rude distractions, he locked the women out and closed the mill.[7] To put an unpopular overlooker in his place, workers at another mill in Bradford in 1890 formed a procession on the factory grounds, playing on tin kettles and a ram's horn.[8] In these instances, workers drew upon repertoires of protest that had traditionally been used to censure those who transgressed community norms.

Textile strikes had long drawn upon community repertoires of mockery. In the Preston strikes of the 1850s, strikers who had turned out called upon itinerant musicians to stand opposite the mill and accompany their dances, which employers interpreted as a form of "ridicule and defiance."[9] Even after the turn of the century, work boycotts could become an occasion for carnival merrymaking. At a village near Burnley, strikers in 1908 lent their

---

5. *Cotton Factory Times*, December 3, 1886, Glossop. The very concept of a strike was imparted, not given automatically: one worker, after spending time in the mill, naively asked colleagues to explain what a strike was. Maggie Newberry, *Reminiscences of a Bradford Mill Girl* (Bradford: Local Studies Department, 1980), p. 49.

6. *Yorkshire Factory Times*, December 15, 1893, p. 5. During the weavers' strike of 1912 in Blackburn, the female workers taunted strike breakers by carrying fireplace blowers on which they beat with pokers. Geoffrey Trodd, "Political Change and the Working Class in Blackburn and Burnley 1880–1914," Ph.D. diss., University of Lancaster, 1978, pp. 306–307.

7. *Yorkshire Factory Times*, May 15, 1891, Great Horton, p. 8.

8. *Yorkshire Factory Times*, June 27, 1890. At a mill in Halifax, the workers formed a circle around an unpopular overlooker at the mill gate and "hooted and hustled him." *Yorkshire Factory Times*, September 30, 1892, Halifax, p. 7. For an instance of rough music at an overlooker's house in Saltaire, see the *Bradford Observer*, June 29, 1894, Saltaire.

9. Henry Ashworth, *The Preston Strike: An Enquiry into Its Causes and Consequences* (Manchester: George Simms, 1854), p. 13. For an example of a handloom weavers' strike during 1823 that drew upon the repertoire of festival wagons, see Frederick James Kaijage, "Labouring Barnsley, 1816–1856: A Social and Economic History," Ph.D. diss., University of Warwick, 1975, p. 320.

stoppage a festival atmosphere when a female participant "masqueraded in man's attire."[10] In mockery of their owner, these revelers also paraded a pig in a cart through the town streets. With such opportunities for entertainment, an incident such as occurred at a Bradford mill in 1893 could only have been expected: officials of the textile workers' union, called to investigate the cause of the stoppage, claimed that many of the merrymakers demonstrating at the mill gate could not cite a grievance. The workers said they had "come out to have 'a little fun.'" The union officials said that "upon inquiry it turned out that few of the women really understood why they were on strike, many of them coming out as sympathizers with the first malcontents."[11]

The British workers thought of their assemblies as a means of signaling their insistence upon bargaining, not just as a means of withdrawing labor. A newspaper account of a stoppage in the Colne Valley during 1891 makes plain the importance workers attached to turning the cessation of work into a visible gesture of disobedience. "The workmen were seen to be making their way to an open space close by their mill," the report stated, "and when anything of this kind takes place all eyes are upon them in wonderment."[12] At a mill in Apperley Bridge in 1893, the weavers were delighted to see that the head of the company "stood stock still when he saw all the weavers outside the mill gates."[13]

The physical arrangement of the British mills often created a stage for workers' demonstrations. The central location of the yard in many mills ensured that a congregation there would be visible to workers and supervisors in every department of the factory. When not used as a site for protest, the mill yard was used by employers and public figures as a platform for addresses. In the Colne Valley, for example, politicians campaigning for

10. *Yorkshire Factory Times*, February 21, 1908.

11. *Yorkshire Factory Times*, June 9, 1893, p. 5. A winder from Bradford who began work during the First World War said of her first experience of a strike, "We had a nice bit of fun." Bradford Heritage Recording Unit, A0067, born 1904.

12. *Yorkshire Factory Times*, July 10, 1891, Milnsbridge and Longwood. Then too, for workers who lacked the courage or know-how to initiate negotiations, assembling in the mill yard at the end of a morning or lunch break forced the owner or manager to inquire into the workers' complaints. At the town of Keighley in 1889, the spinners and doffers at one firm stayed out in the courtyard until the owner, not knowing what the matter was, went out to ask: "None of the older hands daring to say what they wanted, the least girl (a half-timer) spoke as follows: 'We want more wage.' 'Oh, that is it.' 'Aye, it is.' 'But tha' gets enough, doesn't ta.' 'I don't know, but mi' mother doesn't think so.'" *Yorkshire Factory Times*, September 20, 1889.

13. *Yorkshire Factory Times*, June 9, 1893.

office used yards inside the mills as sites for public addresses to workers.[14] A weaver from Yeadon, born in 1861, chose the mill yard as the setting in his autobiography in which to portray the turning point of his spiritual development. There he rejected a job offer from a shady music agent from London and threatened to heave a rock at the man.[15] Well could the central yard, encircled by buildings as if by grandstands, serve as a stage for dramatic confrontation.

The surviving record of evidence in Germany does not easily yield instances before 1914 in which workers turned the mill yard into a theatrical arena for their protests.[16] Yet many examples of conduct come forth that draw on an alternative symbolism: German workers stopped work at their looms and refused to continue until their grievances were corrected. At a weaving mill in Rheydt, for example, weavers stopped work for two days in 1909, but stayed in their shop rooms, to protest against what they viewed as a reduction in piece rates.[17] The workers employed this tactic in Saxony, Bavaria, the Vogtland, the Rhineland, the Münsterland, and the Osnabrück district.[18] Since the workers left whenever owners requested it, this conduct cannot be taken to represent an attempt to occupy the factory by means of a sit-down strike. A police report from the district of Burgsteinfurt said the

14. Robert Brian Perks, "The New Liberalism and the Challenge of Labour in the West Riding of Yorkshire 1885–1914," Ph.D. diss., Huddersfield Polytechnic, 1985, p. 46.

15. Raymond Preston, *Life Story and Personal Reminiscences* (London: Epworth Press, 1930), p. 27.

16. One instance appears in which the workers moved to the mill yard to negotiate for a more liberal interpretation of the piece-rate categories *after* having stopped work in the workrooms the previous day. Staatsarchiv Osnabrück, Rep. 610, Lingen, Nr. 124, August 20, 1902, report on Neuenhaus, Lingen district. Similarly, an employer's journal complained about a congregation of strikers at a weaving yard in Zittau. *Die Deutsche Arbeitgeber-Zeitung*, Dec. 11, 1910. Such gatherings were not only uncommon in Germany but unrecognized among textile workers as a strategy of significance.

17. HSTAD, Regierung Düsseldorf, 24702, October 10, 1909, p. 40. At one mill in Jöllenbeck, at the beginning of a strike in 1907 the female workers spent a day in the mill without working. They entered the workroom on the second day and sat at their machines until managers finally ordered them to leave. Staatsarchiv Detmold, I.U. Nr. 430, May 22, 1907.

18. *Der deutsche Leinenindustrielle*, March 28, 1896, pp. 643–44; Stadtarchiv Steinfurt-Borghorst, B378, July 14, 1892 report; Staatsarchiv Osnabrück, Rep. 610, Lingen, Nr. 125, August 20, 1902; Staatsarchiv Münster, Kreis Steinfurt 1311, February 7, 1891, Werner & Cie; Staatsarchiv Detmold, I.U. Nr. 430, May 3, 1907; *Gladbacher Merkur*, March 21, 1899, Gebrüder Peltzer; *Der Textil-Arbeiter*, April 5, 1901, Chemnitz, workers called trespassers; April 25, 1902, Crimmitschau; January 29, 1909, Mittweida; *Die Textilarbeiter-Zeitung*, June 6, 1908, Lampertsmühle; February 3, 1900, Düren. *Leipziger Volkszeitung*, May 28, 1909, Plauen; *Augsburger Abendzeitung*, July 24, 1912; *Der Christliche Textilarbeiter*, March 10, 1900, Bocholt. For a temporary work stoppage of the same kind, see HSTAD, Regierung Aachen, 1633, p. 302.

inoperative workers had even left "obligingly."[19] Workers sometimes used the sit-down technique after telling the owner that they did not intend to work. Therefore it was not a silent way of striking without verbal communication, nor a way of denying to authorities that a strike was in fact underway.[20] Like their colleagues in Britain, many German workers remained skeptical of employers' claim to authority and were ready to mock it by pranks on the shop floor, such as falsely pulling emergency alarms.[21] Starting a strike by sitting at the machine was not a sign of greater subordination to managerial directives. It simply exemplified the German workers' conception in this period of the stoppage of work.

The tactic of merely sitting at the machine did not represent a less active response than demonstrating in the yard, or one that required less coordination than marching in a body out of the factory. German workers who adopted the tactic of the "passive strike" showed a high degree of discipline. According to police records from Emsdetten, for example, the weavers who initiated a passive strike in 1904 stopped work at their looms "suddenly, according to an arranged signal."[22] These protesters then sat in the workroom all day. A decade later, at another mill in the same town, the weavers repeated this tactic during the morning shift to protest against weft yarn of substandard quality. The owner eventually shut off the steam power and asked the weavers to leave the premises. When the weavers complied, they did not scatter. Having made their point, they had the discipline to return "punctually" to work in a body at the beginning of the afternoon shift.[23] Details such as these indicate that German workers conducted well-orchestrated stoppages. But they hardly drew upon established techniques such as rough music, nor did they regularly mount protests that depended upon a visual display of disobedience in the yard. The German strikes emphasized the precise, timed withdrawal of labor. At some citywide work stoppages, all

19. Staatsarchiv Münster, Kreis Steinfurt, 1311, February 7, 1891.

20. *Leipziger Volkszeitung*, May 28, 1909, Plauen.

21. Staatsarchiv Weimar, Landesregierung Greiz, n Rep. A, Kap. IX a, Nr. 207, 1885–1895, factory inspector reports, p. 108. Female workers ridiculed elections to the employer-organized factory committees by writing in votes for fictitious or mentally handicapped persons. *Christliche Arbeiterin*, June 16, 1906, Mönchengladbach. See Alf Lüdtke, "Cash, Coffee Breaks, Horseplay: *Eigensinn* and Politics Among Factory Workers in Germany Circa 1900," in Michael Hanagan and Charles Stephenson, editors, *Confrontation, Class Consciousness, and the Labor Process* (Westport, Conn.: Greenwood Press, 1986).

22. Stadtarchiv Emsdetten, Nr. 737, February 6, 1904. In some instances the initiators of such a strike agreed among themselves before they entered the workroom that they would file in but not work. HSTAD, Regierung Düsseldorf, 24691, January 20, 1899.

23. Staatsarchiv Münster, Kreis Steinfurt, 1452, January 2, 1914, Emsdetten.

workers in town stopped their work at the same instant. "On May 10th, at nine o'clock in the morning," a factory inspector from Greiz reported, "the strike broke out as if on command in all mechanical weaving mills and in the dyeing and finishing branches."[24] Since workers often began work in the morning with the intention of stopping shortly thereafter, their conduct seemed to affirm the symbolic importance of the act of collectively ceasing the motion of production, rather than merely preventing that motion from starting at all.

The absence of visible workplace demonstrations in the enactment of German strikes made it awkward for some to distinguish between a strike and the contractual withdrawal of labor. Legal-minded German bureaucrats of the time found it so. In the Rhineland, local officials thought that if a large group of workers canceled their employment contract by giving prior notice, they were legally withdrawing their labor and therefore not launching a strike. The Imperial Bureau of Statistics in Berlin had to keep the provincial authorities informed that a mass labor dispute which transpired according to orderly procedures of terminating a labor contract still constituted an event that the officials should report as a strike.[25] The district record keepers in Thüringen may have reflected the prevailing uncertainty about the sighting of a strike in the title of a volume of handwritten enumerations for the period 1882–1906: they called their compilation "Supposed Strikes."[26] In contrast with the British stoppages at the workplace, German protests in the quarter-century before the First World War seem elementary and austere.

---

24. Staatsarchiv Weimar, Landesregierung Greiz, n Rep. A, Kap. IXa, Nr. 207, factory inspector reports 1885–1895, p. 150. The *Reussische Volkszeitung* reported on a strike in Kirchberg in 1907: "At exactly ten o'clock the *Knacken* of the looms and the *Gebrumm* of the other machines was silenced." But the workers did not leave the premises. March 20, 1907.

25. HSTAD, Regierung Düsseldorf, 24692, July 7, 1899. For a parallel case from eastern Germany, see Stadtarchiv Werdau, Rep. II, 2, Nr. 90, Nov. 7, 1899. In reponse to inquiries from authorities in the district of Düsseldorf, the Imperial Bureau of Statistics informed the local authorities that "the workers must have decided in the moment they lay down their work that if their requests are rejected, they will refrain from any further activity for their current employer. . . . Violation of the labor contract and damages suffered by the employer or workers is of course often an accompanying event, but in no way a conceptual prerequisite for a labor dispute to be treated as a 'strike.'" HSTAD, Regierung Düsseldorf, 24692, October 12, 1899. For an example of a work stoppage that local authorities did not consider a "veritable strike," see HSTAD, Landratsamt Mönchengladbach, 99, March 6, 1899, Rheydt.

26. Staatsarchiv Weimar, Landesregierung Greiz, n Rep. A, Kap. IXa, Nr. 165, "Angebliche Arbeitseinstellungen," 1882–1906. When a larger than usual number of workers happened to give notice to quit at a textile firm in Rheydt, the employer inferred—mistakenly—that a strike was underway. *Der Textil-Arbeiter*, April 12, 1907.

How are we to explain the difference between the German and the British forms of protest? Certainly the German workers did not adopt this particular style of action because they lacked acquaintance with forms of crowd action. In the early days of factory development at midcentury, workers also employed rough music (*Katzenmusik*) against their employers, though not in the workplace.[27] A minister reported in this era that the workers in the Wuppertal district treated their employers to this ceremony whenever "it became known that a moral lapse had occurred in an eminent family."[28] The tradition of rough music still enjoyed a rich life in industrial towns of imperial Germany. At a village in the Lausitz in 1886, weavers suffering from a wage reduction subjected the mayor's house to these raucous sounds.[29] Protesters used this repertoire for issues unrelated to the workplace. At a textile town near Mönchengladbach, one hundred people, including workers from the local mills, joined a rough music demonstration in 1902. They banged pot tops and clanged bells for several nights around the home of a carpenter whom they accused of carrying on an indecent sexual liaison.[30] German textile strikers also organized street processions after the cessation of work.[31] Striking weavers at a firm in the Löbau district in 1886 paraded through the streets with their colorful fabrics mounted on poles.[32] German workers had the repertoires for collective demonstrations at hand in the community, but seldom imported them into the workplace.[33]

27. *Der unbefangene Beobachter*, Crimmitschau, August 11, 1848, p. 22.

28. "People especially liked to use this tactic if the sinner belonged to a family who paid its workers poorly and exploited their time and labor capacity, and who were called 'sweaters.'" August Witteborg, *Geschichte der evang.-lutherischen Gemeinde Barmen-Wupperfeld von 1777 bis 1927* (Barmen: Selbstverlag der evang.-lutherischen Gemeinde, 1927), p. 237.

29. *Das deutsche Wollen-Gewerbe*, May 5, 1886, p. 588.

30. The participants called it a *Klatschet-Tierjagen*. HSTAD, Landgericht Mönchengladbach, 10/8. For evidence of the number of residents in Giesenkirchen who worked in textile mills, see the employment listings at Stadtarchiv Mönchengladbach, 1c 3550.

31. One of the earliest references to "factory workers" organizing street demonstrations for higher pay comes from Elberfeld: Zentrales Staatsarchiv Merseburg, Rep. 51E, Nr. 62, Rheinprovinz, Sept. 3, 1830, pp. 47 ff. Also, Staatsarchiv Weimar, Landesregierung Greiz, n Rep. A, Kap. IXa, Nr. 207, factory inspector reports 1885–1895, p. 151; Stadtarchiv Greiz, B 5972, May 22, 1873, report on strike processions, pp. 5–8; Staatsarchiv Detmold, M2 Bielefeld, Nr. 291, pp. 563–564; Klaus Tidow, *Neumünsters Textil- und Lederindustrie im 19. Jahrhundert* (Neumünster: Karl Wachholtz, 1984), p. 68, regarding 1888 strike; for Borghorst, Zentrales Staatsarchiv Merseburg, Rep. 120 BB, VII 1, Nr. 3, Band 3, pp. 134 ff., Dec. 31, 1875, and pp. 137 ff., report of January 4, 1876.

32. Staatsarchiv Dresden, Amthauptmannschaft Löbau, Nr. 3055, May 14, 1886, p. 16. For a demonstration of weavers with flags and chimes, see Landesarchiv Potsdam, Rep. 3B, Regierung Frankfurt I Präs. 327, Guben, 1851.

33. For a commemorative parade organized by textile workers, see *Die Textilarbeiter-Zeitung*, August 20, 1910, Emsdetten.

Nor did the divergence in British and German repertoires of action originate in the legal statutes that applied to protest. To be sure, the laws regarding public assembly in Prussia, and in most other German states, required workers to give local police forty-eight hours' notice of a meeting. Yet the courts ruled that the laws that prevented public meetings of associations without prior announcement did not apply to gatherings of employees at work. The courts reasoned that the participants at meetings on shop property discussed workplace matters, not "public affairs." Therefore the law did not require German workers to give police notice of meetings or assemblies on the mill grounds.[34] On this score the laws governing assembly at work in Germany were no different from those in Britain.

If the difference in the repertoires of action at the workplace cannot be explained by the legal environment, where can we turn to discover their significance? One of the terms workers used to describe their actions provides an initial clue, though not a monolithic response. British textile workers who went on strike often said they had "turned out," a figure of speech which highlighted the crossing of a boundary between inside and outside the mill rather than focusing on the stoppage of labor per se.[35]

A confrontation between workers and employers at a Blackburn weaving mill in 1865 implemented this principle. The insurgent weavers assembled in the mill yard before leaving, but they defined the start of the strike as the moment at which they passed through the main gate and left the premises.[36]

---

34. Stadtarchiv Emsdetten, Nr. 734, *Kammergericht* judgments of September 5, 1903, and July 26, 1904. Provincial authorities unsuccessfully sought to override this ruling. *Das deutsche Wollen-Gewerbe*, January 17, 1904, p. 68. For an example of a meeting held in a German factory without the owner's permission, see *Der Textil-Arbeiter*, January 3, 1902, Crimmitschau. Workers sometimes did not register their meetings at public locales if employers from only one firm were admitted. Stadtarchiv Werdau, Rep. II, Kap. 4, Nr. 7, Bd. 2, March 14, 1904, pp. 139 ff. On workplace meetings, see also Wilhelm Gewehr, *Praktischer Rathgeber für Vereins- und Versammlungsleiter sowie Versammlungsbesucher* (Elberfeld, 1897), p. 34, and Deutscher Textilarbeiterverband, *Leitfaden bei Führung der Geschäfte, in der Agitaton, bei Streiks und Lohnbewegungen* (Berlin: Maurer & Dimmick, 1908), p. 65. For a discussion of the evolution of German laws regarding assembly and association, see Vernon Lidtke, *The Alternative Culture: Socialist Labor in Imperial Germany* (New York: Oxford University Press, 1985), pp. 30–31.

35. *Yorkshire Factory Times*, November 15, 1889, Manningham and Shipley; September 13, 1889, Kirkstall. Striking could also be called "going out." Leeds District Archives, T & M Bairstow, 72, negotiations of July 26, 1913. The term *strike* was not associated only with the defiant stoppage of work, but with individual absence from work for any reason. See Bradford Heritage Recording Unit, A0087, born 1903.

36. Blackburn Library Archives, M31, Nr. 5403, Blackburn Weavers' Minutes, August 16, 1865.

Managers, too, framed the cessation and resumption of work in spatial terms. The director of a factory in Bradford described the readiness of strikers to begin work again with the expression "They were glad to come in."[37] To "come out" became synonymous with going on strike. In their own accounts of work stoppages, workers described the start of a strike with the standard phrase that they "came out" together or "in a body."[38] The phrase "in a body" connoted a highly patterned form of group conduct. Both the middle-class and the working-class press took care to distinguish between actions committed by a "crowd" and those that workers committed "in a body." A crowd, *The Dewsbury Reporter* noted in 1875, moved "without arrangement," even when it seemed a peaceable assemblage, whereas workers organized and coordinated their movements when they acted "in a body."[39] In a word, the spatial form assumed by many strikes was purposeful and methodical.

German workers who struck said they had "ceased their labor" (*die Arbeit eingestellt*). A similar phrase appeared in German dialect speech. The memoirs of Friedrich Storck, a German poet from the Wuppertal who worked in textile mills as a teenager, document the evolution of workers' language. Storck said that in the Wuppertal, a region known as a pioneer in the development of factory workers' movements, the word *strike* (*Streik*) did not acquire currency until after the 1860s.[40] The popular expression of that era was *de Brocken hennschmieten* ("throw down the work"), a colloquialism which survived into the early twentieth century.[41] Modern histori-

---

37. Cited by Elizabeth Jennings, *Sir Isaac Holden* (Bradford: University of Bradford, 1982), pp. 159 ff.

38. Centre for English Cultural Traditions and Language, University of Sheffield, interview tape A72 with Benny Laughlin, describing his participation in the 1912 warpers' strike; B. Riley, *Handbook*, Town Hall, Huddersfield, 1908, p. 18; Archive of General Union of Dyers, Bleachers, and Textile Workers, Yeadon and Guiseley Factory Workers' Union, Minutes, January 19, 1891; *Yorkshire Factory Times*, May 30, 1902, Lockwood, p. 5. For stereotyped use of the term *come out* as a synonym for strikes, see the company records of T & M Bairstow Limited, Leeds District Archives, book 72, workers' speech recorded July 26, 1913; Operative Spinners' Provincial Association, *Fourth Annual Report, 1883* (Bolton: Thomas Abbatt), p. 45; *Cotton Factory Times*, January 22, 1897, Darwen; *Yorkshire Factory Times*, November 22, 1889, Birstall and Oxenthorpe.

39. *The Dewsbury Reporter*, March 13, 1875. The phrase "in a body" reflects a refinement of terms indicating nonriotous groupings. For the earlier distinction between "crowds" and "mobs," see Mark Harrison, *Crowds and History: Mass Phenomena in English Towns, 1790–1835* (Cambridge: Cambridge University Press, 1988), p. 170.

40. Storck said "The word 'strike' was not known in our valley." Friedrich Storck, *Aus der Schule des Lebens* (Elberfeld: G. Lucas, 1910), Part One, p. 178.

41. Ibid., pp. 178–179. This was the same phrase striking weavers used in 1899 in Mönchengladbach when they sat at their looms inside the mill. HSTAD, Regierung Düssel-

cal research confirms that in other regions of Germany, the phrase "cessation of labor" (*Arbeitsniederlegung*) was employed before use of the word *strike* became commonplace.[42]

The German workers' tactic of sitting at the machine indicates that the withdrawal of the owners' command of the conversion of labor power comprised a symbolic statement of its own. The only "language" the employer knew how to interpret, the Social Democratic textile union said, was "the language of the work stoppage."[43] In Britain, by comparison, the exchange of labor as it was embodied in finished products meant that the withdrawal of the conversion of labor power per se at the point of production did not constitute a symbolic end to the employment relation. Instead, workers supplemented this with the crossing of the boundary of the workroom, combined with a visible demonstration of protest in the mill yard, to express their flouting of the owners' authority. British textile workers enacted their protests by responding to the employers' own emphasis on the surveillance of traffic at border zones rather than on the control of the transformation of labor power into labor. They took hold of the employers' use of space as a handle by which they could turn the employers' authority upside down in the theater of the central mill yard.

In both Germany and Britain, the workers' tactics of collective action represented the appropriate counter-symbols to use against the employers' own ways of asserting their authority over the factory. British textile workers did not as a rule sign contracts or other documents when they entered into an employment relation.[44] Custom and implicit agreement, to which the courts referred if called upon, governed workers' association with their employers.[45] Only a few mills posted notices in the workroom about the

---

dorf, 24691, January, 1899. No doubt British workers, too, could refer to the beginning of a strike as "downing tools," but in addition they deployed the customary metaphor of "turning out," absent in Germany.

42. Dieter Schneider et al., *Zur Theorie und Praxis des Streiks* (Frankfurt am Main: Suhrkamp, 1971), p. 7.

43. *Der Textil-Arbeiter*, January 27, 1905, Mönchengladbach.

44. *Yorkshire Factory Times*, March 28, 1902, p. 4; May 30, 1902, Huddersfield; September 18, 1903, Marsden, p. 5; June 3, 1892, p. 5. The *Yorkshire Factory Times* treated the introduction of written agreements as a news event in itself. According to the written contracts in Britain, the owner or the worker had to provide fourteen days' notice if either wanted to end the employment relation. The Yorkshire weavers considered the contracts pointless, however, because the firm might officially keep the weaver on while placing no warp in the loom. *Yorkshire Factory Times*, July 3, 1891, p. 4; May 6, 1898, Ravensthorpe.

45. *Yorkshire Factory Times*, July 26, 1889. The reliance on custom could in some instances provide workers with greater protection. For example, I found instances in which female textile workers left their jobs without notice. Formally they had broken their employ-

terms of employment or about the conduct of the hired hands on the shop floor itself.[46] No wonder, then, that British textile workers did not break the employment relation merely by withdrawing the use of their labor power, for there was no official code giving the owner control on the shop floor over the workers' labor time. Instead, workers reacted by crossing the factories' physical boundaries.[47]

Unlike their British counterparts, German workers signed written contracts when they began employment. As early as midcentury, most German mills had printed rules posted in the shop.[48] After 1891 such posting became obligatory. Workers usually received a personal copy of the factory rules.[49] These ordinances typically told workers how to carry out their work effectively, banned political or religious conversations on the shop floor, and specified the fines that would be levied for misbehavior. According to the provisions of the factory ordinances posted in the mills, stopping work at the loom indicated that workers had "deliberately disobeyed" the factory

---

ment agreement. Yet the courts let them off when the women quoted the obscene language of their overlookers that had provoked their departure—a safeguard difficult to insert into contracts or legislation. See *Textile Mercury*, March 8, 1913, p. 192.

46. United Kingdom, Royal Commission on Labour, PP 1892 XXXV, pp. 250, 265, 270; *Yorkshire Factory Times*, October 18, 1889, Keigley; March 18, 1892, Deighton & Dalton, p. 7; February 5, 1897, Elland; December 20, 1889, J. Skelsey & Sons. Even after 1897, when revisions in the factory acts required owners to provide written warning of the fines to which workers were subject, many mills failed to post notices. *Yorkshire Factory Times*, May 6, 1898, p. 1. For Lancashire, see LRO, Skipton Power-Loom Weavers' Association, DDX 1407, August 5, 1908. Mills lacked such notices in part because workers rejected them. In Bingley, Lockwood, and Leeds, for example, workers objected to the owners posting notices in their workroom. In Bingley, the workpeople struck for the removal of a sign that listed fines for spoiled work—but not against the fines per se. Once the owner removed the notice, they agreed to the fines and returned to work. "Strikes and Lockouts in 1899," PP 1900 LXXXIII, p. 529, strike number 88. For other examples of British workers objecting to the posting of written rules, see *Yorkshire Factory Times*, May 30, 1902, Lockwood.

47. PP 1892 XXXV, p. 160. No doubt instances could be found in which British textile workers stopped their labor and created a disturbance inside their workroom, but this did not comprise a widely enacted, recognized model for strikes.

48. Edward Beyer, *Die Fabrik-Industrie des Regierungsbezirkes Düsseldorf vom Standpunkt der Gesundheitpflege*, p. 134; Germany, *Amtliche Mitteilungen aus den Jahres-Berichten der mit Beaufsichtigung der Fabriken betrauten Beamten* (Berlin: Kortkampf, 1884), p. 381; Karl Emsbach, *Die soziale Betriebsverfassung der rheinischen Baumwollindustrie im 19. Jahrhundert* (Bonn: Röhrscheid, 1982), p. 303.

49. Workers paid a fine of ten pfennigs if they failed to return their copy of the ordinance when they quit. HSTAD, Landratsamt Mönchengladbach, 703, Kloeters & Lamerz, 1897. For other factories that gave workers a copy of the ordinance, see Kreisarchiv Kempen, Gemeindearchiv Breyell, F. Beckmann, 1892, and Esters & Co., 1905; Stadtarchiv Mönchengladbach, Gemeinde-archiv Neersen, 814, Rheinische Velvetfabrik, 1912; HSTAD, Landratsamt Grevenbroich, 271, Peter Sieben, pp. 76 ff., 184.

managers.[50] Such defiance provided grounds for immediate dismissal, according to the provisions of the state industrial labor code.[51] The importance German employers attached to the posting of written rules as a means of enforcing their authority over the labor process can be judged from the composition of the rules. Before 1891, factory owners frequently entitled the factory regulations "laws" (*Gesetze*). On their own initiative, employers had the local police stamp the rules before posting them.[52] In some instances, they entitled their rules "police regulations."[53] Through these tactics German employers could give the impression that conduct on the shop floor was subject to legal scrutiny and punishment.

It seems clear that German workers took a more legalistic view of the employment relation than did their British counterparts—when it was to their immediate advantage. In both Germany and Britain, the workers' newspapers reported that managers typically responded to workers' grievances with the comment, "If you don't like it, you can leave."[54] But workers responded to these taunts in a different way in each country. German workers took such casual challenges as grounds for departing, for they had, literally, been told they could go home if they wanted to do so. In each of the principal textile districts of Germany, the work force left without notice on the grounds that by saying anyone could return home if things did not suit them, factory officials had terminated the employment relation.[55] Individual workers used the same reasoning before the business courts. A bobbin winder told the court in Elberfeld in 1899 that she had left without offering notice because a supervisor had told her, "If you don't want to work

50. The factory rules that owners posted in their mills forbade workers from congregating in the entryways or in the yard of the factory. For example, Westfälisches Wirtschaftsarchiv Dortmund, S 8/41, Arbeitsordnung, 1892, and HSTAD, Landratsamt Grevenbroich, 271, Weberei Carl Rente, 1892, pp. 53 ff.

51. Germany, *Gewerbeordnung für das Deutsche Reich* (München: C. H. Beck, 1909), section 123, Nr. 3.

52. Emsbach, op. cit., p. 303. Before 1891 the employers were not obligated to get police approval of the provisions of their rules.

53. *Das Handels-Museum*, May 12, 1892, p. 245.

54. *Cotton Factory Times*, March 19, 1897; *Yorkshire Factory Times*, June 3, 1892, p. 5; *Der Textil-Arbeiter*, March 19, 1909, Lunzenau.

55. Staatsarchiv Detmold, I.U. 430, May 3, 1907; HSTAD, Regierung Aachen, 1635, May 30, 1900, Düren (Mariaweiler); Stadtarchiv Mönchengladbach, 1c 913, March 7, 1913; Staatsarchiv Münster, Kreis Steinfurt, 1311, August 3, 1892; *Augsburger Neueste Nachrichten*, July 25, 1912; Stadtarchiv Chemnitz, Kap. XI, Sect. I, Nr. 16, April 23, 1866; Staatsarchiv Dresden, Amtshauptmannschaft Chemnitz, Nr. 10, 1889, p. 9; Arbeiter-Sekretariat Luckenwalde, *5. Geschäftsbericht für die Zeit vom 1. Januar bis zum 31. Dezember 1908* (Luckenwalde: Selbstverlag, 1909), p. 11.

for the pay, you should get out of here."[56] In response, she left her machine, never to return.

The legal savvy of German workers can be detected in their treatment of written contracts as well. A spinning mill owner in Rheine complained to a district official in 1908 that workers were acutely aware of their legal situation in the factory during the first hour of their hire, before they had been handed their personal copy of the factory ordinance. During these few minutes, the owner said, the workers believed they were "justified" in committing "the worst kinds of mischief" because they knew they did not yet stand under the legal provisions of a labor contract.[57] Not surprisingly, the "people's bureau" (*Volksbüro*) in that town, set up by Catholic organizations to inform workers of their legal rights in housing and employment, reported frequent inquiries from workers about the terms for concluding labor contracts.[58] In Rheine, weavers in 1891 stopped work instantly when a clerk took down the sign that listed their piece rates. The workers did not ask why the sign had been removed, but they refused to continue until the clerk replaced it—in the absence of a posted agreement about rates, the workers believed that they had no contract.[59]

The German strikers treated a halt to the process of converting labor power into labor as an essential and dramatic challenge to the owner's authority. They oriented their action to the technical violation of the printed factory rules, which specified the employer's authority over conduct on the shop floor. British textile workers, by contrast, considered a visual demonstration of defiance, "coming out" of the mill into an open theater, to be one of the hallmarks of a strike. In each country the workers' actions represented the appropriate counterstatement to daily practices on the shop floor. In German mills, where the rituals for entering the mill and the timing of workers' entry focused on the appropriation of workers' labor power, strikers acted out the withdrawal of labor power as such. In British mills, where owners focused on the appropriation of products and the assertion of control over border spaces, strikers, too, thought in terms of "coming out" and staging visible protests in the mill yard.

For many Germans who reflected on their economy in the middle of the nineteenth century, the treatment of labor as a commodity still appeared

56. HSTAD, Gewerbegericht Elberfeld, Nr. 80/48, March 22, 1899.
57. Stadtarchiv Rheine, 183, January 20, 1908, letter to *Regierungspräsident*.
58. Bistumsarchiv Münster, A38, report for 1913, Rheine.
59. Staatsarchiv Münster, Regierung Münster, 718, February 10, 1891.

monstrous and perverse.[60] Ferdinand Lassalle pointed to industrial conflict in Britain as evidence that the complete objectification of human labor was unrealizable. The melancholy course of strikes in Britain, Lassalle claimed, represented the vain attempt of human beings "to disguise themselves as commodities."[61] In the closing decades of the nineteenth century, however, the specification of labor as a commodity was taken so thoroughly for granted that it guided not only the humdrum enactment of production but the small insurrections workers improvised on the shop floor against the system's indignities. In all likelihood, only a minority of workers could have offered a detailed verbal exposition of their understanding of labor's commodity form. But the eloquent patterning of work stoppages shows, as philosophers and social historians alike have remarked, that although people may not be able to put their knowledge into words, they can put it into action.

THE FORMULATION OF STRIKE DEMANDS

In both the German and the British textile industry, the decade of the 1890s began an upsurge in labor disputes that was sustained until the First World War. Karl Emsbach, in his sample of reports from the textile industry in the Rheinland, found a threefold increase in strikes during the decade 1890–1899 over the averages for the three preceding decades. The trend accelerated in the decade after the turn of the century.[62] In Britain the years from 1888 to 1892, the critical years of development for the New Unionism, also initiated an extended increase in textile strikes.[63] Despite this shared trajectory, however, strike demands at the textile factories of each country reached toward different ends, based on the workers' definition of labor as a commodity. In Germany, textile strikers transcended requests concerning wages and hiring to propose changes of their own in the conditions under which workers carried out the labor activity.

60. "Economically you are a commodity, not a human." *Allgemeine deutsche Arbeiter-Zeitung*, Coburg, Nr. 22, May 31, 1863, p. 130.

61. Dieter Schneider et al., op. cit., p. 26.

62. Emsbach, op. cit., pp. 562–565. Due to the lack of summaries for the decades before the 1890s, however, investigators cannot offer a pithy national measure of the extent to which textile strikes became more frequent. The broad lines of development, however, as laid out in local police reports, are unmistakable.

63. Joseph White, "Lancashire Cotton Textiles," in Chris Wrigley, editor, *A History of British Industrial Relations 1874–1914* (Brighton: Harvester Press, 1982), p. 220.

The German workers went beyond their British counterparts in requesting changes to protect the labor power they entrusted to the employer. They lodged strike demands for technical improvements to prevent accidents at work. In Borghorst, for example, striking weavers requested the introduction of "arrangements for the transport of warps according to the accident prevention regulations" of their company.[64] German strikers also requested the installation of shuttle guards to prevent shuttles from flying off the loom and injuring nearby workers. According to the Imperial Bureau of Statistics in Berlin, demands for safer or healthier working conditions contributed to the outbreak of eleven strikes in textiles from 1901 through 1906 (these are the years for which the official figures can be disaggregated into precise demands).[65]

Unfortunately, the average frequency with which German strikers presented such demands for changes in the organization of work will never be ascertained. Local authorities who submitted strike reports to the Imperial Bureau of Statistics often omitted reference to the demands workers submitted that did not relate to wages or the length of the workday. The officials forwarded only those demands that seemed palpably understandable and that fit into their conventional view of industrial conflict, but the researcher who sifts through police notes or newspaper accounts will find a veritable underground of grievances which the workers themselves incorporated into strike negotiations. Historians who rely on the published government statistics in Germany to enumerate the instigating causes of work stoppages merely recirculate the crass assumptions of German officialdom. In Gummersbach, for example, textile workers in 1900 submitted demands for more light and air in the workplace, for a better canteen, and for cleaner toilets. City officials submitted reports to higher-ups only about the wage demands, however, so only the wage demands entered the published tabulations. Similar misreporting occurred for textile strikes in Saxony, in Luckenwalde, and in the district of Lingen.[66] "The official overview of the results of the

---

64. Stadtarchiv Steinfurt-Borghorst, Akt. B 378.

65. The towns in which these demands originated included Leitelshain, Reichenbach, Krefeld, Crimmitschau, Schwaig, Mesum, Lörrach, Bramsche, and Barmen. They embraced the linen, wool, and cotton industries. Germany, *Statistik des Deutschen Reichs*, Volume 157 (Berlin: Kaiserliches Statistisches Amt, various years), pp. II 103 ff.; Volume 164, pp. II 127 ff.; Volume 188, pp. I 58 ff.

66. Stadtarchiv Gummersbach, 4479, report of May 17, 1900. Compare Germany, *Statistik des Deutschen Reichs*, Volume 141, pp. 62–63; *Der Textil-Arbeiter*, June 20, 1902, Wittgensdorf, with Germany, *Statistik des Deutschen Reichs*, Volume 157, Streiks und Aussperrungen im Jahre 1902, p. II 58; *Der Textil-Arbeiter*, October 14, 1904, Luckenwalde, with Germany, *Statistik des Deutschen Reichs*, Volume 188, Streiks und Aussperrungen im

strike statistics," the Social Democratic *Volkszeitung* concluded in 1892, "is absolutely worthless."[67]

The significant point from a comparative perspective is that German textile workers often formulated such demands in strikes, whereas British workers rarely did. No evidence that British textile workers voiced strike demands for protection against accidents appears in British workers' textile newspapers or in the parliamentary listings.[68] Does the inclusion of demands for workplace safety in German strikes, but their absence in Britain, mean that this issue was of concern only to workers in Germany?

The comments of British workers in the *Yorkshire Factory Times* indicate that they certainly harbored dissatisfaction with unsafe machinery. In my sample of stories from this journal for the years from 1890 through 1893, twenty-seven complaints about unhealthy or dangerous working conditions appeared. Most frequently the workers mentioned the lack of guards to prevent the shuttles from flying out of the loom;[69] they also cited the lack of mesh fencing around some equipment.[70] Yet proposals to correct these problems, in particular the installation of loom guards, were not apt to enter into strike negotiations as they did in Germany. This seems even more curious in view of the British textile workers' legendary obstinacy and readiness to strike over minor arrangements in the workplace that concerned pay.

German textile workers, again unlike British workers, included among their strike demands the building of factory canteens and the cleaning of toilet facilities.[71] At Düren in the Rhineland, for example, the workers at a

Jahre 1904; and Staatsarchiv Osnabrück, Rep. 610, Lingen, Nr. 125, September 16, 1902, with Germany, *Statistik des Deutschen Reichs*, Vol. 157, pp. II 104–105.

67. *Volkszeitung*, May 2, 1892, p. 1.

68. The format of British government reports during the 1890s would have suited the listing of idiosyncratic demands, for officials published concrete descriptions of the points at issue and not merely standardized causes. The lack of appropriate shuttle guards in Britain led weavers in Bradford to improvise: they draped sheets around their looms to deflect the injurious projectiles. *Yorkshire Factory Times*, December 29, 1893, p. 4.

69. *Yorkshire Factory Times*, April 17, 1891, Yeadon; October 2, 1891, Horsforth; November 13, Horsforth; March 17, 1893; April 28, 1893, Bradford; May 19, 1893, Bradford; June 9, 1893, Queensbury.

70. *Yorkshire Factory Times*, October 14, 1892, Bradford; February 24, 1893.

71. Stadtarchiv Gummersbach, 4479, report of May 17, 1900; HSTAD, Regierung Aachen, 1634, February 6, 1899, Düren; *Der Textil-Arbeiter*, June 20, 1902, Wittgensdorf; *Der Christliche Textilarbeiter*, February 24, 1900, Dülken; Historisches Archiv des Erzbistums Köln, 23.2, 2 (2), report from Mönchengladbach, 1900, p. 47. For other instances of demands for canteens, dressing rooms, and bathrooms, see Christlicher Textilarbeiter Deutschlands, *Geschäftsbericht, July 1910 to July 1912*, p. 155, Düren. For an example of extensive negotiations over the condition of toilets, see Wirtschaftsarchiv Baden-Württemberg, Stuttgart, B25-

mill for weaving metal sheets bargained in 1899 for better eating facilities as part of the strike settlement.[72] The male dyers who went on strike in 1899 around the district of Krefeld included among their demands a request that the owner provide dressing rooms in which they could change clothes.[73] In Thüringen, workers pressed for free soap and towels from employers.[74] In Mönchengladbach, striking textile workers in 1900 bargained not only for higher wages but for unsoiled toilets.[75] German workers treated the condition of water closets as a topic meriting separate discussion at their union meetings. At Coesfeld, for example, thirty-seven weavers at a meeting in 1910 signed a petition whose sole object was cleaner toilets.[76]

The circumstance that in strikes only German workers advanced demands for better factory facilities does not imply that only German workers concerned themselves with these amenities. The great majority of British textile workers felt the lack of cloakrooms, cafeterias, and undefiled restrooms, but they did not make this an issue of contestation with employers.[77] Instead, they submitted letters to their newspapers express-

---

319, June 15, 1906. For a demand for better washing facilities submitted along with wage requests, see *Der Textil-Arbeiter,* October 11, 1901. Factory inspectors reported frequent complaints about toilet facilities. HSTAD, Regierung Düsseldorf, 25022, report for 1900, pp. 15 ff. At Gera, the workers had a provision incorporated into the piece-rate agreement of 1905 that guaranteed that the workrooms themselves would be cleaned daily. Stadtarchiv Gera, "Vereinbarungen zu den Akkordlohn-Tarifen," October, 1905.

72. HSTAD, Regierung Aachen, 1634, February 16, 1899.

73. *Gladbacher Merkur,* September 18, 1899.

74. Over eighty firms in the district of the German Textile Workers' Union in Thüringen provided the soap and towels. Verband Deutscher Textilarbeiter, Gau Thüringen, *Tariferläuterungen und Statistisches: Bearbeitet nach Aufzeichnungen der Tarif-Kommission im sächsisch-thüringischen Textilbezirk* (Gera: Alban Bretschneider, 1909), p. 32.

75. Historisches Archiv des Erzbistums Köln, 23.2, 2 (2), July, 1900, report, p. 47.

76. *Die Textilarbeiter-Zeitung,* January 14, 1911, Coesfeld. For other examples of discussions of toilets at union meetings, see *Forster Tageblatt,* August 13, 1899; *Die Textilarbeiter-Zeitung,* July 23, 1910, Bocholt; *Der Textil-Arbeiter,* February 21, 1902, Meerane. The German workers' press adopted a writing style that was all too vivid when it came to the toilets. See, for example, *Der Textil-Arbeiter,* March 18, 1904; April 14, 1905, Dölau. The "free" textile workers' union in Germany developed rating systems of toilet cleanliness and executed statistical surveys of toilet conditions at various mills. See *Der Textil-Arbeiter,* January 15, 1904, Gera, and April 22, 1904, Chemnitz. In Saxony, workers extracted an agreement that employers would clean toilets weekly. Verband Deutscher Textilarbeiter, Gau Thüringen, *Lohnbewegungen der Weber und Weberinnen 1902–1909* (Gera: Alban Bretschneider, 1909), p. 29. But then workers struggled to ensure that the toilets were not merely swept but also scrubbed. *Vorwärts,* Sept. 4, 1909.

77. For an example of a worker's discontent with the lack of a cloakroom but absence of any expectation that the owner should provide one, see Elizabeth Roberts's interview with Mr. C1P, born 1894, Preston, p. 42. An overlooker testified in 1892 that the workpeople grumbled to him, but not to the employer, about dirty, primitive toilets. Royal Commission on Labour, PP 1892 XXXVI, Part II, p. 10.

ing their discontent about toilet and eating facilities. In my *Yorkshire Factory Times* sample for 1890 through 1893, for example, ten complaints about sanitation and two about the absence of canteens appeared.[78] (Remarks about canteens appeared only under unusual circumstances, however: in one case the air in the workroom itself was so noxious people felt they could not safely eat there; in another, the owner punished someone for eating near their loom and spilling crumbs on the cloth.) Thus, the British workers complained informally about toilets, but they did not introduce the state of these facilities into strike negotiations as the Germans did. Nor did the discussion of toilets become a topic for public meetings in Britain, as it was in Germany.

The German strikes and complaints concerning toilet facilities, canteens, and safety all took for granted the owner's responsibility for providing for workers' needs on the shop floor. These strikes assumed that the small rituals of life in the factory—eating, cleaning oneself, going to the toilet—could be treated as confrontations with the owner's authority over the production process.[79] When seen in those terms, apparent details grew into suitable issues to introduce into strike negotiations. Speakers at German union meetings turned them into symbols of the owners' command over the worker.[80] The union secretary in Gera declared it "scandalous" in 1906 that female workers at a mill could clean themselves only by putting water in their mouths and spraying it over their bodies.[81] British workers, by contrast, lacking the notion of the owner's embrace of the expenditure of their labor power, did not dramatize those parts of their *vie intime* that

78. Cf. Bradford Library Archives, Mary Brown Barrett, "In Her Clogs and Her Shawl:. A Working Class Childhood, 1902–1914," p. 56: "We hated having to go to the toilet and were glad to get out again." At a Bradford weaving shed, workers brought camphor with them to avoid nausea from the toilet odors. *Yorkshire Factory Times*, September 20, 1889.

79. Factory inspectors reported that German workers rarely used any facilities, such as bath facilities, that were not required for the labor process, even when the services were free. *Jahresberichte der königlich preussischen Regierungs- und Gewerberäthe, 1898* (Berlin: R. v. Decker, 1899), p. 257. In Barmen the inspector reported that workers said outright that such facilities "served a policing function." *Jahresberichte der königlich preussischen Regierungs- und Gewerberäthe, 1892* (Berlin: T. Burer, 1893), p. 354.

80. Owners in Germany fined workers for dirtying the toilets and for dallying around them. At the C. A. Delius factory near Bielefeld, fines of workers for toilet behavior amounted to fifteen marks a year. Staatsarchiv Detmold, Regierung Minden, I.U. Nr. 425, pp. 106 ff. British textile employers, unlike those in Germany, did not establish fines for dirtying the toilet seats.

81. Arbeiter-Sekretariat, Gera, *Fünfter Geschäfts-Bericht des Arbeiter-Sekretariats Gera* (Gera: Selbstverlag, 1906), p. 17.

transpired within the factory walls as points of contact with their employer.[82]

German textile workers also displayed a tendency to broaden the issues in strike movements to cover many seemingly unrelated points of contention. They extended the conflict to consider the employers' authority over the manufacturing process in multiple ways. According to the reports of the Imperial Bureau of Statistics in Berlin, 44 percent of the strikes that German textile workers launched from 1899 through 1906 included multiple demands (these are the only years for which strikes with more than one ultimatum are distinguishable in published reports). The surviving copies of workers' original demands indicate that strikers sometimes compiled long lists. For example, workers at Schiefbahn in 1905 submitted eleven separate demands, including hourly pay for waiting time, restraints on abusive language, and regular consultation between representatives of management and workers.[83] In Britain, by contrast, in a count of the Board of Trade's strike reports for textiles whose format permits a comparison (the years 1894 through 1900), only 5 percent of strikes included more than one demand.[84]

---

82. Indeed, at some British mills the owner relinquished responsibility for toilet conditions by letting overlookers collect fees from workpeople to hire persons to clean the stalls. *Yorkshire Factory Times*, January 29, 1892, p. 5. Of course, the "contact" with employers through the care of one's body in the factory could become all too literal. Workers at a mill in Thüringen complained that the water they received to wash themselves had already been used by people in the factory's supervisory office. Verband Deutscher Textilarbeiter, Gau Thüringen, op. cit., p. 32.

83. HSTAD, Regierung Düsseldorf, 24699, May 1, 1905, p. 286. For examples of workers presenting nine or ten strike demands, see Wirtschaftsarchiv Baden-Württemberg, Stuttgart, B25-319 May 11, 1906; Staatsarchiv Dresden, Kreishauptmannschaft Zwickau, Nr. 1999, March 12, 1887, p. 134. For examples of five or more demands, see HSTAD, Regierung Düsseldorf, 24701, 1906, Rheydt, p. 223; HSTAD, Regierung Aachen, 1634, Jan. 27, 1900, Düren; HSTAD, Landratsamt Mönchengladbach, 70, April 4, 1906, p. 109; Staatsarchiv Münster, Kreis Steinfurt, 1311, Sept. 12, 1906, Mesum; *Der Christliche Textilarbeiter*, Nov. 4, 1899, Grefrath; Staatsarchiv Dresden, Amthauptmannschaft Glauchau, Nr. 341, July 12, 1910; Staatsarchiv Dresden, Amtshauptmannschaft Chemnitz, Nr. 10, October 27, 1889, p. 112; Staatsarchiv Dresden, Kreishauptmannschaft Zwickau, Nr. 1999, August 5, 1884, p. 121, and Oct. 20, 1889, p. 157; Stadtarchiv Greiz, B Nr. 5977, Kap. IV, Nr. 97, Sept. 13, 1905, pp. 39–42. Even in the course of districtwide strikes over wages, weavers submitted many supplementary demands on a firm-by-firm basis regarding coffee water, repair of cloth defects, payment for reeling, etc. Zentrales Staatsarchiv Merseburg, Rep. 120 BB VII 3, Nr. 32, Aachen, pp. 3–19, 1895.

84. Cross-checks of official British reports with the accounts of strikes in the *Yorkshire Factory Times* reveal no instances in which the Board of Trade omitted subsidiary demands in strike movements.

456 / The Structure of the Workers' Countersigns

It is possible, of course, that the greater incidence of multiple demands in Germany meant only that German workers planned their strikes more carefully or conducted them in a more organized fashion.[85] Were this explanation accurate, strikes in Germany that were initiated with the two weeks' advance notice legally required to terminate the employment relation would revolve around multiple demands more frequently than would more spontaneous strikes begun without sufficient notice. Government statistics are not the last word on the matter, but they lend no support to this hypothesis. For the years 1899 through 1906, the period for which the official German data can be cross-tabulated, textile workers issued multiple demands in 43 percent of the abrupt, illegal strikes. There was no statistically significant difference in Germany between the rate at which textile workers in well-organized, lawful strikes presented multiple demands and the rate at which workers in illegal strikes lodged them.[86]

The variation between Germany and Britain in number of demands lodged probably did not derive from the institutions that factories had in place for mediating workplace conflicts. In both countries, conflict usually broke out in individual mills without turning into district-wide confrontations between the unions and the employers' associations. In Germany, if negotiations at a mill preceded the launching of a strike, workers usually conducted them without assistance from trade union officials. The lack of close union guidance in German textile strikes can be gauged from the circumstance that most of them began without the legal notice necessary to end employment.[87] The so-called worker committees some German mills formed to administer health insurance funds hardly became known for representing the workers' interests in disputes.[88] And in Yorkshire most

85. In her study of strikes in France from 1871 to 1890, Michelle Perrot found that more spontaneous strikers were more likely to lodge only a single demand. *Les Ouvriers en grève* (Paris: Mouton & Co., 1974), p. 344.

86. Of the 313 strikes textile workers initiated in the years 1899 to 1906 with the two weeks' notice necessary to terminate the employment contract, 139 (44 percent) had multiple demands. Of the 362 strikes textile workers undertook in this period without proper notice, 155, or virtually the same portion (43 percent), had multiple demands. Germany, *Statistik des Deutschen Reichs* (Berlin: Kaiserliches Statistisches Amt, 1899–1906). For an autobiographical account of an impromptu strike in which workers articulated more than one demand, see Gewerkschaft Textil-Bekleidung, *Dokumente zu 150 Jahren Frauenarbeit in der Textil- und Bekleidungsindustrie* (Düsseldorf: Courier-Druck, 1981), p. 23: "What we should demand, no one of us knew better than any other, but we knew we wanted to strike!"

87. Ibid. Of 675 strikes in the German textile industry between 1899 and 1906, 362 (54 percent) involved workers who had not legally terminated the employment contract.

88. For the lower Rhine, see HSTAD, Regierung Düsseldorf, 25014, Mönchengladbach Fabrikinspektor, 1892; *Christliche Arbeiterin*, June 16, 1906, Mönchengladbach; *Gladbacher*

strikes broke out before the unions had received word of the dispute.[89] The *Socialist Review* reported in 1910 that in one woolen district, workers launched or threatened half a dozen strikes within three months "without a single Union member being concerned or official intervening."[90]

Still another possible explanation for the greater incidence of multiple demands in Germany is that the German textile workers struck less frequently. By this hypothetical line of argument, fewer strikes would build up a backlog of demands that would then be expressed in a single strike. But in terms of the size of the textile work forces, strikes were actually slightly less frequent during the period from 1899 through 1913 in Britain than in Germany. The annual ratio of strikes to workers was about one to seven hundred in Britain and one to six hundred in Germany.[91]

The tendency of textile workers in Germany to formulate an extensive list of demands rather than to strike over a single issue coincided with another trend: German textile workers included among their strike demands requests that employers reform their governance of the work activity. Strikers at a Chemnitz mill told their employer in 1889 he had to make a "better arrangement of the production techniques" and allow workers to monitor the run-

---

Merkur, August 1, 1899, Fabrik Von Kaubes. For the Wuppertal, see Elisabeth Gottheiner, *Studien über die Wuppertaler Textilindustrie und ihre Arbeiter in den letzten zwanzig Jahren* (Leipzig: Duncker & Humblot, 1903), p. 87; for the Bergisches Land, HSTAD, Landratsamt Gummersbach, 487, May 4, 1890, Bergneustadt. For the Münsterland, see Herbert Erdelen, "Die Textilindustrie in zwei Kreisen (Ahaus und Steinfurt) des Münsterlandes," diss., Freiburg i. Br., 1921, p. 152. Since the committees were often dominated by supervisors, social democratic organizers in some regions discouraged their formation. Staatsarchiv Weimar, Landesregierung Greiz, n Rep. A, Kap. IXa, Nr. 207, factory inspector reports, 1885–1895, p. 152, and Staatsarchiv Weimar, Landesregierung Greiz, n Rep. A, Kap. IXa, Nr. 303, 1896, p. 87, and 1897, p. 159.

89. Ben Turner said, "We seldom heard of the disputes until a day or two had elapsed." *About Myself 1863–1930* (London: Cayme Press, 1930), pp. 116, 125. Turner said the weavers' union approved of only four strikes in more than eight years. Turner's Scrapbook, Kirklees Archives, Sept., 1894. *Yorkshire Factory Times*, September 13, 1889, Morley; June 20, 1890, Kirkheaton; August 15, 1890, Bradford; September 5, 1890, Bradford; September 26, 1890, Shipley; October 2, 1890, Keighley; June 2, 1893, Leeds, p. 1; June 9, 1893, Bradford; August 4, 1893, Luddenden.

If the institutional environment were responsible for differences in the lodging of multiple demands, an analyst might expect significant differences to have arisen in the frequency of multiple demands between Yorkshire and highly unionized Lancashire. Yet in both provinces fewer than 5 percent of strikes involved multiple demands.

90. Henry Wilmott, "The 'Labour Unrest' and the Woollen Trades," *Socialist Review* (November 1910), p. 214.

91. Textile workforces computed from Germany, *Die Deutsche Volkswirtschaft am Schlusse des 19. Jahrhunderts* (Berlin: Puttkammer und Mühlbrecht, 1900), p. 25 and United Kingdom, *Census of England and Wales 1891*, PP 1893–1894 CVI, pp. vii ff.

ning of the engine.[92] In Aachen the weavers demanded that the company create a new job, that of carrying warp beams, to relieve weavers of this burden.[93] Challenges such as this were not simply defensive responses to employers' efforts to introduce new machinery or heavier workloads. At a spinning mill in Viersen, on the lower Rhine, for example, the striking spinners in 1899 listed several demands for the maintenance of machinery. They gave the manager a schedule that stipulated how often he was to carry out preventive maintenance and replace frayed parts on various types of spinning frames.[94] In both Germany and Britain, weavers considered it proper that overlookers dispense warps among the looms in the order in which weavers had finished their previous jobs.[95] At a mill in Eupen, Germany, the weavers even demanded that the overlooker himself, who tended a loom of his own in his spare moments, receive warps in the same order as the ordinary weavers. When the owner disapproved the request, the weavers went on strike.[96] They wanted to override the overlookers' and employers' authority to determine the distribution of work on the shop floor.

How dissimilar are these demands from those of the British? British weavers, like those in Germany, resisted changes in the labor process, such as the change to the two-loom system. Like the German weavers, they struck over the poor quality of raw materials, especially in the cotton industry, because defective materials reduced their piece-rate earnings or caused them to work harder for the same wage. They also struck over the arbitrary sacking of co-workers and, in the spinning departments, over the owners' failure to promote workers in order of seniority from the apprenticeship position of a piecer to the full position of a mule minder. British workers were no less concerned with authority than their German counterparts, but they focused on defending against encroachment rather than challenging

92. Staatsarchiv Dresden, Amthauptmannschaft Chemnitz, Nr. 10, October 30, 1889, pp. 116–117, and Protokoll of Nov. 15, 1889.

93. Zentrales Staatsarchiv Merseburg, Rep. 120 BB VII, Fach. 3, Nr. 32, Feb. 2, 1895.

94. *Der Christliche Textilarbeiter*, June 8, 1899. Textile strikers in the region of Greiz demanded not just fresh air at work but the installation of a new system of ventilation. Staatsarchiv Weimar, Landratsamt Greiz, Nr. 2550, 1895, p. 10. At Anrath striking weavers extracted a promise from the firm in 1902 that overlookers would be on hand to attend broken looms more promptly. *Der Christliche Textilarbeiter*, February 1, 1902, Anrath.

95. For an example of a strike over this issue, see Zentrales Staatsarchiv Merseburg, Rep. 77 2525, Volume 1, Nr. 3, pp. 6 ff., January 1899.

96. *Der Christliche Textilarbeiter*, June 2, 1900, Eupen. In the district of Löbau, weavers also demanded changes in the "arrangement and regulation" of production to reduce waiting time for materials. Staatsarchiv Dresden, Amthauptmannschaft Löbau, Nr. 3055, March 30, 1890.

the governance of production. British textile-factory workers did not propose changes to control the manager's methods of administering production, as did their German counterparts.[97]

British contemporaries believed that some of the strikes over wages disguised textile workers' wishes to change aspects of the manufacturing process. For example, at the Alston wool combing works in Bradford, the director found in 1892 that men who had gone out on strike were glad to come in once he agreed to changes in the organization of work. He concluded that the wages had not been the overriding issue at all; rather, it was "a problem of work operations concerning the disposal of suds and potash."[98] William Drew, an executive of the Yorkshire textile workers' union, testified in 1891 that many strikes over wages were an "excuse," a pretext. Wage demands concealed other concerns, he said, in particular, mismanagement of the looms.[99] Even when British textile workers were both dissatisfied with the technical methods of production and willing to strike, they did not focus on the governance of work as a contestable issue.

Each of these differences between the goals of British and German strikers parallels the differences between their cultural definitions of the commodity of labor. The German concept of the delivery of labor in the form of labor power accentuated the employer's exercise of authority at the point of production to convert this labor capacity into labor.[100] The distinguishing

97. To be sure, British textile workers proposed changes related to the calculation or verification of pay. At a mill in Lockwood, for example, the female weavers in 1902 left the premises and refused to return until the owner agreed to place marks on the warps at ten-foot intervals. By these marks the weavers would be able to check whether the warp spanned a greater distance than the weavers had been told it would. But this demand related to the exchange of products for pay, not to the execution of the labor activity. *Yorkshire Factory Times*, May 30, 1902, p. 5, Lockwood. In the cotton branch, British cotton workers also protested when managers put excessive steam into the air. They suggested limits to the discomforts of work, not improvements in the technique of manufacture proper. See Joseph White, *The Limits of Trade Union Militancy* (Westport, Connecticut: Greenwood Press, 1978), Appendix One, pp. 186–201; Royal Commission on Labour, PP 1890–1891 LXXVII, p. 483, Kirkham and Blackburn.

98. Quoted in Jennings, op. cit., pp. 159 ff.

99. Royal Commission on Labour, PP 1892 XXXV, p. 223. A striking weaver at Sunnyside Mills in Bolton said in 1905 that the wage complaint only cloaked "the real want," which was less specialization in the work process. Zoe Munby, "The Sunnyside Women's Strike," *Bolton People's History*, Volume 1 (March 1984), p. 8. Tom Mann's autobiography provides an interesting parallel case for the dock workers, with wage demands again disguising concern about the organization of the labor process. *Tom Mann's Memoirs* (London: Labour Publishing Company, 1923), p. 110.

100. Thus employers defined a *worker* (*Arbeiter*) as someone "whose activity is controlled by supervisors." Staatsarchiv Dresden, Amthauptmannschaft Löbau, Nr. 3375, factory ordinance, Weberei Gebrüder Hoffmann.

features of German textile workers' strike goals—the greater focus on safety conditions and on hygienic care of the worker's person, the multiplication of grievances in a single strike about the employer's administration of the mill, and the advancement of proposals for changes in the governance of production—all focused on the employer's domination of workers by the exercise of authority at the point of production. British textile strikers did not focus on the small rituals of daily life inside the mill as a point of contact with the employer's authority. Rather, they converted disputes that might have addressed the organization of production into an issue of receiving adequate compensation for products delivered.[101]

German workers' understanding of the labor transaction did not always lead them to reject the owner's authority on the shop floor; sometimes they embraced it. The union of workers employed at home in the sewing industry demanded the erection of central workshops for themselves, though not to boost productivity. Instead, they sought to make employers responsible for providing better working conditions and wanted union and state inspectors to certify and monitor the wages and hours of labor, which would be possible only if workers labored under the employer's supervision.[102] British sewers, by contrast, were far from preferring centralized work.[103] As the example of the home sewers in Germany shows, the specification of labor as a commodity did not inevitably make workers in Germany more rebellious against the capitalist labor transaction or against authority on the shop floor. Factory workers contested employers' authority while home workers embraced it, yet the struggle in both situations started with the presumption that the renter of labor power, entrusted with the disposition over the person of the worker, also bore responsibility for the care of that labor power.[104] Depending on the tactical advantages to be secured, German workers used the prevailing specification of the labor transaction in different ways, but always in a

---

101. For a brief discussion of why workers in the nineteenth century based their demands upon their identities as producers, see Bernard Mottez, *Systèmes de salaire et politiques patronales* (Paris: Centre Nationale de la Recherche Scientifique, 1966), p. 232.

102. Herbert Cohen, "Heimarbeit und Heimarbeiterbewegung in der deutschen Herrenkonfektion," Ph.D. diss., Erlangen, 1926, pp. 78–79.

103. Royal Commission on Labour, PP 1892 XXXVI, Part II, p. 117.

104. "Labor power is the only capital of the worker. . . . It is therefore his first duty to prevent its premature deterioration or even destruction. This is no less the responsibility of the employer, who out of self-interest watches over the health of his subordinates." Walter Höttemann, *Die Göttinger Tuchindustrie der Vergangenheit und Gegenwart* (Göttingen: Göttinger Handelsdruckerei, 1931), p. 105.

manner that reveals consistent differences from the cultural paradigm for conflict in Britain.

OVERLOOKERS' ROLE IN STRIKES

The role of overlookers in Germany helped to sustain German workers' understanding of the labor process as the submission of the labor activity to the employer's domination. When German workers labored under overlookers, they understood themselves as having immediate contact with executants of the employer. In Britain, by contrast, the overlookers' relative independence from the factory owners lent support to the workers' understanding that they transferred their labor as it was embodied in products. The German overlookers' status as agents, not just servants, of the owners prevented them from mediating between workers and owners. By contrast, British overlookers, who boasted that they did not "fawn" on the owners, saw themselves as intermediaries between workers and owners.[105] For example, the rules of the Huddersfield and Dewsbury Power Loom Tuners' Society, issued in 1882, set down as one of the association's goals the "regulating" of relations between workmen and owners.[106] Weavers in Yorkshire and Lancashire could even consult with their overlookers about the chances of obtaining wage concessions or ask for advice about the best timing for a strike.[107] Textile workers in Germany prevented even the lowest supervisors from getting word of a possible strike.[108] The German courts ruled that if an overlooker heard of a planned strike and did not report it to the owner, he had betrayed his duty to the owner and given grounds for immediate dismissal.[109]

The contrast between the roles of overlookers in Germany and in Britain left their marks upon the organization and course of strikes. Overlookers in Britain sometimes supported weavers' strike demands. At Manningham, for

105. *Yorkshire Factory Times,* February 7, 1902, p. 8. A poem published in *Werkmeister-Zeitung* betrays a somewhat different attitude: "If the output is to be a credit to the foreman, then sweat must run from the burning brow. Yet only from above [the owner] can the yield indeed come." January 1, 1892.

106. Kirklees Archives, Rules, Huddersfield and Dewsbury Power Loom Tuners' Society, 1882.

107. For examples of tuners acting as intermediaries, see *Yorkshire Factory Times,* March 20, 1903, and December 6, 1889, p. 6, Huddersfield. For Lancashire, see *Cotton Factory Times,* September 10, 1886, Rochdale.

108. Stadtarchiv Gera, Nr. 2799, pp. 40–41, April 27, 1890.

109. *Das deutsche Wollen-Gewerbe,* December 31, 1905, Beilage zu Nr. 104–105, p. 1663. See the parallel decision for white-collar workers in *Zeitschrift für Textil-Industrie,* October 1, 1913, p. 264.

example, in one of Yorkshire's most famous labor disputes, in 1890 and 1891 the tuners refused to teach silk weaving to the new hires whom the higher management set on to break the weavers' strike. Instead, the tuners walked off the job in support of the striking weavers.[110] Weavers cheered their supervisors' decision with the cry, "Good *owd* overlooker!"[111] In the great weavers' strike of 1883 in the Colne Valley, too, tuners from the district voted against training learners and against filling in on the looms for the striking weavers.[112]

British overlookers also supported weavers' opposition to increases in the number of looms per weaver. For example, the overlookers at a firm outside Bradford in 1891 accused the owner of plotting to shift from two to three looms per weaver. They refused to carry out what they called the owner's "dirty work" of "spotting" for dismissal the least favorite weavers in their sections. This, they charged, would only fit into the owner's plan to begin assigning three looms to each weaver. They ceased work even though the owner did not propose an increase in their own allotments of looms.[113] In Lancashire, too, the overlookers struck in support of workers' demands. In a strike at Nelson in 1891, many of the weaving overlookers left work to force the dismissal of an overlooker who had made immoral propositions to a female subordinate.[114] Overlookers in Lancashire also supported an end to the so-called slate system, in which overlookers posted their workers' earnings to shame the slower ones.[115]

110. Cyril Pearce, *The Manningham Mills Strike, Bradford: December 1890–April 1891* (Hull: University of Hull, 1975), p. 20.

111. *Yorkshire Factory Times*, January 9, 1891, p. 7.

112. *Northern Pioneer*, April 14, 1883, p. 11. The employers' request during the strike that the tuners do weaving reflected a customary expectation: during slowdowns in production, tuners were wont to weave on a loom of their own. A few overlookers did carry out the weaving after the employer threatened them with dismissal. *Yorkshire Factory Times*, November 1, 1889, and December 6, 1889; *Huddersfield Daily Examiner*, April 12, 1883. In 1884 overlookers in Burnley, Lancashire, refused to fill places of weavers who went on strike. When these weaving overlookers went out on strike on their own in 1897 for a higher commission, they issued a leaflet which said, "The masters have set the tacklers and weavers one against the other quite long enough. . . . It is plain to everyone that our interests are identical." Trodd, op. cit., p. 302.

113. *Bradford Daily Telegraph*, May 11, 1891, Horton Bank. This pattern was repeated elsewhere in Yorkshire. When employers at the turn of the century put increasing pressure on weavers in the Colne Valley to take on two looms instead of one, the Huddersfield and Dewsbury Power Loom Tuners' Society censured the employers. *Yorkshire Factory Times*, February 7, 1902, p. 1; March 28, 1902. Tuners in Dewsbury encouraged weavers to join the Textile Workers' Association: *Yorkshire Factory Times*, July 14, 1905, p. 4.

114. Jan Lambertz, "Sexual Harassment in the Nineteenth Century English Cotton Industry," *History Workshop* Issue 19 (Spring 1985), p. 35. The Nelson Society of Powerloom Overlookers dismissed one of its members who allowed his children to work at this shed during the strike. Ibid.

Can we find analogous episodes in Germany where overlookers supported their underlings? In Germany, the professional journal *Der deutsche Meister* reported sympathetically in 1904 on weavers' efforts in Mönchengladbach to resist a move in some branches to the two-loom system.[116] But German overlookers did not make formal statements or take stronger action to support the weavers.[117] In Germany, business journals, textile workers' newspapers, police reports, and factory inspectors' reports appear not to mention such acts of solidarity.

The most telling indicator that overlookers stood closer to the workers in Britain than in Germany lies in the workers' collective actions. In Yorkshire and Lancashire, strikes by subordinates to protest the firing of their overlooker occurred in each of the textile districts and in all branches of the trade, especially among women, but among male workers as well.[118] When companies attempted to replace striking tuners, the *Yorkshire Factory Times*

115. LRO, DDX 1151/19/3, Chorley Power-Loom Overlookers' Association, March 13, 1908. In Lancashire the overlookers' unions voted to strike with weavers against the use of inferior cotton. LRO, DDX 1151/1/3, January 7, 1907.

116. *Der deutsche Meister*, September 7, 1904.

117. Overlookers in Germany, as an arm of the employer, were forbidden to strike. As an appeals court in Dresden reasoned, "If the professional staff resorts to the threat of collectively giving notice, in order through the planned action to force the employer to be more forthcoming, then the staff has grossly violated their duty, inherent in the employment relation, to safeguard the interests of the owner and to refrain from anything that could run against those interests, and has thereby proven themselves guilty of disloyalty in service." The quotation comes from a case involving white-collar workers but applied to the category of professional technical workers as well. *Zeitschrift für die gesamte Textil-Industrie*, October 1, 1913, p. 264. For an analogous case outside of textiles in which an employer could immediately dismiss a technical professional for collaborating with workers, see *Das Gewerbegericht*, September 3, 1903, p. 294, Solingen. So long as they did not strike, however, German overlookers remained free to petition their employers for changes in working conditions. Jürgen Kocka, *Die Angestellten in der deutschen Geschichte, 1850–1980* (Göttingen: Vandenhoeck & Ruprecht, 1981), p. 123. But they exercised this option only when it concerned their own interests. *Die Textilarbeiter-Zeitung*, May 21, 1910, "Kommission der Webermeister," and September 25, 1909, Bocholt; *Der Textil-Arbeiter*, April 29, 1910, p. 134.

118. "Strikes and Lockouts in 1893," PP 1894 LXXXI, strike 694, Halifax; "Strikes and Lockouts in 1894," PP 1895 XCII, strike 966, Leeds; United Kingdom, Royal Commission on Labour, 1891, re strike ca. 1870, op. cit., p. 92; *Yorkshire Factory Times*, Birstall, November 22, 1889; Elland, May 15, 1891; Ravensthorpe, April 29, 1892; Milnsbridge, February 12, 1892; Halifax, June 2, 1893; Luddenden, August 9, 1901; Dewsbury, May 2, 1902; Halifax, June 17, 1898; *Bradford Daily Telegraph*, May 8, 1891. For Lancashire, see J. White, *The Limits*, op. cit., p. 189, and J. White, "Lancashire Cotton Textiles," op. cit., p. 213; *Cotton Factory Times*, January 29, 1897, Colne; PP 1890 68, pp. 574, 580, Manchester; Royal Commission on Labour, PP 1890–1891 LXXVII, Burnley; "Strikes and Lockouts in 1893," PP 1894 LXXXI, p. 77, Wigan, and p. 510, Bolton; "Strikes and Lockouts in 1894," PP 1895 XCII, p. 360, Whittlefield, and p. 481, Stockport; "Strikes and Lockouts in 1897," PP 1898 LXXXVIII, p. 589, Preston. For the early industrial era, see Ashworth, op. cit., p. 13.

reported, "the weight of the evidence is that women weavers will refuse to work with imported overlookers."[119] This newspaper even believed that the ability to retain favorite supervisors in the spinning branch comprised an incentive for workers to join unions. "It's a great pity, to my mind," a correspondent wrote, "that even the spinners do not combine, if for no other reason than to keep a good overlooker."[120] British weavers supported the demands of their tuners for higher commissions.[121] German overlookers received comparatively little support from workers. In Britain, workers' strike support for overlookers was discussed as common knowledge, but in Germany it was considered an extraordinary event. A German supervisor said in 1912 that if an overlooker appealed to underlings for support, "they would laugh at him and declare him insane."[122]

To complete this comparison of overlookers' positions, we must consider the form of union organization pursued by overlookers in the two countries. Although German overlookers could not legally strike, they could unite in collective associations and organize demonstrations.[123] Two major organiza-

---

119. *Yorkshire Factory Times,* December 6, 1912. For Nelson in Lancashire, see *Yorkshire Factory Times,* October 28, 1892. The tuners' society in Bradford resolved at an assembly in 1899 "that the best thanks of this meeting be given to the weavers at Briggella Mills for the gallant stand they have made on behalf of the overlookers." Bradford District Archives, 1/1/6 3D86, July 8, 1899.

120. *Yorkshire Factory Times,* November 17, 1893.

121. *Cotton Factory Times,* April 23, 1897, Oldham.

122. *Zeitschrift für die gesamte Textil-Industrie,* October 31, 1912, p. 967. One example of German weavers striking in support of a fired overlooker did come to light: Zentrales Staatsarchiv Merseburg, Rep. 120, BB VI, No. 164, Band 4, 1899, Mönchengladbach, p. 109.

123. On the staging of demonstrations, see *Der deutsche Meister,* March 1, 1913, and March 15, 1913. Overlookers from the Wuppertal in Germany, during a collective protest in 1910, sought to establish thirty-six looms as their upper limit. *Der Textil-Arbeiter,* 1910, p. 142. German overlookers were not denied the right to bargain over the sale of their labor as a market commodity, only the ability to do so through the threat of collective action. In Yorkshire and Lancashire, strikes by an entire staff of overlookers at weaving mills did not represent a rare event. The tuners' typical grievance was the assignment of an excessive number of looms per tuner. In the twenty-five-year period before the First World War, overlooking disputes occurred in each of the major weaving towns of Yorkshire and in every branch of production, from the fancy woolen trade to cheap worsteds. The largest action by overlookers began during the spring of 1913 in the Bradford district. The overlookers' union in Bradford, which counted 90 percent of the areas' tuners as its members, carried out a general strike to demand a minimum wage of two pounds per week. For tacklers' strikes in Lancashire at Accrington, Church, and Oswaldtwistle, see *Textile Mercury,* July 8, 1899, p. 24, and for Nelson, see *Yorkshire Factory Times,* October 28, 1892. For Yorkshire, see the wagebooks for Taylor and Littlewood, Newsome Mills, August 1894, Kirklees Archives; Minutes of the Huddersfield Power Loom Tuners' Society, January 10, 1912, November 12, 1912, and October 24, 1913, Kirklees Archives; *Textile Mercury,* May 16, 1891, p. 344; *Bradford Daily Telegraph,* May 8, 1891; July 6, 1899. *Yorkshire Factory Times,* June 9, 1905, Dudley Hill.

tions represented the interests of German textile overlookers. The oldest, the German Foremen's Union, founded in 1884, included overlookers from all industries. Before the turn of the century, this group counted over twenty thousand members, including more than one hundred in each of several towns in northwest Germany where textiles predominated: Aachen, Mönchengladbach, Rheydt, Barmen, and Elberfeld.[124] Another association, the German Supervisors' Union, admitted overlookers only from the textile branch. This group, founded by weaving overlookers in 1899 in Mönchengladbach, had over five hundred members in northwest Germany by 1903.[125]

These German overlookers' unions varied in a crucial respect from those in Britain: the lowest loom fixers and the highest foremen united in a single organization.[126] The lowest loom fixers and the highest supervisors in Germany shared the position of salaried servants, in contrast to those below them who received piece rates. German foremen used their organization to support the rights of the lesser overlookers. For example, the German Foremen's Union petitioned to ensure that state officials classified its loom fixers as technical professionals, eligible for the government's pension plan.[127] In each of the major centers of weaving in Yorkshire—Bradford, Leeds, Halifax, Keighley, and Huddersfield—city-wide overlookers' unions developed at the same pace as in Germany. But the British overlookers' unions severed the lower-level overlookers from higher-ups; foremen did not join.[128] The titles of the Yorkshire unions reflected this exclusion: the local associations named themselves Power-Loom Tuners or Power-Loom Overlookers. In contrast to their German counterparts, the British overlookers had an organization in which the

124. Deutscher Werkmeister-Verband, Statistics from 1892. Zentrales Staatsarchiv Merseburg, Rep. 120, BB VII 1, Nr. 25, Bd. 1, p. 19. Membership cannot be broken down by trade on either the city or the national level.

125. *Gladbacher Merkur,* September 26, 1899. Archiv des Freien Deutschen Gewerkschaftbundes, Der Deutsche Meister-Verband, Membership Report, Third Quarter, 1903.

126. Stadtarchiv Bocholt, K2/149, August 1900, statutes of Deutscher Webermeister-Verband. For evidence that not all members had so-called fixed terms *(feste Bezüge)*, see paragraph 133, *Der Textil-Arbeiter,* June 16, 1905. This confirms that loom fixers belonged to this union. See also *Der Christliche Textilarbeiter,* June 8, 1901, "Sonderorganisationen."

127. Archiv des Deutschen Gewerkschaftsbundes, "Stenographischer Bericht über die Verhandlungen des Delegiertentages des Deutschen Werkmeister-Verbandes," 1913, p. 32.

128. In its mill-by-mill survey of members and loom assignments in 1913, the Bradford loom tuners' union counted as members virtually all tuners but in each mill excluded one supervisor, the highest-level foreman. Bradford District Archives, Loom Tuners' Union survey of 1913.

highest foremen, who were tied most closely to the owner, could not put a brake on action directed against the owners. In Germany, by contrast, the overlookers' unions classified the loom fixers, who actually stood near to the status of ordinary workers, as occupants of the same basic position as the employers' closest assistants.

The absence of foremen from overlookers' organizations in Britain also enabled the overlookers to move closer to the position of the textile workers' unions.[129] From their founding in the mid-nineteenth century, the over-lookers' organizations endorsed the principle of providing strike support to weavers if weavers in turn supported the overlookers' cause.[130] In the last quarter of the nineteenth century, affiliation became more explicit. The tuners' societies in the cities of Yorkshire relinquished their status as mere friendly societies and registered as trade unions.[131] By the eve of the First World War, the overlookers' unions in Bradford, the Colne Valley, and the Heavy Woollen District had endorsed the Independent Labour Party. They donated funds and sent representatives to the Labour party's parliamentary council meetings.[132] Even in Halifax, where the overlookers' club was slow to act, some overlookers identified themselves more as laborers than as supervisors. One member of the Halifax society, in a debate during 1909 on a resolution to affiliate with the General Union of Overlookers, a national organization, expressed this view with special clarity. According to the minutes of the union's meeting,

> He said it was the same ol' thing over again, Capital versus Labour. He said if the masters of Halifax wished to reduce overlookers'

129. For an example in which even the mill manager's niece and chief overlooker's daughter volunteered for the weavers' union, see Elizabeth K. Blackburn's autobiography, "In and Out the Windows," Burnley Library Archives, p. 36.

130. LRO, DDX 1128/1/1, Blackburn Overlookers' Society, 1858, 1862.

131. Managers' and Overlookers' Society, Bradford, *Managers' and Overlookers' Society, Centenary Spinning Celebrations, 1827–1927* (Bradford: R. Sewell, 1927), p. 20; *Yorkshire Factory Times*, March 22, 1901, p. 5, and March 17, 1893, p. 4.

132. Managers' and Overlookers' Society, Bradford, op. cit., p. 26. Joanna Bornat, "An Examination of the General Union of Textile Workers 1883–1922," Ph.D. diss., University of Essex, 1981, p. 76; Minutes of the Huddersfield Power Loom Tuners' Society, May, 1905, and December, 1907, Kirklees Archives. The Huddersfield Power Loom Tuners' Society sent delegates to the Labour party parliamentary council meeting in 1905 to decide how many wards ought to be contested "in the interest of Labour." These overlookers' unions also supported the Yorkshire Textile Workers' Federation, which lobbied in Parliament for factory legislation. *Yorkshire Factory Times*, March 22, 1901, p. 5. The *Yorkshire Factory Times* reported in the spring of 1914 that the Yorkshire Tuners' Association planned to put forward Labour candidates for Parliament at Morley, Wakefield, and Holmfirth. March 26, 1914.

wages, this Society could not resist it. Therefore he would support Joining the General Union or he was prepared to go further and amalgamate with the workers of the world.[133]

The collaboration between overlookers and workers extended to Lancashire as well. In 1907, when overlookers in Blackburn, Lancashire, joined the United Textile Workers' Association, a national confederation of textile unions, they justified their decision by citing the "spirit of mutual help and brotherhood that ought to exist among all unionists."[134]

Whereas overlookers' unions in Britain supported their members' interests by fighting for improvements in the factory, their counterpart German unions focused their efforts on the political arena outside the factory. They persuaded the German government to admit them in 1911 to a government pension program similar to one enjoyed by white-collar workers.[135] They advocated that technical professional workers be represented on the government's labor boards.[136] Yet the German overseers' unions did not directly

---

133. Calderdale Archives, TU102/3, June 19, 1909. In Burnley, the overlookers in 1892 urged the formation of a "distinct Labour Party in order to carry forward the full and complete emancipation of labour." Trodd, op. cit., p. 325. The General Association of Powerloom Overlookers supported the Labour Representation Committee, because, it said, other parties are "mixed up and interwoven with capital." General Union of Associations of Powerloom Overlookers, *The Almanack and Guide for 1899* (Manchester: Ashton and Redfern, 1899). Yorkshire overlookers stood close enough to the weavers that they also applied for jobs as dues collectors for the regular textile workers' union, the Textile Workers' Association. *Yorkshire Factory Times*, October 14, 1892, p. 4, Bradford. Overlookers were also elected treasurers of workers' independent mill clubs. *Yorkshire Factory Times*, December 5, 1912. In Yeadon, the tuners never developed their own union, but enlisted with weavers in the Factory Workers' Union. My interview with Edward Mercer, Rawdon, Yorkshire. In the heavy woolen district, some heads of departments, probably outside of weaving, were members of the regular textile workers union. The union chief asked for a raise for them as part of a package of wage demands in 1913. *Yorkshire Factory Times*, May 8, 1913, p. 8. In Lancashire, the manager of an Oldham mill said, "Plenty of overlookers in the weaving trade who have been working weavers are still in the Weavers' Union." *Journal of the British Association of Managers of Textile Works*, Session 1913–1914, Volume 5, p. 17.

134. *Blackburn Times*, March 2, 1907. The textile overlookers played an important role in the founding of the Labour Representation Committee in Lancashire. Trodd, op. cit., p. 303. For Lancashire, see also LRO, DDA 1151/19/3, Chorley Power-Loom Overlookers' Association Minutes, July 11, 1903, support for Labour Representation; LRO, DDX 1151/1/3, Preston Powerloom Overlookers, June 19, 1906, support for Labour Representation. The General Union of Associations of Power-Loom Overlookers endorsed the Labour Representation Committee. *Cotton Factory Times*, April 29, 1904. For the division in political outlooks among overlookers from 1908 to 1920 in Preston, however, see Michael Savage, *The Dynamics of Working-Class Politics* (Cambridge: Cambridge University Press, 1987), p. 155.

135. Heinz Potthoff, *Das Versicherungsgesetz für Angestellte: Vom 20. Dezember 1911.* (Stuttgart: J. Hess, 1912).

136. Franz Potthoff, *Die soziale Frage der Werkmeister* (Düsseldorf: Werkmeister-Buchhandlung, 1910).

confront the issue of raising overlookers' salaries. "In our social program the question of pay is almost completely forgotten," said a speaker at the overlookers' convention in 1911. The first requirement for raising the salaries of overlookers would have been to admit into the union only those who were already able to command a minimum salary, so that all in the union would have some bargaining leverage. Such an entrance requirement the union rejected.[137] The overlookers' societies in Yorkshire and Lancashire, by contrast, imposed a rule that applicants prove they already earned a high wage.[138] British overlookers took on the issue of pay directly, whereas their German counterparts moved to the political arena, a shift which, in the factory itself, upheld the role of German overlookers as servants of the owner.

The forms of association for overlookers in Germany and Britain reflected the basic difference between their perceptions of the overlooker's role in the factory. The German organizations detached the overlookers from the workers and linked them to the highest foremen; they defined their members' status by reference to the exercise of authority. From the German viewpoint, even the lowest loom fixer was unlike a worker, since the loom fixer had to exercise authority over others and made decisions for workers. The British associations for overlookers, by contrast, severed overlookers from the higher foremen close to the owner; they defined their members as workers who delivered a labor product.

The inability of workers in Germany to unite with their immediate supervisors against employers meant that workers' collective action was directed against the employers' domination of the labor process per se. In Britain, the affiliation of workers with their overlookers meant that workers were comparatively insulated on the shop floor itself from regular contact with the employers' authority. They oriented their collective action to a greater degree toward the price at which workers would deliver their materialized labor.

The theory of the capitalist labor process that Marx presented in Volume One of *Kapital* is critical for unraveling the differences between the German and British labor movements—but not for reasons that Marx would ever

---

137. Archiv des Deutschen Gewerkschaftsbundes, "Stenographischer Bericht über die Verhandlungen des Delegiertentages des Deutschen Werkmeister-Verbandes," 1911, p. 94.

138. LRO, DDX 1128/1/1, Blackburn Powerloom Overlookers' Society, February 5, 1862. Kirklees Archives, Minutes of the Huddersfield Power Loom Tuners' Society, September, 1912. For an example of someone rejected due to low salary, see ibid., May, 1907.

have dreamed of. The text reveals the cultural assumptions acquired by German workers in the labor process. Marx's emphasis upon the capitalist's exercise of authority in the factory as a means of extracting surplus forecasts the greater importance German textile workers would place, both in their complaints and in the enactment of strikes, upon aggressively contesting the capitalist's disposition over the labor activity itself.

CONCLUDING REFLECTIONS
ON PART THREE

The reified forms of consciousness that were manufactured at the point of production molded the shape of workers' resistance to the appropriation of their labor. Workers in each country advanced their interests vis-à-vis employers as straightforwardly as they could, but in so doing they confirmed their allegiance to a nationally prevailing concept of labor's commodity form, a concept that ironically united workers and employers in each locale. In *The Rise of Market Culture* William Reddy examined the essential terms of liberal capitalism, in particular the concept of labor as a commodity, as alien, intellectual imports with which nineteenth-century workers never authentically identified. He treated market categories as universalistic tools of scholarly analysis.[139] By illuminating the inconspicuous differences between German and British workers' understanding and use of labor as a commodity, the present study instead suggests that the concept of labor as a commodity represented for workers not just an abstract doctrine but a set of popular repertoires that were linked to the course of industrialization and formed an essential component of popular culture. Rather than juxtapose an ethereal market model to real practices in one country, as Reddy did, we compared practices across countries to detect the impressive, but necessarily incomplete, materialization of market categories in everyday life and tactics of resistance.

The distinctive form of labor as a commodity in each country, as opposed to the alternative specifications operating in other capitalist societies, remained out of view of pointed critique.[140] The cultural order was not immune to radical transformation before the First World War. But change could issue from below only through struggles guided by the definition of labor as a commodity that was, literally, "in place."

---

139. Reddy, op. cit., pp. x–xi. In Reddy's view, workers' self-guided struggles are most accurately portrayed as movements of opposition to market categories, based in part on family and community solidarities. Op. cit., pp. 310–312, 324–325, 330–336; William Reddy, *Money and Liberty in Modern Europe* (Cambridge: Cambridge University Press, 1987), Chapter Five. Workers may have been antagonistic toward commercial culture, but in each country they faithfully borrowed and exploited its terms.

140. Cf. Yorkshire Textile Workers' Deputation, *Official Report of the Yorkshire Textile Workers' Deputation: An Enquiry into the Conditions of the German Woollen Cloth Operatives* (Batley: News Office, 1908).

11   Conclusion: Under the Aegis of Culture

History is just the history of the unceasing overthrow of the
forms of objectivity that shape the life of humankind.
          Georg Lukács, *Geschichte und Klassenbewusstsein*

It is the submission of this book that in the contrasting transitions to capitalist labor markets in Germany and Britain, a different understanding of
the transmission of labor as a commodity emerged in each country, where
it was shared by both its common people and its economic elites; that these
divergent specifications of labor subsequently configured the daily use of
time and space in the developing factories of nineteenth-century Germany
and Britain independently of the immediate economic and technological
circumstances in which manufacturing techniques arose; that once these
nationally diverging models of the conveyance of labor were incarnated at
the point of production, they were reproduced among managers and workers through the execution of work rather than through the reception of a
discourse; and that, by this means, the stipulations of labor as a commodity
acquired an uncanny stability in Germany and Britain throughout the nineteenth century. We have seen, further, that the contrasting German and
British definitions of the exchange of labor provided the cultural schemata
through which workers identified abuses in the workplace, articulated their
demands, and invented tactics for resisting employers' power; that Marx
arrived at the decisive revelations of *Kapital* by mediating between the
opposing German and British experiences of the commodification of labor;
and, finally, that reception of Marx's economic perspective among members
of the labor movements of Germany and Britain depended on whether the
symbolic structures of manufacturing techniques corresponded to Marx's
specification of labor as a commodity. In this extended drama culture played
a causal role first by configuring factory procedures and, once embodied and
reproduced in such practices, by shaping the ideologies of labor movements
and the conduct of struggles between workers and employers. The moment
has arrived to sum up, on a formal level, the method employed in this study
to isolate and specify culture's independent effects.

THE EXPLANATORY METHOD

Rather than make an appeal to culture as the sum of beliefs or implicit background assumptions that together comprised "Britishness" or "Germanness," I condensed the relevant differences between culture in Germany and in Britain into a single principle, the specification of the conveyance of labor as a commodity.[1] I handled this feature in two ways: first as a key for identifying meaningful configurations of practices and, second, as a discrete variable whose causes and consequences could be specified. When I treated culture as an intelligible schema that came to life in a complex of practices, I reasoned from the viewpoint of synchrony; when I treated it as a variable, I reasoned from diachrony. These two approaches employed different comparative strategies.

On the synchronic level, I endeavored to show by judicious comparison that the differences between German and British wool mills in the symbolic patterning of manufacturing techniques could not be explained by the tangible conditions of the immediate business environment. In this part of the inquiry I *excluded* the economic environment as a source of variation between countries. True, factory practices served economic purposes, but the means employed to meet functional demands emerged from the cultural assumptions the agents applied. The German weaving managers' consecration of the "efficiency ratio," for example, served the purpose of measuring the level of production, but it hardly represented a natural or superior adaptation to the conditions of production. To review a second instance, the implementation of "waiting money" in German textiles before 1914 correlated with the workers' distinctive insistence upon payment for the commitment of labor power, rather than conforming to economic features of the German labor market that differed from those in Britain before 1914. The demonstration that culture had a pervasive, but specifiable, influence on industrial technique was complete after the initial, synchronic stage of comparison.

A different set of issues arises and a separate method of analysis must be called into service when one inquires into the historical *origins* of the German and British cultural systems. Culture does not descend from the clouds. Although the growth of the wool textile industries and the imme-

---

1. Whereas this study considers only labor's particular commodity form, other investigators have considered the broader cultural resonance of work in general. Joan Campbell, *Joy in Work, German Work: The National Debate, 1800–1945* (Princeton: Princeton University Press, 1989).

diate circumstances of production in textiles were parallel in Britain and Germany, the national contexts of economic development in the countries as wholes contrast sharply. The conjunctural differences in the way Germany and Britain negotiated the transition from the feudal-corporate organization of work and exchange to factory manufacture in the era of capitalism enabled the agents to import contrasting definitions of labor's commodity form into the factory. On the diachronic level of analysis, therefore, I *included* economic institutions as a context for the emergence of cultural differences at the level of the countries as wholes. In identifying the autonomous causal contribution of culture, we are not required to treat culture as an unmoved mover.

But does this entire study then merely lead to the conclusion that the "economy" generated cultural impressions which subsequently assumed a stable life of their own? For the purpose of stipulating the causal contribution of culture, this is no different in its implications from the viewpoint that supposes that the economy is the active motor of change but that culture does not perfectly reflect economic circumstances, due either to cultural inertia or, if culture is treated as more plastic, due to the incomplete impression made by present economic conditions; nor is it different in its implications from the perspective that asserts that the differences in the national economies, the alleged foundation of social change, were naturally "reflected" in cultural conceptions which were then imported into diverse local undertakings, such as the regionally circumscribed wool industries. From each of these points of view, culture serves as a component, possibly a necessary one, in the creation of institutions, but it is the conduit, even if imperfect, of an original economic logic, not a systematically structuring force in its own right.

In order to override this reductionist interpretation of the findings of this study, wherein cultural differences only mirrored antecedent economic conditions, it is plausible but unsatisfactory to insist dogmatically, as a general rule of social theory, that what we designate the economy could not come into existence except through the medium of culture. Certainly the succession of economic structures cannot serve as the ultimate foundation of cultural change, for the economy has no history of its own apart from its realization in the culture, which gives shape to human practice. But this peremptory culturalist line of argument no longer makes appeal to an evidentiary demonstration; it no longer advances a research program by showing that the study of culture parsimoniously explains a wide range of phenomena that purely utilitarian or adaptive theories of practice do not seem to cover. Not to waste words, the dogmatic culturalist interpretation of the results of the present inquiry into the origins of industrial differences is disenchanting because, if accepted, it means that the evidence marshalled in this study cannot be used to adjudicate between theoretic alternatives. It might well return us to the starting point of choosing an allegiance to a variety of theory based on a priori inclinations.

Perhaps we can apply the conventional method of distinguishing between cause and effect by temporal priority. A survey of the transition to liberal commercialism in each country shows that the definition of labor as a commodity emerged in speculative intellectual ruminations upon economic processes before it was embodied in micro-procedures on the factory shop floor. In their characteristic specifications of labor's commodity form, Adam Smith and Johann Lotz each uncannily foretold the shape of practice in his own country's industrial future. If this sequence of development shows that the definition of labor did not reflect established practice in the factory, does it also show that culture represented a force in its own right for institutional development? By itself, the chronological precedence of distinctive national differences in discourse about labor does not resolve this issue, for it might well be the case that the strategic goal of legitimating a profitable factory system was responsible for sustaining or resurrecting traditions of thought about labor which would not otherwise have been reproduced. Even if cultural definitions of labor display striking continuities, an advocate of utilitarian modes of explanation can still maintain that economic requirements decide which cultural features survive at the national level.

Because of its extensive reliance upon configurational analysis, however, this study enables us to make limited causal inferences from the temporal priority of the cultural template. For the outcome we are analyzing is not an isolated element or a single appurtenance of institutions, but a comprehensive constellation of practices. If the outcome to be explained were a simple trait, such as the affirmation of paternalism, then it might be treated as an accompaniment of factory systems which would have been legitimated in some other fashion in the absence of this feature; or it could be dismissed as a trait that was unsubstitutable, but had it not already been in place, would have been invented to meet the needs of the factory system; or, finally, it could be acknowledged as a resource that the economic agents could not have created, but which they put to the service of a structuring economic logic. But the outcome to be explained, as our synchronic comparison emphasized, was a complete cluster of practices. The tendency toward a patterning of these techniques shows that culture was not just an ingredient or a resource but a structuring principle. In this case, the appearance of the specification of labor in discourse prior to its embodiment in factory procedures is causally definitive; as a system of practice with an internal symbolic logic, culture stands revealed as a positive shaper rather than an accompaniment or passive resource for institutions.

The synchronic comparison of parallel segments of the British and German wool industries shows that practices were configured to form meaningful constellations, but it does not identify in positive fashion the historical genesis of these patterns. It contributes to explaining their initial emergence only by *ruling out* utilitarian accounts of their genesis. But excluding a competing mode of explanation for historical developments does not by default endorse one's own explanation if one's alternative represents not the simple negation of the rival but an entirely different approach. What is more, the differences in the economic environments may not account for the *installation* of differing factory practices, but they could still account for the invention of different specifications of labor before they took on a life of their own. Thus the question for delimiting culture's causal influence is not only whether culture "did" something, but from where that culture came. Even if a specification of labor as a commodity imposed a constitutive logic of its own once it was lodged in the factory, the argument might go, this fact offers slight reason for centering the comparative study of history on culture if national differences in cultural conceptions *originated* as a mere aspect of corresponding economic conditions.

Yet in Britain and Germany the features of the newly emergent discourse about labor that were uncovered in this inquiry debar attempts to see economic circumstances as the cause of the creation of distinctive concepts of labor as a commodity. In Britain the notion that wage workers transfer their labor as it is embodied in a product represented an idealized interpretation, not a mirror image, of the institutions of work in the transition to liberal commercialism. In seventeenth-century Britain, when wage laborers were prevented, at least in official opinion, from offering their labor as a freely marketable ware, and the independent artisan became the exemplary seller of labor, the bulk of the working population was excluded from the paradigm of commercial labor. When labor power became formally marketable in the course of the eighteenth century, Adam Smith, the prototypical philosopher of petty commodity production, recognized in *The Wealth of Nations* a continued divergence between fact and orienting model. Even while Smith employed the model of labor incarnated in a finished ware by a small producer as his paradigm of the circulation of commodities, he acknowledged that nearly all worked in the service of a master, not as independent artificers.[2] In Germany the exclusion of craft work as an imaginary locus for the emergence of labor as a commodity in the first half of the nineteenth century depended on the small urban producers' continued allegiance to a world of corporate production, seemingly in ignorance of the inescapable "reality" of a secular economic transition. Yet the response of the artificers in Germany did not appear out of thin air: unlike their British counterparts, they had in the main lost their guild monopolies only recently, and they confronted the institutionalization of liberal commercialism at a more threatening point on the clock of world development than British artificers did, a point at which it was evidently feasible for centralized factories to supersede craft production.[3] But for this fact to be interpreted and thereby to bear consequences, the agents in Germany had to draw upon the outlying domains of their experience: the imagined past, the global and national economic context, and the projected future. When the manufactory and the textile mill comprised a statistically small portion of employment, they still served as the key site in Germany for the exemplification of capitalist wage labor. The forms of labor as a commodity to which the agents subscribed grew out of the conditions of economic development and exchange, but only as the agents conceived of their relation to them.

That the element of labor became the centerpiece of economic speculation during the transition to commercial liberalism underscores the symbolic process by which the agents established their relation to the commercial world. The young Karl Marx, upon making initial contact with classical political economy, understood that this received body of thought comprised a monumental break with prior reflections on commercial intercourse. Previously wealth had seemed to inhere in natural objects; now, under the sign of capital or, more fundamentally, accumulated labor, agents conceived of it as a form of human subjectivity. As is well known, Marx called Adam Smith "the Luther of political economy," for Smith reoriented belief by showing that development no longer issued from external forces

2. For a compilation of Smith's views on independent manufacture, see Maxine Berg, "Political Economy and the Principles of Manufacture 1700–1800," in Maxine Berg et al., editors, *Manufacture in Town and Country Before the Factory* (Cambridge: Cambridge University Press, 1983), pp. 48–49.

3. For a contemporary discussion of how guild members drew upon the example of mechanization in Britain to reinforce their commitment to corporate regulation in Germany, see *Die Ameise*, October 14, 1833, p. 588.

but arose from the labor of the human subject.[4] The focus on human labor as both the generator and the regulator of value in Smith's eighteenth-century Britain coincided with the consecration of market categories as an effective ideology—that is, as the source of the operative schemata of everyday practice. The agents of commercial life incorporated the conditions of existence into their culture in such a way as to define themselves as the subjects of the economic process, but precisely in so doing they made it possible for themselves to become enmeshed in—and become subject *to*—these economic procedures.[5] The discourse in which the specification of labor's commodity form can first be detected did not just record the landscape of commodities in motion, either straightforwardly or by a natural camera obscura; rather, it performed the symbolic work of constituting people as autonomous subjects even as it enveloped them in a sovereign economic system.[6]

On some of the underlying uniformities identified between the German and British mills—their staffing, the distribution of tasks to overlookers, the general reliance on piece rates for weavers—cultural differences did not impinge. Culture is situated in every institution of society, but not everything is culturally determined. If we admit that the necessity of adapting to the economic environment accounts for certain uniformities between German and British mills—such as the general reliance on piece rates for weavers—do we then fall back on the position that culture was nonetheless determinative "in the last instance"? Such ultimate causes have no observable incarnation in history.[7] But neither has this study retreated to the chicken-and-egg position in which culture and the economy are both necessary for each other's substantiation and the contribution of culture to the constitution of the labor process is limited to one category of prerequisite factors in an inextricable combination of causes. The manner in which culture is seen as making its separate contribution to the historical process differs fundamentally according to whether one is assessing the institution-

---

4. Karl Marx, *Marx/Engels Gesamtausgabe*, Series One, Volume Three (Berlin: Marx-Engels Verlag, 1932), pp. 107–108.

5. Michel Foucault, *The Order of Things* (New York: Vintage Books, 1973), p. 259.

6. Ronald Meek cites evidence that a concern to preserve social relations between human subjects as the foundation of market phenomena gave rise to the eighteenth-century emphasis upon labor as a source of value. Ronald L. Meek, *Economics and Ideology and Other Essays* (London: Chapman and Hall, 1967), pp. 204–205.

7. Raymond Aron, *Introduction to the Philosophy of History* (Boston: Beacon Press, 1962), pp. 252–254; Erik Olin Wright, Andrew Levine, and Elliot Sober, *Reconstructing Marxism* (London: Verso, 1992), "Causal Asymmetries."

alization of practice through contrasting specifications of labor or whether one is considering the origins of those conceptual assumptions. Culture operates in spite of economic similarities in the essentially synchronic comparisons between matched textile factories, so the typical differences in the symbolic orchestration of practice can be attributed to culture *alone* at this stage in the analysis. Only an argument based upon configurational reasoning can advance such a claim to causal exclusivity. Of course the material components of production were indispensable for the incorporation of culture into practice, but the systematic *differences* in the typical meaningful configuration of those resources obeyed nothing but an internal cultural logic. In the comparisons between Germany and Britain as wholes for the sake of identifying the origins of divergent conceptions of labor, culture is seen to operate in an environment of established contrasts in economic institutions. In each country, the agents moved in a cultural milieu that enabled them to isolate certain sectors in the country's economy as the prototypical site for the transmission of labor under liberal commercialism and to simplify and idealize features of the labor transaction.

To filter and interpret the record of evidence, historical investigators bring to bear a theoretical lens formed by their own vantage point in history. Since the researchers themselves stand inside history, the lens they use may comprise a product of the very course of change they are subjecting to examination. This principle offers an explanatory key for the present study. Marx's analysis of the difference between "labor power" and "embodied labor" and his influential emphasis on the ultimate genesis of profit in the conversion of "labor power" developed in response to the experience, shared by German employers and workers in the nineteenth century, of a rapid transition from feudal-corporate institutions of work to the capitalist factory system. As a scholar marked by the German developmental experience and steeped in German economic history, Marx unintentionally replicated in his texts the symbolic forms of everyday practice enacted by German workers and employers. My analysis of the history of economic thought suggests that Marx's position in the German milieu permitted him to recycle the cultural definition of labor as labor power which governed German practice and to present it in the form of a theory. If Marx can be used to analyze the development of German factories, so, too, can the development of German factories be used to analyze Marx.

This principle gives us new means both for theorizing history and for historicizing theory. The late-twentieth-century sociologist who uses Marx's concept of labor power as a tool to analyze the history of factory relations has found a powerful lever, not because the concept necessarily penetrates the hidden essence of capitalism, but thanks to the concept's encapsulation of the particularities of the German experience of industrialization. To this extent, my method may carry subversive implications. In drawing upon the distinction between *embodied labor* and *labor power* I have changed the status of those terms. I converted them from analytic distinctions in the realm of high theory into cultural categories that people used in the inconspicuous procedures of everyday life. Making them a constituent part of sensuous human practice, rather than an outward description of action imposed by the analyst, makes them more "real" but, paradoxically, less objective—for, as realized categories of culture, they become genuine appurtenances of subjects rather than theoretic properties of economic objects.

Having established the cultural formation of the instrumentalities in the workplace, I considered the consequences of those practices for the articulation of grievances and for the adoption of ideologies of exploitation in workers' labor movements. The historical significance of the differences between the cultural construction of labor in German and in British textile factories does not lie in their effects upon economic efficiency, which in all likelihood remained exiguous. Rather, the cultural differences are notable for the differing ways in which they shaped workers' lived experience of the employment relation and thereby provided the underlying assumptions for their union movements. British textile workers focused on the acquisition of products at less than their true market value as the source of exploitation. Without the concept of labor power as a commodity, they did not move from theories about the creation of profit in the market to theories that focused on the extraction of surplus value at the point of production. Their textile unions, which in the 1890s sponsored the rebirth of socialist ideas, focused on the need to redistribute capital and access to the market rather than on the need to remove the subordination of living labor. In Germany, the textile workers' daily experience of the buying and selling of labor power on the shop floor gave them the cultural resources necessary for the positive reception of Marxist economic theory, or at least of a Marxist economic idiom, from the Social Democratic textile union.

In its appropriation of Marx's economic categories as cultural constructs, this inquiry may seem double-edged. In fact, it contains another paradox. Every act of rejection has a moment of reaffirmation. At the same time that this study shows how culture constituted the means of production, it lends qualified support to Marx's emphasis on the importance of the labor activity for the formation of people's understanding of social relations. The respective cultural definitions of labor in Germany and in Britain did not survive through sheer inertia or through the might of intellectuals' discourse. They were sustained by a constellation of practices at the factory—from the small rituals of entering the mill to the fining systems for defective cloth—that gave them palpable form. Culture was enacted, not permanently absorbed. Even within the grey walls of the factory, the meanings that the activity of manufacturing sustains may bear ideological consequences as significant as are its instrumental outcomes. German workers were not duped by Marxist ideologues when they focused on the use of *Arbeitskraft* as the source of the owners' profit, nor did they thereby necessarily discover the essential workings of the capitalist system. Rather, the cultural categories that practices on the shop floor sustained provided German workers with a spontaneous theory of exploitation—a lived truth, if you will—that proved critical for their sympathetic reception of Marxist ideas.

Examining the independent influence of culture on the institutions of the factory solves two problems in labor history with one piece of evidence. It bridges the perplexing divide—established, if not discovered, by E. P. Thompson—between the structured relations of the economy and what Thompson celebrated as the fluid, creative, and heroic formation of political beliefs among workers. The present study identifies the determinate ways in which the symbolic apparatuses of production established the assumptions about labor that workers brought to the arena of politics, but it makes this causal linkage without resorting to economic reductionism. The ideologies of exploitation accepted in the labor movements were fixed, not by the workplace's economic structure, but by the cultural forms inscribed in the micro-practices of production, forms which varied independently of the material or socio-organizational conditions of the manufacturing process.

As a cross-national comparison conceived with a selective question, this investigation has of necessity focused upon a decisive contrast between countries rather than upon variation within them. But this expansive comparison nonetheless affords a perspective from which to study differences within each country in workers' experiences, above all those emerging from the divisions of gender. Consider the inflection of gender distinctions upon the factories' control of intervals of labor in the course of the workday. In Germany, many textile mills granted a special schedule to female workers in charge of households. For example, at lunch time or on the eve of holidays, for the sake of readying the family meal, these women could leave the factory at least half an hour earlier than other workers.[8] The arrangement was consistent with the procedure of partitioning the use of labor power into increments of time that were indefinitely divisible. It also tallied with other rotating or irregular schedules for adult workers in Germany, such as rest pauses whose length alternated according to the day of the week. In Britain, factory owners before the First World War often discussed ways of attracting more workers, especially women, to mill work.[9] They considered giving the mill a more wholesome atmosphere and offering cleaner working conditions. But they did not grant women an extended lunch or single them out for early release on the eve of holidays. This would have fragmented the block of a complete day and slowed the delivery of products. Female textile workers in Britain could instead adjust workdays to their household schedule by sending substitute workers to take their place at the looms. Unlike their German counterparts, they had to offer prompt delivery of products, not necessarily access to their own labor power.[10] These differences in the treatment of women's labor show that the form assumed by labor as a

8. For instance, in the district of the Mönchengladbach factory inspectorate, women in charge of households had extended lunch breaks in forty-three factories. Twelve factories also allowed them to start work a half-hour or more after other workers. Germany, *Jahres-Berichte der königlich preussischen Regierungs- und Gewerberäte und Bergbehörden für 1899* (Berlin: R. v. Decker, 1900), p. 515. After 1891, factory inspectors believed that women in charge of households had a right to a longer lunch break. But this provision, like the laws for donating fines, merely supported practices that had crystallized in the workplace long before. For examples, see HSTAD, Landratsamt Mönchengladbach, 710, 1870s, p. 105; Victor Böhmert, "Die Methode der Lohnstatistik," *Der Arbeiterfreund: Zeitschrift des Central-Vereins in Preussen für das Wohl der arbeitenden Klassen* (Berlin: Otto Janke, 1877), p. 427; Franz Decker, *Die betriebliche Sozialordnung der Dürener Industrie im 19. Jahrhundert* (Köln: Rheinisch-Westfälisches Wirtschaftsarchiv, 1965), p. 71. At factories where the regular midday break amounted to an hour and a half, women with families had no legal claim to longer breaks but many received them. Compare Germany, *Die Gewerbe-Ordnung* (Berlin: Carl Heymanns Verlag, 1910), provision 137, p. 421, with Germany, *Jahres-Berichte der königlich preussischen Regierungs- und Gewerberäte und Bergbehörden für 1894* (Berlin: W. T. Bruer, 1895), pp. 483 ff.; Germany, *Jahres-Berichte der königlich preussischen Regierungs- und Gewerberäte und Bergbehörden für 1895* (Berlin: W. T. Bruer, 1896), pp. 60–61. Women bargained for the flexible schedules in return for working additional hours: Stadtarchiv Gera, Gemeinde Debschwitz, III D 11 0579, 1897, p. 33. The extended breaks were granted even in districts where inspectors reported a surplus of labor: Germany, *Jahres-Berichte der königlich preussischen Regierungs- und Gewerberäte und Bergbehörden für 1900* (Berlin: W. T. Bruer, 1901), p. 12. For early releases on the eve of celebrations, see Landesarchiv Potsdam, Rep. 6B, Kreisverwaltung Cottbus, Nr. 1253, 1902, p. 5.

9. *Yorkshire Factory Times*, November 28, 1912, p. 8; *Textile Mercury*, January 11, 1914, p. 24. For a discussion of women and time schedules in the prewar period, see "The Scarcity of Labour and How to Solve the Difficulty," *Journal of the British Association of Managers of Textile Works* Volume 7 (1915–1916), pp. 61–62.

10. See above, Chapter Two, p. 82. On cross-national differences in women's complaints about changing clothing, see Chapter Three, p. 127.

commodity did not exhaust the determinants of factory life, but operated as a pivotal category that mediated the influence of gender distinctions.[11]

THE FETISHISM OF QUANTIFIED LABOR

The discovery that the apparatuses of production were organized as signifiers of labor's commodity form has important implications for our understanding of the constitution of liberal capitalist society by labor. In his legendary analysis of the fetishism of commodities, the founding charter for Western critical theory, Marx contends that commodity producers grasp their social dependency upon each other only through the moment of exchange.[12] The agents' discovery of the social character of their labor through the trade of products causes human labor to appear under an absurd guise: as the comparative exchange value of products. In Marx's account, not only do the mutual relations of the producers take the misleading form of a social relation between things, but the category of social labor in general disappears from the producers' sight. In his view, liberal capitalism has the peculiarity that it structures social relations by abstract labor at the same time that it effaces abstract labor as a category of social consciousness. Even the classical political economists, by his reading, never identified abstract labor as such but contented themselves with comparing quantities of labor. These brilliant articulators of capitalist logic had "not the least idea, that the merely quantitative difference between kinds of labor presupposes their qualitative unity or equality, therefore their reduction to abstract human labor."[13]

For Marx, the categories of recognition arise from the process of production and exchange depicted only in terms of its most fundamental mechanics. In his discussion of the fetishism of commodities, Marx temporarily suspends his prior characterization of the production process under capitalism and defines it only by the circumstance that articles are produced for the purpose of exchange. Indeed, at this point in his exposition Marx resorts to the counterfactual premise that the economic agents are independent commodity producers who handle the exchange of their own products: "Since the producers do not come into social contact with each other until they

---

11. I have begun a comparative study of the ties between the family and the factory in German and British textile communities. Such a cross-national perspective highlights the articulation of capitalist and gender distinctions and, by contrasting their varying exemplifications in each country, historicizes the concept of gender as well.

12. *Das Kapital* (Berlin: Dietz Verlag, 1980), Volume One, p. 88.

13. Ibid., p. 94 note.

exchange their products, the specific social character of the producer's labor does not show itself except in the act of exchange."[14] This simplification allows Marx to reason from the social horizon of the marketplace, in which officially free and equal owners are associated by exchanging their commodities in terms of values that appear imposed by an objective necessity from without. The experience of production itself, the use of concrete living labor, is not theorized as a process generating the agents' misrecognition of the governing categories of capitalism.

Marx's emphasis upon the generation of the forms of understanding out of the "deep structure" of the exchange of labor gives rise to several questions which the unveiling of the symbolic apparatuses of production on the shop floor can address. The economic agents, in point of fact, are not all independent producers separated except at the moment of exchange: capitalism from its inception required workers to dispose of their living labor by entering into social relations of subordination to employers. Why, then, are the agents' "mutual personal relations" in the performance of labor "disguised under the shape of social relations between products"?[15] Can Marx's simplified model of independent commodity owners who labor in isolation be applied to explain the development of the categories of recognition among dependent wage laborers? The meaningful arrangement of micro-apparatuses on the shop floor suggests that workers acquired the categories of their culture, not from the deep structure of relations of exchange, but from the discernible shape of procedures on the surface of production. Not in the fleeting moment of concluding a wage contract but in the minute details of work itself, in the ongoing experience of systems of payment, accounting, and time discipline, did the dependent British workers learn that human practice revolves around the imagined exchange of labor materialized in a product. Workers in Germany learned to think of their concrete exertions as the expenditure and transmission of a quantity of labor power that appeared to them as a measurable thing with a commercial metric attached to it by the external force of the market. In both countries, the subordination of workers in the factory did not simply appear as the direct personal domination of the employer but came into view as an effect of the impersonal workings of the transmission and circulation of quantified labor. In each country, both workers and employers pursued their interests within shared forms of

14. Ibid., p. 73.
15. Ibid., pp. 91–92.

understanding of labor which neither group alone had created and which confronted both as a prior fact.

Marx's presentation of the fetishism of commodities gives rise to still another issue. In focusing on the fetishization that took place behind people's backs via the market, he depreciated the fetishization of labor as a commodity on the shop floor. In his view, once production is structured to become a mere means of exchanging commodities, the labor process appears to obey natural technical imperatives and relations between producers are structured as instrumental relations. Marx's descriptions of capitalist factories endow the machines themselves with the ability to dictate relations between producers on the shop floor.[16] For Marx, of course, the emergence of technological determinism at the work site is only an effect of the historically unique institutions of capitalism and is in the end, therefore, socially structured. But the use of labor is socially determined at a remove, by the underlying commercial structure which makes of production a mere means for the exchange of commodities. In Marx's account, if the use of labor inside the capitalist factory appears determined by technical imperatives, this is not an illusion but a local reality.[17]

In the realm of the factory itself, Marx mistook as a simple technical outcome or as a set of relations between things what was in truth a set of human relations structured by communication about labor's commodity form. The configuration of procedures on the shop floor in conformity with varying cultural assumptions about labor shows that the fetishism of commodities emerges not just in the marketplace but in the process of production, not just in the exchange of labor but in its use.[18] The factory producers mistook the form of labor as a commodity as an objective force controlling the enactment of their life activity because they were enmeshed in minute procedures structured as signifiers of labor's commodity form. As they engaged in the order of practice, they treated themselves and their fellow agents as if they were things, bearers of objectified labor. This "objectivating attitude" was not a simple correlate of production for

---

16. Ibid., pp. 445–446.

17. *Grundrisse der Kritik der politischen Ökonomie* (Berlin: Dietz Verlag, 1974), p. 716.

18. In effect, Marx's analysis of the fetishism of commodities marks a failure to complete the integration of the British view of exchange of materialized labor with the German view of the employment of labor power. It reverts to the British focus on the exchange of materialized labor among formal market equals as a social process susceptible to theorization, shaped through and through by the abstraction of labor.

exchange, but was sustained by the communicative function of unobtrusive procedures in the execution of work itself.[19]

The disclosure of signifying practices on the shop floor helps to specify the historically unique mode by which culture shaped human activity in nineteenth-century capitalism. At the outset of this study, we saw that Marshall Sahlins aptly demonstrated how noncapitalist societies have used the instrumentalities of production to communicate a symbolic schema.[20] They have incorporated kinship distinctions, which shape society into a functional whole, into the minute procedures of work. But these kinship principles for social relations are also supported by a transcendent cosmology. The principles, received from the gods, stand above production so that the preservation of the social relations based upon them appears as the very motive of production.[21] In the liberal capitalist factory, by contrast, the structuring form of labor as a commodity was neither explicated nor solemnized through transcendent norms or through principles standing above the sensible processes of production and exchange. The reproduction of culture did not rely upon a sacred cosmology to make its preservation appear as an end in itself. The purpose of social life was nothing more than the production of commodities.[22] In noncapitalist societies, the unspoken principles and assumptions of sacred tradition may comprise the undisputed foundation of social life;[23] in the liberal capitalist order, it is not the unspoken parts of enunciated laws or acts of

19. Jürgen Habermas uses the expression "objectivating attitude" to characterize agents' orientation to the exchange value of their labor. *The Theory of Communicative Action* (Boston: Beacon Press, 1987), vol. 2, p. 336. Historians have complained that the study of the texture of everyday life can inadvertently consign one to an atheoretical portrayal of facts. Geoff Eley and Keith Nield, "Why Does Social History Ignore Politics?" *Social History* Volume 5, Number 2 (May 1980), pp. 259–262. By contrast, the present study suggests that the best *Alltagsgeschichte* will become theoretical against its own intentions. The minutiae of everyday experience already contain the fundamental categories that make possible the reproduction of society as a whole.

20. See Chapter One of this work, p. 26.

21. In archaic societies, "the reproduction of traditional relations . . . of the individual to his commune . . . of his relations both to the conditions of labor and to his co-workers, fellow clansmen, etc. . . . is the foundation of development." Marx, *Grundrisse*, op. cit., p. 386.

22. "Thus the old horizon, where the human being always appears as the end of production, regardless of his narrow national, religious, political character, seems to be very lofty when contrasted to the modern world, where production appears as the aim of mankind and wealth as the aim of production." Marx, *Grundrisse*, op. cit., p. 387. Seyla Benhabib, on whom I draw for this interpretation of Marx, explains the implications of the shift from transcendent to immanent legitimation more fully in *Critique, Norm, and Utopia: A Study of the Foundations of Critical Theory* (New York: Columbia University Press, 1986), pp. 110–111.

23. Pierre Bourdieu, *Outline of a Theory of Practice* (Cambridge: Cambridge University Press, 1977), pp. 167–169.

religious ritual but the symbolic form of instrumental practice itself that represents the supreme domain of the culturally undisputed. Nineteenth-century economic theorists and demagogues could put concepts of labor into words for their own, fleeting purposes. But capitalist culture at work did not depend upon its verbal articulation, for the logic of practice did not have to refer to something greater than itself.

The nationally specific understandings of labor as a commodity appeared to the producers in Germany and Britain as natural appurtenances of the capitalist order. Even when spokespersons for the labor movement at the end of the nineteenth century called for the supersession of capitalism, they did not question the particular form in which labor was designated a commodity in their country; that form acted as a reference point for their nationally distinctive visions of socialist society. In noncapitalist societies, that which is unquestionable about social arrangements is merged with the structure of the natural universe. In the nineteenth-century factory, by contrast, the undoubtable fundament was merely the representation of human labor as an objectified and natural thing: the unquestionable procedures of conduct appeared to the agents as if they were attached, not to nature outside of humankind, but to the nature of humankind; not to objects outside of people, but to people as objects. The institutions of the factory are grasped as human creations, but human agency is misrecognized in the guise of quantified human labor. In noncapitalist society, utilitarian action is hidden under the guise of disinterested conduct that conforms to transcendent norms. In this setting the very haziness and incompleteness of the discursive tradition are part of its usefulness, because they make it pliable enough to legitimate unforeseen strategies.[24] In noncapitalist society, practices that appear to serve nothing but noninstrumental goals actually disguise the pursuit of profit. In the nineteenth-century factory, the reverse occurs: the very practices that appear to serve nothing but the pursuit of profit actually conform to a communicative logic. Because the reproduction of the specification of labor as a commodity did not depend upon its legitimation as part of the sacred but could appear as a mode of strictly instrumental conduct, it was less vulnerable to the questioning that occurs with the disenchantment of the modern social world.

24. Ibid., p. 49.

FORMS OF PASSAGE

Comparison of the paths of cultural development in Germany and Britain teaches a paradoxical lesson about the possible advantages of relative under-development for the articulation of economic thought. In Germany the conception of the commodity of labor which proved so suitable for analyz-ing the utilization of labor in the mechanized factory depended not only upon the commercial logic of a free market but upon the cultural model of feudalism. Many historical analyses emphasize the manner in which the exceptionally rapid economic growth in nineteenth-century Germany out-paced cultural change as a result of the relatively late dismantling of the corporate-feudal order there.[25] The present study evaluates the unusually strong feudal template as a helpful resource for the construction of Ger-many's factory institutions in the image of fully realized capitalist catego-ries. The compressed progression from feudalism to the market-industrial order in Germany, far from creating a lag or an imbalance in economic categories, was distilled in a pure capitalist form: it propelled the Germans to place special emphasis on the timed subordination of labor power per se. Thorstein Veblen wisely appreciated the advantages of initial backwardness; at the level of the economic infrastructure, as is well known, he highlighted the benefits of starting with only up-to-date technology, and at the level of cultural resources, he noted that the Germans' unusual combination of ideas from the medieval and mechanical ages created the potential for "an accel-eration of change."[26]

In Britain the precocious development of a unified national market with formally free exchange in finished products bestowed upon the country a pioneering role in economic reasoning. But the development of a set of commercial assumptions centered on labor before labor power itself became a freely marketable commodity led to the installation of practices in the workshops that revolved around the exchange of materialized labor. Nineteenth-century capitalists and political economists in Britain, who em-phasized labor as the generator and regulator of value, did not develop

---

25. Ralf Dahrendorf, *Gesellschaft und Demokratie in Deutschland* (München: R. Piper & Co., 1968); Shulamit Volkov, *The Rise of Popular Antimodernism in Germany* (Princeton: Princeton University Press, 1978); Georg Iggers, *The German Conception of History: The National Tradition of Historical Thought from Herder to the Present* (Middletown, Connecti-cut: Wesleyan University Press, 1983), p. 275; Hans-Ulrich Wehler, *Das deutsche Kaiserreich 1871–1918* (Göttingen: Vandenhoeck & Ruprecht, 1973).

26. Thorstein Veblen, *Imperial Germany and the Industrial Revolution* (New York: Macmillan and Co., 1915), p. 231.

categories for assessing the significance of labor's systematic use in the classical age of the factory. Their commercial ideology of practice remained within the social perspective of exchange relations between juridically equal property owners. The introduction in Germany of officially free market transactions in products only when juridically free markets in labor power were created, and the survival of feudal templates of the appropriation of labor services, together allowed the Germans to incorporate asymmetric social relations at the point of production into the economic specification of the labor transaction. The precipitous introduction of free exchange relations into the feudal-corporate order afforded German political economists a position from which they could critique the social outlooks centered upon the equalitarian sphere of exchange. Marx's penetrating theory of the exploitation of labor power, intriguingly similar to that of other German economists of his time in its treatment of labor power in production, relied upon the peculiar experience of late and rapid development in his homeland as a reference point for the development of critical social theory. As Marx drew upon British assumptions about labor in the sphere of exchange and compounded them with German assumptions about labor at the point of production, he incorporated the combined and uneven development of capitalism across Europe into the very core of his economic theorems.

Britain's early development of an integrated national market and the country's subsequent weakening in the world economy of the twentieth century have prompted vigorous debate about the distinctive features of Britain's movement to a capitalist regime. Many analysts, from Perry Anderson and Tom Nairn to Martin Wiener, have attributed Britain's modern industrial descent to its early and "incomplete" development of a capitalist social order under the auspices of a commercially minded, yet aristocratic, landed elite.[27] Ellen Meiksins Wood has departed from this view in her notable work *The Pristine Culture of Capitalism*. Wood suggests that Britain's industrial fate can be attributed to the consummation of capitalist culture in Britain rather than to the system's unfinished incarnation. In Britain, where free-market principles left entrepreneurs to their own devices, people of business focused upon short-term profit in the consumer

---

27. These authors' recent contributions to the thesis of Britain's incomplete transition to industrial capitalism include Tom Nairn, *The Enchanted Glass: Britain and Its Monarchy* (London: Century Hutchinson, 1988), pp. 239–245; Perry Anderson, "The Figures of Descent," *The New Left Review* Number 161 (January–February 1987), pp. 31, 35; Martin Wiener, *English Culture and the Decline of the Industrial Spirit, 1850–1980* (Cambridge: Cambridge University Press, 1981), pp. 7–10.

goods sectors rather than upon the transformation of technique in heavy industry. In Germany, fewer of the business and political elites converted to the culture of liberal "free enterprise." The Bismarkian state drew upon the authoritarian and military traditions of the precapitalist past to organize technological innovation and to coordinate longterm industrial investment for geopolitical advance. In Wood's opinion, it is not accidental but paradigmatic that state-guided industrialization in Germany proved economically superior to the "pristine culture of capitalism" in Britain.[28]

Likewise, in the present study, the British factory system exemplified "pure" capitalist categories. In the British case the concept of the sale of labor as a commodity was shorn of traditional relations of subordination for its content. In this sense it depended less upon precapitalist forms of labor appropriation than its counterpart in Germany did. Yet, as we have seen, the focus upon the equalitarian realm of product exchange in Britain grew out of the protracted suppression of a market for the transmission of labor power itself after the recognition of a market in goods. The selection of the peculiarly commercial and liberal specification of labor as a commodity in Britain developed as a result of the long survival of the "archaic" corporate administration of wage labor in Britain, not because of a relatively early or clean supersession of the medieval-corporate order. In a word, the pristine cultural outcome emerged from a corrupted transition. In Germany, the protection of contractual relations in industrial wage labor occurred relatively early compared to a recognition of an integrated market in products. The conjuncturally early establishment of a formally free market in labor power in Germany permitted the carryover of feudal relations of domination into the understanding of capitalist wage labor. In my study, Germany's feudal past does not figure as an obstacle to the expression of a purely capitalist culture; rather, the strong legacy of feudal relations of labor defined the fundamental concept of wage labor itself.[29]

28. Ellen Meiksins Wood, *The Pristine Culture of Capitalism* (London: Verso, 1991), pp. 15, 103, 105. Wood's characterization of Germany resembles the classic formulation of Ralf Dahrendorf: "Imperial Germany developed into an industrial, but not into a capitalist society." Op. cit., p. 54.

29. If the focus on the timed conversion of labor power into a product in Germany before 1914 helped to focus attention on the transformation of industrial technique and eventually contributed to German economic superiority, this alters the appreciation of the precapitalist legacy. In Wood's account, the survival of anti-liberal elites and the state-organized pursuit of traditional militaristic ambitions contribute to industrial development as a noncapitalist component of economic institutions. In my analysis, the feudal endowment molds capitalist categories themselves in the hidden abode of the production process. It thereby constructs a

By returning Marx's well-known analysis of the capitalist labor process to its home in German practice, this study helps us to appreciate how the past shaped an economic theory that is alive in the present. Does the contextualization of Marxist categories as the representation of a particular cultural experience also differentiate between past and present by restricting the applicability of Marx's nineteenth-century theory of exploitation to the era in which it originated?

Recent developments in Marxist theory have removed from scholarly discourse that part of Marx's theory which initially derived from the German context, and, in fact, have jettisoned the concept of labor power in toto. In *Kapital,* Marx counted the employer's control over the execution of work as the *first* defining feature of the production process under capitalism.[30] Like nineteenth-century German employers and workers, Marx unified the relations of domination and appropriation at the point of production. Contemporary Marxist theory has disengaged the exercise of authority in the workplace from the appropriation of surplus. John Roemer, among the most influential Marxist economists at present, has offered an intriguing reanalysis of the mechanisms by which surplus is transferred between workers and capitalists. In *A General Theory of Exploitation and Class,* Roemer concludes that surplus labor can be transferred from one class to another if productive assets are unequally distributed among classes, even if the classes with the lesser assets still own the means of production that they employ for their labor.[31] Roemer's demonstration has even led theorists to remove wage labor from the necessary design of capitalism.[32] Adam Przeworski has participated in this analytical shift by turning away from the analysis of the actors' locations in the production process and emphasizing the *distribution* of labor surplus.[33] Erik Olin Wright has also contributed to this continuing realignment of theory. In a revision of his earliest parsing of class categories, Wright eliminated authority over the labor process as a criterion of class position in capitalist relations

peculiar kind of capitalism in social practice from the ground up, not by the external administration of the state.

30. *Das Kapital,* op. cit., pp. 199–200. The capitalist's ownership of the product was for Marx the second defining feature of the capitalist labor process.

31. John Roemer, *A General Theory of Exploitation and Class* (Cambridge, Massachusetts: Harvard University Press, 1982), pp. 104–105.

32. Cf. William H. Sewell, Jr., "A Theory of Structure: Duality, Agency, and Transformation," *American Journal of Sociology* Volume 98, Number 1 (July 1992), p. 25.

33. Adam Przeworski, *Capitalism and Social Democracy* (Cambridge: Cambridge University Press, 1985), pp. 88 ff. and Chapter Four.

of production.[34] The ongoing process by which capitalists rely upon their domination at the work site to extract surplus from living labor power is losing its centrality in the leading Marxist analyses of contemporary economic functions.

This sea-change is telling because it alters the way Marxist theory connects the functioning of the capitalist system to the understandings of the economic agents. In Marx's perspective, the sale of labor power comprises an encounter between the functional requirements of the valorization of labor for the capitalist system on one side and the lived experience of the producers on the other. Labor power for him is both an analytic mold and a category in the producers' social consciousness. The shift of contemporary Marxist analysis away from the experienced moment of the use of labor power means that the operation of the economic system is theorized without reference to its constitutive and governing forms of understanding and experience. To be sure, Marx assumed that only one definition of *labor power* emerges in capitalist culture, in keeping with his premise that its apparent form is an inseparable expression of the essence of the capitalist system. Yet he believed that the lived experience of the monetization of labor is essential both for the system's reproduction and for struggles to change it. The appearance of abstract human labor as a category shaping the practices of production establishes at the outset the cultural foundation for the agents' pursuit of their interests. The present study reaffirmed the constraining effect of the form of abstract labor in the example of the Huddersfield weavers, who were unable to recognize and measure their own activity except under the guise of the objective properties of the fabric itself.[35]

34. Erik Olin Wright, *Classes* (London: Verso, 1987), p. 83. Since the publication of *Classes*, Wright has acknowledged shortcomings in his principles for demarcating class positions, without offering a new general strategy. He has also placed renewed emphasis on the accessory experiences of domination, although not as a basis for establishing class position or for elucidating the reproduction of capitalist economies. Erik Olin Wright et al., *The Debate on Classes* (London: Verso, 1989), pp. 289, 307, 323.

35. If a social analyst attempts to extrapolate from the distribution of resources in the economic system to the agents' recognition and pursuit of class interest, the result is not only crudely reductionist, but, from Marx's viewpoint, the distinguishing feature of conflict in capitalist society is lost. In contrast to precapitalist economies, where struggle between laborers and appropriators can be pursued as direct conflicts over the concrete relations of personal dependence and political inferiority, struggle in bourgeois society is "objectivistically concealed and objectivated through the medium of exchange value." Jürgen Habermas, *The Theory of Communicative Action* (Boston: Beacon Press, 1987), p. 334. In medieval society, Marx explains, "the social relations between individuals in the performance of their labor appear at all events as their own mutual personal relations and are not disguised under the shape of social relations between objects, the labor products. . . . Here the natural form of labor, its particu-

For this comparative study of culture I am interested only in ascertaining what the producers themselves believed was true and in identifying the origins and consequences of their beliefs. This is not a blind strategy of convenience. On the contrary, the truth value of Marxism depends on the interpretations of the producers. Their categories of understanding prompt the development of economic processes, shape the course of change, and continue to alter the relevance of theory. It is not up to theorists to decide with equations from afar whether Marx's definition of the commodity of labor as labor power remains valid at the end of the twentieth century. How the producers themselves interpret the labor process will resolve this fateful question. The history of practice on the shop floor suggests that the concept of labor as a commodity may have long ago lost its position as the center-point of a constellation of practices.

The two decades leading up to the First World War comprise the last days of the classical factory system that was established in the heyday of commercial liberalism. Until the onset of the war, there was little evidence that the cluster of practices based on labor's commodity form was losing its coherence. Yet German and British producers could not inhabit unconnected and uncompared conceptual worlds forever. As they came into tighter contact, they inadvertently reaffirmed their distinctive cultural starting points. In the weaving branch, the diffusion of the so-called pick clock, a technical contrivance mounted on looms in order to count the motions of the shuttle across the warp, caused British managers closely to examine German procedures for executing work. On the very eve of the war, managers in Britain became aware that the philosophy of remunerating weavers by shots in Germany marked the major difference between the two countries' pay systems.[36] In Germany, the concept of pay by shots had preceded the technology of the pick clock, whereas in Britain it happened the other way around.[37] The first batch of pick clocks to arrive in Yorkshire, purchased for inspection and experimentation in 1911 by the Huddersfield employers' association,

---

larity, and not, as in a society based on the production of commodities, its general form is the immediate social form of labor." *Das Kapital*, op. cit., pp. 91–92. My excerpt transposes the sentences in the original.

36. Bradford Technical College, *Quarterly Report of the Department of Textile Industries, City of Bradford Technical College* (Bradford, August 1912), p. 11: "The system of paying for woollen and worsted weaving at so much 'per thousand picks' is general in Germany." For cotton, see *Textile Mercury*, March 16, 1912.

37. See also *Textile Mercury*, March 16, 1912, p. 199. Tentative experiments with pick clocks in Yorkshire began during 1912. Bradford District Archives, Minutes of the Huddersfield and District Woollen Manufacturers' and Spinners' Association, 20 D 81/46.

came from Germany. Before that date, contemporaries claimed, not a single loom in Yorkshire had a pick clock.[38]

Even after they began testing the pick clocks, the British were unsure whether they would restructure their pay scales or would use the clocks just to measure cloth length more precisely.[39] A change in one element of the technical environment did not call into question the overall view of the labor process. The concept of pay by shot in Germany made the usefulness of the pick clock apparent from the start. The slow adoption of pick clocks in Britain resulted not from technical backwardness but from a particular outlook upon labor. The emphasis on measuring production by the length of the output made it difficult for the British to envisage how such clocks could be used until after German industry had provided a complete demonstration. Decades earlier, British technicians had discussed the feasibility and usefulness of assembling pick clocks for looms. A mechanic in Britain had inquired as early as 1879 in the *Textile Manufacturer*, the central forum for technical discussions for British textiles, whether a gadget existed for registering picks as they were inserted. The magazine dismissed the notion of building a pick clock. "We are almost certain that no instrument is in the market specifically intended for this purpose," its technical editors replied, "and if there were, it is a moot point whether there would be a great demand for it."[40] Thoughts of a pick clock disappeared until foreigners reintroduced them.

In the Lancashire cotton district, the idea of remunerating weavers by the total shots inserted appears to have occurred only among managers who, after 1902, installed American-designed Northrop automatic looms with pick clocks.[41] In 1914 only 1 percent of the looms in Britain were of this type.[42] The Gregs of Styal, Cheshire, began to install these new looms in 1909. The surviving account books indicate that the machines alone did not bring about a revised appreciation of weaving. This company placed Northrop looms with pick clocks next to its older weaving equipment. Only weavers on the new machines were paid by thousands of shots, since pick clocks were measuring

38. See also *Yorkshire Factory Times*, February 7, 1908, p. 4; *Textile Mercury*, March 16, 1912, p. 199.

39. *Yorkshire Factory Times*, May 1, 1913, p. 5.

40. *Textile Manufacturer*, February 15, 1879, p. 48.

41. *Journal of the British Association of Managers of Textile Works* Volume IV (1912–1913), p. 46.

42. Behnam Pourdeyhimi, "A Study of the Evolution of the Automatic Loom and Its Diffusion Within the British Cotton Industry," Ph.D. diss., University of Leeds, 1982, p. 173. D. M. Hollins, "The Northrop Loom for Woollens and Worsteds," *Huddersfield Textile Society Journal* (1918–1919), pp. 12–13.

their output.[43] British weavers on the Northrops contested the number of looms each of them would operate as well as the total amount of their wage, but they did not resist the new principles on which their piece earnings were based, another indication that survival of the old piece-rate systems cannot be attributed to organizational inertia or rigidity in industrial relations. The bookkeepers at the Greg firm maintained the accounts for the old and the new machines in the same volume. They awkwardly divided the pages into different sets of columns for the two types, because they calculated the net efficiency only of the new looms. The categories used to measure output and efficiency with the alien technology on new looms were not generalized to the mill as a whole.[44] Their introduction did not lead to revision in the symbolic apparatuses of production for old looms. When the British came into contact with imported technologies, they lost some of the techniques that reproduced their own construct of labor as a commodity. But given the stability in the other parts of the ensemble of practices, the established concept of labor was reproduced.

When the British adopted methods for calculating an efficiency ratio on new looms, their methods did not always conform to the cultural framework in place in Germany. At the firm of Benjamin Thornber and Sons in Burnley, records show that managers began calculating the efficiency of production no later than 1919. Unlike German managers, however, they did not begin with the maximum production possible in a given unit of time. They calculated the hours required to complete a piece of cloth of a fixed length with uninterrupted operation of the loom and then compared this with the actual number of hours used to produce cloth of that length.[45] To be sure, the formula expressed efficiency as a percentage of the maximum possible, as in Germany. Yet fabric partitioned time, not time fabric; British practitioners

43. Manchester Library Archives, C5/2/4. As British firms after the First World War slowly adopted pay per shot, they did not design their scales with a base unit of labor such as one thousand shots. Instead they chose miscellaneous sums (such as 14,551 shots!) whose execution qualified for payment of one penny. The execution of the shots still did not comprise an elementary foundation for the design of the scales. See, illustratively, LRO, DDX 1123/6/2/345, Bolton, 1931.

44. Manchester Library Archives, C5/1/7/3, shows that the bookkeepers sometimes put the data for new and old looms on the same page, but they drew in different layouts of columns on the same page rather than adopt a single scheme applicable to both sets of looms.

45. Burnley Library, Archives, Benjamin Thornber and Sons Ltd., M31, Acc. No. 11498, 1919–1920. I am grateful for the permission granted by the Thornber family to examine the company's books. For an example from the First World War in which a British manager cited an efficiency ratio for the Northrop looms using the German method but, properly, cautioned that the ratio was misleading, see *Journal of the Association of British Managers of Textile Works* Volume VIII (1916–1917), p. 87.

reasoned in this instance from hours per cloth, not, as the Germans did, from cloth per hour.[46] Even when the British analyzed the use of labor in time, then, they sometimes began with the length of cloth, not the motions executed, as labor's denominator, a sign that change did not necessarily push them toward the German perspective of transmission of labor as a commodity.

Whether the systems of industrial practice in Germany and Britain contained endogenous forces for change that would have revealed themselves but for the intervention of the First World War, no one is in a position to determine. In the event, the force summoned to dislocate the systems was the organizational influence of the state, which broke the liberal-capitalist occultism of commodity production. In both Germany and Britain, during the war the state assumed greater responsibility for determining the rate at which workers were paid. In Germany, the workers' receipts from employers for piecework were adjusted to provide additional allowances, regardless of performance, to men for each dependent child.[47] Government intervened to decide not just the social benefits workers received as citizens but the wages they received as wage laborers, which now diverged from the quantity of labor power expended. The state determined not just the amount of pay but the formula by which it was calculated. The purchase of labor as a commodity through the autonomous workings of the market was not circumscribed; rather, it was completely undermined.[48]

46. Likewise, the so-called speed clauses of the Oldham spinning scales, which in effect divided gains in productivity between workers and employers, did not measure length of yarn output per unit of time, but time per unit of length. The design of the scales did not measure the use of a potential, but the progressive cheapening of the product. As a result, industrial commentators did not realize how the division of gains changed as efficiency increased. See the inaccurate analysis in James Winterbottom, "A Criticism of the Oldham and Bolton Lists of Earnings for Mule Spinning," *Journal of the British Association of Managers of Textile Works* Volume VI (1914–1915), pp. 94–95. The history of payment systems suggests that the Oldham scales originated as an attempt to compensate workers assigned to old, slower machinery who delivered less output. H. A. Turner, *Trade Union Growth Structure and Policy* (Toronto: University of Toronto Press, 1962), p. 338 footnote 1. The indicator of motions on the mules was used as a proxy for measuring the product, for its readings were recalibrated and discounted for breakages to equal a hank of yarn. Royal Commission on Labour, PP 1892 XXXVI, Part 4, p. 896.

47. Deutscher Textilarbeiter-Verband, *12. Bericht über die Lage der Textil-Industrie und ihrer Arbeiter in der Kriegszeit*, (Berlin, 1917). On the breakdown of market incentives in German industry during the First World War, see also Rudi Schmiede and Edwin Schudlich, *Die Entwicklung der Leistungsentlohnung in Deutschland* (Frankfurt: Aspekte Verlag, 1976), p. 233.

48. Family wage supplements independent of work performance and wage regulation were enforced in German textiles during the revolutionary crisis of the 1920s. Hauptstaatsarchiv Düsseldorf, 13072, 1920, p. 585; Karl Dörpinghaus, Nachlass in Deutscher Gewerk-

In Britain the breakdown of a market in raw materials and labor is illustrated by the policies of the Cotton Control Board, an association of textile manufacturers appointed in 1917 by the government Board of Trade. The Control Board allocated raw cotton at controlled prices to manufacturers, who were required to purchase a license to operate all their standing machinery. The more equipment the mill owners operated, the greater the levies they owed to the Cotton Control Board; the funds were used to provide unemployment relief for operatives in the industry.[49] The board also controlled wage agreements. When the spinners, weavers, and cardroom workers began negotiations in 1918 for large pay raises, the Cotton Control Board threatened (with great effect) to eliminate unemployment relief.[50] Clearly, the bargaining no longer revolved around the sale of materialized labor, but centered on the collectively managed maintenance of labor power.[51]

The war brought about a fundamental shift in the symbolic apparatuses of production in Britain. Perhaps because manufacturers had to purchase a license for each machine they wanted to run, they began to abandon the custom of locking tardy workers out; instead, they threatened to make latecomers put in a full day of labor by working past quitting time.[52] Government-sponsored costing principles made it superfluous to reckon expenditures on overlookers' labor as an input embodied in the cloth; instead, overlookers received a guaranteed wage whether or not they or their underlings worked.[53] In Germany, workers' struggles in the postwar period were no longer played out through the anonymous

schaftsbund, Bundesvorstand, Archiv, Düsseldorf, "Lebenserinnerungen," p. 11. An analysis of the bureaucratic determination of postwar textile wages by locality and age of the worker, rather than by performance, appears in Constantin Beck, "Die Lohnunterschiede in der württembergischen Metall- und Textil-Industrie," diss., Tübingen, 1927.

49. Alan Fowler, "War and Labour Unrest," in Alan Fowler and Terry Wyke, editors, *The Barefoot Aristocrats* (Littleborough: George Kelsall, 1987), p. 149.

50. Ibid.

51. Unemployment allowances were standardized by age and gender, not fixed to prior earnings. Edwin Hopwood, *A History of the Lancashire Cotton Industry and the Amalgamated Weavers' Association: The Lancashire Weavers Story* (Manchester: Amalgamated Weavers' Association, 1969), p. 82. Overlookers, however, successfully bargained for a percentage of their normal earnings paid directly by the firm whether they worked or not, thereby eroding the accounting methods that calculated their labor as part of the product. Michael Savage, *Control at Work* (Lancaster: University of Lancaster Regionalism Group, Working Paper 7, 1982), p. 31.

52. Leeds District Archives, Bradford Business Science Club, address of November 11, 1915.

53. Savage, *Control at Work*, op. cit., p. 31.

mechanisms of the market, but shifted to the political and state administrative sectors. The revolutionary conflicts over the state constitution and over employee management of factories upon the conclusion of the war allowed struggle between employers and workers to appear for an instant on the ground of their "own mutual personal relations."[54]

The intensifying governmental responsibility for the constitution of the labor process since the First World War suggests that the principle of labor as a commodity has lost its salience as the primary mechanism that both integrates social exchange as a whole and organizes the lifeworld of the producers. Perhaps, then, the disappearance of labor power as a category of human experience in contemporary Marxist theory at the end of the twentieth century was only to have been expected. Perhaps, too, labor power could be rediscovered by scholars as a lived category of nineteenth-century production only through a retrospective inquiry: so long as capitalism appeared as a unitary system with an historical dynamic of its own, researchers would conceive of labor's specification, not as a culturally variable form, but as a universal form of understanding that emanated from the essence of the system. But to investigate the symbolic constitution of practices on the shop floor at the end of the twentieth century, the question may no longer be what form labor takes as a commodity on its own terms, but how that form is intertwined with categories that supplement the role once played by labor alone. As Habermas has emphasized, the commodity of labor has been supplanted by the juridical categories, increasingly salient for citizens and clients of state bureaucracies, that autonomously connect the parts of society apart from the mechanism of exchange value.[55]

Although the effective forms of culture may have changed, the past still offers guidance for the exploration of the institutions of manufacture in the present. From the geometry of the factory portals to the denominators of fabric, labor's commodity form in the nineteenth century did not lie underneath practice but in it. Likewise, for researchers of the present, as for poets and theologians, divinity is contained within life's humblest details. To find the treasure in the concrete, investigators of factories in our own age require neither faith nor dogma, only theory, as Marx's fading categories continue to show us.

54. The phrase of course appears in *Das Kapital*, op. cit., pp. 91–92.
55. Habermas, op. cit., pp. 356–373.

Bibliography

ARCHIVES AND INSTITUTES

Britain

Archive of General Union of Dyers, Bleachers, and Textile Workers, Bradford
Archive of Globe Worsted, Slaithwaite
Archive of Huddersfield Polytechnic Labour Collection
Archives, University of London
Birchcliffe Centre, Hebden Bridge
Blackburn Library Archives
Bolton Library Archives
Bradford District Archives
Bradford Industrial Museum
Bradford Library Archives
Brotherton Collection, University of Leeds
Burnley Library, Archives
Calderdale Archives
Centre for English Cultural Traditions and Language, University of Sheffield
Colne Valley Labour Party Archives, Huddersfield Polytechnic
Goldsmiths' Library, University of London
Institute of Dialect and Folklife Studies, University of Leeds
John Rylands University Library of Manchester Archives
Kirklees Archives
Lancashire Record Office, Preston (cited as LRO)
Leeds District Archives
Manchester Archaeology Unit, University of Manchester
Manchester Library Archives
Oldham City Archives
Public Record Office, London
Royal Commission on Historical Monuments, York
Wakefield Library Headquarters, Local Studies
West Yorkshire Archive Service, Wakefield

France

Archives départementales du Nord
Archives municipales de Roubaix
Bibliothèque nationale, Gr. Fol. Wz 69

Germany

Archiv der Gewerkschaft Textil-Bekleidung, Düsseldorf
Archiv des Deutschen Gewerkschaftsbundes, Düsseldorf
Archiv des Freien Deutschen Gewerkschaftsbundes, Berlin
Archiv des Volkseigenen Betriebs Palla, Meerane
Bistumsarchiv Münster
Firmenarchiv Schoeller, Düren
Gewerkschaft Textil-Bekleidung, Archiv Gronau
Hauptstaatsarchiv Düsseldorf
Historisches Archiv des Erzbistums Köln
Katholische Arbeitnehmerbewegung, Archiv, Krefeld
Kreisarchiv Karl Marx Stadt-Land
Kreisarchiv Kempen
Landesarchiv Potsdam
Rheinisch-Westfälisches Wirtschaftsarchiv zu Köln
Sächsische Landesbibliothek, Dresden
Staatsarchiv Detmold
Staatsarchiv Dresden
Staatsarchiv Münster
Staatsarchiv Osnabrück
Staatsarchiv Weimar
Stadtarchiv Aachen
Stadtarchiv Augsburg
Stadtarchiv Augustusberg
Stadtarchiv Bielefeld
Stadtarchiv Bocholt
Stadtarchiv Borken
Stadtarchiv Chemnitz
Stadtarchiv Cottbus
Stadtarchiv Crimmitschau
Stadtarchiv Düren
Stadtarchiv Emsdetten
Stadtarchiv Euskirchen
Stadtarchiv Forst
Stadtarchiv Gera
Stadtarchiv Glauchau
Stadtarchiv Greiz
Stadtarchiv Greven
Stadtarchiv Grevenbroich
Stadtarchiv Gummersbach
Stadtarchiv Krefeld
Stadtarchiv Mönchengladbach

Stadtarchiv Nordhorn
Stadtarchiv Oerlinghausen
Stadtarchiv Plauen
Stadtarchiv Ratingen
Stadtarchiv Rheine
Stadtarchiv Steinfurt-Borghorst
Stadtarchiv Velbert
Stadtarchiv Viersen
Stadtarchiv Werdau
Stadtarchiv Wuppertal
Stadtarchiv Zwickau
Städtisches Museum Schloss Rheydt
Textilmuseum Apolda
Volkskundliche Kommission für Westfalen, Münster
Westfälisches Industriemuseum Dortmund
Westfälisches Textil-Museum
Westfälisches Wirtschaftsarchiv Dortmund
Wirtschaftsarchiv Baden-Württemberg, Stuttgart
Zentrales Staatsarchiv Merseburg

ORAL ACCOUNTS

Britain

Birthdate of informant is given where known and permission granted.

Bolton Oral History Collection (tapes)
Bornat, Joanna, taped interviews, London (respondents labeled by pseudonym only)
Bradford Heritage Recording Unit (tapes)
Broadbent, Mrs. May, 1896, Midgley, Yorkshire (interview by author)
Brook, Mrs. E., Almondbury, Yorkshire (interview by author)
Bruce, Will, 1879, Bentham Village (tape courtesy of E. R. Pafford and J. H. P. Pafford)
Calderdale Oral History Collection (tapes)
Crowthers, Edward, Midgley, Yorkshire (interview by author)
France, Joe, 1882, Marsden (recording courtesy of the France family)
Healey, Dermot, taped interviews, Oral History Project of the Regional Studies Department, Manchester Polytechnic
Hebden Bridge Oral History Project (tapes)
Jennings, H., taped interview by Bob Turner, Centre for English Cultural Tradition and Language, University of Sheffield
Kirklees Oral History Project (tapes)
Macclesfield Oral History Project
Mercer, Edward, Rawdon, Yorkshire (interview by author)
Murgatroyd, Arthur, 1902, Halifax, Yorkshire (interview by author)
Roberts, Elizabeth, taped interviews, Lancaster University, Centre for North-West Regional Studies
Thompson, Paul, and Thea Thompson, family and work history taped interviews, Essex University

Germany (Author's Interviews)

Beyers, Johannes, Mönchengladbach
Esser, Ludwig, 1905, Hochneukirch
Faeck, Frau, 1905, Neviges
Kortmann, Frau, 1903, Elberfeld
Noisten, Heinrich, 1898, Euskirchen
Penz, Hans, 1895, Barmen
Pollmann, Maria, 1897, Barmen
Putz, Frau, 1900, Elberfeld
Reidegeld, Franz, 1900, Rheine
Schäfer, Frau, 1899, Elberfeld
Scholastika, Lancé, 1897, Düren
Schulters, Gertrud, 1896, Düren
Schnieders, Herr, 1899, Rheine
Sirrenberg, Ewald, 1897, Barmen
Soll, Fritz, Oerlinghausen

PERIODICALS

Allgemeine deutsche Arbeiter-Zeitung
Allgemeine Zeitschrift für Textil-Industrie (Leipzig)
Die Ameise
Arbeiter-Blatt
Der Arbeiterfreund: Zeitschrift des Central-Vereins für das Wohl der
  arbeitenden Klassen
Arbeiterwohl
Arbeiter-Zeitung (Coburg)
Der Arbeitgeber
Der Arbeitsfreund (Chemnitz)
Augsburger Abendzeitung
Augsburger Neueste Nachrichten
T' Bairnsla Folks Annual
Barmer Zeitung
Batley Reporter
Beilage zur Volkswacht (Bielefeld)
Blackburn Labour Journal
Blackburn Times
Blackburn Weekly Telegraph, Yearbook
Blatt für Patent-, Muster- und Zeichenwesen (Berlin)
Bocholter Volksblatt
Bolton People's History
Bradford
Bradford Daily Telegraph
Bradford Labour Echo
Bradford Observer
Burnley Express and Advertiser
Burnley Gazette

Capital and Labour (London)
Centralblatt für die Textil-Industrie (Berlin)
Chemnitzer Freie Presse
Der christliche Arbeiter-Freund
Christliche Arbeiterin
Der Christliche Textilarbeiter
Christlicher Arbeiterfreund
CIBA Review
The Co-operative Magazine and Monthly Herald (London)
Cotton Factory Times
Demokratisches Wochenblatt
Die deutsche Arbeitgeber-Zeitung
Der deutsche Leinenindustrielle
Der deutsche Meister (Mönchengladbach)
Das deutsche Wollen-Gewerbe (Grünberg)
The Dewsbury Reporter
Les Droits de l'homme
L'Écho de la fabrique (Lyon)
L'Egalité: Journal républicain socialiste
Euskirchener Zeitung
Fach-Zeitung: Organ des Niederrheinischen Weber-Verbandes
La Fraternité
La Fraternité universelle
Freie Presse
Freiheit, Arbeit (Köln)
Geraisches Tageblatt
Gewerbe-Blatt für Sachsen
Das Gewerbegericht
Gewerbe- und Kaufmannsgericht (Berlin)
Gladbacher Merkur
Gladbacher Volkszeitung
Gladbacher Zeitung
Le Grand Écho du Nord
Halifax Antiquary Society
Das Handels-Museum
Die Heimat (Emsdetten)
Huddersfield Daily Examiner
Huddersfield Textile Society Journal
Industrie Textile
Journal of the Bradford Textile Society
Journal of the British Association of Managers of Textile Works
Journal of the Department of Textile Industries (Bradford)
Keighley ILP Journal
Keighley News
Köhner Zeitung
The Labour Journal
The Leader (Nelson)
Leipziger Monatschrift für Textil-Industrie

Leipziger Volkszeitung
Magdeburgische Zeitung
Märkische Volksstimme
Maschinenschau: Umschau unter den Maschinen, Apparaten und Utensilien für
    die Textilindustrie
Meeraner Tageblatt
Meine Heimat (Wuppertal)
The Millgate (Manchester)
Mitteilungen des Arbeitgeberverbandes der Textilindustrie zu Aachen
Mitteilungen des Gesamtverbandes der christlichen Gewerkschaften Deutschlands
The Monthly Magazine
Nacht-Eilwagen
Nelson Chronicle
Northern Pioneer (Huddersfield)
Northern Star (Leeds)
The Operative
L'Ouvrier textile
The Pioneer (Burnley)
The Poor Man's Advocate
Poor Man's Guardian (London)
The Power Loom
Preston Pilot
Reichs-Arbeitsblatt (Berlin)
Reussische Volkszeitung
Le Réveil du Nord
Der Rheinische Weber (Mönchengladbach)
Sächsische Industrie
Sächsische Industrie-Zeitung
Sächsisches Volksblatt
Seide (Krefeld)
Shoe and Leather Record
Socialist and N.E. Lancashire Labour News
Le Socialiste
Der Textil-Arbeiter
Der Textilarbeiter-Zeitung
Textil- und Färberei-Zeitung
Die Textil-Zeitung (Berlin, Leipzig)
The Textile Journal
Textile Manufacturer (Manchester)
Textile Mercury (Manchester)
Textile Recorder
Le Travailleur (Lille)
Trier'sche Zeitung
Der unbefangene Beobachter
L'Union sociale
Die Verbrüderung
Viersener Zeitung
Das Volk: Organ des Central-Komitees für Arbeiter

Der Volksstaat
Die Volkswacht (Bielefeld)
Volkswille
Volkszeitung
Vorwärts
Werkmeister-Zeitung (Düsseldorf)
Die Westdeutsche Arbeiter-Zeitung (Krefeld)
Westdeutsche Landeszeitung (Rheydt)
The Workman's Times (Huddersfield)
Yorkshire Dialect Society, Transactions (Bradford)
Yorkshire Factory Times (Huddersfield)
The Yorkshire Inventor and Manufacturer (Bradford)
The Yorkshireman (Bradford)
Zeitschrift für die gesamte Textil-Industrie (Leipzig)
Zeitschrift für Textil-Industrie
Zeitung des Arbeiter-Vereins zu Köln

BOOKS, ARTICLES, DISSERTATIONS

Adelmann, Gerhard. "Die wirtschaftlichen Führungsschichten der rheinisch-west-fälischen Baumwoll- und Leinenindustrie von 1850 bis zum Ersten Weltkrieg." In Herbert Helbig, editor, *Führungskräfte der Wirtschaft im 19. Jahrhundert*, Teil II, 1790–1914. Limburg: C. A. Starke, 1977.

Adelung, Johann. *Grammatisch-Kritisches Wörterbuch der hochdeutschen Mundart*. Part One. Leipzig: J. G. I. Breitkopf, 1793.

Adler, Georg. *Die Geschichte der ersten sozialpolitischen Arbeiterbewegung in Deutschland*. [Orig. published Breslau, 1885.] Frankfurt am Main: Sauer & Auvermann, 1966.

Agnatieff, Michael. "Marxism and Classical Political Economy." In Raphael Samuel, editor, *People's History and Socialist Theory*. London: Routledge & Kegan Paul, 1981.

Allen, G. C. "Methods of Industrial Organization in the West Midlands." *The Economic Journal*, Economic History Series 4 (January 1929).

Allen, Kenneth N. "The Krefeld Silk Weavers in the Nineteenth Century." Ph.D. diss., Stanford University, 1988.

Allgemeine Deutsche Ausstellung auf dem Gebiete der Hygiene und des Rettungswesens. Berlin, 1883.

Althusser, Louis. *Lenin and Philosophy and Other Essays*. New York: Monthly Review Press, 1971.

Althusser, Louis. "Marx et ses découvertes." In Louis Althusser, Etienne Balibar, and Roger Establet, *Lire le capital*. Paris: François Maspero, 1967.

Anderson, Perry. "The Figures of Descent." *The New Left Review* Number 161 (January-February 1987).

Anonymous. *Considerations on the East-India Trade*, 1701. In J. R. McCulloch, editor, *Early English Tracts on Commerce*. [Orig. published 1856.] Cambridge: Cambridge University Press, 1954.

Anonymous. *The Linnen and Woollen Manufactory Discoursed*. London: G. Huddleston, 1698.

Anonymous. *The Workings of Money Capital*. Manchester Library.

Appadurai, Arjun. "Introduction: Commodities and the Politics of Value." In Arjun Appadurai, *The Social Life of Things: Commodities in Cultural Perspective*. Cambridge: Cambridge University Press, 1986.

Appleby, Joyce Oldham. *Economic Thought and Ideology in Seventeenth-Century England*. Princeton: Princeton University Press, 1978.

Appleby, Joyce Oldham. "Ideology and Theory: The Tension Between Political and Economic Liberalism in Seventeenth-Century England." *The American Historical Review* Volume 81, Number 3 (June 1976).

Arbeiter-Sekretariat, Gera. *Geschäfts-Bericht des Arbeiter-Sekretariats Gera*. Gera: Selbstverlag, 1906.

Arbeiter-Sekretariat, Luckenwalde. *2. Geschäftsbericht für die Zeit vom 1. Januar bis zum 31. Dezember 1905*. Luckenwalde: Selbstverlag, 1906.

Arbeiter-Sekretariat, Luckenwalde. *5. Geschäftsbericht für die Zeit vom 1. Januar bis zum 31. Dezember 1908*. Luckenwalde: Selbstverlag, 1909.

Arendt, Hannah. *The Human Condition*. Chicago: University of Chicago Press, 1958.

Aron, Raymond. *Introduction to the Philosophy of History*. Boston: Beacon Press, 1962.

Ashton, T. S. *An Eighteenth-Century Industrialist*. Manchester: Manchester University Press, 1939.

Ashworth, Henry. *The Preston Strike: An Enquiry into Its Causes and Consequences*. Manchester: George Simms, 1854.

Assmann, Klaus. "Verlag—Manufaktur—Fabrik: Die Entwicklung grossbetrieblicher Unternehmensformen im Göttinger Tuchmachergewerbe." In Wilhelm Abel, editor, *Handwerksgeschichte in neuer Sicht*. Göttingen: Otto Schwartz & Co., 1978.

Association for the Dissemination of the Knowledge of the Principles of an Equitable Labour Exchange. *Production the Cause of Demand*. Birmingham: Radcliffe & Co., 1832.

Aubin, Hermann, and Wolfgang Zorn, editors. *Handbuch der deutschen Wirtschafts- und Sozialgeschichte*. Volume 1. Stuttgart: Union Verlag, 1971.

Ausschuss über Petitionen von Webern und Spinnern. *Bericht des volkswirtschaftlichen Ausschusses über Petitionen von Webern und Spinnern*. Protokoll der 184. Sitzung, Dresden, March 12, 1849.

Autorenkollektiv. *Grundlinien des ökonomischen Denkens in Deutschland*. Volume One. Berlin: Akademie-Verlag, 1977.

Aveling, Edward. *The Students' Marx: An Introduction to the Study of Karl Marx' "Capital."* London: Swan Sonnenschein & Co., 1907.

Aylmer, G. E. "Gentlemen Levellers?" *Past & Present* Number 49 (November 1970).

Aymard, Maurice. "La transizione dal feudalesimo al capitalismo." In Ruggiero Romano and Corrado Vivanti, editors, *Storia d'Italia. Annali I: Dal feudalesimo al capitalismo*. Torino: Giulio Einaudi, 1978.

Baader, Ottilie. *Ein steiniger Weg: Lebenserinnerungen einer Sozialistin*. [Orig. published 1921.] Berlin: J. H. W. Dietz, 1979.

Babbage, Charles. *On the Economy of Machinery and Manufactures.* London: Charles Knight, 1835.

Bahr, Betsy. "New England Mill Engineering: Rationalization and Reform in Textile Mill Design, 1790–1920." Ph.D. diss., University of Delaware, 1987.

Bailey, Samuel. *A Critical Dissertation on the Nature, Measures, and Causes of Value; Chiefly in Reference to the Writings of Mr. Ricardo and His Followers.* London: R. Hunter, 1825.

Baker, Robert. *The Factory Acts Made Easy: Or, How to Work the Law Without the Risk of Penalties.* Leeds: H. W. Walker, 1854.

Balgarnie, Robert. *Sir Titus Salt.* London: Hodder & Stoughton, 1878.

Ballod, Karl. "Die Produktivität der industriellen Arbeit." *Jahrbuch für Gesetzgebung, Verwaltung und Volkswirtschaft im Deutschen Reich.* Volume 34, new series. Leipzig: Duncker & Humblot, 1910.

Balser, Frolinde. *Sozial-Demokratie 1848/49–1863.* Volume One. Stuttgart: Ernst Klett Verlag, 1962.

Barbon, Nicholas. *An Apology for the Builder.* London: For Cave Pullen, 1685.

Barker, Arthur. *The Management of Small Engineering Workshops.* Manchester: John Heywood, 1899.

Barker, Bernard. "Anatomy of Reformism: The Social and Political Ideas of the Labour Leadership in Yorkshire." *International Review of Social History* Volume 18, Part 1 (1973).

Barkhausen, Ernst. *Die Tuchindustrie in Montjoie, ihr Aufstieg und Niedergang.* Aachen: Aachener Verlags- und Druckerei-Gesellschaft, 1925.

Barmen. *Beiträge zur Statistik der Stadt Barmen.* Volume 2. Barmen, 1906.

Bauer-Mengelberg, Käthe. "Zur Theorie der Arbeitsbewertung." *Archiv für Sozialwissenschaft und Sozialpolitik* Volume 55, Number 3 (1926).

Baum, Gustav. *Entwicklungslinien der Textilindustrie mit besonderer Berücksichtigung der bautechnischen und maschinellen Einrichtungen der Baumwoll-Spinnereien und Webereien.* Berlin: M. Krayn, 1913.

Bealey, Frank, and Henry Pelling. *Labour and Politics 1900–1906.* London: Macmillan & Co., 1958.

Beau, Horst. *Das Leistungswissen des frühindustriellen Unternehmertums in Rheinland und Westfalen.* Köln: Rheinisch-Westfälisches Wirtschaftsarchiv, 1959.

Bebel, August. *Aus meinem Leben.* Part One. Stuttgart: J. H. W. Dietz Nachf., 1910.

Bebel, August. *Gewerkschafts-Bewegung und politische Parteien.* Stuttgart: J. H. W. Dietz, 1900.

Beck, Constantin. "Die Lohnunterschiede in der württembergischen Metall- und Textil-Industrie." Diss., Tübingen, 1927.

Beer, M. *Early British Economics.* London: George Allen & Unwin, 1938.

Beer, M. *A History of British Socialism.* London: George Allen & Unwin, 1940.

Behagg, Clive. "Controlling the Product: Work, Time, and the Early Industrial Workforce in Britain, 1800–1850." In Gary Cross, editor, *Worktime and Industrialization: An International History.* Philadelphia: Temple University Press, 1988.

Behagg, Clive. "The Democracy of Work, 1820–1850." In John Rule, editor, *British Trade Unionism 1750–1850.* London: Longman, 1988.

Behagg, Clive. "Secrecy, Ritual and Folk Violence: The Opacity of the Workplace in the First Half of the Nineteenth Century." In Robert D. Storch, editor, *Popular*

Culture and Custom in Nineteenth-Century England. London: Croom Helm, 1982.

Beier, A. L. *Masterless Men: The Vagrancy Problem in England 1560–1640.* New York: Methuen, 1985.

Bein, Louis. *Die Industrie des sächsischen Voigtlandes. Zweiter Theil: Die Textil-Industrie.* Leipzig: Duncker & Humblot, 1884.

Bellers, John. *Essays About the Poor, Manufactures, Trade, Plantations, and Immorality.* London: T. Sowle, 1699.

Bendix, Reinhard. *Work and Authority in Industry.* Berkeley: University of California Press, 1956.

Benhabib, Seyla. *Critique, Norm, and Utopia: A Study of the Foundations of Critical Theory.* New York: Columbia University Press, 1986.

Berdahl, Robert, et al., editors. *Klassen und Kultur.* Frankfurt am Main: Syndikat, 1982.

Berg, Maxine. "Political Economy and the Principles of Manufacture 1700–1800." In Maxine Berg, Pat Hudson, and Michael Sonenscher, editors, *Manufacture in Town and Country Before the Factory.* Cambridge: Cambridge University Press, 1983.

Berg, Maxine, et al. *Manufacture in Town and Country Before the Factory.* Cambridge: Cambridge University Press, 1983.

Bergmeyer, Bernhard. "Das Baumwollgewerbe im Münsterlande." Diss., Bonn, 1921.

Bergmann, Jürgen. *Das Berliner Handwerk in den Frühphasen der Industrialisierung.* Berlin: Colloquium Verlag, 1973.

Bernays, Marie. "Auslese und Anpassung der Arbeiterschaft der geschlossenen Grossindustrie: Dargestellt an den Verhältnissen der 'Gladbacher Spinnerei und Weberei' A.G. zu Mönchengladbach." *Schriften des Vereins für Sozialpolitik,* Volume 133. Leipzig: Duncker & Humblot, 1910.

Bernays, Marie. "Berufsschicksale moderner Industriearbeiter." *Die Frau* Volume 18, Number 3 (December 1910).

Bernays, Marie. "Zur Psychophysik der Textilarbeit." *Archiv für Sozialwissenschaft und Sozialpolitik,* Volume 32. Tübingen: J. C. B. Mohr, 1911.

Bernhard, Ludwig. *Die Akkordarbeit in Deutschland.* Leipzig: Duncker & Humblot, 1903.

Bernhardi, Theodor. *Versuch einer Kritik der Gründe, die für grosses und kleines Grundeigentum angeführt werden.* St. Petersburg: Kaiserliche Akademie der Wissenschaften, 1849.

Bernier, P.-D. *Essai sur le tiers-état rural.* [Orig. published 1892.] Genève: Slatkine-Megariotis Reprints, 1974.

Bernstein, Eduard. *Ferdinand Lassalle: Eine Würdigung des Lehrers und Kämpfers.* Berlin: P. Cassirer, 1919.

Bernstein, Eduard. *Von der Sekte zur Partei.* Jena: Eugen Diederichs, 1911.

Beyer, Edward. *Die Fabrik-Industrie des Regierungsbezirkes Düsseldorf vom Standpunkt der Gesundheitspflege.* Oberhausen: Spaarmann, 1876.

Biagini, Eugenio F. "British Trade Unions and Popular Political Economy, 1860–1880." *The Historical Journal* Volume 30, Number 4 (1987).

Biernacki, Richard. "The Cultural Construction of Labor: A Comparative Study of Late Nineteenth-Century German and British Textile Mills." Ph.D. diss., University of California, Berkeley, 1988.

Binns, Isaac. *From Village to Town*. Batley: E. H. Purchas, n.d. [ca. 1882].

Bittner, Emil. *Die Fabriks-Buchführung für Webereien*. Leipzig: Hartleben, 1902.

Blanchard, Ian. "Labour Productivity and Work Psychology in the English Mining Industry." *The Economic History Review*, second series, Volume XXXI, Number 1 (1978).

Blanning, T. C. W. *The French Revolution in Germany: Occupation and Resistance in the Rhineland 1792–1802*. Oxford: Clarendon Press, 1983.

Blatchford, Robert. *Merrie England: A Series of Letters to John Smith of Oldham—a Practical Working Man*. [Orig. published 1894.] New York: Monthly Review Press, 1966.

Blaug, Mark. *Ricardian Economics: A Historical Study*. New Haven: Yale University Press, 1958.

Bleakly, W. "Desirable Textile Inventions." *Journal of the British Association of Managers of Textile Works* Volume 4 (1912–1913).

Blum, Jerome. *The End of the Old Order in Rural Europe*. Princeton: Princeton University Press, 1978.

Blumberg, Horst. *Die deutsche Textilindustrie in der industriellen Revolution*. Berlin: Akademie-Verlag, 1965.

Böhle, Cilly. *Die Idee der Wirtschaftsverfassung im deutschen Merkantilismus*. Jena: Gustav Fischer, 1940.

Böhmert, Victor. "Die Methode der Lohnstatistik." *Der Arbeiterfreund: Zeitschrift des Central-Vereins in Preussen für das Wohl der arbeitenden Klassen*. Berlin: Otto Ianke, 1877.

Böhmert, Victor. "Weberlöhne einer Fabrik in Meerane." *Zeitschrift des königlich sächsischen statistischen Bureaus* Volume XXIII. 1877.

Bökelmann, Curt. *Das Aufkommen der Grossindustrie im sächsischen Wollgewerbe*. Heidelberg: J. Hörning, 1905.

Bornat, Joanna. "An Examination of the General Union of Textile Workers 1883–1922." Ph.D. diss., University of Essex, 1981.

Bosselmann, Otto. *Die Entlöhnungsmethoden in der südwestdeutsch-luxemburgischen Eisenindustrie*. Berlin: Leonhard Simion, 1906.

Bossenga, Gail Margaret. "Corporate Institutions, Revolution, and the State: Lille from Louis XIV to Napoleon." Ph.D. diss., University of Michigan, 1983.

Botero, Giovanni. *A Treatise Concerning the Causes of the Magnificencie and Greatness of Cities*. London: R. Ockould, H. Tomes, 1606.

Both, Otto. *Die Bandweberei*. Hannover: Max Jänecke, 1907.

Botzet, Hans. "Die Geschichte der sozialen Verhältnisse in Krefeld und ihre wirtschaftlichen Zusammenhänge." Diss., Köln, 1954.

Bourdieu, Pierre. *Distinction: A Social Critique of the Judgment of Taste*. Cambridge, Massachusetts: Harvard University Press, 1984.

Bourdieu, Pierre. *Language and Symbolic Power*. John Thompson, editor. Cambridge: Polity Press, 1991.

Bourdieu, Pierre. *The Logic of Practice*. Cambridge: Polity Press, 1990.

Bourdieu, Pierre. *Outline of a Theory of Practice*. Cambridge: Cambridge University Press, 1977.

Bourdieu, Pierre. "Scientific Field and Scientific Thought." In Comparative Study of Social Transformations Working Paper Number 32, University of Michigan, November, 1989.

Bourdieu, Pierre, and M. de Saint Martin. "Le Patronat." *Actes de la recherche en sciences sociales* Number 20–21 (March-April 1978).

Bourdieu, Pierre, and Loïc Wacquant. *An Invitation to Reflexive Sociology.* Chicago: University of Chicago Press, 1992.

Bousquet, G.-H. *Esquisse d'une histoire de la science économique en Italie des origines à Francesco Ferrara.* Paris: Marcel Rivière, 1960.

Bowles, Samuel. "The Production Process in a Competitive Economy: Walrasian, Neo-Hobbesian, and Marxian Models." *The American Economic Review* Volume 75, Number 1 (March 1985).

Bowley, Marian. "Some Seventeenth Century Contributions to the Theory of Value." *Economica* Volume XXX, Number 118 (May 1963).

Bradbury, Fred. *Worsted Preparing and Spinning.* Volume One. Halifax: F. King & Sons, 1910.

Bradford Chamber of Commerce. "Weavers' Standard Wage List." *Bradford Chamber of Commerce 46th Annual Report.* Bradford, 1896.

Bradford Technical College. *Quarterly Report of the Department of Textile Industries, City of Bradford Technical College.* Bradford, August 1912.

Bradford Technical College. *Report of the Department of Textile Industries, City of Bradford Technical College.* Bradford, July 1917.

Brady, Robert. *The Rationalization Movement in German Industry.* New York: Howard Fertig, 1974.

Brants, Victor. *Tisserand d'usine de Gladbach.* In Société d'Economique Sociale, editor, *Les Ouvriers de deux mondes,* 3. Série, 6. Fascicule. Paris: Au Siège de la Société Internationale, 1902.

Brauer, Theodor. *Produktionsfactor Arbeit.* Jena: Gustav Fischer, 1925.

Brauns, Heinrich. *Katholische Sozialpolitik im 20. Jahrhundert: Ausgewählte Aufsätze und Reden von Heinrich Brauns.* Hubert Mockenhaupt, editor. Mainz: Matthias-Grünewald-Verlag, 1976.

Bray, John. *Labour's Wrongs and Labour's Remedy.* Leeds: David Green, 1839.

Bredt, Johannes Victor. *Die Lohnindustrie dargestellt an der Garn- und Textilindustrie von Barmen.* Berlin: von Bruer & Co., 1905.

Brendgens, Willi. *Die wirtschaftliche, soziale und communale Entwicklung von Viersen.* Viersen: Gesellschaft für Druck und Verlag, 1929.

Brenner, Robert. "The Agrarian Roots of European Capitalism." In T. H. Aston and C. H. E. Philpin, editors, *The Brenner Debate: Agrarian Class Structure and Economic Development in Pre-Industrial Europe.* Cambridge: Cambridge University Press, 1985.

Brenner, Robert. *Merchants and Revolution.* Princeton: Princeton University Press, 1993.

Breuilly, John. "Arbeiteraristokratie in Grossbritannien und Deutschland: Ein Vergleich." In Ulrich Engelhardt, editor, *Handwerker in der Industrialisierung.* Stuttgart: Klett-Cotta, 1984.

Brigg, Mary, editor. "Journals of a Lancashire Weaver." *The Record Society of Lancashire and Cheshire* Volume CXXII (1982).

British Association for the Advancement of Science, Manchester Meeting of 1887. *On the Regulation of Wages by Means of Lists in the Cotton Industry.* Manchester: John Heywood, n.d.

Brockway, Fenner. *Britain's First Socialists: The Levellers, Agitators and Diggers of the English Revolution*. London: Quartet Books, 1980.

Brodnitz, Georg. *Vergleichende Studien über Betriebsstatistik und Betriebsformen der englischen Textilindustrie*. Halle: Habilitationsschrift Universität Halle-Wittenberg, 1902.

Brooker, Keith. "The Northhampton Shoemakers' Reaction to Industrialization: Some Thoughts." *Northhamptonshire Past and Present* Volume VI, Number 3 (1980).

Brose, Eric Dorn. *Christian Labor and the Politics of Frustration in Imperial Germany*. Washington, D.C.: The Catholic University of America Press, 1985.

Brown, A. F. J. *Essex at Work 1700–1815*. Chelmsford: Tindal Press, 1969.

Brown, E. H. Phelps. "The Labour Market." In Thomas Wilson and Andrew S. Skinner, editors, *The Market and the State: Essays in Honour of Adam Smith*. Oxford: Clarendon Press, 1976.

Budde, A., J. Child, A. Francis, and A. Kieser. "Corporate Goals, Managerial Objectives, and Organizational Structure in British and West German Companies." In *Organization Studies*, Volume 3. Berlin: W. de Gruyter, 1982.

Bullen, Andrew. "Pragmatism Versus Principle: Cotton Employers and the Origins of an Industrial Relations System." In J. A. Jowitt and A. J. McIvor, editors, *Employers and Labour in the English Textile Industries, 1850–1914*. London: Routledge, 1988.

Burawoy, Michael. *The Politics of Production*. London: Verso, 1985.

Burkard, Karl-Josef. *Thomas Hodgskins Kritik der politischen Ökonomie*. Hannover: SOAK Verlag, 1980.

Burnley, James. *Phases of Bradford Life*. London: Simpkin, Marshall & Co., 1889.

Burscheid, Peter. *Textilarbeiterschaft in der Industrialisierung: Soziale Lage und Mobilität in Württemberg*. Stuttgart: Klett-Cotta, 1978.

Bursian, Hans. "Über den Einfluss des 'Kapitals' von Karl Marx auf die Magdeburger Arbeiterbewegung, 1869–1871—Forschungsprobleme und Ergebnisse." *Beiträge zur Geschichte der deutschen Arbeiterbewegung*. Volume 10. Berlin: Institut für Marxismus-Leninismus, 1968.

Burton, Francis G. *The Commercial Management of Engineering Works*. Manchester: Scientific Publishing Co., 1899.

Busch, Johann Georg. *Abhandlung von dem Geldumlauf in anhaltender Rücksicht auf die Staatswirtschaft und Handlung*. Volume One. Hamburg: C. E. Bohn, 1780.

Bythell, Duncan. *The Handloom Weavers*. Cambridge: Cambridge University Press, 1969.

Calhoun, Craig. *The Question of Class Struggle*. Chicago: University of Chicago Press, 1982.

Campbell, Joan. *Joy in Work, German Work: The National Debate, 1800–1945*. Princeton: Princeton University Press, 1989.

Campe, Joachim Heinrich. *Wörterbuch der deutschen Sprache*. Part One. Braunschweig: In der Schulbuchhandlung, 1807.

Camps, Heinrich. *Geschichte und Entwicklung des Bezirks Westfalen des Zentralverbandes Christlicher Textilarbeiter Deutschlands*. Münster: Bezirkssekretariat Christlicher Textilarbeiter, 1924.

Canning, Kathleen. "Class, Gender, and Working-Class Politics: The Case of the German Textile Industry, 1890–1933." Ph.D. diss., The Johns Hopkins University, 1988.

Canning, Kathleen. "Gender and the Politics of Class Formation: Rethinking German Labor History." *American Historical Review* Volume 97, Number 3 (June 1992).

Canton, Hiram. "The Preindustrial Economics of Adam Smith." *The Journal of Economic History* Volume 45 (December 1985).

Carpanetto, Dino, and Giuseppe Ricuperati. *Italy in the Age of Reason 1685–1789.* London: Longman, 1987.

Carpenter, Kenneth E. *Dialogue in Political Economy: Translations from and into German in the Eighteenth Century.* Boston: Harvard University Printing Office, 1977.

Carpenter, Kenneth E., editor. *The Framework Knitters and Handloom Weavers: Their Attempts to Keep Up Wages.* New York: Arno Press, 1972.

Catling, Harold. *The Spinning Mule.* Newton Abbot: David & Charles, 1970.

Cauwès, Paul. *Précis du cours d'économie politique.* Volume One. Paris: L. Larose et Forcel, 1881.

Cayley, E. S. *On Commercial Economy.* London: James Ridgway, 1830.

Chabert, Alexandre. "Aux Sources du socialisme anglais." *Revue d'histoire économique et sociale* No. 4 (1951).

Chalonder, W. H., and A. E. Musson. *Industry and Technology.* London: Vista Books, 1963.

Chapman, Sydney J. *The Lancashire Cotton Industry: A Study in Economic Development.* Manchester: Manchester University Press, 1904.

Chassagne, Serge. "La Diffusion rurale de l'industrie cotonnière en France, 1750–1850." *Revue du Nord* Volume 61, Number 240 (January-March 1979).

Child, John, and Alfred Kieser. "Organizational and Managerial Roles in British and West German Companies: An Examination of the Culture-Free Thesis." In Cornelis Lammers and David Hickson, editors, *Organizations Alike and Unalike: International and Interinstitutional Studies in the Sociology of Organizations.* London: Routledge and Kegan Paul, 1979.

City of Bradford Technical College. *Report of the Department of Textile Industries.* Bradford, July, 1917.

Claeys, Gregory. *Machinery, Money and the Millennium: From Moral Economy to Socialism, 1815–60.* Cambridge: Polity Press, 1987.

Clagg, H. A., Allan Fox, and A. F. Thompson. *A History of British Trade Unions Since 1889.* Oxford: Clarendon Press, 1964.

Clapham, J. H. *A Concise Economic History of Britain from the Earliest Times to 1750.* Cambridge: Cambridge University Press, 1957.

Clapham, J. H. "The Decline of the Handloom in England and Germany." *Journal of the Bradford Textile Society* Volume 11 (1905).

Clapham, J. H. *The Woollen and Worsted Industries.* London: Methuen & Co., 1907.

Clark, Alice. *Working Life of Women in the Seventeenth Century.* [Orig. published 1919.] New York: Augustus Kelley, 1968.

Clark, David. *Colne Valley: Radicalism to Socialism.* London: Longman, 1981.

Clark, Sylvia. "Chorlton Mills and Their Neighbors." *Industrial Archaeology Review* Volume II, Number 3 (Summer 1978).

Clark, W. A. Graham. House of Representatives Committee on Interstate and Foreign Commerce. *Lace Industry in England and France*. Washington, D.C.: Government Printing Office, 1909.

Clay, C. G. A. *Economic Expansion and Social Change: England 1500–1700*. Volume II. Cambridge: Cambridge University Press, 1984.

Clements, R. V. "British Trade Unions and Popular Political Economy 1850–1875." *Economic History Review* Volume 14, Number 1 (August 1961).

Coats, A. W. "Changing Attitudes to Labour in the Mid-Eighteenth Century." *The Economic History Review*, second series, Volume XI, Number 1 (August 1958).

Cohen, Abner. *Two-Dimensional Man*. Berkeley: University of California Press, 1974.

Cohen, Herbert. "Heimarbeit und Heimarbeiterbewegung in der deutschen Herrenkonfektion." Diss., Erlangen, 1926.

Cohen, Isaac. *American Management and British Labor*. Westport, Connecticut: Greenwood Press, 1990.

Cole, Robert. *Work, Mobility, and Participation: A Comparative Study of American and Japanese Industry*. Berkeley: University of California Press, 1979.

Coleman, D. C. *Courtaulds: An Economic and Social History*. Oxford: Clarendon Press, 1969.

Coleman, D. C. "Labour in the English Economy of the Seventeenth Century." *The Economic History Review*, second series, Volume VIII, Number 3 (April 1956).

Coleman, James S. *Foundations of Social Theory*. Cambridge, Massachusetts: Harvard University Press, 1990.

Collins, Henry. "The Marxism of the Social Democratic Federation." In Asa Briggs and John Saville, editors, *Essays in Labour History 1886–1923*. Hamden, Conn.: Archon Books, 1971.

Collins, Henry, and Chimen Abramsky. *Karl Marx and the British Labour Movement*. London: Macmillan & Co., 1965.

Colquhoun, P. *A Treatise on Indigence, Exhibiting a General View of the National Resources for Productive Labour*. London: J. Hatchard, 1806.

Colson, C. *Cours d'économie politique*. Volume 2. Paris: Gauthier-Villars, 1901.

Comaroff, Jean. *Body of Power, Spirit of Resistance*. Chicago: University of Chicago Press, 1985.

Comaroff, John L., and Jean Comaroff. "The Madman and the Migrant: Work and Labor in the Historical Consciousness of a South African People." *American Ethnologist* Volume 14 (1987).

Connerton, Paul. *How Societies Remember*. Cambridge: Cambridge University Press, 1989.

Conrady, Alexander. *Die Rheinlande in der Franzosenzeit 1750–1815*. Stuttgart: J. H. W. Dietz, 1922.

Cooper, J. P. "Economic Regulation and the Cloth Industry in Seventeenth-Century England." *Transactions of the Royal Historical Society*, fifth series, Volume 20. London: Printed for The Society by Butler & Tanner, 1970.

Cooper, L. *Great Men of Yorkshire West Riding*. London: The Bodley Head, 1955.

Copley, Stephen. *Literature and the Social Order in Eighteenth-Century England*. London: Croom Helm, 1984.

Corns, Thomas N. *Uncloistered Virtue: English Political Literature, 1640–1660*. Oxford: Clarendon Press, 1992.

Cornthwaite, Robert. *Cotton Spinning: Hints to Mill Managers, Overlookers and Technical Students.* Manchester: John Heywood, ca. 1905.

Crankshaw, W. P. "The Internal Books of a Weaving Mill." *Journal of the British Association of Managers of Textile Works* Volume 4 (1912–1913).

Crouzet, François. *The First Industrialists: The Problem of Origins.* Cambridge: Cambridge University Press, 1985.

Crozier, Michel. *The Bureaucratic Phenomenon.* Chicago: University of Chicago Press, 1964.

Dahrendorf, Ralf. *Gesellschaft und Demokratie in Deutschland.* München: R. Piper & Co., 1968.

Dal Pane, Luigi. *Economia e società a Bologna nell'età del Risorgimento.* Bologna: Zanichelli, 1969.

Daniels, S. J. "Moral Order and the Industrial Environment in the Woolen Textile Districts of West Yorkshire, 1780–1880." Ph.D. diss., University College, London, 1980.

Decker, Franz. *Die betriebliche Sozialordnung der Dürener Industrie im 19. Jahrhundert.* Köln: Rheinisch-Westfälisches Wirtschaftsarchiv, 1965.

Defoe, Daniel. *The Great Law of Subordination Consider'd.* [Orig. published 1724.] In Stephen Copley, editor, *Literature and the Social Order in Eighteenth-Century England.* London: Croom Helm, 1984.

Dehn, R. M. *The German Cotton Industry.* Manchester: Manchester University Press, 1913.

Delsalle, Paul. "Tisserands et fabricants devant les Prud'Hommes." Diss., University of Lille, 1984.

Dentith, Simon. "Political Economy, Fiction and the Language of Practical Ideology in Nineteenth-Century England." *Social History* Volume 8, Number 2 (May 1983).

Dertouzos, Michael, Richard Lester, and Robert Solow. *Made in America: Regaining the Productive Edge.* Cambridge, Massachusetts: The M.I.T. Press, 1989.

Deutscher Handwerker- und Gewerbe-Congress. *Entwurf einer allgemeinen Handwerker und Gewerbe-Ordnung für Deutschland: berathen und beschlossen von dem Handwerker- und Gewerbe-Congress zu Frankfurt am Main im Juli und August 1848.* Hamburg, 1848.

Deutscher Textilarbeiterverband. *Jahrbuch des deutschen Textilarbeiterverbandes, 1910.* Berlin: Karl Hübsch, 1911.

Deutscher Textilarbeiterverband. *Jahrbuch des deutschen Textilarbeiterverbandes, 1911.* Berlin: Karl Hübsch, 1912.

Deutscher Textilarbeiterverband. *Jahrbuch des deutschen Textilarbeiterverbandes, 1913.* Berlin: Karl Hübsch, 1914.

Deutscher Textilarbeiterverband. *Leitfaden bei Führung der Geschäfte, in der Agitation, bei Streiks und Lohnbewegungen.* Berlin: Maurer & Dimmick, 1908.

Deutscher Textilarbeiterverband. *Lohnbewegungen der Weber und Weberinnen 1902–1909.* Gera: Alban Bretschneider, 1909.

Deutscher Textilarbeiterverband. *Protokoll des ersten deutschen Textilarbeiter-Kongresses.* Berlin: Deutscher Textilarbeiterverband, 1891.

Deutscher Textilarbeiterverband. *Protokoll der Verhandlungen der 6. ordentlichen General-Versammlung des Verbandes aller in der Textilindustrie beschäftigten*

Arbeiter und Arbeiterinnen Deutschlands. Berlin: Deutscher Textilarbeiterverband, 1902.

Deutscher Textilarbeiterverband. *Protokoll der vierten ordentlichen General-Versammlung des Verbandes aller in der Textil-Industrie beschäftigten Arbeiter und Arbeiterinnen.* Berlin: Deutscher Textilarbeiterverband, 1898.

Deutscher Textilarbeiterverband. *Soziale Gegensätze oder die Lage der Textilarbeiter in Augsburg.* Berlin: Carl Hübsch, 1907.

Deutscher Textilarbeiterverband. *Die Tuch-Konferenz in Crimmitschau 26. und 27. Februar 1910: Unterhandlungs-Bericht.* Berlin: Carl Hübsch, 1910.

Deutscher Textilarbeiter-Verband. *12. Bericht über die Lage der Textil-Industrie und ihrer Arbeiter in der Kriegszeit.* Berlin: Deutscher Textilarbeiterverband, May, 1917.

Deutscher Textilarbeiter-Verband, Filiale Neumünster. *Jahresbericht für das Geschäftsjahr 1912.* Hamburg: Verlagsgesellschaft deutscher Konsumvereine, 1913.

Deutscher Textilarbeiterverband, Gau Thüringen. *Tariferläuterungen und Statisches.* Gera: Alban Bretschneiderm, 1909.

Deutscher Textilarbeiterverband, Hauptvorstand/Arbeiterinnensekretariat. *Mein Arbeitstag—mein Wochenende.* Berlin: Textilpraxis, 1931.

Deutscher Werkmeister-Verband. *Stenographischer Bericht über die Verhandlungen des Verbandstages, 1913.* Düsseldorf: Deutscher Werkmeister-Verband, 1913.

Deutschmann, Christoph. *Der Weg zum Normalarbeitstag.* Frankfurt: Campus Verlag, 1985.

Dewerpe, Alain. "Politiques, économiques et industrialisation en Italie du Nord pendant la période française." In Gérard Gayot and Jean-Pierre Hirsch, editors, *La Révolution française et le développement du capitalisme.* Lille: Revue du Nord, 1989.

Diefendorf, Jeffrey M. *Businessmen and Politics in the Rhineland, 1789–1834.* Princeton: Princeton University Press, 1980.

Dietel, Ernst. *Die Greizer Wollindustrie.* Berlin: Wilhelm Pilz, 1915.

Dieterici, W. *Über Preussische Zustände, über Arbeit und Kapital.* Berlin: Ernst Siegfried Mittler, 1848.

Dietz, Walter. *Die Wuppertaler Garnnahrung: Geschichte der Industrie und des Handels von Elberfeld und Barmen 1400 bis 1800.* Neustadt an der Aisch: Ph. C. W. Schmidt, 1957.

Dietzgen, Joseph. "Dass der Sozialist kein Monarchist sein kann." *Der Volksstaat,* August 13 and August 15, 1873.

Dilks, H. "The Value of Graphical Charts in Weaving Mill Management." *Journal of British Association of Managers of Textile Works* Volume VII (1915–1916).

DiMaggio, Paul. "Interest and Agency in Institutional Theory." In Lynne Zucker, editor, *Institutional Patterns and Organizations: Culture and Environment.* Cambridge, Massachusetts: Ballinger Publishing Co., 1988.

Dipper, Christof. *Die Bauernbefreiung in Deutschland 1790–1850.* Stuttgart: W. Kohlhammer, 1980.

Dipper, Christof. "Revolution und Reaktion im Jakobinismus." *Quellen und Forschungen aus italienischen Archiven und Bibliotheken.* Tübingen: Max Neimeyer Verlag, 1979.

Dithmars, Justus Christoph. *Einleitung in die Oeconomische Policei- und Cameral-Wissenschaften.* Franckfurth an der Oder: J. J. Friedel, 1745.

Dittrich, Erich. "Zur sozialen Herkunft des sächsischen Unternehmertums." In H. Kretzschmar, editor, *Neues Archiv für sächsische Geschichte und Altertumskunde,* Volume 63. Dresden: Baensch-Druckerei, 1943.

Dlubek, Rolf. "Die Rolle des 'Kapitals' bei der Durchsetzung des Marxismus in der deutschen Arbeiterbewegung." In *Beiträge zur Marx-Engels Forschung.* Berlin: Dietz Verlag, 1968.

Dlubek, Rolf, and Hannes Skambraks, editors. *"Das Kapital" von Karl Marx in der deutschen Arbeiterbewegung: 1867 bis 1878.* Berlin: Dietz Verlag, 1967.

Dobb, Maurice. *Studies in the Development of Capitalism.* London: George Routledge & Sons, 1946.

Dobson, B. A. *Some Difficulties in Cotton Spinning.* Bolton: G. S. Heaton, 1893.

Dobson, E. Philip, and John B. Ives. *A Century of Achievement: The History of James Ives & Company Limited.* London: William Sessions, 1948.

Dodd, E. E. *Bingley: A Yorkshire Town Through Nine Centuries.* Bingley: T. Harrison & Sons, 1958.

Dodd, Gerald. *Days at the Factories: Or, the Manufacturing Industry of Great Britain Described.* London: Charles Knight, 1843.

Doherty, John, editor. *The Poor Man's Advocate; Or, a Full and Fearless Exposure of the Horrors and Abominations of the Factory System in England, in the Year 1832.* Manchester: J. Doherty, 1833.

Donham, Donald. *History, Power, Ideology: Central Issues in Marxism and Anthropology.* Cambridge: Cambridge University Press, 1990.

Dore, Ronald. *British Factory, Japanese Factory.* Berkeley: University of California Press, 1973.

Dore, Ronald. *Taking Japan Seriously.* London: Athlone Press, 1987.

Dornig, Hermann. *Die Praxis der mechanischen Weberei.* Leipzig: A. Hartleben, 1895.

Dörstling, Gustav. *Die Arbeitgeber und die Löhne der Arbeiter.* Chemnitz, 1847.

Douglas, Mary. *Implicit Meanings.* London: Routledge & Kegan Paul, 1975.

Douglas, Mary. *The World of Goods.* New York: Basic Books, 1979.

Duffield, Neil. "Bolton Socialist Club." *Bolton People's History* Volume 1 (March 1984).

Dumont, Louis. *From Mandeville to Marx.* Chicago: University of Chicago Press, 1977.

Dutton, H., and J. E. King. *"Ten Percent and No Surrender": The Preston Strike, 1853–54.* Cambridge: Cambridge University Press, 1981.

Duveau, Georges. *La Vie ouvrière sous le second empire.* Paris: Librairie Gallimard, 1946.

Eccarius, J. Georg. *Eines Arbeiters Widerlegung der national-ökonomischen Lehren John Stuart Mills.* Berlin: Buchhandlung des 'Vorwärts,' 1888.

Eisenberg, Christiane. *Deutsche und englische Gewerkschaften.* Göttingen: Vandenhoeck & Ruprecht, 1986.

Elbaum, Bernard, and Frank Wilkinson. "Industrial Relations and Uneven Development: A Comparative Study of the American and British Steel Industries." *Cambridge Journal of Economics* Volume 3, Number 3 (September 1979).

Elbourne, Edward. *Factory Administration and Accounts*. London: Green & Co., 1914.

Elementi di economia pubblica. In *Scrittori classici italiani di economia politica*, Parte Moderna, Tomo XI. Milano: G. G. Destefanis, 1804.

Eley, Geoff, and Keith Nield. "Why Does Social History Ignore Politics?" *Social History* Volume 5, Number 2 (May 1980).

Emsbach, Karl. *Die soziale Betriebsverfassung der rheinischen Baumwollindustrie im 19. Jahrhundert*. Bonn: Röhrscheid, 1982.

Encyklopädisches Wörterbuch. Volume I. Zeitz und Naumburg, 1793.

Engelhardt, Ulrich. *"Nur vereinigt sind wir stark": Die Anfänge der deutschen Gewerkschaftsbewegung 1862/63 bis 1869/70*. Volume One. Stuttgart: Ernst Klett, 1977.

Engels, Friedrich. *The Condition of the Working-Class in England*. [Orig. published in German in 1845.] London: George Allen and Unwin, 1892.

Engels, Friedrich. "Zur Geschichte der preussischen Bauern." *Marx/Engels Werke*, Volume 21. Berlin: Dietz Verlag, 1962.

Engels, Friedrich. "Outline for a Critique of National Economics." In *Marx/Engels Gesamtausgabe*. Berlin: Marx-Engels-Verlag, 1930.

Engels, Friedrich, Paul Lafargue, and Laura Lafargue. *Correspondance*. Paris: Editions Sociales, 1956.

Engels, Wilhelm. *Ablösungen und Gemeinheitsteilungen in der Rheinprovinz*. Bonn: Ludwig Röhrscheid, 1957.

Engrand, Charles. "Concurrences et complémentarités des villes et des campagnes: Les Manufactures picardes de 1780 à 1815." *Revue du Nord* Volume 61, Number 240 (January-March 1979).

Ephraim, Hugo. "Organisation und Betrieb einer Tuchfabrik." *Zeitschrift für die gesamte Staatswissenschaft* Volume 61 (1905).

Erämetsä, Erik. "Adam Smith als Mittler englisch-deutscher Spracheinflüsse." In Suomalainen Tiedeakatemia, editor, *Toimituksia: Annales*, Series B. Helsinki: Suomalainen Tiedeakatemia, 1961.

Erdelen, Herbert. "Die Textilindustrie in zwei Kreisen (Ahaus und Steinfurt) des Münsterlandes." Diss., Freiburg i. Br., 1921.

Erlacher, Georg. *Briefe eines Betriebsleiters über Organisation technischer Betriebe*. Hannover: Gebrüder Jänecke, 1903.

Eyraud, François, and Frédérique Rychener. "A Societal Analysis of New Technologies." In Peter Grootings, editor, *Technology and Work: East-West Comparison*. London: Croom Helm, 1986.

"Ein Fabrikant." *Praktische Darstellung der Oberlausitzer Leinwand-Fabrikation nebst ihren Mängeln*. Herrnhut: J. D. Schöpfischen Buchhandlung, 1837.

Faccarello, Gilbert. "L'Evolution de l'économie politique pendant la Révolution: Alexandre Vandermonde ou la croisée des chemins." In *Französische Revolution und Politische Ökonomie*. Trier: Schriften aus dem Karl-Marx-Haus, 1989.

Fairbairn, William. *Treatise on Mills and Millwork*. London: Longmans, Green, 1861.

Fanfari, Amintore. *Storia del lavoro in Italia dalla fine del secolo XV agli inizi del XVIII*. 2d ed. Milano: A. Giuffrè, 1959.

"A Farmer." "On Taken-Work." *The Monthly Magazine* (May 1799).

Feinendegen, Reinhard. *Der niederrheinische Adel der Neuzeit und sein Grundbesitz.* Bonn: Ludwig Röhrscheid, 1961.

Fenet, P. A., editor. *Recueil complet des trauvaux préparatoires du Code civil.* Volume 14. [Orig. published 1827.] Osnabrück: Otto Zeller, 1968.

Ferrara, Francesco. *Oeuvres économiques choisis.* Paris: Marcel Rivière, 1938.

Finley, M. I. *The Ancient Economy.* Berkeley: University of California Press, 1985.

Firth, Gary. "The Bradford Trade in the Nineteenth Century." In D. G. Wright and J. A. Jowitt, editors, *Victorian Bradford.* Bradford: Bradford Metropolitan Council, 1982.

Fischer, Wolfram. *Handwerksrecht und Handwerkswirtschaft um 1800.* Berlin: Duncker & Humblot, 1955.

Fitton, R. S., and A. P. Wadsworth. *The Strutts and the Arkwrights 1758–1830.* Manchester: Manchester University Press, 1958.

Fix, Théodore. "De la Mesure de la valeur." *Journal des Economistes* Volume 9 (1844).

Fleischer, Johann Georg. *Philosophisch-Politische Abhandlung von den Naturalfrohndiensten.* Frankfurt am Main: J. G. Fleischer, 1775.

Flinn, M. W., editor. *The Law Book of the Crowley Ironworks.* London: Bernard Quaritch, 1957.

Flohr, Bernd. *Arbeiter nach Mass.* Frankfurt am Main: Campus, 1981.

Forti-Messian, Anna-Lucia. "La Législation du travail en Lombardie à l'époque napoléonienne." *Annales Historiques de la Révolution Française*, Volume 49. Paris, 1977.

Foster, A. R. *Weaving Mill Management.* Manchester: John Heywood, ca. 1908.

Foucault, Michel. *Discipline and Punish.* New York: Vintage Books, 1979.

Foucault, Michel. *The Order of Things.* New York: Vintage Books, 1973.

Fourquin, Guy. *Lordship and Feudalism in the Middle Ages.* London: George Allen & Unwin, 1976.

Fowler, Alan. "War and Labour Unrest." In Alan Fowler and Terry Wyke, editors, *The Barefoot Aristocrats.* Littleborough: George Kelsall, 1987.

Fowler, Alan, and Lesley Fowler. *The History of the Nelson Weavers Association.* Nelson: Burnley, Nelson, Rossendale & District Textile Workers Union, 1989.

Funk, V. *Arbeiter-Katechismus.* Giessen: Emil Roth, 1881.

Fuoco, Francesco. *Saggi economici,* Prima Serie I. Pisa: Presso Sebastiano Nistri, 1825.

Fuoco, Francesco. *Saggi economici,* Prima Serie II. Pisa: Presso Sebastiano Nistri, 1827.

Furet, F., C. Mazauric, and L. Bergeron. "The Sans-Culottes and the French Revolution." In *New Perspectives on the French Revolution.* New York: John Wiley & Sons, 1965.

Furniss, Edgar S. *The Position of the Laborer in a System of Nationalism: A Study in the Labor Theories of the Later English Mercantilists.* Boston: Houghton Mifflin, 1920.

G., H. S. *Autobiography of a Manchester Cotton Manufacturer.* Manchester: John Heywood, 1887.

Gadian, David. "Class Formation and Class Action in North-West Industrial Towns, 1830–1850." In R. J. Morris, editor, *Class, Power and Social Structure in British Nineteenth-Century Towns.* Leicester: Leicester University Press, 1986.

Galiani, Ferdinando. *On Money*. [Orig. published 1751.] Ann Arbor: University Microfilms International, 1977.

Gallie, Duncan. *Social Inequality and Class Radicalism in France and Britain*. Cambridge: Cambridge University Press, 1983.

Galloway, Robert. *Annals of Coal Mining and the Coal Trade*, second series. London: The Colliery Guardian Company, 1904.

Ganilh, M. *Dictionnaire analytique d'économie politique*. Paris: Imprimerie de Fain, 1826.

Garlan, Yvon. "Le Travail libre en Grèce ancienne." In Peter Garnsey, editor, *Non-Slave Labour in the Greco-Roman World*. Cambridge: Cambridge Philological Society, 1980.

Garside, W., and H. F. Gospel. "Employers and Managers: Their Organizational Structure and Changing Industrial Strategies." In C. Wrigley, editor, *A History of British Industrial Relations*. Brighton: Harvester, 1982.

Gaskell, Peter. *The Manufacturing Population of England*. London: Baldwin and Cradock, 1833.

Gauvorstand des Textilarbeiterverbands. *Arbeitszeit und Löhne in der Textilindustrie der Niederlausitz*. Berlin: Franz Kotzke, 1909.

Geertz, Clifford. *The Interpretation of Cultures*. New York: Basic Books, 1973.

General Union of Associations of Powerloom Overlookers. *The Almanack and Guide for 1899*. Manchester: Ashton and Redfern, 1899.

Gera-Greizer Kammgarnspinnerei. *50 Jahre Gera-Greizer Kammgarnspinnerei 1890–1940*. Gera: Karl Basch & Co. 1940.

Gerlier, Pierre. *Des Stipulations usuraires dans le contrat du travail*. Paris: V. Giard et E. Brière, 1907.

Germany. *Die deutsche Volkswirtschaft am Schlusse des 19. Jahrhunderts*. Berlin: Puttkammer und Mühlbrecht, 1900.

Germany. *Gewerbeordnung für das Deutsche Reich*. München: C. H. Beck, 1909.

Germany. *Jahres-Berichte der königlich preussischen Regierungs- und Gewerberäthe und Bergbehörden*. Berlin, various years.

Germany. *Jahres-Berichte der mit Beaufsichtigung der Fabriken betrauten Beamten*. Berlin, various years.

Germany. *Statistisches Jahrbuch für das Deutsche Reich*. Berlin: Kaiserliches Statistisches Amt, 1909.

Germany. *Statistik des Deutschen Reichs*. Volumes 141, 157, 164, 188, 214. Berlin: Kaiserliches Statistisches Amt, various years, 1899–1906.

Germany. *Die Gewerbe-Ordnung*. Berlin: Carl Heymanns Verlag, 1910.

Germany, Enquete-Kommission. *Reichs-Enquete für die Baumwollen- und Leinen-Industrie: Stenographische Protokolle über die mündliche Vernehmung der Sachverständigen*. Berlin: Julius Sittenfeld, 1878.

Germany, Kaiserliches Statistisches Amt. *Streiks und Aussperrungen im Jahre 1900*. Berlin: Puttkamer & Mühlbrecht, 1901.

Germany, Reichskanzler-Amt. *Ergebnisse der über die Verhältnisse der Lehrlinge, Gesellen und Fabrikarbeiter auf Beschluss des Bundesrathes angestellten Erhebungen*. Berlin: Carl Heymann, 1877.

Gewehr, Wilhelm. *Praktischer Rathgeber für Vereins- und Versammlungsleiter sowie Versammlungsbesucher*. Elberfeld, 1897.

Gewerkschaft Textil-Bekleidung. _Dokumente zu 150 Jahren Frauenarbeit in der Textil- und Bekleidungsindustrie._ Düsseldorf: Courier-Druck, 1981.

Gille, Bertrand. _Recherches sur la formation de la grande entreprise capitaliste: 1815–1848._ Paris: S.E.V.P.E.N., 1959.

Glaser, J. C. _Die allgemeine Wirtschaftslehre oder Nationalökonomie._ Berlin: E. H. Schroeder, 1858.

Glover, Frederick James. "The Rise of the Heavy Woollen Trade of the West Riding of Yorkshire in the Nineteenth Century." _Business History_ Volume 4, No. 1 (December 1961).

Godelier, Maurice. _The Mental and the Material: Thought, Economy and Society._ London: Verso, 1986.

Göhring, Martin. _Die Feudalität in Frankreich vor und in der grossen Revolution._ Berlin: Emil Ebering, 1934.

Goldenberg, Charles. _De la Nature juridique des contrats de travail._ Paris: V. Giard & E. Brière, 1908.

Goldstrom, Max. "Popular Political Economy for the British Working Class Reader in the Nineteenth Century." In Terry Shinn and Richard Whitley, editors, _Expository Science: Forms and Functions of Popularisation._ Dordrecht: D. Reidel, 1985.

Gonner, E. C. K. "The Progress of Inclosure During the Seventeenth Century." _The English Historical Review_ Volume XXIII (1908).

Gordon, Andrew. _The Evolution of Labor Relations in Japan._ Cambridge: Harvard University Press, 1985.

Gottdiener, Mark. "Ökonomie, Ideologie und Semiotik." _Zeitschrift für Semiotik._ Volume 10, Numbers 1–2 (1988).

Gottheiner, Elisabeth. _Studien über die Wuppertaler Textilindustrie und ihre Arbeiter in den letzten zwanzig Jahren._ Leipzig: Duncker & Humblot, 1903.

Gourvish, T. R. "British Business and the Transition to a Corporate Economy: Entrepreneurship and Management Structures." In R. P. T. Davenport-Hines and Geoffrey Jones, editors, _Enterprise, Management and Innovation in British Business, 1914–1980._ London: Frank Cass, 1988.

Graach, Hartmut. "Labour und Work." In Sprachwissenschaftliches Colloquium Bonn, editor, _Europäische Schlüsselwörter: Wortvergleichende und wortgeschichtliche Studien._ München: Max Hueber Verlag, 1964.

Graul, Hugo. _Das Eindringen der Smithschen Nationalökonomie in Deutschland und ihre Weiterbildung bis zu Hermann._ Halle-Saale: Paul Malok, 1928.

Gray, John. _Lectures on the Nature and Use of Money._ London: Longman, Brown, Green, and Longmans, 1848.

Gray, John. _The Social System._ London: Longman, Rees, Orme, Brown, and Green, 1831.

Gray, Paul. "The Deconstructing of the English Working Class." _Social History_ Volume 11, Number 3 (October 1986).

Graziani, Augusto. _Storia critica della teoria del valore in Italia._ Milano: U. Hoepli, 1889.

Greif, Wilfrid. _Studien über die Wirkwarenindustrie in Limbach in Sachsen._ Karlsruhe: G. Braunsche Hofbuchdruckerei, 1907.

Grigorovici, Tatiana. _Die Wertlehre bei Marx und Lassalle._ Wien: Ignaz Brand & Co., 1910.

Grimm, Jacob, and Wilhelm Grimm. *Deutsches Wörterbuch von Jacob Grimm und Wilhelm Grimm*. Leipzig: S. Hirzel, 1854.

Grinda, Klaus. *"Arbeit" und "Mühe": Untersuchungen zur Bedeutungsgeschichte altenglischer Wörter*. München: Wilhelm Fink, 1975.

Gross, Reiner. *Die bürgerliche Agrarreform in Sachsen in den ersten Hälfte des 19. Jahrhunderts: Untersuchung zum Problem des Übergangs vom Feudalismus zum Kapitalismus in der Landwirtschaft*. Weimar: Hermann Böhlaus Nachfolger, 1968.

Gruner, Anton. *Mechanische Webereipraxis sowie Garnnumerierungen und Garnumrechnungen*. Leipzig: A. Hartleben, 1898.

Gudeman, Stephen. *Economics as Culture: Models and Metaphors of Livelihood*. London: Routledge & Kegan Paul, 1986.

Guignet, Philippe. *Mines, manufactures, et ouvriers du Valenciennois au XVIIIe siècle*. New York: Arno Press, 1977.

Guitto, Luigi. *La fabbrica totale*. Milan: Feltrinelli Economica, 1979.

Gullickson, Gay L. *Spinners and Weavers of Auffay*. Cambridge: Cambridge University Press, 1986.

Günther, Ernst. *Die Entlöhnungsmethoden der bayrischen Eisen- und Maschinen-Industrie*. Berlin: Leonhard Simion, 1908.

Gurr, Duncan, and Julian Hunt. *The Cotton Mills of Oldham*. Oldham: Oldham Cultural and Information Services, 1989.

Habermas, Jürgen. *Theorie des kommunikativen Handelns*. Frankfurt am Main: Suhrkamp, 1981.

Habermas, Jürgen. *Theory and Practice*. Boston: Beacon Press, 1974.

Habermas, Jürgen. *The Theory of Communicative Action*. Volume Two. Boston: Beacon Press, 1985.

Hagan, Gustav. "Zum sachlichen und sprachlichen Einfluss der englischen politischen Ökonomie auf dei deutsche im 18. und 19. Jahrhundert." Diss., Humboldt-Universität, Berlin, 1968.

Hale, Matthew. *A Discourse Touching Provision for the Poor*. London: H. Hills, 1683.

Hall, Charles. *The Effects of Civilization on the People in European States*. London: T. Ostell, 1805.

Hamerow, Theodore S. *Restoration, Revolution, Reaction: Economics and Politics in Germany, 1815–1971*. Princeton: Princeton University Press, 1958.

Hamilton, Gary, Nicole Woolsey Biggart, and Marco Orrù. "Organizational Isomorphism in East Asia." In Walter W. Powell and Paul J. DiMaggio, editors, *The New Institutionalism in Organizational Analysis*. Chicago: University of Chicago Press, 1991.

Hammond, J. L., and Barbara Hammond. *The Skilled Labourer*. London: Longman, 1979.

Handelskammer Mönchengladbach. *Jahresbericht, 1896*. Mönchengladbach: V. Hütter, n.d.

Handelskammer Mönchengladbach. *Jahresbericht, 1897*. Mönchengladbach: V. Hütter, n.d.

Hannavy, John, and Chris Ryan. *Working in Wigan Mills*. Wigan: Smiths Books, 1987.

Hansen, Joseph. *Die Rheinprovinz 1815–1915*. Volume I. Bonn: A. Marcus & E. Webers Verlag, 1917.

Hanssen, Georg. "Ueber den Mangel an landwirtschaftlichem Arbeitspersonal." *Archiv der politischen Oekonomie und Polizeiwissenschaft.* Heidelberg: C. F. Winter, 1844.

Harris, Marvin. *Cultural Materialism: The Struggle for a Science of Culture.* New York: Vintage Books, 1980.

Harrison, Mark. *Crowds and History: Mass Phenomena in English Towns, 1790–1835.* Cambridge: Cambridge University Press, 1988.

Harrison, Mark. "The Ordering of the Urban Environment: Time, Work and the Occurrence of Crowds, 1790–1835." *Past and Present* Number 110 (February 1986).

Hart, Keith. "On Commoditization." In Esther N. Goody, editor, *From Craft to Industry: The Ethnography of Proto-Industrial Cloth Production.* Cambridge: Cambridge University Press, 1982.

Hasek, Carl W. *The Introduction of Adam Smith's Doctrines into Germany.* New York: Columbia University, 1925.

Haupt, Heinz-Gerhard. "Frankreich: Langsame Industrialisierung und republikanische Tradition." In Jürgen Kocka, editor, *Europäische Arbeiterbewegungen im 19. Jahrhundert.* Göttingen: Vandenhoeck & Ruprecht, 1983.

Haushofer, Max. *Der Industriebetrieb.* München: E. Koch, 1904.

Haynes, J. *Great Britain's Glory; Or, an Account of the Great Numbers of Poor Employ'd in the Woollen and Silk Manufactories.* London: J. Marshall, 1715.

Heaton, Herbert. "The Assessment of Wages in the West Riding of Yorkshire in the Seventeenth and Eighteenth Centuries." *The Economic Journal* Volume XXIV, No. 94 (June 1914).

Heaton, Herbert. *The Yorkshire Woollen and Worsted Industries.* Second edition. Oxford: Clarendon Press, 1965.

Hecking, Eugen. *100 Jahre J. Hecking.* Neuenkirchen: self-published, 1958.

Heighton, William. *An Address to the Members of Trade Societies and to the Working-Classes Generally.* London: Co-Operative Society, 1827.

Heinsius, Theodor. *Volksthümliches Wörterbuch der deutschen Sprache.* Hannover: Hahn, 1818.

Henning, Friedrich-Wilhelm. *Dienste und Abgaben der Bauern im 18. Jahrhundert.* Stuttgart: Gustav Fischer, 1969.

Hermann, Friedrich. *Staatwirtschaftliche Untersuchungen.* München: Anton Weber, 1832.

Hermann, Friedrich. *Staatswirtschaftliche Untersuchungen.* München: Fleischmann, 1870.

Herzig, Arno. "Vom sozialen Protest zur Arbeiterbewegung: Das Beispiel des märkisch-westfälischen Industriegebietes 1780–1865." In Heinrich Volkmann and Jürgen Bergmann, editors, *Sozialer Protest: Studien zu traditioneller Resistenz und kollektiver Gewalt in Deutschland vom Vormärz bis zur Reichsgründung.* Opladen: Westdeutscher Verlag, 1984.

Heuss, Adam. *Wanderungen und Lebensansichten.* Jena: Friedrich Frommann, 1845.

Heylin, Henry Brougham. *The Cotton Weaver's Handbook: A Practical Guide to the Construction and Costing of Cotton Fabrics.* London: Charles Griffen & Co., 1908.

Hicks, John. *A Theory of Economic History.* Oxford: Clarendon Press, 1969.

Hill, Christopher. "A Bourgeois Revolution?" In J. G. A. Pocock, editor, *Three British Revolutions: 1641, 1688, 1776*. Princeton: Princeton University Press, 1980.

Hill, Christopher. *The Century of Revolution 1603–1714*. Edinburgh: Thomas Nelson and Sons, 1961.

Hill, Christopher. "The Poor and the People." *The Collected Essays of Christopher Hill*. Amherst: University of Massachusetts Press, 1986.

Hill, Christopher. "Pottage for Freeborn Englishmen: Attitudes to Wage Labour in the Sixteenth and Seventeenth Centuries." In C. H. Feinstein, editor, *Socialism, Capitalism and Economic Growth: Essays Presented to Maurice Dobb*. Cambridge: Cambridge University Press, 1967.

Hill, Christopher. *Society and Puritanism in Pre-Revolutionary England*. New York: Schocken Books, 1964.

Hill, Christopher. *The World Turned Upside Down*. New York: Viking Press, 1972.

Hill, Harold. "Influences Arising from the Employment of New and Improved Machines." *Official Record of the Annual Conference of the Textile Institute Held at Bolton, June, 1927*. Leeds: Chorley & Pickersgill, 1927.

Hillier, Bill, and Julienne Hanson. *The Social Logic of Space*. Cambridge: Cambridge University Press, 1984.

Hinrichs, Ernst. "Feudalität und Ablösung: Bemerkungen zur Vorgeschichte des 4. August 1789." In Eberhard Schmitt, editor, *Die Französische Revolution*. Köln: Kiepenheuer & Witsch, 1976.

Hinton, James. *Labour and Socialism*. Amherst: University of Massachusetts Press, 1983.

Hinze, Kurt. *Die Arbeiterfrage zu Beginn des modernen Kapitalismus in Brandenburg-Preussen 1685–1806*. [Orig. published 1927.] Berlin: de Gruyter & Co., 1963.

Hirsch, Jean-Pierre. *Les Deux Rêves du commerce: Entreprise et institution dans la région lilloise, 1780–1860*. Paris: Ecole des Hautes Etudes en Sciences Sociales, 1991.

Hirsch, Jean-Pierre. "Négoce et corporations." In *La Révolution française et le développement du capitalisme*. Lille: Revue du Nord, 1989.

Hirsch, Jean-Pierre. "Revolutionary France, Cradle of Free Enterprise." *American Historical Review* Volume 94, Number 5 (December 1989).

Hobsbawm, E. J. *Industry and Empire: An Economic History of Britain Since 1750*. London: Weidenfeld and Nicolson, 1968.

Hobsbawm, E. J. "Karl Marx and the British Labour Movement." In *Revolutionaries: Contemporary Essays*. London: Weidenfeld and Nicolson, 1973.

Hobsbawm, E. J. "The Seventeenth Century in the Development of Capitalism." *Science and Society* Volume XXIV, Number 2 (Spring 1960).

Hobsbawm, Eric, editor. *Labour's Turning Point 1880–1900*. London: Lawrence & Wishart, 1948.

Hobson, Samuel G. *Pilgrim to the Left*. London: E. Arnold & Co., 1938.

Hodgskin, Thomas. *Labour Defended Against the Claims of Capital*. [Orig. published 1825.] London: Labour Publishing Company, 1922.

Hodgskin, Thomas. *Popular Political Economy*. [Orig. published 1827.] New York: Augustus Kelley, 1966.

Hoffmann, Ludwig. *Die Maschine ist nothwendig*. Berlin: Naucksche Buchhandlung, 1832.

Hoffmann, Wilhelm. *Vollständiges Wörterbuch der deutschen Sprache.* Volume One. Leipzig: A. M. Colditz, 1853.

Hofstede, Geert. *Culture's Consequences: International Differences in Work-Related Values.* Beverly Hills: Sage Publications, 1980.

Holbrook-Jones, Mike. *Supremacy and the Subordination of Labour.* London: Heinemann Educational Books, 1982.

Holderness, B. A. *Pre-Industrial England: Economy and Society 1500–1750.* London: J. M. Dent & Sons, 1976.

Holdsworth, W. S. *A History of English Law.* Volume IV. Boston: Little, Brown and Company, 1924.

Holdsworth, W. S. *A History of English Law.* Volume XI. Boston: Little, Brown and Company, 1938.

Hollander, J. H. "The Development of Ricardo's Theory of Value." In John Cunningham Wood, editor, *David Ricardo: Critical Assessments.* London: Croom Helm, 1985.

Hollins, D. M. "The Northrop Loom for Woollens and Worsteds." *Huddersfield Textile Society Journal* 1918–1919 session.

Hollis, Patricia. *The Pauper Press.* London: Oxford University Press, 1970.

Hölters, Hermann. "Die Arbeiterverhältnisse in der niederrheinischen Baumwollindustrie mit besonderer Berücksichtigung der männlichen Arbeiter." Diss. Heidelberg, 1911.

Honeyman, Katrina. *Origins of Enterprise.* Manchester: Manchester University Press, 1982.

Hopkin, Deian. "The Membership of the Independent Labour Party, 1904–1910." *International Review of Social History* Volume 20, Part Two (1975).

Hopwood, Edwin. *A History of the Lancashire Cotton Industry and the Amalgamated Weavers' Association: The Lancashire Weavers Story.* Manchester: Amalgamated Weavers' Association.

Horkheimer, Max. *Eclipse of Reason.* New York: Oxford University Press, 1947.

Horster, Paul. *Die Entwicklung der sächsischen Gewerbeverfassung, 1780–1861.* Crefeld: Wilhelm Greven, 1908.

Hoskins, W. G. *Industry, Trade and People in Exeter 1688–1800.* Manchester: Manchester University Press, 1968.

Hoth, Wolfgang. *Die Industrialisierung einer rheinischen Gewerbestadt, dargestellt am Beispiel Wuppertal.* Köln: Rheinisch-Westfälisches Wirtschaftsarchiv, 1975.

Höttemann, Walter. *Die Göttinger Tuchindustrie der Vergangenheit und Gegenwart.* Göttingen: Göttinger Handelsdruckerei, 1931.

Howe, Anthony. *The Cotton Masters, 1830–1860.* Oxford: Clarendon Press, 1984.

Howell, George. *Labour Legislation, Labour Movements, and Labour Leaders.* London: T. Fisher Unwin, 1902.

Hubert-Valleroux, P. *Le Contrat de travail.* Paris: Rousseau, 1895.

Hudson, Pat. *The Genesis of Industrial Capital.* Cambridge: Cambridge University Press, 1986.

Hülffe, J. A. *Die Technik der Baumwollspinnerei.* Stuttgart: J. G. Cotta, 1863.

Hull, Charles Henry, editor. *The Economic Writings of Sir William Petty.* Cambridge: Cambridge University Press, 1899.

Hüllmann, Karl Dietrich. *Historische und staatswissenschaftliche Untersuchungen über die Natural-Dienste der Gutsunterthanen nach fränkisch-deutscher Ver-*

fassung: Und die Verwandlung derselben in Geld-Dienste. Berlin: Friedrich Nicolai, 1803.

Hume, L. J. "Jeremy Bentham on Industrial Management." *Yorkshire Bulletin of Economic and Social Research* Volume 22, Number 1 (May 1970).

Hundert, E. J. "The Making of *Homo Faber*: John Locke Between Ideology and History." *Journal of the History of Ideas* Volume XXXIII, Number 1 (January–March 1972).

Hundert, E. J. "Market Society and Meaning in Locke's Political Philosophy." *Journal of the History of Philosophy* Volume XV, Number 1 (January 1977).

Hurst, Gerald. *Closed Chapters*. Manchester: Manchester University Press, 1942.

Hüser, Karl. *Mit Gott für unser Recht: Ein Beitrag zur Geschichte der Gewerkschaftsbewegung im Münsterland*. Paderborn: Gewerkschaft Textil-Bekleidung, 1978.

Hutchison, T. W. "Berkeley's *Querist* and Its Place in the Economic Thought of the Eighteenth Century." *British Journal for the Philosophy of Science* Volume IV, No. 13 (May 1953).

Hutchison, T. W. *On Revolutions and Progress in Economic Knowledge*. Cambridge: Cambridge University Press, 1978.

Hyndman, H. M. *The Economics of Socialism*. London: The Twentieth Century Press, 1909.

Hyndman, H. M. *Further Reminiscences*. London: Macmillan & Co., 1912.

Hyndman, H. M. *The Historical Basis of Socialism in England*. [Orig. published 1883.] London: Garland Publishing, 1984.

Hyndman, H. M. *The Record of an Adventurous Life*. London: Macmillan & Co., 1911.

Iggers, Georg. *The German Conception of History: The National Tradition of Historical Thought from Herder to the Present*. Middletown, Connecticut: Wesleyan University Press, 1983.

Ipsen, Adolf. *Neumünster: ein holsteinischer Fabrikort in seiner Entwicklung während der Jahre 1852–1863*. Kiel, 1863.

Isenburg, Robert. "Untersuchungen über die Entwicklung der bergischen Wollenindustrie." Diss. Heidelberg, 1906.

Ittenson, Josef. *Das Kalulations-Buch des Baumwollwebers: Für die Praxis Bearbeitet*. Leipzig: Gustav Weigel, 1908.

Jacoby, Sanford. *Employing Bureaucracy*. New York: Columbia University Press, 1985.

Jaffe, James. *The Struggle for Market Power: Industrial Relations in the British Coal Industry, 1800–1840*. Cambridge: Cambridge University Press, 1991.

Jakob, Ludwig. *Grundsätze der National-Ökonomie oder National-Wirthschaftslehre*. Halle: Ruffscher Verlag, 1805.

Jakob, Ludwig. *Grundsätze der National-Ökonomie; oder, Theorie des National-Reichtums*. Halle: Friedrich Ruff, 1825.

Jakob, Ludwig Heinrich. *Ueber die Arbeit Leibeigner und freyer Bauern in Beziehung auf den Nutzen der Landeigenthümer*. St. Petersburg: Akademie der Wissenschaften, 1814.

James, Margaret. *Social Problems and Policy During the Puritan Revolution 1640–1660*. London: Routledge & Kegan Paul, 1966.

Jarman, T. L. *Socialism in Britain: From the Industrial Revolution to the Present Day*. London: Victor Gollancz, 1972.

Jenkins, D. T., and J. C. Malin. "European Competition in Woollen and Cloth, 1870–1914: The Role of Shoddy." *Business History* Volume 32, Number 4 (October 1990).

Jenkins, D. T., and K. G. Ponting. *The British Wool Textile Industry 1770–1914*. London: Heinemann Educational Books, 1982.

Jennings, Elizabeth. "Sir Isaac Holden." Diss., University of Bradford, 1982.

Jewitt, Llewellynn. *The Wedgwoods: Being a Life of Josiah Wedgwood*. London: Virtue Brothers and Co., 1865.

Jewkes, John, and E. M. Gray. *Wages and Labour in the Lancashire Spinning Industry*. Manchester: Manchester University Press, 1935.

Johann Junkers, 100 Jahre 1852–1952. Rheydt: N.p., 1952.

Johnstone, Russell D. *The Textile Industry in Meltham Fifty Years Ago*. Leeds: Institute of Dialect and Folk Studies, University of Leeds.

Jones, Gareth Stedman. *Languages of Class*. Cambridge: Cambridge University Press, 1983.

Jones, P. M. *The Peasantry in the French Revolution*. Cambridge: Cambridge University Press, 1988.

Jorke, Wolf-Ulrich. "Rezeptions- und Wirkungsgeschichte von Lassalles politischer Theorie in der deutschen Arbeiterbewegung." Diss., Bochum, 1973.

Joyce, Patrick. *Visions of the People: Industrial England and the Question of Class 1848–1914*. Cambridge: Cambridge University Press, 1991.

Joyce, Patrick. *Work, Society and Politics*. London: Methuen, 1980.

Joynes, James L. *Wage-Labour and Capital*. London: The Modern Press, 1886.

Jubb, Samuel. *The History of the Shoddy-Trade*. Batley: J. Fearnsides, 1860.

Judt, Tony. *Marxism and the French Left*. Oxford: Clarendon Press, 1986.

Jung, E. *Die Berechnung des Selbstkostenpreises der Gewebe*. Berlin: Julius Springer, 1917.

Jung, Johann Heinrich. *Versuch eines Lehrbuchs der Fabrikwissenschaft*. Nürnberg: Grattenauer, 1785.

Kahn-Freund, Otto. "Blackstone's Neglected Child: The Contract of Employment." *Law Quarterly Review* Volume 93 (October 1977).

Kaijage, Frederick James. "Labouring Barnsley, 1816–1856: A Social and Economic History." Ph.D. diss., University of Warwick, 1975.

Kaufhold, Karl Heinrich. *Das Gewerbe in Preussen um 1800*. Göttingen: Otto Schwartz & Co., 1978.

Kautsky, Karl. *Karl Marx' ökonomische Lehren*. Berlin: J. H. W. Dietz, 1980.

Keane, John. "Work and Interaction in Habermas." *Arena* Number 38 (1975).

Kellenbenz, Hermann. "The Organization of Industrial Production." In *The Cambridge Economic History of Europe*. Volume V. Cambridge: Cambridge University Press, 1977.

Kellett, J. R. "The Breakdown of Gild and Corporation Control over the Handicraft and Retail Trade of London." *The Economic History Review*, second series, Volume X, Number 3 (April 1958).

Kelsall, Keith. *Wage Regulation Under the Statute of Artificers*. London: Methuen & Co., 1938.

Kennedy, John G., and Robert Edgerton, editors. *Culture and Ecology: Eclectic Perspectives*. Washington, D.C.: American Anthropological Association, 1982.

Kenney, Annie. *Memories of a Militant*. London: Edward Arnold & Co., 1924.

Kenney, Rowland. *Westering: An Autobiography*. London: J. M. Dent and Sons, 1939.

Kermann, Joachim. *Die Manufakturen im Rheinland 1750–1833*. Bonn: Ludwig Röhrscheid, 1972.

Kershaw Lees & Co. *Weaving Prices Paid*. Stockport, 1854.

Kesselbauer, Günther. "Einige Probleme des Kampfes der preussischen Bourgeoisie zur Durchsetzung der kapitalistischen Produktionsverhältnisse 1789 bis 1806." *Jahrbuch für Wirtschaftsgeschichte* Teil II/III (1964).

Keynes, J. M. *The General Theory of Employment Interest and Money*. New York: Harcourt, Brace & World, 1936.

Kiesewetter, Hubert. *Industrialisierung und Landwirtschaft*. Köln: Böhlau Verlag, 1988.

Kimball, Janet. *The Economic Doctrines of John Gray 1799–1883*. Washington, D.C.: Catholic University of America Press, 1948.

Kimeldorf, Howard. *Reds or Rackets?* Berkeley: University of California Press, 1988.

Kindleberger, C. P. "The Historical Background: Adam Smith and the Industrial Revolution." *The Market and the State: Essays in Honour of Adam Smith*. Oxford: Clarendon Press, 1976.

King, J. E. "Utopian or Scientific? A Reconsideration of the Ricardian Socialists." *History of Political Economy* Volume 15, Number 3 (1983).

Kirby, M. W. "The Lancashire Cotton Industry in the Inter-War Years." *Business History* (July 1974).

Kirkness, Alan. *Geschichte des deutschen Wörterbuchs 1838–1863*. Stuttgart: S. Hirzel, 1980.

Kisch, Herbert. "The Crafts and Their Role in the Industrial Revolution: The Case of the German Textile Industry." Ph.D. diss., University of Washington, 1958.

Kisch, Herbert. *From Domestic Manufacture to Industrial Revolution: The Case of the Rhineland Textile Districts*. Oxford: Oxford University Press, 1989.

Kisch, Herbert. "The Textile Industries in Silesia and the Rhineland: A Comparative Study in Industrialization." *Journal of Economic History* Volume 19, No. 4 (December 1959).

Knäbel, A. *Die Tuchfabrikation und der Zeugdruck*. Leipzig: Karl Scholtze, 1882.

Kocka, Jürgen. *Die Angestellten in der deutschen Geschichte, 1850–1980*. Göttingen: Vandenhoeck & Ruprecht, 1981.

Kocka, Jürgen. "Craft Traditions and the Labour Movement in Nineteenth-Century Germany." In Pat Thane et al., editors, *The Power of the Past*. Cambridge: Cambridge University Press, 1984.

Kocka, Jürgen. "Einführung und Auswertung." In Ulrich Engelhardt, editor, *Handwerker in der Industrialisierung*. Stuttgart: Klett-Cotta, 1984.

Kocka, Jürgen. "Entrepreneurs and Managers in German Industrialization." *The Cambridge Economic History of Europe*. Volume VII, Part I. Cambridge: Cambridge University Press, 1978.

Kocka, Jürgen. "Problems of Working-Class Formation in Germany: The Early Years, 1800–1875." In *Working-Class Formation: Nineteenth-Century Patterns in Western Europe and the United States*. Princeton: Princeton University Press, 1986.

Koehne, Carl. *Arbeitsordnungen im deutschen Gewerberecht*. Berlin: Siemenroth und Troschel, 1901.

Kopf, Eike. "Die Ideen des 'Kapitals' von Karl Marx werden zur materiellen Gewalt: Zur Wirkungsgeschichte des 'Kapitals' in Deutschland bis 1872." *Wissenschaftliche Zeitschrift der Friedrich-Schiller-Universität Jena*, Gesellschafts- und Sprachwissenschaftliche Reihe, Volume 17, Number 2 (1968).

Körner, Hermann. *Lebenskämpfe in der Alten und Neuen Welt*. Volume I. New York: L. W. Schmidt, 1865.

Koselleck, Reinhard. *Preussen zwischen Reform und Revolution*. Stuttgart: Klett, 1975.

Kraus, Christian Jakob. *Staatswirtschaft*. Volume I. Breslau: G. Schletter, 1837.

Kress, Siegfried. "Die Bauten der sächsischen Kattundruck-Manufaktur." Diss., Technische Hochschule Dresden, 1958.

Kriedte, Peter. "Proto-Industrialisierung und grosses Kapital: Das Seidengewerbe in Krefeld und seinem Umland bis zum Ende des Ancien Regime." *Archiv für Sozialgeschichte* Volume 23 (1983).

Kriedte, Peter. *Eine Stadt am seidenen Faden*. Göttingen: Vandenhoeck & Ruprecht, 1991.

Kriedte, Peter, Hans Medick, and Jürgen Schlumbohm. *Industrialisierung vor der Industrialisierung*. Göttingen: Vandenhoeck und Ruprecht, 1977.

Krupp, Meta. "Wortfeld 'Arbeit.'" In Sprachwissenschaftliches Colloquium Bonn, editor, *Europäische Schlüsselwörter: Wortvergleichende und wortgeschichtliche Studien*. München: Max Hueber Verlag, 1964.

Kuczynski, Jürgen. *Die Geschichte der Lage der Arbeiter in England von 1640 bis in die Gegenwart*. Second edition. Berlin: Tribüne, 1954.

Kufahl, Ludwig. "Ueber die Anlage von Fabrikgebäuden." *Zeitschrift für praktische Baukunst*, Volume 4. Berlin: Allgemeine deutsche Verlags-Anstalt, 1844.

Kühnis, Silva. *Die wert- und preistheoretischen Ideen William Pettys*. Winterthur: P. G. Keller, 1960.

Laclau, Ernesto, and Chantal Mouffe. *Hegemony and Socialist Strategy*. London: Verso, 1985.

Laitin, David. *Hegemony and Culture*. Chicago: The University of Chicago Press, 1986.

Lakatos, Imre. "Falsification and the Methodology of Scientific Research Programmes." In Imre Lakatos and Alan Musgrave, editors, *Criticism and the Growth of Knowledge*. Cambridge: Cambridge University Press, 1970.

Lambertz, Jan. "Sexual Harassment in the Nineteenth Century English Cotton Industry." *History Workshop* Issue 19 (Spring 1985).

Landau, Johann. "Die Arbeiterfrage in Deutschland im XVII. und XVIII. Jahrhundert und ihre Behandlung in der deutschen Kameralwissenschaft." Diss., Zürich, 1915.

Landes, David. *Revolution in Time: Clocks and the Making of the Modern World*. Cambridge, Massachusetts: Belknap Press, 1983.

Landes, David. "The Structure of Enterprise in the Nineteenth Century: The Cases of Britain and Germany." In Comité International des Sciences Historiques, editor, *Rapports V: Histoire contemporaine*. Uppsala: Slmwvist & Wiksell, 1960.

Landes, David. "What Do Bosses Really Do?" *The Journal of Economic History* Volume XLVI, Number 3 (September 1986).

Lassalle, Ferdinand. *Reden und Schriften*, Volume 3, ed. Eduard Bernstein. Berlin: Verlag des 'Vorwärts,' 1893.

Laski, Harold. *The Rise of Liberalism: The Philosophy of a Business Civilization*. New York: Harper and Brothers, 1936.

Laslett, Peter. *The World We Have Lost*. London: Methuen and Co., 1971.

Lave, Jean. *Cognition in Practice*. Cambridge: Cambridge University Press, 1988.

Laybourn, Keith. "The Attitude of the Yorkshire Trade Unions to the Economic and Social Problems of the Great Depression, 1873–1896." Ph.D. diss., Lancaster University, 1973.

Laybourn, Keith. "'The Defence of the Bottom Dog': The Independent Labour Party in Local Politics." In D. G. Wright and J. A. Jowitt, editors, *Victorian Bradford*. Bradford: Bradford Metropolitan Council, 1982.

Lazonick, William. *Business Organization and the Myth of a Market Economy*. Cambridge: Cambridge University Press, 1991.

Lazonick, William. *Competitive Advantage on the Shop Floor*. Cambridge, Massachusetts: Harvard University Press, 1990.

Lazonick, William. "Production Relations, Labor Productivity, and Choice of Technique." *The Journal of Economic History* Volume XLI, Number 3 (September 1981).

Lee, J. J. "Labour in German Industrialization." *The Cambridge Economic History of Europe*. Volume VII, Part I. Cambridge: Cambridge University Press, 1978.

Lefebvre, Georges. *Les Paysans du Nord pendant la révolution française*. Bari: Editori Laterza, 1959.

Le Goff, Jacques. *Du Silence à la parole: Droit du travail, société, Etat 1830–1989*. Third edition. Quimper: Calligrammes, 1989.

Lehmann, Hermann. "Die Wollphantasiewaren im nordöstlichen Thüringen." *Schriften des Vereins für Socialpolitik* Volume 40, Part Two (1889).

Leigh, Evan. *The Science of Modern Cotton Spinning*. London: Simpkin, Marshall and Co., 1873.

Lenger, Friedrich. *Zwischen Kleinbürgertum und Proletariat*. Göttingen: Vandenhoeck & Ruprecht, 1986.

Leonard, Heinrich. *Wilhelm Bracke: Leben und Wirken*. Braunschweig: H. Rieke & Co., 1930.

Leroy-Beaulieu, Paul. *Traité théorique et pratique d'économie politique*. Volume 2. Paris: Guillaumin, 1900.

Letwin, William. *The Origins of Scientific Economics*. London: Methuen and Co., 1963.

Levenstein, Adolf. *Die Arbeiterfrage*. München: Ernst Reinhardt, 1912.

Lewenhak, Sheila. *Women and Trade Unions*. London: Ernest Benn, 1977.

Lewis, J. Slater. *The Commercial Organization of Factories*. London: E. & F. N. Spon, 1896.

Lidtke, Vernon. *The Alternative Culture: Socialist Labor in Imperial Germany*. New York: Oxford University Press, 1985.

Lie, John. "Embedding Polanyi's Market Society." *Sociological Perspectives* Volume 34, Number 2 (Summer 1991).

Lindsay, Jean. "An Early Factory Community: The Evans' Cotton Mill at Darley Abbey Derbyshire, 1783–1810." *Business History Review* Volume 34, Number 3 (1960).

Lipson, Ephraim. *The Economic History of England.* Volume III. London: Adam and Charles Black, 1948.

Litterer, Joseph. *The Emergence of Systematic Management as Shown by the Literature of Management from 1870–1900.* New York: Garland Publishing, 1986.

Löbner, Otto. *Praktische Erfahrungen aus der Tuch- und Buckskin-Fabrikation.* Grünberg: Das deutsche Wollen-Gewerbe, 1892.

Locke, John. *Some Considerations of the Consequences of the Lowering of Interest, and Raising the Value of Money.* [Orig. published 1696.] In Patrick Hyde Kelly, editor, *Locke on Money,* Volume One. Oxford: Clarendon Press, 1991.

Löhr, August. *Beiträge zur Würdigung der Akkordlohnmethode im rheinisch-westfälischen Maschinenbau.* Mönchengladbach: Volksvereins-Verlag, 1912.

Lotmar, Philipp. *Der Arbeitsvertrag nach dem Privatrecht des Deutschen Reiches.* Volume I. Leipzig: Duncker & Humblot, 1902.

Lotmar, Philipp. *Der Arbeitsvertrag nach dem Privatrecht des Deutschen Reiches.* Volume II. Leipzig: Duncker & Humblot, 1908.

Lotz, Johann Friedrich Eusebius. *Revision der Grundbegriffe der Nationalwirtschaftslehre.* Volume One. Leipzig: Sinner, 1811.

Lowenthal, Esther. *The Ricardian Socialists.* [Orig. published 1911.] Clifton, New Jersey: Augustus M. Kelley, 1972.

Lown, Judy. *Women and Industrialization.* Cambridge: Polity Press, 1990.

Lüdtke, Alf. "Arbeitsbeginn, Arbeitspausen, Arbeitsende." In Gerhard Huck, editor, *Sozialgeschichte der Freizeit.* Wuppertal: Peter Hammer Verlag, 1980.

Lüdtke, Alf. "Cash, Coffee Breaks, Horseplay: *Eigensinn* and Politics Among Factory Workers in Germany Circa 1900." In Michael Hanagan and Charles Stephenson, editors, *Confrontation, Class Consciousness, and the Labor Process.* Westport, Conn.: Greenwood Press, 1986.

Lueder, August. *Über Nationalindustrie und Staatswirtschaft.* Part One. Berlin: Heinrich Frölich, 1800.

Lukács, Georg. *Geschichte und Klassenbewusstsein.* Darmstadt: Hermann Luchterhand, 1977.

Lukács, Georg. *History and Class Consciousness.* Cambridge, Massachusetts: The M.I.T. Press, 1971.

Lütge, Friedrich. *Geschichte der deutschen Agrarverfassung vom frühen Mittelalter bis zum 19. Jahrhundert.* Second edition. Stuttgart: Eugen Ulmer, 1967.

Luzzatto, Gino. *An Economic History of Italy from the Fall of the Roman Empire to the Beginning of the Sixteenth Century.* London: Routledge & Kegan Paul, 1961.

McCulloch, J. R. Commentary to *An Inquiry into the Nature and Causes of the Wealth of Nations.* Volume One. Edinburgh: Adam Black and William Tait, 1828.

McCulloch, J. R., editor. *Early English Tracts on Commerce.* [Orig. published 1856.] Cambridge: Cambridge University Press, 1954.

McCulloch, J. R., editor. *A Select Collection of Scarce and Valuable Tracts on Money.* London: Political Economy Club, 1856.

Machtan, Lothar. "'Es war ein wundervolles Gefühl, dass man nicht allein war': Streik als Hoffnung und Erfahrung." In Wolfgang Ruppert, editor, *Die Arbeiter*. München: C. H. Beck, 1986.

Macintyre, Stuart. *A Proletarian Science*. Cambridge: Cambridge University Press, 1980.

McKelvie, D. "Some Aspects of Oral and Material Tradition in an Industrial Urban Area." Ph.D. diss., University of Leeds, 1963.

Mackie, John. *How to Make a Woollen Mill Pay*. London: Scott Greenwood & Co., 1904.

Mackrell, J. Q. C. *The Attack on "Feudalism" in Eighteenth-Century France*. London: Routledge & Kegan Paul, 1973.

McLeod, Hugh. *Class and Religion in the Late Victorian City*. London: Croom Helm, 1974.

McNally, David. *Political Economy and the Rise of Capitalism*. Berkeley: University of California Press, 1988.

Macpherson, C. B. "Harrington's 'Opportunity State.'" In Charles Webster, editor, *The Intellectual Revolution of the Seventeenth Century*. London: Routledge & Kegan Paul, 1974.

Macpherson, C. B. *The Political Theory of Possessive Individualism*. Oxford: Oxford University Press, 1962.

Macpherson, C. B. *The Rise and Fall of Economic Justice and Other Papers*. Oxford: Oxford University Press, 1985.

Macpherson, C. B. "Servants and Labourers in Seventeenth-Century England." *Democratic Theory: Essays in Retrieval*. Oxford: Clarendon Press, 1973.

Maier, Charles S. "The Factory as Society: Ideologies of Industrial Management in the Twentieth Century." In R. J. Bullen et al., editors, *Ideas into Politics*. London: Croom Helm, 1984.

Malcolmson, Robert. *Life and Labour in England 1700–1780*. London: Hutchinson, 1981.

"Manager." *Examples of Engineering Estimates, Costs and Accounts, for the Use of Young Engineers*. Huddersfield: C. F. Maurice, n.d.

Managers' and Overlookers' Society, Bradford. *Managers' and Overlookers' Society, Centenary Spinning Celebrations, 1827–1927*. Bradford: R. Sewell, 1927.

Mandel, Ernest. *The Formation of the Economic Thought of Karl Marx*. New York: Monthly Review Press, 1971.

Mangoldt, Hans. *Grundriss der Volkswirtschaftslehre*. Stuttgart: J. Engelhorn, 1863.

Mangoldt, Hans. *Grundriss der Volkswirtschaftslehre*. Stuttgart: Julius Maier, 1871.

Mann, Julia de Lacy. *The Cloth Industry in the West of England from 1640 to 1880*. Oxford: Clarendon Press, 1971.

Mann, Julia de Lacy. "Clothiers and Weavers in Wiltshire During the Eighteenth Century." In L. S. Pressnell, editor, *Studies in the Industrial Revolution*. London: Athlone Press, University of London, 1960.

Mann, Tom. *Tom Mann's Memoirs*. London: Labour Publishing Company, 1923.

Marcroft, William. *Management of a Company's Cotton Mill*. Oldham: Tetlow, Stubbs & Co., 1878.

Marsden, Richard. *Cotton Weaving: Its Development, Principles, and Practice*. London: George Bell & Sons, 1895.

Marshall, Alfred. *Principles of Economics.* Volume One. London: Macmillan & Co., 1895.

Marshall, J. D. "Colonisation as a Factor in the Planting of Towns in North-West England." In H. J. Dyos, editor, *The Study of Urban History.* London: Edward Arnold, 1968.

Marshall, Leslie. *The Practical Flax Spinner.* London: Emmott & Co., 1885.

Martini, Alexis. *La Notion du contrat de travail.* Paris: Editions des "Juris-Classeurs," 1912.

Marx, Karl. *Capital.* New York: International Publishers, 1967.

Marx, Karl. *Collected Works.* London: Lawrence & Wishart, 1975–78.

Marx, Karl. *Exzerpte und Notizen.* Berlin: Dietz Verlag, 1986.

Marx, Karl. *Grundrisse der Kritik der politischen Ökonomie.* Berlin: Dietz Verlag, 1974.

Marx, Karl. *Das Kapital.* Berlin: Dietz Verlag, 1980.

Marx, Karl. *Kritik des Gothaer Programms.* Moskau: Verlag für fremdsprachige Literatur, 1941.

Marx, Karl. *The Poverty of Philosophy.* Originally published 1847. New York: International Publishers, 1963.

Marx, Karl. *Theorien über den Mehrwert.* Stuttgart: J. H. W. Dietz, 1919–1921.

Marx, Karl, and Friedrich Engels. *Briefwechsel mit Wilhelm Bracke 1869–1880.* Berlin: Dietz Verlag, 1963.

Marx, Karl, and Friedrich Engels. *Gesamtausgabe.* Series One, Volume Three. Berlin: Marx-Engels Verlag, 1932.

Marx, Karl, and Friedrich Engels. *Marx-Engels Werke.* Berlin: Dietz Verlag, 1959–1990.

Mathias, Peter. *The Transformation of England.* New York: Columbia University Press, 1979.

Matoré, Georges. *Le Vocabulaire et la société sous Louis-Philippe.* Genève: Slatkine Reprints, 1967.

Matsukawa, Shichiro. "An Essay on the Historical Uniqueness of Petty's Labour Theory of Value." *Hitotsubashi Journal of Economics* Volume 5, Number 2 (January 1965).

Matsukawa, Shichiro. "Sir William Petty: An Unpublished Manuscript." *Hitotsubashi Journal of Economics* Volume 17, Number 2 (February 1977).

Matthias, Erich. "Kautsky und der Kautskyanismus." *Marxismus-Studien,* second series. Berlin: Institut für Marxismus-Leninismus, 1957.

Mattutat, H. "Das Prämiensystem in der Augsburger Textil-Industrie." *Soziale Praxis,* Volume 5 (1895–1896).

Matzerath, Horst. "Industrialisierung, Mobilität und sozialer Wandel am Beispiel der Städte Rheydt und Rheindahlen." *Probleme der Modernisierung in Deutschland.* Opladen: Westdeutscher Verlag, 1979.

Maucher, Herbert. *Zeitlohn Akkordlohn Prämienlohn.* Darmstadt: Druck- und Verlags-Gesellschaft Darmstadt, 1965.

Maurice, Marc. "Méthode comparative et analyse sociétale: Les Implications théoriques des comparisons internationales." In *Sociologie du travail* Volume 31, Number 2 (1989).

Maurice, Marc. *The Social Foundations of Industrial Power.* Cambridge: M.I.T. Press, 1986.

Maurice, Marc, François Sellier, and Jean-Jacques Silvestre. *The Social Foundations of Industrial Power*. [Orig. published 1982.] Cambridge, Massachusetts: The M.I.T. Press, 1986.

Medick, Hans. "Freihandel für die Zunft." In *Mentalitäten und Lebensverhältnisse: Beispiele aus der Sozialgeschichte der Neuzeit,* Festschrift für Rudolf Vierhaus. Göttingen: Vandenhoeck & Ruprecht, 1982.

Meek, Ronald L. *Economics and Ideology and Other Essays*. London: Chapman and Hall, 1967.

Meek, Ronald L. "Ideas, Events and Environment: The Case of the French Physiocrats." In Robert V. Eagly, editor, *Events, Ideology and Economic Theory*. Detroit: Wayne State University Press, 1968.

Mende, Michael. "Männer des Feuers und der eisernen Kraft." In Wolfgang Ruppert, editor, *Die Arbeiter*. München: C. H. Beck, 1986.

Menger, Anton. *The Right to the Whole Produce of Labour*. Introduction by H. S. Foxwell. [Orig. published 1899.] New York: Augustus Kelley, 1962.

Messenger, Betty. *Picking Up the Linen Threads: A Study in Industrial Folklore*. Austin: University of Texas Press, 1978.

Meyer, H. *Einrichtung und Betrieb einer Seidenstoff-Fabrik*. Zürich: Juchli & Beck, 1908.

Meyknecht, Ernst. "Die Krisen in der deutschen Woll- und Baumwollindustrie." Diss., München, 1928.

Michel, Hans. *Die hausindustrielle Weberei*. Jena, 1921.

Mill, James. *Elements of Political Economy*. Third edition. London: Henry Bohn, 1844.

Mill, John Stuart. *Essays on Some Unsettled Questions of Political Economy*. Second edition. London: Longmans, Green, Reader & Dyer, 1874.

Mill, John Stuart. *Principles of Political Economy*. London: Longmans, Green & Co., 1920.

Minchinton, W. E. "Introduction." *Wage Regulation in Pre-Industrial England*. Newton Abbot: David & Charles, 1972.

Mirus, Leon. "Die Futterstoffweberei in Elberfeld und Barmen." Diss., Leipzig, 1909.

Dammer, Otto, editor. *Handbuch der Arbeiterwohlfahrt*. Volume II. Stuttgart: Enke Verlag, 1903.

Moll, Alex. *950 Jahre Oerlinghausen*. Oerlinghausen: Loewe, 1986.

Monz, Heinz. *Karl Marx: Grundlagen der Entwicklung zu Leben und Werk*. Trier: NCO-Verlag Neu, 1973.

Moody, F. W. "Some Textile Terms from Addingham in the West Riding." *Transactions, Yorkshire Dialect Society* Volume 8 (1950).

Moore, Barrington. *Social Origins of Dictatorship and Democracy*. Boston: Beacon Press, 1966.

Mooser, Josef. *Ländliche Klassengesellschaft 1770–1848: Bauern und Unterschichten, Landwirtschaft und Gewerbe im östlichen Westfalen*. Göttingen: Vandenhoeck & Ruprecht, 1984.

Mooser, Josef. "Maschinensturm und Assoziation: Die Spinner und Weber zwischen sittlicher Ökonomie, Konservatismus und Demokratie in der Krise des Leinengewerbes in Ravensberg, 1840–1870." In Karl Ditt and Sidney Pollard, editors, *Von der Heimarbeit in die Fabrik*. Paderborn: Ferdinand Schöningh, 1992.

Morgan, Roger. *The German Social Democrats and the First International 1864–1872*. Cambridge: Cambridge University Press, 1965.

Most, Johann. *Kapital und Arbeit: "Das Kapital" in einer handlichen Zusammenfassung*. Frankfurt am Main: Suhrkamp Verlag, 1972.

Mottez, Bernard. *Systèmes de salaire et politiques patronales*. Paris: Centre Nationale de la Recherche Scientifique, 1966.

Muir, Augustus. *The History of Bowers Mills*. Cambridge: W. Heffer, 1969.

Müller, Alfred. "Die Lohnbemessungsmethoden in der Chemnitzer Textilindustrie." Diss., Marburg, 1924.

Müller-Wiener, Wolfgang. "Die Entwicklung des Industriebaus im 19. Jahrhundert in Baden." Diss., Karlsruhe, 1955.

Munby, Zoe. "The Sunnyside Women's Strike." *Bolton People's History* Volume 1 (March 1984).

Münch, Ernst. "Feudalverhältnis—Feudalherrschaft—Feudalstaat." *Jahrbuch für Geschichte des Feudalismus* Volume 14 (1990).

Munro, J. E. Crawford. *Sliding Scales in the Coal Industry*. London: John Heywood, 1885.

Munro, J. E. Crawford. "Sliding Scales in the Iron Industry." Address to the Manchester Statistical Society, December 9, 1885, Manchester Library.

Nahrgang, Alfred. "Die Aufnahme der wirtschaftspolitischen Ideen von Adam Smith in Deutschland zu Beginn des XIX. Jahrhunderts." Diss., Frankfurt am Main, 1933/34.

Nairn, Tom. *The Enchanted Glass: Britain and Its Monarchy*. London: Century Hutchinson, 1988.

Napoleoni, Claudio. *Smith Ricardo Marx*. Oxford: Basil Blackwell, 1975.

Nasmith, Frank. *Recent Cotton Mill Construction and Engineering*. Manchester: John Heywood, 1909.

Nath, Raghu, editor. *Comparative Management: A Regional View*. Cambridge, Massachusetts: Ballinger Publishing Co., 1988.

Newberry, Maggie. *Reminiscences of a Bradford Mill Girl*. Bradford: Local Studies Department, 1980.

Nolan, Mary. "Economic Crisis, State Policy, and Working-Class Formation in Germany, 1870–1900." In Ira Katznelson and Aristide R. Zolber, editors, *Working-Class Formation*. Princeton: Princeton University Press, 1986.

North, Roger. *A Discourse of the Poor Shewing the Pernicious Tendency of the Laws Now in Force*. London: M. Cooper, 1753.

Norton, George Pepler. *Textile Manufacturers' Book-keeping*. Bradford: Brear & Co., 1894.

Noyes, P. H. *Organization and Revolution: Working-Class Associations in the German Revolutions of 1848–1849*. Princeton: Princeton University Press, 1966.

Oakley, Allen. *The Making of Marx's Critical Theory*. London: Routledge & Kegan Paul, 1983.

Oakley, Allen. *Marx's Critique of Political Economy*. Volume I. London: Routledge & Kegan Paul, 1984.

Oberschall, Anthony. *Empirical Social Research in Germany, 1848–1914*. New York: Mouton & Co., 1965.

Offermann, Toni. "Mittelständisch-kleingewerbliche Leitbilder in der liberalen Handwerker- und handwerklichen Arbeiterbewegung der 50er und 60er Jahre des 19. Jahrhunderts." In Ulrich Engelhardt, editor, *Handwerker in der Industrialisierung*. Stuttgart: Klett-Cotta, 1984.

Ogg, David. *England in the Reigns of James II and William III*. Oxford: Clarendon Press, 1955.

Olivier-Martin, François. *L'Organisation corporative de la France d'ancien régime*. Paris: Librairie du Recueil Sirey, 1938.

Operative Spinners of England, Ireland, and Scotland. *A Report of the Proceedings of a Delegate Meeting of the Operative Spinners of England, Ireland and Scotland, Assembled at Ramsey, Isle of Man*. Manchester: M. Wardle, 1829.

Orth, F. *Der Werdegang wichtiger Erfindungen auf dem Gebiete der Spinnerei und Weberei*. Berlin: Verein Deutscher Ingenieure, 1922.

Ortner, Sherry B. "Patterns of History: Cultural Schemas in the Foundings of Sherpa Religious Institutions." In Emiko Ohnuki-Tierney, editor, *Culture Through Time: Anthropological Approaches*. Stanford: Stanford University Press, 1990.

Ortner, Sherry B. "Theory in Anthropology Since the Sixties." *Comparative Studies in Society and History* Volume 26, Number 1 (January 1984).

Owen, Robert. *Report to the County of Lanark of a Plan for Relieving Public Distress*. Glasgow: Wardlaw & Cunninghame, 1821.

Paas, Rolf. "Die Beeinflussung der sozialen und wirtschaftlichen Lage der Weber durch die Mechanisierung der deutschen Textilindustrie." Diss., Universität Köln, 1961.

Palgrave, Sir Robert Harry Inglis. *Palgrave's Dictionary of Political Economy*. London: Macmillan & Co., 1917.

Pankhurst, Richard. *William Thompson*. London: Watts & Co., 1954.

Parker, Harold T. *The Bureau of Commerce in 1781 and Its Policies with Respect to French Industry*. Durham, North Carolina: Carolina Academic Press, 1979.

Pauling, N. J. "The Employment Problem in Pre-Classical English Economic Thought." *The Economic Record* Volume XXVII, Number 52 (1951).

Payne, Peter L. "Industrial Entrepreneurship and Management in Great Britain." *The Cambridge Economic History of Europe*. Volume VII, Part I. Cambridge: Cambridge University Press, 1978.

Pearce, Cyril. *The Manningham Mills Strike, Bradford: December 1890-April 1891*. Hull: University of Hull, 1975.

Peard, Charles. *The Woollen Labourer's Advocate*. London: Printed for the author and sold by J. Dormer, 1733.

Pelling, Henry, editor. *The Challenge of Socialism*. London: Adam & Charles Black, 1968.

Peltzer, Artur. "Die Arbeiterbewegung in der Aachener Textilindustrie von der Mitte des 19. Jahrhunderts bis zum Ausbruch des Weltkrieges." Diss., Universität Marburg, 1924.

Perkin, Harold. *The Origins of Modern English Society 1780–1880*. London: Routledge & Kegan Paul, 1969.

Perkins, J. A. "Dualism in German Agrarian Historiography." *Comparative Studies in Society and History* Volume 28, Number 2 (April 1986).

Perks, Robert Brian. "The New Liberalism and the Challenge of Labour in the West Riding of Yorkshire 1885–1914." Ph.D. diss., Huddersfield Polytechnic, 1985.

Perrot, Michelle. *Les Ouvriers en grève*. Paris: Mouton & Co., 1974.

Perrot, Michelle. "The Three Ages of Industrial Discipline in Nineteenth-Century France." In John M. Merriman, editor, *Consciousness and Class Experience in Nineteenth-Century Europe*. New York: Holmes & Meier, 1979.

Petitcollot, Maurice. *Les Syndicats ouvriers de l'industrie textile dans l'arrondissement de Lille*. Lille: Coopérative "La Gutenberg," 1907.

Petry, Franz. *Der soziale Gehalt der Marxschen Werttheorie*. Jena: Gustav Fischer, 1916.

Petty, Sir William. *The Petty Papers*. Volume I. New York: Augustus Kelley, 1967.

Petyt, William. *Britannia Languens; Or, A Discourse of Trade*. London: For T. Dring and S. Couch, 1680.

Petzold, Herbert. "Die Bielefelder Textilindustrie." Diss., Rostock, 1926.

Pfuhl, E. *Die Jute und ihre Verarbeitung*, 3 volumes. Berlin: J. Springer, 1888–1891.

Phelps Brown, E. H. "The Labour Market." In Thomas Wilson and Andrew S. Skinner, editors, *The Market and the State: Essays in Honour of Adam Smith*. Oxford: Clarendon Press, 1976.

Pierson, Stanley. *British Socialists: The Journey from Fantasy to Politics*. Cambridge, Massachusetts: Harvard University Press, 1979.

Pigott, Stanley. *Hollins: A Study in Industry*. Nottingham: William Hollins & Co., 1949.

Platt Brothers and Company. *Particulars and Calculations Relating to Cotton Ginning, Opening, Carding, Combing, Preparing, Spinning, and Weaving Machinery*. Manchester: Platt Brothers, ca. 1918.

Plattner, Stuart. "Markets and Marketplaces." In Stuart Plattner, editor, *Economic Anthropology*. Stanford: Stanford University Press, 1989.

Plössl, Elisabeth. *Weibliche Arbeit in Familie und Betrieb: Bayerische Arbeiterfrauen 1870–1914*. München: Schriftenreihe des Stadtarchivs, 1983.

Pocock, J. G. A. "Early Modern Capitalism—The Augustan Perception." In Eugene Kamenka and R. S. Neale, editors, *Feudalism, Capitalism and Beyond*. Canberra: Australian National University Press, 1975.

Polanyi, Karl. *The Great Transformation*. Boston: Beacon Press, 1957.

Pollard, Sidney. "Capital Accounting in the Industrial Revolution." *Yorkshire Bulletin of Economic and Social Research* Volume 15, Number 2 (November 1963).

Pollard, Sidney. "England: Der unrevolutionäre Pionier." In Jürgen Kocka, editor, *Europäische Arbeiterbewegungen im 19. Jahrhundert*. Göttingen: Vandenhoeck & Ruprecht, 1983.

Pollard, Sidney. "Factory Discipline in the Industrial Revolution." *The Economic History Review*, second series, Volume XVI, Number 2 (1963).

Pollard, Sidney. "The Factory Village in the Industrial Revolution." *The English Historical Review* Volume 79, Number 312 (July 1964).

Pollard, Sidney. *The Genesis of Modern Management*. London: Edward Arnold, 1965.

Poni, Carlo. "All'origine del sistema di fabbrica: Tecnologia e organizzazione produttiva dei mulini da seta nell'italia settentrionale (sec. XVII–XVIII)." *Rivista Storica Italiana* Volume LXXXVII, fascicolo III (September 1976).

Poni, Carlo. "Mass gegen Mass: Wie der Seidenfaden rund und dünn wurde." In Robert Berdahl et al., editors, *Klassen und Kultur*. Frankfurt am Main: Syndikat, 1982.

Pönicke, Martin Herbert. *Die Geschichte der Tuchmacherei und verwandter Gewerbe in Reichenbach i. V. vom 17. bis Anfang des 19. Jahrhunderts.* Plauen: Franz Neupert, 1929.

Poollitt, A, presider. "The Scarcity of Labour and How to Solve the Difficulty." *Journal of the British Association of Managers of Textile Works* Volume 7 (1915–1916).

Porta, Pier Luigi, editor. *David Ricardo: Notes on Malthus's "Measure of Value."* Cambridge: Cambridge University Press, 1992.

Porter, Roy. *English Society in the Eighteenth Century.* London: Penguin Books, 1982.

Potthoff, Franz. *Die soziale Frage der Werkmeister.* Düsseldorf: Werkmeister-Buchhandlung, 1910.

Potthoff, Heinz. *Das Versicherungsgesetz für Angestellte vom 20. Dezember 1911.* Stuttgart: J. Hess, 1912.

Pourdeyhimi, Behnam. "A Study of the Evolution of the Automatic Loom and Its Diffusion Within the British Cotton Industry." Ph.D. diss., University of Leeds, 1982.

Powell, Walter W., and Paul J. DiMaggio, editors. *The New Institutionalism in Organizational Analysis.* Chicago: University of Chicago Press, 1991.

Der praktische Maschinen-Constructeur. *Bau- und Betriebs-Anlage für Spinnereien und Webereien.* Leipzig: Baumgärten, 1875.

Preston, Raymond. *Life Story and Personal Reminiscences.* London: Epworth Press, 1930.

Price, Richard. "The New Unionism and the Labour Process." In Wolfgang J. Mommsen and Hans-Gerhard Husung, editors, *The Development of Trade Unionism in Great Britain and Germany, 1880–1914.* London: George Allen & Unwin, 1985.

Price, Richard. "Structures of Subordination in Nineteenth-Century British Industry." In Pat Thane et al., editors, *The Power of the Past.* Cambridge: Cambridge University Press, 1984.

Projektgruppe Entwicklung des Marxschen Systems. *Der 4. Band des "Kapital"?* Berlin: Verlag für das Studium der Arbeiterbewegung, 1975.

Prosser, J. E. *Piece-Rate, Premium and Bonus.* London: Williams & Norgate, 1919.

Proudhon, Pierre-Joseph. *Système des contradictions économiques, ou philosophie de la misère.* Second edition. Paris: Garnier Frères, 1850.

Przeworski, Adam. *Capitalism and Social Democracy.* Cambridge University Press, 1985.

Pugh, Arthur. *Men of Steel, by One of Them.* London: Iron and Steel Trades Confederation, 1951.

Puschner, Uwe. *Handwerk zwischen Tradition und Wandel.* Göttingen: Otto Schwartz & Co., 1988.

Quandt, Georg. *Die Niederlausitzer Schafwollindustrie in ihrer Entwicklung zum Grossbetrieb und zur modernen Technik.* Leipzig: Duncker & Humblot, 1895.

Quataert, Jean. "Workers' Reactions to Social Insurance: The Case of Homeweavers in the Saxon Oberlausitz in the Late Nineteenth Century." *Internationale Wissenschaftliche Korrespondenz zur Geschichte der deutschen Arbeiterbewegung* Volume 20, Number 1 (1984).

Quentin, C. *Ein Wort zur Zeit der Arbeiter-Koalitionen*. Düsseldorf: J. H. C. Schreiner, 1840.

Rachel, Hugo. *Das Berliner Wirtschaftsleben im Zeitalter des Frühkapitalismus*. Berlin: Rembrandt-Verlag, 1931.

Radcliffe, William. *Origin of the New System of Manufacturing Commonly Called "Power-Loom Weaving."* Stockport: J. Lomax, 1828.

Rainone, Corrado. *Pensiero e strutture socio-economiche europee e italiane nell'epoca risorgimentale 1748–1861*. Milano: A. Giuffrè, 1975.

Ramsay, G. D. "Industrial Laisser-Faire and the Policy of Cromwell." *The Economic History Review* Volume XVI, Number 2 (1946).

Ramsay, G. D. *The Wiltshire Woollen Industry in the Sixteenth and Seventeenth Centuries*. London: Frank Cass & Co., 1965.

Randall, Adrian. *Before the Luddites*. Cambridge: Cambridge University Press, 1991.

Rau, Karl Heinrich. *Grundsätze der Volkswirtschaftslehre*. Heidelberg: C. F. Winter, 1826.

Rau, Karl Heinrich. *Grundsätze der Volkswirtschaftslehre*. Volume I, 5th edition. Heidelberg: C. F. Winter, 1847.

Raudin, Johann. *Praktisches Handbuch der Tuchfabrikation*. Leipzig: G. Basse, 1838.

Rebber, Wilhelm. *Fabrikanlagen: Ein Handbuch für Techniker und Fabrikbesitzer*. Second edition. Leipzig: B. F. Voigt, 1901.

Rebel, Hermann. "Reimagining the *Oikos*: Austrian Cameralism in Its Social Formation." In Jay O'Brien and William Roseberry, editors, *Golden Ages, Dark Ages*. Berkeley: University of California Press, 1991.

Reddy, William. "Entschlüsseln von Lohnforderungen: Der *Tarif* und der Lebenszyklus in den Leinenfabriken von Armentières, 1889–1904." In Robert Berdahl et al., editors, *Klassen und Kultur*. Frankfurt am Main: Syndikat, 1982.

Reddy, William. "Modes de paiement et contrôle du travail dans les filatures de coton en France, 1750–1848." *Revue du Nord* Volume LXIII, Number 248 (January–March 1981).

Reddy, William. *Money and Liberty in Modern Europe*. Cambridge: Cambridge University Press, 1987.

Reddy, William. *The Rise of Market Culture*. Cambridge: Cambridge University Press, 1984.

Reddy, William. "Skeins, Scales, Discounts, Steam, and Other Objects of Crowd Justice in Early French Textile Mills." *Comparative Studies in Society and History* Volume 21, Number 1 (January 1979).

Reddy, William. "The Structure of a Cultural Crisis: Thinking About Cloth in France Before and After the Revolution." In Arjun Appadurai, editor, *The Social Life of Things*. Cambridge: Cambridge University Press, 1986.

Reddy, William. "The Textile Trade and the Language of the Crowd at Rouen: 1752–1871." *Past & Present* Number 74 (February 1977).

Reichel, Ortrud. "Zum Bedeutungswechsel der Worte 'Werk' und 'Wirken' in as, ahd, und mhd Zeit." Diss., Tübingen, 1952.

Reiser, Nicolas. *Die Betriebs- und Warenkalkulation für Textilstoffe*. Leipzig: A. Felix, 1903.

Reulecke, Jürgen. "Die Entstehung des Erholungsurlaubs für Arbeiter in Deutschland vor dem Ersten Weltkrieg." In Dieter Langewiesche and Klaus

Schönhoven, editors, *Arbeiter in Deutschland: Studien zur Lebensweise der Arbeiterschaft im Zeitalter der Industrialisierung.* Paderborn: Schöningh, 1981.

Reynolds, J., and K. Laybourn. "The Emergence of the Independent Labour Party in Bradford." *International Review of Social History* Volume 20, Part 3 (1975).

Rheinisch-Westfälisches Wirtschaftsarchiv zu Köln. *Kölner Unternehmer und die Frühindustrialisierung im Rheinland und in Westfalen 1835–1871.* Köln: Rheinisch-Westfälisches Wirtschaftsarchiv zu Köln, 1984.

Ricardo, David. *On the Principles of Political Economy and Taxation.* Third edition. London: John Murray, 1821.

Ricardo, David. *The Works and Correspondence of David Ricardo.* Piero Sraffa, editor. Volume IV. Cambridge: Cambridge University Press, 1951.

Riley, B. *Handbook, Sixteenth Independent Labour Party Conference.* Huddersfield, 1908.

Rimmer, W. G. *Marshalls of Leeds: Flax-Spinners 1788–1889.* Cambridge: Cambridge University Press, 1960.

Roberts, David. *Paternalism in Early Victorian England.* New Brunswick, New Jersey: Rutgers University Press, 1979.

Roemer, John. *A General Theory of Exploitation and Class.* Cambridge, Massachusetts: Harvard University Press, 1982.

Roesler, Carl Friedrich Hermann. *Zur Kritik der Lehre vom Arbeitslohn: Ein volkswirtschaftlicher Versuch.* Erlangen: Ferdinand Enke, 1861.

Rogers, James E. Thorold. *A History of Agriculture and Prices in England.* Volume V: *1583–1702.* Oxford: Clarendon Press, 1887.

Rogers, James E. Thorold. *Six Centuries of Work and Wages: The History of English Labour.* London: George Allen & Unwin, 1884.

Rohr, Werner. "Die Geschichte der Arbeiterbewegung in Nordhorn." Diss., Universität Bremen, 1981.

Rohrscheidt, Kurt von. *Vom Zunftzwange zur Gewerbefreiheit.* Berlin: Carl Heymanns Verlag, 1898.

Roll, Eric. *A History of Economic Thought.* New York: Prentice-Hall, 1942.

Roncaglia, Alessandro. *Petty: The Origins of Political Economy.* Armonk, New York: M. E. Sharpe, 1985.

Roscher, W. "Die Ein- und Durchführung des Adam Smith'schen Systems in Deutschland." *Berichte über die Verhandlungen der königlich sächsischen Gesellschaft der Wissenschaften zu Leipzig.* Philologisch-historische Classe Volume 9. Berlin: Akademie-Verlag, 1867.

Roscher, Wilhelm. *Geschichte der National-Oekonomik in Deutschland.* München: R. Oldenbourg, 1874.

Roscher, Wilhelm. *Grundlagen der Nationalökonomie.* Stuttgart: J. G. Cotta, 1922.

Rosdolsky, Roman. *Zur Entstehungsgeschichte des Marxschen "Kapital."* Volume One. Frankfurt: Europäische Verlagsanstalt, 1968.

Rose, Mary. *The Greggs of Quarry Bank Mill: The Rise and Decline of a Family Firm, 1750–1914.* Cambridge: Cambridge University Press, 1986.

Rossi, P. *Oeuvres complètes.* Volumes I and II. Fifth edition. Paris: Guillaumin, 1884.

Rotteck, Carl, and Carl Welcker, editors. *Das Staats-Lexikon.* Volume One. Altona: J. F. Hammerich, 1834.

Rule, John. *The Experience of Labour in Eighteenth-Century Industry.* London: Croom Helm, 1981.

Rule, John. *The Labouring Classes in Early Industrial England, 1750–1850.* London: Longman, 1986.

Rule, John. "Some Social Aspects of the Cornish Industrial Revolution." In Roger Burt, editor, *Industry and Society in the South-West.* Exeter: University of Exeter, 1970.

Ruppert, Wolfgang. *Die Fabrik.* München: Verlag C. H. Beck, 1983.

Russell, David. "The Pursuit of Leisure." In D. G. Wright and J. A. Jowitt, editors, *Victorian Bradford.* Bradford: Bradford Metropolitan Council, 1982.

Sabean, David. "Intensivierung der Arbeit und Alltagserfahrung auf dem Lande—ein Beispiel aus Württemberg." *Sozialwissenschaftliche Informationen für Unterricht und Studium* Volume 6, Number 4 (1977).

Sabel, Charles, and Jonathan Zeitlin. "Historical Alternatives to Mass Production: Politics, Markets and Technology in Nineteenth-Century Industrialization." *Past & Present* Number 108 (August 1985).

Sagnac, P. *Le Rhin français pendant la révolution et l'empire.* Paris: Félix Alcan, 1917.

Sahlins, Marshall. *Culture and Practical Reason.* Chicago: University of Chicago Press, 1976.

Sahlins, Marshall. *Historical Metaphors and Mythical Realities.* Ann Arbor: University of Michigan Press, 1981.

Sahlins, Marshall. *Islands of History.* Chicago: University of Chicago Press, 1985.

St. Clair, Oswald. *A Key to Ricardo.* London: Routledge & Kegan Paul, 1957.

Ste. Croix, G. E. M. de. *The Class Struggle in the Ancient World.* Ithaca: Cornell University Press, 1981.

Saint Jacob, P. de. *Les Paysans de la Bourgogne du Nord au dernier siècle de l'ancien régime.* Paris: Société "Les Belles Lettres," 1960.

Sanders, Daniel. *Wörterbuch der deutschen Sprache.* Volume I. Leipzig: Otto Wigand, 1860.

Sartorius, Georg. *Elemente des National-Reichtums.* Part One. Göttingen: Johann Röwer, 1806.

Sartorius, Georg. *Handbuch der Staatswirtschaft, zum Gebrauche bei akademischen Vorlesungen nach Adam Smiths Grundsätzen ausgearbeitet.* Berlin, 1796.

Savage, Michael. *Control at Work.* Lancaster: University of Lancaster Regionalism Group, Working Paper 7, 1982.

Savage, Michael. *The Dynamics of Working-Class Politics.* Cambridge: Cambridge University Press, 1987.

Saxonhouse, Gary, and Gavin Wright. "Stubborn Mules and Vertical Integration: The Disappearing Constraint?" *Economic History Review* 40, No. 1 (February 1987).

Say, Jean Baptiste. *Catéchisme d'économie politique.* Paris: Guillaumin, 1881.

Say, Jean Baptiste. *Cours complet d'économie politique pratique.* Volume I. Second edition. Paris: Guillaumin, 1852.

Scheller, Ernst F. *Vorstellung und Begriff der wirtschaftlichen Arbeit.* Erlangen: M. Krahl, 1936.

Schildt, Gerhard. *Tagelöhner, Gesellen, Arbeiter.* Stuttgart: Klett-Cotta, 1986.

Schissler, Hanna. *Preussische Agrargesellschaft im Wandel: Wirtschaftliche, gesellschaftliche und politische Transformationsprozesse von 1763 bis 1847.* Göttingen: Vandenhoeck & Ruprecht, 1978.

Schloss, David F. *Methods of Industrial Remuneration*. London: Williams and Norgate, 1892.

Schlumbohm, Jürgen. "Seasonal Fluctuations and Social Division of Labour: Rural Linen Production in the Osnabrück and Bielefeld Regions and the Urban Woollen Industry in the Niederlausitz c. 1770–c. 1850." In Maxine Berg et al., editor, *Manufacture in Town and Country Before the Factory*. Cambridge: Cambridge University Press, 1983.

Schmid, Karl. *Die Entwicklung der Hofer Baumwoll-Industrie 1432–1913*. Leipzig: A. Deichertsche Verlagsbuchhandlung, 1923.

Schmiede, Rudi, and Edwin Schudlich. *Die Entwicklung der Leistungsentlohnung in Deutschland*. Frankfurt: Aspekte Verlag, 1976.

Schmoller, Gustav. *Umrisse und Untersuchungen zur Verfassungs-, Verwaltungs- und Wirtschaftsgeschichte*. Leipzig: Duncker & Humblot, 1898.

Schneider, David M. "Notes Toward a Theory of Culture." In Keith H. Basso and Henry A. Selby, editors, *Meaning in Anthropology*. Albuquerque: University of New Mexico Press, 1976.

Schneider, Dieter, et al. *Zur Theorie und Praxis des Streiks*. Frankfurt am Main: Suhrkamp, 1971.

Schneider, Michael. *Die Christlichen Gewerkschaften 1894–1933*. Bonn: Neue Gesellschaft, 1982.

Schneider, Walter. *Die Apoldaer Wirkwarenindustrie bis zum Jahre 1914*. Jena: Gustav Fischer, 1922.

Schönhoven, Klaus. "Localism—Craft Union—Industrial Union: Organizational Patterns in German Trade Unionism." In Wolfgang J. Mommsen and Hans-Gerhard Husung, editors, *The Development of Trade Unionism in Great Britain and Germany, 1880–1914*. London: George Allen & Unwin, 1985.

Schorske, Carl. *German Social Democracy 1905–1917*. New York: John Wiley and Sons, 1955.

Schröter, Alfred, and Walter Becker. *Die deutsche Maschinenbauindustrie in der industriellen Revolution*. Berlin: Akademie-Verlag, 1962.

Schulz, Günther. "Die betriebliche Lage der Arbeiter im Rheinland vom 19. bis zum beginnenden 20. Jahrhundert." *Rheinische Vierteljahrsblätter* Jahrgang 50 (1986).

Schumpeter, Joseph. *History of Economic Analysis*. New York: Oxford University Press, 1954.

Schwanke, Hans-Peter. "Architektur für Stadt, Gesellschaft und Industrie: Das Werk der Krefelder Architekten Girmes & Oediger 1892–1933." Diss., Bonn, 1987.

Schwarz, L. D. "Income Distribution and Social Structure in London in the Late Eighteenth Century." *Economic History Review* Volume XXXII, Number 2 (May 1979).

Schwarz, L. D. *London in the Age of Industrialisation*. Cambridge: Cambridge University Press, 1992.

Scott, Joan Wallach. *Gender and the Politics of History*. New York: Columbia University Press, 1988.

Scott, N. K. "The Architectural Development of Cotton Mills in Preston and District." Master's thesis, University of Liverpool, 1952.

Sée, Henri. *Economic and Social Conditions in France During the Eighteenth Century*. New York: Cooper Square Publishers, 1968.

Seidel, Jutta. *Wilhelm Bracke: Vom Lassalleaner zum Marxisten*. Berlin: Dietz Verlag, 1966.

Seilhac, Léon de. *La Grève du tissage de Lille*. Paris: Arthur Rousseau, 1910.

Sella, Domenico. *Crisis and Continuity: The Economy of Spanish Lombardy in the Seventeenth Century*. Cambridge, Massachusetts: Harvard University Press, 1979.

Senior, Nassau William. *An Outline of the Science of Political Economy*. [Orig. published 1836.] New York: Farrar & Rinehart, 1939.

Stephan, Cora. *"Genossen, wir dürfen uns nicht von der Geduld hinreissen lassen!"* Frankfurt am Main: Syndikat, 1977.

Seward, David. "The Devonshire Cloth Industry in the Early Seventeenth Century." In Roger Burt, editor, *Industry and Society in the South-West*. Essex: University of Essex, 1970.

Sewell, William H., Jr. "How Classes Are Made: Critical Reflections on E. P. Thompson's Theory of Working-Class Formation." In Harvey J. Kaye and Keith McClelland, editors, *E. P. Thompson: Critical Perspectives*. Philadelphia: Temple University Press, 1990.

Sewell, William H., Jr. "A Theory of Structure: Duality, Agency, and Transformation." *American Journal of Sociology* Volume 98, Number 1 (July 1992).

Sewell, William H., Jr. *Work and Revolution in France*. Cambridge: Cambridge University Press, 1980.

Sharp, Buchanan. *In Contempt of All Authority: Rural Artisans and Riot in the West of England, 1586–1660*. Berkeley: University of California Press, 1980.

Shelton, George. *Dean Tucker and Eighteenth-Century Economic and Political Thought*. London: Macmillan, 1981.

Sheppard, M. G., and John L. Halstead. "Labour's Municipal Election Performance in Provincial England and Wales 1901–13." *Society for the Study of Labour History* Bulletin Number 39 (Autumn 1979).

Sheppard, William. *Englands Balme*. London: J. Cottrel, 1657.

Shuttle, Timothy. *The Worsted Small-Ware Weavers' Apology*. Manchester: James Schofield, 1756.

Sider, Gerald. *Culture and Class in Anthropology and History*. Cambridge: Cambridge University Press, 1986.

Sigsworth, E. M. *Black Dyke Mills*. Liverpool: Liverpool University Press, 1958.

Sigsworth, E. M. "The Woollen Textile Industry." In Roy Church, editor, *The Dynamics of Victorian Business*. London: George Allen & Unwin, 1980.

Simon, Daphine. "Master and Servant." In John Saville, editor, *Democracy and the Labour Movement*. London: Lawrence and Wishart, 1954.

Simon, Manfred. *Handwerk in Krise und Umbruch*. Köln: Böhlau Verlag, 1983.

Sington, Theodore. "Plan for a Continental Cotton Mill." In *Cotton Mill Planning and Construction*. Manchester: published by the author, 1897.

Sismondi, Simonde. *De la Richesse commerciale*. Volume One. Genève: J. J. Paschoud, 1803.

Skambraks, Hannes. *"Das Kapital" von Marx—Waffe im Klassenkampf*. Berlin: Dietz Verlag, 1977.

Small, Albion. *The Cameralists: The Pioneers of German Social Polity*. Chicago: The University of Chicago Press, 1909.

Smelser, Neil J. "Culture: Coherent or Incoherent." In Richard Münch and Neil J. Smelser, editors, *Theory of Culture*. Berkeley: University of California Press, 1992.

Smelser, Neil J. *Social Change in the Industrial Revolution*. Chicago: The University of Chicago Press, 1959.

Smith, Adam. *An Inquiry into the Nature and Causes of the Wealth of Nations*. [Orig. published 1776.] Chicago: University of Chicago Press, 1976.

Smith, Adam. *Lectures on Justice, Police, Revenue and Arms*. Edited by Edwin Cannan. Oxford: Clarendon Press, 1896.

Smith, Adam. *Untersuchung über die Natur und die Ursachen des National-reichtums*. Translated by Christian Garve. Breslau: Wilhelm Korn, 1794.

Smith, Dempster, and Philip C. N. Pickworth. *Engineers' Costs and Economical Workshop Production*. Manchester: Emmott & Co., 1914.

Smith, Jonathan. "The Strike of 1825." In D. G. Wright and J. A. Jowitt, editors, *Victorian Bradford*. Bradford: Bradford Metropolitan Council, 1982.

Smith, L. "The Carpet Weavers of Kidderminster 1800–1850." Diss., University of Birmingham, 1982.

Smith, Thomas. "Peasant Time and Factory Time in Japan." *Past and Present* Number 111 (May 1986).

Snowden, Philip. *Socialism and Syndicalism*. Baltimore: Warwick & York.

Soboul, Albert. *The French Revolution, 1787–1799*. New York: Vintage Books, 1975.

Soboul, Albert. "Problèmes du travail en l'an II." *Annales historiques de la révolution française* Number 144 (July–September 1956).

Soboul, Albert. *Les Sans-culottes parisiens en l'an II*. Paris: Clauvreuil, 1958.

Sonenscher, Michael. "Le Droit du travail en France et en Angleterre à l'époque de la révolution." In Gérard Gayot and Jean-Pierre Hirsch, editors, *La Révolution française et le développement du capitalisme*. Lille: Revue du Nord, 1989.

Sonenscher, Michael. *Work and Wages: Natural Law, Politics and the Eighteenth-Century French Trades*. Cambridge: Cambridge University Press, 1989.

Sperber, Jonathan. *Popular Catholicism in Nineteenth-Century Germany*. Princeton: Princeton University Press, 1984.

Spicer, Robert S. *British Engineering Wages*. London: Edward Arnold & Co., 1928.

Spiethoff, Arthur. *Die wirtschaftlichen Wechsellagen: Aufschwung, Krise, Stockung*. Volume 2. Tübingen: J. C. B. Mohr, 1955.

Stadtarchiv Mönchengladbach. *Die Fabrikordnung der Firma F. Brandts zu Mönchengladbach, Ausgabe von 1885*. 1974. Mönchengladbach: Stadtarchiv Mönchengladbach.

Steffen, Gustaf F. *Studien zur Geschichte der englischen Lohnarbeiter*. Stuttgart: Hobbing & Büchle, 1901.

Steinberg, Hans-Josef. *Sozialismus und deutsche Sozialdemokratie*. Hannover: Verlag für Literatur und Zeitgeschehen, 1967.

Steitz, Walter, editor. *Quellen zur deutschen Wirtschafts- und Sozialgeschichte im 19. Jahrhundert bis zur Reichsgründung*. Darmstadt: Wissenschaftliche Buchgesellschaft, 1980.

Steuart, Sir James. *An Inquiry into the Principles of Political Oeconomy*. Edited by Andrew Skinner. Edinburgh: Oliver & Boyd, 1966.

Stewart, Mary Lynn. *Women, Work, and the French State*. Kingston: McGill-Queen's University Press, 1989.

Stone, Lawrence. "The Bourgeois Revolution of Seventeenth-Century England Revisited." In Geoff Eley and William Hunt, editors, *Reviving the English Revolution*. London: Verso, 1988.

Stone, Lawrence. "The Results of the English Revolutions of the Seventeenth Century." In J. G. A. Pocock, editor, *Three British Revolutions: 1641, 1688, 1776*. Princeton: Princeton University Press, 1980.

Storck, Friedrich. *Aus der Schule des Lebens*. Part One. Elberfeld: G. Lucas, 1910.

Straubel, Rolf. "Verlage und Manufakturen im Textilgewerbe der preussischen Provinzen Magdeburg und Halberstadt 1763–1800." *Jahrbuch für Geschichte des Feudalismus*, Volume 14. Berlin: Akademie-Verlag, 1990.

Strauss, E. *Sir William Petty: Portrait of a Genius*. London: Bodley Head, 1954.

Styles, John. "Embezzlement, Industry and the Law in England, 1500–1800." In Maxine Berg, Pat Hudson, and Michael Sonnenscher, editors, *Manufacture in Town and Country*. Cambridge: Cambridge University Press, 1983.

Supple, B. E. *Commercial Crisis and Change in England 1600–1642*. Cambridge: Cambridge University Press, 1959.

Swain, John T. *Industry Before the Industrial Revolution: North-East Lancashire c. 1500–1640*. Manchester: Manchester University Press, 1986.

Swaysland, Edward J. C. *Boot and Shoe Design and Manufacture*. Northhampton: Joseph Tebbutt, 1905.

Swidler, Ann. "Culture in Action: Symbols and Strategies." *American Sociological Review* Volume 51, No. 2 (April 1986).

Takeshi, Inagami. "The Japanese Will to Work." In Daniel Okimoto and Thomas Rohlen, editors, *Inside the Japanese System*. Stanford: Stanford University Press, 1988.

Tann, Jennifer. *The Development of the Factory*. London: Cornmarket Press, 1970.

Tanner, Duncan. "Ideological Debate in Edwardian Labour Politics: Radicalism, Revisionism and Socialism." In Eugenio F. Biagini and Alastair J. Reid, editors, *Currents of Radicalism: Popular Radicalism, Organised Labour and Party Politics in Britain, 1850–1914*. Cambridge: Cambridge University Press, 1991.

Tarlé, E. *L'Industrie dans les campagnes en France à la fin de l'ancien régime*. Paris: Edouard Cornély, 1910.

Taussig, F. W. *Wages and Capital: An Examination of the Wages Fund Doctrine*. New York: D. Appleton and Co., 1896.

Tawney, R. H. *Religion and the Rise of Capitalism*. [Orig. published 1926.] New York: New American Library, 1954.

Tawney, R. H., editor. *Studies in Economic History: The Collected Papers of George Unwin*. London: Macmillan and Co., 1927.

Tawney, R. H., and Eileen Power. *Tudor Economic Documents*. London: Longmans, Green and Co., 1924.

Temple, William. *A Vindication of Commerce and the Arts*. [Orig. published 1758.] Reprinted in Stephen Copley, editor, *Literature and the Social Order in Eighteenth-Century England*. London: Croom Helm, 1984.

Thal, Erich. *Die Entstehung und Entwicklung der Halbwoll- und Wollindustrie im M.-Gladbacher Bezirk bis zum Jahre 1914*. Mönchengladbach: W. Hütter, 1926.

Therborn, Göran. *The Ideology of Power and the Power of Ideology.* London: New Left Books, 1980.

Thirsk, Joan, and J. P. Cooper. *Seventeenth-Century Economic Documents.* Oxford: Clarendon Press, 1972.

Thomas, Keith. "The Levellers and the Franchise." In G. E. Aylmer, editor, *The Interregnum: The Quest for Settlement 1646–1660.* London: Macmillan & Co., 1972.

Thomas, Keith. "Work and Leisure in Pre-Industrial Society." *Past & Present* Number 29 (1964).

Thompson, E. P. "Homage to Tom Maguire." In Asa Briggs and John Saville, editors, *Essays in Labour History.* London: Macmillan & Co., 1960.

Thompson, E. P. *The Making of the English Working Class.* New York: Vintage Books, 1963.

Thompson, E. P. "The Moral Economy of the English Crowd in the Eighteenth Century." *Past & Present* Number 50 (February 1971).

Thompson, E. P. "The Peculiarities of the English." In Ralph Miliband and John Saville, editors, *The Socialist Register.* New York: Monthly Review Press, 1965.

Thompson, E. P. *The Poverty of Theory and Other Essays.* New York: Monthly Review Press, 1978.

Thompson, E. P. "Time, Work-Discipline, and Industrial Capitalism." *Past and Present* Number 38 (December 1967).

Thompson, E. P. *Whigs and Hunters: The Origin of the Black Act.* New York: Pantheon Books, 1975.

Thompson, E. P. *William Morris: Romantic to Revolutionary.* New York: Pantheon Books, 1976.

Thompson, Noel W. *The Market and Its Critics.* London: Routledge, 1988.

Thompson, Noel W. *The People's Science: The Popular Political Economy of Exploitation and Crisis 1816–1834.* Cambridge: Cambridge University Press, 1984.

Thompson, William. *An Inquiry into the Principles of the Distribution of Wealth.* [Orig. published London, 1824.] New York: Burt Franklin, 1968.

Thompson, William. *Labour Rewarded.* London: Hunt & Clarke, 1827.

Thomson, J. K. J. *Clermont-de-Lodève 1633–1789.* Cambridge: Cambridge University Press, 1982.

Thrupp, Sylvia. "The Gilds." *The Cambridge Economic History of Europe.* Volume III. Cambridge: Cambridge University Press, 1965.

Thun, Alphons. *Die Industrie am Niederrhein und ihre Arbeiter.* Leipzig: Duncker & Humblot, 1879.

Thünen, Johann Heinrich von. *Der isolirte [sic] Staat.* Part II. [Orig. published 1842.] Berlin: Wiegandt, Hempel & Parey, 1875.

Tidow, Klaus. *Neumünsters Textil- und Lederindustrie im 19. Jahrhundert.* Neumünster: Karl Wachholtz, 1984.

Tillett, Anthony, et al., editors. *Management Thinkers.* Harmondsworth: Penguin Books, 1970.

Timmermann, Walter. *Entlöhnungsmethoden in der Hannoverschen Eisenindustrie.* Berlin: Leonhard Simion, 1906.

Tipton, Frank. *Regional Variations in the Economic Development of Germany During the Nineteenth Century.* Middletown, Connecticut: Wesleyan University Press, 1976.

Torr, Dona. *Tom Mann and His Times.* Volume One. London: Lawrence & Wishart, 1956.

Torrens, Robert. *An Essay on the Production of Wealth.* London: Longman, Hurst, Rees, Orne, and Brown, 1821.

Trénard, L. "The Social Crisis in Lyons on the Eve of the French Revolution." In Jeffry Kaplow, editor, *New Perspectives on the French Revolution.* New York: John Wiley & Sons, 1965.

Tribe, Keith. *Genealogies of Capitalism.* London: Macmillan & Co., 1981.

Tribe, Keith. *Governing Economy: The Reformation of German Economic Discourse 1750–1840.* Cambridge: Cambridge University Press, 1988.

Tribe, Keith. *Land, Labour and Economic Discourse.* London: Routledge & Kegan Paul, 1978.

Trodd, Geoffrey. "Political Change and the Working Class in Blackburn and Burnley 1880–1914." Ph.D. diss., University of Lancaster, 1978.

Troeltsch, Walter. *Die Calwer Zeughandlungskompagnie und ihre Arbeiter.* Jena: Gustav Fischer, 1897.

Tryon, T. *Some General Considerations Offered, Relating to Our Present Trade. And Intended for Its Help and Improvement.* London: J. Harris, 1698.

Tsuzuki, Chushichi. *H. M. Hyndman and British Socialism.* Oxford: Oxford University Press, 1961.

Tsuzuki, Chushichi. *Tom Mann, 1856–1941.* Oxford: Clarendon Press, 1991.

Tully, James. *A Discourse on Property: John Locke and His Adversaries.* Cambridge: Cambridge University Press, 1980.

Turner, Ben. *About Myself 1863–1930.* London: Cayme Press, 1930.

Turner, Ben. *A Short Account of the Rise and Progress of the Heavy Woollen District Branch of the General Union of Textile Workers.* N.p.: Yorkshire Factory Times Press, 1917.

Turner, Ben. *Short History of the General Union of Textile Workers.* Heckmondwike: Labour Pioneer, 1920.

Turner, H. A. *Trade Union Growth Structure and Policy.* Toronto: University of Toronto Press, 1962.

Turner, Terence. "'We Are Parrots,' 'Twins Are Birds': Play of Tropes as Operational Structure." In James Fernandez, editor, *Beyond Metaphor.* Stanford: Stanford University Press, 1991.

Uhlmann, Wolfgang. "Die Konstituierung der Chemnitzer Bourgeoisie während der Zeit der bürgerlichen Umwälzung von 1800 bis 1871." Diss., Pädagogische Hochschule Dresden, 1988.

Ujihara, Shojiro. "Essai sur la transformation historique des pratiques d'emploi et des relations professionnelles au Japan." *Sociologie du travail* Volume 33, Number 1 (1991).

Unger, Emil. *Entscheidungen des Gewerbegerichts zu Berlin.* Berlin: Carl Heymann, 1898.

United Kingdom. *Census of England and Wales 1891.* Volume III. London: H.M.S.O., 1893.

United Kingdom. *Parliamentary Debates*. Series Four, Volume 43, 1896 July 17–August 6.

United Kingdom. Parliamentary Papers. Various years.

United Kingdom. *Textile Trades, Huddersfield*. London: H.M.S.O., 1914.

Unwin, George. *Industrial Organization in the Sixteenth and Seventeenth Centu ries*. Oxford: Clarendon Press, 1904.

Ure, Andrew. *Philosophy of Manufactures*. London: Charles Knight, 1835.

Urwick, L., and E. F. L. Brech. *The Making of Scientific Management*. London: Isaac Pitman & Sons, 1957.

Utz, Ludwig. *Moderne Fabrikanlagen*. Leipzig: Uhlands technischer Verlag, 1907.

Utz, Ludwig. *Die Praxis der mechanischen Weberei*. Leipzig: Uhlands technischer Verlag, 1907.

van den Heuvel, Gerd. *Grundprobleme der französischen Bauernschaft 1730–1794*. München: R. Oldenbourg Verlag, 1982.

Vardar, Berke. *Structure fondamentale du vocabulaire social et politique en France, de 1815 à 1830*. Istanbul: Imprimerie de la Faculté des Lettres de l'Université d'Istanbul, 1973.

Vaughan, Rice. *A Discourse of Coin and Coinage*. [Orig. published 1675.] In J. R. McCulloch, editor, *A Select Collection of Scarce and Valuable Tracts on Money*. London: Political Economy Club, 1856.

Veblen, Thorstein. *Imperial Germany and the Industrial Revolution*. New York: Macmillan & Co., 1915.

Verband Deutscher Textilarbeiter. *Tariferläuterungen und Statistisches: Bearbeitet nach Aufzeichnungen der Tarif-Kommission im sächsisch-thüringischen Textilbezirk*. Gera: Alban Bretschneider, 1909.

Verband Deutscher Textilarbeiter. *Die Tuch-Konferenz in Crimmitschau, 26. und 27. Februar 1910. Verhandlungs-Bericht*. Berlin: Carl Hübsch, 1910.

Verband Deutscher Textilarbeiter, Gau Brandenburg. *Die Lohn- und Arbeitsbedingungen in der Niederlausitzer Tuchindustrie 1908–1909*. Berlin: Franz Kotzke, 1909.

Vernant, Jean-Pierre. *Myth and Thought Among the Greeks*. London: Routledge & Kegan Paul, 1983.

Versammlung deutscher Gewerbetreibender. *Bericht über die Verhandlungen in der Versammlung deutscher Gewerbetreibender in Leipzig am 7. Oktober 1844*. Leipzig: Friedrich Nies, 1844.

Das Versicherungsgesetz für Angestellte: Vom 20. Dezember 1911. Stuttgart: J. Hess, 1912.

Vester, Michael, et al., editors. *Gibt es einen "Wissenschaftlichen Sozialismus"?* Hannover: SOAK Verlag, 1979.

Vickers, W. Farrar. *Spin a Good Yarn*. Leeds: MT Co., 1978.

Vikerman, Charles. *Woollen Spinning: A Text-Book for Students in Technical Schools and Colleges and for Skillful Practical Men in Woollen Mills*. London: Macmillan & Co., 1894.

Vogel, Barbara. *Allgemeine Gewerbefreiheit: Die Reformpolitik des preussischen Staatskanzlers Hardenberg 1810–1820*. Göttingen: Vandenhoeck & Ruprecht, 1983.

Voigt, F. Hermann. *Die Weberei in ihrer sozialen und technischen Entwicklung und Fortbildung.* Weimar: Bernhard Friedrich Voigt, 1882.

Volkov, Shulamit. *The Rise of Popular Antimodernism in Germany.* Princeton: Princeton University Press, 1978.

Volta, Riccardo dalla. *Le forme del salario.* Firenze: Fratelli Bocca, 1893.

vom Stein, Helmut. *Die industrielle Entwicklung der Stadt Wermelskirchen seit Anfang des neunzehnten Jahrhunderts.* Düsseldorf: G. H. Nolte, 1939.

von Frauendorfer, Sigmund. *Agrarwirtschaftliche Forschung und Agrarpolitik in Italien.* Berlin: Paul Parey, 1942.

von Frauendorfer, Sigmund. *Ideengeschichte der Agrarwirtschaft und Agrarpolitik im deutschen Sprachgebiet.* Volume I. München: Bayerischer Landwirtschaftsverlag, 1957.

von Justi, Johann Heinrich Gottlob. *Gesammelte politische und Finanzschriften über wichtige Gegenstände der Staatskunst, der Kriegswissenschaften und des Kameral- und Finanzwesens.* Volume One. [Orig. published 1761.] Aalen: Scientia Verlag, 1970.

von Rohrscheidt, Kurt. *Vom Zunftzwange zur Gewerbefreiheit.* Berlin: Carl Heymanns Verlag, 1898.

von Schulze-Gävernitz, Gerhart. *The Cotton Trade in England and on the Continent.* London: Simpkin, Marshall, Hamilton, Kent & Co., 1895.

von Schulze-Gävernitz, Gerhart. *Der Grossbetrieb: Ein wirtschaftlicher und sozialer Fortschritt.* Leipzig: Duncker & Humblot, 1892.

von Sonnenfels, J. *Grundsätze der Staatspolizey, Handlung und Finanzwissenschaft.* München: J. B. Strobel, 1801.

von Zwiedineck-Südenhorst, Otto. *Beiträge zur Lehre von den Lohnformen.* Tübingen: H. Laupp, 1904.

Vopelius, Elisabeth. *Die altliberalen Ökonomen und die Reformzeit.* Stuttgart: Gustav Fischer, 1968.

Wadsworth, Alfred P., and Julia de Lacy Mann. *The Cotton Trade and Industrial Lancashire 1600–1780.* Manchester: Manchester University Press, 1931.

Walzer, Michael. *The Revolution of the Saints: A Study in the Origins of Radical Politics.* Cambridge, Massachusetts: Harvard University Press, 1965.

Watts, John. "Essay on Strikes." *British Association for the Advancement of Science: The Workman's Bane and Antidote.* Manchester: A. Ireland, 1861.

Webb, Beatrice. *The Co-operative Movement in Great Britain.* London: S. Sonnenschein, 1891.

Webb, Sidney. *Socialism in Great Britain.* London: Swan Sonnenschein & Co., 1890.

Webb, Sidney. *The Works Manager To-Day.* London: Green & Co., 1914.

Webb, Sidney, and Beatrice Webb. *The History of Trade Unionism.* London: Longmans, Green & Co., 1894.

Webb, Sidney, and Beatrice Webb. *Industrial Democracy.* [Orig. published 1897.] New York: Augustus Kelley, 1965.

Weber, Max. *Economy and Society.* Berkeley: University of California Press, 1968.

Weber, Max. *Gesammelte Aufsätze zur Soziologie und Sozialpolitik.* Tübingen: J. C. B. Mohr, 1924.

Weber, Max. "Kritische Bemerkungen zu den vorstehenden 'Kritische Beiträgen.'" In Max Weber, *Die protestantische Ethik II*, edited by Johannes Winckelmann. Gütersloh: Gerd Mohn, 1982.

Weber, Max. *The Protestant Ethic and the Spirit of Capitalism*. New York: Charles Scribner's Sons, 1958.

Weber, Max. *The Sociology of Religion*. Boston: Beacon Press, 1963.

Wehler, Hans-Ulrich. *Das deutsche Kaiserreich 1871–1918*. Göttingen: Vandenhoeck & Ruprecht, 1973.

Weigand, Friedrich Ludwig Karl. *Deutsches Wörterbuch*. Fifth edition, revised by Hermann Hirt et al. Giessen: A. Topelmann, 1909–10.

Weiss, Rudolf. "Entlöhnungsmethoden und ihre Anwendung in der Textilindustrie." Diss., München, 1925.

Wendel, Hugo. *The Evolution of Industrial Freedom in Prussia 1845–1849*. Allentown, Pennsylvania: H. R. Haas, 1918.

Westerfield, Ray Bert. *Middlemen in English Business Particularly Between 1660 and 1760*. New Haven: Yale University Press, 1915.

Wettstein-Adelt, Minna. *3 1/2 Monate Fabrik-Arbeiterin*. Berlin: J. Leiser, 1893.

White, Hayden. *Metahistory*. Baltimore: Johns Hopkins University Press, 1973.

White, Joseph. "Lancashire Cotton Textiles." In Chris Wrigley, editor, *A History of British Industrial Relations 1874–1914*. Brighton: Harvester Press, 1982.

White, Joseph. *The Limits of Trade Union Militancy*. Westport, Connecticut: Greenwood Press, 1978.

Wiedemann, Konrad. *Arbeit und Bürgertum: Die Entwicklung des Arbeitsbegriffs in der Literatur Deutschlands an der Wende zur Neuzeit*. Heidelberg: Carl Winter, 1979.

Wiener, Martin. *English Culture and the Decline of the Industrial Spirit, 1850–1980*. Cambridge: Cambridge University Press, 1981.

Wilkinson, Dyke. *Rough Roads: Reminiscences of a Wasted Life*. London: Sampson Low, Marston, & Co., 1912.

Willard, Claude. *Les Guesdistes*. Paris: Editions Sociales, 1965.

Williams, Charles. "Cotton Mill Costings." *Journal of the National Federation of Textile Works Managers Associations* Volume V (1925–26).

Williams, D. H. *Costing in the Wool Textile and Other Industries*. Manchester: Emmott & Co, 1946.

Williams, D. H. "Some Suggestions for Factory Organization and Efficiency." *Huddersfield Textile Society Journal* (1918–1919).

Williams, D. H. *Textile Factory Organization and Management*. London: Emmott & Co., 1934.

Willis, Paul E. *Human Experience and Material Production: The Culture of the Shop Floor*. Birmingham: Centre for Contemporary Cultural Studies, 1975.

Willis, Paul E. *Learning to Labor*. New York: Columbia University Press, 1977.

Wilmott, Henry. "The 'Labour Unrest' and the Woollen Trades." *Socialist Review* (November 1910).

Wilson, C. H. "Trade, Society and the State." *The Cambridge Economic History of Europe*. Volume IV. Cambridge: Cambridge University Press, 1967.

Wilson, Joseph. *Joseph Wilson: His Life and Work*. London: Lund Humphries & Co., [1923].

Winch, Donald. "The Emergence of Economics as a Science 1750–1870." In Carlo Cipolla, editor, *The Industrial Revolution 1700–1914: The Fontana Economic History of Europe.* New York: Barnes & Noble, 1976.

Winkel, Harald. *Die Ablösungskapitalien aus der Bauernbefreiung in West- und Süddeutschland.* Stuttgart: Gustav Fischer Verlag, 1968.

Winterbottom, James. "A Criticism of the Oldham and Bolton Lists of Earnings for Mule Spinning." *Journal of the British Association of Managers of Textile Works* Volume VI (1914–15).

Wirtz, Rainer. "Die Ordnung der Fabrik ist nicht die Fabrikordnung." In Heiko Haumann, editor, *Arbeiteralltag in Stadt und Land.* Berlin: Argument-Verlag, 1982.

Wischer, Franz. "Die Organisationsbestrebungen der Arbeiter in der Krefelder Seiden- und Samtindustrie." Diss., Universität Köln, 1920.

Wischermann, Clemens. "An der Schwelle der Industrialisierung 1800–1850." In Wilhelm Kohl, editor, *Westfälische Geschichte.* Volume 3. Düsseldorf: Schwann, 1984.

Witteborg, August. *Geschichte der evang.-lutherischen Gemeinde Barmen-Wupperfeld von 1777 bis 1927.* Barmen: Selbstverlag der evang.-lutherischen Gemeinde, 1927.

Wood, Ellen Meiksins. *The Pristine Culture of Capitalism.* London: Verso, 1991.

Wood, G. H. "The Statistics of Wages in the Nineteenth Century." *Journal of the Royal Statistical Society* Volume 73 (1910).

Wood, George S. "The Theory and Practice of Piecework." *Huddersfield Textile Society Session 1910–1911.* [Huddersfield: Huddersfield Textile Society, 1911.]

Woodward, Donald. "Wage Rates and Living Standards in Pre-Industrial England." *Past & Present* Number 91 (May 1981).

Woollen and Worsted Trades' Federation. *Systems of Cost Finding for the Textile Trade.* Bradford, 1921.

Worthington, J. *One Day in My Early Working Life.* 1918, Bolton Library.

Wright, Erik Olin. *Class Structure and Income Determination.* New York: Academic Press, 1979.

Wright, Erik Olin. *Classes.* London: Verso, 1987.

Wright, Erik Olin. "What Is Middle About the Middle Classes?" In John Roemer, editor, *Analytical Marxism.* Cambridge: Cambridge University Press, 1986.

Wright, Erik Olin, Andrew Levine, and Elliot Sober. *Reconstructing Marxism.* London: Verso, 1992.

Wright, Erik Olin, et al. *The Debate on Classes.* London: Verso, 1989.

Wrobel, Brigitte. *Geschichte der Arbeiterbewegung des Kreises Zittau: Chronik 1830–1945.* Zittau: Kommission zur Erforschung der Geschichte der örtlichen Arbeiterbewegung, 1972.

Wrong, Dennis. "The Oversocialized Conception of Man in Modern Sociology." *American Sociological Review* Volume 26, Number 2 (April 1961).

Wunderlich, Frieda. *Farm Labor in Germany 1810–1945.* Princeton: Princeton University Press, 1961.

Wurm, Christian Friedrich Ludwig. *Wörterbuch der deutschen Sprache von der Druckerfindung bis zum heutigen Tage.* Volume One. Freiburg in Breisgau: Herder, 1858.

Wuthnow, Robert. *Meaning and Moral Order*. Berkeley: University of California Press, 1987.

Wuttke, Robert. *Gesindeordnungen und Gesindezwangsdienst in Sachsen bis zum Jahre 1835*. Leipzig: Duncker & Humblot, 1893.

Wutzmer, H. "Die Herkunft der industriellen Bourgeoisie Preussens in den vierziger Jahren des 19. Jahrhunderts." In Hans Mottek et al., editors, *Studien zur Geschichte der industriellen Revolution in Deutschland*. Berlin: Akademie-Verlag, 1960.

Yarmie, Andrew. "Captains of Industry in Mid-Victorian Britain." Diss., King's College, 1975.

Yarranton, Andrew. *England's Improvement by Sea and Land*. London: R. Everingham, 1677.

Yorkshire Textile Workers' Deputation. *Official Report of the Yorkshire Textile Workers' Deputation: An Enquiry into the Conditions of the German Woollen Cloth Operatives*. Batley: News Office, 1908.

Zachmann, Karin. "Der Mechanisierungsprozess in der deutschen Textilindustrie im Zeitraum von 1870 bis 1914." *Beiträge zur Wirtschaftsgeschichte*, Number One. Dresden: Technische Universität Dresden, 1988.

Zeeh, Bruno. *Die Betriebsverhältnisse in der sächsischen Maschinenstickerei*. Borna-Leipzig: Verlag Noske, 1909.

Zeitlin, Jonathan. "The Emergence of Shop Steward Organization and Job Control in the British Car Industry: A Review Essay." *History Workshop* Number 10 (Autumn 1980).

Zentralverband Christlicher Textilarbeiter Deutschlands. *Geschäftsbericht*. 1906–1908, 1908–1910, 1910–1912, 1912–1914.

Zunkel, Friedrich. *Der Rheinisch-Westfälische Unternehmer 1834–1879*. Köln: Westdeutscher Verlag, 1962.

Index

Abstract labor: link between product and, 59–60, 215–16, 252, 337; of small tailors, 242n135. *See also* Labor

Accounting: accepted elements of, 162; for British/German labor transfers, 78–84; British/German method of time, 105–21; for costs of German overlookers, 155–57

Agnatieff, Michael, 346

Agriculture: French feudal, 327–28; social relations of German feudal, 299–305, 308–9

Althusser, Louis, 42n2, 383n112, 384

American employment practices, 14–15

Anderson, Perry, 488

"The Apotheosis of Labour" (*Textile Mercury*), 392

Arbeit, 310. *See also* Labor

Arbeitskraft. *See* Labor power (*Arbeitskraft*)

Armstrong, Clement, 216

Artisan, 290

Association of Blast-Furnacemen, 86

Association of Iron and Steel Workers, 86

Authority: German worker resistance to, 468–69; hiring/dismissal, 171–74; implications of fining systems to, 190–91, 193–94; of overlookers, 166–97; protests against employer, 441

Bailey, Samuel, 248–49

Barbon, Nicholas, 221

"Barracks" language, 183

Batley Chamber of Commerce (1912), 80

Bean Ing mills, 134

Bebel, August, 413

Beccaria, Cesare, 319

Behagg, Clive, 241

Bendix, Reinhard, 14, 92

Bernhardi, Theodor, 252, 277–78

Biggart, Nicole Woolsey, 15, 145

Blackburn Labour Journal, 407

Blackstone, Sir William, 229–30, 256

Blatchford, Robert, 408

Bolton cotton trade, 140

Bonus system, 427n179

Bookkeeping systems. *See* Accounting

Born, Stephen, 413

Botero, Giovanni, 215

Bourdieu, Pierre, 21–24, 207, 485n23

Boycotts, 438. *See also* Strikes

Bradford Independent Labour Party, 408

Bradford Labour Echo (newspaper), 408, 410

Bradford Socialist Vanguard (journal), 406

Bray, John, 398, 412

Bremer, Julis, 417

British mills: adoption of efficiency ratio by, 494–95;

of fines, 426–29; on function of unions, 404–5; on offensive pay practices, 376; on sanitation complaints, 454; on unsafe machinery issue, 452; on "waiting time," 368; on worker complaints, 179–84, 191

Yorkshire mills: dismissal authority in, 173; labor transfer practice in, 81–82; overlooker's compensation in, 152–53, 155, 156–60; piece-rate system in, 46–52, 54–55; practice of latching doors at, 105–6; production norms established in, 206; social control of, 194–95; social expectations of overlookers in, 187–88; socialist movement within, 403, 406; strikes in, 437–38; unions from, 361, 422–23. *See also* British mills

Zwiedineck-Südenhorst, Otto von, 257

Compositor: Fog Press
Printer: BookCrafters, Inc.
Binder: BookCrafters, Inc.
Text: 10/13 Aldus
Display: Aldus